Pro SQL Server 2005
High Availability

■■■

Allan Hirt

Apress®

Pro SQL Server 2005 High Availability

Copyright © 2007 by Allan Hirt

ISBN-13: 978-1-4302-1180-8

ISBN-13: 978-1-4302-0374-2 (eBook)

Lead Editors: Jim Huddleston, Dominic Shakeshaft

Technical Reviewer: Vidya Vrat Agarwal

Editorial Board: Steve Anglin, Ewan Buckingham, Gary Cornell, Jonathan Gennick, Jason Gilmore, Jonathan Hassell, Chris Mills, Matthew Moodie, Jeffrey Pepper, Ben Renow-Clarke, Dominic Shakeshaft, Matt Wade, Tom Welsh

Project Manager: Kylie Johnston

Copy Edit Manager: Nicole Flores

Copy Editors: Jennifer Whipple, Kim Wimpsett, Ami Knox

Assistant Production Director: Kari Brooks-Copony

Production Editor: Laura Esterman

Compositor: Linda Weidemann, Wolf Creek Press

Proofreader: Elizabeth Berry

Indexer: Julie Grady

Artist: April Milne

Cover Designer: Kurt Krames

Manufacturing Director: Tom Debolski

For information on translations, please contact Apress directly at 2855 Telegraph Avenue, Suite 600, Berkeley, CA 94705. Phone 510-549-5930, fax 510-549-5939, e-mail info@apress.com, or visit http://www.apress.com.

The source code for this book is available to readers at http://www.apress.com in the Source Code/ Download section.

*This book is dedicated to the memory of James Huddleston,
who passed away unexpectedly during the writing and editing
process of this book. He was one of my biggest champions at Apress,
and you would not be reading this if it were not for him.*

Contents at a Glance

Foreword xix
About the Author xxi
About the Technical Reviewer xxiii
Acknowledgments xxv
Preface xxvii

PART 1 ■ ■ ■ The Building Blocks of High Availability

■ CHAPTER 1   The Business of Availability 3
■ CHAPTER 2   Pay Now or Pay Later 27

PART 2 ■ ■ ■ Always On: SQL Server Technology

■ CHAPTER 3   Backup and Restore 41
■ CHAPTER 4   Failover Clustering: Preparing to Cluster Windows 107
■ CHAPTER 5   Failover Clustering: Clustering Windows 131
■ CHAPTER 6   Failover Clustering: Windows Server Cluster Administration 205
■ CHAPTER 7   Failover Clustering: Preparing to Cluster SQL Server 2005 225
■ CHAPTER 8   Failover Clustering: Clustering SQL Server 2005 249
■ CHAPTER 9   Failover Clustering: SQL Server 2005 Failover Clustering Administration . . . 321
■ CHAPTER 10   Log Shipping 363
■ CHAPTER 11   Database Mirroring 425
■ CHAPTER 12   Replication 479
■ CHAPTER 13   Making Your Data Available 529

PART 3 ■ ■ ■ Administration for High Availability

■ CHAPTER 14   Designing High Availability Solutions 553
■ CHAPTER 15   24x7 Database Administration 579
■ CHAPTER 16   24x7 Database Maintenance 673
■ CHAPTER 17   Disaster Recovery 713

■ INDEX 725

v

Contents

Foreword xix

About the Author xxi

About the Technical Reviewer xxiii

Acknowledgments xxv

Preface xxvii

PART 1 ■■■ The Building Blocks of High Availability

CHAPTER 1   The Business of Availability 3

The Building Blocks of Availability 4

    People 4

    Training 5

    Processes 6

The Cost of Availability 13

Defining Downtime 14

Nines 15

The Data Center Mentality 16

    Planning the Data Center 17

    Securing the Data Center 19

    Power 21

    Cabling, Networking, and Communications 22

    Outsourcing Server Hosting and Maintenance 23

    Technology 25

Summary 25

CHAPTER 2   Pay Now or Pay Later 27

The Genesis of a Solution 27

    What Is the Business Problem You Are Solving? 27

    Has This Been Done Before? 28

    What Other Mission-Critical Systems Have Been Implemented? 28

    Are You Biting Off More Than You Can Chew? 28

    Are You Governed By Law or a Regulatory Body? 28

    Do You Understand the End-User Requirements? 29

Money Changes Everything 29
Keep Your Friends Close and Your Enemies Closer 29
Service Level Agreements 31
    Service Level Targets 31
    Availability Service Level Agreements 32
    Performance Service Level Agreements 33
    Operational Level Agreements 34
Compromise 35
Time Is of the Essence 36
Support Agreements 36
Applications, Application Development, and Availability 38
Summary 38

PART 2 ▪▪▪ Always On: SQL Server Technology

▌CHAPTER 3   **Backup and Restore** 41

Understanding Backup and Restore Basics 41
    Describing the Types of SQL Server Database Backups 41
    Backing Up a Table 46
    Mirroring Backups 46
    Describing the Recovery Models 47
    Understanding SQL Server Database Recovery 51
    Backing Up and Restoring Full-Text Indexes 51
    Backing Up and Restoring Analysis Services 52
    Setting the Recovery Interval 52
    Using Media Retention 53
    Attaching and Detaching Databases 54
    Querying Backup and Restore Information 54
    Understanding Backup File Compatibility 54
    Understanding Systemwide Options for Backing Up to Tape 57
Planning Your Backup and Restore Strategy 58
    Understanding SLAs and Recovery 58
    Dealing with Human Error 58
    The "Need" for Zero Data Loss 59
    Understanding the Link Between Disk Design, Database Layout,
        Retention, Performance, and Backups 59
    Knowing Your Application 60
    Backing Up to Disk, to Tape, or over the Network 61
    Checking the Availability of Your Backups 61
    Testing the Backups 62
    Synchronizing Your Backups and Restores 63

Understanding Your Recoverability Paths 64
Managing the Transaction Log Through Backups 67
Implementing the Plan. 68
Ensuring SQL Server Agent Is Started 69
Knowing Your Backup Requirements and Their Relation to
    Backup Frequency 69
Implementing Backup Security 69
Checking Database Status 70
Monitoring Backup Media and Backup Status 72
Using the Database Maintenance Plan Wizard 73
Backing Up SQL Server Databases 75
Restoring SQL Server Databases 84
Performing Piecemeal Restores. 95
Backing Up and Restoring Analysis Services Databases. 96
Automating the Retention Policy 103
Deploying Custom Backup and Restore Scripts 104
Summary 106

CHAPTER 4   **Failover Clustering: Preparing to Cluster Windows** 107

What Is Clustering? 107
Network Load Balancing Cluster 107
Server Cluster. 108
Planning for a Windows Server Cluster 116
The Windows Server Catalog 116
Networking 120
32-bit and 64-bit Windows. 122
Mixing Windows Versions 122
Disk Configuration 122
Security Configuration for a Server Cluster. 127
Geographically Dispersed Clusters 129
Summary 130

CHAPTER 5   **Failover Clustering: Clustering Windows**. 131

Step 1: Installing and Configuring Hardware and the Operating System 131
Step 2: Creating and Configuring the Cluster Service Account. 132
Creating the Cluster Service Account 132
Adding the Cluster Service Account to Each Node. 135
Step 3: Configuring Networking for a Server Cluster 141
Configuring the Public Network 141
Configuring the Private Cluster Network 145
Setting Network Priorities 148

Step 4: Configuring the Shared Disks 149
    Step 4a: Sector Aligning the Disks................................ 149
    Step 4b: Formatting the Disks 152
    Step 4c: Verifying the Disk Configuration 155
Step 5: Running the Microsoft Cluster Configuration Validation Wizard....... 156
Step 6: Adding the First Node to a New Server Cluster 166
    Using Cluster Administrator 166
    Using the Command Line 175
Step 7: Adding Other Nodes to the Server Cluster 175
    Using Cluster Administrator 175
    Using the Command Line 180
Performing Post-Installation Tasks 188
    Configuring Cluster Networks..................................... 188
    Resizing the Quorum Log 190
    Creating a Clustered Microsoft Distributed Transaction Coordinator.... 191
    Testing the Server Cluster 200
Summary 203

▌CHAPTER 6   Failover Clustering: Windows Server Cluster Administration 205

Remote Connectivity 205
Antivirus Programs and Clustering..................................... 205
Changing the Cluster Service Account Password......................... 206
Disk Management for a Windows Server Cluster 211
Summary 224

▌CHAPTER 7   Failover Clustering: Preparing to Cluster SQL Server 2005 225

New Features of SQL Server 2005 Failover Clustering 227
Planning SQL Server 2005 Failover Clustering Instances 228
    Number of Instances on a Single Windows Failover Cluster........... 228
    Clustered SQL Server Instance Names 228
    Clustering Analysis Services...................................... 230
    Clustering Other SQL Server Components 230
    SQL Writer and Failover Clustering 230
    SQL Server Browser Service...................................... 230
    Dependencies... 231
    Combining SQL Server 2005 and Exchange on the
       Same Windows Server Cluster 231
    Security.. 232
    Installing SQL Server 2005 Failover Clustering Instances
       Side-by-Side with SQL Server 2000 234

Installing Local Instances and Clustered Instances on the
    Same Hardware 237
Disk Configuration 237
Configuration Considerations for Multiple SQL Server Instances
    on the Same Windows Server Cluster 238
Upgrading to SQL Server 2005 Failover Clustering 245
Upgrading Analysis Services 2005 in a Clustered Environment 245
Summary 247

CHAPTER 8   **Failover Clustering: Clustering SQL Server 2005** 249

Step 1: Ensure the Windows Failover Cluster Is Configured Properly 249
Step 2: Create the SQL Server 2005 Failover Clustering
    Service Accounts and Groups 250
    Creating the SQL Server Service Accounts 250
    Creating the SQL Server–Related Cluster Groups 251
    Adding the SQL Server Service Accounts to the Cluster Groups. 253
    Adding the Cluster Groups to Each Node 255
Step 3: Rename the Cluster Resource Group 256
Step 4: Install .NET Framework 2.0 256
Step 5: Install SQL Server 2005 259
    New Installation: Setup 260
    New Installation: Command Line 291
    In-Place Upgrade: Setup 295
Performing Post-Installation Tasks 304
    Installing SQL Server Service Packs, Patches, and Hotfixes 304
    Adding Additional Disks As Dependencies 304
    Changing the Affect the Group Property of the SQL Server or
        Analysis Services Resource. 308
    Setting the Preferred Node Order for Failover. 309
    Installing the Management Tools on the Other Nodes 310
    Removing the BUILTIN\Administrators Account 313
    Testing the Failover Cluster 316
    Upgrade Only: Changing the Service Accounts 318
Summary 320

CHAPTER 9   **Failover Clustering:**
SQL Server 2005 Failover Clustering Administration 321

Querying Failover Clustering Properties 321
Using SQL Server 2005 Surface Area Configuration with
    Clustered Instances 325

Starting, Stopping, and Pausing Clustered SQL Server Services 329

    SQL Server Configuration Manager 330

    SQL Server Surface Area Configuration. 331

    Cluster Administrator. 331

    Command Line. 332

Renaming a Failover Clustering Instance of SQL Server 334

Changing the Service Accounts Used by a Failover Clustering Instance 337

Changing the IP Address of a Failover Clustering Instance 339

Assigning a Static IP Port to a Failover Clustering Instance 340

Rebuilding master on a Failover Clustering Instance. 342

Adding or Removing a Node 343

    Using Setup 343

    Using the Command Prompt. 349

Uninstalling a Failover Clustering Instance 350

    Using Setup 351

    Command Prompt 355

Changing Domains. 355

    Changing the Domain with No IP Address Changes. 355

Summary 361

■CHAPTER 10   **Log Shipping**. 363

How Log Shipping Works 363

Best Uses for Log Shipping. 365

    Disaster Recovery and High Availability 365

    Intrusive Database Maintenance 366

    Migrations and Upgrades 366

Log Shipping Considerations 367

    Location of the Primary and Secondary. 367

    Full Database Restoration on the Secondary 367

    Sending Transaction Logs to More Than One Secondary 368

    Transaction Size 368

    Transaction Log Backup Frequency and Size. 368

    Copy Frequency and Transaction Log Backup Location 368

    Network Latency and Network Speed. 369

    Networks, Domain Connectivity, and Log Shipping 369

    Log Shipping Between Versions of SQL Server 369

    Code Page/Sort Order/Collation 370

    Directory or Share Permissions 370

    Synchronizing Database Logins 370

    Objects That Reside Outside the Database. 370

    Log Shipping and Maintaining Consecutive LSNs 370

    Log Shipping and Backup Plans. 371

Database Maintenance, Updates, and the Secondary 371
Applications and Role Changes 372
SQL Server Functionality vs. Custom Log Shipping 372
Configuring Log Shipping 373
Create the Backup Share(s) 373
SQL Server Built-in Functionality 386
Custom Log Shipping 403
Postconfiguration Tasks 403
Administering Log Shipping 404
Monitoring Log Shipping 404
Modifying Log Shipping 408
Changing the Monitor Server 408
Disabling Log Shipping 410
Removing Log Shipping 412
Adding Another Secondary to the Log Shipping Plan 418
Manually Killing Database Connections 420
Performing a Role Change 421
Summary 423

█**CHAPTER 11**   **Database Mirroring** 425

How Database Mirroring Works 425
Transaction Safety 426
Mirroring State 426
Database Mirroring Modes 427
Best Uses for Database Mirroring 430
Disaster Recovery and High Availability 430
Migration to New Hardware 430
Reporting 430
Database Mirroring Considerations 430
High Performance Mode vs. High Safety Mode 430
Edition and Version Configuration 431
Location of the Principal, Mirror, and Witness 431
Mirror Database Recovery Model 432
Database Restoration and Configuration on the Mirror 432
Server Sizing 432
Disk Design and Performance 432
Networks, Domain Connectivity, and Database Mirroring 433
Code Page/Sort Order/Collation 433
Security 433
Distributed Transactions 433
Transaction Size 434
Transaction Logs and Database Mirroring 434

Synchronizing Database Logins 434
Objects that Reside Outside the Database 434
Database Mirroring and Maintaining Consecutive LSNs 434
Database Maintenance, Updates, and the Mirror. 435
Applications and Database Mirroring Failover 435
Configuring Database Mirroring 436
Step 1: Back Up and Restore the Database 436
Step 2: Set Up Database Mirroring 436
Step 3: Configure Network Load Balancing or a DNS Alias
(Optional). 454
Administering Database Mirroring 454
Monitoring Database Mirroring. 454
Controlling Database Mirroring. 470
Altering the Database Mirroring Configuration 472
Removing Database Mirroring 473
Failing Over from the Principal to the Mirror. 475
Full-Text Indexes 477
Redirecting Clients to the Mirror 477
Summary 478

■CHAPTER 12   **Replication**. 479

How Replication Works 479
Snapshot Replication. 480
Merge Replication 481
Transactional Replication 482
Understanding the Replication Agents. 485
Replication Considerations 486
The Application 487
Component Location, Network Latency, and Network Speed. 487
Disk Performance and Sizing 488
Making Replication Highly Available 488
SQL Server Agent and Replication. 488
Database Schema 488
Push or Pull Subscriptions 491
Security. 491
Configuring Replication 492
Step 1: Configuring the Distributor 492
Step 2: Configuring the Publication 506
Step 3: Subscribing to the Publication. 516
Administering Replication 524
Backing Up Databases Involved with Replication. 524
Monitoring Replication. 525
Summary 528

█CHAPTER 13   **Making Your Data Available** 529

The Application 529
    Making Third-Party Applications Available 530
    Making Custom Applications Available 530
    Getting In on the Ground Floor 532
Partitioning Your Data 533
    Creating Objects on a Specific Filegroup 533
    Partitioning Databases and Indexes with Transact-SQL 534
    Partitioned Views 536
    Data Dependent Routing 538
Database Snapshots 540
    Creating a Database Snapshot 543
    Database Snapshot Administration 544
Using Multiple Read-Only Databases 549
Summary 550

PART 3 ████ Administration for High Availability

█CHAPTER 14   **Designing High Availability Solutions** 553

What High Availability Technology Should You Use? 553
Comparing the SQL Server High Availability Technologies 554
    Failover Clustering vs. Other Technologies 556
    Log Shipping vs. Other Technologies 558
    Database Mirroring vs. Other Technologies 558
    Replication vs. Other Technologies 559
Combining the SQL Server High Availability Technologies 560
    Failover Clustering with Other Technologies 560
    Log Shipping with Other Technologies 563
    Database Mirroring with Other Technologies 565
    Replication with Other Technologies 566
Designing Your Solution 566
    Performance 566
    Sizing Processor and Memory and Purchasing Servers 567
    Sizing, Purchasing, and Designing Disk Subsystems 569
    Keywords 571
    How Features and Functionality Affect Deployment 571
    Designing with Disaster Recovery in Mind 571
Example Solution for an Existing Environment 572

Example Solution for a New Deployment 573
    First Things First 573
    Requirements.. 573
    The Architecture... 574
    Planning and Deployment 574
    Administration 575
Example Solution for Disk Configuration for a Failover Cluster............ 576
    Requirements.. 576
    Planning and Deployment 577
Summary 578

CHAPTER 15   **24x7 Database Administration** 579

Testing and Change Management...................................... 579
Installing and Configuring SQL Server................................. 579
    Installing SQL Server....................................... 579
    Configuring SQL Server Instances 584
    Setting Memory Values...................................... 587
    Configuring Databases 588
SQL Server Security... 594
    Securing the Instance 594
    Securing the Application and Databases........................ 602
    Dedicated Administrator Connection 603
Monitoring SQL Server 604
    What Should You Monitor?................................... 604
    Using a Monitoring Application to Monitor SQL Server 612
    Using Performance Monitor to Monitor SQL Server 613
    Using SQL Server Dynamic Management Views to
        Monitor SQL Server 617
    Getting Notified of Problems................................. 618
Attaching and Detaching Databases 638
    Detaching a Database via SQL Server Management Studio 640
    Attaching a Database via SQL Server Management Studio........... 641
Using SSIS to Transfer Logins and Objects............................. 645
Abstracting a Name Change During a Server Switch...................... 658
    Using Network Load Balancing 658
    Using a DNS Alias to Abstract a Server Name Change 670
Summary 672

CHAPTER 16   **24x7 Database Maintenance** 673

Performing Database Maintenance 673
    Creating SQL Server Agent Jobs 673
    Performing Routine Maintenance.............................. 686

Performing Server and Instance Maintenance 690
    Handling Physical Disk Fragmentation 690
    Performing Maintenance to the Server Itself 690
    Disabling Automatic Windows Updates. 691
    Applying a SQL Server 2005 Service Pack 692
Importing and Exporting Data. 703
    Using bcp to Import and Export Data. 703
    Using SSIS to Import and Export Data 704
Summary 712

CHAPTER 17   Disaster Recovery 713

Expect the Unexpected 713
Preparing for Disaster Recovery. 713
    Data Loss 714
    Plan in Advance 714
    Data Center Access 715
    Have More Than One Plan 715
    Documentation and the Run Book 715
    Staffing and Chain of Command 718
    Supplies and Contingencies 719
    Test the Disaster Recovery Plans. 720
    Check Your Support Contract 720
When Disaster Strikes 721
    Assessing the Situation. 721
    Contacting Support 721
    Implementing the Plan 721
    Maintaining Your Cool 722
    Shadowing and Documenting. 722
When the Dust Settles. 722
SQL Server Disaster Recovery Features 723
Summary 724

INDEX 725

Foreword

My name is Mark Souza and I am a director of program management for the SQL Server product team in Redmond, Washington. I manage the external facing customer and partner programs. These teams spend three weeks a month away from our Redmond labs, working with our customers on the most mission-critical, highly scalable SQL Server systems all over the world. For example, we have assisted many mainframe migrations for systems such as insurance claims processing and airline reservations to be successfully deployed on Microsoft SQL Server, and guided multiple high-end trading systems that can scale to more than 100,000 database transactions per second. If these types of systems go down for even a short period of time, it could be front-page news. It is critical that all these customers learn how to design, build, and deploy highly available systems.

Microsoft SQL Server 2005 has incorporated significant enhancements to help customers do just that. There are many complementary technologies to help, such as replication, log shipping, failover clustering, and now database mirroring. There are also many engine-based features such as online indexing, online restore, and partitioning that provide the foundation of day-to-day maintenance online.

In all of the years I have been working with customers, one of the silliest questions I have ever asked them is "What would you like your availability of your application to be?" The answer is always the same: "I would like it up 100% of the time!" That is the way I would answer the question if asked of me. Of course when they realize the cost and complexities of coming close to this goal—never mind the mean time to failure of hardware, the probability of a software bug, the stringent change control process required, and the requirement for the perfectly written application—their requirement for uptime decreases slightly from the desired 100%.

I have known Allan Hirt for nearly ten years. I used to work with him when he worked for Microsoft. Allan was a SQL Server consultant in the field working with customers. Even back then Allan was "the HA guy." He not only enjoyed working with customers directly, but also loved spending time with the developers, discussing and writing about high availability. I also hire Allan today to work side by side with my team on several of our high-end engagements. I can recommend this book not only because Allan knows a lot about SQL Server and high availability but the chapters were reviewed by and had input from members of the SQL Server development team and the internal groups managing the SQL Server implementations used by Microsoft.

I always encourage all of my high-end customers who need 24x7 systems to not only learn as much as they possibly can about high availability in general, but also about any products and service offerings available. Knowledge of the tools, features, and processes will help ensure your high availability success. Don't expect technology and technology alone to provide high availability for you. That is the main reason I recommend reading this book. I won't promise you that after reading the book you'll have all the relevant experience you need, but I do guarantee you that the knowledge you do gain will create a solid foundation for you to build high availability systems using Microsoft SQL Server technology.

Mark Souza

Director of Program Management for Customer and ISV Programs,
Microsoft SQL Server Product Team

About the Author

ALLAN HIRT has been working with SQL Server longer than he'd care to admit. His first exposure was while working as an intern at SQL Solutions before it was purchased by Sybase. Since then his journey has led him to work for various companies over the years (including a stint at Microsoft), and he has been consulting directly for clients for nearly ten years. He has worked with clients of all sizes, from a few people all the way up to enterprise-class organizations with a multinational presence. He has authored many popular documents over the years, including the SQL Server 2000 and SQL Server 2005 failover clustering white papers for Microsoft, some articles for *SQL Server Magazine,* and parts of the SQL Server 2000 Resource Kit. He is the primary author of the book *Microsoft SQL Server 2000 High Availability* (Microsoft Press, 2003). He has also delivered training (including custom courses) on various SQL Server topics and has been a frequent speaker at SQL Server user groups, webcasts, podcasts, and conferences such as Tech Ed and SQL PASS.

About the Technical Reviewer

 **VIDYA VRAT AGARWAL** is a Microsoft .NET purist and an MCPD, MCTS, MCT, MCSD.NET, MCAD.NET, and MCSD. He works with Lionbridge Technologies Inc. (NASDAQ: LIOX) and his business card reads Subject Matter Expert (SME). He is also a lifetime member of the Computer Society of India (CSI). He started working on Microsoft .NET with its beta release. He has been involved in software development, evangelism, consulting, corporate training, and T3 programs on Microsoft .NET for various employers and corporate clients.

He lives with his beloved wife, Rupali, and lovely daughter, Vamika ("Pearly"). He believes that nothing will turn into a reality without them. He is the follower of the concept "no pain, no gain" and believes that his wife is his greatest strength. He is a bibliophile. When he is not working on technical stuff he likes to play with his one-and-half-year-old daughter and also likes reading spiritual and occult science books. He blogs at http://dotnetpassion.blogspot.com.

Acknowledgments

First and foremost, I'd like to thank Apress and everyone I worked with: Laura Esterman, James Huddleston, Kylie Johnston, Dominic Shakeshaft, Jennifer Whipple, and Kim Wimpsett. I appreciate their seemingly never-ending patience with me and hope they are willing to work with me again on a revision of this book for the next version of SQL Server in a few years. I think sometimes they wanted to kill me (especially when I blew through deadlines), but all of the struggles were worth it in the end. I promise if I get another opportunity I'll make a realistic schedule! They worked very hard with me on this book, and I truly do appreciate their contributions.

Next I'd like to thank all of my reviewers. Without them, you also wouldn't see the text as it appears. I like to think I feel the pulse of what people want based on what I've heard, seen, and experienced over the years, but you don't know until people give you honest feedback. And boy was the feedback honest. I apologize in advance if I forgot anyone in this list, but here goes: Bob Beauchemin, Aftab Chopra, Larry Clark, Trevor Dwyer, Kevin Farlee, James Herring, Wolfgang Jekel, Leon Krancher, Chong Lee, Rod Le Quesne, Ross LoForte, Sean McCown, Sanjay Mishra, Max Myrick, Marius Pederson, Mark Pohto, Christopher Smith, Eric Stoever, and Jens Sussmeyer.

A special heartfelt thank-you goes out to Mark Souza, who graciously agreed to write the forward to this book. I consider him a friend and was pleasantly surprised when he agreed to do it. I've known Mark since my days at Microsoft and appreciate him taking some time away from his busy schedule to do it. There are very few people as intimate with SQL Server as Mark is. A little tidbit about Mark: his first manager at Microsoft was also my first manager when I worked at Microsoft. It's a small world.

Finally, I'd like to thank my friends, family, and bandmates (did I also forget to mention in all of this madness I am a musician with a fairly active rehearsal and gigging schedule, too?) for putting up with me during this year-long project. I've been largely unavailable at times, didn't answer the phone, dropped from sight . . . you name it. Now that the book is done, I can get back to more of a "normal" life and finish a few projects I've put on the back burner, such as the big band album I've been threatening to write, arrange, and record for 15 years. It'll be nice not to have to write text for a while. Writing music will be a nice change of pace.

Preface

The journey leading to this book started after writing *Microsoft SQL Server 2000 High Availability* (Microsoft Press, 2003). With that original book, I was the primary author and the coauthors wrote a smaller percentage of it. The problem was that not only was I managing the schedule for the book and getting them to write, but when I got their writing, I had to make it sound like the rest of the book written by me. So I was managing a ton of things concurrently, making for a very draining process by the time it was done.

That process also led to me making some compromises to get the book out the door. While I know a lot of people felt it was very good, the perfectionist in me knew I could do better. Soon after it hit the shelves, some of what was written had changed due to some late findings, and I could never update that text to revise that edition. At that point, I wasn't sure I wanted to even touch it because it had been a hard process, and I swore that I'd never write a book again. Since you are reading this, I clearly lied to myself. However, I did take a long hiatus from a lot of things: writing, speaking, webcasts—you name it. I was fried on all things SQL Server high availability.

Inevitably I started to get the itch to get out there again—maybe do some writing and some speaking. The first major thing I attempted was the "SQL Server 2005 Failover Clustering" white paper for Microsoft, which was published in late summer 2006. As I was writing the white paper I thought more and more about doing the updated version of the high availability book, but I still was not sure it was something I wanted to tackle. I wasn't even sure anyone would be interested in it, let alone want to publish it. Of course, if I did it, I wanted to right the wrongs of the previous book. A good example is that I was summarily skewered on the replication chapter (I hope I redeem myself this time around). That was my first lesson in humility: reading online reviews. People may like the rest of it, but they'll latch onto the part they do not like and you have to get over it.

In early 2006, I developed a rough outline of content and started to do some polling of people to see if it resonated with them and if what I wanted to do was on target. I made the decision that this project, should it go forward, would be a solo effort; it would succeed or fail by my own proverbial keyboard. I knew this version would be as big as, if not bigger than, the last version. I was correct. However, I was unwilling to compromise my vision of the book just to do it. I wanted to ensure that everything got the proper coverage and that the text and content had a more logical flow. There were things I wanted to say that I couldn't last time around and had to find a publisher that was willing to get on board with this lunacy. Ironically, what put me over the edge to really push to find a publisher was visiting client sites and finding the old book sitting on their bookshelves. Once they figured out I was the guy who wrote the book they had sitting there (and maybe even had me sign it; note: I am not a rock star), I realized that I let those negative reviews taint my view of the book. People did seem to like it.

I have to credit a friend of mine, Greg Moss, for pointing me in the direction of Apress, which obviously signed up for this mishegas. He made the suggestion, I sent an e-mail to Apress, and the process started from there. Their concern was more around the timeline and whether I could deliver this much content on the schedule I had put forth.

I missed nearly every deadline that was set. Originally the book was supposed to be done in late 2006, which then slipped to spring 2007. The writing was finally finished in May 2007, with editing and proofing completed in early June.

You try to think of all of the things that could impact your ability to meet a schedule, but I really had someone who wasn't in my corner. Just as I was getting started on the book, I found out I had a kidney stone. That set me back a little bit. Then I was assigned to a project that consumed many, many hours beyond the normal workday, and that ate into my writing time. Trust me when I tell you that it's hard to write in a hotel room at 10 p.m. when you are mentally exhausted. I could have written something, but it would have been junk, and I would not want to be associated with a paperweight that killed trees for no reason. Then there was also a month where my home Internet connection was down. The pièce de résistance sums up my frustrations in getting this book done: on a flight home from Chicago to Boston in the early fall of 2006, the passenger in front of me leaned his seat back and broke my laptop screen. I was working on the book at the time. I was without my primary laptop for about a month, which slowed down the process. Was someone trying to tell me I shouldn't have attempted to write the book? Add to all of this that I needed to get some sleep and try to have a semblance of a life. It was a difficult year from start to finish. It has certainly been a long road to get to this point, but I am really proud of the work you are holding in your hands.

I hope you enjoy this book as much as I enjoyed putting it together for you. Those who know me say they can hear my "voice" throughout the book, and that means I've achieved my ultimate goal. I did not want to write a stuffy computer book; I wanted you to smile, maybe laugh, but definitely think. I even expect you to probably disagree with me on some things. Had I done a typical features-function book, it would be useless in my opinion. You need the how-to, but you also need the why. I hope I achieved the balance.

Happy reading!

Downloading the Code

All of the examples in this book can be found at both the Source Code/Download section of the Apress web site (http://www.apress.com/book/download.html) and at my new web site (http://www.sqlha.com).

Contacting the Author

To contact me with any questions, comments, suggestions for future versions of the book, and so on, use the contact form at http://www.sqlha.com or e-mail me directly at sqlhabook@sqlha.com.

PART 1
■ ■ ■
The Building Blocks of High Availability

Anyone putting servers into a production capacity expects them to be available. When your implementations become mission critical, you need what is known as *high availability*. Achieving high availability for any solution is ultimately the combination of people, processes, and technology. The first part of this book introduces high availability, how to achieve it, and how to determine your high availability requirements. This part does not contain a lot of technology-specific information—that is what the rest of the book covers—but provides the conceptual foundation to design, implement, and manage highly available solutions that use SQL Server 2005 as the back end.

CHAPTER 1

■ ■ ■

The Business of Availability

We live in a connected world that is seemingly *on*—or more accurately, *online*—24 hours a day, seven days a week (otherwise known as *24x7*). Whether you are checking e-mail on your cellular phone, sitting in a coffee shop browsing the Internet, or doing some shopping via a wireless connection, the need and desire to access vast amounts of information has never been greater in any other point in modern history. The world is literally a click away.

However, this demand for information anywhere at any time means that somewhere in the world a set of servers must be up and running 24x7 to support access to data. End users may take it for granted that they will always be able to access information; but you know that achieving around-the-clock availability for systems is by no means a trivial task. The question ultimately arises—when the system goes down, what is the end result? Is it lost revenue? The possibility of a lost life? Something else? Unfortunately, there is always a cost associated with downtime, and some costs have more dire consequences than others.

World events such as the terrorist attacks on the U.S. Pentagon and the World Trade Center in New York, Hurricane Katrina in New Orleans, and the tsunami in Asia are excellent indicators of how devastating catastrophic events can be. No amount of preparation could have prevented these tragedies, but they demonstrate that planning for the worst-case scenario is absolutely necessary, and that minutes versus days and weeks makes a difference on many levels—economic, social, technological, and financial.

The ripple effect of September 11, 2001 (despite the human tragedy, which will never be erased), could have been much worse since it struck so many businesses. Many of those businesses that were affected were in the financial industry or linked to it and could have disrupted the entire financial industry on a global basis for an extended period of time. Many of the companies maintained contingency plans with facilities elsewhere, which ultimately allowed business to get back to relative normal sooner rather than later; otherwise, that ripple effect would have been crippling and may have taken quite some time to recover from. This is also known as *business continuity*, which is what you want for your business: to go on. Aside from a tragic event like 9/11, a single disk failure in one server at your company could cause downtime that could cause a catastrophic impact on your business.

If you think business continuity is just an IT problem, it is not. There are so many other aspects to a normal routine being able to continue after a disaster. Some industries mandate that there are plans in place, such as the health-care industry. Laws sometimes require continuity. Some examples can be found at `http://www.gartner.com/DisplayDocument?doc_cd=128123`. At some point, with no cash flow and no way to get back in business, businesses fail and go bankrupt.

Some people naïvely assume that achieving availability is only a technology problem. It is as "simple" as spending some fixed amount of money, acquiring hardware, setting it up in a data center, hooking up some disks, and letting it run, right? Wrong! If it was that easy, you would not be reading this book. Availability is *business*-driven, not technology-driven, since there is always an economic reason why you actually need to achieve some form of availability. Technology only represents the physical aspect, or implementation, of the availability chain.

How you achieve availability is multidimensional: are you isolating against a "local" failure, or a more global problem? A local failure—when a problem occurs in your data center—is where *high availability* comes into play. For example, if a memory chip goes bad in one of your primary database servers, having hardware that supports the ability to replace it on the fly would be a way to mitigate a local failure and possibly maintain full availability (with reduced performance, of course) of the database system to the application or applications it is serving.

If the primary data center burns down, or the failure is less isolated, it becomes *disaster recovery*. While disaster recovery is closely related and tied to high availability, it is a completely different exercise to plan and account for. Another way to think about high availability versus disaster recovery is that high availability tends to be based on some sort of measure during what you consider "normal" business, whereas disaster recovery is measured on something "abnormal." Disaster recovery is discussed in more detail in Chapter 17.

The easiest way to think of both high availability and disaster recovery is to equate them to insurance policies; if you never have a problem, they will not be invoked. Upper management may even complain that money was wasted. That makes sense if you think about it; it is hard to quantify the pain if you are not actually feeling it, but it only takes one outage to convert the nonbelievers to the religion of availability.

Playing the what-if game may seem pointless to some, but the reality is that it is a matter of *when* you will have a problem, not *if*; so if you put the right mix of people, processes, and technology into place, the impact felt should be minimal and the end result should be one where you will not suffer much.

The Building Blocks of Availability

Even with technology in the mix, availability first and foremost stems from people and processes. This may be the last thing most of you want to see taking up space so early on in a technology book, but the fact remains that it is the truth. Without people, you cannot plan, implement, and manage; without processes, things will fail faster than the blink of an eye. Chaos and flying by the seat of your proverbial pants is a surefire way to lower your availability, not increase it. Investing in both people and processes should be fundamental to any organization actually wanting to attain high availability, not one that just pays it lip service.

People

It is not an exaggeration to say that without good people, nothing happens—or more accurately, nothing happens right. Giving an unqualified or incompetent person a job is not the way to hire your staff. Having the right people in the right place with the right experience can potentially mean the difference between minutes and days of downtime.

I am often asked if a person who has the certification of Microsoft Certified IT Professional: Database Administrator, MCSE, or MCDBA is the best candidate. Like many things in life, it all depends. If someone with the relevant experience has the certification, he most likely went through the process to make himself more marketable (since certification is perceived as showing you know what you are doing) or to further validate and make official what it is he does on a day-to-day basis. The certification may mean little to him, other than maybe getting him a higher base salary because someone else values it.

If someone who has just graduated from college and has never used SQL Server before goes through Get Your Cert Fast Inc.'s cram course on what to study, or just attends a few training classes, he or she is by no means the best candidate for the job. Nothing can substitute for actual real-world experience in designing, planning, implementing, managing, monitoring, and maintaining systems. Certifications are valid; but never make your staffing decisions based on that alone. Putting your production environment in the hands of the Microsoft Certified IT Professional: Database Administrator with no experience is akin to playing Russian roulette: you may hit the empty chamber and the person will work out, or you may get the loaded chamber where his or her inexperience may hurt you. How much risk can you assume?

Ideally, the best candidates will ultimately have that perfect mix of book learning, relevant experience (maybe not in the number of years, but in the actual experience they have gained), and experience working with others who have mentored them and helped them absorb traits such as strong communication skills, as well as the elusive ability to troubleshoot and prioritize, all while reacting to any emergency thrown their way.

More relevant to the topic at hand, do you want some neophyte who has never faced adversity or true pressure running your disaster-recovery procedures? Keep in mind that there is a different mindset of just maintaining your servers on a day-to-day basis than there is with knowing that you need to have business continuity. In more cases than not, it is always better to hire a candidate who has 12 years of relevant experience with no certification who knows the difference, and then hire your certified junior person and have him or her soak up the experience of the veteran. There is nothing worse than having a young hotshot who thinks he or she knows it all, because that brazen overconfidence based on some minor experience or book knowledge can be a dangerous thing.

You are looking to run a marathon, not finish the race winded. Both types of workers have a place in your organization. But many companies do not want highly paid and experienced senior-level administrators doing day-to-day work when they can get someone at a third of the cost. You have to realize what end of the spectrum the people you are hiring are on and where they will fit into your organization. To maintain availability, you need local expertise you trust, and quite frankly, good DBAs are not easy to come by.

The bottom line: hire quality people and your chance for success goes up exponentially. The same applies to network administrators, storage engineers, and anyone else you may hire.

Training

Training represents a way for companies and people to grow their skills in a formalized environment. Unfortunately, many implementations of the corporate training program leave a sour taste for most of the users and nonusers of the system put in place. Most companies are supposed to allow their employees a yearly allotment of training and development, but all too often the employees who most need the training are never able to attend because they are busy running the business. It is very rare to encounter a company enlightened enough to hire the "extra" worker necessary to allow the senior technologists running the day-to-day IT infrastructure to train others on the system in case they're unavailable, let alone learn something new.

Putting such an infrastructure in place allows these employees to not only attend classes and conferences, but to also come back and present what they have learned. Staffing levels need to be designed around support for continuing education commitments. Ultimately, the business needs to ask itself a simple question: what is the cost to the business in the future if that DBA's skills lapse? It is a double-edged sword.

In a mission-critical environment with extremely high availability requirements, it is absolutely crucial that everyone involved with managing the systems stays up-to-date with their skill sets. If at all possible, they should stay ahead of the curve and be allowed to look at beta releases of software. This requires a serious commitment on the part of the employer, but one that should pay great dividends.

What I often see happen is that individuals who work a zillion hours per week and barely have time for family and friends, let alone training, spend their own time on learning it. This is a slippery slope because then the business can "expect" that it is acceptable. It is not. Training should occur on the clock. Burning your employees out and destroying any hope of a work/life balance lowers morale and, ultimately, retention rates. Training should always be a positive benefit for your employees and a reward (maybe a week out of the office for a change of scenery) for all the hard work they put in day in and day out.

If sending employees out to training or conferences is not a possibility, remember that training can also come in other forms. Mentoring and activities such as "brown bag" lunches to share knowledge and experiences can go a long way. Many software companies offer on-demand training over the Internet. For a junior employee, there is no better learning than on-the-job with mentoring. Formal training has its place, but you do not learn how to manage a 24x7 environment by sitting in a classroom. It is always an eye-opening experience the first time you are involved in a server-down situation; and for junior employees to be involved in the recovery process or to observe it will only further prepare them to be able to do their jobs.

Another method of training that works well is to have peers and senior-level technologists create lab exercises for the more junior employees. This requires having some dedicated hardware. For example, set up a specific solution (such as a cluster), and then break it on purpose. Have the trainees then go through the process of troubleshooting and see whether they can fix the issue, find all the issues, and see how long it takes. These are the types of skills that could prove crucial in an outage.

Not all things that are educational in a corporate environment need to be on a one-to-one or small-group basis. For example, one of the things you will need to do is hold "fire drills" where you test your failure scenarios. Going through the drill, you learn quite a bit about not only what is possibly broken in the process and needs to be fixed, but whether people truly know their roles and whether everyone is communicating as expected. The business needs to learn and grow as well.

Note Do not forget to develop the soft skills of your employees. Maintaining their technical skills is ultimately important and critical for the tasks at hand, but knowing how to communicate is an equally important skill to have. In a disaster recovery situation, cooler heads will prevail; and if there is a breakdown of command and communication, you will only lengthen your availability outage.

Processes

Along with having the right people, there is another key piece to the puzzle: process. Process is something many IT workers have acquired a hatred for over their years in IT. Ironically, the ones who curse and fight it at every step have the most to gain from it. If you delve into the issues around the "annoyance" of processes, more often than not it is not the actual processes themselves, but their delivery.

Consider the following questions:

- Was the underlying purpose for the process clearly explained?

- Was the purpose presented in a way that made it clear and compelling?

- When the process was created, was I consulted for input? And was my input included in the final process when relevant?

- Are there obvious exceptions to the process that the process left "open" and did not attempt to solve?

- Are there steps of the process that ultimately hurt the business from the point of view of the members of my team?

When these types of surrounding concerns are properly addressed, processes can become much more of a friend than an enemy. These processes can help by allowing workers to find out how other workers resolved a problem. This type of information can prove critical in an outage where the problem has been seen before. Reinventing the wheel is not something you ever want to do.

The secret to a successful set of implemented policies is enabling the proper communication to ensure the process works for everyone. There is nothing more damaging to a company than poorly defined or thought out (or nonexistent) processes that are ignored or used in such an inconsistent way that they are ineffective. That definitely leads to outages, chaos, and confusion. In a worst-case scenario, management may react in a way that seems contrary to what is needed, which may lead to critical failures. Management may make this type of decision based on *published* policies versus what is actually *practiced*. The two should stay in sync. Unfortunately, the policies that are actually practiced may have been developed as a result of resistance to the published policies, or they may have evolved and adapted to the working conditions through necessity (not unlike Darwin's theory!).

Even the most skilled and qualified of workers cannot combat processes that are that horribly broken. I have no hard statistics to back up my claim. I am only drawing upon my experiences and those of others I know. It is a pattern I have seen over and over again in my travels and experiences in all sorts of environments and in different roles. The size of the company or IT department does not matter, but it is safe to say that the larger the environment, the more glaring and magnified the problems.

The three biggest types of process breakdown seem to occur around communication, change management, and testing.

Communication

Arguably the No. 1 factor that contributes to downtime is communication, or lack thereof. While this is obviously in part a people problem and could be discussed in that light, it is also related to process and how things work in your environment. Communication is the central hub of a well-oiled organization. Poor communication inhibits availability and creates barriers to success.

The communication issue is multilayered and complex to deal with if there are problems within your organization. Why? There is communication within a specific team, and then there is communication with other groups, which can even be extended to include contact with customers or end users. Both types of communication are crucial, especially when you are in a 24x7 environment.

Intergroup Communication

For better or for worse, most environments (mostly larger ones) have a clear division of powers in an IT organization. This has some obvious benefits, such as concentrating areas of expertise within a single group instead of having it dispersed; but in some cases it can complicate matters. For example, many companies have separate groups of network administrators, system administrators, and storage administrators, in addition to a complement of DBAs and other types of administrators. These groups are usually started with the best of intentions to serve a specific need since it is easier to grow domain expertise with a focused group of individuals. Where it breaks down is when some things actually need to get done and some form of compromise must be achieved. Each group may have its own work style, policies, procedures, standards, and other preferences that will conflict with another group's. In the end, too many hands in the pot can make something that should be simple become something that takes an act of Congress or Parliament to approve due to partisan posturing where everyone stands their ground and no one is willing to compromise. Everyone needs to work together as a team, not as little fiefdoms trying to one-up each other. For example, if you have different groups (storage, backup operators, DBAs, and possibly even a few others) involved in the backup (and eventual restore) process, it is unrealistic and time-consuming if everyone points to the DBAs as being the only group responsible for restoring the backup in the event of a problem. The reality is that the DBAs are absolutely necessary, but the central IT group owns the network-based backup solution backing up the SQL Server databases, and the backup operators have already moved the archive tape offsite. How can the fingers point to the DBAs as the problem if it is taking hours, since it will take quite a few other groups to do their jobs before the DBA can even think about restoring the database?

If you cannot work together as a team under normal circumstances, how can you expect to do it in a server-down situation? When the dust settles, everyone has to play by the same set of rules as determined by your organization, and having standards that everyone must adhere to (despite the technology being different) should put everyone in their respective places. You are all managing the same goal. It stands to reason that problems are only magnified when the pressure is on, and most likely you will experience a lot of confusion and pain. Cross-group communication strategies that work need to be devised and implemented.

Intragroup Communication

Even within a group, such as the DBAs or the network administrators, there may be no unity of purpose. This usually occurs due to assumptions, poor documentation, or lack of vision in the group as to its overall goals and deliverables. There is no way a single group can be effective if there are a million different agendas going on and people not communicating properly with one another. If the DBAs cannot do their job, how can they expect to meet the availability goals before them? A good manager will foster a positive environment where all of the petty, catty behavior is left at the door and everyone has a hand in (and can be rewarded by) the success of the group as a whole.

Individuals are important, but what does it matter if Bob takes care of the backups when Sue is ill? That is what should happen, but often does not. Poor intragroup communication can often lead to the blame game where someone wants to pass the buck ("it was not my responsibility"). That is unacceptable in IT shops small and large. Every individual should be responsible; otherwise, what is the point of hiring them?

Setting End-User Expectations

End-user expectations are viewed in a somewhat different light in Chapter 2, but for this discussion, the purpose is simple: if there is going to be downtime, communicate it to all who need to be "in the know." For example, if you are going to be taking a maintenance window for your servers and this affects, say, an online store where people normally have the ability to shop around the clock, make sure that a friendly message is put up on the web server that says something like the following:

> Thank you for visiting our online store. We are temporarily down for maintenance and will be back up for your shopping pleasure at 04:00 GMT.

This may seem like an obvious thing to do, but it really is not to some. Think of it another way: if you as a consumer go to a web page and get an error, you will try to visit a few more times and at some point move on, right? It is human nature. While that may be fine for you—you found what you want elsewhere—what that means is that the online retailer may have lost a customer, possibly permanently. Lost business is not a good thing. Putting up user-friendly messages lets people know what is going on, that you are still in control, and the situation is being handled. On top of it all, you may retain your customers since you are telling them when they can come back, not unlike a store posting its hours outside the door.

You should also treat your internal business customers the same way you would treat external ones since proper notification allows those affected to make the appropriate plans. If you do not, all of a sudden you may have some manager breathing down your neck because his or her application, database, web server, and so on, was unavailable when he or she needed it. When managers are unhappy, you are unhappy. So if you need to take a system down to apply an update, give business users a heads up with decent lead time so they can plan ahead, and definitely let them know how long the outage will be. I cannot tell you how many times in the past ten years I have been onsite with a customer and suddenly the resource we are accessing is unavailable. Why? Someone rebooted the server and did not let anyone know, or some other similar event happened.

What this all boils down to is providing good customer service whether your customers are sitting in their houses buying widgets, or sitting in a cubicle in your office building trying to do their jobs. From your perspective, the attitude you must have is that what you do as an individual affects much more than yourself; one action you take may affect an undetermined number of people.

Testing

A failure in many environments—and it is glaring in the change management process—is testing. *Testing* is not just testing the application itself, but everything involved in the whole ecosystem that makes up the solution. Arguably, testing the application is most important. For example, I cannot tell you how many times at this point I have heard "So we upgraded from SQL Server 2000 to SQL Server 2005 and we are seeing (insert issue here, most likely related to performance)." I then always ask if they tested the application with SQL Server 2005 before upgrading, to which more often than not the reply is no. "We assumed it would work just fine since the upgrade went smoothly." Sometimes they actually do some testing, but none of it is under actual or simulated production loads, or with data (both in size and makeup) that is representative of production.

The bottom line is that one should never assume that things will "just work" since an oversight can become costly. You do not want to find out that what you thought would be a simple two-week effort based on an assumption will actually be a four-month effort.

Coming from a quality assurance background, I know how important testing is and how much it is impacted by many factors. If your development cycle runs long but the ship date cannot change, what gets squeezed? Most likely it is the testing time, or the amount of coverage within the application that is tested is reduced to get the product out the door. I understand the bottom line, but if the product blows up in production, causing you to spend weeks or months patching it just to get it usable, is it worth it? It not only causes problems with future development projects, but there are most likely large numbers of dissatisfied customers who will change back to the old version of the product or find another vendor because your new offering is unreliable and does not meet their business needs. You cannot afford either of these occurrences. Plan the appropriate amount of time for testing and building quality into the product.

You may not think of it this way, but testing is one of your first weapons for achieving availability. Will things work as advertised or promised? If the application does not work, it could mean downtime due to retooling. Too often, the focus is on testing: what has changed instead of what is important to the business. Focus on ensuring that your application's core deliverables are not affected, instead of trying to test underlying functionality that you may or may not be using. This customer-focused testing will pay off in the long run. To be quite honest, it is not, nor should it be, the IT department's job to first figure this out. By then, it is too late. IT most likely does not know much, if anything, about the application itself yet is tasked with supporting it. This means that if you are deploying your back end with certain technology, it is imperative at the testing stages to test to see whether the application will work with the technology in question and what will happen should a disaster strike. This also means the IT staff and the application developers and support staff must be in contact from the beginning. With third-party applications, you may not have the ability to do as much extensive testing and customization as you would with your own applications. This does not absolve you from testing them properly in your target environment.

For example, if you are deploying mirroring at the database level (a feature of SQL Server 2005 that will be discussed in Chapter 11), what happens in the failure of the primary server and the switch to the mirror? Not only will you learn about application behavior and how you may need to change the application to deal with the server change, but administrators or DBAs can also test their processes to ensure they work.

Change Management

Change management is the process where updates to applications, such as schema changes, or fixes, such as service packs, are applied in a way that causes minimal or no interruption in service to the business and/or end users. Production should never be the first place you roll out a change. Very few companies have an operationally mature change management process—if there is even a change management process at all. Change management is never important to a company until it has an outage and realizes that it could have been prevented with a proper change management process. The excuses are always plentiful (and sometimes entertaining):

"It worked on my machine."

"We do not have the budget for test or staging servers, so we just apply changes directly to production and hope for the best."

"We assumed it would just work since the patch came from our vendor who we trust."

Do any of these apply to you now? If so, how many of these excuses have you encountered after an update fails in production? I would venture to guess that most of you have heard excuses at some point in your career. This happens every day somewhere in IT Land. And outages due to updates to servers and applications, for the most part, can be prevented. The lack of change management is a gap in preparation for availability and can cause you tremendous grief and aggravation. Change management needs to be a way of life.

Note To assist you in change management and other aspects of your organization, there are existing frameworks you can refer to. The most well-known is called Information Technology Infrastructure Library (ITIL). Microsoft has a few subsets of ITIL—the Microsoft Operations Framework (MOF), `http://www.microsoft.com/technet/itsolutions/cits/mo/mof/default.mspx`, which is geared toward IT professionals, and the Microsoft Solutions Framework (MSF), `http://www.microsoft.com/technet/itsolutions/msf/default.mspx`, which is geared more toward development. Both are similar and are meant to be a set of best practices to guide you in continually managing your environments, as change never stops.

Set Up Multiple Environments

One of the key things that you must do to ensure that you have a successful change management process is to establish other environments, in addition to production that will create separation and, in certain cases, redundancy. Those environments are development, testing, and staging.

Development and testing are pretty self-explanatory, but are often not implemented in an optimal way. In a best-case scenario, the development and testing environments will be isolated from one another. Some companies may implement solutions such as virtual machines and allow each developer to have his or her own environment, but all changes are rolled up centrally. All change processes and technologies deployed in development and testing should prove out what will eventually be performed in production. What you have in development and production in terms of environments should in some way reasonably resemble what production will look like. How can you expect to be successful if what you are developing in no way, shape, or form looks or acts like the end target? For example, if the intent is to have your target application work on a clustered system, you would simulate a cluster (or have a real one) in your development and testing environments. Developing for clusters is similar, yet different, than developing for a stand-alone server. Never assume it is someone else's problem.

Depending on your solution in production, having a facsimile in development, testing, and/or staging could be an expensive proposition. In most places I travel, development usually does not get this setup. It is unfortunate that the company does not see that failing to invest early leads to problems during implementation. For example, in development, the solution and all of its components are configured only on one server. In production, they will be spread out over multiple servers: a web server, an application server, a middleware server, and a database server. When the solution is deployed, much to the shock of no one, the installation fails because the solution is designed to work as a one-box solution only, without taking into account the complexity of decoupling all of the components. I know I have seen this in action, have you?

Staging is the ultimate key to IT success. This is usually an environment that is an almost, if not exact, copy of your production that no one but IT uses. This is the last place where any changes can be tested before rolling them out in production. I understand that most companies can barely afford what it takes to have one copy of production for high availability or disaster recovery, let alone more. But how many times have you seen where a production environment needs to be rolled back to a previous state because no testing of a fix has been done anywhere else?

If you have a staging environment, in the event that your production hardware fails, and assuming that clients can be redirected to this other environment and data is somehow synchronized, it could possibly be used for some sort of short-term disaster scenario (although this is discouraged; you should have a proper disaster recovery solution). This is an example of how investing in a staging environment can be viewed as more than just some servers that are sitting there and have no other purpose than to test changes that may only happen twice a year.

Beyond rolling out application-based changes, a staging environment is most important for proving out operating-system and application-specific patches such as hotfixes and service packs (see Chapter 16). Take the example of a failover cluster, which is a specific implementation both at the hardware and software levels. Rolling out patches to such an environment is not necessarily the same as doing it to a stand-alone server and may have its own gotchas associated with it. Applied improperly, you are looking at downtime, and at worst, full system recovery in certain cases. Is that something you want to do for the first time in production? Once again I will say this: buying systems is not cheap. But how much is your uptime worth to you?

Implementing Change Management

Change management is hard to do if you have never done it before. It requires quite a bit of discipline. Whatever you employ for change management *must* be flexible enough to handle emergency situations where things need to get done immediately. I have seen where change management can also get in the way during server-down situations, while people are waiting for upper management to sign off on something. This is a simple equation:

$$\text{Minutes going by} = \text{downtime} = \text{consequences}$$

Implementing basic change has four main aspects:

- Locking down the production environment so that changes can't be made or can't be made without proper approval

- Creating an approval process for changes that includes test sign-off for those changes

- Creating a test process that provides the business confidence that testing reasonably covers what is done in production

- Creating a process to track proposed changes and their status, as well as their results, in terms of success or needed improvements over time

Hopefully the DBA is involved with all aspects of the database implementation, from the application on up through the implementation plans at an early stage in the process. If not, it is a change management problem waiting to happen since the DBA will have no clue how things work or why things are being done the way they are and will likely have to question changes for the wrong reasons.

Most environments will have one group of DBAs for development and testing and another for staging and production. The information flow needs to be uninhibited between the two groups and, arguably, DBAs should be rotated so that they are always kept fresh and have the opportunity to see all aspects of the business.

Remember that changes to the servers and components under SQL Server—from development up through production—impact the availability of your SQL Servers.

Here are some best practices for change management as they relate to highly available database environments:

- Make backups of all databases (including the SQL Server system databases) prior to attempting any change. You may need them if the application of the change or update fails and you need to revert to a previous state.

- Make backups of all databases (including the SQL Server system databases) after a successful update. These will be your new baseline full backups of the databases.

- Change management should be based on forms filled out by the appropriate parties—either electronic or paper-based. The form should at a minimum include what the change is, why it needs to be done, who will be performing the task, the steps to execute the change, and what the plan is if something goes wrong; and it should have places for signatures (real or electronic) of people empowered to approve the change. This provides accountability for all involved and a way to look back if something goes wrong later so you can track what changes have been done.

- Application developers should never assume that applying changes are only an IT problem. Developers should package all application changes (including database schema changes) in easy-to-deploy packages that can be rolled back without having to reinstall the entire application or server. If they do not, have them witness how painful it is to apply the changes and see if they like it. I will bet that they will go back and change their code to be more IT-friendly.

- Use version control for any code written, as well as key components such as baseline databases. I have been in too many environments in my career where at some point it is discovered that the wrong version of a script was run against the database, or the wrong DLL was deployed in a build, but due to lack of proper version control, there is no way to go back and deploy a previous version of whatever went wrong, or even build it since the source tree only contains updated source code and the old source that built the DLL no longer exists. This is also an issue when a problem is introduced in a later version and regression testing needs to be done, and the only way to get older versions is through source control.

- When testing changes, record how long it takes to apply the changes from soup to nuts. If you are working against a maintenance window, this information is crucial. Assuming the testing was done on similarly configured hardware, the timing should be fairly accurate for the rollout in production. If the production environment takes significantly more or less time during any step, this is a good indicator of an area where the test environment is not sufficiently similar to the production environment.

- Make sure all steps to apply changes are well-documented. If they are not, reject the application of the change until they are. There should be *no* ambiguity as to what should be done, and no assumptions should be made, as you may have no control over who actually applies the changes. It may be that junior DBA hired yesterday.

- Always have contingency/fallback plans in place and ready to go. Risk mitigation is the key to change management. While most of the time whatever you are rolling out will be successful, you will encounter at some point a time when your update fails. You need to then find a way to quickly troubleshoot and complete what it is you are trying to achieve.

- Set a go/no go point, and stick to it. The go/no go point is when you meet with all parties involved beforehand to ensure that everything is lined up for the update to be a success, and if the implementation is taking too long and the maintenance window is drawing to a close, a call can be made to cancel the update and the rollback process can be started.

- Once the change is rolled out successfully, test. Even if the change deployed is a patch to Windows, which may have nothing to do with your application, you should have testers on hand (or be able to remotely log in, even if it is 2 a.m.) to ensure that what was rolled out did not affect the application. You do not want to roll out a hotfix on a Friday night, only to discover on Monday morning that no one can connect to the application.

- Do a postmortem after the update is applied even if it is successful. There are always lessons that can be learned and applied to future updates that may be similar, and the lessons, whether painful or positive, should be used as reference material for future work that may need to be done in the future. For example, if something happens that has a workaround, there is a chance someone may encounter that again. If you only have a postmortem and do not document the findings, it is a missed opportunity.

The Cost of Availability

On the surface, there seems to be only one cost to achieving availability: the financial cost of implementing the solution. That is certainly important and will partially drive the process to varying degrees; but there is another cost that must be taken into consideration. What does it mean if the business incurs a system-down event? This answer *should* directly influence the actual cost of the system and is discussed in detail in Chapter 2.

For example, assume that you work for a company that sends specialty automobile parts to dealerships all over the world. You are linked via a business-to-business (B2B) system where your customers order on a web page and can view your current inventory. You are located in Chicago, where your standard workday hours are not the same as those in Tokyo, Frankfurt, or Cairo because you are not in the same time zone. With this system, you are nearly able to process each request instantaneously, and since putting it in place, your profits have soared 300%, and most orders are seeing a 12-hour turnaround from order placement to fulfillment, when it used to take nearly three to five days. Financially, you are now making on average $100,000 per day in orders, which translates into just under $8,500 per hour. The company has blossomed from one that nets $500,000 per year and just covered its expenses, with a little room for growth, to one that is now seeing profits of $15,000,000 annually.

Based on pure numbers alone, for every hour of that B2B system being down, you are losing a serious amount of income that may go elsewhere and never come back since other companies carry similar merchandise. One of the basic rules of any business, whether it is consulting or selling auto parts, is that relationships are everything. Damage relationships and you'll spend more time, effort, and money replacing the customers you lost or trying to woo back the spurned.

Another example is a crucial hospital system dealing with patient care. The system provides essential information about patient history and drug allergies. If the system goes down and there is an emergency, the time lost could mean the difference between life and death. Seconds count.

A final example is one that everyone has most likely experienced: waiting to pay by credit card at a store. How many times have you been in a store, walked up to the sales clerk, and gone through the transaction, but when it comes to authorizing your payment, the system is down, busy, or unavailable? This gets magnified even more at the holiday shopping season when lines are long and additional time in line means the queue gets longer, customers become irate . . . the list goes on.

Defining Downtime

Downtime is much more than the failure of a database or SQL Server instance and the length of time it takes to come back up. Downtime includes the events that occur, the repercussions afterward, and the dependencies that go along with everything involved. SQL Server is usually only one component in the whole solution that needs to be accounted for. Downtime can be affected by numerous things, and you must plan for an appropriate budget for mitigation. This budget must include but is not limited to the following:

- Proper staffing

- Hardware acquisition

- Software licensing

- Support costs

- Yearly improvements (both software and hardware, including hardware refreshes, software upgrades, software license renewal, etc.)

- Disaster recovery

Downtime in isolation is only an amount of time. When talking about system and application availability, there are two main types of downtime that you need to define in terms of how your organization works: *planned downtime* and *unplanned downtime*. Beyond that, there is also the concept of *perceived unavailability*.

Planned downtime is the simplest to understand. It is when you have a known outage that is taken into account and hopefully well-communicated to all who need to know. For example, most environments have scheduled outages to perform maintenance on servers that will disrupt overall availability. Usually these outages happen during low-usage times, such as the early morning hours during the weekend, and can be short or long in nature depending on the work that needs to be done and/or the agreements that dictate how long the servers can be kept "offline," meaning even if the server or application is up, it may not be available to end users.

Unplanned downtime is exactly what I am trying to help you prevent in this book: when things go down without warning and you have no idea why. This is the worst-case scenario that no one wants but that happens to everyone at some point in their careers. I cannot state enough that there are no 100% guarantees against unplanned downtime, even if you follow all the advice and best practices in this book and seek out the guidance of others who know what they are doing. But you can certainly have the plans in place to mitigate it if it happens.

Perceived unavailability is arguably the trickiest to define and plan for. It may have elements with aspects of both planned and unplanned downtime, or it may have its own characteristics brought on by other factors. The easiest definition is when the end users can connect to the application or solution, which includes SQL Server as the back end, or directly to the database but do not get results in a time frame they expect. This may appear as perceived unavailability to the end user.

A good example of perceived unavailability is when an application is having performance issues, causing problems such as locking and blocking at the database level, or slower performance due to disk I/O being saturated from other requests to the database. Another good example is when SQL Server is up and running but the web server that processes the requests is down. To the DBA, there is no problem—SQL Server is up and running—but the users cannot access their data, so they are complaining to your help desk or management and all of a sudden the spotlight is on you.

Perceived unavailability can be prevented more often than not and is discussed further in this book as topics such as service level agreements (SLAs) and proactive monitoring are introduced. However, no matter what you do, if this type of situation occurs, you cannot help that the perception from end users will always be the same, whether it is a true outage, slow performance, or not even SQL Server's fault.

Nines

With both high availability and disaster recovery, you may have heard the term *nines* floating around. The concept is a simple one: a *nine* is the number of nines in a percentage that will represent the uptime of a system, network, solution, and so on. Based on that definition, 99.999% is *five nines of availability*, or the measure that the application is available 99.999% of the year. But how should a nine be interpreted in the real world, which is definitely not the absolute value of what 99.999% translates into in minutes?

Before you figure out what level of nines you need, you must determine whether your planned downtime counts toward your overall availability number. When defining availability, I always like to include both planned and unplanned downtime. Leaving out planned downtime gives you a skewed picture of your actual availability in the time frame you are measuring. For example, it is easy to say you achieved 99.999% uptime this year in a report to upper management. What you might have failed to mention is that your application and systems were only mission critical from 9 a.m. to 5 p.m. in your environment, and you had no outages *in that time frame between 9 and 5.*

Calculating the number of minutes allowed by each level of nines is straightforward: take the number of hours per year (365 days × 24 hours × 60 minutes, or 525,600 minutes per year), and then multiply your percentage desired. Simply put

$$\text{Minutes Allowed to Be Down} = 525{,}600 - (\text{percentage} \times 525{,}600)$$

Table 1-1 shows the amount of time associated with the most popular levels of nines.

Table 1-1. *Nines and the Downtime Associated with Them*

Nines Percentage	Number of Minutes of Downtime (Yearly)
90.0	52,560 (876 hours)
99.0	5,256 (87.6 hours)
99.9	525.6 (8.76 hours)
99.99	52.6
99.999	5.26

You may already be thinking to yourself that 5.26 minutes of downtime *per year* is impossible, and you would nearly be correct. It can be achieved, but the amount of effort and money you will spend to acquire, plan, deploy, manage, and maintain such a solution is exponential with each additional nine and may not be worth it in the end.

The reality is that while five nines is nice to have, most companies are able to perform the necessary business and IT activities (including maintenance) and achieve three to four nines. Even three to four nines can be difficult for some of the most seasoned IT organizations. Four nines, or 52.6 minutes, equates to just more than 4.38 minutes of downtime per month. Is your organization currently able to achieve that? Maybe, but three nines equates to approximately 43.8 minutes of downtime per month. That is arguably a more realistic number to strive for, especially if you have no experience with mission-critical systems to begin with.

Out of the gate, if you have a lack of experience and you call the Availability Fairy to come in and sprinkle fairy dust over your servers, I would be surprised if you got more than three nines. I may be kidding around a little here, but three nines is nothing to sneeze at. It is an achievement if you are coming from a place where you previously had hours of downtime. Bottom line: work up to more nines. Shooting for the moon is noble, but it could prove costly and fail miserably. Be realistic about what you can and cannot do. Do not be afraid to communicate that to upper management either, and make sure they are in the loop as to the limitations of what can and cannot be done since their planning and responses may depend on it.

Why did I bring up management? There is something to be said for the CEO/CFO/CIO/COO/CTO (who will be referred to in the rest of this book in examples or scenarios as the *CxO*) who may want or demand to have five nines but then does not commit to the expense of the human and actual cost associated with it. Management, for obvious reasons, might want to make magnanimous announcements such as "we will achieve five nines" and announce it to the world in some blustery press release if what you are doing is externally facing, but it is up to the groups who are tasked with implementing to push back where appropriate. If you do not push back and get everyone on the same page as to what can actually be done, there could be even worse consequences down the road (up to and including people being fired).

Note Never forget that you are only as good as your weakest link. Take SQL Server—when it is installed in a stable platform, you may be able to achieve three to four nines right there. But when is SQL Server the only component of a solution? Never. So if SQL Server is the back end of a BizTalk solution that involves the network, a storage area network (SAN), web servers, BizTalk application servers, and the rest of the ecosystem supporting it (including people and processes), how available is each one of those components? If your web servers are down and they are the front end to the users, is SQL Server really up? Technically it is, but it most likely is not servicing any transactions since nothing is coming in. This helps frame the content of Chapter 2, where you will see that the number of nines you need is driven by many factors, and you will learn how to define your availability criteria.

If you want to calculate your actual availability percentage, the calculation is the following:

$$\text{Availability} = (\text{Total Units of Time} - \text{Downtime})/\text{Total Units of Time}$$

For example, there are 8,760 hours (365 days $\times$ 24 hours) in a calendar year. If your environment encounters 100 hours of downtime during the year (which is 8⅓ per month), this would be your calculation:

$$\text{Availability} = (8760 - 100)/8,760$$

The answer is .98858447, or 98.9% system uptime, which is nothing to sneeze at. To say your systems are only down 1.1% of your calendar year would be an achievement for some environments.

The Data Center Mentality

Whether you are a small company with one server or a large enterprise with thousands, the same guiding principles apply to making your systems available. Obviously the scale of execution and the inevitable budget considerations will most likely be different. The problem, however, is that no one has an unlimited budget. So what do you do?

To start forming your data center mentality, look at what has already been presented. Start with your people and your processes because technology alone will not solve things. No matter how automated you are, you still need human beings somewhere behind the scenes. Automation is going to be key in maintaining availability, but technology itself is not the panacea. High availability should never be a turnkey mentality (despite what some vendors may tell you when they are selling you a solution). The primary reason is that the worst form of downtime comes from problems that arise unexpectedly. These problems, by their very nature, are going to come from left field where nobody will have expected them. As a result, the automation is not going to have a custom-coded handling routine for them. However, the right people following a good and tested set of processes are the match for any problem.

The data center mentality when it comes to systems is a whole different mindset. How many development or test servers do you have in your environment that are down for one reason or another with no ETA, or are down intermittently because some developer made a change in code and then had to reboot it, which in turn kicked everyone else off? That just cannot be allowed to happen in a 24x7 production environment. People lose their jobs over these things, and I have seen it happen.

Availability is serious business that has equally serious consequences that must be in place. The old adage "if you can't stand the heat, get out of the kitchen" definitely applies here. Anyone who has been in the industry for any length of time has his favorite server-down story, which usually involves many long hours away from family, friends, and life in general. The story at the time was not funny, but looking back, it is amusing to think that it could have happened. In most cases, the signs of impending doom are obvious in hindsight and overlooked for one reason or another.

In many companies, and especially in ones with Windows-based applications, some systems start out as someone's desktop, but through some process that seems to happen naturally, that machine all of a sudden has some central role and becomes a production server without really having been properly planned to become one. That "server" winds up staying in Bob, Raheel, or Miko's cubicle and is vulnerable to everything from the cleaning crew unplugging it to use the vacuum cleaner to someone accidentally bumping into it and resetting it. This is absolutely a situation that does not lend itself to making that server a highly available system and preventing downtime.

The rest of this section will examine the things your company needs to take into consideration to ensure that your data centers and servers are availability and disaster ready.

Planning the Data Center

One of the most difficult things is actually planning your data center. A lot of the reason has to do with obsolescence: how long do you expect to use the data center? The amount of time is directly related to capacity planning. Miss your estimate and you may run out of capacity sooner, which brings its own host of problems. When talking about data center capacity, it is much more than just physical room for servers and racks; it is electric consumption, air conditioning, noise control, physical security, and so on.

The first thing you need to do when planning a data center, or reevaluating a current data center and its design, is to figure out capacity. How long do you plan on having this data center in operation? How much growth is the company experiencing, and does the lifespan of the data center meet the growth pattern? Oftentimes this is what gets people in trouble. For example, you should know the number of servers on average you are adding per month to the data center.

This example is the "simplistic" approach and must be done no matter what. A more detailed approach would examine your IT organization and branch out from there. For example, a retailer who exclusively sells online may have quite different needs than one who has a chain of "brick and mortar" stores (possibly in addition to an online presence).

Taking the next step, what is the data center going to house? Is it going to house critical infrastructure, or just servers? Some of both? The bottom line is that you need to know what you are designing for. Keep in mind that technology will change the landscape, but you need to change with it. A few years ago you may have bought 4U database servers that were racked, and now you are considering blade servers with just as much (or more) computing power that take up less physical space. However, you keep the same 10/100 network backbone and do not upgrade its capacity. Does that make sense? Maybe it does, maybe it does not, but it all needs to be evaluated.

Here are some decision points to consider:

Choose your data center location: This is multidimensional; there are geographic region considerations as well as local considerations. Unfortunately, as weather-related disasters can happen and will continue to happen, if the data center is located in a part of the world that is susceptible to potentially catastrophic natural disasters such as hurricanes and earthquakes, you must take this into consideration when planning, and take the appropriate measures. Whether that means reinforcing the building to ensure that the servers do not fall down during an earthquake, or somehow waterproofing the room, weather is not a server's best friend.

The other main aspect of location—where the server is located in a building—is not always straightforward. You must know the building's layout. For example, you wouldn't knowingly place your data center in a basement under the water pipes of the building or where there is not enough clearance for the racks. The basement seems like a good idea until the main water valve bursts, right? You must do your homework, as what may be an ideal location from a space perspective may not be right for other reasons.

Size your data center appropriately: Capacity management is more than sizing a server with processors, disk, and memory. It applies to building out your data center, too. Much like when you buy your hardware, you have a certain life expectancy of the solution. Do you want to keep the data center for five years? Ten? Indefinitely? If the answer is indefinitely and you are a rapidly growing company, you may hit your capacity sooner rather than later without proper planning.

Install climate control: Whether you live in a tropical climate or in Alaska, your data center must account for it. Servers generate heat, and lots of it. The more servers, the more heat is generated. This should be taken into account when sizing your data center and figuring out how long it will be in service. You should not have to replace your climate control system midway through the life of the data center. Servers do not perform well in heat, and their proverbial lives are reduced when there is not enough air cooling the data center. Some systems may actually perform faster when cooler. You also need to ensure that the design of the data center allows for proper air flow above and below the systems (including in the racks themselves), and the air flow should be even in all parts of the data center. You do not want any one spot being too hot or too cold.

Rack your systems: Putting your servers in racks saves space, but make sure that the racks you buy can actually fit in the data center you are going to use. Make sure that there is enough room above and below for air flow, and that there is sufficient room for cabling; so measure your dimensions of the doors and room prior to purchase.

Install fire suppression systems: Fire suppression is necessary, but make sure you install a system that will not damage your servers or endanger human lives. There should be visual cues (such as a blinking light) as well as audible clues (such as loud alarms) in the data center to ensure that any workers in the data center can exit the room safely. The data center is usually a loud place, so without those measures, there could be the potential loss of human life.

Document the physical server installations: This may seem painfully obvious, but there is nothing worse in diagnosing a hardware problem than trying to figure out not only which rack and space the server is in, but what hardware is configured in it, and where the connections such as fiber cables to a shared storage array are plugged in.

All of the previous points will influence how your data center is built and constructed and can ultimately be easily quantified in terms of money; but there is more to building a data center than the physical aspects. Spending millions of dollars only to skimp on some other aspect of your data center deployment is akin to shooting yourself in the foot. The points listed are only part of what needs to be taken into account in the design of the data center itself.

Securing the Data Center

If there is any one thing that needs attention from the beginning of the design of any application, system, or location, it is security. Security has many levels: physical security of the facility and access to the servers themselves, right down to how applications and clients interact with the solution. Certainly external threats such as denial of service attacks against web servers need to be defended against, but arguably the biggest threats to security come from the inside. Corporate espionage or disgruntled employees (or former employees who somehow still have access) are much more damaging, and by the time the damage is discovered, it is most likely too late. There are certain precautions that can help.

Keep Systems in the Data Center

If a system is relied upon by more than one person, you should most likely move it into the data center. How many applications start out as non–mission critical and are located on someone's workstation or a development/test server, and then for one reason or another it becomes something the business cannot live without? That is a good thing, but the location of the server is still in someone's office where it can easily be tampered with. As crazy as this may sound, this scenario still happens every day. I hear the stories time and time again. Do you want the cleaning staff to accidentally unplug the server so they can vacuum? That would cause an availability outage that not only could be prevented but should never happen in the first place. Even worse is when the DBAs, the help desk, or other administrators get a call saying the system is down when they never knew it existed in the first place. That is never a situation anyone wants to find themselves in, as the blame game will start to be played full force.

Control Access

Make sure access to the data center and server room is tightly controlled. Formalize plans around who will have access to the data center, what they can touch, when they can touch it, and how they will be able to get in and out with a trace of who was actually in the data center. Even if it is as simple as a sign-in and sign-out list on a clipboard, it is better than nothing. Ideally, there would be electronic pass cards or other advanced technologies such as biometrics that would more accurately track the comings and goings in the server room.

You should maintain a backup key to the door (i.e., a way to get in) if the electronic security measures are not working. Achieving this level of security can get difficult if third-party vendors or repair people need to come in and perform some service or install new equipment, but there should be formalized processes on how those people are allowed into the actual server room. In the case of third-party vendors, most companies have some sort of an escort policy where the visitor must be with an employee at all times.

Install Surveillance Equipment

Along with processes around who gets in and out of the data center and how that happens, you should have a visual record of it. Did a server go missing last weekend? Who really was in the data center? Electronic measures such as pass cards unfortunately can be circumvented or impersonated if someone is really good at doing such devious things. If you have still pictures or some form of video, it is easier to actually *see* who was there. Implement a formalized retention policy around how long surveillance pictures or video will be retained.

Lock and Secure Server Racks

Do not let everyone and their uncle have keys to all racks and server locks. Locks may be low-tech, but they are a great deterrent to thieves and others who have malicious intent or might sell the equipment for a quick buck. Only the owners of the system as well as those responsible for maintenance should have the keys and the ability to remove the systems from racks and be able to access sensitive parts, such as the fiber cables leading from your SQL Server to the SAN.

Enable Remote Administration

Back in the stone age of server administration, more often than not, all work done on the server, either at an operating system level or physically to the server itself, was done in the data center. Times have changed, and third-party products such as Citrix or the built-in Terminal Services feature of Windows allow administrators to access the servers and do their work without physically having to be in the data center. With SQL Server 2005, you have tools such as Management Studio that allow you to do most DBA-related tasks remotely. The more remote management solutions can be implemented, the less risk there is to the physical (not logical) environment. Securing the *logical environment*, meaning the operating system and the applications running on top of it, is a whole different task.

Secure Your Data and Backups

When it comes down to it, no matter what the application is on top, you are accessing data that has some corporate value. Secure it properly by restricting access and adding encryption if necessary. The same goes for your SQL Server database backups. Once you make the backup, make sure it is placed in a secure area (who is preventing someone from taking it and restoring it elsewhere?) and is encrypted.

Having said that, a major issue when it comes to hiring the right staff for managing your database environment that I hear all the time is summed up in the following question: how can you prevent DBAs and/or administrators from viewing data that may be sensitive or confidential? The answer is simple: do not hire people you do not trust. While security will be discussed all throughout this book and data security is a subset of that discussion, this requirement is much more basic than that. Only hire people that you trust will not do anything malicious with any data they may have access to. This type of security has nothing to do with accessing servers and data with accounts configured with the least amount of privileges possible. Technology solutions can help in terms of securing data, but you can never guarantee that it will do the entire job. Sometimes DBAs or administrators have to view data to do their jobs.

To match any technology solution for minimizing access to sensitive data, there should be corporate policy measures to bolster your security. For example, there could be a policy that lists penalties, such as payment of any financial damages if someone leaks information, loss of their job, or other severe penalties that match the damage incurred. Assuming the penalties are stiff, they should serve as a deterrent to anyone who wants to try to do something harmful.

What makes all of this harder is that some IT organizations are outsourcing operations to contractors, third-party hosting providers, or remote offshore organizations. The same rule applies: hire well and you will have no problems. Just because you may not see these people and they are not employees who are "full" members of your organization does not absolve you from having control over the hiring process, who touches your environment, and the penalties associated with anything that happens as a result. Any outsourced employees should be held to the same standard as full-fledged, salaried employees.

Audit Logs for Security

Most applications such as SQL Server and operating systems such as Windows have ways of auditing security. While a user *could* be impersonated, the only surefire way to track something is to be vigilant and see who is on the server and what they are doing. Auditing within SQL Server itself can add overhead, but when someone does something malicious, you will want to know what was done, who it was done by, and what the extent of the damage is. Along with auditing logs, you should arguably have some way to trace a connection back to a particular workstation/NIC/IP address.

Caution Applications should *never* be coded to have system administrator (SA) access within SQL Server because someone can come in through your firewall who knows the user account with SA privileges and its password, and then proceed to wreak havoc on your SQL Server instance. Do not find this out after it is too late. Ask questions of your developers early and force them to code to a least-privileged user.

Devise and Enforce Corporate Password Policies

Never use a master password that can access all systems. This may seem obvious, and a data center staffer managing a lot of servers may hate me for saying this, but if this password gets out, someone may get a backdoor into a system. Most software such as SQL Server requires domain-level service accounts, and changing these accounts is a huge pain and may even cause downtime. But what is the cost if someone who should not accesses sensitive data? A few seconds of downtime to cycle the SQL Server service is generally a small price to pay. Another consequence of using a single service account is that if all of your SQL Servers use the sqladmin account in a particular domain, you will have one massive outage to change the password for each instance. That has to factor into your overall availability picture.

Caution Depending on how your password security is devised, you may affect your availability. For example, Windows has the ability to ensure password expiration after a certain number of days. Resetting this password may affect the availability of applications such as SQL Server that may use domain-based Active Directory accounts that need to be reset. These types of things must be taken into account when solutions are devised and implemented.

Isolate Users and Administrators

Some environments require that a master administrator account is created and has access to all servers. Other than this possible user, all other users, logins, and administrators should strive to be unique to isolate any potential problems.

Power

Without power, systems cannot run. It is as simple as that. Therefore, you have to make sure that there is no interruption in power to your servers. The following are some things to help you mitigate power issues in your data centers:

Ensure you are deploying the right power for the equipment: There is nothing funny about putting a 110 volt plug into a 220 volt power source and vice versa. Standardize on how things will be plugged in, deploy that, and make sure every acquisition adheres to that standard.

Make sure all electrical lines are grounded and conditioned: Grounding is essential for computers. Some older buildings may not have grounded wiring and must be rewired to support grounding. To ensure that all things that are in the data center are powered evenly, and that there will be no sudden power spikes that could fry internal components of your servers, use power conditioners to provide even power to all of your servers. Conditioning also prevents undervolting, which could damage the system by not providing enough power.

Deploy backup power supplies: Each server and separate disk storage should have some sort of uninterruptible power supply (UPS) attached to it to allow it at a bare minimum to be shut down gracefully in the event of a data center power failure. Some data centers will implement central UPS solutions that will work with all equipment used in the data center.

Plan for an extended power outage: A UPS will only protect the device it is connected to and will provide a short amount of emergency power to it, not the whole data center. Depending on how much power the UPS provides and the time it takes to shut down the servers, the UPS may or may not provide enough protection. During the concerns over Y2K, many companies bought large diesel-powered generators to power their data centers in the event that the power went off at 12:01. You should consider deploying a similar solution to power your business if it needs such availability requirements.

Buy a battery backup solution: Battery backup is most common with storage devices such as SANs. With SQL Server, this becomes especially important since once the data goes through and the hardware handshakes with SQL Server saying in essence "I've got your data," there is a period of time (even if it is milliseconds) before the cache is flushed and written to the physical disk. If the power goes out and you have no battery backup, you may potentially lose data or corrupt disks.

Monitor equipment batteries: Remember to check the batteries in your controllers and other components that contain them, and make sure that they are replaced before they fail. If a battery dies on a key component, you may cause worse problems than you can even imagine.

Cabling, Networking, and Communications

One of the major components of your data center is the miles and miles of cabling that connect everything together. Properly cabling a data center to support your network and communications infrastructure can pose significant challenges since you will have power cables, network cables, fiber cables, and more. These tips will assist you in the process:

Keep all cabling neat: There is nothing worse than trying to troubleshoot a hardware problem only to discover when looking at the back of a rack of servers a rat's nest of cables. You cannot trace a cable from its source and destination that way. Do due diligence and cable your systems, networks, and storage properly. You may be under the gun to get things done quickly, but that is no excuse for sloppy work. In the event of a failure due to a cable problem, it is much easier to pull and replace when it is not tangled up with 1,000 others. Time spent doing things right at this point pays huge dividends later.

Properly label all cables: Along with neatly putting cables into components, buy a labeling machine and label both ends of the cable. If you are going to spend thousands, or even millions, on your data center, investing $50 on a labeler is one of the biggest bargains in your budget and can even be used for other purposes such as labeling your servers. You may also want to consider using color coding for each cable that corresponds to its purpose. For example, all network cables will be blue, all crossover cables yellow, and so on. If a single cable needs to be replaced for some reason or is knocked loose, one of both of these methods will make it easy to identify them.

Install phone lines in the data center itself: Whether it is your employees needing to talk to someone internally, or a third-party vendor needing to call some people while he or she is in the data center, you need a phone installed. Although it is arguably outdated, you may also want to consider standard analog phone lines in addition to a digital phone system in case the digital phone system fails; this would enable modems in servers or laptops to dial out of the data center. For the über-paranoid, install a pay phone or locate your data center near one. Pay phones operate on completely separate circuits that almost always stay up during emergencies.

Have backup communications systems in place: In the event of a power outage or another type of emergency where phone systems may be down, make sure you can communicate. Whether you use walkie-talkies, pagers, or some other device that meets your needs, do not assume that your primary communication system will always be working. For example, if you only have one phone in the data center and there is no cellular phone reception, you may have an inability to solve your crisis and keep management informed. If you have redundant communications, your coworker can be talking on one line on a phone to tech support while you are on another line talking to management.

Employ redundant networks: In the event of a main network failure, you should have the ability to switch to an alternate source to have traffic flow in and out with little to no downtime. If your main network fails, every single server in your data center, and subsequently all of your company's productivity from the top on down to end users, will be halted. Yes, this is expensive, but a network blip can also cause more havoc than just reducing productivity. It may introduce instability into such things as applications (depending on how they handle such failures), and could cause a whole chain of events to happen. This scenario, however, may not take care of a wide area network (WAN), which involves multiple sites that are located across the globe. A redundant network will only protect the network in the location it is deployed.

Include the network in capacity planning: Imagine this scenario: your data center has plenty of free rack space. You buy a new set of servers for your new SharePoint installation, get them racked, and shockingly discover you are out of network ports or the necessary amps to run them. Need I say more? The best test is the "9 a.m. test" where you turn everything on at once and see what happens. You can oversaturate everything in your data center very quickly.

Outsourcing Server Hosting and Maintenance

Given the costs of implementing, maintaining, and staffing a data center, companies are increasingly hosting their servers in a third-party owned data center that may or may not be near to where the company is actually located. If this situation is one you are currently in, or one you are considering, the following points should help you in implementing a data center, whether you are just leasing space with your engineers onsite or you are fully outsourcing everything. Pick your hosting company wisely—your availability will depend on it.

Ensure that your employees can access your servers: What access will the hosting company actually give you if your administrators show up onsite? Is there a limit to how many of your employees can actually be in the data center at one time? Does the hosting company restrict access to its facility at certain hours, or do you have 24x7 access? You need to look beyond the monetary cost you may save on paper to see if any of the answers to these questions will actually increase your downtime in a server-down situation. Also, know how much it will cost to go to the data center. Is it a plane ride? Do you need hotels and rental cars?

Know how long it takes to get to the third-party facility: If for cost reasons your third-party data center is not close to where your company is located, know how long in both worst-case and best-case scenarios it takes to actually get there. In a normal situation where you are going to just do some scheduled maintenance, time may not be as much of the essence, but in a server-down situation, seconds, minutes, and hours will count, depending on what SLAs you have in place. Third-party data centers will most likely have their own staff and can certainly act as your "eyes and ears," but you should always know what it takes when your staff needs to be onsite.

Qualify the hosting company: If the hosting company will also be responsible for multiple tasks, including administering your systems, what support agreements do they have in place with their vendors and how will they affect you? For example, if they have a contract with a network provider that states the network provider will have a repair person onsite within 24 hours when you need to be up in minutes, is that acceptable? Are their own policies and procedures in line with your overall availability goals, and will they happily accept whatever corporate policies, procedures, and standards you want them adhere to, or will they reject them?

Tip A good rule of thumb is that the hosting company should be capable of and already delivering to existing customers one more nine than necessary. This will give you a sense of confidence that it can meet your needs. Ask for references.

Consider turnaround time: If you decide to go with a third party, most likely you are bound to its infrastructure and rules for fixing problems, especially if it is the primary caregiver for your equipment. If the engineers cannot meet your SLAs and are not up to what you would consider to be a high enough level of expertise, those are warning flags. Make sure your agreements specify how long it will take if you call and issue a trouble ticket, that you have direct access to a qualified engineer, and that you don't have to go through a tiered and gated system. If you're talking to the wrong person, it will only delay getting things fixed in a server-down situation.

Put procedures in place to monitor third-party work: How do you know whether your requests, for example, to apply a SQL Server service pack, are getting done? Out of sight should not mean out of mind. You are entrusting your servers to people you may not have daily interaction with, so there needs to be a formalized process in place to foster communication around these types of activities.

Ensure all equipment is secure: If your servers are in a hosting company, are you the only customer? If not, where are your servers in relation to other companies? And if there are other companies in the data center, what policies or other measures are in place to prevent them from touching your servers?

Technology

Availability is straightforward from a pure technology perspective and can be summed up in one word: redundancy. For example, if you have one server as your primary database server, buy another and configure it as a "backup" (so to speak). But that is not all you need to do. Providing the right redundancy is far more complex than just buying another server and putting it on the network. Redundancy, to some degree, *is* the key to almost everything that will be presented in this book; and *how much* redundancy you need is dictated by how you will ultimately define your availability criteria.

Summary

Availability is not something you will achieve overnight and is not something that can be achieved by throwing money and technology at it. Downtime, especially unplanned downtime, is a matter of when, not if, you will encounter it, so investing the proper resources to mitigate that risk will be necessary. Do not think of the upfront cost, because over time it is amortized. Think of the peace of mind you will have knowing you will be able to handle most disasters that come your way. Chapter 2 will walk you through other aspects of preparing for availability, so come along on the rest of the journey to see how to make SQL Server 2005 highly available.

■ ■ ■

CHAPTER 2

Pay Now or Pay Later

Now that you understand the basics of availability and the relevant concepts, it is time to roll up your sleeves and begin the work of creating highly available systems. That work begins not with network cards, hard drives, or even SQL Servers, but with people sitting in a room and determining what exactly you want to achieve. If you skip this part of the planning process for availability, you *will* feel the pain down the road.

The Genesis of a Solution

Everything that winds up in production begins somewhere as an idea in someone's mind. This is true whether it is a redundant power supply in a server or a full-blown infrastructure to support a mission-critical application. Ideas are great, but they need to be properly explored to end up with the right result. The right result is one that supports a business need, not a technological one. Technology is the physical implementation. So before I talk technology, consider the following questions.

What Is the Business Problem You Are Solving?

This is where most companies get fouled up. They do not have a clear vision of what it is they want to achieve. The end game is the prize, not personal glory. Quite often, a CxO gets caught up in the hype of something—a piece of software, a hot technology, the latest buzzwords—and decides that to keep up with competitors, or to go ahead, they *must* implement it, and implement it now. Back up the bus, corporate soldier! Do you actually need it? And what problem of yours is that technology solving? Will it possibly make your lives more difficult in other ways, or do you care about that?

There have been many times I have gone onsite to a customer where an existing technical solution had been overengineered or a new one had already been determined before all of the requirements were established (which should determine what you implement). From the perspective of most people, the solution implemented is only a technical problem and the people implementing it approach it in that way; but the reality is that the IT needs to match the business need. Unfortunately, a lot of what I wind up doing at some companies is undoing some of the existing work, or retrofitting it to make it work for the actual business need. Do not put yourself in that situation. You need to sit down and really think about things before you go down the wrong implementation path.

For example, your company needs to implement some sort of customer management system that will enable the field personnel to work more smoothly with the folks back at the home office. Also, customers' needs need to be fulfilled more easily, and this should drive up sales and customer satisfaction. Now that you have answered the most fundamental question, which will guide nearly every aspect of the implementation, it is time to ask some more questions. Technology should not even be a large consideration at this stage.

Has This Been Done Before?

Some of you may be scratching your head with this question, but how many times have you worked somewhere (either as an employee or as a consultant) where you are three-fourths of the way down the implementation road, only to find out that some other division of the company has a similar solution up and running? And on top of that, you realize that what you are doing will not interface with the rest of the company infrastructure.

Your lack of due diligence could cost the company a lot of time and money that could be better spent on other projects. Never, ever reinvent the wheel. If the business problem you are trying to solve has been tackled elsewhere, is that solution appropriate? Can you just adopt it as is? Or if it is not completely suitable in all ways, can it be extended/customized for your needs? The more you can reuse existing solutions, the quicker it will be to implement, especially if the solution is already highly available. Having said that reuse is good, the flip side may rear its ugly head—going out of your way to save a buck or reuse systems can also become a drain on the project and a money pit. You need to weigh your options carefully.

What Other Mission-Critical Systems Have Been Implemented?

As well as avoiding reinventing the wheel, you need to do your homework. If you have previously deployed a large-scale system that required high availability, talk to the people involved with that project and read the documentation. What problems did they encounter? How did they solve them (if they could)? Can you leverage anything from that project or the post implementation review, or, even better, adopt the standards set forth by that project? How is that system running today? What would they do differently if they were going to start over today? Across your company, all solutions should (as much as they can) act, feel, and behave similarly from a pure infrastructure perspective. A lot of differences among solutions leads to confusion for the administrators later on.

Are You Biting Off More Than You Can Chew?

So you have a vision. Terrific! But is your vision a bit *too* grand? There is sometimes a reason why someone is the idea person—they think big, but fall short on what it actually takes to implement the plan. The people who will do the work have to keep this person realistic. For example, never attempt both a full migration to SQL Server 2005 as well as a consolidation without testing the waters first. Come up with your steps, and then perform them on a subset of your databases or SQL Server instances. Gather your lessons learned, and then tackle the bigger picture once you know what it will really take to get to your end state.

Are You Governed By Law or a Regulatory Body?

Many industries are regulated by professional organizations or governmental bodies. Some companies also strive to adhere to industry standards such as the International Standards Organization (ISO) 9000/9001/14000 or Sarbanes-Oxley (SOX). These are ultimately requirements that trickle down into your specific requirements for the solution you deploy.

Many times this not only factors in on how you do business, but on how you archive data and how long it needs to be retained or what levels of security are needed in accessing and archiving your data. For example, physical disk space is relatively cheap these days, but how are you going to manage 20 years worth of data (which may amount to terabytes or petabytes of data) as well as your current data set, all while performing secure backups (and storing them somewhere on disk) and proactive maintenance without affecting your end users and overburdening your administrators? Are you overwhelmed just thinking about that? In matters like this, you will not have a choice but to find a way to deal with the rules you must abide by.

Do You Understand the End-User Requirements?

You know all of your employees are clamoring for something to make their jobs easier, but do you actually know what they want in terms of features and functions—even down to how the interface should appear? If you answered no to any aspect, do your homework. Spend time determining the end-user requirements with the actual end users, or at least a focus group of them. There is no point in deploying a multimillion-dollar global solution if the users will hate it and not adopt it. The information gathered from the end users should form the basis of any application requirements documents you will base your solution on, whether they are technical or not. Never proceed with a design until you have signed off on these requirements, as this will lead to additional work for everyone involved and most likely delays to all aspects of the solution from the application itself to the infrastructure if everyone is not on the same page from the start. Changing streams during the project leads to higher costs and exposes your poor planning.

Money Changes Everything

Everything that winds up in production may start as an idea in someone's mind, but to become real it needs money (and, of course, people to do the work). Money is the unspoken, ugly secret that controls every project you have worked on, currently work on, and will work on until you retire. If budgets were unlimited, no one would ever have downtime and all system designs and operations would be perfect—at least in theory. The human element always tends to spoil the perfect glass house.

The budget is one of the first things, if not the only, attached to your new project, and it will determine a lot of what you will be able to achieve, at least from a hardware acquisition standpoint. It is incumbent upon you to know as much of the facts up front about what it will take to implement your system when you are asked how much money you need. Never have I worked for an employer or with a client where they had carte blanche on the cost. It is possible some company out there has such deep pockets they do not care, but I have yet to find one—even in larger companies. Everyone worries about the cost. This will be your first compromise point when you start designing your system. How do you achieve the availability you need with the budget you are given? This is why you need to set realistic requirements, goals, and SLAs.

There is a point where you need to stand up for yourself and tell management the truth if they are not willing to compromise on requirements or budget—that what they want to do is impossible. All goals need to be in-line with one another. You know what you need to implement, and there is sometimes a big gulf between want and need. The company may *want* five nines of availability, but can it afford to achieve it? If the answer is no, they need to go back to the drawing board and figure out what they actually need, given the resources that will be available. Compromise is definitely in order. You may not ultimately get what you want, but you will hopefully get what you need to get the job done. Otherwise no one will be happy with the end result.

Keep Your Friends Close and Your Enemies Closer

There is always some risk associated with whatever you embark upon in life and at work. You know if you follow your requirements and guidelines you should have a successful implementation, but it will take work to navigate the pitfalls. The reality is that you still cannot avoid risk. Risk is the whole basis of why you are even reading this book. Deploying highly available systems is all about mitigating the threats that are lurking to take your servers down. In some ways, knowing your weaknesses is better when developing plans for high availability. What you do not know may actually harm you, and in a worst-case scenario, cost you your job.

You must realize from the start that you will never come up with 100% certainty of all the permutations and scenarios to mitigate. For the ones that you come up with, you need to prioritize them and assign probabilities to them. For example, it is less likely that a large earthquake would hit New York City than a blackout (such as the power grid blackout of a few years back). Table 2-1 shows some example risks and possible mitigations. You may have seen some of these or have solutions of your own.

Table 2-1. *Sample Risks and Their Mitigations*

Risk	Solution
A disk fails in a shared storage array	Have spare disks on hand; if the array supports hot swapping, change the disk at the time of failure
A backup fails upon restore	Test backups daily or on a scheduled basis to ensure that the backup is good and can be restored in the case of an emergency
Rolling blackouts cut power	Have UPS units and a diesel power generator
A key aspect of SQL Server is not being monitored	Take the appropriate steps to make sure that whatever is being ignored is given the proper attention
The company has layoffs	Make sure that no one person is a single point of failure on your team

There are things that you may not be able to mitigate—these are barriers to availability. A *barrier* is just what it sounds like—a roadblock that you have no way to remove, and possibly no way to work around. While it can be classified as a risk, and in time may be able to be mitigated, depending on how severe the barrier is, it may put your implementation and availability in jeopardy. To mitigate a barrier takes more resources than simply having an extra disk on hand. Barriers generally fall into four categories:

People: For example, too many head chefs in the kitchen and not enough line cooks is a systemic problem with no easy fix. Hiring is usually not the answer, as that is not only a budgetary concern but a fundamental change to corporate culture.

Process: As you can probably tell from Chapter 1, process is important in all aspects of IT, but what do you do when there is none, or the process exists but it is broken? Again, it needs to become a systemic change. There is no easy short-term fix.

Budget: Along with process, an underfunded project or budget is something that can be a real killer. Similarly, if the staff feels like they are being underpaid and overworked and get insufficient raises year after year, what incentive do they have to work? Low team morale can have a devastating impact on productivity and quality of work.

Time: This one goes along withsetting reasonable expectations. If you have a multi-terabyte database with a disaster recovery requirement of being up in 30 minutes, you better have a large budget, a cracking staff, and a lot of experience. Restoring a multi-terabyte database, unless it is from a hardware-based backup, can potentially take *hours*. Another good example is not managing time properly and causing conflicts in matters such as maintenance tasks. If you are working with a certain maintenance window, and something in it goes long, it means that other things may not get done. What problems will this cause as time goes on? Certain tasks will always take a fixed amount of time. You cannot add hours to the day.

Service Level Agreements

One of the hardest things to hammer out is what level of service you actually need. This is definitely the next step after you determine what you are actually trying to achieve. SLAs are formal statements that detail what is expected in terms of what will actually be done, as well as the timing. There have been many times I've walked into a company and asked what their SLAs are, only to get a response like "What do you mean?" or "We do not have any documented SLAs." The harsh reality is that without your SLAs, you might as well stick your finger in the wind and determine what it is you need to design and implement. You may have guessed my tactic by now, but you have to be 100% realistic in what you are trying to achieve. It is better to pad and come in better than your expectation than to completely blow it. Keep your IT organization and business honest.

SLAs cover a lot of ground, but the two most popular aspects are availability and performance. Other issues include management. Each solution (or system in some cases) should have its own SLA, which may fall under a master management SLA that has overriding principles. SLAs are generally defined as agreements between the solution owner and the IT organization.

There are also variations of SLAs called operational level agreements (OLAs), and service level targets (SLTs) that will also factor in as well.

Service Level Targets

Before you put any kind of formal agreements into place, you have to have some idea of what you want to achieve. There are many different aspects of your implementation that need service level targets:

- Security
- Performance
- Service
- Data loss

For example, you may state goals such as the following:

- For availability, switching to your primary standby solution should take no more than five minutes during core business hours.
- If a disaster strikes, the core business (list the items defined as part of the core business) must be up and running within six hours.
- You can tolerate five minutes of data loss.

However, are those targets realistic? As you may have guessed, you need to put the right people in a room to discuss these goals and revise the targets appropriately. If you currently do not have the operational capacity to only experience five minutes of data loss, do you really think you will get it tomorrow by stating it? No, but targets help guide you through the rest of the process, even before they are formalized, and they help you figure out what you should agree to and what you should not sign yourself up for. Keep in mind that once you agree, it could be your neck on the chopping block.

Availability Service Level Agreements

Availability SLAs answer these three questions:

- How much uptime do you require?

- What is the maximum amount of time that is allowed for disaster recovery in a server-down situation?

- What are the specific availability objectives (e.g., data loss allowed) required for my implementation?

These are three seemingly simple questions, but actually arriving at the answers is complex, since there are so many factors. The answers will absolutely dictate the architecture and technologies used in the solution and impact the budget accordingly. Your availability SLAs ultimately cannot be out of line with your budget.

Consider this example: I have had many customers over the years say to me either on an engagement or during a question-and-answer session at a conference that they cannot tolerate any data loss. While this may seem more like a requirement (and is one), it really is an agreement between IT and a business that there will be no data lost. This is achieved by the implemented technology coupled with the application design.

Zero data loss makes sense at a 10,000-foot view, and makes even more sense in some industries, such as financial. But is zero data loss actually realistic? In most instances, the answer is no. First, there is technology involved. Somewhere in your solution, latency will be encountered, whether the data is moving across the network from the end user to the servers, or is written from the server to the disk subsystem where it may sit in the cache first.

Assuming you can actually determine where data loss occurs, are you prepared to spend the money it takes to achieve zero or near-zero data loss? Most customers are not able to spend what it takes to achieve near-zero data loss, especially if there is no budget for extreme high availability. Buying a lottery ticket is a better bet.

When going through the process of determining your availability SLAs you must consider your capabilities and be realistic about your availability needs.

What Are Your Capabilities?

As you assess what availability you can achieve, a big part of that is knowing what your staff can and cannot do and where their weaknesses are. This is definitely an important "need to know" point. If part of the implementation involves a skill set and/or a technology you currently do not have in-house, and it will be new to you, do you need to send people out for training? Even after training, will they have the right tools to do the job? Can you afford to send them out for training? Do you need to augment your staff with consultants? Do you need to hire new employees with the right expertise? How will hiring a full-time employee or consultant, or getting your employees trained impact your budget and the timeline for other projects currently in process?

What Are Your Availability Needs?

When you are solving a business problem, more often than not a monetary budget is attached to it, even before requirements are determined and SLAs are put into place. It is most likely a fixed cost that will take an act of heaven to get expanded. You know what you have to work with, and you also should know the capabilities of your administrators, engineers, and developers. Throwing out "we require five nines of availability" without thought is irrational. It may look good on the glossy marketing sheet ("Our systems achieve 99.999% uptime" in great, bold letters with a font size of 48), but is most likely going to be the biggest nightmare for your administrators and budget.

Do you know what level of availability you are already able to achieve in your IT organization? Chances are you have implemented individual servers and whole solutions elsewhere in your organization and you know how well (or poor) they fare. If your existing production SQL Servers average 90% availability, do you think this new system will be better? If you cannot currently achieve the level of availability you already know you need, assess why, and fix the problems (which are most likely people or process related) before requiring that a new solution have higher availability that deep down you know you will not be able to meet.

Another aspect of being realistic is knowing your working hours. Your CxO may demand that you have 24x7 availability, but what are your core working hours? The truth is that you may have differing levels of availability depending on what time of the day it is or what day of the week it is.

Consider this example: You are part of a company based in Chicago. Your business is primarily dealing with customers in the United States Monday through Friday during normal business hours. This means that at around 8 or 9 a.m. Eastern Standard Time, which is 7 or 8 a.m. Chicago time, to around 6 or 7 p.m. Pacific Standard Time, which is 8 or 9 p.m. Chicago time, your servers must be up and have five nines of availability. This means that for a period of roughly 15 hours a day, your servers absolutely must be up and running. However, that means there are nine hours a day, and the entire weekend, where there is much less work going on with the servers. That makes the environment and planning ultimately much more manageable.

On the flip side, take the example of a global company with offices in Tokyo, Bangalore, and various locations in Europe and North America. The application being used is SAP. Since the time zones are wildly different, the systems need to be available close to 24 hours a day, seven days a week. Outages may not affect one geographic location, but they may certainly affect another. How will you deal with that?

Note Availability SLAs are required for each individual component (such as disk subsystems, the SQL Server installation itself, the network, etc.) as well as an overall SLA for the entire solution. Your solution is only as available as its weakest component, so your overall SLA will most likely be the same as the component with the lowest availability. This speaks to the points made in Chapter 1 about perceived availability—if most of the system is up but key parts are down, is your whole solution really available?

Performance Service Level Agreements

What is the point of a highly available system if it is not also highly performing? Once again, there are many factors that will determine the performance SLAs. A big component of determining the performance SLAs will occur during the end-user interviews: what performance do they expect? Of course the answer is something akin to "*Fast!*" but what is the *real* requirement? A one-second response for 80% of the queries? A subsecond response? Minutes?

If the architecture calls for disconnected or remote users, how does that factor into performance SLAs? Obviously someone who is limited to, say, a dialup connection will no way be able to achieve the speed of those with a direct connection on the corporate LAN. As with availability SLAs, keep any performance SLAs realistic. Setting pie-in-the-sky SLA numbers of subsecond response times when you issue reports on a frequent basis that will scan multi-terabytes of data is only setting yourself up for end-user dissatisfaction. It is your job to also set the realistic expectations with the end users as to what performance will actually be, since it is really an agreement between IT, the business, and the end users. The discussion goes both ways.

Hardware and system design and, specifically with SQL Server, your disk design, will also factor into how slow or fast you will be able to get work done and processed. Another factor is preventative maintenance such as index rebuilds to maintain performance. Performance SLAs are usually determined before any of these are in place. So whatever is determined as your performance SLA should be revisited once the hardware and the design on top of it is in place and sufficient tuning and testing has been done to determine the actual performance of the system. Periodic SLA reviews should also be conducted as agreed upon by involved parties.

Performance and system design is covered in Chapter 14.

Note Similar to availability SLAs, your solution will only perform as well as its weakest component. Your performance SLAs should reflect this fact. Performance and availability must be measured consistently and accurately. An organization should standardize its definitions and calculations for these metrics; otherwise, there is little or no credibility when the achieved results are reported.

Operational Level Agreements

Operational level agreements are similar to SLAs and tied to them, however they have a very different purpose. An OLA is a formal agreement between the service organizations (usually internal, though it may involve external if you have some of your IT department outsourced) that specifies how they will work together to achieve the service level requirements that are detailed in the SLA. If you do not implement OLAs, most likely you will not have success with SLAs, and there will be a lot of finger-pointing.

At its most basic level, an OLA is a more technically focused document than an SLA, which has specific guidelines. The OLA is really a definition of how your IT organization will support the IT effort. Think about it. If you have separate storage, network, and DBA groups, do they work well together now without any formal documents or agreements? Even if they do, is it just in normal circumstances? The reality is that when everything goes to hell in a handbasket, human nature tends to make people panic, run around like chickens with their heads cut off, and forget any kind of rational thought. Calm, cool, and collected is not the hallmark of most disaster scenarios. In the midst of chaos, OLAs can help bring order.

OLAs are hard to implement and not always necessary but in most cases are absolutely vital for success. Some of your barriers to success for implementing OLAs will include issues such as different management for different groups, lack of time, and lack of interest since everyone is looking out for themselves.

An OLA should answer the basics: who, what, why, and how. The following questions cover most of the items that should be documented in an OLA:

What is the objective? I hate to state the obvious, but you have to define what it is you are trying to achieve. Are you protecting the new CRM solution? Your SAP implementation? A specific aspect of SAP?

Who is responsible for delivering the SLA? Before you get into the specifics of responsibilities, you need to define who will do the work. You should list roles (such as senior DBA), the group they come from, and, optionally, specific personnel by name. If you list personnel by name, you will have to revisit this document often to ensure it is up-to-date since people come and go over time. You do not want to find yourself in a situation where you go to test your disaster recovery procedures or actually implement them and not only has Bob or Mary left the company but the position (and role in the actions) has been eliminated, leaving a glaring hole.

What are the services one group will provide to another? In conjunction with responsibility is what one group will do for another. For example, the DBAs will provide database expertise in the areas of (insert items here). If it is determined that there seems to be an issue with the disk subsystem, the storage group will be contacted and the two will work together to resolve the issue and correlate information.

What are the hours defined for each group? Different groups may have different operating hours, and those should be defined. That means that off-hours contact information must be provided in the event of an emergency so that the OLA can be met.

What is each person or group responsible for? Defining the roles that each person or group is responsible for is key for the success of the OLA. Any ambiguity and the finger-pointing can begin. If there is a shared responsibility where more than one entity must work with another to achieve the end result, define that. That way if one party does not hold up its end of the bargain, there is accountability. You should define the exact steps if possible.

What are the priorities and escalation structures? On paper, everyone is supposedly on the same team and should be working together, but that does not guarantee there is any guidance for that to actually happen, or even happen in a nonchaotic fashion. If you have multiple failures, what is the priority order of things to fix? Who will be the leader of the task to oversee all groups? What is the escalation structure if someone is not doing their job or is out? Who will take over? Defining these will reduce or eliminate finger-pointing. You do not want to spend two hours fixing a problem that is not even defined when the main problem is getting worse.

What are any penalties? Unfortunately, consequences sometimes need to be defined. If group A fails to perform its duties, which in turn causes group B to fail, is there any recourse?

What are the response times? One of the key aspects of any formal agreement is response time. If all of the roles and responsibilities are defined between groups properly, it should be easy to state how long it should take for one group to react to another. Remember: every moment of downtime affects the business.

Compromise

For the last few pages I have gone on about things such as SLAs, requirements, budgets, and risks. In an absolute fantasy world, everything would get done with no conflict. In the real world you and I live and work in, getting things done is a matter of compromise, or more specifically, picking and choosing your battles. If the end state is the same as the vision, congratulate yourself—you have achieved something most cannot.

This begs the obvious question: how do you compromise when *everything* is important? Security, availability, scalability, budget, risks, requirements—what stays, what goes, what gets watered down, and what gets morphed into the "future enhancements" bucket? Unfortunately, achieving compromise in the corporate world usually boils down to politics. People can get entrenched at this point. "It's my requirement, and I refuse to budge." Meanwhile, the clock is ticking. The CxO has already promised the system will be live in 120 days, and you know you have at least 180 days worth of work. In companies that communicate well, these issues usually get resolved fairly quickly, as everyone has been around the block. Some companies, and I have worked in and with a few, love to have meetings and then conduct further meetings about meetings.

This is where a strong project leader (or formal project manager), as well as a project sponsor, will come into play. For large mission-critical projects—and even smaller ones that may not have as much visibility are just as mission-critical to someone—both roles need to be filled. The project sponsor is a higher-up in the company (such as the CxO) who is your champion and can make or break the project. If you make him or her happy and look good, you have it made. The buck literally stops with that person, and they can be the difference between getting that extra $10,000 or not.

A project leader needs to be able to make the tough calls and decisions (and be empowered to do so by the sponsor) and have the ability to veto things in progress or flat out say no to other things. Many people are good technologists but horrible leaders. A strong person at the helm will make the life of the technologist that much easier, since he or she will deal with anything that would distract the technologist from doing his or her job and increase the chance of success. Just as you would not put a DBA with no production experience as the lead on a 24x7 implementation, you should not have project leaders who are ineffective. They can be as much of a roadblock to getting things done as any other factor.

Time Is of the Essence

It is a bit early in the book to really talk about how long it is going to take to go from conception to birth of your solution, but in terms of the timeline of events, along with determining your budget, risks, SLAs, and requirements, you need to figure this out and deliver on it. In my experience, the physical implementation, that is, the technology part, is usually the easiest aspect. Everything else is what takes up the greatest amount of time.

A few years ago, I was assisting a client in implementing their mission-critical CRM system. It was their first mission-critical project with SQL Server. We spent a good three months planning the implementation, and the actual execution took only a few hours. (In reality, it was a bit more than that, but we were not tasked with installing the operating system or racking the servers in the data center.) After we were done, one of the people I was working with looked at me and said, rather anticlimactically, something to the effect of "So that was it?" Implementation should never be lengthy or painful if you have done your planning. Planning is sometimes painful, but that is to be expected. There is always work to be done, such as setting up monitoring and such, but you should have this experience more often than not.

I would be remiss if I did not briefly address a topic you may or may not be familiar with (and most of you should be): scope creep. In fact, I do not think in all my years working as a professional in this industry I have ever worked on a project or engagement that had zero scope creep. *Scope creep* is when you are well into the process (stage is irrelevant) of performing whatever task you have been saddled with and someone decides to change the way things are done, or introduce some new wrinkle or aspect that completely makes you have to revisit and revise work already done. Those are never happy moments for anyone involved. The time frame to complete the task usually never changes, only the parameters of how you get there.

So how do you mitigate scope creep? Well, it is not easy. Planning and getting the initial scope right (or close to right) from the get-go is the best way. If you are thrown a curve ball during the work process, you will arguably be able to handle things easier the more correct things are up front. However, as with other aspects of planning, even the best of planning cannot overcome a lot of obstacles. So if you face a massive amount of scope creep, at some point, things will break down; it won't matter how good your planning was to start with.

Some aspects of scope creep pop up during the course of a project and could never have been known during the planning phase—for example, if your company acquires another company midway through your implementation and that company is governed by rules you must now adhere to. If this new company requires that all of your backups be encrypted and you have no solution in place in your company, that one aspect may completely invalidate the solution you have in place already.

Support Agreements

By this point you should have your requirements, budget, SLAs, and so on completed and you are looking at planning and then buying hardware. Great! However, I see this time and time again at companies: purchasing support contracts with your vendors that do not match your availability needs. That is akin to making plans to build the Parthenon, but then deciding to hire the cut-rate contractor to save a buck and thereby adding risk to the project. What usually happens is that it takes one or two long outages for a company to realize the true value of a good and proper support contract, but by then, the horses have left the barn. It may be too little, too late. Support contracts are also sometimes known as *underpinning contracts*, and help to bind the SLA.

Yes, I am well aware that cost is an issue here. Low-hour response time (such as four hours) to come onsite is not cheap. And top-level phone support where you do not have to sit in a queue is not free. But you get what you pay for. You cannot run a 24x7 application with pay-per-incident support. You need to know that should the ship tip over, you can be on the phone with a qualified engineer within minutes.

This should extend to *all* of your vendors: hardware and software. You need to purchase the right level from all of them, not a mix. What is the point of buying the top-level of support from Microsoft only to find out your problem is at the hardware level and those guys will not show up for 24 hours. There goes your two-hour recovery SLA and your availability numbers.

After you buy your support contracts, make sure that you know how the support works. Some vendors may require you to have a point of contact person (or people) that they are authorized to deal with. Others may not. Nearly all of them will want the support contract number or some other identifier that will prove that who the person is calling is really who he says he is. This information should be kept in a safe, secure, and known place. The last thing you want is someone calling support and not being authorized to talk to the engineer, or not having the right information. Time is something you do not have in a server-down situation.

Make sure you know the terms of your support agreements. Do not do *anything* that may void them. Consider this example: your third-party software does not allow customization of the database schema. Despite that, someone in your company makes the implementation decisions to extend the schema because you need an additional column of information and a custom application on top of it to deal with querying information. All of a sudden, you have a problem with your custom application based on some schema issue due to the change. You call the vendor for support and they void your contract because you did not adhere to their stated rules. Do not put yourself in that position.

I see customers wanting to circumvent and bend rules all the time when it comes to implementations. Vendors do not put these rules out there because they want to make your life difficult. For Microsoft, aside from the documentation that ships with the product, always check the Knowledge Base at `http://support.microsoft.com` since it may contain updated information or rules that you may need to follow.

One other thing you need to always be aware of is the actual life cycle of the software you are implementing or have already implemented. You should know when it will no longer be supported by the vendor. Seemingly innocuous, this one detail could prove to be a big barrier when you are three years into production, have an issue, and call the vendor's support line, only to find that the product was decommissioned a year ago. That is unlikely since most mainstream support for a product in the enterprise space usually runs a few years, but it is better to be safe than sorry. The end of life support needs to be taken into account for planning and the planned lifespan of these systems. Planned obsolescence is built into nearly every hardware and software platform whether we like it or not.

Where you especially need to be aware of a product's life cycle is if you are implementing it later in its life cycle. If its support ends in one year but you want three years of life, you may need to upgrade sooner rather than later, or work with your vendor to ensure extended life support. Many vendors will offer support beyond the stated date of the end of support, but you will most likely pay dearly for it.

Tip For the life cycles of Microsoft products, go to the web site `http://support.microsoft.com/lifecycle/`. Each individual product's life cycle may vary by country, so make sure you select the country where you live.

Applications, Application Development, and Availability

It bears repeating that availability is not just an IT problem. If you are going to implement a custom-developed solution, you must make sure that well before the implementation and support phase, which is the focus of this book, your developers are trained in how to make applications available, scalable, and secure. Most applications are not designed with availability in mind (let alone scalability and security), and it shows when IT struggles to implement and support it.

I have seen all too often that IT organizations need to piece the solution together with proverbial rubber bands and paper clips to get it to work with the availability features of the platform, and they have to give escalated security since they are system administrators on the developer's workstation. Some features, such as failover clustering, which will be described in Chapters 4 through 9, have their own programming interface, which allows the application itself to detect an outage should the service go down and start up again.

If you are implementing a third-party application, know what features of the underlying platform are and are not supported. For example, if you need to create a warehouse or reporting database, is replication supported or not? If not, it rules out one way you can achieve populating the other database. The same thing goes with any other feature such as failover clustering, mirroring, and so on.

A red flag when it comes to application development and availability is server names and/or database names hard-coded into the application itself. It severely limits what can be done to make that application available at the platform level and will make disaster recovery a nightmare to implement. In this day and age, the application layer should be able to support such things through configurable files or options that are stored outside of the database.

Summary

Planning mission-critical, highly available systems is quite a bit of work. It requires a lot of information, patience, perseverance, and compromise on the part of all parties involved. Even after all the hard work, there will still be risks that you may not be able to deal with—in fact, I can guarantee it. But if you can keep scope creep and noise down to a minimum, you have a fighting chance to deal with what is already on your plate without having to react to something coming from left field. Risk mitigation is the prime directive for highly available systems, and your failure to mitigate risk will cost you down the road. The more work you do before you even touch any technology, the better off you will be.

Now that you understand the basics of achieving availability, which has both everything and nothing to do with technology, it is time to move on to the technical aspects of availability as they relate to SQL Server 2005.

PART 2

■ ■ ■

Always On: SQL Server Technology

Now that you've learned how to think about and plan for a highly available environment, it's time to delve into the technologies for implementing SQL Server 2005 high availability: backup and restore, failover clustering, log shipping, database mirroring, and replication. This part will also cover where, when, and how to use each technology, explain the trade-offs inherent in implementation, and show examples of highly available deployments.

CHAPTER 3

∎∎∎

Backup and Restore

Availability and disaster recovery begin with a sound backup and restore policy. Without good and *tested* backups, anything else you do—failover clustering, database mirroring, replication—means nothing. The other technologies are ways to increase your availability or provide a switch process in a disaster, but they do not—nor will they ever—replace SQL Server backups. This chapter will take you through those options, as well as strategies for implementing a solid backup and restore strategy based on my experience over the years. Backup and restore could easily be its own book, so I will do my best to encapsulate everything in one chapter.

Understanding Backup and Restore Basics

Before you start to plan and implement a backup and restore plan, you must understand how SQL Server implements backup and restore within the product.

Describing the Types of SQL Server Database Backups

You first have to know the options available to make backups of your databases. You must understand that all native SQL Server backups listed in this chapter take place while the database is up and active. There is *no* reason to ever shut down SQL Server to make backups. I have seen documentation that states this incorrectly, and it makes my blood boil every time. Backups that occur while the database is fully online will impact the database from a performance perspective since you are reading the data from the database to the backup device at the same time it is servicing requests; however, if architected properly, it should at worst have only minimal impact on your business.

Whether you are backing up to tape or disk, the media is called a *device* in SQL Server terminology. Each backup must use a device. A single backup device can contain multiple backups (of multiple types); however, I do not recommend you go down that path, because if you have one backup device containing multiple backup files, it is not as easy to restore a database as it is with a 1:1 ratio from backup to device. It is easiest to think of a device as a file, and when it contains multiple files, it is more like an archived file (such as a ZIP file) where you can have multiple files and extract each individually later. In addition, you will have one massive file for all your backups. For example, if your database is 500GB in size and you have four full database backups in the device, you are looking at 2TB of disk space for that one file. That is not very portable.

Note A native SQL Server backup is neither compressed nor encrypted. A SQL Server backup is just a plain-text file written to your disk or tape. To compress or encrypt your SQL Server backups, you must use third-party tools.

Full Database Backup

A *full* database backup is exactly what it sounds like—it is a point-in-time backup of your whole database. It backs up all data and objects that reside within the database, but it will not back up objects (such as jobs or SQL Server logins) that reside outside the database. With versions prior to SQL Server 2005, if you executed a full database backup, you couldn't make any other backups (such as a transaction log backup) of that database until the full backup was complete. SQL Server 2005 allows you to do two concurrent backups at the same time. For example, you could be doing a full backup and a transaction log backup at the same time or a differential and a transaction log at the same time. However, if you exceed two, the third backup will fail. Most situations will not dictate that you run backups in parallel, and you might experience very high disk input/output (I/O) if you do this, but it is nice to know that it is possible.

■**Note** The full backup does not truncate or back up a transaction log, which is a common misunderstanding of how a full backup works. See the upcoming section "Transaction Log Backup" for more information.

The full backup process is straightforward:

1. When the backup command is issued, SQL Server *checkpoints* the database, which writes all *dirty pages* (ones that have changed since loaded into memory) to disk. This ensures that all committed transactions up to the point of the backup command will be backed up as part of the full backup.

2. SQL Server makes a mark in the transaction log to denote the point where the full backup begins. This is important because in the recovery process, SQL Server will use this mark to help validate what combinations of files can (or cannot) be used to restore the database from the full backup.

3. The data is then read out of the database files to the backup file, which is a plain-text file that is created on disk or tape.

4. When the full backup is complete, SQL Server makes another mark in the transaction log.

A full backup is arguably the most popular kind of backup and is the basis for all backup and restore strategies. If all you ever do is perform full backups, you are only as good as your last tested full backup that is known to be good. For example, if you have a failure at 2 p.m. Wednesday and you have a backup from midnight that you have tested, you will lose 14 hours of data if you restore your database from that full backup. Fourteen hours of data loss might be in your SLA tolerance, but in my experience, 14 hours of data loss is generally not acceptable for customers, whether they are small or a large enterprise. The person who allowed it to happen should most likely polish up his or her résumé.

Differential Database Backup

A *differential* database backup with SQL Server might not be what you actually think it is. A differential database backup contains only the changes made to the database since the last full backup. If you do a full backup at midnight on Sunday and then perform a differential at midnight every other day of the week, each differential backup will contain the changes between that day and Sunday, not between that day and the prior differential backup. A differential database backup does not take the place of a full backup, but you can use it as part of an overall strategy to get you to a closer point in time faster, as well as to lighten the load of the system if you are unable to perform a full backup every day.

A differential database backup is possible because SQL Server keeps track of the extents that have changed in an internal bitmap contained within the data files. When a full backup is made, the bitmap is reset. One bit is used per *extent*, which is eight physically contiguous 8KB pages (64KB), so a single 8KB page can map to about 4GB of data.

If you use differential backups in addition to doing full database backups (with no other types of backups in the mix), you are only as good as your last good tested full backup as well as the differential backup associated with that full backup. For example, assume that for space reasons you cannot afford to make a full backup every night. At midnight, you perform a full backup on Sunday, and a differential is done every other day of the week except Sunday. A failure occurs at 2 p.m. Monday. You then need to restore the full backup plus the last differential, which would give you 14 hours of data loss that you might or might not be able to get back.

Transaction Log Backup

A *transaction log* backup, like a full backup, is exactly what it sounds like—it is a backup of your current transaction log. From a recovery standpoint, no backup is more critical than a transaction log because it allows you to recover to a more granular point in time. If you are doing frequent transaction log backups, you can restore to the last transaction log, which might be only minutes out, instead of hours or days, thereby minimizing your data loss. To apply a transaction log, your database must be restored WITH NORECOVERY or WITH STANDBY. WITH NORECOVERY puts your database in a pure loading state where it cannot be accessed for client connections. WITH STANDBY puts your database in a loading state where clients can access the database for read-only purposes, but when a transaction log is loaded, the database needs exclusive access to load the log, so it would be unavailable for client use.

Although there is only one way to do a transaction log backup, there is a special term for backing up the last transaction log. It is known as backing up the "tail" of the log. It is important to note that there is no difference between the tail of the log and a normal transaction log backup; the tail of the log is just a term. You generally back up the tail of the log when the database is at a point where it is seeing minimal to no usage and when you are most likely looking to bring a standby online at the same point using that last transaction log. In this case, the tail of the log is the portion of the log that has not been backed up yet. This last transaction log backup is important, because it will allow you to recover to the last transaction recorded in the transaction log. In a disaster scenario where you might not have access to the database for whatever reason (hardware failure, database failure, disk corruption, and so on), you might not be able to access the tail of the log and will be able to recover only to the last transaction log available to you. If you are able to access the database but you think there is damage, you might not want to back up the tail of the log because it might be an incomplete snapshot of what has transpired since the last transaction log backup.

To understand how a transaction log backup works, you need to be aware of how the transaction log works. On the surface, you create and use one or more physical log files with your data file or files. In the transaction log, SQL Server writes a sequential string of records. Each record is assigned a unique log sequence number (LSN). The LSN chain must never be broken because it affects your recoverability options. The transaction log itself is just a large text file and is not like a database data file that can use a 64KB read-ahead. The transaction log is essentially the living record of your database and what happens in it. This record includes all transactions; all inserts, updates, and deletes of data (as well as all Data Definition Language [DDL] code, including creation of objects); all extent and page allocations/deallocations; and all rollbacks.

SQL Server takes the physical log file and divides it internally into many virtual log files (VLFs), which have no fixed size. There can be an infinite number of virtual log files, but SQL Server does its best to have only as few as needed. The more VLFs, the slower your database will be. The transaction log is a wraparound file, meaning that when it reaches the end of the file, depending on what has transpired, it will start writing from the beginning of the file again. If you have not truncated your log, it will increase the log file to accommodate the space needed for the LSNs. If the log can no longer grow, you will see a 9002 error. As the transaction log is used, SQL Server keeps track of the minimum LSN (MinLSN) so that whenever the log is truncated, all LSNs before the MinLSN will be flushed. This is a bit of an oversimplification of the process since you just need a basic understanding of how this works. Figure 3-1 shows an example of VLFs, and Figure 3-2 shows an example of the wraparound.

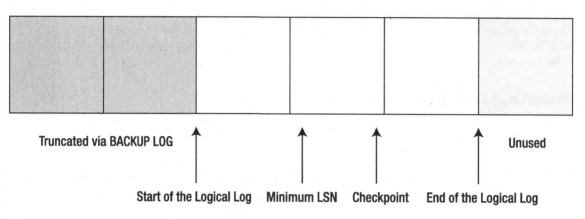

Figure 3-1. *Transaction log with six VLFs*

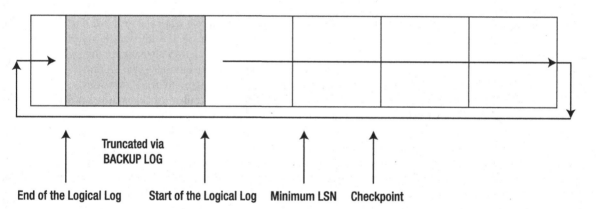

Figure 3-2. *Transaction log wraparound*

Note   What confuses many customers is that although a truncation occurs after the transaction log backup (or other command that just truncates the log without doing a backup) is completed, it does *not* actually shrink the log file if it has grown. It just deletes LSNs that are no longer needed. To reclaim space, you will need to deal with the physical operation of shrinking the file in conjunction with doing operations that truncate the contents of the transaction log. The ability to truncate the transaction log and reclaim space is one of the key components of enabling reuse of the same transaction log space through the wraparound previously documented.

SQL Server issues a checkpoint to the transaction log every time a backup of any kind is made to the database. The checkpoint flushes the pages from memory to the physical disk. This means that at any given point, you have modified data pages in your buffer cache in your server's physical memory that have not been physically written to the hard disk. The checkpoint tells SQL Server that all pages prior to this mark have been committed to disk. You should never have to issue a manual CHECKPOINT command. A checkpoint is issued every time SQL Server is stopped and started, a manual CHECKPOINT command is issued, or the number of log records meets the number of records SQL Server estimates it can process as specified in the recovery interval setting. In simple recovery mode, this can also occur when the log is 70% full. During the checkpoint process, the following things occur:

1. A record in the log marks the beginning of the checkpoint.

2. Information (such as the first LSN written by the checkpoint) is written about the checkpoint in checkpoint log records.

3. All the space prior to the MinLSN is marked for reuse so that when a truncation occurs (that is, a transaction log backup), the space will be reclaimed.

4. All dirty data and log pages are flushed to disk.

5. A record in the log marks the end of the checkpoint.

File and Filegroup Backups

File and *filegroup* backups are based on full and differential backups. If your database architecture uses multiple files and filegroups, although you can do a standard full or differential backup, you now have the option of doing a more granular backup, which might make recovery much easier. Although you can do a file/filegroup backup from a full database backup, the advantage of doing a file/filegroup backup explicitly is that backing up a multiterabyte database to a single file will be a daunting task to manage after it is generated. Using a file/filegroup strategy will allow you to deal with smaller chunks and make your allotted backup window much easier.

A file- and filegroup-based strategy works the same as a full or differential backup (you can back up the entire database or just part of it), except you are required to take transaction log backups to make the file/filegroup consistent at the time you restore since you might restore only one file that might have been backed up at a different time than another. A file or filegroup strategy can help you more so from an administrative standpoint since it tends to work better with very large databases (VLDBs)—you can back up parts of your database instead of having to do the whole process all at once. However, it does add the complexity a bit on the restore side, so you do need to think about whether it is the right methodology for your backups.

Third-Party Software–Based Backup

Many third-party backup programs are widely used in IT shops. For any program to work properly with SQL Server, it must be coded to the SQL Server 2005 Virtual Device Interface (VDI), which is an application programming interface (API) provided by Microsoft to allow third-party hardware and software vendors to interface directly with SQL Server. If it is not coded to the VDI, it is not a SQL Server–compliant backup program. The VDI did not change from SQL Server 2000, so if your preferred backup software vendor wrote its software properly for SQL Server 2000, it should also work correctly with SQL Server 2005. However, always consult your backup vendor to see whether it supports SQL Server 2005 with the version of the product you currently own.

■**Note** For more information about the SQL Server 2005 VDI, download the API and its corresponding documentation from http://www.microsoft.com/downloads/details.aspx?familyid=416f8a51-65a3-4e8e-a4c8-adfe15e850fc&displaylang=en.

How can a third-party program benefit you over doing backups with SQL Server itself? In some instances, it can provide an enterprise solution that not only backs up your SQL Server databases but also nearly everything in your environment (Exchange, all files on a server, and so on). In essence, it allows you to standardize how things are done across the board.

Another way that third-party programs can benefit you is that they can extend the functionality of a regular SQL Server backup. For example, some popular packages allow you to compress and encrypt your backups as they are being made, which in turn allows you to save a lot of disk space. Others can speed up the backup process through their own special optimizations—something you do not get out of the box with a native SQL Server backup. If you are backing up to tape, some programs have the ability to manage the tape libraries and hardware that drive it, which is necessary for backups that will exceed the capacity of a single tape. If you used SQL Server, you would have to employ someone to switch tapes. That isn't very practical.

However, do not employ a third-party program for the sake of using it. By that, I mean just because some external program exists to help you with your backups does not mean you should use it. Sometimes the keep it simple, stupid (KISS) method is best. Purchase and deploy another program for your SQL Servers only if either the features it provides give you an advantage over regular normal SQL Server backups and help you better meet your SLAs as well as other requirements set forth for the solution or it is already used as a corporate standard in your environment and you must adopt it.

Hardware-Assisted Backup

One challenge that faces most growing environments is that at some point, your database is so large that a traditional backup strategy might no longer work well for you, even if you employ third-party products to assist you. What can you do? This is one problem that throwing money at can help. Certain storage vendors allow you to do a hardware-assisted, or split-mirror, backup. It is out of scope of this chapter to get into each vendor-specific implementation of hardware-assisted backups. If you are interested in a particular storage vendor and their solutions, I recommend you contact them directly.

Backing Up a Table

SQL Server does not have the ability to back up only a single table through the traditional backup mechanism. This was a feature of SQL Server through version 6.5 but was removed in subsequent versions. Although some have requested that this feature be put back in the product, to date it has not been. The only way to make a backup of your table is to use a tool such as the command-line bulk-loading tool BCP or something like SQL Server Integration Services (SSIS) to generate a file that contains the contents of your table or tables.

Mirroring Backups

New in SQL Server 2005 is the ability to mirror your backup media. This means when SQL Server is writing the backup of your database, it is not only streamed to multiple devices at the same time (which is already possible) but that you are actually creating a mirrored media set. Each mirror requires a separate physical device. For example, if you currently write your backup to a single file on disk, you can now write it at the same time to another disk. If you lose disk A, SQL Server will know about the backup on disk B. This protects you since the database engine ensures that the mirrors are identical because of synchronized writes to the backup devices.

In many ways, this is similar to RAID 1 (disk mirroring) for your backups. If you lose a disk or tape from a mirrored media set because of either hardware damage or other error, you cannot use the mirror for other backups. As long as one complete half of the mirror is accessible, SQL Server can read from the media set. If portions of both mirrored media sets are damaged, the entire media set is unusable, and you have no backups.

Describing the Recovery Models

Another aspect of SQL Server 2005 database architecture that is important to understand is *recovery models*. Recovery models were introduced in SQL Server 2000. The recovery model is set per database, controls the level of logging done by the database, and affects your availability in a recovery scenario. The amount of logging might also potentially affect the performance of your database. The recovery model is set at database creation time, and you can find it on the Options page of the New Database dialog box, as shown in Figure 3-3.

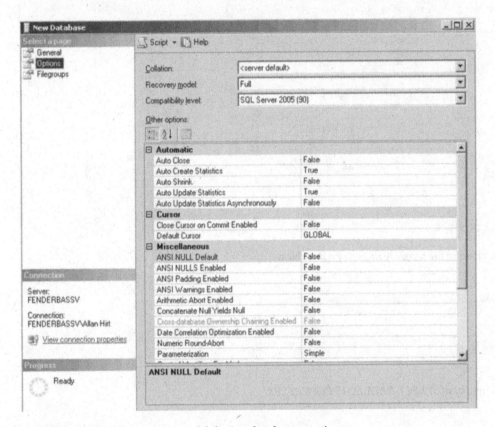

Figure 3-3. *Setting the recovery model during database creation*

After the fact, you can see the recovery model of a database by selecting the properties of the database and then selecting the Options page, as shown in Figure 3-4. You can also see the recovery model by issuing the query SELECT DATABASEPROPERTYEX ('*database_name*', 'Recovery'), where *database_name* is the name of your database. Figure 3-5 shows an example.

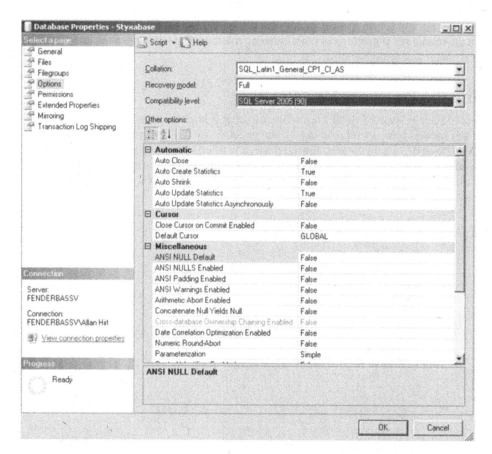

Figure 3-4. *Viewing the recovery model of a database*

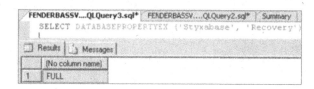

Figure 3-5. *Results of SELECT DATABASEPROPERTYEX*

Another way of seeing the recovery model for a database is to issue the following query against the master database:

```
SELECT [name], [recovery_model], [recovery_model_desc]
FROM sys.databases
```

Figure 3-6 shows some example output.

	name	recovery_model	recovery_model_desc
1	master	3	SIMPLE
2	tempdb	3	SIMPLE
3	model	1	FULL
4	msdb	3	SIMPLE
5	Styxabase	1	FULL
6	DBCLONE	1	FULL
7	DBADB	1	FULL
8	LiteSpeedLocal	1	FULL
9	Styxabase2	1	FULL
10	Styxabase3	1	FULL
11	Styxabase4	1	FULL
12	Styxabase6	1	FULL

Figure 3-6. *Querying the system tables to see the recovery model*

Full

The Full recovery model is the default setting for all user-created databases. Full logs every operation that writes to the log completely and gives you the best recovery options including schemes
that include transaction log backups and restores. All recovery options are possible if you are set to
Full. This is the most important factor in making Full the recommended recovery model for production databases.

Note Although Full recovery is the recommended setting for all production (and nonsystem) databases, you
must be aware of one consequence: your transaction log will grow as large as you allow it and possibly fill up your
disk if you do not perform proper maintenance of the transaction logs. This means you must have a plan in place
to back up your transaction logs on a regular basis to maintain a reasonable transaction log file size. If you have
this plan, your transaction log size even with Full recovery should not be significantly larger than using another
recovery model. If you do not back up your transaction log, it might wind up dwarfing your main data file in size,
and it will make the startup of SQL Server slow to recover that database since it has to trawl through the entire
transaction log to bring that database online.

Bulk-logged

The Bulk-logged recovery model is somewhat similar to Full, but most operations are minimally
logged. This means only the extents that are modified are actually logged in the database. You
cannot back up the tail of the log after you have done a bulk operation when in Bulk-logged
mode. Keep in mind that not all operations are minimally logged with Bulk-logged (for example,
a DROP INDEX statement's index page deallocation). The list of operations that are minimally
logged are as follows:

- All bulk import operations (BCP, BULK INSERT, and so on).

- All WRITETEXT and UPDATETEXT statements that insert or append data using the data types of
  text, ntext, and image. (Note that WRITETEXT and UPDATETEXT are depreciated in SQL Server
  2005 and are replaced with the UPDATE using the WRITE clause.)

- All UPDATE statements that use the WRITE clause.

- All SELECT INTO statements.

- All CREATE INDEX statements.

- All `ALTER INDEX REBUILD` statements.
- All `DBCC DBREINDEX` statements. (`DBCC DBREINDEX` has been depreciated in SQL Server 2005 and is replaced by `ALTER INDEX`.)
- `DROP INDEX` new heap rebuild.

The best use for Bulk-logged is a database that is doing frequent bulk data loads since it provides the best size-to-performance ratio. Although you can take transaction log backups with Bulk-logged, if there are bulk operations, you can restore only to the end of the last log backup that does not have the bulk-logged operations. You also do not have the option of using marked transactions or restoring to a specific point in time.

Should you perform a bulk operation, make sure you back up your transaction log prior to and immediately following the operation.

Simple

Simple recovery mode gives you the least recovery options. Logging takes place in the same way as Bulk-logged, but the log self-truncates and clears on its own. The log file arguably should not grow much if at all from its initial size. You do not have the ability to make transaction log backups with Simple, so you are only as good as your last full or differential backup.

Choosing a Recovery Model

Unless you have a good reason to use Simple, always use Full for your production databases. There should be no exceptions to this rule. Sometimes you might need to switch to Bulk-logged, but that should be infrequent if at all. If you have the capacity from a performance perspective, you should be able to handle even bulk operations with Full set on your database. Simple is commonly found in development and test environments where you do not need the same level of recoverability as you do in production.

Changing the Recovery Model for a Database

If you want to change the recovery model from one to another, it is entirely possible. To do it in SQL Server Management Studio, change the recovery model on the Options page of the Database Properties dialog box, as shown in Figure 3-4, and click OK. To change it via a Transact-SQL statement, issue one of these commands:

```
-- Set the database context to the right database
USE database_name
GO
-- Set the recovery model to Full
ALTER DATABASE database_name SET RECOVERY FULL
GO
-- Set the recovery model to Bulk-logged
ALTER DATABASE database_name SET RECOVERY BULK_LOGGED
GO
-- Set the recovery model to Simple
ALTER DATABASE database_name SET RECOVERY SIMPLE
GO
```

Before you change the recovery model, you must understand the implications of doing this. If you change from either Full or Bulk-logged to Simple, you will break the LSN chain, and you will need to generate a new backup set (which might be a full or differential database backup or a complete file or filegroup backup). If you change from Full to Bulk-logged, you will not lose continuity of the transaction log, but heed the behavior differences described earlier. The same goes from Bulk-logged to Full. If you switch from Simple to Full or Bulk-logged, you should make a transaction log backup as soon as the change has taken place.

Understanding SQL Server Database Recovery

Now that you understand the types of backups and the recovery models, you need to know how SQL Server recovers a database. First you need to understand the difference between restoring and recovery. *Restoring* a database is the process of using full/differential backup files and their subsequent transaction files to roll the database forward to a certain point. *Recovery* is the overall set of processes that SQL Server runs to ensure that the database is in a consistent state when it is brought online, which might include such processes as rolling back uncommitted transactions. A restore has three main phases: data copy, redo, and undo.

Data Copy Phase

During the data copy phase of restore, the contents of the database, files, or pages being restored are initialized. The data is copied from the files (or tapes) to the destination and, where necessary, SQL Server resets the contents of the database, files, or pages to the right bits of data from the backup. The oldest file used in the backup set of files (also known as the *roll-forward set*) will contain the LSN for the redo phase.

Redo Phase

The redo phase is also known as the *roll-forward phase*. This is when the transaction logs are processed to ensure the consistency of your databases. If you specified a specific point in time to recover to (date or marked transaction), this will be done in the redo phase. Even with all things rolled forward that have been committed, there might still be some uncommitted transactions.

Tip New in SQL Server 2005 is the concept of a fast recovery. Prior to SQL Server 2005, the database was unavailable until the whole recovery phase was complete. You can now access a database after the redo phase completes. This is a feature of Enterprise Edition only and is especially useful with failover clustering.

Undo Phase

Undo is the last step in ensuring the consistency of your database. In this phase, any changes made by uncommitted transactions are undone, or *rolled back*. At the end of undo, no more backup files can be processed, and the database is brought online. Undo will not be done if WITH NORECOVERY is specified.

Backing Up and Restoring Full-Text Indexes

If you perform a standard full or differential backup, the full-text catalogs will be backed up as part of the backup process automatically. If you are doing file- or filegroup-based backups, it's a bit different. You must explicitly write a Transact-SQL statement to back up the full-text catalog either as a full or as a differential; I'll show this later in the sections "Backing Up SQL Server Databases" and "Restoring SQL Server Databases."

If the full-text catalogs exist in a different filegroup from where your data is, it will affect your restore order. If you restore the data first and bring it online before restoring the full-text indexes, the two main problems are that full-text queries will fail since the indexes have yet to be restored and the AUTO or UPDATE POPULATION options are not run until the index is restored. If you restore the full-text indexes first, you won't have any problems since nothing can happen if the data is not restored. In both cases, if after restoration the data and full-text catalog are out of sync, they will be made consistent as soon as both are online.

Backing Up and Restoring Analysis Services

If you are using Analysis Services, you must back up your Analysis Services databases like you would if you were using a standard SQL Server database. Should your Analysis Services database contain remote partitions, you can also back those up, but you will have to copy those backups made on the remote servers to another location if you want your backups in one location. Backing up Analysis Services consists of backing up to a file on your disks. Depending on how you configure your Analysis Services database, it will contain different content, as shown in Table 3-1.

Table 3-1. *Differences in Content of Analysis Services Backups*

Usage	Backup Contents
Hybrid OLAP (HOLAP) partitions and dimensions	Metadata, aggregations
Multidimensional OLAP (MOLAP) partitions and dimensions	Metadata, aggregations, and source data
Relational OLAP (ROLAP) partitions and dimensions	Metadata

Setting the Recovery Interval

SQL Server has an option that controls how often the database issues a checkpoint. This option is recovery interval and is set per database, not for the whole SQL Server instance, via sp_configure. Here's an example:

```
USE database_name
GO
EXEC sp_configure 'recovery interval', '5'
GO
```

The recovery interval option's measure is minutes, and the default value is 0. The 0 value means that SQL Server takes care of when the checkpoint happens (see earlier in the chapter around how checkpoints work). Do not change this value unless you think your performance is affected by frequent checkpoints of the database. If you change the value to 60 minutes or more, you need to also run the statement RECONFIGURE WITH OVERRIDE. The value takes effect immediately without stopping and starting the SQL Server services.

■**Note** If you change the value of recovery interval, your database recovery time will take that many times longer to complete. So if you change the value to 5 as shown in the earlier code example, recovery will take nearly five times longer to complete than if you left the default value of 0. This might not be beneficial if you have SLAs to meet, so keep the value for this parameter as small as possible. Change this value with extreme caution.

Using Media Retention

At an instance level, you can set how long SQL Server will retain a backup set. *Retaining* means that within SQL Server, you cannot delete it (but it will not prevent you from doing anything physically on your media). This option is media retention and is considered an advanced configuration option within SQL Server. It is set in days, and the values can be from 0 (the default) to 365.

Note As of the February 2007 SQL Server Books Online update, the topic "Setting Server Configuration Options" denotes that setting media retention requires a restart of the database engine. However, if you click through to its detail page ("media retention Option"), it clearly states that a restart is not necessary.

SQL Server Management Studio

To set media retention using SQL Server Management Studio, follow these steps:

1. Start SQL Server Management Studio.

2. Select the instance name, right-click, and select Properties.

3. Select the Database Settings page of the Server Properties dialog box, as shown in Figure 3-7. Enter a value for Default Backup Media Retention (in Days).

4. Click OK.

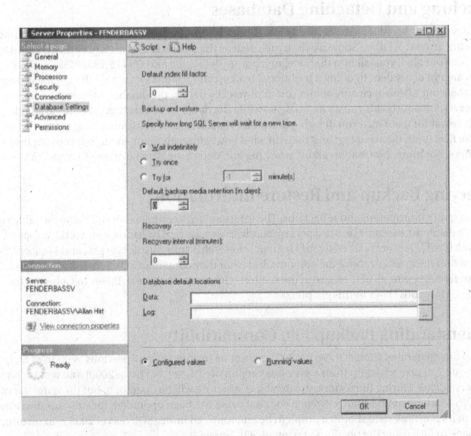

Figure 3-7. *Database Settings page of Server Properties*

Setting media retention in a Query Window

To be able to set this configuration option, enter the following commands in order:

```
USE master
go
sp_configure 'show advanced options', 1
go
reconfigure with override
go
```

If you do not run these commands, you will see the following error:

```
Msg 15123, Level 16, State 1, Procedure sp_configure, Line 51
The configuration option 'media retention' does not exist,
or it may be an advanced option.
```

To configure the value for media retention, use the following sample syntax. The example sets the value to 100 days.

```
sp_configure 'media retention', 100
go
reconfigure with override
go
```

Attaching and Detaching Databases

Since it was introduced in SQL Server 7.0, attaching and detaching databases has become another tool in the arsenal of DBAs. Some like to try to use it as their backup and restore strategy. I hate to burst your bubble if you fall into this category, but sp_detach_db and CREATE DATABASE ... FOR ATTACH are not equivalent to doing a traditional backup and restore. Detaching the database does what it sets out to do—it cleanly allows you to physically detach the database and its files from SQL Server. Obviously this causes an outage—while the database is detached, it is not available to SQL Server for use. Once you detach, you can then make copies at the operating system level of those files (both data and log) and then do what you want with them, including copying them elsewhere. For more information about attaching and detaching databases, see Chapter 15.

Querying Backup and Restore Information

You can query information about backups. The information is contained in the following tables in the msdb database: backupfile, backupfilegroup, backupmediafamily, backupmediaset, backupset, logmarkhistory, restorefile, restorefilegroup, restorehistory, suspect_pages, and sysopentapes. You can find information about the columns and what they contain in SQL Server Books Online. You can find an example of their use in the section "Querying the System Tables to Generate the Backup Commands" later in this chapter.

Understanding Backup File Compatibility

Backup files generated from SQL Server 2005 cannot be restored by any previous version of SQL Server. You can take a backup from a previous version of SQL Server (7.0 or 2000) and restore it with SQL Server 2005. During the restore, the database structure will be upgraded, but the *database compatibility level* will not be changed. Once your database has been upgraded, the only surefire way to revert to its previous state should a problem be encountered under SQL Server 2005 is to restore your backup files using the previous version of SQL Server.

A database's compatibility level does not affect another database. The compatibility level is set per database and "forces" the database engine to behave (as much as it is possible in the version of SQL Server that you are using) like that version of SQL Server you set. In the case of SQL Server 2005, it emulates the previous version (such as SQL Server 2000 or 8.0) as best it can. The compatibility level you set is *not* a guarantee that your SQL Server 2005 database will fully function and act like it did in your previous version, even if you set the compatibility level to that version of SQL Server. Unlike SQL Server 2000, there is no SQL Server 6.0 or 6.5 compatibility level listed in the Management Studio interface, as shown in Figure 3-8. The minimum compatibility level accessible in Management Studio is SQL Server 7.0. To change the compatibility level, you should put the database in single-user mode prior to changing it to ensure that it will not affect any queries or users currently connected to the database.

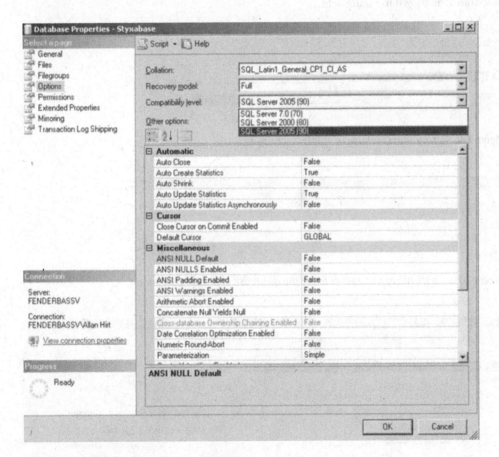

Figure 3-8. *Compatibility level for a database*

Tip If you still have databases under SQL Server 2000 running at a compatibility level older than SQL Server 7.0, I highly suggest you start testing now to ensure that it will work under a later compatibility level. If it does not work, you might have to make changes to your application to accommodate SQL Server 2005. The sad truth is that SQL Server 6.*x* is at least ten years old in terms of technology, so if you have legacy applications that have not been touched in that long, you have other issues outside the scope of SQL Server (such as application remediation) that you will most likely need to address.

Setting the Compatibility Level in SQL Server Management Studio

To set the compatibility level in SQL Server Management Studio, follow these steps:

1. Start SQL Server Management Studio.

2. Expand Databases, select the database that will be changed, right-click, and select Properties. The Properties dialog box will now be displayed. Select the Options page, as shown in Figure 3-4.

3. Under Other Options, scroll down until you see State. Expand it. Change Restrict Access to SINGLE_USER, as shown in Figure 3-9. Click OK. You will be asked to confirm, as shown in Figure 3-10. Click Yes. The Properties dialog box will close, and the database will reflect its new status, as shown in Figure 3-11.

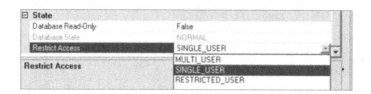

Figure 3-9. *Setting the database in single-user mode*

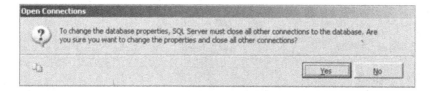

Figure 3-10. *Confirming the option to set the database in single-user mode*

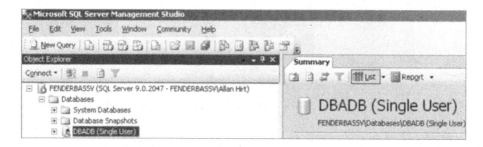

Figure 3-11. *Database reflects single-user mode status*

4. Expand Databases, select the database that will be changed, right-click, and select Properties. The Properties dialog box will now be displayed. Select the Options page, as shown earlier in Figure 3-4.

5. Select the proper compatibility level from the drop-down list, as shown earlier in Figure 3-9.

6. Under Other Options, scroll down until you see State. Expand it. Change Restrict Access to MULTI_USER. Click OK. You will again be prompted with the same dialog box from Figure 3-10. The Properties dialog box will close, and the database will now accept more than one connection.

Setting the Compatibility Level in a Query Window

If you want to script the compatibility level change, you set it via the stored procedure sp_dbcmptlevel. The stored procedure uses the following parameters:

- @dbname, which is the name of the database.

- @new_cmptlevel, which is the version of SQL Server that you are trying to force SQL Server to act like for the database specified by @dbname. The valid values for @new_cmptlevel are 60 (SQL Server 6.0), 65 (SQL Server 6.5), 70 (SQL Server 7.0), 80 (SQL Server 2000), and 90 (SQL Server 2005). The values 60 and 65 are formally depreciated in SQL Server 2005, so do not rely on them. As you can tell, they have already been removed from SQL Server Management Studio. In fact, if you configure a value of 60, you run the risk of causing errors in SQL Server Management Studio and SQL Server Management Objects (SMO), which do not support the value of 60.

To set the compatibility level in a query window, follow these steps:

1. Start a query window in SQL Server Management Studio (or use your favorite query tool such as sqlcmd).

2. Ensure that the context is set to the master database.

3. Set the database in single-user mode with the following command:

```
ALTER DATABASE database_name SET SINGLE_USER
```

4. Run the system stored procedure sp_dbcmptlevel. An example is as follows:

```
exec master.dbo.sp_dbcmptlevel
    @dbname = 'database_name',
    @new_cmptlevel = '80'
```

5. Reset the database to allow multiple connections with the following command:

```
ALTER DATABASE database_name SET MULTI_USER
```

Understanding Systemwide Options for Backing Up to Tape

You might have noticed in Figure 3-7 that there are some systemwide tape options you can set on the Database Settings page of your server properties. These options are available only on this page and cannot be set via a Transact-SQL command. These options are useful only if you are employing a tape as your backup method. Chances are your tape backup will span multiple tapes, and this is how you'll mainly use these options. The options are as follows:

- *Wait Indefinitely*: This is the default and best option. SQL Server will wait forever until you insert a new backup tape.

- *Try Once*: If a new backup tape is not ready for use when SQL Server needs it, SQL Server will time out.

- *Try for Minutes*: If you select this option, you must also select a numeric value up to 2147483647. This will tell SQL Server to wait the specified number of minutes before it will time out.

Planning Your Backup and Restore Strategy

One of the questions I am most often asked by clients is, "What is the best backup plan to implement for our databases?" The answer is always, "It depends." I take all the considerations in the following sections into account (as well as anything else that might be specific to that customer) and work with the customer to devise the right strategy. Rarely do I implement the same strategy more than once.

Understanding SLAs and Recovery

Most administrators (either system administrators or DBAs) responsible for ensuring that backups are made tackle a backup strategy in the wrong way. They first think about the technology they are going to use and how long the backup is actually going to take to generate a file or go to tape. Those are definitely important considerations, but the one issue more than any other that will govern your backup strategy is your recoverability goal. In other words, what is your target SLA for a normal recovery, and what is your agreed upon time to recover in a full disaster scenario? Answering those questions will dictate how you devise your backup strategy.

If you think back to the previous chapters, how much is your data worth to the business? How much does every hour of downtime cost the business? If you are losing $100,000 an hour when your production database is down, it is a pretty safe bet that a restore that takes ten hours to complete (not counting any application testing or checks that need to be done after the restore is complete) is going to be unacceptable to upper management.

So, how do you translate the business requirement of backing up quickly from a bare-metal restore into a technology-based solution without breaking the bank? It is not easy and, more often than not, is impossible. You will have to pay for a robust solution that might have you up and running in less than an hour. The unfortunate reality is that just like everything else when it comes to designing something that is highly available, unless you have deep pockets, you are going to have to make trade-offs somewhere. Only *you* know the trade-offs that are acceptable in your environment and acceptable by your management.

Where you must start is by asking yourself the question, "What is my goal for recovery?" Then break the answer into both high availability and disaster recovery scenarios. The reality is that in most high availability scenarios, you will be using some other technology to meet your primary availability goal. Backups usually come into play with two main scenarios—human error, which happens when data was deleted or changed and you need to go back to what it was before the error, or some hardware/software/environmental failure, which happens when you must recover from backups. Both need to factor into your backup and recovery plan.

Dealing with Human Error

The most common and hardest challenge you need to protect against is what I like to call the "oops" scenario—one caused by human error. Some have also referred to this scenario as *fat fingering*. Picture this: It is 3:59 p.m. Your DBA issues a massive UPDATE statement on a million-row table. The statement executes successfully; only you realize two hours later that he updated the wrong table affecting how your customer-facing web site is now behaving. How do you recover to the point right before the "oops"?

The answer is not clear-cut. When was your last transaction log backup? If you are in simple recovery mode, you are out of luck unless you can easily issue an UPDATE statement to revert the data to its original state or use a backup system that might be at an older point since you have no transaction log backups. In addition, because of the way the wraparound works, the record of the changes are most likely already gone from the log. You will be able to recover only to your last full and/or differential backup in this scenario.

If you have your transaction logs, you will be able to recover to the transaction log prior to the problem, which might mean a small amount of data loss. If all your transaction logs are available, you might be able to recover to the exact point of the data change, but this requires a third-party tool to allow you to read the current transaction log (as well as possibly your transaction log backups) and step through each individual transaction. SQL Server does not provide any native tools for reading the transaction log. If you decide to employ such a method, only experienced DBAs who know what they are doing should use the tool; otherwise, you might incur even more damage to your data.

This example illustrates how important it is to make frequent transaction log backups. Unless you do not care about your business's data, transaction logs could mean the difference between surviving human errors or losing crucial data you might never see again.

The "Need" for Zero Data Loss

If there is any one statement I hear more than any other when it comes to availability from customers, it is, "I cannot tolerate any data loss." Not only in 9.9 times out of 10 is this not true, but in any kind of availability technology, you should count on some data loss. Although this is a topic that should arguably be introduced after discussing each technology individually, your data loss is directly related to your last backup. Look at the examples shown earlier: For the full backup, could you tolerate losing that 14 hours of data? Is that within your tolerance allowed in your SLAs? Do you have a method of reconstructing the 14 hours of data from another system even if it will take time? These are the types of questions you need to be asking yourself as you are devising your backup and restore plans as they relate to your SLAs.

A more robust and frequent backup strategy leads to less data loss in a recovery. The rate of your data change will dictate this to some degree as well. If your data is barely changing on an hourly or daily basis, less frequent backups can be absolutely appropriate. To say you need to do transaction log backups every five minutes when you have only ten records inserted an hour might be overkill . . . or it might not be. However, if you are updating, inserting, or changing thousands of records per minute, your exposure with less frequent backups is glaring: a minute's worth of data could mean thousands of dollars to the business.

Understanding the Link Between Disk Design, Database Layout, Retention, Performance, and Backups

Most administrators do not realize that a backup strategy starts way before you even run a Transact-SQL statement or a utility. Your backups will in many ways be influenced by how you have your databases configured on your disk. I know some of you are scratching your heads right now, but hear me out. I cannot tell you how many times I have seen one of the following disk architectures at clients or at places I have worked in my career:

- All data and log files are in the same directory, which is not optimal from an availability standpoint, but it might (or might not) work for performance depending on how busy your database is and the resulting disk I/O that comes from it. On top of that, the backups are also made to the *same* directory, and at some point, your disk space runs out.

- The SQL Server instance hosts multiple databases—some sit on the same set of disk spindles, and some are different. However, all databases are backed up at the same time to the same disk, which saturates disk I/O both on the server and at the location that stores the backups.

- The database uses multiple files and filegroups, but the backup and restore plans do not take this into account.

- A hardware-based backup solution through snapshots is purchased, but your vendor does not support multiple databases per disk, so you have a 1:1 ratio from database to LUN. This can get challenging in a disk design.

The two biggest downfalls I see with customers when it comes to backups is either a lack of space or diminished performance because of performing backups to the same drive(s) where the data and log files exist. The lack of space issue I have seen at nearly every customer's location for the past ten years. Why? The answer is surprisingly simple: when databases are deployed, not much thought has gone into sizing the disk subsystem to account for backups and, specifically, multiple backups. They did not take into account retention of backups and the space that those backup files will consume.

When it comes to database backup retention, you must think about that up front. A backup plan will include how long you actually have to keep the backups around in some form or another. I am not just talking about doing this for archival purposes: in my experience, it is much easier and speeds up the recovery process if you keep a certain amount of database backups stored on local disks (either directly in the server or through a connected disk subsystem). The logic is simple: the more distance between you and your files, the longer it will take.

As for performance, this one can almost be summed up in the following question: how could you think that placing all of your files on a single drive won't affect performance? You're going to have your databases—which arguably are doing some form of work for your business, and most likely 24x7—sitting on the same spindles where you now need to not only do that work but where you need to read data out for a backup *and* write a backup file to the same disk. Mysteriously your performance tanks at the same time your backup happens. I've seen this at various customer locations. Do you see where this is going? Now, if you have a million disk spindles powering your SQL Server installations, you might not notice anything, but for the rest of us, I would say in most cases you will run into disk contention. Add to this the fact that you now have a single point of failure—if your drive goes, so goes all your data and your backups. Backups are about giving you availability options.

The most important question you must ask is, "How much is the data stored in your databases worth to the business?" Without quantifying that, you can never devise the proper backup solution.

Knowing Your Application

A common problem I see, which is prevalent with packaged applications that you can purchase, is understanding how they support the backup and restore of their application and its databases. You might have the most efficient, top-of-the line plan that works with all your other applications that were built in-house, but if the vendor does not support it, you will need to devise a scheme that is supported. This means it might not fit into the nice, neat world of a single unified backup strategy across your enterprise. Your IT organization needs to be flexible to handle this case. I have seen too many organizations try to force their solution upon something, and ultimately they find themselves wasting time, money, and resources trying to get it to work. Your eyes need to be wide open when evaluating and purchasing packaged software, since you are also buying the administration requirements that come along with it. If you are not ready to accept the terms, I suggest you reevaluate your purchase.

A good case in point is Microsoft's BizTalk. It has a specific way of doing its backups that requires it to do log marks and back up to a local disk or a share. It is deployed via stored procedures that BizTalk provides. It does not allow much (if any) integration with external backup software you might use elsewhere. This caused an issue at one of my clients. One of the ways that we solved the problem was a bit of a hybrid: I took the supplied BizTalk stored procedures, renamed them (so that the originals remained and any work I did was separate), and recoded parts of them to integrate with the third-party backup solution. Although this solved the problem, it creates the problems of having custom code you need to maintain and having to check whether there is an update from Microsoft, and if you have a support issue, Microsoft might make you use the standard procedures. These things happen all the time, but check with your vendor to see the implications of going with such a custom solution. I do not recommend it. Always use what the vendor provides if possible before making life harder for yourself.

Backing Up to Disk, to Tape, or over the Network

SQL Server has historically bucked the trend of many other RDBMS vendors such as Oracle and IBM, even going back to the 4.21a days. Other popular RDBMS systems on various platforms have generally used a tape-based system as the primary form of backup media. The most popular, and arguably best, method of backing up SQL Server has always been directly to a backup file on disk. Tape has always been an option in SQL Server, but because disk costs have significantly come down over the years, using tape as the primary form of backup media has made less and less sense. Since Windows NT 4.0, I have seen an increase in popularity of enterprise backup software that will pull the backup across the network to a central server. All approaches are valid and have pros and cons, but which one is best for you?

As documented earlier, backing up to disk and the wrong disk architecture can prove fatal. If you are going to back up to disk, make sure your backups are physically separate from your data and log files; otherwise, you have a single point of failure. What should happen even if you back up to disk is that another process comes along at some point and copies or moves the files to some central storage for archival purposes. This also frees up space on the local disk. Most companies implement SQL Server backups in this manner.

Backing up directly to tape is good if you are limited on disk space, but this has potential problems. First, I have seen way too many times where a single tape is reused (and not even rotated), so there is a chance every time you do a backup, you are overwriting the old one. If you are doing direct to tape, make sure the administrator responsible has a valid rotation for the tapes and it is being enforced. Second, tape is inherently more unreliable than disk, so it makes it imperative to test the backup after it is made. Media reliability is king with tape. Third, if these tapes are being moved off-site, how will you get them if you need them? And what is the lag time associated with that? This point also goes for disk-based backups that are archived and moved off-site. If you have a disaster today at noon and need last night's backup, what is the process of getting it, and how long will it take? If you had the backup on the local disk (or an attached SAN), you would have access to it instantly. These are the types of questions you need to think about when choosing your backup media. Last, but not least, you need to think of both the bandwidth of streaming to tape as well as the wear and tear of the heads of the tape machine. You might be able to write to disk faster than tape, and since a tape drive has mechanical parts, at some point it will fail.

Backing up across the network using software that integrates with the VDI mentioned earlier is similar to backing up to tape (regardless of what media is on the other end—disk or tape), but this time you have the added complexity of network bandwidth. Generally, you are sharing the same network pipe as all your other traffic, so if you are going to back up your SQL Server databases over the network, you might want to consider a dedicated network or VLAN just for backup traffic. One customer of mine backed up nearly 200GB in about eight hours. That is not exactly going from 0 to 60 in four seconds. You need to decide whether the performance you will get on your network and the impact it has on your network is acceptable. My recommendation is to do what I said earlier: back up to disk and then have an agent grab the generated backup files so you will not be impacting any SQL Server work. You are just pulling files at the operating system level.

I cannot stress enough that there is no right or wrong answer whether to use disk, tape, network, or some combination of them. You need to weigh the pros and cons for yourself and your environment and make the best decision for you.

Checking the Availability of Your Backups

One question that is never answered by most IT shops is, "How available are my backup files?" Sure, everyone usually *makes* the backups, but are the backup files actually available for your use when you need them? If you have trouble answering that question, then the answer is a resounding "no!" You need to take into account a few scenarios. Retention on disk is your first step to the availability of your backups. It is always quicker to restore from something that is right there than try to have to get it from somewhere else. A hardware-assisted backup serves the same purpose here—if the split mirror is available, it is even quicker than restoring from a local disk backup because the synchronization that happens at the disk level starts to happen immediately.

Even if you do local disk or split mirror backups, you cannot store every backup locally. That would require an infinite amount of disk space and, quite frankly, is unrealistic. The next scenario would cover this—what happens if your local disk backups become unavailable or the backup you need is no longer on-site and easily available? You must have a process that takes this into account.

If you have archived your backups to disk or tape to an off-site location, how do you get them? How long will it take? Who is responsible for that process? Keep in mind that no matter how long that process takes, it is the DBA who will ultimately be held accountable for the restore and the time it takes. If you have a four-hour SLA but the process between the backup administrators and the DBAs is broken and it takes three to get the tape and mount it and another two hours to get the backup file to disk (assuming no problems with the tape), you have already blown your SLA before you have even restored the database.

A final key to the availability of your backup files is determining what exactly is the driving factor or purpose for your backups—disaster recovery? The "oops"/fat finger problem? If it is for either one of those, you need that nearline, immediately available backup file that is recent. If the backups are for archive purposes, your SLA is going to be much different than if it is for a problem. For example, if you have a need to restore an old database of sales data from 2002, it is realistic to assume that the restore of the archived backup will not be instantaneous. That backup is probably on some tape in an off-site facility. However, you will most likely need the last week, month, quarter, or year handy.

Remember, when it comes to your backups and restores, every second counts, and this is yet another reason why your backup and retention strategies must be managed to your restore, not the backups themselves.

Testing the Backups

I said it in the first paragraph of this chapter, and I will say it again: if you do not test your backups, you have no backups. You have backup files sitting on physical media. There is a big difference between the two. Most people fall in the latter camp: they do backups but never test them. Unfortunately, few companies I have been at except for one or two over the years actually test their backups, even randomly. I have been onsite with customers who have unfortunately had to go back one month to find a valid backup. People have lost their jobs because of things like this, so do not become a statistic.

The only true way to test a backup is to do a full restore. This is a serious commitment that generally requires an instance dedicated for restores and enough disk space to do the restores. Most IT departments are unwilling or unable (because of budget or resource constraints) to do this commitment. The next best thing is to do a RESTORE VERIFYONLY. RESTORE VERIFYONLY does not actually restore a database but is as close as it gets without doing an actual restore. By default, it does not verify the data itself inside the backup. However, if you enable page checksums on the database you are backing up and you use the WITH CHECKSUM option of BACKUP and RESTORE (or RESTORE VERIFYONLY) introduced in SQL Server 2005, not only is the checksum validated on the backup media, but the checksum is validated on every database page as it is read for backup or as the restore processes the page. This is as close to a verification as you will get in SQL Server 2005 to ensuring that your data is the same. To enable page checksums for your database, execute the following command:

```
ALTER DATABASE database_name SET PAGE_VERIFY CHECKSUM
```

RESTORE VERIFYONLY has been enhanced in SQL Server 2005 to do some additional checks to see whether there are any potential data errors. This process checks the following:

- Checks that the backup set is complete
- Checks that the backups are readable

- Checks some of the header fields of the database pages to simulate writing of the data
- Performs a checksum if one is on the backup media
- Checks for enough disk space on the destination drive or drives

RESTORE VERIFYONLY will not do the same level of checks as doing a DBCC CHECKDB, but it should give you sufficient confidence in your backups. You can find examples of RESTORE VERIFYONLY in the section "Restoring SQL Server Databases."

Synchronizing Your Backups and Restores

A trend I've seen with nearly every one of my customers for the past two to three years is the need to synchronize database backups and restores. Their applications use more than one database (and might also span multiple applications or SQL Server instances), and all of those databases must be restored to the same consistent point. You would think this would be something simple to accomplish, but nothing could be further from the truth. SQL Server does not have a default mechanism for allowing you to say that databases are related.

You must understand up front that even if you could get all your backups to generate at the same time, this does not mean that from a transactional consistency or data standpoint the multiple databases are actually at the same point in time. You know your application and databases (assuming no third-party or packaged applications for the moment). You know that when you insert data into table A, actions X, Y, and Z take place in other tables or databases, which might exist in other instances of SQL Server. Your backup and restore plans must take this into account. After a restore, you will manually need to check data and possibly deal with issues such as orphaned records. The truth is that you will most likely have to do that anyway to see where your last bit of data is, but when multiple databases are involved, doing data consistency checks becomes that much more difficult. You must put a plan together for testing your application and its data thoroughly after a restoration occurs; otherwise, the many hours you just spent restoring your SQL Server environment might go up in smoke because there was data you were not aware of that needed to be there. The fiefdoms cannot be in play at this time. Checking the data is a coordinated effort across groups. Sometimes if some data is missing, it still exists within other systems inside (or outside) your company, so your plan needs to also take that into account—if you need to re-create data, you need to know how you will do it.

The only way to synchronize databases within SQL Server is to use a marked transaction in your applications. Doing so will allow you to recover databases to that marked transaction across all databases. However, this assumes you are using the Full recovery model as well on the databases. A *marked transaction* is pretty much what it sounds like—in your application, you use a distributed marked transaction using the BEGIN TRANSACTION ... WITH MARK syntax, which creates a named transaction mark across all the transaction logs for the databases. The following example will create a marked transaction named MyMark across three databases. Note that you actually have to do generate a transaction to create the mark; a simple SELECT statement that reads data as part of a transaction will not do an INSERT, UPDATE, or DELETE and will not mark that database unless some work is done to the database.

```
BEGIN TRANSACTION MyMark WITH MARK
INSERT INTO DB1.dbowner.MyTable(Column1, Column2) VALUES (1, 'Two')
INSERT INTO DB2.dbowner.AnotherTable
(Column1, Column2) VALUES (3, 'Four')
INSERT INTO AnotherInstance.DB3.dbowner.AnotherTable
(Column1, Column2) VALUES (1, 'Two')
COMMIT TRANSACTION MyMark
```

If you cannot build consistency into your application, you can force a marked transaction log mark across multiple databases. BizTalk employs a similar mechanism in its backup scheme. First, you would need to create a stored procedure for each database that will need to be marked, which will actually place the named transaction. This can be a "dummy" statement that updates just a single record with the same value each time. This is an example:

```
CREATE PROCEDURE dba_MarkTLog
     @MarkName as nvarchar(50)
AS
BEGIN TRANSACTION @MarkName WITH MARK
UPDATE dbname.database_owner.dummytable SET column = 1
COMMIT TRANSACTION
GO
```

Second, you would need a procedure to execute the marks as part of a single transaction. Since the BEGIN TRANSACTION ... COMMIT TRANSACTION is essentially a *two-phase commit* (a transaction that's not committed in one location until it is complete in the other), it makes sure the mark is placed across all databases at the same time; otherwise, it is rolled back.

```
CREATE PROCEDURE dba_MarkAllDBs
     @MarkName as nvarchar(50)
AS
BEGIN TRANSACTION @MarkName WITH MARK
EXEC dbname.database_owner.dummytable.proc_MarkTLog @MarkName
EXEC anotherinstance.dbname.database_owner.dummytable.dba_MarkTLog @MarkName
COMMIT TRANSACTION
GO
```

To cross instance names, you need privileges (such as a linked server or executing under a login that had rights on each instance). The problem with doing log marks outside an application transaction is that although you could definitely restore your databases to the named log mark in all databases, it still will not guarantee that from a data perspective your databases are all at the same point. It will just ensure they are restored to the same point in time. To do a restore of a transaction log, you use the STOPATMARK or STOPBEFOREMARK clause of the RESTORE statement.

Another variation similar to using named transaction log marks is to use the STOPAT clause of RESTORE. STOPAT takes a specific date and time and rolls your database forward only to that point in time. For example, the following statement will restore a database and its log file to the same point:

```
RESTORE DATABASE MyDB
FROM MyBackupDevice
WITH NORECOVERY, STOPAT = '1/1/06 12:00 AM'

RESTORE LOG MyDBLog
FROM MyLogDevice
WITH RECOVERY, STOPAT = '1/1/06 12:00 AM'
```

Understanding Your Recoverability Paths

In a recovery scenario where you need to use backups, one trick to keeping calm is to know the options available to you—not only what backups are on hand or what is on tape (or archived offsite), but what paths can you go down to restore the database. Consider the following scenario: you make a full backup once a week on Sunday at midnight, daily differentials every other day at midnight, and transaction log backups every 15 minutes. The following are two examples of how to deal with a failure and a recovery using backups.

Example 1

At 9:52 a.m. Tuesday, your server, which is stand-alone, suffers a catastrophic failure to the internal disks. After working on the system for an hour, the Windows administrators determine that it is impossible to recover the system, and it will need to be reformatted and rebuilt.

If the backups were stored only on those internal disks, shame on you. Your backups are gone. However, lucky for you, your company makes copies of the backups every hour to a central share. Since your server failed at 9:52 a.m., this means the last backup files available to you would be the ones copied off at 9 a.m. This might (or might not) include the 9 a.m. transaction log file. Assuming the worst-case scenario, you can recover to 8:45 a.m. assuming all the backups are on the share—which they are. This means you will have roughly one hour of data loss that you might or might not be able to piece together from other places.

Here are all the backups you have available to you: the Sunday full, the Monday differential, and all transaction logs up until 8:45 a.m. Tuesday. You have two main possibilities when it comes to restoring your database:

- Restore the full backup, the differential backup, and all transaction log backups after the differential backup.

- Restore the full backup and all transaction log backups after the full backup.

If the full backup takes 20 minutes and the differential takes 8, that means you are restoring either 36 (1 full, 1 differential, and 34 transaction log backups) or 129 (1 full backup, 128 transaction logs) files, respectively. Although 129 files seem like a lot of files, it might or might not be quicker. This is where your testing will have paid off, since you will know the most optimal version for restoring.

Example 2

The server still encounters a failure at 9:52 a.m. However, damage seems to have been done only to the Windows disks, which also happen to contain the SQL Server executables but not the databases or the backups. That means you can restore your environment possibly to the point of failure. First, you must rebuild (or restore, depending on what is done) Windows and reconfigure SQL Server. That will most likely take an hour or two—you are already at noon. Once Windows and SQL Server are functional, you can now go about restoring the databases.

You have three options available to you:

- Attach the database.

- Restore the full backup, the differential backup, and all transaction log backups after the differential backup up to and including 9:45 a.m.

- Restore the full backup and all transaction log backups after the full backup up to and including 9:45 a.m.

Believe it or not, assuming that there has been no damage to the file system that contains the existing .mdf, .ndf, and .ldf files, attaching the database files will be your quickest and best option. You will most likely have to fix some things, such as jobs (any object that sat outside that database will need to be re-created) and logins, and possibly run UPDATE STATISTICS, but the biggest part of your pain is always the database itself. Attaching in this case saves you a lot of the pain since a restore of a large database can take hours.

If for some reason the attach fails, that means you are restoring either 40 (1 full, 1 differential, and 38 transaction log backups) or 133 (1 full backup, 132 transaction logs) files, respectively.

Querying the System Tables to Generate the Backup Commands

To save yourself work in a disaster, you can query the tables listed in the section "Querying Backup and Restore Information" earlier in this chapter to derive the files and syntax needed for restoring your database. Automating this and running the query often and saving the output through a SQL Server Agent job can save you a great deal of time. To help you, I have created a stored procedure named dba_GenerateBackupCommands that does this. It queries both backupset and backupmediafamily in the msdb database and is a simple example of what you can do. Modify the code to fit your needs. The stored procedure has two parameters:

- @backuptype, which is a number that tells the stored procedure the commands to generate. The value 1 is for a full backup only, 2 is for a full plus all transaction logs, 3 is for a full plus a differential, and 4 is for a full plus differential and transaction logs.

- @dbname, which is the name of the database you are generating the syntax for and is encased in single quotes.

A sample execution is as follows, and Figure 3-12 shows its resulting output. You can then copy and paste those commands into a file or directly send the output of the query to a file.

```
dba_GenerateBackupCommands
    @backuptype = 4,
    @dbname = 'Styxabase'
```

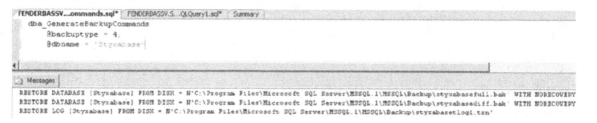

Figure 3-12. *Output of running* dba_GenerateBackupCommands

Tip To download the code for the stored procedure dba_GenerateBackupCommands, go to the Apress web site at http://www.apress.com. I made a conscious decision not to put long passages of code in this book not only to save space (this thing is big enough), but I did not expect you to retype nine pages of code!

Another example that I had to use recently was to query the system tables to see the order of log files I had to restore. What happened was that I accidentally set two separate transaction log backup jobs on a production database that I was log shipping to migrate to new hardware. (Yes, even authors screw up from time to time.) The jobs ran at the same time, so it was a race to the finish to see what would complete first. Since I knew the name of the full backup file, the first step I had to take was to figure out which backups could come after it. I queried the backupmediafamily table to get the media_set_id for the specific backup file I used. The query is as follows:

```
SELECT [media_set_id]
FROM msdb.dbo.backupmediafamily
WHERE [physical_device_name] = 'backup_file_name'
```

When you get the media_set_id, use the number in the next query that uses the backupset table. Since I had differential backups on the source that I no longer had access to, I knew I had to narrow it down to the transaction log backups that have a type of L in backupset. The last LSN from the previous file has to match the first LSN of the next file. The query I ran is as follows:

```
select b.[physical_device_name], a.[first_lsn], a.[last_lsn]
from msdb.dbo.backupset a, msdb.dbo.backupmediafamily b
where a.[media_set_id] > result_from_last_query
and a.[media_set_id] = b.[media_set_id]
and a.[database_name] = 'db_name'
and a.[type] = 'L'
```

Figure 3-13 shows an example execution with the consecutive LSNs.

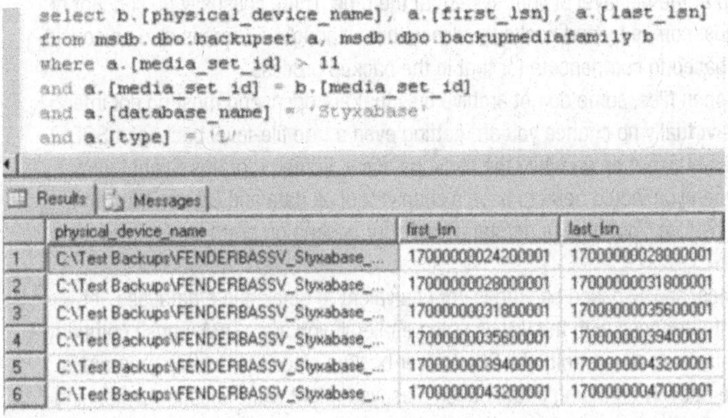
```
select b.[physical_device_name], a.[first_lsn], a.[last_lsn]
from msdb.dbo.backupset a, msdb.dbo.backupmediafamily b
where a.[media_set_id] > 11
and a.[media_set_id] = b.[media_set_id]
and a.[database_name] = 'Styxabase'
and a.[type] = 'L'
```

	physical_device_name	first_lsn	last_lsn
1	C:\Test Backups\FENDERBASSV_Styxabase_...	17000000024200001	17000000028000001
2	C:\Test Backups\FENDERBASSV_Styxabase_...	17000000028000001	17000000031800001
3	C:\Test Backups\FENDERBASSV_Styxabase_...	17000000031800001	17000000035600001
4	C:\Test Backups\FENDERBASSV_Styxabase_...	17000000035600001	17000000039400001
5	C:\Test Backups\FENDERBASSV_Styxabase_...	17000000039400001	17000000043200001
6	C:\Test Backups\FENDERBASSV_Styxabase_...	17000000043200001	17000000047000001

Figure 3-13. *Output of query*

Managing the Transaction Log Through Backups

It should go without saying, but your log file should be sized appropriately from the start and, if necessary, have a reasonable automatic growth set for it. You should not see frequent log growths; otherwise, you did not size it properly. A good rule of thumb is to make it twice as big as your largest table's clustered index since in the event of an index rebuild, SQL Server will not only need to make sure it can perform the rebuild that is logged but also keep track of the changed pages just in case the operation needs to be rolled back.

To maintain the size of your transaction log, the easiest way is to perform frequent enough transaction log backups to flush the completed transactions from the log file. A transaction log backup will not shrink the actual transaction log file. By performing frequent transaction log backups, you should maintain the same size of the transaction log file or files you are using. The reality is that you need transaction log backups for point-in-time recovery, so they will now serve a dual purpose.

However, you might run into cases where a backup won't solve your problem. The most common problem I see is physically running out of space on disk.

OS-BASED FILE-LEVEL BACKUPS AND BACKING UP SERVERS WITH SQL SERVER INSTANCES

One of the things I run into quite frequently with customers is the following question from non-DBA administrators who are the ones tasked with backing up SQL Server, "Why can't I use my operating system imaging software to make a point-in-time backup of my SQL Server instances?" The answer is sadly easy: it is not a SQL Server backup in the way a traditional SQL Server backup is defined. The imaging programs or OS-based backups (network or local) generally make a snapshot backup at the file level of your system at the time. There is usually no concept of application-specific considerations—it just comes by and backs up files with no "thought." There is also no consideration that SQL Server is transactional based to compensate for that in the backup process.

Some programs allow backups of open files, some do not archive files that are open, and most do not interface with the SQL Server VDI, so there is virtually no chance you are getting even a true file-level backup of SQL Server unless SQL Server and its services are shut down while the backups occur. Some programs might indirectly interface with the VDI through VSS, but then you would need to have a snapshot of all data and log volumes done at the same time to ensure a consistent restore. You must understand how your backup program works to see whether it does this.

In my experience, 9.9 out of 10 times, an OS-based backup is not equivalent to detaching a database, let alone a true SQL Server backup, unless it interfaces with the VDI as noted earlier. If you are a DBA whose company insists on such a backup strategy and refuses to do a traditional SQL Server backup since the backup program is coming along and attempting to grab the actively changing data and log files, you might want to consider heading for the door . . . and quickly. You do not want to be around for the disaster when it happens since you might not have a valid backup of your SQL Server databases. Having said all of this, most popular enterprise-class backup software has a plug-in or option that is specifically coded to the VDI and can be used to back up SQL Server, so you might have to educate your company on using the software properly to perform SQL Server backups.

A great use of backup programs with SQL Server is to allow SQL Server to perform the backups to disk, preferably to a stable, known location. Then at a scheduled time, that program can come along and grab the SQL Server backup files and archive them to another location such as a large storage array on the back end for nearline storage or to tape for off-site archiving. This is the most common usage of a backup program with SQL Server in my experience.

The subject of backing up the operating system is also a strange topic when it comes to SQL Server since in most cases SQL Server is on a dedicated server for use just with SQL Server. You need to evaluate your company's needs, but if your SQL Server goes down, what are you more concerned about—your data or the configuration of the server itself? By no means am I saying to ignore the configuration of the server and the SQL Server instance. You should have it well documented. Consider this example: You make a backup of the operating system. The server goes down (for whatever reason), and you need to get it back up and running. It takes one hour to locate the backup, 50 minutes to do the restore, and 30 minutes to perform baseline tests. In most cases, I find that doing a bare-metal installation will take the same or less time. The installation media is usually easier to locate than the backup. Windows generally takes 30–60 minutes to install, and my guess is your company has a base image that it can throw on a server possibly quicker than that. SQL Server should take about the same when all is said and done. The choice is up to you—I think it is valid to back up your operating system, but is it efficient for your IT organization versus doing a reinstall? That is a question I cannot answer for you.

Implementing the Plan

When it comes to backup and restore, most of the difficulty is usually at the planning stage. The actual implementation and technology is much more straightforward, but it does take a bit of work to get it right.

Tip Create a SQL Server Agent job (jobs are covered in depth in Chapter 16) that contains all the syntax to do your restore from your SQL Server backup file or files (depending on your strategy). This will ensure that in the heat of the moment during a disaster, no one will screw up typing the command. If it is a job, all you need to do is execute it and let it run.

Ensuring SQL Server Agent Is Started

One of the key steps you can take to ensure your backups work is to check to see that the SQL Server Agent is up and running. Without it, none of your scheduled backups will work. This might seem like a no-brainer, but I have definitely seen where it was not. SQL Server does not start and stop the SQL Server Agent automatically only when it needs to run a scheduled task. It must be on all the time.

Knowing Your Backup Requirements and Their Relation to Backup Frequency

As you have ascertained by now, everyone's needs are different, and each system or environment might have its own set of requirements. At a bare minimum, do a full backup as frequently as you need it. If your database is small enough, you can even do a full backup every day. However, that might be excessive in terms of drive space. If your database is larger and/or you want to speed up your nightly backups, I suggest doing a weekly or biweekly full and doing differentials on the other days. Then you need to consider your transaction log backups, which all goes back to your data loss SLAs and business requirements. I usually start with 15-minute intervals and go up or down depending on my customer's needs. If you have a fast enough disk subsystem and your transactions are small, you can possibly even get your transaction log backups down to being done every minute, but that is unrealistic. Most of my customers have not done transaction log backups more frequently than five minutes (with rare exceptions over the years). If their data is not changing much, I might put them at 30 minutes or 1 hour, but I usually never recommend much beyond that.

I have implemented file or filegroup backups infrequently, although many could benefit from it. Most databases I encounter do not use partitioning or have a disk configuration that would provide the best availability and performance you could get from a file/filegroup database design. It is definitely a specific strategy that works in certain instances, but it is not a common scenario with most of my current clients. I think as more and more databases become VLDBs, this situation will change since one of the only ways to deal with large databases is to back them up in manageable chunks.

Implementing Backup Security

People seem to forget security when it comes to backups. This manifests itself in different ways. Just when I thought I had seen it all, I was at a client site where one of the DBAs had recently left the company. That should not cause problems under normal circumstances since it is the corporate policy in most workplaces to change passwords and such to which that person might have had access. Unfortunately, this client removed the accounts this person had access to from each individual database. This should not have been major, but what happened was that the jobs that performed the backups were associated with that user, so the jobs no longer had access to the databases. This left that customer exposed for nearly a month before they realized no backups were being done. Needless to say, that is a problem. Do not let this happen to you. Have policies in place that prevent these types of events, and use accounts that are not directly associated with any one single user.

In addition to security around administrative accounts, you must secure the directories that will contain the database backups. This is even more imperative when your data is already highly confidential, such as with data stored in financial or government systems. Unless you use some form of third-party backup solution to encrypt your backup as it is generated, the resulting backup is essentially a plain-text file sitting on the file system that could be parsed. Anyone with access to the directory containing the backup file can essentially load it into their favorite text editor and try to read it. Certain tools give you the ability to read the transaction log, so you might even have someone who could load a transaction log into a tool and see what happened transaction by transaction. Clearly you want none of this to happen. At the least, secure the access to the Windows directory at the Windows level and allow access only to those who need it. Remember to add the SQL Server service accounts to access that directory. Another option you have is to encrypt the directory at the file system level, but you would need to take into account the performance hit you might take when reading and writing from that directory.

External people and companies might be involved with your backups. If you trust your DBAs but your servers are hosted by a company and their operators are responsible for getting the backups to tape and archiving them, do you trust them? Are they bonded? Or if you need to move your backups containing sensitive data off-site, do you trust the truck driver or the facility housing the backups? You can obviously take security to a ridiculous level, but these questions just emphasize the point that you need to worry about security at all levels when it comes to your backups.

When performing a restore, you should take similar care when deciding who has access to do that functionality. You do not want anyone who does not have the right clearance (if you are dealing with sensitive data) to be able to restore a database. I am not going to presume to tell you who in your organization should and should not have access, but suffice it to say that evaluation will need to take place when you put your policies in place.

Tip SQL Server has a database-level role db_backupoperator that allows only the user associated with that role to execute a backup of that database. So if you want to allow your Windows administrators to back up your database without having more rights than they need, consider creating a user in the database with just this role. There is no equivalent role for the restoration of a database at the instance level, so the person executing that task will need to have some sort of higher-level access to the instance to restore the database.

Checking Database Status

Before you try to restore your database or transaction log, it is always a good idea to check to see whether what you are trying to do is possible. If your database is in a state where it cannot be backed up, why even attempt it? Or if you were not expecting the database to be in a state where it could not be backed up, you can investigate why. You can go about this task in two ways.

SQL Server Management Studio

Checking the status of your database in SQL Server Management Studio is simple. Just expand Databases, and its status will appear next to the database name. If the database is online and operational and is not in a special state such as single user, nothing will appear next to its name. Figure 3-14 shows an example of databases with different states next to them.

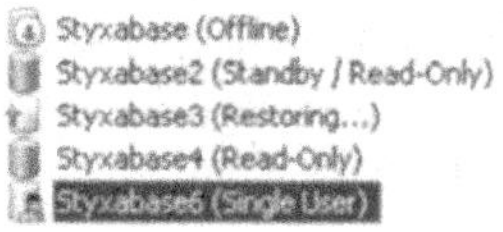

Styxabase (Offline)
Styxabase2 (Standby / Read-Only)
Styxabase3 (Restoring...)
Styxabase4 (Read-Only)
Styxabase6 (Single User)

Figure 3-14. *Database state examples*

Transact-SQL

In the past, you may have used the function DATABASEPROPERTY to query properties of your individual databases. You should use the function DATABASEPROPERTYEX in SQL Server 2005 to query database properties. Although you can still use DATABASEPROPERTY within SQL Server 2005, it is recommended that you use only DATABASEPROPERTYEX.

No matter what type of backup you are restoring, you should execute the command SELECT DATABASEPROPERTYEX ('*database_name*', 'Status'), where *database_name* is the name of your database. If the values EMERGENCY, OFFLINE, RECOVERING, RESTORING, or SUSPECT appear, investigate why that is before you go and take a corrective course of action, since each of these denotes that there is some sort of issue or the database is already in the middle of a restore process.

If you are restoring a transaction log, first check whether the recovery model is set to Simple since it does not allow a transaction log to be loaded. You learned how to show the recovery model earlier in the section "Describing the Recovery Models." Next check whether the database is in a state where transaction logs can be applied. If you restored the database using WITH NORECOVERY, execute the command SELECT DATABASEPROPERTYEX ('*database_name*', 'Status'), where *database_name* is the name of your database. The query should return a value of RESTORING, as shown in Figure 3-15.

Figure 3-15. *Sample execution of DATABASEPROPERTYEX with a database in NORECOVERY*

If you restored the database WITH STANDBY and if you execute the same statement, you will see that the database has a value of ONLINE, which is not actually the case because although you can technically use the database for read-only purposes, it is not fully online to both read and write to. If you get a value of ONLINE, you must then run the query DATABASEPROPERTYEX ('*database_name*', 'IsInStandby'). If this returns a value of 1, your database has been restored WITH STANDBY. If it returns a value of 0, your database truly is online, and no transaction logs can be restored.

Another way you can see the status is by querying sys.databases.

Note There is a bit of an inconsistency with the implementation of DATABASEPROPERTYEX. Microsoft seems to have collapsed the DATABASEPROPERTY options of IsEmergencyMode, IsInRecovery, IsOffline, IsRestoring, and IsSuspect into the option Recovery for DATABASEPROPERTYEX, but the option IsInStandby is still its own option to check. Table 3-2 maps the options and values from DATABASEPROPERTY to their counterparts in SQL Server 2005's DATABASEPROPERTYEX.

Table 3-2. *Comparison of DATABASEPROPERTY and DATABASEPROPERTYEX As They Relate to Individual Database Status*

DATABASEPROPERTY Option	Value	DATABASEPROPERTYEX Option	Value
No equivalent—must issue query SELECT [recovery_model_desc] FROM sysdatabases WHERE [name] = 'database_name'	BULK_LOGGED, FULL, or SIMPLE	Recovery	BULK_LOGGED, FULL, or SIMPLE
IsDetached	1 (True)	No equivalent	Detaching a database in SQL Server 2005 appears like you dropped the database and no longer exists in sys.databases.
IsEmergencyMode	1 (True)	Status	EMERGENCY
IsInLoad	1 (True)	Status	RESTORING
IsInRecovery	1 (True)	Status	RECOVERING
IsInStandby	0 (False), 1 (True), NULL	IsInStandby	0 (False), 1 (True), NULL
IsOffline	0 (False), 1 (True)	Status	ONLINE (maps to 0), OFFLINE (maps to 1)
IsSuspect	1 (True)	Status	SUSPECT

Monitoring Backup Media and Backup Status

Another consistent problem I see at too many sites is the lack of monitoring (which is a topic I will formally address in Chapter 15). When it comes to backups, you must closely monitor whether your backups are succeeding. This is as simple as seeing the history of the job, as shown in Figure 3-16. An even better option is to automate that process and to use the built-in notification mechanisms of SQL Server or some third-party monitoring tool to inform you of the status of the backups. Do not discover too late that your backups have been failing for weeks. Not only are you blowing your SLA and OLA, but the amount of exposure with regard to data loss that you will have is tremendous. Do *you* want to be the one telling the business that if SQL Server failed today, you would need to go back to a backup (which might or might not be tested) that was created three weeks ago?

Similarly, one common cause of failure for backups is that the resulting backup location on disk is full. This is yet another thing I see at nearly every customer's site. Most customers do not have enough disk space as is (and they know it), so it is paramount to monitor your servers for the amount of free space to allow time for proper remediation if you start to fill your disks. Nothing is worse than discovering 30 days later that you have no backups because your disk is full or you never rotated the tape and the same tape was written over.

Having a proper retention plan will also help you manage that precious disk space since you should know at any time how much space is being used and what is being stored on disk. The usage will go up as time goes on, but it should not magically fill up leaving everyone scratching their heads about why all of a sudden you are out of disk space. You need to have a careful balance between quick recoverability (having local backups ready to use), the business (having backups for emergencies), and IT (managing the implementation).

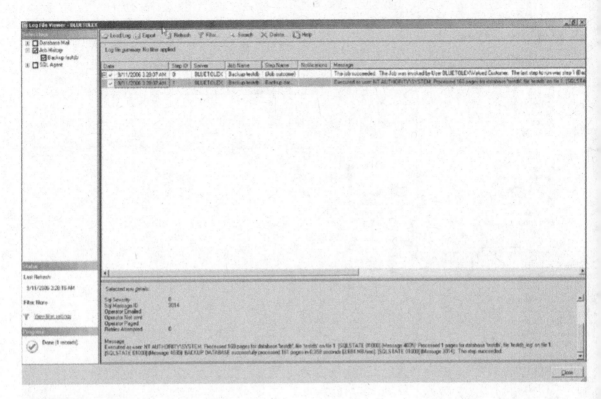

Figure 3-16. *Checking the status of a backup job*

Using the Database Maintenance Plan Wizard

In my opinion, an enterprise-class deployment of SQL Server should never use the Database Maintenance Plan (DBMP) Wizard to set up maintenance, including backups. I am constantly amazed how
often I see this. Now, don't get me wrong: the DBMP Wizard is an excellent feature of SQL Server and
really helps the small- to mid-sized IT shops and stand-alone businesses where there is little to no
SQL Server expertise. When you are managing hundreds (or thousands) of databases across tens or
hundreds of SQL Server instances, though, you need to do it yourself by creating jobs and using
Transact-SQL.

What the DBMP does is essentially create an SSIS package that is called by a SQL Server Agent
job. To see the details, you need to actually look at the maintenance plan. To modify the parameters
of the maintenance plan, you need to do it in the maintenance plan itself, which takes a few clicks
(selecting the maintenance plan, selecting the proper task, and then modifying it). To me, this is
much less flexible and you have less visibility into what is happening. Instead of seeing the
Transact-SQL BACKUP command in a SQL Server Agent job shown in Figure 3-17, you see what is displayed in Figure 3-18. I find it easier to decipher Transact-SQL than to debug a maintenance plan.
In the heat of the battle where you are trying to get your database restored, the DBMP job is not
going to help you much. I find it is much better to code and implement things on your own.

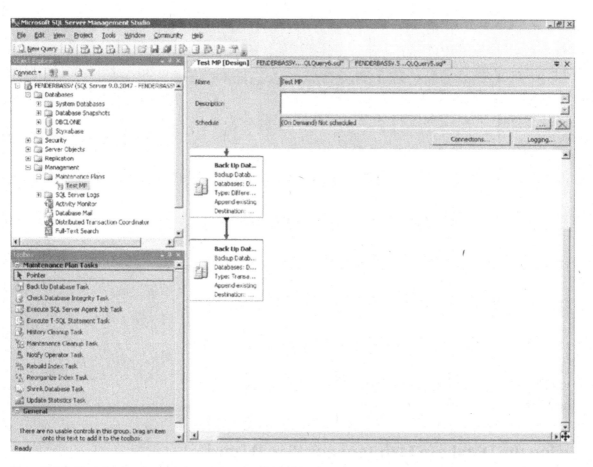

Figure 3-17. *What the database maintenance plan looks like*

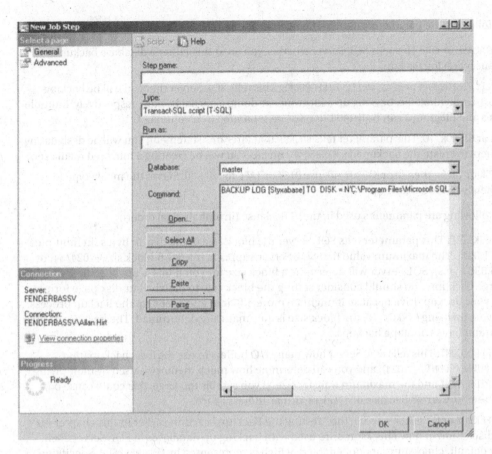

Figure 3-18. *Job step with Transact-SQL*

Backing Up SQL Server Databases

The following sections will cover how to back up SQL Server databases either via a Transact-SQL statement or in SQL Server Management Studio. Full database backups default to a file extension of .bak, transaction log backups usually have an extension of .trn, and differential backups usually have an extension of .dif.

Note Ensure that the user who will be executing the backup has the right permissions and access to the device, whether tape or disk.

Transact-SQL

The BACKUP statement has two main variations: BACKUP DATABASE and BACKUP LOG. BACKUP DATABASE is for doing a full or differential backup of the database, and BACKUP LOG is for backing up the transaction log. The parameters used by both are similar (if not the same) in most cases.

The following are parameters used in the main portion of the BACKUP statement:

- DATABASE or LOG: This tells SQL Server whether you are doing either a database backup or a transaction log backup.

- FILE, FILEGROUP, or READ_WRITE_FILEGROUPS: This tells SQL Server that you will be backing up an individual file, backing up a filegroup, or doing a partial backup, respectively. Multiple files and filegroups can be listed but must be separated by a comma (,).

- TO or MIRROR TO: This parameter tells BACKUP that after this statement, you will be designating where to create the backup file. MIRROR TO means you will be creating a mirrored media set.

- DISK or TAPE: After TO or MIRROR TO, use DISK or TAPE to tell SQL Server the media type to where you are backing up.

The following are parameters used in the WITH clause (in alphabetical order):

- BLOCKSIZE: This parameter tells SQL Server the block size of the disk in bytes (in multiples of 1,024). The maximum value that SQL Server supports is a 64KB block size (1024*64, or 65,536 bytes). SQL Server will determine a block size for you if this is not specified, but for large backups, you should consider setting the block size to match your disk page format of your backup drive because it might be more efficient and speed up the backup process. If you are using MIRROR TO, the block size is automatically determined. The best use of this parameter is with tape backups.

- BUFFERCOUNT: This tells SQL Server how many I/O buffers to use during a backup (that is, BUFFERCOUNT = 1024), and you can determine how much memory is used by multiplying BUFFERCOUNT and the maximum transfer size. If you set this too large, this could cause out-of-memory errors because of a lack of virtual address space.

- CHECKSUM or NO_CHECKSUM: See the "Testing the Backups" section earlier in this chapter for a discussion of how checksums are used with backing up databases in SQL Server 2005. By default, checksums are not enabled, which is represented by NO_CHECKSUM. Specifying CHECKSUM can give you a nice validation of your backup and is something you should consider, especially if you are not testing your backups that are generated. However, keep in mind that because additional checks are happening, the backup might take longer to generate.

- COPY_ONLY: COPY_ONLY is new to SQL Server 2005. A backup that is specified with the COPY_ONLY parameter is one that will not affect your LSN sequence. It cannot be used to seed a backup strategy and can be used only to create full or transaction log backups. If DIFFERENTIAL is specified in a BACKUP statement containing COPY_ONLY, COPY_ONLY is ignored, and a differential backup is created. If you create a transaction log backup using COPY_ONLY, it will not truncate the transaction log and will still have the behavior of not affecting the LSN chain. A COPY_ONLY backup can be used in scenarios where, for example, you want to create a point-in-time read-only copy of the database via a backup but do not want to affect any other backup plans you might have in place.

- DESCRIPTION: This parameter contains up to a 255-character explanation encased in single quotes of what is in the backup.

- DIFFERENTIAL (BACKUP DATABASE only): This parameter indicates that the type of backup performed will be a differential database backup. As noted earlier, a differential backup contains the delta between the last full backup and the time when the differential backup is started.

- EXPIREDATE: This parameter tells SQL Server to set a date when the backup media set will no longer be valid and can be overwritten from a SQL Server perspective. SQL Server cannot prevent one of your administrators from erasing or overwriting a file. If EXPIREDATE is not configured, SQL Server will default the expiration date to the SQL Server configuration option media retention, which was described earlier in this chapter. If SKIP is used as part of the WITH clause, EXPIREDATE is ignored. The value must be in a valid date format encased in single quotes.

- FORMAT or NOFORMAT: FORMAT tells SQL Server to create a new media set and not append the backup to an existing media set. If you are using the same device name or tape, it will overwrite any existing header and backup sets. FORMAT implies using SKIP, so you do not need to expressly use SKIP when using FORMAT. NOFORMAT is the default behavior and preserves existing headers and backup sets.

- INIT or NOINIT: If you want to overwrite an existing backup set with the same name, use INIT. INIT will keep the media header. If you specify NOINIT, the backup made will be appended to the backup set. NOINIT is the default behavior.

- MAXTRANSFERSIZE: This option (set in bytes up to 4,194,304—4MB, with a minimum of 65,536 bytes) tells SQL Server the largest amount that can be transferred in one chunk to the backup media (that is, MAXTRANSFERSIZE = 4194304).

- MEDIADESCRIPTION: This is an optional description of the media set and can be up to 255 characters encased in single quotes.

- MEDIANAME: This is an optional name for the entire media set and can be up to 128 characters encased in single quotes.

- MEDIAPASSWORD: This parameter will set a password for the entire media set. If it is specified, the password will be required before you create a backup set on the media set and before you restore the database. The password is entered only in plain text and thus cannot be considered secure. According to Microsoft, this parameter will be removed in a future version of SQL Server, so if you are using it now, you might want to consider other ways to secure your backups.

- NAME: This parameter specifies a name for the backup set and can be up to 128 characters encased in single quotes.

- NO_LOG or TRUNCATE_ONLY (BACKUP LOG only): These options are functionally the same and have been the historical way of truncating the transaction log going back to the 4.21a days, but Microsoft is putting all DBAs on notice that these will be removed in a future version of SQL Server after 2005. See the "Transaction Log Backup" section earlier in this chapter for the caveats (such as breaking the LSN chain) when truncating the transaction log, especially if you are in Full or Bulk-logged recovery mode.

- NORECOVERY or STANDBY (BACKUP LOG only): This is new functionality to SQL Server 2005. When you are backing up a transaction log, if you specify one of these, it will put the database into the state you specify once the transaction log backup is complete. If you are using STANDBY, you must also set a valid standby file (for example, STANDBY = 'c:\undofile'), which contains all rolled-back changes to the database that might have to be undone as a result of a RESTORE LOG.

- NO_TRUNCATE (BACKUP LOG only): This tells a transaction log backup not to truncate the transaction log and to try the transaction log backup no matter what state the database is in. The reason you would use this type of transaction log backup is if your database might be damaged and you want to get a transaction log backup. The transaction log backup will fail with this option if the database is in either the OFFLINE or EMERGENCY state.

- PASSWORD: This parameter will set a password for the backup set. If it is specified, the password will be required during the restoration of the database. The password is entered only in plain text and thus cannot be considered secure. According to Microsoft, this parameter will be removed in a future version of SQL Server, so if you are using it now, you might want to consider other ways to secure your backups.

- RESTART: This is no longer a valid option in SQL Server 2005 but is included for compatibility with older versions that used this.

- RETAINDAYS: This parameter sets the number of days before the backup media set can be overwritten.

- REWIND or NOREWIND (tape backup only): REWIND means that SQL Server will rewind the tape as part of the backup process. NOREWIND means that the tape will be kept open by SQL Server after the backup is complete. If you are performing multiple backups to the same tape, this is useful, but it also means that until a REWIND or UNLOAD is issued in the same session or SQL Server is shut down, the tape drive will not be available to any other process on your server. REWIND is the default option.

- SKIP or NOSKIP: If you want to bypass the default checks that a backup does when the process is initiated (backup set expiration and the NAME as specified earlier), use SKIP. NOSKIP is the opposite (and the default BACKUP behavior)—all normal checks are performed.

- STATS: Specifying STATS will show you the percentage complete of the backup you are performing. By default, SQL Server will update you every 10%, but if you want something different, you must specify a percentage as to when you want to be updated (that is, STATS = 3). However, as shown in the later example, it is not an exact science even if you specify a value. This is to be expected. STATS can be useful when you are backing up large databases.

- STOP_ON_ERROR or CONTINUE_AFTER_ERROR: If you are worried about the integrity of your backups, you should consider using STOP_ON_ERROR, which is the default behavior. If SQL Server encounters a page checksum that cannot be verified, the backup will fail. If you do not care about page checksum errors or torn pages, specify CONTINUE_AFTER_ERROR. Using CONTINUE_AFTER_ERROR might be the only way to capture the tail of the log if your database is damaged and can be used in place of NO_TRUNCATE.

- UNLOAD or NOUNLOAD (tape backup only): UNLOAD means that when the backup is complete, the tape is rewound and ejected. NOUNLOAD tells the backup command to leave the tape loaded in the tape drive, so you would have to manually remove it. This option remains in place until your session has ended. UNLOAD is the default option.

Creating a Backup Device

The following statement creates a backup device. Note the use of the word *dump* in sp_addumpdevice, which is the original name for the BACKUP command in versions prior to SQL Server 7.0. For the list of all options, see the topic "sp_addumpdevice (Transact-SQL)" in SQL Server Books Online. A device can be used for either the data or log.

```
sp_addumpdevice
    @devtype = 'disk',
    @logicalname = 'MyDataBackupDevice'
    @physicalname = 'c:\Backups\MyDataBackupDevice.bak'
```

Performing a Full Database Backup to a Backup Device

This statement backs up a database to a disk file:

```
BACKUP DATABASE MyDB TO MyDataBackupDevice
```

Performing a Full Database Backup to Disk

This statement backs up a database to a disk file:

```
BACKUP DATABASE MyDB TO DISK = 'C:\Backups\MyDB.bak'
```

Performing a Full Database Backup to Tape

This statement backs up a database to a tape device:

```
BACKUP DATABASE MyDB TO TAPE = '\\.\tape0'
```

Performing a Differential Database Backup

This statement backs up a database to a disk file:

```
BACKUP DATABASE MyDB TO DISK = 'C:\Backups\MyDB.dif' WITH DIFFERENTIAL
```

Performing a Backup to Mirrored Media Set

This statement backs up a database to single-family mirrored media set. Note the use of FORMAT, which tells the command to create a new media set, and the use of MEDIANAME, which names the media set.

```
BACKUP DATABASE MyDB
TO DISK = 'C:\Backups\MyDB1.bak'
MIRROR TO DISK = 'D:\Backups\MyDB2.bak'
WITH MEDIANAME = 'MyDB Mirror Media Set'
```

Setting a Backup Expiration

SQL Server allows you to set when a backup set expires, and the setting can be overwritten. You control this with the EXPIREDATE clause. The RETAINDAYS clause tells SQL Server how many days are allowed before the backup media set can be overwritten.

```
BACKUP DATABASE MyDB
TO DISK = 'C:\Backups\MyDB
WITH RETAINDAYS = 10, EXPIREDATE = '01/01/2007'
```

Performing a File Backup

The following are examples of backing up a database using a file-based backup strategy. Remember that you still need to do a transaction log to keep the backups synchronized.

```
BACKUP DATABASE MyDB
FILE = 'MyDBDataFile1.mdf'
FILEGROUP = 'PRIMARY'
TO DISK = 'C:\Backups\MyDBDataFile1.bak'

BACKUP DATABASE MyDB
FILE = 'MyDBDataFile2.ndf'
FILEGROUP = 'Secondary'
TO DISK = 'C:\Backups\MyDBDataFile2.bak'
```

Performing a Filegroup Backup

The following are examples of backing up a database using a file-based backup strategy. Remember that you still need to do a transaction log to keep the backups synchronized.

```
BACKUP DATABASE MyDB
FILEGROUP = 'Secondary'
TO DISK = 'C:\Backups\MyDBDataFile1.bak'
```

Performing a Full-Text Index Backup

Run a separate full-text backup only if your full-text catalogs are in a separate filegroup from your data. You can do both full and differential backups of full-text catalogs, as well as a file or filegroup backup.

```
BACKUP DATABASE MyDB
FILE = 'MyFTSCatalog'
TO DISK = 'C:\Backups\MyFTSBackup.bak'
```

Performing a Transaction Log Backup to a Device

This statement backs up the transaction log to a device:

```
BACKUP LOG MyDB TO MyLogBackupDevice
```

Performing a Transaction Log Backup to Disk

This statement backs up a database to a disk file:

```
BACKUP LOG MyDB TO DISK = 'C:\Backups\MyDBTL.trn'
```

Backing Up the Tail of the Log

If you are performing the final transaction log backup for a variety of reasons (log shipping switch, and so on), you can add the NORECOVERY or STANDBY clause. NORECOVERY will put the database in a loading state, and STANDBY will place the database in a state where it is allowed to restore transaction logs and service read requests when it is not loading transaction logs.

```
BACKUP LOG MyDB
TO DISK = 'C:\Backups\MyDBTrnLog.trn'
WITH NORECOVERY

BACKUP LOG MyDB
TO DISK = 'C:\Backups\MyDBTrnLog.trn'
WITH STANDBY = 'c:\Backups\StandbyFile.bak'
```

Truncating the Transaction Log

In the event that other methods such as creating disk space, backing up the tail of the log, and shrinking the log file itself fail in trying to make the transaction log smaller, you might be forced into truncating the transaction log, which will flush the older LSNs out. Enter one of the following commands, where *database_name* is the name of the database you are truncating the log of. NO_LOG and TRUNCATE_ONLY are synonyms; you do not need to execute both—choose one.

```
BACKUP LOG database_name WITH NO_LOG
BACKUP LOG database_name WITH TRUNCATE_ONLY
```

■**Caution** Be aware that if you truncate the transaction log with these statements, you will break the LSN chain and affect your point-in-time recoverability. You must now generate a new full backup and transaction logs to be able to have point-in-time recoverability.

Backing Up and Viewing Status

SQL Server allows you to see the progress of your backup. Use the STATS option, and set it to a percentage after which you will be updated. The following is an example, with a sample output in Figure 3-19:

```
BACKUP DATABASE MyDB
TO DISK = 'C:\Backups\MyDB1.bak'
WITH STATS = 10
```

```
14 percent processed.
24 percent processed.
34 percent processed.
44 percent processed.
54 percent processed.
64 percent processed.
74 percent processed.
84 percent processed.
94 percent processed.
Processed 160 pages for database 'Styxabase6', file 'Styxabase' on file 1.
100 percent processed.
Processed 2 pages for database 'Styxabase6', file 'Styxabase_log' on file 1.
BACKUP DATABASE successfully processed 162 pages in 0.294 seconds (4.489 MB/sec).
```

Figure 3-19. *Output of using WITH STATS*

SQL Server Management Studio

To back up a database with SQL Server Management Studio, follow these steps:

1. Start SQL Server Management Studio.

2. Select the database you want to back up, right-click, select Tasks, then select Back Up, as shown in Figure 3-20.

   In the Back Up Database dialog box, as shown in Figure 3-21, you have quite a few options. The Database drop-down list allows you to select the database you will be backing up. Backup Type allows you to select a full, differential, or transaction log backup. You can then select whether you will be doing a database or file/filegroup backup.

Figure 3-20. *Selecting the Back Up database option*

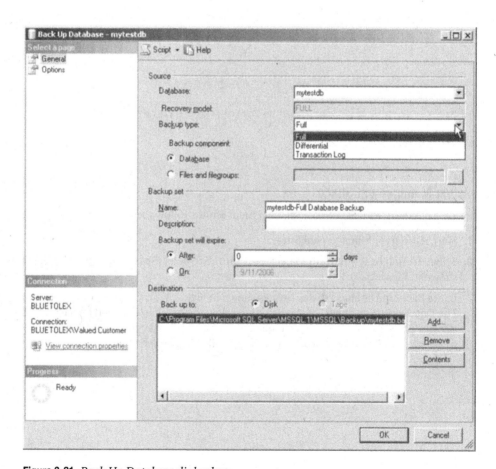

Figure 3-21. *Back Up Database dialog box*

If you click Contents, you will see what is contained in the backup device. Figure 3-22 shows an example.

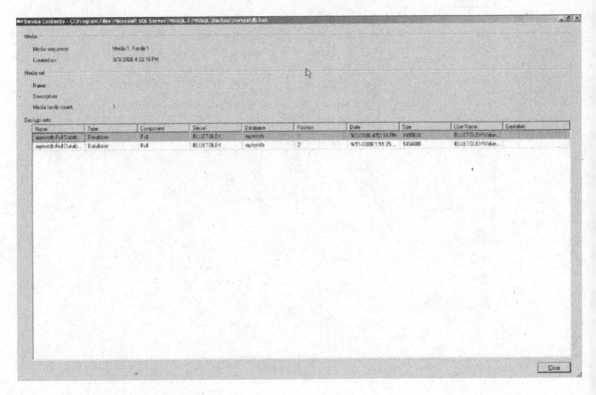

Figure 3-22. *Device Contents dialog box*

3. Select the Options page, as shown in Figure 3-23.

4. When the backup is complete, click OK. Figure 3-24 shows a success message.

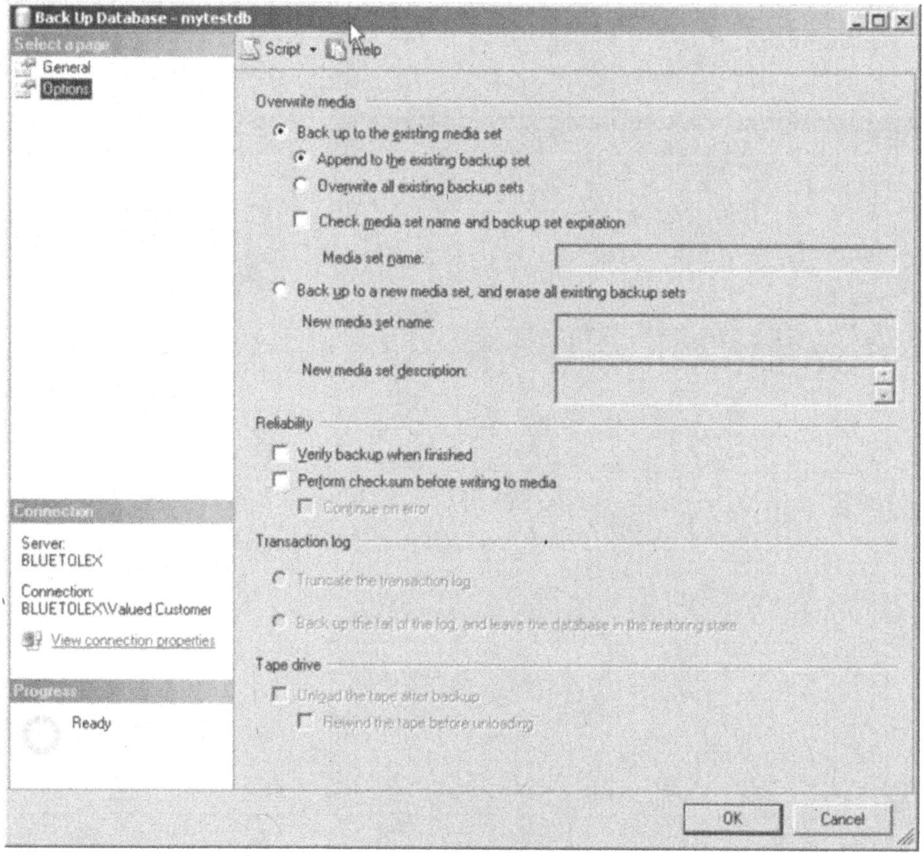

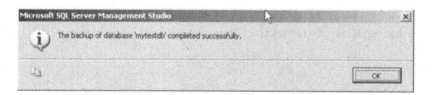

Figure 3-23. *Options page for backing up a database*

Figure 3-24. *Successful database backup*

Restoring SQL Server Databases

The following sections will cover how to restore SQL Server databases either via a Transact-SQL statement or in SQL Server Management Studio.

Note The restore process restores only what is in the backup file. There might be objects, such as logins, that you might need to synchronize or re-create. Any objects that sit outside the database (that is, SQL Server Agent Jobs, maintenance plans, and so on) must be re-created manually or from scripts you have saved.

Transact-SQL

As with the BACKUP statement, RESTORE has six variations: RESTORE (DATABASE or LOG), RESTORE FILELISTONLY, RESTORE HEADERONLY, RESTORE LABELONLY, RESTORE REWINDONLY, and RESTORE VERIFYONLY. The parameters used by all are similar (if not the same) in most cases.

The following are parameters used in the main portion of the RESTORE statement:

- DATABASE or LOG: This tells SQL Server whether you are doing either a database restore or a transaction log restore.

- FILE, FILEGROUP, PAGE, or READ_WRITE_FILEGROUPS: This tells SQL Server that you will backing up an individual file, backing up a filegroup, backing up a page, or doing a partial backup, respectively. Multiple files and filegroups can be listed but must be separated by a comma (,). A page has the format of 'filename:page', and multiple pages can be separated by commas.

- FROM DISK, FROM TAPE, or FROM DATABASE_SNAPSHOT: This parameter tells RESTORE from where to restore the database or log. You can restore from a backup contained on disk, from a backup contained on tape, or from a database snapshot (which will be described in Chapter 13).

The following are parameters used in the WITH clause (in alphabetical order):

- CHECKSUM or NO_CHECKSUM (valid with all RESTORE variations except RESTORE REWINDONLY): See the "Testing the Backups" section earlier in this chapter for a discussion of how checksums are used with restoring databases in SQL Server 2005. By default, checksums are not enabled, which is represented by CHECKSUM. Specifying NO_CHECKSUM disables the default behavior and will not validate checksums. I do not recommend doing this.

- ENABLE_BROKER (valid with RESTORE only): If you are using SQL Server Service Broker, this option in the WITH clause tells SQL Server to start Service Broker in its enabled mode so any messages can be sent immediately. Service Broker is disabled by default during a restore unless ENABLE BROKER is specified.

- ERROR_BROKER_CONVERSATIONS (valid with RESTORE only): If you are using SQL Server Service Broker, this option in the WITH clause tells SQL Server to send an error message stating that the database is attached or restored. Service Broker is then disabled until the restore is complete and reenabled.

- FILE: This is an integer that is specified if you are doing a restore from a media set that contains more than one backup set. By default, SQL Server will set a value of 1 to restore the first backup set if this is not explicitly set. This is also another good reason to have each media set contain only one backup set.

- KEEP_REPLICATION: This is an important option if you are using replication with your databases that are configured with log shipping. You need to use this in every RESTORE statement. This works only if the database is recovered WITH STANDBY, the warm standby has the same name as the original server, and msdb and master are synchronized with the primary. For more about replication, see Chapter 12.

- LOADHISTORY (valid only with RESTORE VERIFYONLY): This option in the WITH clause tells SQL Server to populate the msdb backup history tables.

- MEDIANAME: This is an optional name for the entire media set and can be up to 128 characters encased in single quotes. If you do not specify MEDIANAME, the check that is done to verify the media set name is skipped.

- MEDIAPASSWORD: This parameter will specify the password you set for the media set during the backup. If a password is set and is not part of the RESTORE statement, the RESTORE will fail.

- MOVE (valid only with RESTORE and RESTORE VERIFYONLY): Specifying this in the WITH clause allows you to change the location of the data and log files. This is an important statement, since the path you are restoring to on your destination might not be the same. If you are restoring a database, it will default to the path and filenames that were stored in the backup that are associated with that database.

- NEW_BROKER (valid with RESTORE only): If you are using SQL Server Service Broker, this option in the WITH clause tells SQL Server to create a new service_broker_guid in sys.databases. The broker is enabled, and no messages are sent to any remote endpoints.

- PARTIAL (RESTORE DATABASE only): If you are doing a piecemeal restore (that is, not restoring all filegroups), this will tell SQL Server to use the primary filegroup, so specifying FROM FILEGROUP = 'PRIMARY' is not necessary, but you will still need to list all other filegroups you want to do as part of the piecemeal restore.

- PASSWORD: If a password was set for the backup set during the backup operation, it will need to be specified for the restore.

- RECOVERY, NORECOVERY or STANDBY: Using one of these options in the WITH clause tells SQL Server to put the database in a specific state (as described earlier in this chapter). STANDBY requires that you specify the location for your standby files, which were known as *undo files* in SQL Server 2000.

- REPLACE (valid only with RESTORE): This option in the WITH clause tells SQL Server to overwrite the database even if it already exists with the same name and its files with the backup contained in the backup file or device you specify. Use this option with caution, and make sure this is what you really want to do.

- RESTART: This option in the WITH clause tells SQL Server to restart the restore process if it was interrupted.

- RESTRICTED_USER: Similar to the database-level option, this option in the WITH clause tells SQL Server that after the database is restored, only logins and users assigned to the db_owner, dbcreator, or sysadmin role can access the database. This replaces DBO_ONLY in previous versions of SQL Server. This is valid only if you are explicitly specifying RECOVERY or it is implied.

- REWIND or NOREWIND (tape restore only): REWIND means that SQL Server will rewind the tape as part of the restore process. NOREWIND means that the tape will be kept open by SQL Server after the restore is complete. If you are performing multiple restores from the same tape, this is useful, but it also means that until a REWIND or UNLOAD is issued in the same session or SQL Server is shut down, the tape drive will not be available to any other process on your server. REWIND is the default option.

- STATS: Specifying STATS will show you the percentage complete of the restore you are performing. By default, SQL Server will update you every 10%, but if you want something different, you must specify a percentage for when you want to be updated (that is, STATS = 3). However, as shown in the later example, it is not an exact science even if you specify a value. This is to be expected. STATS can be useful when you are backing up large databases.

- STOPAT: If there is a specific date and time you want to roll your databases forward to, use STOPAT.

- STOPATMARK or STOPBEFOREMARK: If you are using named transactions or know the LSN, you can specify the exact point to which to roll the database forward. STOPATMARK and STOPBEFOREMARK also have optional AFTER clauses, which are valid with RESTORE LOG. AFTER is a datetime and tells SQL Server to stop either exactly before or after the LSN or mark specified. If AFTER is not specified, it will always stop just before the LSN or mark.

Note When you use STOPAT, STOPATMARK, or STOPBEFOREMARK, if the mark, LSN, or time you specify is after the last transaction log backup, the database is left in an unrecovered state equivalent to specifying NORECOVERY.

- STOP_ON_ERROR or CONTINUE_AFTER_ERROR: This option in the WITH clause tells SQL Server either to abort the restore if an error is found or to continue restoring the database even though an error has occurred. If you use CONTINUE_AFTER_ERROR, I recommend you look at all logs to see what error occurred and inspect your data to see that what you expect to be there is actually there. You do not want to use an option like CONTINUE_AFTER_ERROR if you do not know what to look for in your data. Damaged backups are something you should not be playing around with.

- UNLOAD or NOUNLOAD (tape restore only): UNLOAD means that when the restore is complete, the tape is rewound and ejected. NOUNLOAD tells the restore command to leave the tape loaded in the tape drive, so you would have to manually remove it. This option remains in place until your session has ended. UNLOAD is the default option.

Restoring a Database from a Full Backup on Disk

This statement restores a database from a full backup contained in a backup file on disk:

```
RESTORE DATABASE MyDB
FROM DISK = 'C:\Backups\MyDB.bak'
WITH RECOVERY
```

Restoring a Database from a Device

This statement restores a database from a full backup contained in a backup device that has a single backup:

```
RESTORE DATABASE MyDB
FROM MyFullBackupDevice
WITH RECOVERY
```

Restoring a Database from Tape

This statement restores a database from a full backup contained on tape:

```
RESTORE DATABASE MyDB
FROM TAPE = '\\.\tape0'
WITH RECOVERY
```

Moving the Location of the Data and Log Devices

This example shows how to restore a database and change the location of the data and log files during the restore. This is helpful if you are reconfiguring your database or restoring it on another server that might not have the same drive configuration. You must know the name of each device (such as MyDBData) to be able to move the physical files.

```
RESTORE DATABASE MyDB
FROM DISK = 'C:\Backups\MyDB.bak'
WITH MOVE 'MyDBData' TO 'D:\SQL Data\MyDBData.mdf',
MOVE 'MyDBLog' TO 'E:\SQL Logs\MyDBLog.ldf'
WITH RECOVERY
```

Resuming a Restore

This example shows how you can resume a restore that was interrupted:

```
RESTORE DATABASE MyDB
FROM DISK = 'C:\Backups\MyDB.bak'
WITH RESTART
```

Restoring a Database from a Full Backup and a Differential Backup

This statement restores a database from a full backup contained in a backup file on disk:

```
RESTORE DATABASE MyDB
FROM DISK = 'C:\Backups\MyDB.bak'
WITH NORECOVERY
```

```
RESTORE DATABASE MyDB
FROM DISK = 'C:\Backups\MyDBDiff.dif'
WITH RECOVERY
```

If the device has multiple backups in it, you need to know the file number of the backup to restore. For example, say you have a device that has four backups—a full, a differential, and two transaction logs. If you want to restore from a device and use, in this case, the full and differential that have file numbers of 1 and 2, respectively, the following syntax works:

```
RESTORE DATABASE MyDB
FROM MyDBBackupDevice
WITH NORECOVERY
```

```
RESTORE DATABASE MyDB
FROM MyDBBackupDevice
WITH FILE = 2, RECOVERY
```

Restoring a Database from a Full Backup and a Transaction Log Backup

This example shows you how to use transaction logs as part of a restore. All backups (full, differential, file/filegroup full or differential, transaction log) must be restored with NORECOVERY or STANDBY until the last transaction log RESTORE statement.

```
RESTORE DATABASE MyDB
FROM DISK = 'C:\Backups\MyDB.bak'
WITH NORECOVERY
```

```
RESTORE LOG MyDB
FROM DISK = 'C:\Backups\MyDBTL1.trn'
WITH NORECOVERY
```

```
RESTORE LOG MyDB
FROM DISK = 'C:\Backups\MyDBTL2.trn'
WITH RECOVERY
```

Restoring a File

This example shows the restoration of a single database file. Since you are restoring a file that might be out of sync with the others, you must restore all transaction log backups made after the file backup to synchronize the database to the latest point in time.

```
RESTORE DATABASE MyDB
FILE = 'MyDBFile2'
FROM DISK = 'C:\Backups\MyDB.bak'
WITH NORECOVERY

RESTORE LOG MyDB
FROM DISK = 'C:\Backups\MyDBTL1.trn'
WITH NORECOVERY

RESTORE LOG MyDB
FROM DISK = 'C:\Backups\MyDBTL2.trn'
WITH RECOVERY
```

Restoring a Filegroup

Similar to a file restore, this example shows how to restore a filegroup and roll it forward using transaction log backups:

```
RESTORE DATABASE MyDB
FILEGROUP = 'Secondary'
FROM DISK = 'C:\Backups\MyDB.bak'
WITH NORECOVERY

RESTORE LOG MyDB
FROM DISK = 'C:\Backups\MyDBTL1.trn'
WITH NORECOVERY

RESTORE LOG MyDB
FROM DISK = 'C:\Backups\MyDBTL2.trn'
WITH RECOVERY
```

Restoring to a Point in Time

You can roll the database forward to a single point in time in a few ways. The first is to restore to a specific time using the STOPAT clause:

```
RESTORE DATABASE MyDB
FROM DISK = 'C:\Backups\MyDB.bak'
WITH NORECOVERY

RESTORE LOG MyDB
FROM DISK = 'C:\Backups\MyDBTL1.trn'
WITH NORECOVERY

RESTORE LOG MyDB
FROM DISK = 'C:\Backups\MyDBTL2.trn'
WITH STOPAT = 'January 1, 2007 10:01 AM', RECOVERY
```

Another method is to use the transaction log marks. You can either use STOPATMARK to recover up to and including the log mark point or use STOPBEFOREMARK, which will recover the database to the point in time right before the log mark:

```
RESTORE DATABASE MyDB
FROM DISK = 'C:\Backups\MyDB.bak'
WITH NORECOVERY
```

```
RESTORE LOG MyDB
FROM DISK = 'C:\Backups\MyDBTL1.trn'
WITH NORECOVERY

RESTORE LOG MyDB
FROM DISK = 'C:\Backups\MyDBTL2.trn'
WITH STOPATMARK = 'MyDBMark10', RECOVERY
```

Restoring a Page

You have the ability to restore a page in SQL Server 2005. If you encounter an 824 error, you may want to consider a page-level restore if you have the right backups and processes in place.

First, you want to check what is in the msdb..suspect_pages table. You want to check for an event_type of 1, 2, or 3, which corresponds to an 824 error, bad checksum, or a torn page, respectively. The query would look like the following:

```
SELECT *
FROM msdb..suspect_pages
WHERE (event_type = 1)
     OR (event_type = 2)
     OR (event_type = 3)
```

■**Tip** For more information about suspect_pages, see the topic "Understanding and Managing the suspect_pages Table" in SQL Server 2005 Books Online.

Once you understand which pages have a problem, back up the transaction log to get the tail. You can then restore the page from your most recent full backup. If you have multiple pages, they can be listed in the PAGE clause via commas. This is a sample statement:

```
RESTORE DATABASE MyDB
PAGE = '1:51'
FROM DISK = 'C:\Backups\MyDB.bak'
WITH NORECOVERY
```

After the restore of the page(s), apply the proper sequence of differential and/or transaction log backups (including the tail of the log that you just backed up prior to the page restore) to roll the database forward to the most current point.

Finally, take a new backup of your database and transaction log after so you have a new (and clean) start to a restore chain.

Executing RESTORE VERIFYONLY

This is a sample execution of RESTORE VERIFYONLY. I described its uses earlier in this chapter.

```
RESTORE VERIFYONLY MyDB FROM DISK = 'C:\Backups\MyDB.bak'
```

Executing RESTORE REWINDONLY

If you back up directly to tape and have tape devices that were left open because of executing BACKUP or RESTORE with NOREWIND, use RESTORE REWINDONLY to rewind and close the tape device. To close the device and unload the tape, use this:

```
RESTORE REWINDONLY FROM '\\.\tape0' WITH UNLOAD
```

To close the device and not unload the tape, use this:

```
RESTORE REWINDONLY FROM '\\.\tape0' WITH NOUNLOAD
```

Executing RESTORE FILELISTONLY

To see what files are in a backup set or device, use the RESTORE FILELISTONLY syntax. To see what information is brought back, consult the SQL Server Books Online "RESTORE LABELONLY (Transact-SQL)" topic. Here's an example:

```
RESTORE FILELISTONLY FROM DISK ='C:\MyBackupDevice.bak'
```

Executing RESTORE HEADERONLY

To see the header information about the backup set, use RESTORE HEADERONLY. To see what information is brought back, consult the SQL Server Books Online "RESTORE HEADERONLY (Transact-SQL)" topic. Here's an example:

```
RESTORE HEADERONLY FROM DISK = 'C:\MyBackupDevice.bak'
```

Executing RESTORE LABELONLY

To see information about the backup media itself, use the RESTORE LABELONLY syntax. To see what information is brought back, consult the SQL Server Books Online "RESTORE LABELONLY (Transact-SQL)" topic. Here's an example:

```
RESTORE LABELONLY FROM DISK = 'C:\MyBackupDevice.bak'
```

SQL Server Management Studio

Start SQL Server Management Studio, select the database you want to restore, right-click, select Tasks, select Restore, and then select either Database, Files and Filegroups, or Transaction Logs, as shown in Figure 3-25.

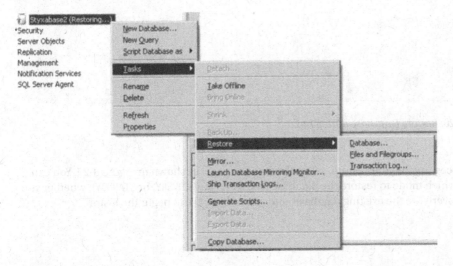

Figure 3-25. *Restore option*

Database Restore

Follow these steps to restore a database using SQL Server Management Studio:

1. In the Restore Database dialog box, as shown in Figure 3-26, select the files or filegroup to restore by checking the box next to the name. If you want to restore the database as a different name, enter that in the To Database drop-down/entry field. If you are restoring from a device instead of the database, select From Device, and click the ellipsis to select the file. You can also select a point in time by specifying a value for To a Point in Time.

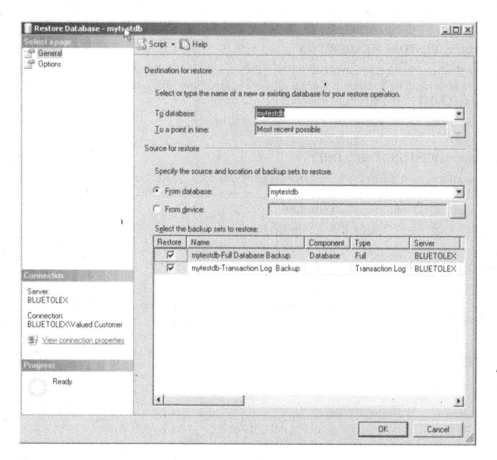

Figure 3-26. *Restore Database dialog box*

2. If it is necessary for your restore, select the Options page, as shown in Figure 3-27. You can choose which mode to restore the database (RECOVERY, NORECOVERY, or STANDBY), whether you want to overwrite the existing database, and so on. Click OK to begin the restore.

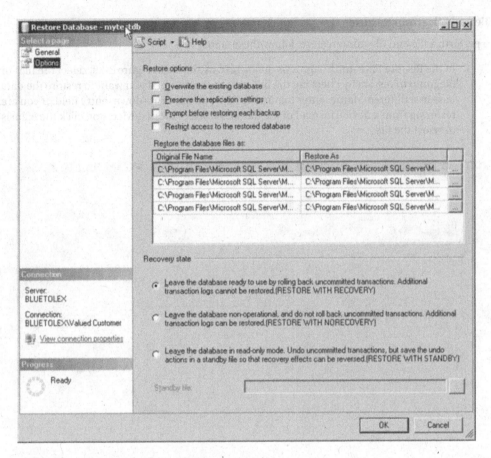

Figure 3-27. *Options page for a database restore*

3. When the restore is complete and successful, you should see a message similar to the one in Figure 3-28.

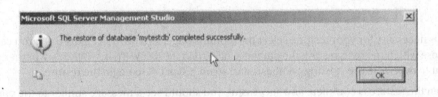

Figure 3-28. *Successful database restore*

File and Filegroup Restore

To perform a file and filegroup restore, follow these steps:

1. In the Restore Files and Filegroups dialog box, as shown in Figure 3-29, select the files or filegroup to restore by checking the box next to the name. If you want to restore the database as a different name, enter that in the To Database drop-down/entry field. If you are restoring from a device instead of the database, select From device, and click the ellipsis to select the file.

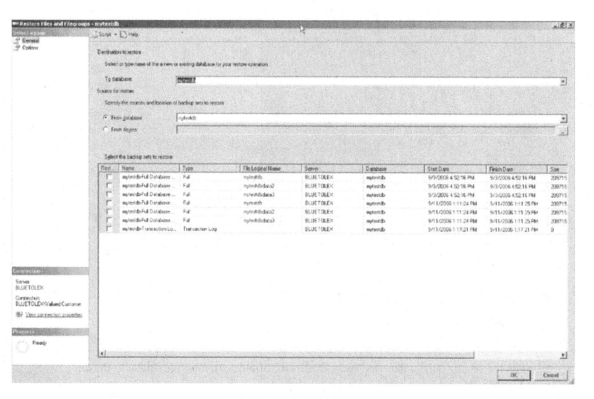

Figure 3-29. *General page for restoring files and filegroups*

2. If it is necessary for your restore, select the Options page, as shown in Figure 3-30. You can choose which mode to restore the database (RECOVERY, NORECOVERY, or STANDBY), whether you want to overwrite the existing database, and so on. Click OK to begin the restore.

3. When the restore is complete and successful, you should see a message similar to the one in the earlier Figure 3-28.

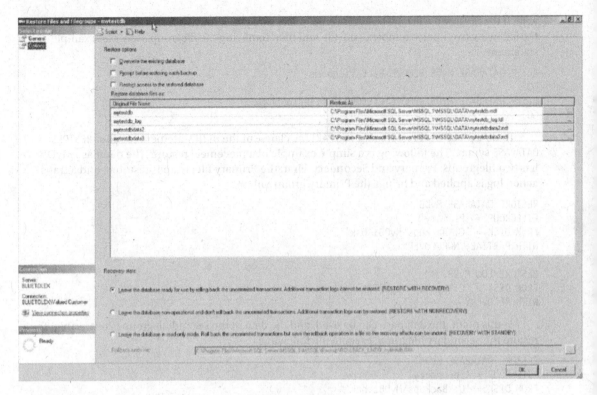

Figure 3-30. *Options page for restoring files and filegroups*

Performing Piecemeal Restores

Another enhancement to backup and restore in SQL Server 2005 is the ability to allow filegroups to be restored after an initial and partial restore of the primary filegroup and some of the other filegroup(s). What was known as a *partial restore* in SQL Server 2000 is now known as a *piecemeal restore* in SQL Server 2005. Filegroups that have not yet been restored are denoted as Offline and cannot be used. This restore strategy will allow you to get the essential portions of your database up and running and then allow you to restore the rest as time goes on. This minimizes your downtime since the rest of the restores might not affect others (that is, they might contain historical data). In SQL Server 2000, this could be done by using a full backup only, but in SQL Server 2005, this can be any combination of valid backups. If your recovery model does not support a certain type of backup (such as Simple and transaction log backups), you cannot use that backup as part of your piecemeal restore. In a perfect world, your data should be partitioned in such a way that your data is completely separated and no data is spread out across multiple filegroups. If some of your filegroups are read-only, those are easier to handle.

There are two scenarios for a piecemeal restore: online and offline. An *offline* piecemeal restore allows you to bring the database online after a partial restore, but you cannot have any deferred transactions. All things that are brought online must be brought online to completion, and anything that does not have to come online as part of the initial restore can be brought online after. An *online* piecemeal restore is similar, except it allows deferred transactions, which is crucial for consistency.

If you apply a transaction log but the filegroup is offline, any transactions that need to be applied to that filegroup are known as *deferred* transactions and will be applied when the filegroup is brought online. A transaction will stay in a perpetually deferred state until that filegroup is dealt with. If the filegroup will never be recovered, make sure you remove it from the database by doing the following two things: removing the file and then removing the filegroup. Here's an example statement:

```
ALTER DATABASE MyDB REMOVE FILE filename
GO
ALTER DATABASE MyDB REMOVE FILEGROUP filegroupname
GO
```

To do a piecemeal restore, use the PARTIAL clause of the WITH statement for your RESTORE DATABASE syntax. The following is a simple example of a piecemeal restore. The database MyDB has two filegroups: Primary and Secondary. First, the Primary filegroup is restored, and a transaction log is applied and brings the Primary group online.

```
RESTORE DATABASE MyDB
FILEGROUP = 'Primary'
FROM DISK = 'C:\Backups\MyDB1.bak'
WITH PARTIAL, NORECOVERY

RESTORE LOG MyDB
FROM DISK = 'C:\Backups\MyDBTL1.trn'
WITH RECOVERY
```

At this point, the database can be used, and the data in the second filegroup is not usable. To restore the Secondary filegroup, execute the following:

```
RESTORE DATABASE MyDB
FILEGROUP = 'Secondary'
FROM DISK = 'C:\Backups\MyDB2.bak'
WITH RECOVERY
```

Note An online piecemeal restore is a feature of SQL Server 2005 Enterprise Edition only.

Backing Up and Restoring Analysis Services Databases

Analysis Services databases and cubes should also be backed up. As with the SQL Server relational engine, you can back up and restore them in two ways: coding or through Management Studio. All code for Analysis Services is in the form of XML. It is slightly different, however, from a traditional SQL Server backup. You do have the ability to compress your backups. Analysis Services backups default to a file with the extension of .abf. To execute a backup or restore command in Analysis Services, you must be a system administrator or database administrator.

Note Backing up an Analysis Services database does not back up the sources (databases, files, and so on) for the Analysis Services database. Those must be accounted for separately.

Backup Code

Analysis Services does not use Transact-SQL like the relational engine of SQL Server. It uses XML for Analysis (XMLA). It has fewer options than its equivalent command in SQL Server has. The options available are as follows:

- Object: This tells backup which database to back up. You set the DatabaseID property.

- File: This is the backup file that will be created.

- Security: This tells the backup whether to also back up the security definitions of your Analysis Services database. This can be set to SkipMembership, CopyAll, or IgnoreSecurity. SkipMembership includes security definitions but does not include membership definitions in the backup file. CopyAll puts both security and membership definitions in the backup file. IgnoreSecurity puts no security information in the backup file.

- ApplyCompression: This tells the backup to compress the file after it is generated.

- AllowOverwrite: This tells the backup to overwrite the existing backup file if it exists.

- Password: If a password is specified, the file is encrypted using the password. It is important to note that if ApplyCompression and Password are left blank, the Analysis Services backup file will store all usernames and passwords in connection strings in clear text.

- BackupRemotePartitions: This parameter allows you to create a remote backup file for each data source that has a partition of the Analysis Services database.

- Locations: You must specify this parameter if you use BackupRemotePartitions. You must specify a Location element with a File property set to the UNC path and filename of the remote backup file. You must also set the DataSourceID property to the identifier or the remote data source defined in your Analysis Services database.

Here is an example:

```
<Backup xmlns="http://schemas.microsoft.com/analysisservices/2003/engine">
  <Object>
    <DatabaseID>ASTest</DatabaseID>
  </Object>
  <File>ASTest.abf</File>
</Backup>
```

Using SQL Server Management Studio to Back Up Analysis Services Databases

To use SQL Server Management Studio to back up Analysis Services databases, follow these steps:

1. Start SQL Server Management Studio, and connect to the Analysis Services installation, as shown in Figure 3-31.

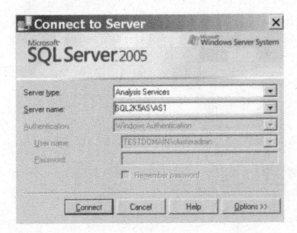

Figure 3-31. *Connecting to Analysis Services*

2. Expand Databases, select the database you want to back up, right-click, and select Back Up, as shown in Figure 3-32.

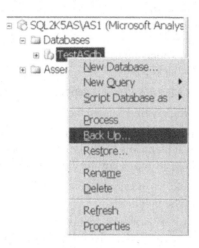

Figure 3-32. *Selecting Back Up*

3. In the Backup Database dialog box, click Browse to select where the backup file will be placed. Enter a name for the backup file. Figure 3-33 shows an example. If you want to over-write an existing backup file with the same name, select Allow File Overwrite. If you want to compress the backup, select Apply Compression. If you want to encrypt the backup file, select Encrypt Backup File, and enter a password. Figure 3-34 shows an example. Click OK.

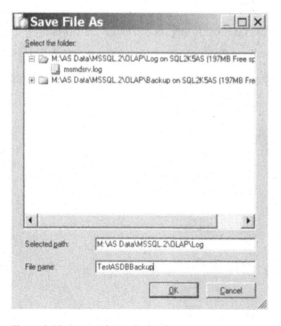

Figure 3-33. *Save File As dialog box*

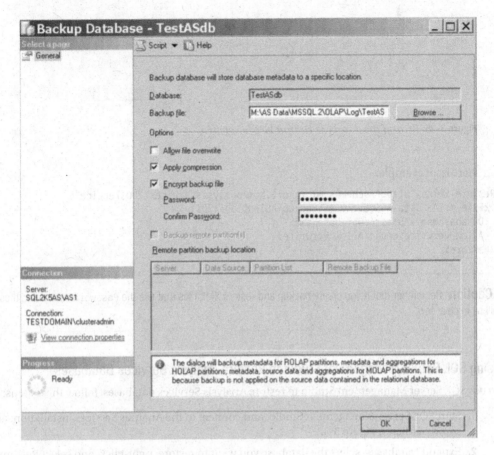

Figure 3-34. *Backup Database dialog box*

Restore Code

For a full explanation of all of the options, see the SQL Server Books Online "Restore Element (XMLA)" topic. It has fewer options than its equivalent command in SQL Server has. The options available are as follows:

- `DatabaseName`: This tells backup which database to create/restore during the restoration process.

- `File`: This is the backup file that will be used.

- `Security`: This tells the restore whether to also restore the security definitions of your Analysis Services database. This can be set to `SkipMembership`, `CopyAll`, or `IgnoreSecurity`, which all have the same implication as their counterparts for the backup.

- `AllowOverwrite`: This tells the restore to overwrite the existing backup file if it exists. If you do not select this, you might see an error similar to the one in Figure 3-35.

- `Password`: This is the password used to encrypt the backup.

- `Locations`: This parameter must be specified if you used `BackupRemotePartitions`. You must specify a `Location` element with a `File` property set to the UNC path and filename of the remote backup file. You must also set the `DataSourceID` property to the identifier or the remote data source defined in your Analysis Services database.

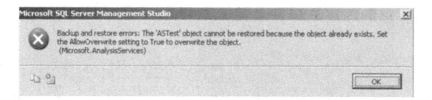

Figure 3-35. *Error if the database cannot be overwritten*

Here is an example:

```
<Restore xmlns="http://schemas.microsoft.com/analysisservices/2003/engine">
  <File>M:\AS Data\MSSQL.2\OLAP\Backup\ASTest.abf</File>
  <DatabaseName>ASTest</DatabaseName>
  <AllowOverwrite>true</AllowOverwrite>
</Restore>
```

■**Caution** Remember that if you create backup and restore XML files that use the `Password` parameter, those will be in clear text.

Using SQL Server Management Studio to Restore Analysis Services Databases

To use SQL Server Management Studio to restore Analysis Services databases, follow these steps:

1. Start SQL Server Management Studio, and connect to the Analysis Services installation, as shown earlier in Figure 3-32.

2. Expand Databases, select the database you want to restore, right-click, and select Restore, as shown in Figure 3-36. If the database does not exist, right-click Databases, and select Restore.

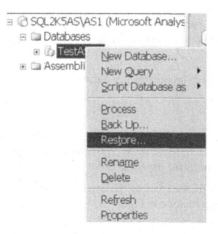

Figure 3-36. *Selecting Restore*

3. In the Restore Database dialog box, as shown in Figure 3-37, select the database to restore (if you are overwriting an existing database). Click Browse to open the Locate Database Files dialog box, as shown in Figure 3-38. Select the backup file to use, and click OK. The backup file will now display, as shown in Figure 3-39. Select the proper options for your restore in the Restore Database dialog box. If you are restoring remote partitions, click Partitions, as shown in Figure 3-40, and configure as necessary. Click OK.

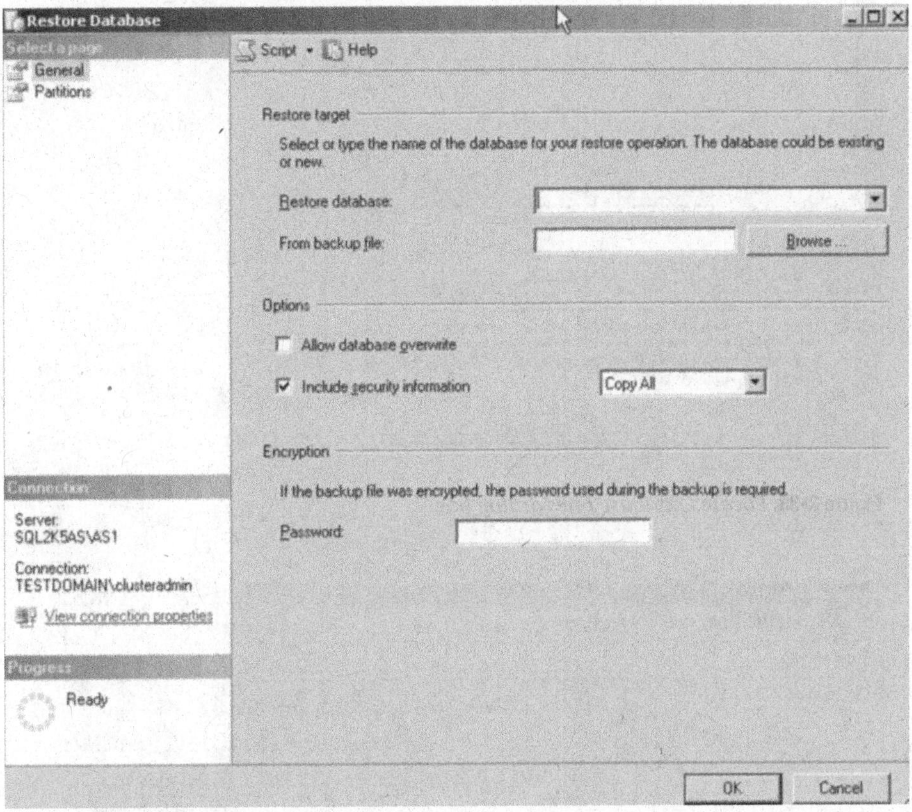

Figure 3-37. *Restore Database dialog box*

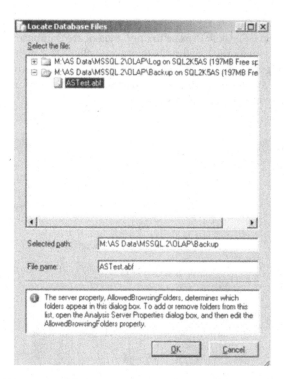

Figure 3-38. *Locate Database Files dialog box*

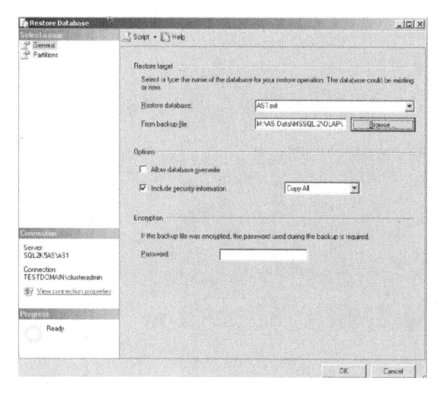

Figure 3-39. *The backup file*

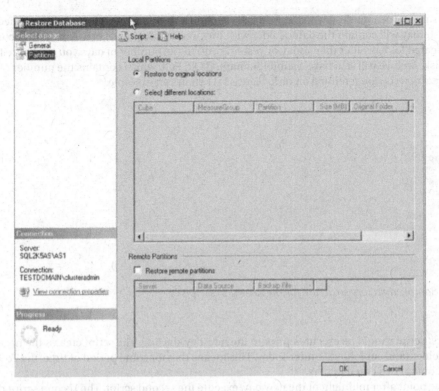

Figure 3-40. *Partitions page*

Automating the Retention Policy

SQL Server has no built-in way of deleting backup files. This means that if you are backing up to disk, you will manually have to delete the files. However, manual intervention always has risks since you might delete something that you do not want to remove from disk. To get around this, you will have to code and implement your own solution. For a few clients of mine, I have coded solutions using Windows Management Instrumentation (WMI) code and VBScript. I have included an example of WMI code on the Apress web site that will satisfy a retention policy and automatically delete files. The code is fully functional and serves as an example of what you can do for your own solutions.

Tip To learn more about WMI, you can refer to one of the many decent books and web sites available. One of the most helpful is Microsoft's TechNet Script Center, which has numerous examples. You can find it at http://www.microsoft.com/technet/scriptcenter/default.mspx.

The code is comprised of two scripts, and both in conjunction perform the whole task. The scripts manage a retention policy where you retain two full backups on disk as well as N number of days of other backups (transaction log and differential) on disk. The process will use a directory named Today, which contains all the backups for the current day. Under that folder will be another folder that has today's date in the MM-DD-YYYY format, where MM is the month, DD is the day, and YYYY is the year. Underneath the dated folder are two directories—User, which will contain all user database backups made on that date, and SystemDBs, which contains the system database backups.

At the same level of the Today folder, you will also find a Yesterday as well as a folder named Archive. Yesterday will contain the dated folder with the previous day's backups. Archive will contain all the dated folders older than today or yesterday up to the number of days you configure to retain on disk. Archive will also have a subfolder named Old Full, which contains the number of full database backups you are retaining on disk. Figure 3-41 shows an example.

Figure 3-41. *Sample directory structure for the retention scripts*

The first script should be executed prior to the new day starting. The script creates the next day's new folder (and subfolders) under Today. This means that for some period of time, the Today folder will contain two dated folders.

At some point after midnight of the new day, execute the second script. The second script does the bulk of the work. First, it checks to see whether the dated folder from yesterday (which has not been moved yet from the *Today* folder) has a full backup. If it does, it moves that backup to Old Full and, if necessary, deletes one of the older full backups. After that, the oldest directory that is one day beyond the retention policy is deleted. Yesterday's directory is moved from Today to Yesterday, and the folder in Yesterday is moved to Archive.

■**Tip** You can find the WMI code for these scripts on the Apress web site at `http://www.apress.com`.

Deploying Custom Backup and Restore Scripts

To demonstrate how you can create your own backup code, go to the Apress web site to see some custom backup and restore stored procedures (as well as instructions on how to use them) I wrote as examples. The code would take too much space in this chapter and distracts from the other information presented here.

BACKING UP YOUR DATABASES THE MICROSOFT WAY

One question many people often ask is, "How does Microsoft do it?" In other words, how does Microsoft deploy and manage its own technology? In Microsoft's internal IT department, it deploys and manages many SQL Server databases. How many? As of this writing, the number of databases is somewhere from 17,000 to 18,000 across 800 instances. To manage those databases, Microsoft averages about six DBAs (sometimes augmented by up to three others). That means each DBA is responsible for roughly 100–120 servers per internal customer or a group of internal customers (known as a *business unit*). These servers might not be exclusively SQL Server—there might be some IIS and file servers as well. This means Microsoft's DBAs multitask. However, the mix is that out of the total amount of servers each is responsible for, approximately 50% are SQL Server.

The databases consume about 10–15TB of total storage. This amount is just for the *data*—not logs or backups. Each SQL Server instance contains an average of 22 databases. Doing the math, if you assume that each of the six DBAs has an equal amount of those nearly 18,000 databases, each has to monitor, maintain, and "feed" nearly 3,000 databases. Obviously, this means a lot of automation and solid processes are in place. There would be chaos otherwise.

These more dedicated resources are the main hands on the ground. To keep them from being bombarded with the average day-to-day requests, another team is responsible for the first-line support and deals not only directly with customers but with issues such as alerts from MOM, triage, and basic tasks such as one-off backups, on-demand system checks, and escalation to the DBAs. This gives the DBAs the ability to be free from the burden of an on-call/pager rotation (which I'm sure many of you reading this not only have to participate in but is the bane of your existence). Other DBAs who are available for off-hour escalations, but this is becoming less frequent as time goes on.

You can also imagine that having to back up 18,000 databases is not a trivial task. The sheer amount of storage to do this would be quite massive. To make things easier, Microsoft currently uses Quest's SQL LiteSpeed product to speed up backups and compress them so they take up much less space on disk. The backups are retained on disk for one day, kept on-site for two weeks on tape, and then, depending on the SLA and retention policy for each database or system, moved off-site for final storage.

Microsoft uses a series of custom backup stored procedures and jobs to achieve its backups to disk:

- `SQLBackupAll`: This stored procedure performs the full database backup.

- `SQLBackupDiffAll`: This stored procedure performs a differential database backup. This is employed only if the customer's requirements use a differential backup.

- `SQLBackupTranAll`: This stored procedure performs a transaction log backup.

- `SQLBackupChecker`: This stored procedure checks to see whether a backup has been performed recently (measured in a specified amount of hours) and alerts whoever is responsible for monitoring the backup processes if one has not been made.

- `SQLCleanupMsdbBackupHistory`: This stored procedure cleans up backup history from the tables in `msdb`.

Tip Microsoft generously provided the code for these stored procedures; you can find them at `http://www.apress.com` along with full instructions on how to use them as well as scripts to deploy them in your environment.

Summary

Whatever you do to implement availability and disaster recovery, remember that having no backups—or, more specifically, no tested backups—equates to no availability or recoverability. There is no middle ground on this point. Backups are not just used for availability and recoverability—they can be used to create development, test, and staging environments and to facilitate other things, such as reporting databases, depending on your needs. To think of backups as one-dimensional is nearsighted. If you do one thing well in your availability implementation, it should be a rock-solid, robust backup and restore plan that matches your documented SLAs and OLAs. Once you do this, any of the other technologies you implement (discussed in the upcoming chapters) will be able to give you much more availability than if you did not have the foundation of reliable backups.

CHAPTER 4

■ ■ ■

Failover Clustering: Preparing to Cluster Windows

Two stacked layers ultimately make up a clustered installation of SQL Server: Windows and SQL Server itself. This chapter will describe what a Windows server cluster is, how it works, and how to plan a server cluster. This is the first of three chapters about clustering that are mostly Windows-focused with a strong SQL Server slant since the ultimate goal is to implement a SQL Server 2005 failover cluster.

Note Some of the concepts and tasks in the next three chapters might be unfamiliar to those who are mostly focused on SQL Server and DBA-type work. A lot of the information might not directly relate to your day-to-day duties, but it is extremely important when implementing clusters. Make sure you work with the appropriate individuals and organizations within your own IT departments to ensure that you accomplish the tasks presented in these chapters; otherwise, you will most likely have problems implementing SQL Server 2005 failover clustering.

What Is Clustering?

The basic concept of a cluster is easy to understand, as it relates to a server ecosystem; a *cluster* is two or more systems working together in concert to achieve a common goal. Under Windows, two main types of clustering exist: scale-out/availability clusters known as *Network Load Balancing* (NLB) clusters, and strictly availability-based clusters known as *server clustering*. The latter is the focus of Chapters 4, 5, and 6. The SQL Server portion of clustering will be covered in Chapters 7, 8, and 9.

Network Load Balancing Cluster

An NLB cluster adds availability as well as scalability to TCP/IP-based services, such as web servers, FTP servers, and COM+ applications (should you still have any deployed). An NLB implementation using the built-in feature of Windows is one where multiple servers (up to 32) run independently of one another and do not share any resources. Client requests come into the farm of servers and can be sent to any of the servers since they all provide the same functionality. The algorithms deployed know which servers are busy, so when that request comes in, it is sent to a server that can handle it. In the event of an individual server failure, NLB knows about the problem and can be configured to automatically redirect the connection to another server in the NLB cluster.

■**Caution** An NLB cluster cannot be configured on the same hardware with a Windows server cluster. In some scenarios, SQL Server and Analysis Services can utilize NLB, but those will be covered in upcoming chapters of the book where applicable.

Server Cluster

A Windows server cluster's purpose is to help you maintain client access to applications and server resources even if you encounter some sort of outage (human error, natural disaster, software failure, server failure, etc.). The whole impetus of availability behind a server cluster implementation is that client machines and applications do not need to worry about which server in the cluster is running the resource; the name and IP address of whatever is running is *virtualized*. This means the application or client connects to a single name or IP address, but behind the scenes, whatever you are using could be running on any server that is part of the cluster. To allow virtualization of names and IP addresses, a server cluster provides or requires redundancy of nearly every component—servers, network cards, networks, and so on. This redundancy is the basis of all availability in the server cluster. However, the one single point of failure in any server cluster implementation is the single *shared cluster disk array*, which is a disk subsystem that is attached to and accessible by all servers of the server cluster.

■**Note** Through Windows Server 2003 and SQL Server 2005, failover clustering is exclusively a SQL Server term used to describe clustering at the SQL Server level. You might also see documented references to Microsoft Cluster Server (MSCS). MSCS and a server cluster are the same thing. A SQL Server failover cluster is built on top of a Windows server cluster; Windows server clustering is the foundation. In future versions of the Windows Server line, a server cluster will be known as *failover clustering*, the same term used for the SQL Server clustering feature.

Depending on your data center and hardware implementation, a server cluster can be implemented within only one location or across a distance. A server cluster implemented across a distance is known as a *geographically dispersed cluster*. A server cluster does not provide scale-out abilities, but the solution can scale up as much as the operating system and hardware will allow.

Clustering SQL Server 2005 requires Windows 2000 Advanced Server with Windows 2000 Server Service Pack 4, Windows 2000 Datacenter Server with Windows 2000 Server Service Pack 4, Windows Server 2003 Enterprise Edition with Windows Server 2003 Service Pack 1 or later, or Windows Server 2003 Datacenter Edition with Windows Server 2003 Service Pack 1 or later.

■**Note** A clustered SQL Server cannot be implemented using Windows Compute Cluster Server 2003; and a Windows failover cluster cannot be configured on the same hardware with Windows Compute Cluster Server 2003. For more information, see the sidebar "SQL Server 2005 and Windows Compute Cluster Server 2003."

How a Server Cluster Works

A server cluster works on the principle of a *shared-nothing* configuration; however, this is a bit of a misnomer. A shared-nothing cluster is one where only a single server can utilize a particular resource at any given time. Multiple servers, otherwise known as *nodes*, participating in the cluster might ultimately be able to own that resource. (Depending on the configuration, some resources might not be able to be owned by all nodes.) Therefore, the shared component must be able to be used by each server that might ultimately own that resource, so it is a 1:1 ownership role from resource to node. Depending on the operating system and version of SQL Server you are using, you will have a different maximum number of nodes available to you, as described in Table 4-1.

Table 4-1. *Number of Cluster Nodes*

SQL Server Edition	Windows Server 2000 Advanced Server	Windows Server 2000 Datacenter Server	Windows Server 2000 Advanced Server Limited Edition (64-bit)	Windows Server 2003 (Enterprise or Datacenter Edition)
SQL Server 2000 Enterprise Edition	2	4	0	4
SQL Server 2000 Enterprise Edition 64-bit (IA64 only)	0	0	8	8
SQL Server 2005 Standard Edition	2	2	2	2
SQL Server 2005 Enterprise Edition	2	4	8	8

For an application like SQL Server to work properly in a Windows server cluster, it must be coded to the clustering application programming interface (API) of the Windows Platform SDK (software development kit), and it must have at least three things: one or more disks configured in the server cluster, a clustered network name for the application that is different from the Windows server cluster name, and one or more clustered IP addresses for the application itself, which are not the same as the IP addresses for either the nodes or the Windows server cluster. That combination has historically been known as a *virtual server*, but since the release of Microsoft Virtual Server, that terminology is no longer valid and will not be used anywhere in this book to refer to a clustered SQL Server instance.

A clustered application has individual *resources*, such as an IP address, a physical disk, and a network name, which are then contained in a *cluster resource group*, which is similar to a folder on your hard drive that contains files. The cluster resource is the lowest unit of management in a server cluster. The resource group is the unit of failover in a cluster; you cannot fail over individual resources. Resources can also be a *dependency* of another resource (or resources) within a group. If a resource is dependent upon another, it will not be able to start until the top-level resource is online.

SQL Server requires a 1:1 ratio from instance to resource group. That means you can install only one instance of SQL Server (either SQL Server 2000 or SQL Server 2005) per resource group. Resources such as disks cannot be shared across resource groups and are dedicated to that particular instance of SQL Server residing in a resource group.

Once SQL Server is installed in the cluster, it uses the underlying cluster semantics to ensure its availability. The Windows server cluster uses a *quorum* that not only contains the master copy of the server cluster's configuration but also serves as a tiebreaker if all network communications fail between the nodes. If the quorum fails or becomes corrupt, the server cluster shuts down and will not be able to be started until the quorum is repaired.

You can implement two types of server clusters under Windows depending on the type of quorum used:

- *A standard server cluster*: Uses a traditional quorum device placed on a dedicated shared disk attached to the cluster.

- *A Majority Node Set (MNS) server cluster*: Does not require a dedicated drive and drive letter to maintain quorum. It uses a directory on the local system drive for the quorum and can be found at %SystemRoot%\Cluster\MNS.%ResourceGUID%$\%ResourceGUID%$\MSCS. This directory and its contents should never be modified. For one node to be able to access the quorum to update the cluster database on another node, a share is set up as \\%NodeName%\ %ResourceGUID%$. For the cluster to remain up and running, the majority of nodes must be operational. The calculation is simple: take the total number of nodes you have, divide it by 2, and add 1. Table 4-2 has the calculations for you. If the number of nodes exceeds the total amount allowed, the resources in an MNS cluster will gracefully shut down, and you will manually need to force quorum to bring them back online to allow the minority of nodes to run the resources.

Table 4-2. *MNS Nodes and Tolerated Node Failures*

Total # of Nodes	# of Node Failures Allowed
1	0
2	0
3	1
4	1
5	2
6	2
7	3
8	3

For SQL Server, the most common method of implementing clustering is to use a traditional Windows server cluster, which uses a disk (and a drive letter) for the quorum. Although using an MNS implementation would save a drive letter, a clustered SQL Server still requires a shared disk subsystem, so you get no benefit of each node being completely autonomous. In addition to that, you do not want to have to manually force quorum to keep availability if the majority of nodes fails. In a traditional quorum server cluster, unless all nodes go down or something is configured improperly, all resources should fail to an available node no matter how many nodes go down.

The cluster has two primary networks:

- A *private cluster network*: Sometimes known as the *intracluster network*, or more commonly, the *heartbeat*. It is a dedicated network that is segregated from all other network traffic and is used for the sole purpose of running internal processes on the cluster nodes to ensure that the nodes are up and running and, if not, to initiate failover. The private cluster network does not detect process failure. The intervals these checks happen at are known as *heartbeats*.

- A *public network*: The network that connects the cluster to the rest of the network ecosystem and allows clients, applications, and other servers to connect to the server cluster.

Finally, two other processes support the semantics of a server cluster and are coded specifically by the developer of the cluster-aware application:

- The *LooksAlive* process is a basic lightweight test that basically goes out to the application and says "Are you there?" By default, this runs every five seconds.

- The *IsAlive* process is a more in-depth application-level check that can include application-specific calls. For SQL Server, this is a Transact-SQL query that issues SELECT @@SERVERNAME. This query is not configurable, and IsAlive requires that the Cluster Service account has access to SQL Server to issue this query. IsAlive has no mechanism for checking to see whether your database is actually online and usable; it knows only if SQL Server (and the master database) is up and running. By default, this runs every 60 seconds.

Figure 4-1 represents a simple server cluster implementation.

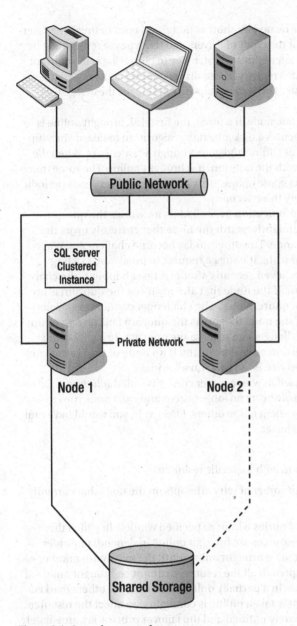

Figure 4-1. *Sample server cluster*

How does all of this work to ensure the availability of SQL Server?

The actual Cluster Service has a few processes that run in it: an event processor, a database manager, a node manager, a global update manager, a communication manager, and a resource (failover) manager. The resource manager communicates directly with a resource monitor that talks to a specific application DLL that makes an application cluster-aware. The communication manager talks directly to the Windows Winsock layer (a component of the Windows networking layer).

All nodes "fight" for ownership of resources, and an arbitration process governs which node owns which resource. In the case of disks (including the quorum in a traditional server cluster), three SCSI commands are used under the covers: reserve to obtain or maintain ownership, release to allow the disk to be taken offline so it can be owned by another node, and reset to break the reservation on the disk. For more information about the types of drivers and the types of resets done by them, see the section "Hardware and Drivers" later in this chapter. Key to clustering is the concept of a disk signature, which is stored in each node's registry. These disk signatures must not change; otherwise, you will encounter errors. The Cluster Disk Driver (clusdisk.sys) reads these registry entries to see what disks the cluster is using.

When the cluster is turned on (assuming one node at a time), the first disk brought online is the quorum. To do this, the failover cluster executes a disk arbitration algorithm to take ownership of that disk on the first node. It is first marked as Offline and goes through a few checks. When the cluster is satisfied that there are no problems with the quorum, it is brought online. The same thing happens with the other disks. After all the disks come online, the Cluster Disk Driver sends periodic reservations to keep ownership of the disk every three seconds.

If for some reason the cluster loses communication over all of its networks, the quorum arbitration process begins. The outcome is straightforward: the node that currently owns the reservation on the quorum is the defending node. The other nodes become challengers. When the challenger detects that it cannot communicate, it issues a request to break any existing reservations it owns via a buswide SCSI reset. Seven seconds after this reset happens, the challenger attempts to gain control of the quorum. If the node that already owns the quorum is up and running, it still has the reservation of the quorum disk. The challenger cannot take ownership and it shuts down the Cluster Service. If the node that owns the quorum fails and gives up its reservation of it, after ten seconds, the challenger can reserve the quorum, bring it online, and subsequently take ownership of other resources in the cluster. If no node of the cluster can gain ownership of the quorum, the Cluster Service is stopped on all nodes.

The situation you never want to find yourself in with a server cluster is called *split brain*. This is when all nodes lose communication and the heartbeats no longer occur and each node tries to become the primary node of the cluster independent of the others. Effectively, you would have multiple clusters thinking they are the CEO of the cluster.

The failover process is as follows:

1. The resource manager detects a problem with a specific resource.

2. The resource goes through a specified number of retry attempts on the node that currently owns it.

3. Each resource has a specific number of retries within a specified window in which that resource can be brought online. The resources are brought online in dependency order. This means the resources will attempt to be brought online until the maximum number of retries in that window has been attempted. If all the resources cannot be brought online at this point, the group might come online in a partially online state with the others marked as offline. However, if any resource that is taken offline is configured to affect the resource group, the failover manager is immediately notified and the failover process is immediately notified. If the resources are not configured to affect the group, they will be left in an offline state leaving you with a partially online group.

4. If the failover manager is contacted, it determines based on the configuration of the resource group who the best owner will be. The new owner is notified, and the resources are attempted to be brought online—effectively, the process starts over again. If that node cannot bring the resources online, another node (if there is one configured) might become the owner. If all potential owners cannot start the resources, the resource group as a whole is left in an offline state.

Figure 4-2 shows the cluster during the failure process.

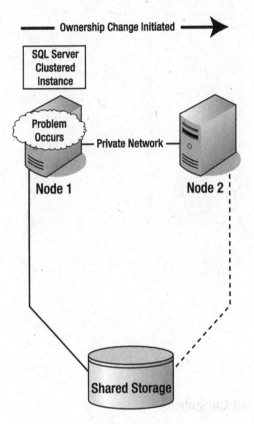

Figure 4-2. *Cluster during the failure process*

Figure 4-3 shows the cluster after the failover process.

5. If a node fails, the failover manager is notified. The failover manager determines which groups (and, subsequently, resources) are owned by the failed node. The resource manager tells the failover manager that the node is offline and the groups need to be moved to another node. The failover manager goes through the arbitration process to find the best owner and attempts to bring the resources online on another node.

From a SQL Server perspective, each of its resources has a similar arbitration process. If a dependency of a SQL Server resource fails, it can cause the parent resource to fail, and vice versa. For example, if you have a disk failure, it will cause SQL Server to fail, and then the group will fail over to another node. If the disk is not bad and the failure is because of, say, a host bus adapter (HBA) card failure, the SQL Server resource group will restart successfully on the other node. If SQL Server fails the LooksAlive and IsAlive processes and its thresholds, it will cause a failure.

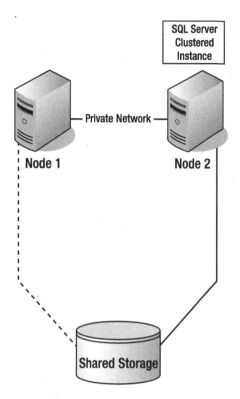

Figure 4-3. *Cluster after the failover process*

Client Connections and Clustered SQL Server–Based Applications

As noted earlier, the IP address and name of an application are "virtualized" so that the connection does not need to worry about which node owns the resources you are using. The clustered application, in this case SQL Server, will appear as a regular SQL Server to the end user or application. All clients will access the IP address and name configured during the SQL Server installation. The individual nodes and the Windows server cluster names and IP addresses will not be used at all. For example, say you have the following configuration:

- The two nodes of DENNIS, with an IP address of 197.100.101.5, and TOMMY with an IP address of 197.100.101.6

- A Windows server cluster with the name STYX with an IP address of 197.100.101.7

- A clustered SQL Server default instance with the name ROBOTO with an IP address of 197.100.101.8

Your clients and applications will connect to ROBOTO or 197.100.101.8 (and its associated TCP/IP port), not any of the other names or IP addresses.

How your application behaves in a failover will differ depending on how it is coded. During the failover process from one node to another, the resources are stopped on one node and started on another. From a SQL Server perspective, this means that all client connections will need to deal with a stop and a start of the SQL Server service since the client connections will be dropped and broken.

The best way to handle the stop and start is to use a cluster-aware application. SQL Server itself is a cluster-aware application, as are many of its tools such as Management Studio. A cluster-aware application is one that is coded to the clustering API, which is part of the Windows Server 2003 Platform SDK. A cluster-aware application detects the failover of the back-end service and gracefully reconnects without interruption to the end user. If you are coding your own applications, this is a capability you want to think about building in from the start.

Tip You can find the latest version of the Platform SDK by going to `http://www.microsoft.com/downloads` and searching for *Platform SDK*.

Most applications are not coded to be cluster-aware. Since there is a stop and a start of SQL Server, the best approach, if you do not want to code to the Platform SDK, is to put some sort of retry logic into the application that will poll to see whether SQL Server is up, and then automatically reconnect when SQL Server comes back up after the failover. Some web-based applications might not need to take into account that the back end is clustered. In many cases, a simple refresh of the browser will do. Sometimes a middle-tier or queuing application such as Microsoft BizTalk when incorporated into an overall solution might also help abstract a clustered SQL Server failover, but that is something that would need to be evaluated based on your requirements. A final approach could be implementing some sort of time-out value in the application and then returning a friendly message to the end user.

What you do not want to do is something that will impede an application from being able to connect to a clustered back end after a failover. Years ago I was working with a client who encountered a failover of their SQL Server on a cluster. The SQL Server failed-over just fine, but for some reason, the client could not get the application to reconnect. As it turns out, the application was ODBC-based and was using a persistent connection to the database back end. When the SQL Server instance failed-over, the connections knew nothing about it. The client had to reset the persistent connection.

An important point to remember is that an application that requires some form of state, or memory, of the user's session will have to be taken into account in the context of a clustered SQL Server back end. SQL Server will always remain consistent in a failover since in the stop and start process, the transaction logs will be rolled back or forward depending on what is there. Incomplete transactions will be rolled back, and any transactions that are not yet committed will be rolled forward. All committed transactions will already be in the database. Your user databases will be in the same state as they were at the point of failure. This is why it is important to always code and use transactions within your statements to ensure database consistency.

Ports are another issue in terms of client connectivity. Both SQL Server 2000 and SQL Server 2005 by default will dynamically be assigned a port number. The first instance will generally take the well-known 1433, but if it is in use, another will be used. If you have more than one instance of SQL Server running, they will all have unique port values. The SQL Server native client knows this. However, from a pure security standpoint, setting a static port is the best way to ensure consistency, and you can avoid known ports such as 1433 that might be security risks. This means the application will need to know about static port. However, if the static port is unavailable in the event of a failover to another node, SQL Server will use another port. Make sure you take this into account in your overall planning. I explain how to set a manual port number for a clustered SQL Server 2005 instance in Chapter 9.

One step you will definitely have to take is to test your application against a clustered SQL Server back end to see how it will behave. Part of measuring your availability is to understand the impact to your end users when something like a failover event happens. Knowing the behavior of your application when you implement a server cluster will help you manage expectations of your end users and assist in troubleshooting any problems.

SQL SERVER 2005 AND WINDOWS COMPUTE CLUSTER SERVER 2003

There is another way to configure Windows—Windows Compute Cluster Server 2003. Windows Compute Cluster Server 2003 is a version of Windows optimized for *high-performance computing*. High-performance computing is a solution where you take a cluster of standard servers that can all function together to achieve the same purpose, but if one server is maximized, the load can be taken up by a server that has cycles available. It makes difficult tasks, such as complex calculations, easier since the work can be done in parallel across many different nodes at the same time. This has been very popular in academic computing and is now gaining steam in the corporate world.

Windows Compute Cluster Server 2003 is comprised of two main components: the Compute Cluster operating system and a Compute Cluster Pack that sits on top of it. The operating system is a stripped-down version of Windows Server 2003. If you have an existing installation of Windows Server 2003 Standard Edition or Windows Server 2003 Enterprise Edition with at least Windows Server 2003 Service Pack 1, you can install the Compute Cluster Pack on top of those. The technology used in Windows Compute Cluster Server 2003 is completely different from a server cluster or an NLB cluster.

SQL Server is not currently designed to work with Windows Compute Cluster Server 2003. The support is not built into the version of the operating system or SQL Server (either 2000 or 2005). This means you cannot use Windows Compute Cluster Server 2003 to scale out your SQL Server implementations for things such as distributed transactions. Keep checking the Microsoft web sites regarding both Windows Compute Cluster Server and SQL Server to see whether this changes.

SQL Server can be installed on servers that will be configured with Windows Compute Cluster Server 2003. What you must do is create a named instance of SQL Server prior to configuring the Compute Cluster Pack with a name of *computecluster* since that is the name of the MSDE instance that Windows Compute Cluster Server 2003 requires. Although you will not be able to take advantage of Compute Cluster Server's features for SQL Server, this will allow you to use the SQL Server instance for something other than Windows Compute Cluster Server 2003.

Planning for a Windows Server Cluster

Before you attempt to install and configure a server cluster, you must deal with quite a few prerequisites to ensure that by the time you install SQL Server, the Windows base upon which it sits is stable and functioning properly. Most problems that occur during a SQL Server installation stem from a missed configuration step at the Windows level.

The Windows Server Catalog

The most important step in planning your cluster is ensuring your intended server cluster solution is listed on the Windows Server Catalog, as described in the Microsoft Knowledge Base article 309395 (http://support.microsoft.com/?id=309395). Prior to Windows Server 2003, the Windows Catalog was called the Windows Hardware Compatibility List (HCL). The reason for this list is simple: the listings ensure that you are going to deploy a known, good, tested, and certified combination of hardware and drivers for your server cluster deployments.

Note Here is the bottom line: if you do not implement a server cluster that is listed as a cluster solution or geographically dispersed cluster solution, you do not have a supported solution in the eyes of Microsoft. It is imperative that you work with your hardware vendor to ensure that the hardware it is selling you matches an entry in the Windows Server Catalog. If the company cannot provide a link to the solution, do not buy it. For reference, keep the following Microsoft Knowledge Base articles handy: 327518, "The Microsoft SQL Server Support Policy for Microsoft Clustering" (http://support.microsoft.com/kb/327518), and 303395, "The Microsoft Support Policy for Server Clusters, the Hardware Compatibility List, and the Windows Server Catalog" (http://support.microsoft.com/kb/309395/).

Where the problems come in is when people want to start deviating from the Windows Server Catalog. A cluster is not a recipe where you take a pinch of this and an ounce of that. For example, you cannot mix and match nodes from different server manufacturers, and you cannot match a model number from one certified cluster solution with one from another solution if it is not the same one in the solution you are looking to implement—even if it is the same vendor who makes the server. Just because the items are *individually* in the Windows Server Catalog, it does not mean that a server from cluster configuration A, a server made by another manufacturer from cluster configuration B, and a storage device from the multicluster list are together a supported solution. Table 4-3 lists the only deviations allowed.

Table 4-3. *Allowed Deviations from the Windows Server Catalog for Cluster Solutions*

Component	Aspect	Deviations Allowed
Server	Model number	Number of processors, RAM (unless it is below minimum requirements for running Windows), number of network cards (with a minimum of two physically separate network cards), processor speed with a differential allowed of up to 500MHz.
HBA card	Driver version	Check with vendor for an updated driver that is certified for use in a server cluster. Do not implement a later version if it is not certified.
Multipath software (MPIO)	Driver version	See deviations allowed for HBA.
Storage controller	Firmware version	See deviations allowed for HBA.
Geographically dispersed cluster software components	Driver and software versions	No deviations allowed.
Multisite interconnect for geographically dispersed clusters	Network technology	No deviations allowed, and latency must be under 500 milliseconds per round-trip.

To access the Windows Server Catalog, follow these steps:

1. Open a web browser window, and navigate to http://www.microsoft.com/windows/catalog/server/default.aspx?subID=22&xslt=hardwarehome, as shown in Figure 4-4.

2. Under Hardware Testing Status as shown in Figure 4-4, click Cluster Solutions.

Figure 4-4. *The Windows Server Catalog main page*

3. When the Cluster Solutions page is displayed, you can then search by server name, HBA name, or storage name as shown in Figure 4-5. You can also drill down by category (Cluster Solution or Geographically Dispersed Cluster Solution as shown in Figure 4-5), by company, or by compatibility as shown in Figure 4-6.

4. As shown in both Figures 4-5 and 4-6, the results will be displayed on the right-hand side of the browser window. Click the link, and the details of each cluster solution will be displayed.

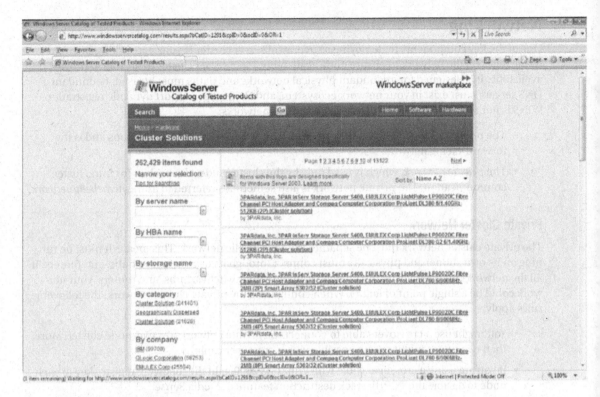

Figure 4-5. *Selecting a cluster solution*

Figure 4-6. *Selecting a cluster solution by company or compatibility*

Networking

One of the key components to deploying a successful server cluster is your networking since clustering relies on the network to ensure node availability. For a server cluster to be able to provide the availability it is designed for, redundant physical networks and paths must be used. Redundant DNS servers must exist in your network ecosystem, and DNS must support dynamic registration. WINS is not required. A server cluster uses two main networks:

- The *public network*, which is the one used mainly by clients and applications and is the forward-facing network.

- The *private network*, which is used only by the cluster nodes themselves for intracluster communication. The private network is also sometimes referred to as the *heartbeat network*.

Private Cluster Network

The private cluster network must be separate from the public network. This means it must be running on its own subnet and physically must connect through its own switches, hubs, and routers. If all the networks on your cluster are plugged into the same switches, hubs, and routers, your network could be a single point of failure. When configuring the private cluster network, the following rules apply:

- You might use a crossover cable to connect the private network of a two-node cluster. More than two nodes might not be possible with a crossover cable.

- If you are using a crossover cable with Windows 2000, add the following registry key to each node to disable the TCP/IP stack destruction feature of Media Sense:

```
HKEY_LOCAL_MACHINE\System\CurrentControlSet\Services\Tcpip\Parameters
Value Name: DisableDHCPMediaSense
Data Type: REG_DWORD
Data: 1
```

■**Caution** Do not add this registry key for any edition of Windows Server 2003.

- Do not configure a gateway or DNS server in the TCP/IP settings for the network adapter used for the private cluster network.

- Disable NetBIOS for all network adapters that are participating in the private cluster network.

- The private cluster network needs to have redundancy, whether it is another physical network or the public network providing the backup.

- The private cluster network cannot have a network latency of greater than 500 milliseconds.

- The private cluster network can use the following blocks of IP addresses:

  - 10.0.0.0 to 10.255.255.255 (Class A)

  - 172.16.0.0 to 172.31.255.255 (Class B)

  - 192.168.0.0 to 192.168.255.255 (Class C)

- Although it might support higher speeds from the physical network, the private cluster network does not require high bandwidth.

Public Network

The public network does not have as many strict rules imposed on it as the private network, but there are still some considerations:

- You might configure more than one public network as long as you have the IP addresses available and slots to put additional network cards in the servers.

- You must configure both a gateway and a primary and secondary DNS for each network adapter configured for use with the public network.

- If no other network provides redundancy for the private cluster network, the public network must be configured within Cluster Administrator to be able to do all cluster communications.

- Each network (and this includes the private cluster network) must be configured as a distinct subnet that differs from all other networks being used. The same subnet mask is fine, but, for example, configuring two networks to use 195.222.x.x would be invalid.

Network Cards

You must have a minimum of two physically separate network cards in the servers that will participate as nodes in a server cluster. One network card will be used for the public network and another for the private network. Many motherboards in servers now include network cards. It is recommended that you use real network cards and not built-in network ports on the motherboard.

Unlike other aspects of the solution that are dictated by the specific cluster solution listing in the Windows Server Catalog, network cards are not bound in that way. For redundancy and fault tolerance, some might be inclined to use teamed network cards. Although this is allowed on any external-facing network, it is completely unsupported to use teamed network cards on the private network.

If you do implement teaming for any externally facing network, make sure you use the proper network card drivers from the manufacturer and configure them properly. If you encounter a problem and contact Microsoft Product Support Services (PSS), Microsoft might require you to disable teaming if the problem is related to teaming.

If the network cards you have purchased have teaming and you do want to use them for the private cluster network, instead of teaming them, what you might want to do is configure the other network port as the redundant backup for the private cluster network. This will not protect you from a full network card failure, but it will provide redundancy if something happens to the primary port and the network cards are still functioning.

■Note All network adapters should be set with the actual speed and duplex of the network to which it is connected. Never allow the settings to autosense the network configuration.

Dedicated TCP/IP Addresses

When deploying a SQL Server failover cluster, you need to reserve a minimum of six TCP/IP addresses, and you might need more depending on your deployment. Although you might employ Dynamic Host Configuration Protocol (DHCP) to assign dynamic TCP/IP addresses to desktops and some servers, clustering requires static TCP/IP addresses. The TCP/IP addresses you must reserve are as follows:

- One for each cluster node, for a minimum of two. If you have an eight-node cluster, you will need eight.
- One for the private network on each cluster node, for a minimum of two.
- One for the Windows server cluster virtualized Windows TCP/IP address.
- One for the SQL Server failover cluster for the virtualized SQL Server TCP/IP address.

If you are using the Microsoft Distributed Transaction Coordinator (MSDTC), it will also require its own dedicated TCP/IP address.

32-bit and 64-bit Windows

With SQL Server 2005, you have the option of choosing a 32-bit environment (x86) or a 64-bit environment (AMD's AMD64, Intel's EMT64T technology, or Intel's Itanium IA64). All can be clustered, but you cannot mix 32-bit and 64-bit nodes in the same Windows server cluster. All nodes must be of the same type. For example, if you are looking to upgrade an existing 32-bit server cluster to 64-bit, you will need to migrate to new hardware and use a method such as restoring backups to get the environment up. You cannot join the 64-bit node to the 32-bit cluster and perform an in-place upgrade.

If you do need a clustered 32-bit SQL Server instance but want to have only 64-bit hardware, you can install a clustered 32-bit SQL Server instance on an x64-based Windows server cluster. This is called *running in Windows-on-Windows 64 (WOW) mode*. You cannot run a clustered 32-bit SQL Server instance in WOW mode on IA64. This support was first introduced with SQL Server 2000 Service Pack 4, and SQL Server 2005 continues this support.

Mixing Windows Versions

Microsoft does not support mixing versions of Windows in the same server cluster. This means all nodes must be at the same operating system version, so you could not have a mixed Windows 2000 Server and Windows Server 2003 cluster where two nodes are of one operating system and the other two are another operating system version. One exception to this rule is when you are in the midst of an in-place operating system upgrade where the servers are nodes of a server cluster. It is meant to be temporary and is not supported in production indefinitely.

Disk Configuration

Disks are the most important configuration point for your databases. There are specific considerations when implementing a cluster that do not apply to nonclustered environments.

Note At TechEd 2006, Microsoft unveiled the SQL Server 2005 Always On program (`http://www.microsoft.com/sql/alwayson/default.mspx`), which is an umbrella that brings all the SQL Server availability technologies under one banner. Part of the Always On program is a partner program for storage solution partners. This specific portion of Always On is known as the SQL Server Storage Solution Review Program. The storage vendors must adhere to a specific set of requirements. Besides looking at the Windows Server Catalog, look at the Always On web site to see whether your storage vendor is listed, and then ask which solutions are branded for Always On. You can find information about this program and the requirements at `http://www.microsoft.com/sql/alwayson/overview.mspx`. Purchasing a solution that is both in the Windows Server Catalog and is Always On branded is about as good as it gets in terms of guarantees from Microsoft that it will provide the best protection for your SQL Server databases.

Hardware and Drivers

Making sure you have the right disk subsystem for your needs is important, but you must consider aspects during the planning and purchase stages. For example, are you going to be using an existing shared disk storage array or buying a new one? Whether it is new or existing, the requirements stay the same.

No matter what type of shared storage array and technology you plan on using with your server cluster, underneath the covers at the driver level, they have to support SCSI commands. To be exact, in Windows Server 2003 these are as follows:

- SCSI-3 SPC-2 Compliant
  - Reserve(6)
  - Release(6)
  - Logical Unit Reset
  - Unique IDs (device identification page 83h with identifier type 2 or 3)

To ensure high availability for your disk access, you must employ some sort of MPIO. This is always a vendor-provided solution, not one that comes from Microsoft. Part of achieving multiple paths is to configure each cluster node with at least two HBAs. MPIO requires specific drivers to work. Storage vendors can code two kinds of HBA drivers:

- *Miniport*: This is a driver that directly interfaces with scsiport.sys to communicate with Windows and contains the hardware-specific information for the fiber HBA card. This type of driver is also known as SCSIport.

- *Storport*: This type of driver was introduced with Windows Server 2003. It bypasses scsiport.sys to communicate with Windows, and it implements the scsiport.sys functionality within the driver itself. This is the preferred type of driver.

Depending on the type of driver implemented and the operating system, the mechanism used to manage the disk will vary and will cause different levels of interruption at the shared disk array layer. For Windows 2000 Server, a SCSI bus reset is used to break reservations to a target. The RTM version of Windows Server 2003 with a miniport driver also uses a SCSI bus reset to break reservations. The RTM version of Windows Server 2003 with a storport driver does a logical unit (LUN) reset to break reservations, meaning it will first try to break reservations at the LUN level and will then progress to target and finally to the bus.

Windows Server 2003 with Windows Server 2003 Service Pack 1 uses unique IDs to better identify the disks to be able to do enhanced arbitration with fewer resets, thus minimizing disruptions to the disk bus. Check with your storage vendor to see whether it supports unique IDs on LUNs.

Windows supports many different kinds of shared disk arrays. As of Windows Server 2003 Service Pack 1, there is full support for iSCSI-based arrays. Service Pack 1 is also friendlier to disk subsystems because it enables no bus reset floods if the underlying LUN supports a unique identifier. All shared disk arrays must be accessed via block level. The array must of course be part of a cluster solution in the Windows Server Catalog.

Be careful when connecting multiple servers to your shared storage. Some vendors do not support mixing multiple operating systems on certain shared storage enclosures, and doing so might put your solution in an unsupported state depending on the terms of your contract with your hardware vendor. The old version of the Windows Server Catalog had a separate section under Storage that was called the Multi-Cluster list. This no longer exists in the current version. The best way to see if your storage solution is supported with your servers is to search the Cluster Solutions and search by storage name.

To ensure that disks on a shared disk subsystem can be seen and used only by the intended servers, you must employ both zoning and masking at the disk subsystem level. Zoning isolates interactions between the cluster node and the storage volumes. Zoning is usually implemented at the controller or switch and must be configured prior to installing clustering. Masking, or LUN (volume) masking, allows you to define a specific relationship between a LUN and the host at the controller level. When configured properly, no other host (in this case, a server) will be able to access the LUN or be able to manipulate it in any way. Hardware-based zoning and masking are recommended.

Sizing the Disks for the Quorum and Microsoft Distributed Transaction Coordinator

Both the quorum disk and the disk used for MSDTC are generally sized fairly small. The quorum recommendation is generally 500MB at a minimum size or as big as 2GB. MSDTC is a different story. If you are not heavily using MSDTC, this can be a small drive. However, if you are using MSDTC, such as with a BizTalk implementation, this could be a fairly heavily used drive, and you will need to perform tests to size the clustered disk appropriately and provide the right amount of disks and level or RAID behind it to ensure that it is highly performing.

Cluster Disk Configuration Considerations for SQL Server

The most difficult part of configuring a server cluster for use with any version of SQL Server is the disk configuration. The main reason is simple: each disk must be presented with a drive letter. That limits you to a maximum of 26 drive letters. The reality is that to start with, you have fewer than 26 drives available. Figure that one is taken up by your internal drive and one is taken up by a CD or DVD drive, and factor in any mapped drives that your company uses. So, at a bare minimum, figure that you have at most 25 drive letters available for use.

When configuring disks for use with the server cluster, all must be basic disks, not dynamic disks, and formatted with NTFS. Under the 64-bit editions of Windows Server 2003 that support clustering, all shared disks must be configured as master boot record (MBR) partition-style disks; 32-bit users do not need to worry about MBR because it is used automatically. The other type of disk partition style is a globally unique identifier (GUID) partition table (GPT). GPT is specific to Itanium-based Windows Server 2003 installations.

Tip If you want to use dynamic disks, you might use a third-party software program such as Symantec's Storage Foundation, but if you encounter problems at the disk level, that third-party vendor will be your primary point of support for your disk issues. Refer to Microsoft Knowledge Base Article 237853, "Dynamic Disk Configuration Unavailable for Server Cluster Resources" (http://support.microsoft.com/?id=237853) for full details on dynamic disks with a server cluster.

Each instance of SQL Server or Analysis Services you will be adding to the cluster will require its own dedicated drives. When drives are created, they are placed in a resource group, and they cannot be shared across resource groups. A single SQL Server installation on a Windows server cluster uses its own resource group; you cannot put more than one SQL Server installation in the same resource group. If you are proposing to implement more than one instance of SQL Server on your cluster, it will take careful planning to get it right so that each instance has the right number of drives. You will most likely want to do things such as split out your data from your log and your user databases from the system databases such as tempdb.

When you are formatting and carving up your drives, do not place more than one logical drive on a single LUN. Although in Windows Explorer it appears as two drives, in reality, it is seen as only one. So you cannot implement more than one SQL Server instance on your cluster, even though it has two logical drive letters on it. Figure 4-7 shows a LUN presented to Windows with two logical drives (IG and I) on top of it in Disk Management.

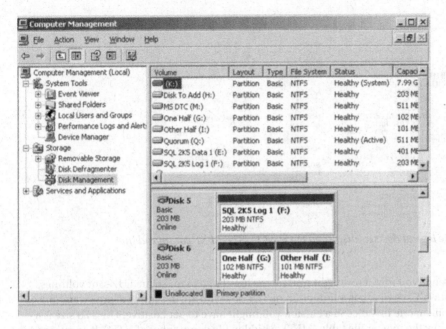

Figure 4-7. *Two logical disks on one physical disk in Disk Management*

Figure 4-8 shows how the two logical drives (G and I) appear as a single disk resource in Cluster Administrator even though to the OS it is technically two drives.

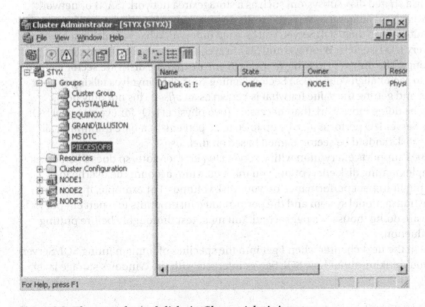

Figure 4-8. *The same logical disks in Cluster Administrator*

Figure 4-9 demonstrates how the disks would be displayed if you queried the cluster to see what resources were configured.

```
X:\>cluster resource
Listing status for all available resources:

Resource               Group               Node          Status
--------------------   -----------------   ----------    ----------
Disk Q:                Cluster Group       NODE1         Online
Disk E:                EQUINOX             NODE1         Online
SQL IP Address1<EQUINOX> EQUINOX                   NODE1        Online
SQL Network Name<EQUINOX> EQUINOX                  NODE1           Online
SQL Server             EQUINOX             NODE1         Online
SQL Server Agent       EQUINOX             NODE1         Online
SQL Server Fulltext    EQUINOX             NODE1         Online
Disk F:                GRAND\ILLUSION      NODE1         Online
Disk H:                CRYSTAL\BALL        NODE1         Online
SQL Network Name <CRYSTAL> CRYSTAL\BALL          NODE1         Online
SQL IP Address 1 <CRYSTAL> CRYSTAL\BALL          NODE1         Online
SQL Server <BALL>      CRYSTAL\BALL        NODE1         Online
SQL Server Agent <BALL> CRYSTAL\BALL            NODE1        Online
Disk M:                MS DTC              NODE1         Online
MS DTC IP Address      MS DTC              NODE1         Online
MS DTC Network Name    MS DTC              NODE1         Online
MS DTC                 MS DTC              NODE1         Online
Disk G: I:             PIECES\OF8          NODE1         Online
Cluster IP Address     Cluster Group       NODE1         Online
Cluster Name           Cluster Group       NODE1         Online
```

Figure 4-9. *The same logical disks as displayed via the CLUSTER.EXE command line*

Another challenge you might (or might not) face is how large to make the LUNs, or volumes, presented to Windows. Each disk has a limitation of 2TB, so if you are designing a large warehouse and want it to live all on one instance in a cluster, you might have to get creative. The 2TB size is a limitation imposed by the master file table (MFT), a hidden file component of NTFS. It applies to both 32- and 64-bit environments and assumes a 4KB block size.

When formatting data disks for use with SQL Server in NTFS, you should use 64KB as the block size if you are doing a mix of read and write, or 8KB if you are doing mostly writes. Do not accept the default, which is 4KB. This means that in reality, you would have less than 2TB available to you.

When you are using a shared disk subsystem such as a storage area network (SAN) or network attached storage (NAS), each manufacturer implements its disk solution a bit differently. This means its interaction with Windows, and then SQL Server, will be a tad different. What you ultimately want to happen is that for every I/O issued by Windows and SQL Server, there is one corresponding I/O on the hardware side of things. The only way to achieve this is to ensure that the disks are sector aligned. (Chapter 5 covers how to sector align your disks.) Sector aligning your disks involves talking to your hardware manufacturer and getting the value for what is known as an *offset*. This not only helps ensure that you will not be doing more work than necessary (two physical I/Os for every logical I/O issued), but boosts SQL Server I/O performance by up to 20 to 25 percent. At a bare minimum, all SQL Server data and log disks should be sector aligned based on their use.

Windows Server 2003 supports encryption with a server cluster; therefore, so does SQL Server 2005. If you plan on implementing disk encryption, you must take into account the overhead of encryption and how it might impact performance on your disk volumes. For example, if you are running a high-volume transactional system and the performance hit amounts to 5 percent per I/O, it could be costly if you are doing thousands per second. You must test thoroughly before putting such a system into production.

I discuss this more in the next chapter when I get into the specifics of implementing SQL Server 2005, but this will get you thinking about how SQL Server interacts with the Windows storage layer.

Note Never use software RAID on disks configured for use in a server cluster. Always use hardware-based RAID.

Mount Points and SQL Server 2005

SQL Server 2005 supports the use of *mount points* in a cluster. A mount point is a directory on an existing disk that can be used to "mount" another disk without the need for another drive letter. The caveat to using clustered mount points with SQL Server is that they must be attached to a drive with a drive letter. So SQL Server 2005 will not solve the problem of you potentially running out of drive letters.

Note You do have the ability to install SQL Server 2000 and SQL Server 2005 side by side in a Windows server cluster. It is not a valid configuration to use mount points with SQL Server 2005 and do a side-by-side implementation with SQL Server 2000 on a cluster. SQL Server 2000 does not support the use of mount points and cannot be configured on a Windows server cluster that has mount points configured at all. This is documented in the Microsoft Knowledge Base article 819546, "SQL Server 2000 and SQL Server 2005 Support for Mounted Volumes" (http://support.microsoft.com/kb/819546/en-us).

Security Configuration for a Server Cluster

A server cluster requires that all nodes have Active Directory or Windows domain connectivity, and there must be redundant domain controllers. A single domain controller is a single point of failure that could bring down your cluster if it goes offline. If you are using some form of other authentication in your environment and do not have an existing Windows domain or Active Directory configuration, you must create one for use with the cluster nodes and join the nodes to the domain. If you do not, you cannot implement SQL Server failover clustering. If your company has multiple Active Directory or domain implementations, choose one and have all nodes join. You cannot have nodes that cross domains; all nodes must be in the same domain.

You need to configure two sets of domain accounts for a failover cluster implementation: one for the Windows-level cluster administrator service account that starts the Windows server cluster and then the accounts specific to the SQL Server 2005 implementation. All accounts and groups must be created at the Active Directory level and then added to the individual nodes with the proper permissions, as described in Chapter 5.

Many companies institute a domain policy that states that after a certain period, a user's password expires. If it is domainwide, it means that after a certain number of days, the password will expire. This is not good for mission-critical applications that need high availability. A change in password will most likely cause an interruption in service.

Tip If you utilize security policy templates that lock down aspects and rights on each server you deploy, make sure those policies do not conflict with the rights needed for the service accounts on a cluster. If they do, your cluster implementation will fail. I have seen this while engaged with a customer who was implementing clustering, so make sure you work with the group that controls server security and, if need be, create a new security template for your cluster implementations. This will save you many hours of troubleshooting headaches.

Cluster Nodes As Domain Controllers

It is strongly not recommended to configure the cluster nodes themselves as domain controllers. Most of you already have a domain with which to add the nodes, but for those of you who do not (and these would be the only servers that need it), buy two additional servers and make them your domain controller and the backup domain controller. If you need to make your nodes domain controllers, here are some challenges you might run into:

- When you configure one node as a domain controller, you will need to configure another node (or the only other node in a two-node cluster) as a domain controller as well as to serve as a backup. If you configure only one, it is a single point of failure.

- Since the cluster nodes would be the domain controllers, they will also need to function as DNS servers and point to each other for primary DNS resolution and to themselves for secondary.

- Some additional overhead (130MB to 140MB of memory) is associated with running a domain controller and you will see increased network traffic and overall activity since the domain controllers need to be in constant communication with each other and need to replicate.

- When domain controllers are configured, they perform the functions as defined by the Operations Master Roles. By default, they exist on the first domain controller. If one node fails, the specific Operations Master Roles of that node will not be available, so you should not allow Operations Master Roles to run on any cluster node.

- This configuration needs thorough testing before deploying it in production.

Cluster Administrator Service Account

The Windows-level cluster administrator service account must have the following properties:

- The account must be created in the domain. Name it something appropriate (such as "Cluster Administrator" with a login name of "clusteradmin").

- The domain account should not be and does not need to be a domain administrator.

- The domain account must be added to the Local Administrators group on every node.

- The Local Administrators group on each node must have the following rights:

  - Debug Programs

  - Impersonate a Client After Authentication

  - Manage Auditing and Security Log

Note If you have an overall Group Policy that updates the Impersonate a Client After Authentication right, the cluster administrator account must be expressly added to that Group Policy. The cluster administrator account cannot just be added to the Local Administrators group. If the cluster administrator account is not added to the Group Policy you configured, Windows Management Instrumentation (WMI) access for that node might no longer be available since the local policy settings will be overwritten.

- The domain account that has been added to the local node must have the rights specified in Table 4-4. If the Local Administrators group has these rights, they do not need to be expressly granted to the cluster administrator login itself.

Table 4-4. *Rights Needed for the Cluster Administrator Service Account*

Windows Right	Windows 2000 Server	Windows Server 2003
Act as Part of the Operating System	Yes	Yes
Adjust Memory Quotas for a Process	No	Yes
Back Up Files and Directories	Yes	Yes
Increase Quotas	Yes	No
Increase Scheduling Priority	Yes	Yes
Load and Unload Device Drivers	Yes	No
Lock Pages in Memory	Yes	No
Log on a Service	Yes	Yes
Restore Files and Directories	Yes	Yes

Firewalls and the Windows Server Cluster

For Windows failover clustering to work in an environment that incorporates firewalls, you might need to open certain ports in addition to the ports required for SQL Server or Analysis Services. When opening these ports, make sure you properly secure them to guarantee that a denial of service attack cannot affect the private network that is crucial for cluster health. The known User Datagram Protocol (UDP) ports you need to open from a Windows failover clustering perspective are as follows:

- *135*: This is the port used by the remote procedure call (RPC) endpoint mapper.

- *139*: This is the port used by the NetBIOS session service.

- *445*: This is the port used by Windows file sharing (SMB).

- *3343*: This is the port used by the cluster network driver and what the private heartbeat network uses to communicate. If this is down, you can potentially bring your whole server cluster down.

- *5000 to 5099*: Although you might not need to open up all these ports, some of these might need to be opened to allow remote RPC connectivity to Cluster Administrator. If they are not open, you might see a 1721 error in the Event Log. The actual Cluster Service needs at least 100 ports for communicating through RPCs. When other services such as SQL Server 2005 are using some of the ports, there might not be enough ports open for the cluster to function properly.

- *8011 to 8031*: If the cluster nodes are separated via a firewall, these ports must be opened to allow RPC connectivity between the nodes. If these are not opened, errors that refer to a "Sponsor" will be found in the cluster log. As with the previous point, the reason this might occur is that there are not enough ports required for clustering to allow RPC communication between a node that is trying to join the cluster and its sponsoring node.

Geographically Dispersed Clusters

If you plan on implementing a server cluster that spans considerable distance, this requires a specialized solution that appears in the Windows Server Catalog as a geographically dispersed cluster as noted in the section "The Windows Server Catalog." You cannot implement this yourself; you will need to work with your preferred hardware vendor to configure this type of cluster. Implementing a geographically dispersed cluster is much more complex than a standard server cluster that is housed in a single data center. You will have to take the following into account:

- Both the private and public networks connecting the nodes have to appear as a single, non-routed LAN that must guarantee a 500-millisecond or less round-trip response time. If your latency is greater than that, it does not adhere to the guidelines. You can use behind-the-scenes technology such as virtual LANs (VLANs), but the cluster interconnect itself must appear as a standard LAN to the servers.

- Mirroring your disks is a key component of a geographically dispersed cluster. This means you need a copy of your shared disk subsystem in the other location; the split nodes over the two locations do not share the same disk subsystem. The quorum must be mirrored synchronously; it cannot be done asynchronously. The single disk semantics must be maintained. You can mirror your SQL Server disks either synchronously or asynchronously, but obviously it is better that they are mirrored synchronously. Keep in mind that when things are mirrored at the disk level, they are done at the block or page. There is no concept of transaction as there is within SQL Server itself. One of the reasons to employ a certified geographically dispersed cluster is that the vendor has tested the solution with programs such as SQL Server and Exchange and most likely has a specific way of configuring for that application. With SQL Server, you must absolutely guarantee that there will be no torn pages written to the disk. A *torn page* is when the bits written to the disk are in the wrong state at the disk level and SQL Server detects the abnormality. A torn page can, and usually does, mean data loss. Qualified solutions should be able to prevent torn pages.

Note Use the Microsoft Knowledge Base article 280743, "Windows Clustering and Geographically Separate Sites," (http://support.microsoft.com/kb/280743) as a reference when dealing with your vendor. Never implement a solution that does not appear in the Windows Server Catalog as a geographically dispersed cluster. Although you might have the right technology, such as mirroring disks between sites, already configured, this does not mean what you have will work in a clustered scenario.

Summary

It is important to understand what you are implementing before you actually configure clusters. Microsoft's server cluster serves as the base for SQL Server's failover clustering feature, and both are designed from an availability standpoint. Once you do understand, there is a lot of planning and prework to do to ensure that the failover cluster is configured properly. Once you have done your planning, you can move onto the implementation phase for your Windows server cluster.

CHAPTER 5

∎∎∎

Failover Clustering:
Clustering Windows

Once you understand what clustering is, how it works, its potential benefits, and the prerequisites needed, and you have decided to use it, you can progress to the installation phase. It is extremely important from a SQL Server standpoint to get the Windows configuration correct; otherwise, you could potentially have an unstable SQL Server 2005.

∎**Note** Although SQL Server 2005 can be clustered on either Windows 2000 Advanced Server or Windows 2000 Datacenter Server with Windows 2000 Service Pack 4, the next two chapters will focus on implementing and administering a server cluster with Windows Server 2003. Where applicable, I provide links for Windows 2000 Server information.

Step 1: Installing and Configuring Hardware and the Operating System

The first step is the easiest: get your hardware in-house, and configure what needs to be done outside the Windows and SQL Server aspects. Make sure that in each node, all the hardware is identical (such as HBAs), and make sure all firmware and BIOS levels for the components match the versions in the Windows Server Catalog or the updated certified versions as specified by the hardware vendor. Once you've done that, you can install the proper version of Windows on your servers.

∎**Tip** To see the latest recommendations and hotfixes for Windows Server 2003–based server clusters, consult Microsoft Knowledge Base article 895092, "Recommended Hotfixes for Windows Server 2003–Based Server Clusters" (http://support.microsoft.com/kb/895092/en-us). For Windows 2000 Server with Service Pack 4–based server clusters, see the Microsoft Knowledge Base article 895090, "Recommended Hotfixes for Windows 2000 Service Pack 4–Based Server Clusters" (http://support.microsoft.com/kb/895090/en-us).

Step 2: Creating and Configuring the Cluster Service Account

The Windows server cluster requires a single domain-based account to be used as its service account. If you will be implementing more than one server cluster in your environment, you can technically use this account for all clusters. Using one account might not be the right thing to do, not only from a security standpoint but also from an availability standpoint. If you need to reset the password, do you want it to affect one cluster or all of them?

Creating the Cluster Service Account

To create the service account used for a server cluster, follow these steps:

1. Log on to one of the servers as an administrator who has rights to add accounts to the domain.

2. From Administrative Tools, start the Active Directory Users and Computers tool, as shown in Figure 5-1.

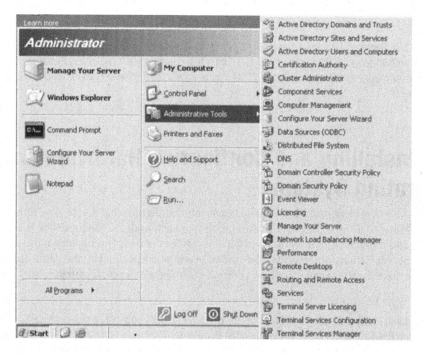

Figure 5-1. *Selecting the Active Directory Users and Computers tool*

3. In the pane on the left, expand the domain, right-click Users, and select New ➤ User, as shown in Figure 5-2.

4. In the New Object – User dialog box, you must enter at least a first name or a last name, as well as the user logon name, as shown in Figure 5-3. Click Next.

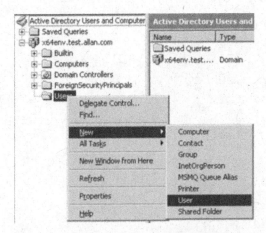

Figure 5-2. *Selecting the menu option to create a new user*

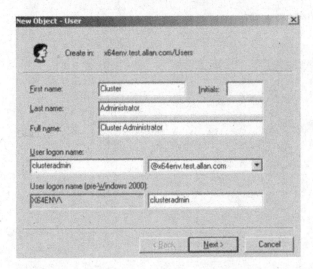

Figure 5-3. *Creating the cluster service account*

5. Enter a password for the account in the Password box, and enter it again in the Confirm Password box. Deselect the option User Must Change Password at Next Logon, and if your security policy allows it, select the Password Never Expires option, as shown in Figure 5-4. Click Next.

6. Click Finish to complete the account creation process, as shown in Figure 5-5.

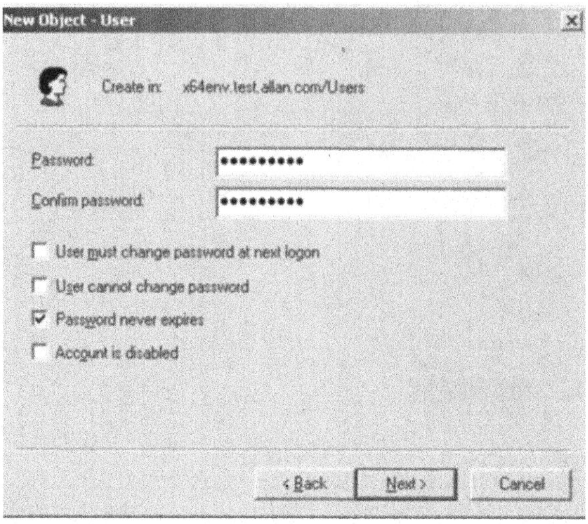

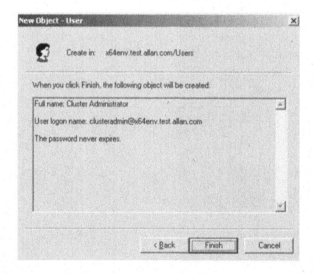

Figure 5-4. *Creating the account password*

Figure 5-5. *Completing the account creation*

7. To verify that the account was created, select Users in the left pane of Active Directory Users and Computers. The account you just created will be displayed on the right side, as shown in Figure 5-6.

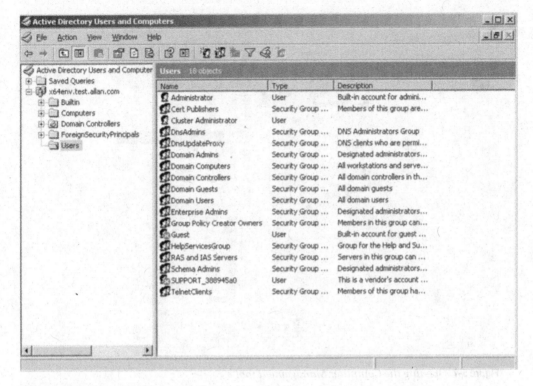

Figure 5-6. *Verifying the account creation*

Adding the Cluster Service Account to Each Node

To add the cluster service account to each node, follow these steps:

1. Log on to one of the servers, which will be a node in the cluster with an account that has the administrative access to add and modify users.

2. From Administrative Tools, start the Computer Management tool, as shown in Figure 5-7.

3. Expand Local Users and Groups, and select Groups, as shown in Figure 5-8.

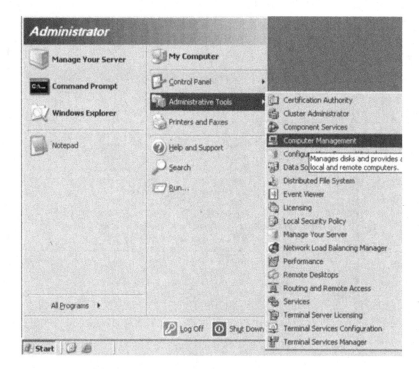

Figure 5-7. *Opening the Computer Management tool*

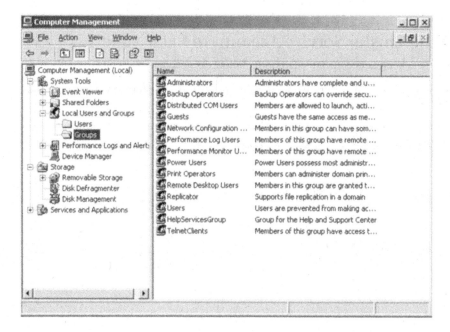

Figure 5-8. *Selecting Groups*

4. In the right pane, select Administrators and the Add to Group option, as shown in Figure 5-9; alternatively, double-click Administrators.

Figure 5-9. *Selecting the Add to Group option*

5. In the Administrators Properties dialog box, click Add, as shown in Figure 5-10.

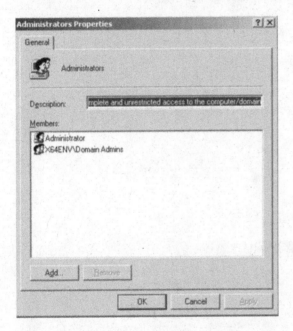

Figure 5-10. *Administrators Properties dialog box*

6. In the Select Users, Computers, or Groups dialog box as shown in Figure 5-11, verify that the From This Location value is set to the domain. If it's not, click Locations, then in the Locations dialog box, select the correct domain, as shown in Figure 5-12. Click OK in the Locations dialog box to return.

7. Enter the name of the cluster service account you created earlier in the Enter the Object Names to Select box, as shown in Figure 5-13. Click Check Names.

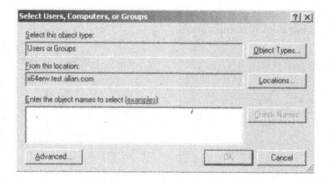

Figure 5-11. *Select Users, Computers, or Groups dialog box*

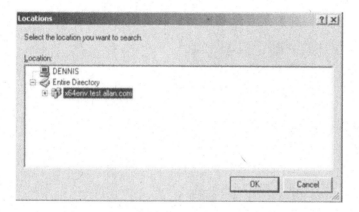

Figure 5-12. *Locations dialog box*

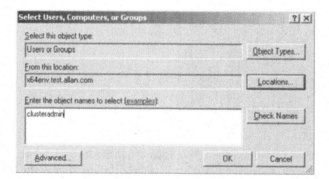

Figure 5-13. *Entering the name to check in the domain*

The account will be validated against the domain, and the result will look like Figure 5-14. Click OK.

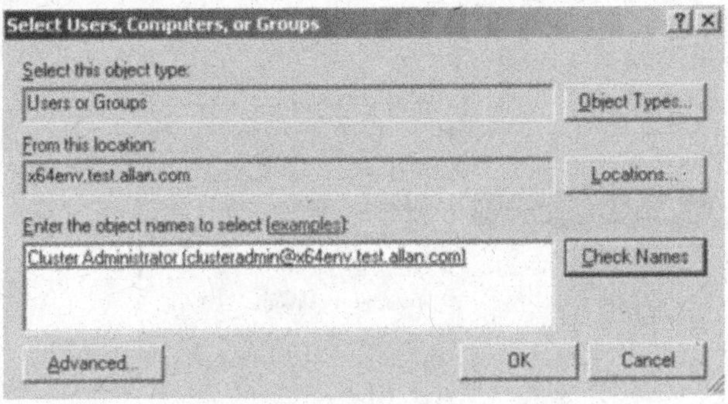

Figure 5-14. *Results of the name validation*

8. The Administrators Properties dialog box will now reflect the addition of the account, as shown in Figure 5-15. Click Apply and then OK.

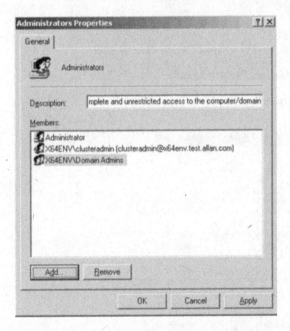

Figure 5-15. *Administrators Properties after adding the cluster administrator*

9. From Administrative Tools, select Local Security Policy, as shown in Figure 5-16.

10. Expand Local Policies, and select User Rights Assignment, as shown in Figure 5-17.

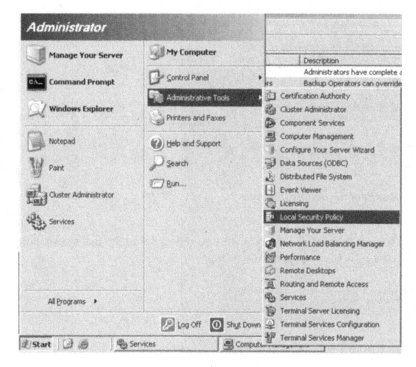

Figure 5-16. *Opening Local Security Policy*

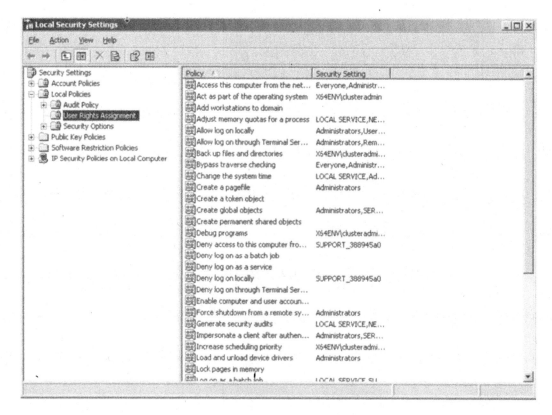

Figure 5-17. *Selecting User Rights Assignment*

11. Refer to the section "Cluster Administrator Service Account" in Chapter 4 to see which policies need to be assigned to the cluster service account. If the policy is already granted to the Administrators group, you do not need to add it to the cluster service account since the account is already part of the local Administrators group. If you need to add a policy, right-click it in the right pane, and select Properties, as shown in Figure 5-18; alternatively, double-click it. The properties page for the specific policy will be shown and will be similar to the one displayed in step 5. Follow steps 6–8 to add the cluster administrator to the local security policy. Repeat this step for all policies.

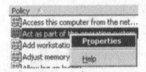

Figure 5-18. *Opening a policy*

12. Exit Local Security Policy when the task is complete.

13. Log off from the node on which you are working.

14. Log on to another node, and repeat steps 2–13 until you've added the cluster service account to every node that will participate in the Windows server cluster.

Step 3: Configuring Networking for a Server Cluster

You must plan your disk configuration for a clustered implementation carefully according to the rules listed in Chapter 4.

Configuring the Public Network

To configure the public network, follow these steps:

1. Log on to one of the servers that will serve as a node in the server cluster.

2. From Control Panel, right-click Network Connections, and select Explore, as shown in Figure 5-19.

3. Right-click the network card you want to configure in the right pane, and select Rename, as shown in Figure 5-20.

   Enter a name for the public network that is easy to identify such as **Public Network**, and hit Enter. You'll see the new name, as shown in Figure 5-21.

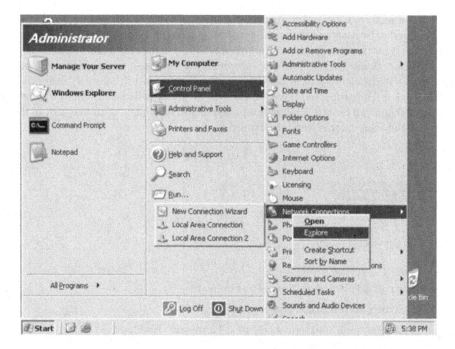

Figure 5-19. *Selecting Network Connections*

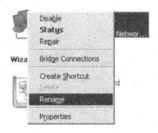

Figure 5-20. *Selecting Rename*

Figure 5-21. *Renamed network card*

4. Right-click the network card you just renamed, and select Properties; alternatively, double-click it. The properties for the network card will look like Figure 5-22.

5. Select Internet Protocol (TCP/IP), and click Properties; alternatively, double-click Internet Protocol (TCP/IP). The Internet Protocol (TCP/IP) Properties dialog box will now be displayed, as shown in Figure 5-23.

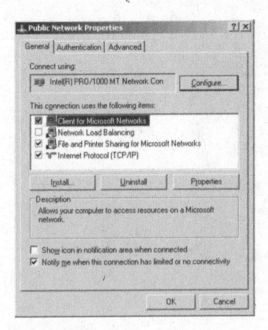

Figure 5-22. *Network card properties*

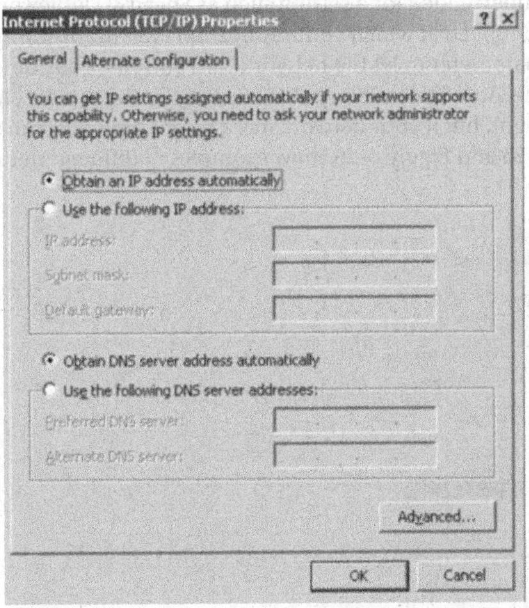

Figure 5-23. *Internet Protocol (TCP/IP) Properties dialog box*

6. Click the Use the Following IP Address option, and enter a static IP address, a valid gateway in Default Gateway, and a primary and secondary DNS server in Preferred DNS Server and Alternate DNS Server. When finished, it should look something like Figure 5-24. Click OK.

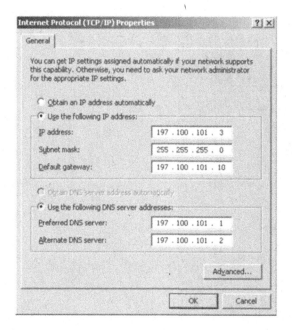

Figure 5-24. *Example TCP/IP properties for a public cluster network*

7. Select the Advanced tab. Under Property, look for a setting such as Speed & Duplex or External PHY, where you can set the speed at which communications will occur through the network card. Do not set this parameter to let the network card automatically detect the speed. Some manufacturers call this Auto Detect, some Auto Sense. For the private cluster network, 10Mbps should be sufficient, but if your network has a bigger pipe, you can select a faster setting. Click OK. Figure 5-25 and Figure 5-26 show examples of different network cards and their settings for speed.

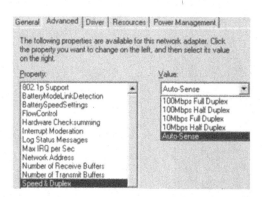

Figure 5-25. *Setting the speed of the public network, example 1*

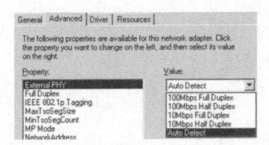

Figure 5-26. *Setting the speed of the public network, example 2*

8. Click OK to close the network card's properties.

9. Repeat steps 3–8 for every public network that will be used in the cluster.

10. Repeat steps 1–9 for every node in the cluster. Make sure that the network cards are named the same way across all nodes for all networks to avoid confusion.

Configuring the Private Cluster Network

To configure the private cluster network, follow these steps:

1. Log on to one of the servers that will serve as a node in the server cluster.

2. From Control Panel, right-click Network Connections. The Network Connections window will now be displayed.

3. Right-click the network card you want to configure in the right pane, and select Rename. Enter a name for the private network that is easy to identify such as **Heartbeat**, and hit Enter. The new name will be reflected, as shown in Figure 5-27.

Figure 5-27. *Renamed private cluster network example*

4. Right-click the network card you just renamed, and select Properties; alternatively, double-click it. The properties for the network card will now be shown.

5. Select Internet Protocol (TCP/IP), and click Properties; or, double-click Internet Protocol (TCP/IP). The Internet Protocol (TCP/IP) Properties dialog box will now be displayed.

6. Click the Use the Following IP address option, and enter a static IP address that is a valid subnet, as listed in Chapter 4. Do not enter a value for a gateway or any values for DNS. The result will look similar to Figure 5-28.

7. Click Advanced. In the Advanced TCP/IP Settings dialog box, select the WINS tab, and under NetBIOS Setting, select the option Disable NetBIOS Over TCP/IP, as shown in Figure 5-29. Click OK.

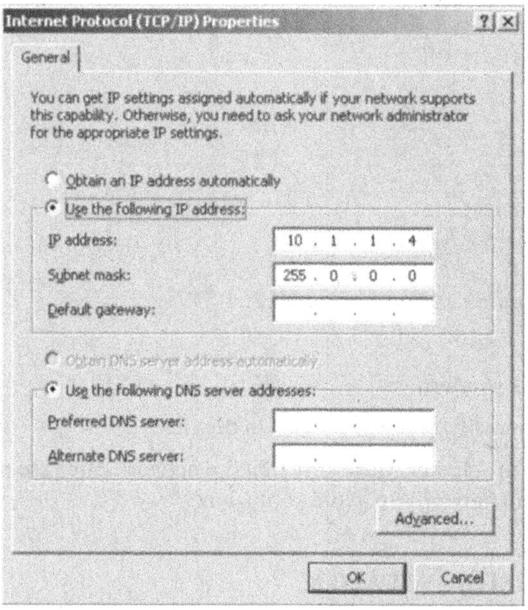

Figure 5-28. *Private cluster network example TCP/IP settings*

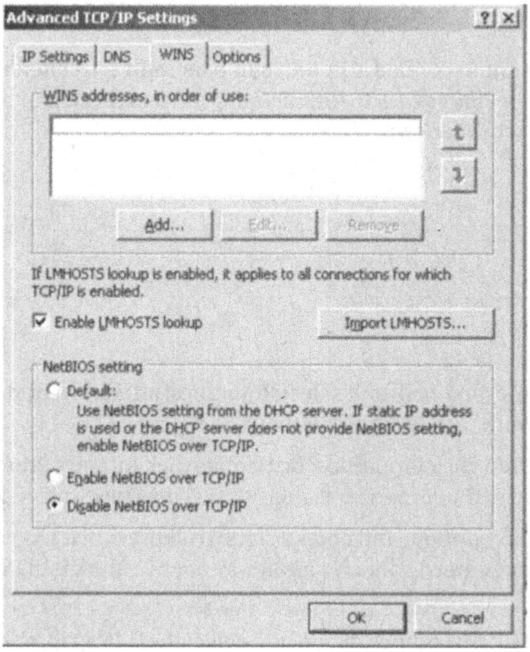

Figure 5-29. *Advanced TCP/IP Settings dialog box for the private cluster network*

8. In the network card's Properties dialog box, deselect all options such as Client for Microsoft Networks and File and Printer Sharing for Microsoft Networks except for Internet Protocol (TCP/IP). Figure 5-30 shows an example. Click OK.

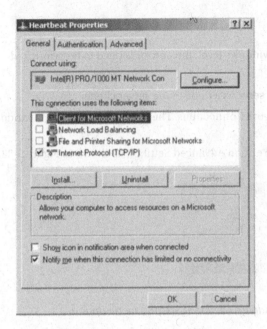

Figure 5-30. *Deselected network options*

9. Select the Advanced tab. Under Property, look for a setting such as Speed & Duplex or External PHY, where you can set the speed at which communications will occur through the network card. Do not set this to the default of Auto Sense. For the private cluster network, 10Mbps should be sufficient, but if your network has a bigger pipe, you can select a faster setting. Click OK. Figure 5-31 shows an example.

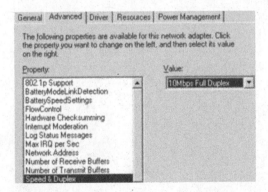

Figure 5-31. *Private network set to 10Mbps*

10. Repeat steps 3–9 for every private cluster network that will be used in the cluster.

11. Repeat steps 1–10 for every node in the cluster. Make sure that the network cards are named the same way across all nodes for all networks to avoid confusion.

Setting Network Priorities

For the networking to work properly at the Windows level, the networks need to be prioritized properly:

1. Log on to one of the servers that will serve as a node in the server cluster.

2. From Control Panel, right-click Network Connections. The Network Connections window will now be displayed.

3. From the Advanced menu, select the option Advanced Settings, as shown in Figure 5-32.

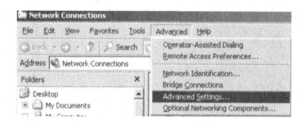

Figure 5-32. *Network Connections window's Advanced Settings menu option*

4. In the Advanced Settings dialog box, make sure that all the public networks are listed above all the private cluster networks, as shown in Figure 5-33. If they are not, select the network that is misplaced in Connections, and use the up or down arrows to put it in the right place in the order. You can prioritize which public network and private network takes precedence over another one.

5. Repeat steps 1–4 for every node in the cluster.

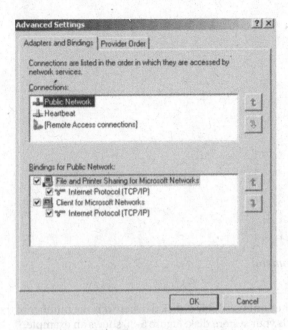

Figure 5-33. *Advanced Settings dialog box*

Step 4: Configuring the Shared Disks

This section documents how to configure the disks on your shared disk array. There are many chapters in this book that talk about how to configure disks for a specific feature of SQL Server. Chapters 4, 7, and 14 will be most helpful with clustering, but make sure you read the disk requirements for any feature you may want to use before embarking on the actual task of configuration because you will need to take many factors into account to have a good disk subsystem for your SQL Server databases.

■**Caution** Do not use Disk Management to recognize the disks since it does not have the ability to sector align them.

Step 4a: Sector Aligning the Disks

The following instructions show the steps for sector aligning Windows Server 2003, but you can use these steps with Windows 2000 Server if you get the DISKPAR.EXE tool from the *Microsoft Windows 2000 Server Resource Kit* by Microsoft Corporation (Microsoft Press, 2000).

1. Make sure all nodes except the first node of the cluster are powered down and not connected to the SAN at the moment.

2. Open a command window, and type **diskpart**. You will see the display shown in Figure 5-34.

3. At the DISKPART> prompt, enter the command **list disk**. This will show the disks that Windows sees and are available for use. The disk will have a number associated with it, as shown in Figure 5-35.

```
C:\>diskpart

Microsoft DiskPart version 5.2.3790.1830
Copyright (C) 1999-2001 Microsoft Corporation.
On computer: TOMMY

DISKPART>
```

Figure 5-34. *Starting DISKPART*

```
DISKPART> list disk

  Disk ###  Status       Size     Free     Dyn  Gpt
  --------  ----------   -------  -------   ---  ---
  Disk 0    Online         10 GB  8033 KB
  Disk 1    Online        511 MB   511 MB
  Disk 2    Online        511 MB   511 MB
  Disk 3    Online       3067 MB  3067 MB
  Disk 4    Online       2039 MB  2039 MB
  Disk 5    Online       4095 MB  4095 MB
  Disk 6    Online       1022 MB  1022 MB
  Disk 7    Online       3067 MB  3067 MB
  Disk 8    Online       5114 MB  5114 MB
```

Figure 5-35. *Using the list disk command*

4. At the DISKPART> prompt, enter the command **select disk d**, where *d* is the number of the disk that you want to use. Disk 0 is your system disk. Figure 5-36 shows an example.

```
DISKPART> select disk 1

Disk 1 is now the selected disk.
```

Figure 5-36. *Using the select disk command*

5. At the DISKPART> prompt, enter the command **create partition primary align=o**, where *o* is the proper offset provided by your storage vendor. Do not enter an arbitrary number because only the vendor knows the correct value. This command will create a partition that consumes the whole LUN. Figure 5-37 shows an example. If you do not want to use the whole LUN, use the command create partition primary size=*n* align=*o*, where *n* is the size of the partition in megabytes (MB).

```
DISKPART> create partition primary align=128

DiskPart succeeded in creating the specified partition.
```

Figure 5-37. *Aligning the disk and using the whole LUN*

If you then run a list disk command, you will see that some of the disk is allocated and some of it is not, as shown in Figure 5-38.

6. To make it easier to identify the drive when you format it in Computer Management, at the DISKPART> prompt, enter the command **assign letter=l**, where *l* is a valid letter of the alphabet. Figure 5-39 shows an example.

7. To verify that the partition was created properly, enter the command **list partition** at the DISKPART> prompt. You should see something similar to Figure 5-40.

To verify that the drive letters have been assigned, enter the command **list volume**. You will see output similar to Figure 5-41.

```
DISKPART> list disk

  Disk ###   Status        Size       Free     Dyn  Gpt
  --------   ---------   --------   --------   ----  ----
  Disk 0     Online         10 GB    8033 KB
  Disk 1     Online        511 MB       0 B
  Disk 2     Online        511 MB       0 B
* Disk 3     Online       3067 MB    1012 MB
  Disk 4     Online       2039 MB    2039 MB
  Disk 5     Online       4095 MB    4095 MB
  Disk 6     Online       1022 MB    1022 MB
  Disk 7     Online       3067 MB    3067 MB
  Disk 8     Online       5114 MB    5114 MB
```

Figure 5-38. *Showing the partially used LUN*

```
DISKPART> assign letter=q

DiskPart successfully assigned the drive letter or mount point.
```

Figure 5-39. *Assigning a drive letter*

```
DISKPART> list partition

  Partition ###   Type              Size     Offset
  -------------   --------------   -------   -------
* Partition 1     Primary           511 MB    128 KB
```

Figure 5-40. *Showing the partition information*

```
DISKPART> list volume

  Volume ###  Ltr  Label          Fs      Type        Size     Status     Info
  ----------  ---  -----------    -----   ---------   -------  ---------   ------
  Volume 0     D   BRMECD2XFRE    CDFS    DVD-ROM      167 MB  Healthy
  Volume 1     C                  NTFS    Partition     10 GB  Healthy     System
  Volume 2     Q                  RAW     Partition    511 MB  Healthy
  Volume 3     M                  RAW     Partition    511 MB  Healthy
  Volume 4     H                  RAW     Partition   2055 MB  Healthy
  Volume 5     I                  RAW     Partition   1028 MB  Healthy
  Volume 6     J                  RAW     Partition   1004 MB  Healthy
  Volume 7     K                  RAW     Partition   4095 MB  Healthy
  Volume 8     L                  RAW     Partition   1022 MB  Healthy
  Volume 9     N                  RAW     Partition   3067 MB  Healthy
* Volume 10    O                  RAW     Partition   5114 MB  Healthy
```

Figure 5-41. *Showing the drive mappings*

8. Repeat steps 1–7 until all disks are created properly and aligned.

9. At the DISKPART> prompt, enter the command **exit**, and then close the command window.

Tip If you do not want to run DISKPART interactively, you can run it from a command line that uses a preconfigured text file. For example, diskpart /s myscript.txt > output.txt will run DISKPART with commands in the file myscript.txt and will put any output in the file output.txt.

Step 4b: Formatting the Disks

Two methods of formatting the disks were just added to Windows via DISKPART: you can use Computer Management, or you can use the FORMAT command in a command window.

Formatting Disks via Computer Management

To format disks via Computer Management, follow these steps:

1. From Administrative Tools, start the Computer Management tool.

2. Select Disk Management. All the disks you created in DISKPART will now display in the right pane. Figure 5-42 shows an example.

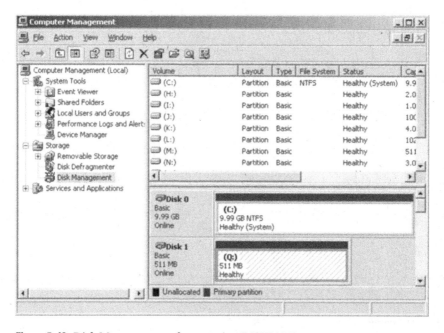

Figure 5-42. *Disk Management after running DISKPART*

3. In the lower half of the right pane, select the disk to format by right-clicking and selecting Format, as shown in Figure 5-43.

4. In the Format dialog box for the disk selected, enter a descriptive name in the Volume Label field, select NTFS as the file system, and select the proper cluster size in the Allocation Unit Size drop-down. If the disk is going to be used for SQL Server data or might be used for SQL Server data, it should be 64KB. If the disk will be used purely for SQL Server logs or backups and no data files will ever be placed on the drive, you can use 4096. If your drive will be used for data and will be purely a write with no read, use 8192. I do not recommend doing a quick format. Do not select the Enable File and Folder Compression option. Figure 5-44 shows an example. Click OK.

5. At the prompt shown in Figure 5-45, click OK.

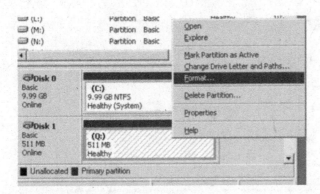

Figure 5-43. *Selecting the Format option*

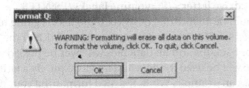

Figure 5-44. *Example Format dialog box*

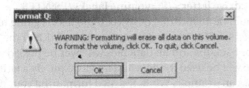

Figure 5-45. *Format disk verification*

When the formatting process is complete, the display will be updated, as shown in Figure 5-46.

6. Repeat steps 3–5 for all other disks on the shared disk array.

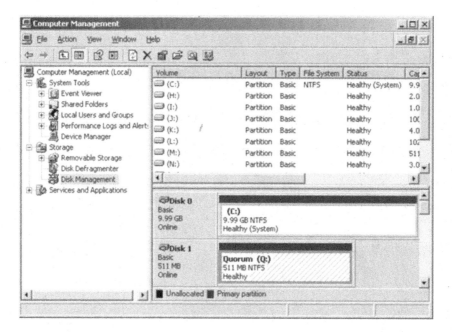

Figure 5-46. *Completed disk format*

Formatting the Disks via the Command Line

To format disks via the command line, follow these steps:

1. Open a command window.

2. At the command prompt, enter **format <drive letter> /V:<volume label> /FS:NTFS
   /A:<cluster size>**, where your values would be 4096, 8192, or 64KB. If the disk is going to be
   used for SQL Server data or might be used for SQL Server data, it should be 64KB. If the disk
   will be used purely for SQL Server logs or backups and no data files will ever be placed on
   the drive, you can use 4096. If your drive will be used for data and it will be purely a write
   with no read, use 8192. Figure 5-47 shows an example. When finished formatting your disks,
   close the command window.

```
C:\>format H: /V:Data1 /FS:NTFS /A:64K
The type of the file system is RAW.
The new file system is NTFS.

WARNING, ALL DATA ON NON-REMOVABLE DISK
DRIVE H: WILL BE LOST!
Proceed with Format (Y/N)? y
Verifying 2055M
Creating file system structures.
Format complete.
    2104448 KB total disk space.
    2091200 KB are available.
```

Figure 5-47. *Formatting the disks in a command window*

Step 4c: Verifying the Disk Configuration

Now that the disks are formatted and added to the first node, you must verify that they are working properly and that every node in the cluster can see and use the disks:

1. Start Windows Explorer.

2. Select one of the disks you just created and formatted.

3. Create a file, such as a text document, and open it to verify that you can both read and write to the disk.

4. Repeat steps 2 and 3 until all disks are tested.

5. Power down the node.

6. Power up another server in the cluster that will become a node.

7. Repeat steps 1–6 until all nodes are verified to be able to read and write to the shared disks. If the drives are not showing up immediately, you might have to start Computer Management and assign the disk letters or use DISKPART (as demonstrated earlier) so they are recognized properly in Windows Explorer. If you do not know which drive letter should go with the specific partition, power down the node you are working on, return to the original node, and write them down. To use Computer Management to assign a drive letter, perform these steps:

    a. Select Disk Management.

    b. In the lower-right pane, right-click the disk, and select the option Change Drive Letter and Paths, as shown in Figure 5-48.

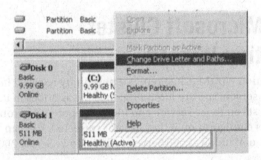

Figure 5-48. *Selecting the Change Drive Letter and Paths option*

    c. In the Change Drive Letter and Paths dialog box, as shown in Figure 5-49, click Add.

    d. In the Add Drive Letter or Path dialog box, as shown in Figure 5-50, select the Assign the Following Drive Letter option, and in the drop-down list, select the proper letter. Click OK.

    e. Repeat steps b through d for each drive.

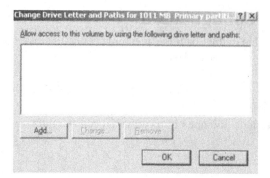

Figure 5-49. *Change Drive Letter and Paths dialog box*

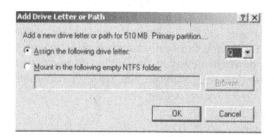

Figure 5-50. *Add Drive Letter and Paths dialog box*

Step 5: Running the Microsoft Cluster Configuration Validation Wizard

Microsoft's Cluster Configuration Validation Wizard (ClusPrep) is a new utility released in February 2007 that assists you in verifying the servers you are intending on using as nodes in the cluster. ClusPrep runs a focused set of tests on those servers and identifies potential problems with either the hardware or the Windows configuration if they are not corrected. You can run ClusPrep against all clusterable versions of Windows 2000 Server and Windows Server 2003.

ClusPrep validates the following:

- At least two separate network cards exist per server.
- Each network card has a unique IP address on a separate subnet.
- Each server can communicate with all other intended nodes of the server cluster.
- The shared disks that will be used for your cluster are accessible from all machines, are visible only once, and are uniquely identifiable.
- The network and disk I/O latencies are within spec.
- The disk bus reset or LUN reset.
- SCSI reserve/release, reservation, breaking, and reservation defense mechanisms.
- Online/offline to simulate failover.

You can also run ClusPrep on an already configured cluster to provide an inventory of what is on the cluster, do network testing, and validate the configuration. Here is what ClusPrep catalogs:

- Domain membership and role of the server
- Processor architecture
- That all systems are patched to the same levels (service packs, hotfixes, QFEs)
- That all systems have the same Windows version, and that version supports server clustering
- System drivers
- Analysis of unsigned drivers
- Inventory of plug-and-play devices
- A complete list of all running processes and services
- Information about memory
- Information about the HBAs and network adapters
- A list of environment variables
- BIOS information

Installing ClusPrep

Follow these instructions to install ClusPrep. It needs to be installed on only one node of the cluster.

Note ClusPrep is a 32-bit utility, and it must be run from a 32-bit machine. If you are trying to validate a 64-bit x64 or IA64-based cluster, install it on a 32-bit machine, and run it remotely. ClusPrep can be installed on Windows XP with Windows XP Service Pack 2 (or later) and all 32-bit versions of Windows Server 2003.

---

1. Download ClusPrep from the Microsoft Download Center (http://www.microsoft.com/ downloads).

2. After downloading clusprep.exe, run the executable. When the Welcome to the Microsoft Cluster Configuration Validation Wizard Setup dialog box is displayed, click Next (see Figure 5-51).

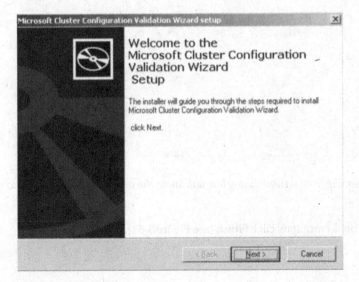

Figure 5-51. *Welcome dialog box*

3. On the License Agreement dialog box, read the license agreement, select I Agree (as shown in Figure 5-52), and click Next. The installation will begin.

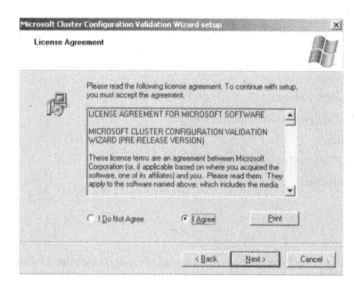

Figure 5-52. *License Agreement dialog box*

Progress will be displayed in the bar of the dialog box, as shown in Figure 5-53.

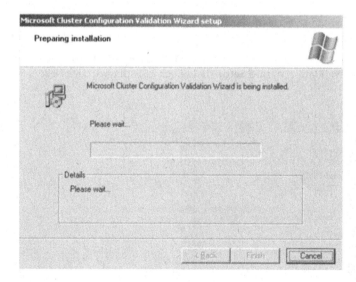

Figure 5-53. *The Preparing Installation dialog box will show the progress of the installation.*

4. When the installation is complete, click Finish (see Figure 5-54).

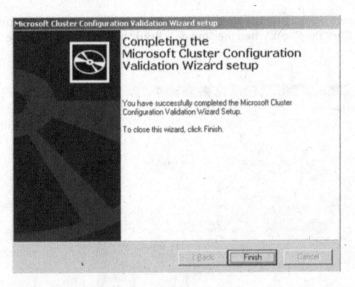

Figure 5-54. *Successful installation of ClusPrep*

Using ClusPrep

Follow these instructions to run ClusPrep against your cluster nodes:

1. Start ClusPrep. When the Welcome to the Microsoft Cluster Configuration Validation Wizard dialog box appears, click Next (see Figure 5-55).

Figure 5-55. *Welcome dialog box*

2. Make sure your storage is configured as per the instructions on the Storage Preparation for Testing dialog box. Click the Check When the Storage Is Ready box, as shown in Figure 5-56. Click Next.

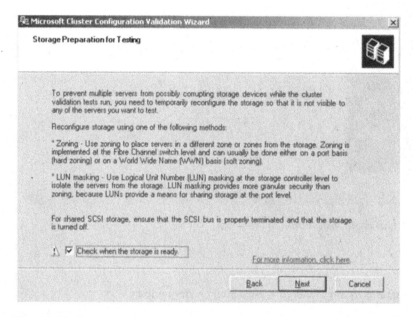

Figure 5-56. *Storage Preparation for Testing dialog box*

3. On the Domain Name dialog box, select the name of the domain that contains your nodes, as shown in Figure 5-57. Click Next.

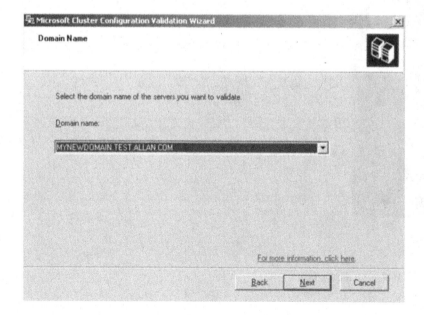

Figure 5-57. *Domain Name dialog box*

4. On the Server Names dialog box, enter the name of one of the nodes in Server Name, and click Add. The name will now be displayed in the Selected Servers area. Figure 5-58 shows an example.

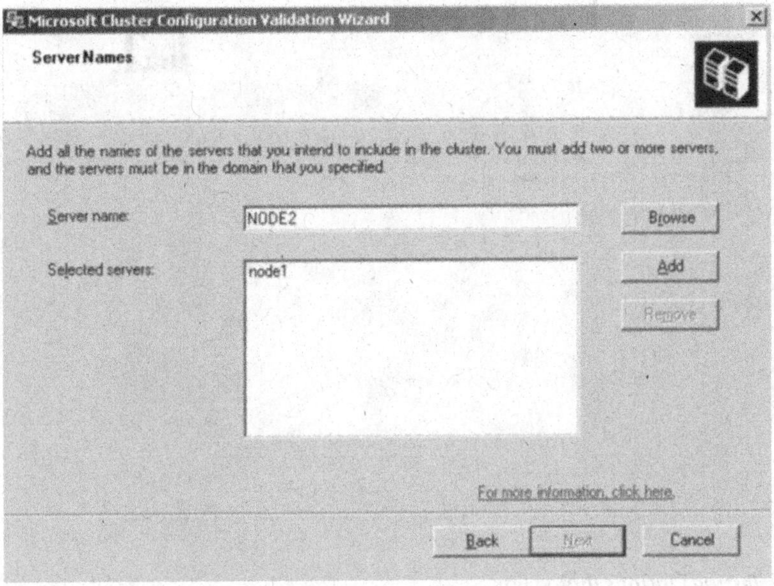

Figure 5-58. *Server Names dialog box*

When the process is complete, all nodes will be shown in Selected Servers, as shown in Figure 5-59. Click Next.

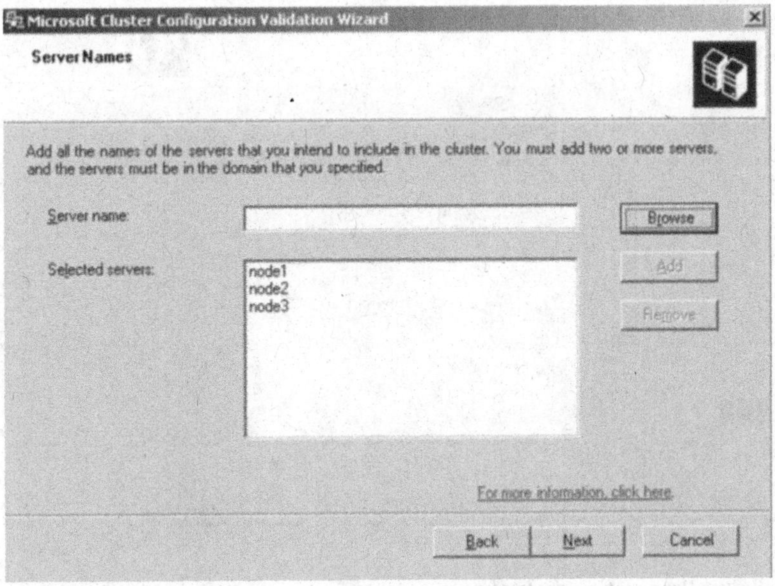

Figure 5-59. *All nodes are added and ready to proceed.*

5. On the Testing Options dialog box, select whether to run only a few tests or everything, as shown in Figure 5-60. My suggestion is to run every test.

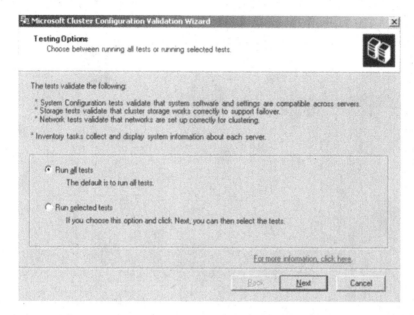

Figure 5-60. *Testing Options dialog box*

6. On the Server Preparation dialog box (as shown in Figure 5-61), click Next when it is complete.

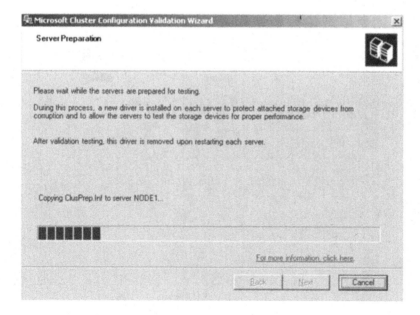

Figure 5-61. *Server Preparation dialog box*

7. On the Storage Management Secure dialog box, configure the storage as per the instructions. Select the check box, as shown in Figure 5-62.

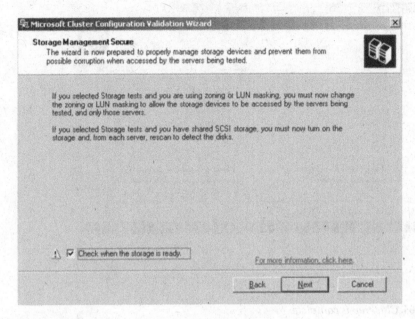

Figure 5-62. *Storage Management Secure dialog box*

When you are ready, click Next. ClusPrep will now analyze your nodes. During the analysis, you will see the progress, as shown in Figure 5-63.

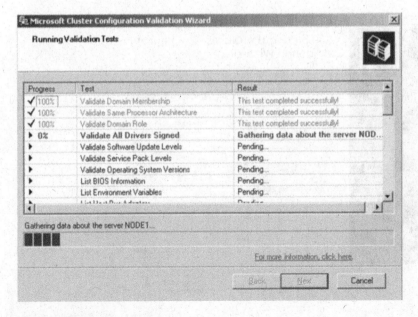

Figure 5-63. *ClusPrep progress*

When the process is complete, click Next, as shown in Figure 5-64.

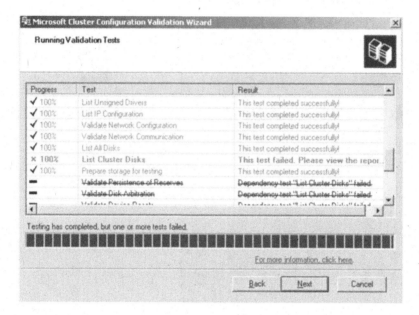

Figure 5-64. *ClusPrep is complete.*

8. Once ClusPrep has completed, you can either view the report immediately by clicking View Report or view it later by clicking Finish and then viewing it from the location displayed in the example dialog box shown in Figure 5-65.

Figure 5-65. *The ClusPrep process is ready to display your reports.*

Figures 5-66 and 5-67 show some example report output. If there are any problems, you must correct them at this time. Do not proceed with errors because you will create an unstable base for your SQL Server failover clustering installations.

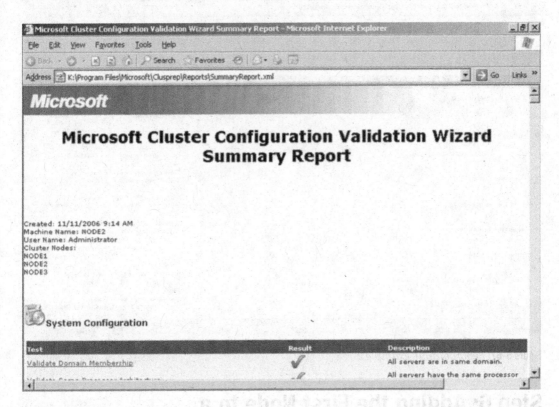

Figure 5-66. *Report output, example 1*

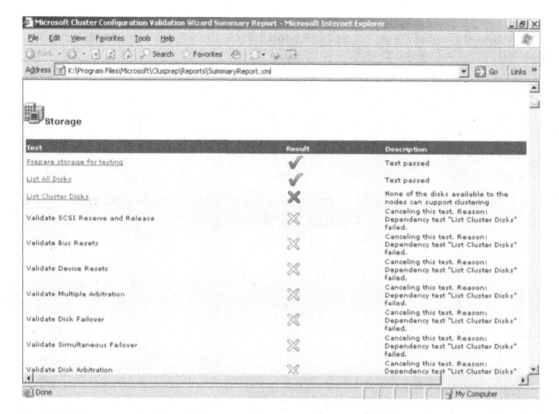

Figure 5-67. *Report output, example 2*

Step 6: Adding the First Node to a New Server Cluster

When configuring the Windows server cluster, do it one node at a time, starting with the first node. You can configure a cluster in two ways: either through a graphical interface within Windows called Cluster Administrator or via the command line.

Tip Make sure all nodes except the first one to join the cluster are powered down at this point. Do not proceed if more than one node is powered up. You should always be physically on the server to install the cluster software. If you absolutely must use Terminal Services or Remote Desktop, you must log on with the /CONSOLE switch.

Using Cluster Administrator

To use Cluster Administrator to add the first node to the server cluster, follow these steps:

1. Log on to the node you want to configure as your first node with an account that has administrative privileges.

2. From Administrative Tools, start Cluster Administrator, as shown in Figure 5-68.

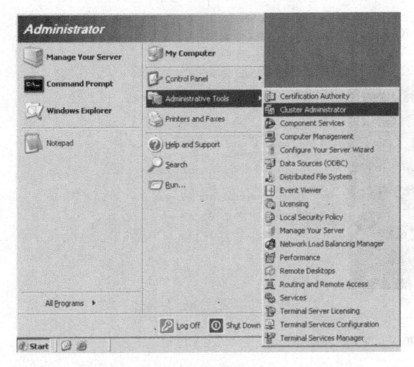

Figure 5-68. *Starting Cluster Administrator*

3. In the Open Connection to Cluster dialog box, select the Create New Cluster option in the Action drop-down (as shown in Figure 5-69), and click OK.

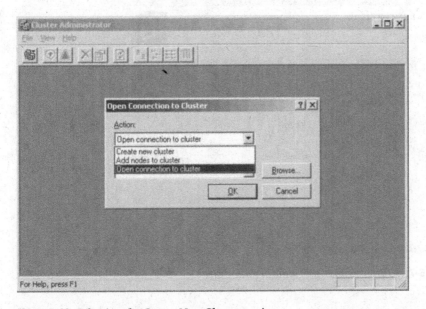

Figure 5-69. *Selecting the Create New Cluster option*

4. Click Next on the Welcome to the New Server Cluster Wizard dialog box, as shown in Figure 5-70.

Figure 5-70. *New Server Cluster Wizard*

5. On the Cluster Name and Domain dialog box, make sure the right domain is selected in the Domain drop-down. Enter a name for the cluster in the Cluster Name text box. Figure 5-71 shows an example. Click Next.

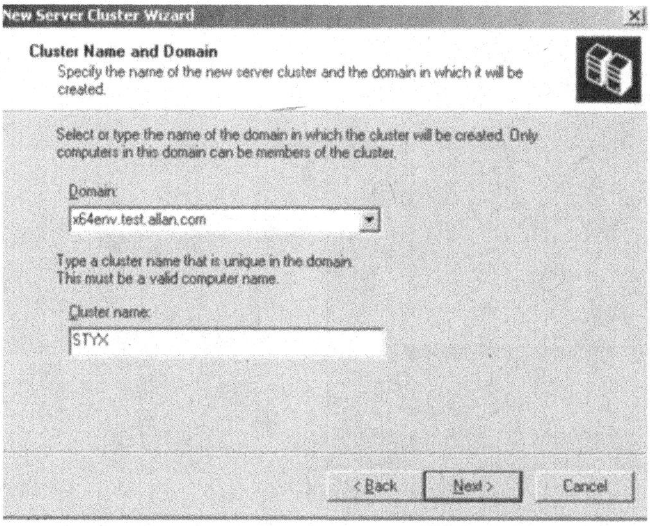

Figure 5-71. *Cluster Name and Domain dialog box*

6. On the Select Computer dialog box, the name of the node you are logged on to should appear in the Computer Name text box. If not, enter it manually. Figure 5-72 shows an example. Click Next.

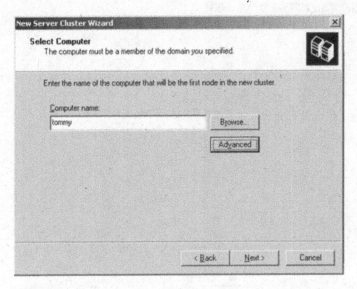

Figure 5-72. *Select Computer dialog box*

7. The wizard will now analyze your configuration. If there are no problems, you should see the display shown in Figure 5-73.

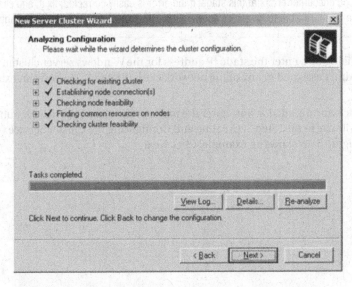

Figure 5-73. *No problems during analysis*

If you would like to view the log in your default text editor, click View Log. To see the detail for this step, click Details. Figure 5-74 shows an example. Click Next.

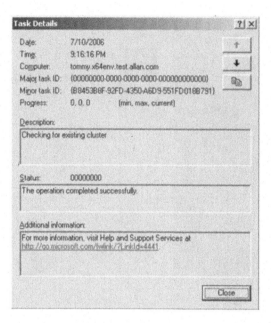

Figure 5-74. *Result of clicking Details*

Caution Do not proceed if you encounter errors at this stage. If the error is easily corrected, fix it, and click Reanalyze. If the error will take a bit more work to fix, click Cancel, resolve the issue, and start the wizard again.

---

8. On the IP Address dialog box, enter the static IP address for the Windows server cluster. This cannot be the IP address assigned to any of the network cards. Figure 5-75 shows an example. Click Next.

9. On the Cluster Service Account dialog box, enter the name of the cluster service account you configured previously in the "Step 2: Creating and Configuring the Cluster Service Account" section. Figure 5-76 shows an example. Click Next.

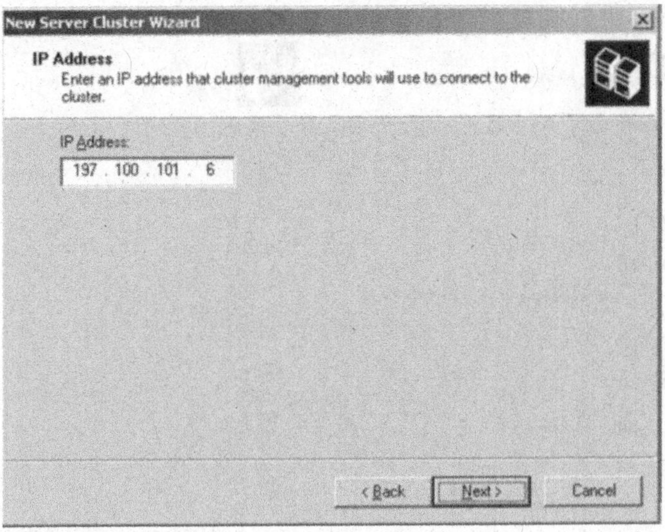

Figure 5-75. *Entering the IP address*

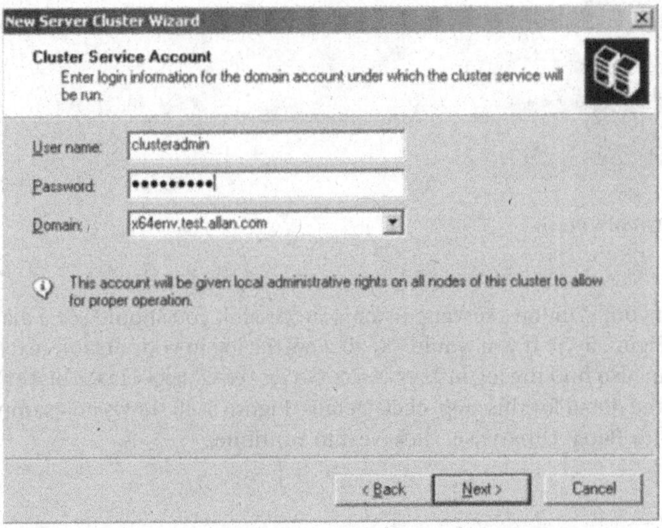

Figure 5-76. *Entering the cluster administrator account*

10. On the Proposed Cluster Configuration dialog box, click Quorum, as shown in Figure 5-77.

11. On the Cluster Configuration Quorum dialog box, use the drop-down list to select the drive where you want to place the quorum if you are creating a traditional Windows server cluster, or select Majority Node Set if you are configuring an MNS cluster. Figure 5-78 shows an example. Click OK, and then click Next on the Proposed Cluster Configuration dialog box to start the configuration process.

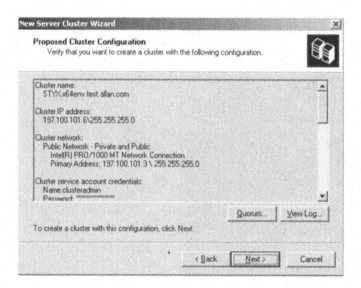

Figure 5-77. *Proposed Cluster Configuration dialog box*

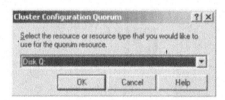

Figure 5-78. *Setting the quorum*

12. If the configuration of your Windows server cluster is successful, you should see a dialog box similar to the one in Figure 5-79. If you would like to view the log in your default text editor, click View Log. You can also find the log in %SystemRoot%\System32\LogFiles\Cluster\ ClCfgSrv.Log. To see the detail for this step, click Details. Figure 5-80 shows an example. If this fails, you can click Retry. Otherwise, click Next to continue.

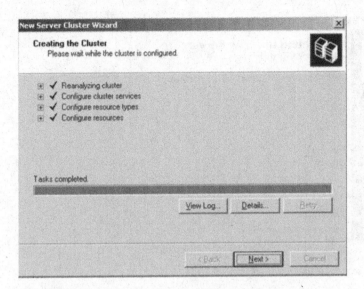

Figure 5-79. *Successful Windows server cluster configuration*

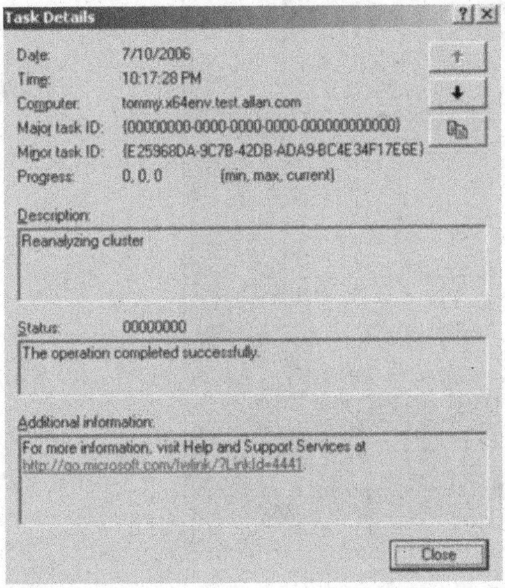

Figure 5-80. *Result of clicking Details*

13. Click Finish on the Completing the New Server Cluster Wizard dialog box, as shown in Figure 5-81.

The new cluster will be shown in Cluster Administrator. Figure 5-82 shows an example. Do not power down the first node.

Figure 5-81. *Finishing the configuration process*

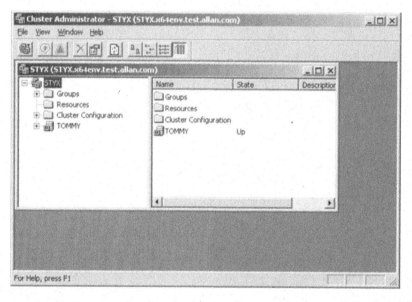

Figure 5-82. *The new server cluster in Cluster Administrator*

Tip To configure a Windows 2000 server cluster in a similar fashion, read the document found at http://www.microsoft.com/technet/prodtechnol/windows2000serv/howto/clustep.mspx.

Using the Command Line

To use the command line to add the first node to the server cluster, follow these steps:

1. Open a command window.

2. At the command prompt, enter the command **cluster clustername /create /ipaddress:clusterip /user:clustersrvaccount /password:pwd /node:firstnodename /verbose** where *clustername* is the name of your server cluster, *firstnodename* is the name of the first node of the cluster, *clusterip* is the IP address of the server cluster, *clustersrvaccount* is the name of the domain account used to administer the server cluster, and *pwd* is the password of the cluster service account. Using the /verbose switch allows you to see the output as it is run and is optional. Figure 5-83 shows an example.

```
C:\>cluster STYX /create /ipaddress:197.100.101.6 /user:clusteradmin /password:p
assword /node:tommy /verbose
```

Figure 5-83. *Example of a command to create a new Windows server cluster*

When the configuration is complete and successful, you will see output similar to Figure 5-84. If you are creating an MNS cluster, you must convert the quorum resource to an MNS quorum. If you are not, you can stop here.

```
Configuring resources
    tommy: Starting cluster resources. (step 7 of 12)
    tommy: Starting cluster resources.
    tommy: Resource 'Disk K:' brought online successfully. (step 1 of 1)
Configuring resources
    tommy: Starting cluster resources. (step 8 of 12)
    tommy: Starting cluster resources.
    tommy: Resource 'Disk L:' brought online successfully. (step 1 of 1)
Configuring resources
    tommy: Starting cluster resources. (step 9 of 12)
    tommy: Starting cluster resources.
    tommy: Resource 'Disk N:' brought online successfully. (step 1 of 1)
Configuring resources
    tommy: Starting cluster resources. (step 10 of 12)
    tommy: Starting cluster resources.
    tommy: Resource 'Disk O:' brought online successfully. (step 1 of 1)
Configuring resources
    tommy: Starting cluster resources. (step 11 of 12)
    tommy: Starting cluster resources. (step 12 of 12)
Configuring cluster services
    tommy: Creating a cluster with this node. (step 2 of 2)
Done.
```

Figure 5-84. *Complete and successful Windows server cluster configuration*

Step 7: Adding Other Nodes to the Server Cluster

Once you've added the first node successfully to create the cluster, you must add the other nodes. Once you've joined all nodes to the cluster, it is recommended that you reboot all nodes.

Using Cluster Administrator

To use Cluster Administrator to have other nodes join the server cluster, follow these steps:

1. Power up a node to be joined to the cluster.

2. Start Cluster Administrator, which is located under Administrative Tools. You do not need to run Cluster Administrator from the node that you will be joining. It can be run on the first node.

3. From the File menu, select New ➤ Node. An alternate method is to select File ➤ Open Connection to start the Open Connection to Cluster dialog box. In the dialog box, select the Add Nodes to Cluster option on the Action drop-down list, and make sure the right cluster name is represented. Click OK. Figure 5-85 shows an example.

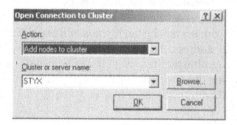

Figure 5-85. *Open Connection to Cluster dialog box*

4. On the Welcome to the Add Nodes Wizard dialog box, as shown in Figure 5-86, click Next.

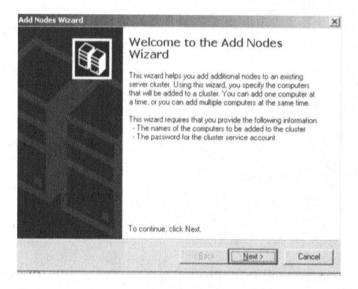

Figure 5-86. *Welcome to the Add Nodes Wizard dialog box*

5. On the Select Computers dialog box, enter the name of the node that you are adding in the Computer Name text box, as shown in Figure 5-87. Conversely, you can click Browse and find it that way. Click Add. The node name will be placed in the Selected Computers list.

You can repeat this step and add all remaining nodes. Figure 5-88 shows an example.

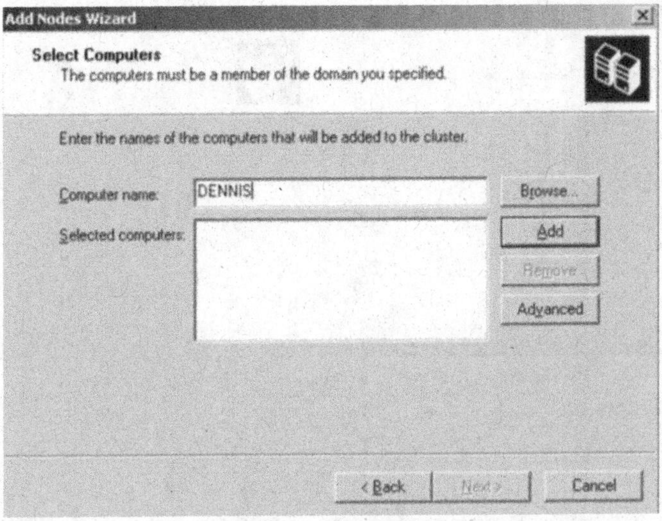

Figure 5-87. *Entering the name of the node to add to the cluster*

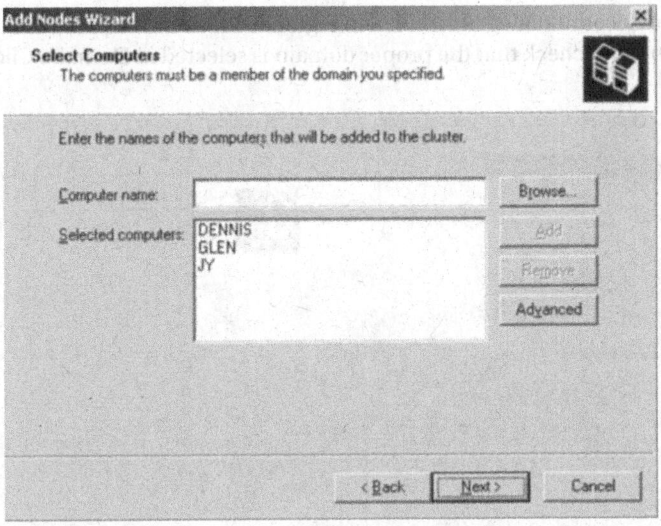

Figure 5-88. *All nodes to be added to the cluster*

6. The wizard will now analyze your configuration. If there are no problems, you should see the display shown in Figure 5-89. If you would like to view the log in your default text editor, click View Log. Click Next.

■ **Caution** Do not proceed if you encounter errors at this stage. If the error is easily corrected, fix it, and click Reanalyze. If the error will take a bit more work to fix, click Cancel, resolve the issue, and start the wizard again. Any problems introduced into your server cluster configuration from the start will most likely have dire consequences down the road.

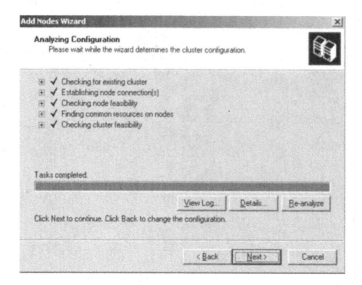

Figure 5-89. *No problems during analysis*

7. On the Cluster Service Account dialog box shown in Figure 5-90, enter the password of the cluster service account, and check that the proper domain is selected in Domain. Click Next.

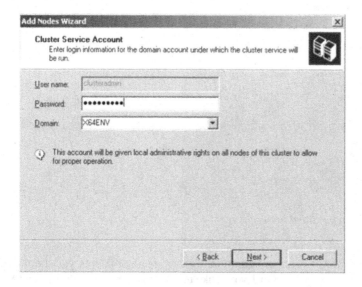

Figure 5-90. *Cluster Service Account dialog box*

8. On the Proposed Cluster Configuration dialog box, as shown in Figure 5-91, click Next.

9. If the process is successful, the Adding Nodes to the Cluster dialog box will look similar to Figure 5-92. The Reanalyzing Cluster step will have a warning next to it.

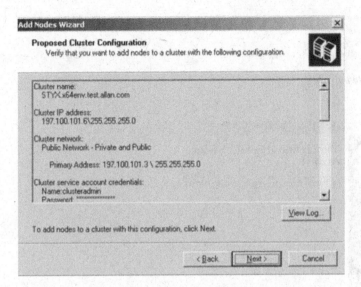

Figure 5-91. *Proposed Cluster Configuration dialog box*

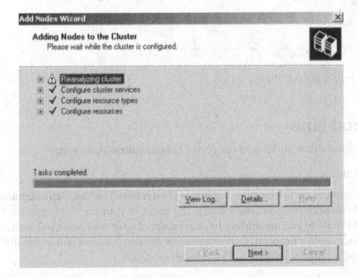

Figure 5-92. *Adding Nodes to the Cluster dialog box*

If you open the tree, you will see that what caused it is a Status 0x00138f message where the cluster resource could not be found on the nodes that were being added. Figure 5-93 shows an example. Click Next.

10. Click Finish on the Completing the Add Nodes Wizard dialog box, as shown in Figure 5-94.

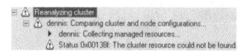

Figure 5-93. *Example warning*

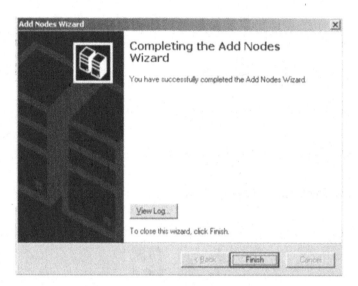

Figure 5-94. *Finishing the node additions*

Using the Command Line

To use the command line to have other nodes join the server cluster, follow these steps:

1. Open a command window.

2. At the command prompt, enter the command **cluster clustername /addnode:nodename / password:password /verbose** where *clustername* is the name of your server cluster, *node-name* is the name of the node you are adding to your server cluster, and *password* is the password of the cluster service account. Using the /verbose switch allows you to see the output as it is run and is optional. Figure 5-95 shows an example.

```
C:\>cluster STYX /addnode:DENNIS /password:password
```

Figure 5-95. *Example of a command to create a new Windows server cluster*

When the configuration is complete and successful, you will see output similar to Figure 5-96.

3. To further verify that the node is added successfully to the server cluster, view it in Cluster Administrator. Figure 5-97 shows an example.

```
Preparing to add nodes to a cluster:
   Cluster name = STYX
   Node name    = DENNIS
Analyzing.................................................................
...........................................................
Adding nodes to the cluster..............................................
...........................................................
Done.
```

Figure 5-96. *Complete and successful Windows server cluster configuration*

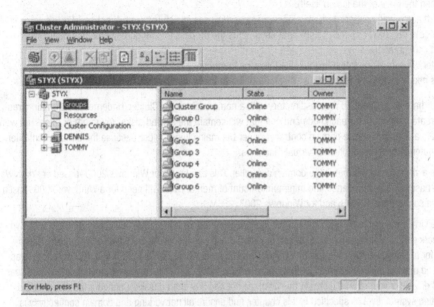

Figure 5-97. *Newly added node in Cluster Administrator*

USING VMWARE AND MICROSOFT VIRTUAL SERVER TO CREATE A SERVER CLUSTER

One of the best uses of software-based server virtualization is the ability to test scenarios where you might not otherwise have the hardware to achieve the end result. SQL Server failover clustering is one of the best examples of this: you do not always have the budget to have clusters everywhere. Both the Microsoft Virtual Server product as well as the VMware line of products allow you to cluster Microsoft-based environments. Microsoft does support clustering in production environments, but if you plan on using VMware or any other virtualization product, read the Microsoft Knowledge Base article 897615 (http://support.microsoft.com/kb/897615/en-us) carefully. I would never recommend that you use a clustered VMware or Virtual Server–based installation in production because you most likely need something much more robust and because that configuration will never really be in the Windows Server Catalog per se.

If you plan on implementing Virtual Server or VMware-based server cluster for testing or demonstration purposes, make sure you have a large and fast hard drive (7,200 rpm or faster, even in laptops) since I/O contention will be an issue with multiple virtual machines running at once. As of this writing, with laptops, only 2.5-inch drives come with 7,200 rpm. Many laptops use the smaller 1.8-inch drives that run at 4,200 rpm. Each virtual machine will take up many gigabytes of space, so I recommend something along the lines of a drive that is at least 60GB–100GB in space. You can obviously buy an external USB 2.0 or FireWire (400 or 800) drive as well, but if this is intended as a portable solution, it might not be ideal.

In addition, when virtualizing clusters, you must have a lot of memory available to you. Remember that SQL Server 2005 at a bare minimum recommends 512MB of memory for the server on which it will be running. When I have implemented clusters under VMware, I have been able to give those virtual machines only 384MB of memory, but you will see warnings during the SQL Server installation. At a minimum, you need to have three virtual machines: a domain controller and two cluster nodes, so you will need enough memory on your machine to handle running all three at once, taking into account the overhead needed by either VMware or Virtual Server, as well as anything else needed to run on your machine at the same time. I recommend having at least 1.5GB of memory. Most laptops max out at 2GB of memory (some support 4GB, but the cost of memory is prohibitive—and most likely more than the price of the laptop itself).

Microsoft has a white paper at `http://www.microsoft.com/technet/prodtechnol/ virtualserver/deploy/cvs2005.mspx` that documents the process to configure Microsoft Virtual Server in a clustered configuration.

To cluster VMware Workstation images, the following instructions reflect how to do it with version 5.5. Version 6.0 is nearly identical and the steps will also work with the newer version:

1. On your hard drive, create a master directory with a name such as My Cluster. Underneath that main directory, create a directory for each node and one that will contain the shared disks. You might or might not want to create a directory for the domain controller under the main cluster folder because the domain controller could potentially be used for other virtual machines.

2. Create a virtual machine that is the domain controller. This can be either Windows 2000–based or Windows 2003–based. In my experience, the minimum amount of memory you will need for a Windows 2000–based domain controller is 128MB, and for Windows 2003, 256MB.

3. Create virtual machines for each node in the directory created for it in step 1, and configure them with two "network cards." When configuring the primary hard drive, size it somewhere between 8GB and 10GB to allow for expansion and further use (the OS will take up somewhere between 2GB and 4GB of space). I recommend making the OS/"internal" virtual hard drive IDE, not SCSI because you will need as many SCSI-based virtual drives for your shared disks. At this point, do not add any shared disks. Configure the server at the operating system level as specified in this chapter, and ensure all networking and domain connectivity is working properly. Remember that depending on the amount of memory you have available to you, you might be able to create only a two-node server cluster. The following screenshot shows an example base VMWare virtual machine configuration.

4. Now it is time to add your shared virtual SCSI disks. Power down all nodes. As with planning for a real failover clustering implementation, you will need a minimum of three shared disks: one for SQL Server (per instance), one for the quorum (if you are doing a traditional quorum-based cluster), and one for MS DTC. To add the disks in VMware Workstation, perform the following steps:

a. Select the virtual machine that represents the first node of the cluster. Open the Virtual Machine Settings dialog box, shown in the following screenshot, by selecting Edit Virtual Machine Settings from the VMware main screen; or select Settings under the VM menu; or hit Ctrl+D.

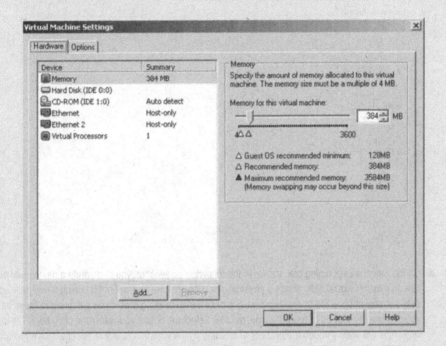

b. Click Add.

c. In the first dialog box of the Add New Hardware Wizard, shown in the following screenshot, click Next.

d. For Hardware Types, select Hard Disk and click Next, as shown in the following screenshot.

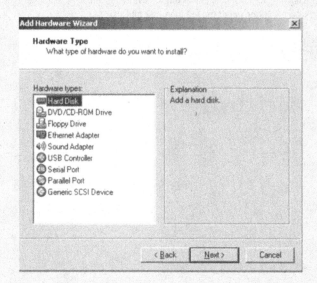

e. On the Select a Disk dialog box, shown in the following screenshot, you can create a new virtual disk, use an existing virtual disk, or use a physical disk. Chances are you will not be using a real disk, so your only two real options are to create a new one or reuse an existing one. If you are going to reuse an existing one, it must be of the SCSI type, not IDE. Select the option you want, and click Next. The next few steps will walk through the process of creating a new virtual disk. If you select to use an existing virtual disk, you will be prompted for the location of the existing virtual disk.

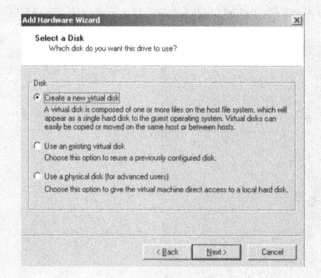

f. On the Select a Disk Type dialog box, select SCSI, as shown in the following screenshot, and click Next.

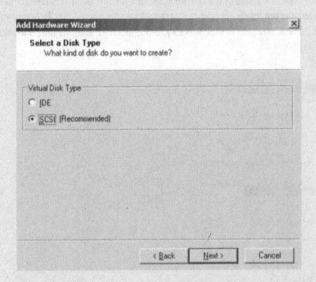

g. On the Specify Disk Capacity dialog box, shown in the following screenshot, enter the size of the virtual SCSI disk. If this is a test system, you might not need to make them as large as production, but size the disks appropriately for their use. For performance reasons, you might want to allocate the full disk size now, but it is not a requirement. The virtual disks will grow as they need to.

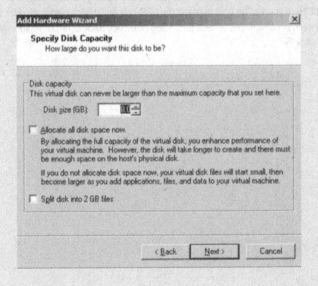

h. On the Specify Disk File dialog box, as shown in the following screenshot, enter the name for the virtual SCSI disk. By default, it will take the name of the operating system you are using. It is best to name it something logical, such as **quorum.vmdk**. To ensure it is placed into the shared disk directory you created in step a, select Browse, navigate to that directory, and select it (or enter its full path before the disk name). Click Finish to continue.

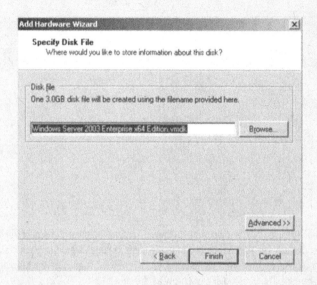

If you click Advanced on the Specify Disk File dialog box, you will see Specify Advanced Options, as shown in the screenshot. Here you will be able to select the SCSI bus and device designation for the virtual disk (if you want such control). If you access this dialog box, click Back to return to Specify Disk File, or if you are done, click Finish.

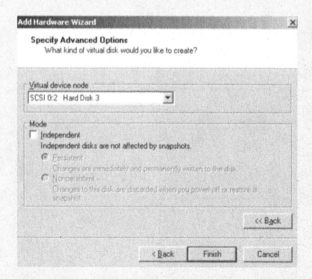

The disk will now be displayed on the Virtual Machine Settings dialog box.

i. Repeat steps b through h until you've added all disks.

5. Power up the first cluster node, and format the disks as described in the section "Step 4: Configuring the Shared Disks" in this chapter. Once you've done this, power down the first node.

6. Navigate to the directory containing the first node and its associated files. Open the node's configuration file, which has the extension .vmx in a text editor. Copy all the lines that specify the shared disk configuration to the configuration files of the other nodes. The lines will look similar to the following:

```
scsi0:0.present = "TRUE"
scsi0:0.filename = "E:\VMs\x64 Cluster\Shared Disks\quorum.vmdk"
```

7. In each node's configuration file, add the following line:

```
disk.locking = "FALSE"
```

8. Your VMware virtual machine "hardware" configuration is now complete. Follow the rest of the instructions for installing a Windows server cluster to configure the Windows server cluster as if you were working on real hardware. You might want to use Disk Management to format your disks since you are not connected to a real shared storage array and since aligning the disks will not matter. The following screenshot shows a sample VMware configuration as it appears in the VMware environment:

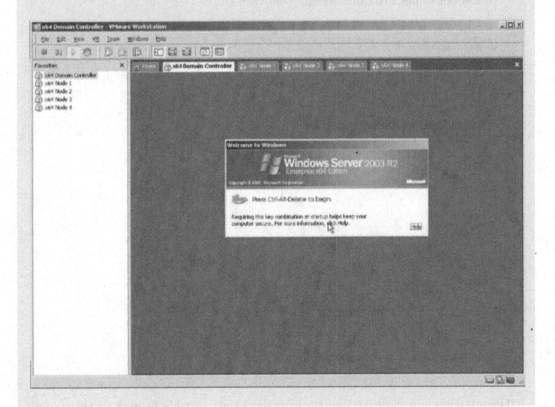

Performing Post-Installation Tasks

After performing the initial installation steps, you must execute some tasks to finish configuring your Windows server cluster.

Configuring Cluster Networks

Earlier you configured the network priorities within Windows. Now you must prioritize the networks within the server cluster. The networks are the reverse here: the private cluster network should be above the externally facing networks.

1. From Administrative Tools, start Cluster Administrator.

2. Right-click the cluster name in the left pane, and select Properties.

3. In the cluster's Properties dialog box, select the Network Priority tab. If the public network appears above the private cluster network in the Networks Used for Internal Cluster Communications box, select the private network, and click Move Up until it is in the proper place. If you have more than one private network, repeat this step. The end configuration should look similar to the one in Figure 5-98. Click OK.

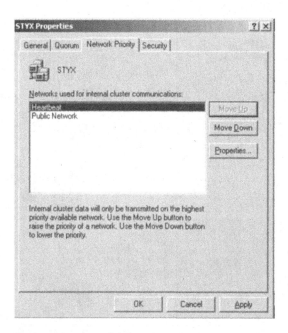

Figure 5-98. *Network Priority configuration*

If there is only one dedicated private cluster network and one public network, you must configure the public network to serve as the backup for the private cluster network.

1. From Administrative Tools, start Cluster Administrator.

2. Expand Networks, right-click the name of the public network, and select Properties, as shown in Figure 5-99.

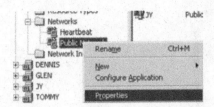

Figure 5-99. *Selecting the properties of the public network*

3. On the properties dialog box for the public network, verify that it is set to All Communications (Mixed Network). Figure 5-100 shows an example. If there are two or more dedicated private cluster networks, this might be set to Client Access Only (Public Network). Click OK.

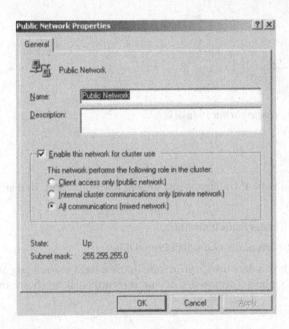

Figure 5-100. *The properties of the public network*

4. Right-click the private cluster network, and select Properties.

5. Verify that the private cluster network is set to Internal Cluster Communications Only (Private Network), as shown in Figure 5-101. Click OK.

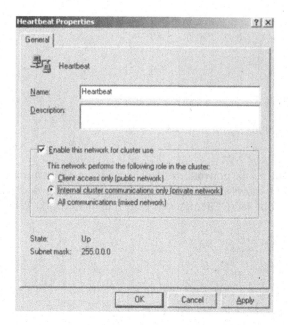

Figure 5-101. *The properties of the private cluster network*

Resizing the Quorum Log

By default, the cluster log is sized to 4096KB, or 4MB. That is insufficient for production. To resize the quorum log, follow these steps:

1. From Administrative Tools, start Cluster Administrator.

2. Right-click the cluster name in the left pane, and select Properties.

3. In the cluster's Properties dialog box, select the Quorum tab. In the Reset Quorum Log At text box, enter a fairly large number based on the size of your quorum's disk, as shown in Figure 5-102. Click OK.

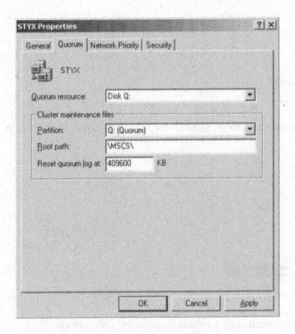

Figure 5-102. *Resizing the quorum log*

Creating a Clustered Microsoft Distributed Transaction Coordinator

Some might contend that configuring the Microsoft Distributed Transaction Coordinator is optional, but some features of SQL Server utilize it. It is better to be safe than sorry, so my recommendation is to configure this before you install SQL Server.

Creating the MS DTC Resources

To create the MS DTC resources, follow these steps:

1. Start Cluster Administrator.

2. In the left pane, expand Groups. Right-click the group that contains the dedicated disk for use with MS DTC, and select Rename, as shown in Figure 5-103.

Figure 5-103. *Selecting the Rename option*

Enter the new name for the resource group as something logical, such as **MS DTC**, and hit Enter. Figure 5-104 shows an example.

Figure 5-104. *MS DTC group renamed*

3. Right-click the newly renamed resource group, select New, and then select Resource, as shown in Figure 5-105.

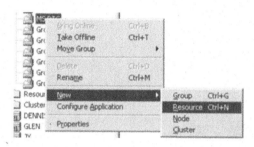

Figure 5-105. *Selecting the option to create a new resource in the MS DTC group*

4. In the New Resource dialog box, enter an appropriate name for the IP resource that will be associated with MS DTC such as **MS DTC IP Address**. In the Resource Type drop-down list, select IP Address. In the Group drop-down list, make sure the right resource group is selected. Figure 5-106 shows an example. Click Next.

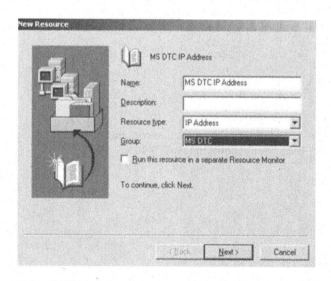

Figure 5-106. *Creating the IP resource for MS DTC*

5. In the Possible Owners dialog box, verify that all nodes of the server cluster are listed as possible owners of this resource. If a node is not listed on the right side, select it from the Available Nodes list, and click Add. Figure 5-107 shows an example. Click Next.

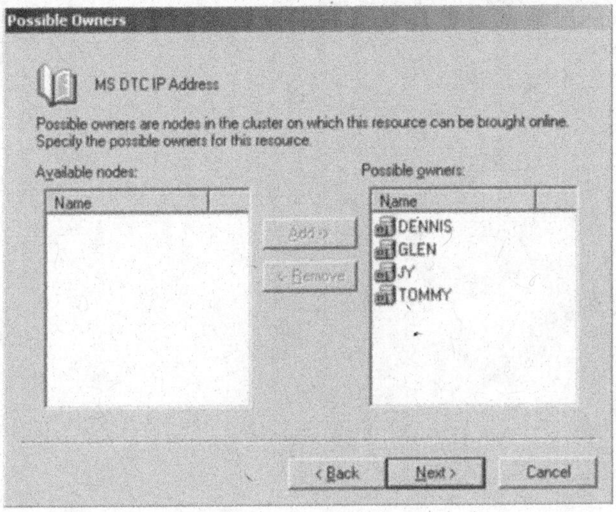

Figure 5-107. *Verifying resource ownership*

6. In the Dependencies dialog box, select the drive from Available Resources, and click Add to add it to the Resource Dependencies list. When finished, it should appear similar to Figure 5-108. Click Next.

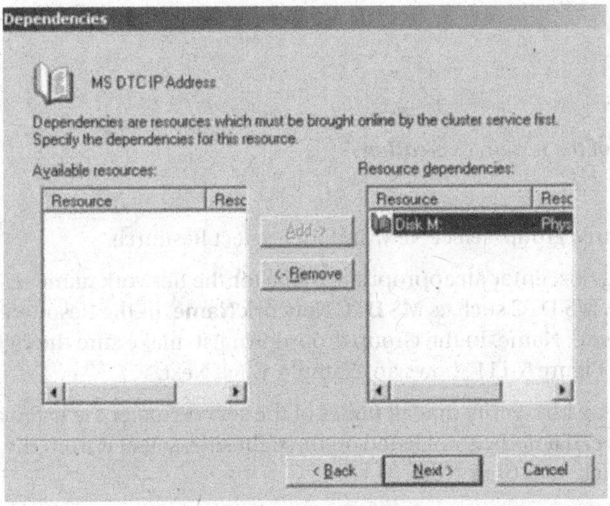

Figure 5-108. *Adding the disk as a dependency of the resource*

7. In the TCP/IP Address Parameters dialog box, enter a static IP in the Address input box, and select the proper public network to use. Figure 5-109 shows an example. Click Finish.

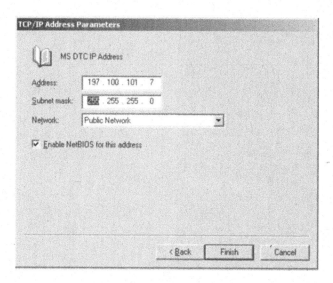

Figure 5-109. *Assigning the IP address*

If the resource is created, you will see the message box in Figure 5-110 appear. Click OK. The resource now appears in the resource group and has a state of Offline.

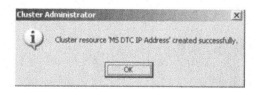

Figure 5-110. *Confirmation of the resource's creation*

8. Right-click MS DTC's resource group, select New, and then select Resource.

9. In the New Resource dialog box, enter an appropriate name for the network name resource that will be associated with MS DTC such as **MS DTC Network Name**. In the Resource Type drop-down list, select Network Name. In the Group drop-down list, make sure the right resource group is selected. Figure 5-111 shows an example. Click Next.

10. In the Possible Owners dialog box, verify that all nodes of the server cluster are listed as possible owners of this resource. If a node is not listed on the right side, select it from the Available Nodes list, and click Add. Click Next.

11. In the Dependencies dialog box, select the MS DTC IP address from Available Resources, and click Add to add it to the Resource Dependencies list. When finished, it should appear similar to Figure 5-112. Click Next.

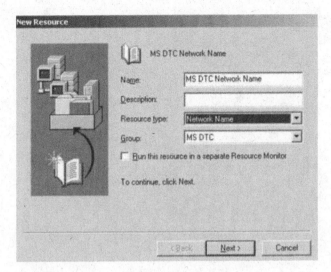

Figure 5-111. *Creating the Network Name resource for MS DTC*

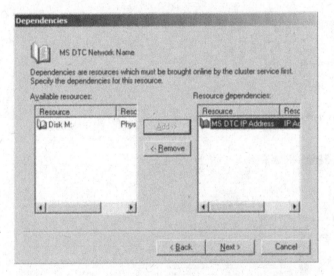

Figure 5-112. *Dependencies for the MS DTC network name*

12. In the Network Name Parameters dialog box, enter a name for MS DTC that will be used by other applications. Figure 5-113 shows an example. Click Finish.

    If the resource is created, you will see the message box in Figure 5-114 appear. Click OK. The resource now appears in the resource group and has a state of Offline.

13. Right-click MS DTC's resource group, select New, and then select Resource.

14. In the New Resource dialog box, enter an appropriate name for the MS DTC resource itself such as **MS DTC**. In the Resource Type drop-down list, select Distributed Transaction Coordinator. In the Group drop-down list, make sure the right resource group is selected. Figure 5-115 shows an example. Click Next.

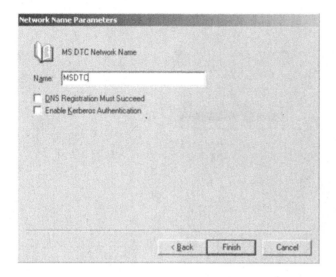

Figure 5-113. *Dependencies for the MS DTC network name*

Figure 5-114. *Confirmation of the resource's creation*

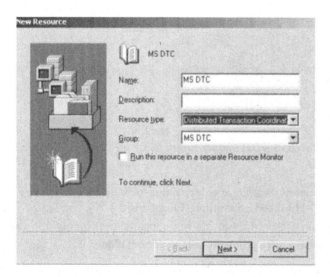

Figure 5-115. *Creating the resource for MS DTC*

15. In the Possible Owners dialog box, verify that all nodes of the server cluster are listed as possible owners of this resource. If a node is not listed on the right side, select it from the Available Nodes list, and click Add. Click Next.

16. In the Dependencies dialog box, select the physical disk and the MS DTC network name from Available Resources, and click Add to add them to the Resource Dependencies list. When finished, it should appear similar to Figure 5-116.

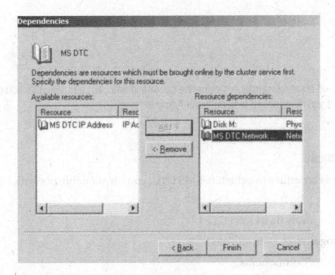

Figure 5-116. *Dependencies for MS DTC*

Click Finish. If the resource is created, you will see the message box in Figure 5-117 appear. Click OK. The resource now appears in the resource group and has a state of Offline.

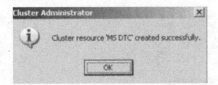

Figure 5-117. *Confirmation of the resource's creation*

17. Start the newly created resources by right-clicking the MS DTC group and selecting Bring Online, as shown in Figure 5-118.

Figure 5-118. *Bringing the resources online*

All resources should now have a status of Online, as shown in Figure 5-119.

Name	State
Disk M:	Online
MS DTC IP Address	Online
MS DTC Network N...	Online
MS DTC	Online

Figure 5-119. *All resources are online.*

■**Tip** The CD-ROM has a script named createclusterdtc.bat using the command line `cluster.exe` that you can use to create the MS DTC resources if you do not want to use Cluster Administrator.

Enabling Network MS DTC Access

To ensure that external processes can utilize the clustered MS DTC, you must enable network MS DTC access. Follow these steps:

1. Log on to the node that currently owns MS DTC.

2. Open Add or Remove Programs in Control Panel.

3. Click Add/Remove Windows Components.

4. Select Application Server, as shown in Figure 5-120. Click Details.

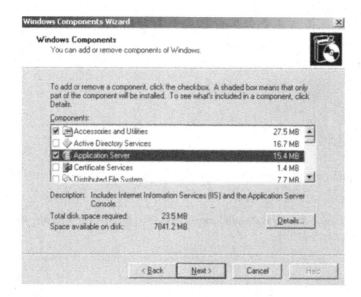

Figure 5-120. *Selecting Application Server*

5. In the Application Server dialog box, make sure that the Enable Network DTC access option is checked, as shown in Figure 5-121. Click OK.

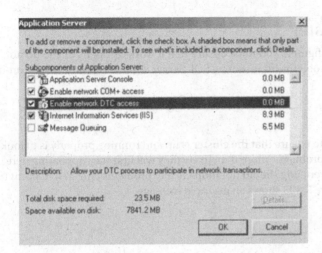

Figure 5-121. *Enabling network DTC access*

6. Click Next. You might be prompted for your Windows installation media, so you should have it nearby or on an accessible network share.

7. Click Finish on the Completing the Windows Components Wizard dialog box, as shown in Figure 5-122.

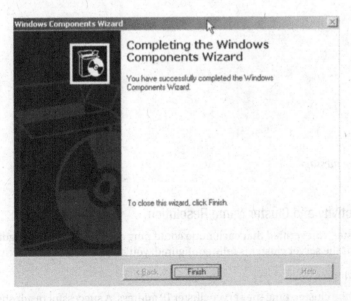

Figure 5-122. *Completing the Windows Components Wizard dialog box*

8. Stop MS DTC by right-clicking the cluster group and selecting the option Bring Offline.

9. Restart MS DTC by right-clicking the cluster group and selecting the option Bring Online.

Testing the Server Cluster

Once the server cluster is fully configured, you must ensure that it works properly. If you do not, a failure to test might result in big problems for installing SQL Server and the stability of your production platform.

Reviewing the Event Log

One of the easiest things to check to ensure that the cluster is up and running properly is to look at the Event Log. If there are serious problems, more than likely they will first start appearing here. All the messages that appear in the Event Log should not indicate any problems and should point to the cluster working properly. Figure 5-123 shows an example message.

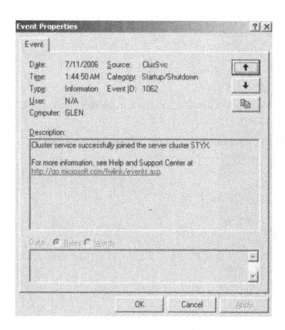

Figure 5-123. *Sample event log message*

Verifying Network Connectivity and Cluster Name Resolution

Before you installed the cluster, you verified that each node could ping each IP address configured on the other nodes. Now that the server cluster is fully configured, you must verify its connectivity:

1. Open a command window.

2. From every node in the cluster, ping the server cluster IP address. A successful result should be similar to the one shown in Figure 5-124.

```
C:\>ping 197.100.101.6

Pinging 197.100.101.6 with 32 bytes of data:

Reply from 197.100.101.6: bytes=32 time=3ms TTL=128
Reply from 197.100.101.6: bytes=32 time=1ms TTL=128
Reply from 197.100.101.6: bytes=32 time<1ms TTL=128
Reply from 197.100.101.6: bytes=32 time=14ms TTL=128

Ping statistics for 197.100.101.6:
    Packets: Sent = 4, Received = 4, Lost = 0 (0% loss),
Approximate round trip times in milli-seconds:
    Minimum = 0ms, Maximum = 14ms, Average = 4ms
```

Figure 5-124. *Pinging the cluster IP address successfully*

3. From a server or computer outside of the cluster nodes, ping the server cluster IP address to ensure that it can be reached from computers that are not part of the cluster itself.

4. From every node in the cluster, ping the server cluster name. This will prove that the name of the cluster can be resolved. A successful result should be similar to the one shown in Figure 5-125.

```
C:\>ping styx

Pinging styx.x64env.test.allan.com [197.100.101.6] with 32 bytes of data:

Reply from 197.100.101.6: bytes=32 time<1ms TTL=128
Reply from 197.100.101.6: bytes=32 time<1ms TTL=128
Reply from 197.100.101.6: bytes=32 time<1ms TTL=128
Reply from 197.100.101.6: bytes=32 time<1ms TTL=128

Ping statistics for 197.100.101.6:
    Packets: Sent = 4, Received = 4, Lost = 0 (0% loss),
Approximate round trip times in milli-seconds:
    Minimum = 0ms, Maximum = 0ms, Average = 0ms
```

Figure 5-125. *Pinging the cluster name address successfully*

5. From a server or computer outside the cluster nodes, ping the server cluster IP name to ensure that it can be reached from computers that are not part of the cluster.

6. From Cluster Administrator on every node, connect to the server cluster you configured.

Validating Resource Failover

All nodes should be able to access the resources in the cluster. The easiest way to verify this is to force a failover of the resources to another node:

1. Start Cluster Administrator.

2. In the left pane, expand Groups, right-click a cluster group, select the Move Group option, and finally select a node to move the resource group, as shown in Figure 5-126.

   If the failover is functioning properly, the owner of the resources will change to the new node name, as shown in Figure 5-127.

3. Repeat step 2 to move the resource to all other nodes of the server cluster.

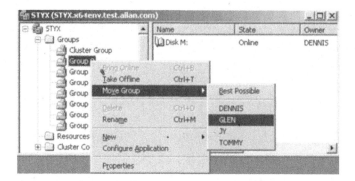

Figure 5-126. *Manually failing over a resource group to another node*

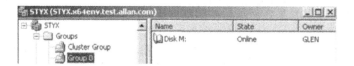

Figure 5-127. *A resource reflecting its new owning node*

Checking Disk Semantics

When a server cluster is working properly, only the node that owns the resource should have access to it. To verify that the disks cannot be accessed by any other node, perform the following steps:

1. Start Cluster Administrator.

2. For each resource group that contains a disk, go to that node, and make sure you can access it from Windows Explorer.

3. On all other nodes of the cluster that do not own the disk resource, start Windows Explorer, and try to access the disk. It should yield a result like the one in Figure 5-128. If you are able to access the disk from another node, your configuration is not correct, and you will have to troubleshoot.

4. Following the procedures in the previous "Validating Resource Failover" section, manually fail the disk resources to the other nodes, and repeat step 3.

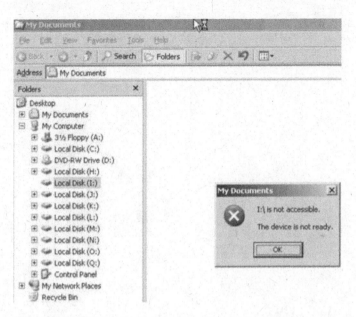

Figure 5-128. *The result of a node not owning the disk resource*

Summary

Without a solid foundation, you cannot build a house. In a similar fashion, if you do not get the Windows server cluster portion correct, you cannot successfully implement a clustered SQL Server implementation on it. You must do a lot of planning and prework to ensure that the server cluster is configured properly. According to some Microsoft Product Support statistics, more than 70% of all calls regarding SQL Server clusters have nothing to do with SQL Server. The reality is that most configurations that fail at some point stem from a missed configuration point or some human error due to poor administration.

Now that the cluster is installed, you must learn how to administer it.

CHAPTER 6

■■■

Failover Clustering: Windows Server Cluster Administration

This describes the various tasks and topics you will need to perform or think about when administering a Windows server cluster. The main tools you will use are Cluster Administrator, which was improved in Windows Server 2003 Service Pack 1 to be multithreaded, and the command-line CLUSTER.EXE. CLUSTER.EXE can do everything Cluster Administrator can do with the advantage that every task can be fully scripted. This chapter will not cover every single administrative task but instead will cover the most common, and in some cases it will include both the graphical and command-line versions.

Remote Connectivity

You can use a Remote Desktop Connection to connect to clustered nodes for the remote administration of the nodes. One problem you might encounter in using a Remote Desktop Connection to administer a server cluster is that if you are doing disk manipulations (such as using Disk Management) or if a failover occurs, you might see odd behavior; for example, the drive letters might not be able to be accessed or might show up with a "?" where the drive letter used to be.

Note SQL Server 2005 is not supported on clustered Windows Server 2003 servers where Terminal Server (the actual feature) is also installed and configured. This applies to SQL Server 2000 as well.

Antivirus Programs and Clustering

Installing some sort of antivirus program is standard for most server builds for nearly every client I have visited for the past five to six years, including SQL Servers. The reality with SQL Server is that most SQL Server instances are well behind a firewall and far away from where any public access can get at the server and do something malicious such as install malware. SQL Servers are also generally dedicated to SQL Server and are not used for any other purpose like Web servers, file servers, or print servers. In most cases, the recommendation is to not put antivirus programs on SQL Servers. It is incumbent upon you to assess what the risk is of possibly not putting antivirus on your SQL Servers. Some things you do might expose risk, such as mailing alerts from SQL Server, which might mean there is some sort of inbound and outbound mail traffic on the server.

With clustering, both at a Windows and a SQL Server level, things are a bit more complex. Most antivirus programs are not cluster-aware, and some antivirus programs can actually interfere with the regular operations of a server cluster. In the event that you need to troubleshoot your cluster where antivirus software is installed, you might need to uninstall (and not just disable) the software. Microsoft Product Support Services might require this during a support call. This policy is defined in the Microsoft Knowledge Base article 250355, "Antivirus Software Might Cause Problems with Cluster Services" (http://support.microsoft.com/kb/250355/en-us).

If you require that antivirus programs be installed on the nodes of the cluster, you must set up exclusions after the program is installed on each node. Setting these exclusions will ensure that in the case that some resource fails over to another node, that resource will not be scanned and impede the resource from being started. Can you imagine an antivirus program having to scan a 1TB data file for SQL Server? That will take some time and definitely affect your availability, effectively negating why you implemented a cluster in the first place.

The exclusions you should set are as follows:

- The quorum directory (\MSCS) on the shared disk configured as the quorum or the local directory used in a Majority Node Set cluster.

- The directory used by the clustered Microsoft Distributed Transaction Coordinator (\MSDTC), which can be found on the shared disk configured with MSDTC.

- All SQL Server data and log files. These files will have extensions of .mdf and .ndf for data and .ldf for logs.

Changing the Cluster Service Account Password

Under Windows 2000 Server, changing the cluster service account's password required planned downtime. The steps are not complex: gracefully shut down all services running on the cluster, stop the cluster service on all nodes, manually change the password of the Cluster Service in the Services applet, and then bring everything back up. With Windows Server 2003, changing the password is a completely online operation using the command-line CLUSTER.EXE with the /changepassword option. The /changepassword option with no switches will update the password at the domain controller as well as on all nodes of the cluster. By default, if one or more of the nodes is unavailable, you will receive an error similar to the one in Figure 6-1.

```
Verifying cluster node availability...
Node GLEN of cluster STYX is Down.
All nodes in all clusters must be Up or Paused to support the password
change operation.

Unable to proceed with the password change operation.

System error 5037 has occurred (0x000013ad).
All cluster nodes must be running to perform this operation.
```

Figure 6-1. *Error occurring when a node is down*

You can use five options when changing the password, and you can combine them:

- /skipdc: If you have already changed the password at the domain level and just need to change it on the cluster nodes so that the cluster service works properly, use this option. If you do not use this option, the password will also be updated at the domain.

- /force: This switch will force CLUSTER.EXE to proceed with the password change even if nodes of the cluster are unavailable.

- /test: Before doing the actual password change, this switch will check to see whether the password is able to be changed on the nodes as well as at the domain (if you are not using /skipdc).

Note You must run your statement with /test prior to committing your change because the actions taken when invoking /changepassword are committed immediately and cannot be rolled back if the password is not updated correctly at the domain controller.

- /quiet: This switch will suppress all output except errors.
- /verbose: This switch will show all output. I recommend using /verbose because it will give you the most information.

Here are some sample statements:

- cluster /cluster:clustername /changepassword:*newpassword,currentpassword* /test /verbose: This tests that the password can be changed successfully. Figure 6-2 shows a sample.

```
C:\>cluster /cluster:STYX /changepassword:newp@ssw0rd,pas$w0rd /test /verbose

Cluster Name = STYX

                          Service Account
Node          ID   State  In Use/Stored
---------------------------------------------------------------
JY            4    Up     clusteradmin@x64env.test.allan.com
                          x64env\clusteradmin
GLEN          3    Up     clusteradmin@x64env.test.allan.com
                          x64env\clusteradmin
TOMMY         1    Up     clusteradmin@x64env.test.allan.com
                          x64env\clusteradmin
DENNIS        2    Up     clusteradmin@x64env.test.allan.com
                          x64env\clusteradmin

Verifying cluster node availability...
Verifying support for password change operation...
Verifying that all clusters use the same service account...
```

Figure 6-2. *Running /changepassword with the /test option*

Note If your password requires an ampersand (&), you must use quotes around your new password, such as cluster /cluster:CLUSTER1 /changepassword:"mynewpas$word&7893",*currentpassword*. If you enter an invalid password for *currentpassword*, you will see a system error of 86, as shown in Figure 6-3.

```
Changing password on domain controller...
Failed to change password on the domain controller.
System error 86 has occurred (0x00000056).
The specified network password is not correct.
```

Figure 6-3. *Error when entering an invalid current cluster service password*

- cluster /cluster:clustername /changepassword:*newpassword,currentpassword* /verbose: This example changes the password and commits the changes. Figure 6-4 shows a sample.
- cluster /cluster:clustername /changepassword:*newpassword,currentpassword* /skipdc /verbose: This example changes the password and commits the changes to the cluster nodes only. Figure 6-5 shows a sample.
- cluster /cluster:clustername /changepassword:*newpassword, currentpassword* /force /verbose: This example forces a changed password while a node is down. Figure 6-6 shows a sample.

```
C:\>cluster /cluster:MYSRVCLU /changepassword:password1,password /verbose

Cluster Name = MYSRVCLU
                                Service Account
Node          ID   State      In Use/Stored
----------------------------------------------------------------
CLUNODE2      2    Up         clusteradmin@testdomain.allan.com
                              testdomain.allan.com\clusteradmin
CLUNODE1      1    Up         clusteradmin@testdomain.allan.com
                              testdomain.allan.com\clusteradmin

Verifying cluster node availability...
Verifying support for password change operation...
Verifying that all clusters use the same service account...

Changing password on domain controller...

Changing password on cluster MYSRVCLU...
The password change on node CLUNODE1 of cluster MYSRVCLU succeeded.
The password change on node CLUNODE2 of cluster MYSRVCLU succeeded.
```

Figure 6-4. *Running /changepassword and committing the changes*

```
C:\>cluster /cluster:STYX /changepassword:Mypa$sword,pas$w0rd /skipdc /verbose

Cluster Name = STYX
                                Service Account
Node          ID   State      In Use/Stored
----------------------------------------------------------------
JY            4    Up         clusteradmin@x64env.test.allan.com
                              x64env\clusteradmin
TOMMY         1    Up         clusteradmin@x64env.test.allan.com
                              x64env\clusteradmin
DENNIS        2    Up         clusteradmin@x64env.test.allan.com
                              x64env\clusteradmin
GLEN          3    Up         clusteradmin@x64env.test.allan.com
                              x64env\clusteradmin

Verifying cluster node availability...
Verifying support for password change operation...
Verifying that all clusters use the same service account...

Skipping password change on domain controller.

Changing password on cluster STYX...
The password change on node TOMMY of cluster STYX succeeded.
The password change on node DENNIS of cluster STYX succeeded.
The password change on node GLEN of cluster STYX succeeded.
The password change on node JY of cluster STYX succeeded.
```

Figure 6-5. *Running /changepassword with the /skipdc option*

```
C:\>cluster /cluster:MYSRVCLU /changepassword:password2,password1 /force /verbose

Cluster Name = MYSRVCLU
                                Service Account
Node          ID   State      In Use/Stored
----------------------------------------------------------------
CLUNODE2      2    Down       <null>
                              <null>
CLUNODE1      1    Up         clusteradmin@testdomain.allan.com
                              testdomain.allan.com\clusteradmin

Verifying cluster node availability...
Node CLUNODE2 of cluster MYSRVCLU is Down.
Ignoring.
Verifying support for password change operation...
Verifying that all clusters use the same service account...

Changing password on domain controller...

Changing password on cluster MYSRVCLU...
The password change on node CLUNODE1 of cluster MYSRVCLU succeeded.
The password change was not issued on node CLUNODE2 of cluster MYSRVCLU.
```

Figure 6-6. *Running /changepassword with the /force option*

Tip If your cluster service account is used on more than one server cluster, you can change multiple clusters at the same time by adding the cluster name to the /cluster switch. For example, use cluster /cluster: CLUSTER1,CLUSTER2 /changepassword:*newpassword, currentpassword*.

If a node is down or unavailable during the password changing, you will see the error shown in Figure 6-7 when you start the node, and you will see the error shown in Figure 6-8 in the Event Log.

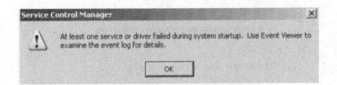

Figure 6-7. *Error when starting the node after the password has been changed at the domain before updating the password for the Cluster Service*

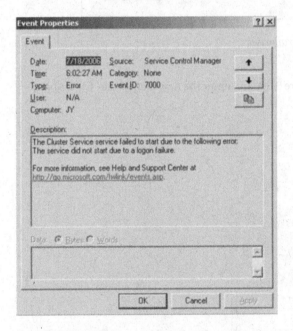

Figure 6-8. *Event log error when the Cluster Service cannot start*

To manually change the password on a node that is unavailable during the /changepass operation, follow these instructions:

1. Log on to the node that has the service failure.

2. From Administrative Tools, start Services.

3. Right-click Cluster Service, and select Properties, as shown in Figure 6-9; alternatively, double-click Cluster Service.

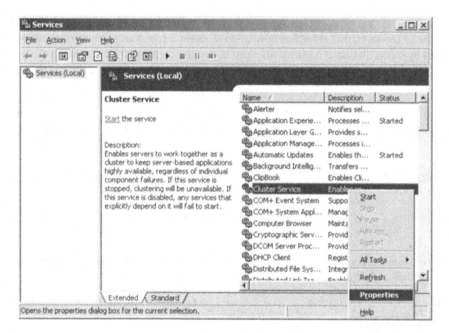

Figure 6-9. *Selecting the Cluster Service properties*

4. Select the Log On tab, as shown in Figure 6-10, and enter the new credentials. Click Apply.

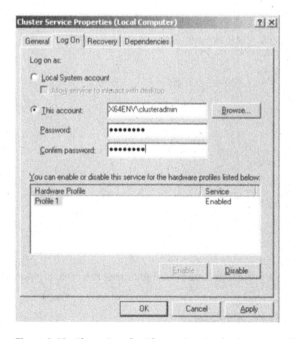

Figure 6-10. *Changing the Cluster Service login properties*

5. Select the General tab, as shown in Figure 6-11. Click Start.

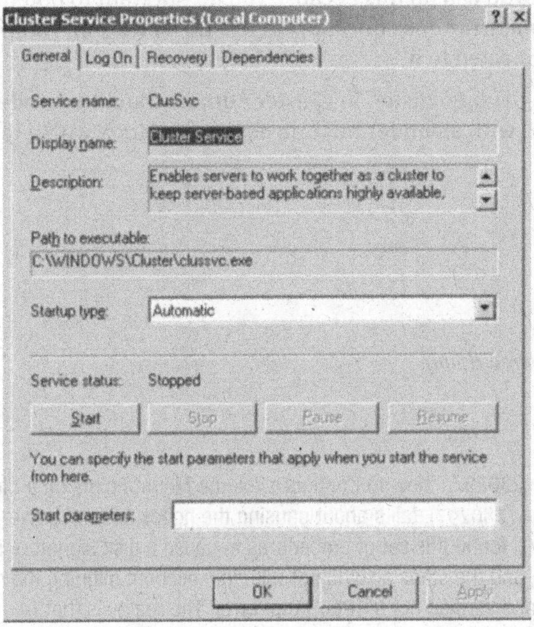

Figure 6-11. *Starting the Cluster Service*

6. Once the Cluster Service successfully starts, click OK.

7. Exit Services.

Disk Management for a Windows Server Cluster

One of the more Windows-related tasks that you might have to perform in the life cycle of your SQL Server failover clustering implementation is some sort of disk-related task. The following sections will cover what will arguably be the most common scenarios.

■**Caution** Most of the tasks described here will affect the availability of SQL Server, so they should be planned for with an outage window or configured when the cluster is first installed if possible. Messing around at the disk layer is not work that should be taken lightly because if the task is done incorrectly you could do more harm than good. Make sure you always make backups prior to doing anything that will involve manipulating the shared disk array.

Configuring Mount Points for Use with SQL Server 2005 Failover Clustering

One of the newly supported features with SQL Server 2005 is the ability to use clustered mount points. This allows you to add a physical disk resource as a junction point under an existing disk resource, where it appears somewhat like a folder:

1. Create the disk space on your shared disk array with the appropriate zoning and masking. Most will support creating the LUN while servers are up and connected. Please check with your array's vendor to ensure that you can do this because you do not want to potentially ruin your disk configuration. If your array does not support live LUN creation, you will have to shut down the servers connected to it.

2. Power down all nodes except one in your cluster. In Cluster Administrator, the nodes should look similar to Figure 6-12, with all nodes but one having a white *X* with a red circle around it.

Figure 6-12. *All but one node is powered down.*

■**Note** The Microsoft Knowledge Base Article 280297, "How to Configure Volume Mount Points on a Clustered Server" (http://support.microsoft.com/kb/280297), talks about pausing the nodes and not powering them down during the creation of mount points. I found this set of procedures to cause a disk signature issue, as shown in Figure 6-13, with my test harness, and the steps also do not take into account aligning the disk. The steps included in this section were tested and verified not to return that error. The reality is that from a risk standpoint, you need to plan downtime to do operations such as this, so it is better to power down the other nodes while doing disk manipulation anyway.

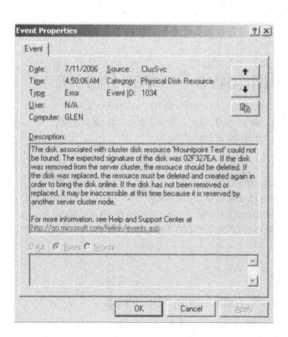

Figure 6-13. *Error if nodes are paused and not shut down*

3. Open Windows Explorer, and connect to the drive where you want to place the mount point. Create a folder on that drive that will house the mount point. Figure 6-14 shows an example.

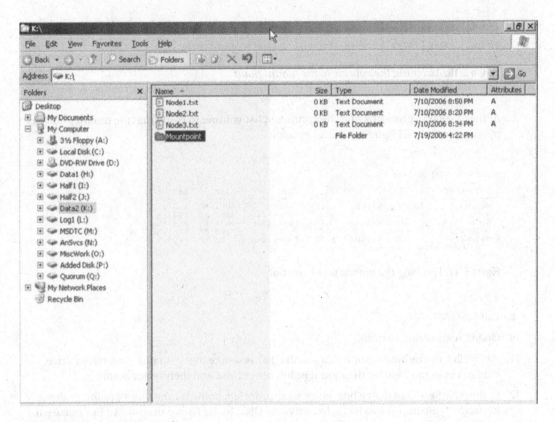

Figure 6-14. *The mount point directory*

4. Open a command window, and start DISKPART. Following the instructions in steps 3 through 5 in the section on how to sector align the disks in Chapter 5, align the disk that will be mounted in the folder created in step 3 of this section.

5. Format the disk you just aligned but do not assign it a drive letter.

6. Start DISKPART. At the DISKPART> prompt, enter the command **list volume** to see all the valid volumes. Select the volume that will be used as the mount point with select volume *n*, where *n* is the number of the volume as shown in Figure 6-15.

```
DISKPART> list volume

  Volume ###  Ltr  Label       Fs     Type       Size     Status    Info
  ----------  ---  ----------- -----  ---------  -------  ---------  --------
  Volume 0    D    SQLENTSEL   CDFS   CD-ROM      891 MB  Healthy
  Volume 1    C                NTFS   Partition  8182 MB  Healthy    System
  Volume 2         New Volume  NTFS   Partition  6128 KB  Healthy
  Volume 3    K    Data2       NTFS   Partition   101 MB  Healthy
  Volume 4         New Volume  NTFS   Partition    10 MB  Healthy

DISKPART> select volume 4

Volume 4 is the selected volume.
```

Figure 6-15. *Listing and selecting the volume*

7. At the DISKPART> prompt, enter the command **assign mount=path**, where *path* is the mount point folder created in step 3. Figure 6-16 shows an example.

```
DISKPART> assign mount = K:\Mountpoint
DiskPart successfully assigned the drive letter or mount point.
```

Figure 6-16. *Assigning the volume to the mount point*

8. At the DISKPART> prompt, enter the command **list volume** to verify that the mount point displays properly. See Figure 6-17 as an example.

```
DISKPART> list volume

  Volume ###  Ltr  Label        Fs     Type        Size     Status     Info
  ----------  ---  -----------  -----  ----------  -------  ---------  --------
  Volume 0    D    SQLENTSEL    CDFS   CD-ROM       891 MB  Healthy
  Volume 1    C                 NTFS   Partition   8182 MB  Healthy    System
  Volume 2         New Volume   NTFS   Partition   6128 KB  Healthy
  Volume 3    K    Data2        NTFS   Partition    101 MB  Healthy
* Volume 4         New Volume   NTFS   Partition     10 MB  Healthy
     K:\Mountpoint\
```

Figure 6-17. *Verifying the mount point creation*

9. Exit DISKPART.

10. Open Cluster Administrator.

11. Right-click the resource group that has the disk resource that contains the lettered drive that serves as the base for the mount point, select New, and then select Resource.

12. In the New Resource dialog box, enter an appropriate name for the mount point. In the Resource Type drop-down list, select Physical Disk. In the Group drop-down list, make sure the right resource group is selected. Figure 6-18 shows an example. Click Next.

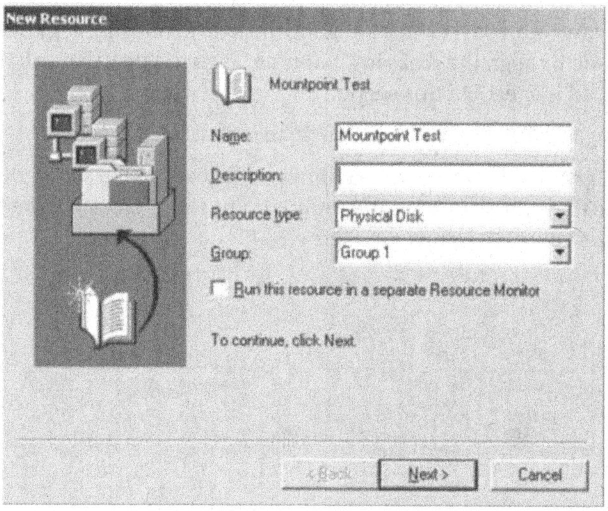

Figure 6-18. *Creating the mount point resource*

13. In the Possible Owners dialog box, verify that all nodes of the server cluster are listed as possible owners of this resource. If a node is not listed on the right side, select it from the Available Nodes list, and click Add. Click Next.

14. On the Dependencies dialog box, select the drive from Available Resources, and click Add to add it to the Resource Dependencies list. When finished, it should appear similar to Figure 6-19. Click Next.

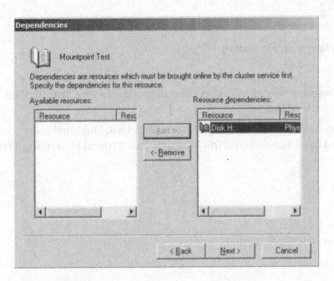

Figure 6-19. *Adding the disk as a dependency of the resource*

15. In the Disk Parameters dialog box, verify the proper disk is selected. Figure 6-20 shows an example. Click Finish.

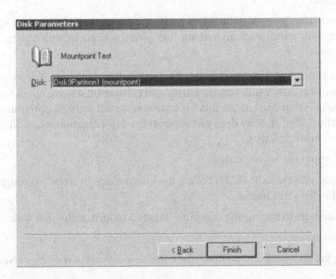

Figure 6-20. *Assigning the mount point*

If the resource is created, you will see the message box in Figure 6-21 appear. Click OK. The resource now appears in the resource group and has a state of Offline.

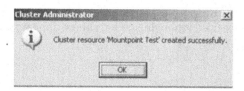

Figure 6-21. *Confirming the resource's creation*

16. Start the newly created resource by right-clicking the group and selecting Bring Online. The disk will now have a state of Online.

17. In Windows Explorer, the new mount point is ready for use and will look similar to Figure 6-22. Test that you can write and read from the new mount point by creating a text file and opening it.

Figure 6-22. *Confirming the resource's creation*

18. Power up one of the other nodes. Test that you can fail the lettered drive with the new mount point to that node and that you can read and write files from it.

19. Repeat step 18 for all nodes in the server cluster.

Adding a New Disk to the Cluster

If you run out of capacity on one of the drives associated with SQL Server or Analysis Services and you do not want to configure a mount point, you can add another physical drive letter if one is available.

1. Create the disk space on your shared disk array with the appropriate zoning and masking. Most will support creating the LUN while servers are up and connected. Please check with your array's vendor to ensure that you can do this because you do not want to potentially ruin your disk configuration. If your array does not support live LUN creation, you will have to shut down the servers connected to it.

2. Power down all nodes except one in your cluster.

3. Open a command window, and start DISKPART. Follow the instructions in steps 3 through 7 on how to sector align the disks in Chapter 5.

4. Follow the instructions on how to format the disks in Chapter 5 to format the new disk.

5. Open Cluster Administrator.

6. Right-click the resource group where you want to place the new disk resource, select New, and then select Resource.

7. In the New Resource dialog box, enter an appropriate name for the mount point. In the Resource Type drop-down list, select Physical Disk. In the Group drop-down list, make sure the right resource group is selected. Figure 6-23 shows an example. Click Next.

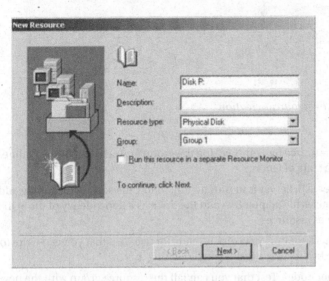

Figure 6-23. *Creating the new drive resource*

8. On the Possible Owners dialog box, verify that all nodes of the server cluster are listed as possible owners of this resource. If a node is not listed on the right side, select it from the Available Nodes list, and click Add. Click Next.

9. In the Dependencies dialog box, do not make this resource dependent on anything. Click Next.

10. In the Disk Parameters dialog box, verify the proper disk is selected. Figure 6-24 shows an example. Click Finish.

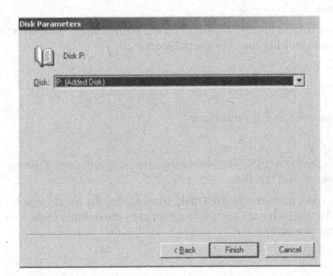

Figure 6-24. *Assigning the disk*

If the resource is created, you will see the message box in Figure 6-25 appear. Click OK. The resource now appears in the resource group and has a state of Offline.

Figure 6-25. *Confirming the resource's creation*

11. Start the newly created resource by right-clicking the group and selecting Bring Online. The disk will now have a state of Online.

12. If this drive is added after SQL Server is in production, follow the section on adding additional disks as dependencies in Chapter 8 to add the drive as a dependency of the SQL Server or Analysis Services resource.

13. In Windows Explorer, check that the new disk is ready for use. Test that you can write to and read from the new drive by creating a text file and opening it.

14. Power up one of the other nodes. Test that you can fail the resource group with the new mount point to the node you just turned on and that you can read and write files from it.

15. Repeat step 14 for all nodes in the server cluster.

Expanding Disks via DISKPART

When you initially create your disk within Windows from the attached LUN—and if you did not format the full capacity of the drive—as long as your shared disk array supports it, you can expand the capacity to the maximum size of the drive with DISKPART. Check with your vendor to see whether this method is supported.

1. Power down all nodes except one in your cluster.

2. Open Cluster Administrator.

3. Right-click the group that contains the disk resource you will be expanding, and select the option Take Offline. It should look like the example in Figure 6-26.

Figure 6-26. *An offline group in Cluster Administrator*

4. Open a command window, and start DISKPART. Follow the instructions in steps 3 through 7 in Chapter 5 on how to sector align the disks.

5. At the DISKPART> prompt, enter the command **list disk**. The resulting list will show you which disks are fully used and which ones are not, as denoted by the number in the Free column. Figure 6-27 shows an example.

```
Disk ###   Status        Size      Free     Dyn  Gpt
--------   ------        ----      ----     ---  ---
Disk 0     Online        10 GB   8033 KB
Disk 1     Online       511 MB      0 B
Disk 2     Online       511 MB      0 B
Disk 3     Online      3067 MB   1012 MB
Disk 4     Online      2039 MB   8033 KB
Disk 5     Online      4095 MB      0 B
Disk 6     Online      1022 MB      0 B
Disk 7     Online      3067 MB      0 B
Disk 8     Online      5114 MB      0 B
Disk 9     Online      1020 MB      0 B
Disk 10    Online      1020 MB      0 B
```

Figure 6-27. *Seeing which disks have free space*

6. At the DISKPART> prompt, enter the command **select disk d**, where *d* is the number of the disk you want to use.

7. At the DISKPART> prompt, enter the command **detail disk**. This command will show all the attributes of the disk, but what you are looking for is the drive letter associated with the disk to verify that it is the disk you want to expand. You can find it under the Ltr column. Take note of the volume number, which is found in the ### column. Figure 6-28 shows an example.

```
DISKPART> detail disk

VMware, VMware Virtual S SCSI Disk Device
Disk ID: 96E7A829
Type    : SCSI
Bus     : 0
Target  : 2
LUN ID  : 0

Volume ###  Ltr  Label      Fs     Type      Size      Status    Info
----------  ---  -----      --     ----      ----      ------    ----
Volume 5    H    Data1      NTFS   Partition 2055 MB   Healthy
```

Figure 6-28. *Result of the detail disk command*

8. At the DISKPART> prompt, enter the command **select volume v**, where *v* is the number of the volume that contains the drive letter you want to expand. Figure 6-29 shows an example.

```
DISKPART> select volume 5
Volume 5 is the selected volume.
```

Figure 6-29. *Result of the select volume command*

9. To expand the full complement of the LUN, at the DISKPART> prompt, enter the command **extend**. If you want to use only a portion of that unused space, use the command extend size=s, where *s* is the amount you want to expand the disk. Figure 6-30 shows an example.

```
DISKPART> extend
DiskPart successfully extended the volume.
```

Figure 6-30. *Result of the expand command*

10. At the DISKPART> prompt, enter the command **list disk**. The disk you chose to expand should now reflect the new size.

11. Right-click the group that contains the disk resource you will be expanding, and select the option Bring Online.

12. Test that the disk is still functioning properly by accessing the disk through Windows Explorer, writing a text file, and opening that file.

13. Power up one of the other nodes. Test that you can fail the resource group with the new expanded disk to the node you just turned on and that you can read and write files from it.

14. Repeat step 13 for all nodes in the server cluster.

These are some of the errors you might see if something goes wrong in the expanding process:

- Figure 6-31 shows the error if you accidentally try to extend the LUN to another disk.

```
DISKPART> extend disk=5

Cannot extend a basic volume to a different disk.
Please use extend without specifying a disk.
```

Figure 6-31. *Expansion error across disks*

- Figure 6-32 shows the error if the expand process fails and you cannot expand the volume.

```
DISKPART> extend

DiskPart failed to extend the volume.
Please make sure the volume is valid for extending.
```

Figure 6-32. *Failure to expand error*

- Figure 6-33 shows the error when the volume is not able to be expanded.

```
DISKPART> extend

The volume you have selected may not be extended.
Please select another volume and try again.
```

Figure 6-33. *The volume is unable to be expanded.*

- Figure 6-34 shows the error if you select a size greater than the amount of space available for expansion.

```
DISKPART> extend size=512

The volume size you have selected is too large for the disk.
Either select a disk with more free space, or specify a smaller volume.
```

Figure 6-34. *The size is greater than the space available for expansion.*

Changing the Quorum Disk

At some point you might want to change the disk that the quorum is configured on if you are using a traditional server cluster.

Tip This set of instructions also works if you configured your server cluster to use Majority Node Set and you want to now use another disk for the quorum.

Cluster Administrator

To use Cluster Administrator to change which disk the quorum uses, follow these steps:

1. Open Cluster Administrator.

2. Select the cluster group that contains the disk that will become the new quorum.

3. In the right pane, right-click the disk resource, select Change Group, and then select Cluster Group, as shown in Figure 6-35. You might also drag and drop the resource to the Cluster Group if you do not want to use a menu selection.

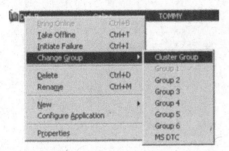

Figure 6-35. *Changing the resource's group*

4. At the confirmation dialog box, click Yes. Figure 6-36 shows a sample.

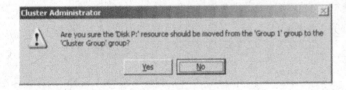

Figure 6-36. *Move disk confirmation #1*

5. In the Move Resources dialog box, click Yes. Figure 6-37 shows a sample.

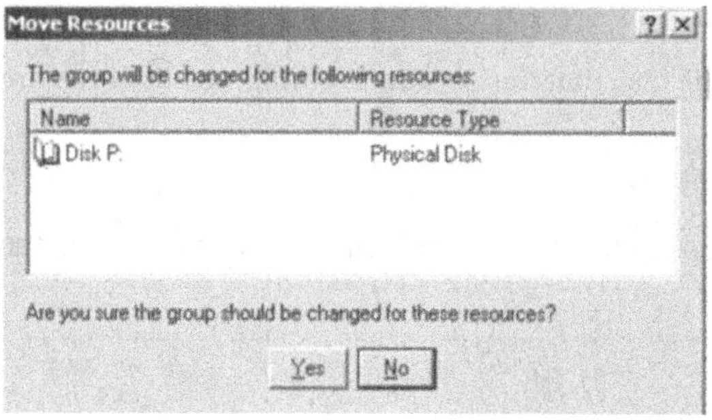

Figure 6-37. *Move disk confirmation #2*

Note If the disk resource is not owned by the same node as the Cluster Group resource group, you will see the error shown in Figure 6-38. Fail the cluster group containing the new quorum disk to the same node that owns Cluster Group, and restart the process.

Figure 6-38. *Move disk error*

6. Verify that the disk is now in the Cluster Group, as shown in Figure 6-39.

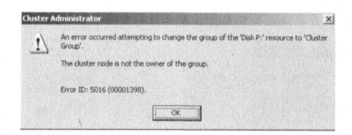

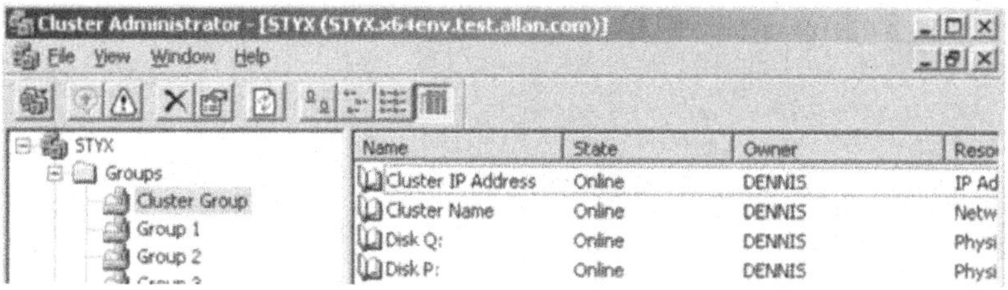

Figure 6-39. *Disk after moving groups*

7. Select the cluster name in the left pane, right-click the name of the server cluster, and select Properties.

8. Select the Quorum tab. In the Quorum Resource drop-down list, select the drive you moved to the Cluster Group, and resize the quorum log to an appropriate size. Figure 6-40 shows an example. Click Apply, and then click OK.

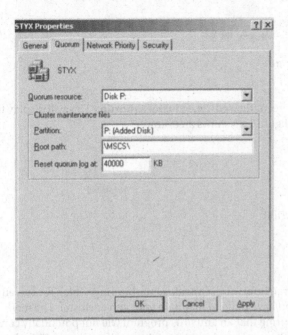

Figure 6-40. *Changing the quorum disks*

9. If the disk has no issues, you can move it to another resource group to repurpose it. If the disk is no longer needed or damaged, delete the resource from the cluster. To delete it, right-click the disk resource, and select Delete.

Command Line

To use the command line to change which disk the quorum uses, follow these steps:

1. Open a command window.

2. Move the disk resource, which will now contain the quorum. To do this, enter the command **cluster /cluster:clustername resource resourcename /move:groupname**, where *clustername* is the name of your Windows server cluster, *resourcename* is the name of the resource, and *groupname* is the name of the cluster resource group that is the destination. Figure 6-41 shows an example.

```
C:\>cluster /cluster:STYX resource "Disk P:" /move:"Cluster Group"
Moving resource 'Disk P:' to group 'Cluster Group'...
Resource              Group              Node            Status
-------------------   ----------------   -------------   --------
Disk P:               Cluster Group      DENNIS          Online
```

Figure 6-41. *Moving a resource via the command line*

3. To create the new quorum, enter the command **cluster /quorum:resourcename / maxlogsize:logsizeinkb**, where *resourcename* is the name of the disk resource you moved in the previous step and *logsizeinkb* is the size of the log in kilobytes (KB). Figure 6-42 shows an example.

```
C:\>cluster /quorum:"Disk P:" /maxlogsize:40000
```

Figure 6-42. *Creating the new quorum*

4. To verify that the quorum is now reconfigured, type **cluster /quorum**. This will display the current quorum configuration. Figure 6-43 shows an example.

```
C:\>cluster /quorum
Quorum Resource Name Device                                    Max Log Size
Disk P:              P:\MSCS\                                   40960000
```

Figure 6-43. *Verifying the new quorum*

Summary

Administering a server cluster is fairly straightforward. Outside of monitoring, which is covered in Chapter 15, there should be very little you have to do to maintain your server cluster. The main things you need to watch out for are ensuring that an antivirus program will not potentially corrupt your cluster and correctly changing the cluster service account password if necessary. This chapter concludes the trilogy of chapters dedicated to the Windows portion of clustering. At this point you are ready to tackle the next portion—SQL Server.

CHAPTER 7

■ ■ ■

Failover Clustering: Preparing to Cluster SQL Server 2005

The previous three chapters have focused on the Windows portion of clustering. This chapter and the next two focus on SQL Server failover clustering that is built on top of a Windows server cluster. Before you implement the SQL Server portion, carefully read this chapter. Just as Chapter 4 served as your guide for planning your implementation of the Windows portion, this chapter will walk you through SQL Server–specific design considerations so that you can make informed implementation decisions about your SQL Server 2005 failover clustering installations.

THE "I HATE SQL SERVER FAILOVER CLUSTERING" SYNDROME

I run into a surprising amount of resistance when assisting my clients in implementing clustered SQL Servers. After years of doing it, I have narrowed down the reasons that people hate clustering. You may or may not agree with me, and if you do, you may even fall into one of the categories discussed here:

Category One

Many customers have had a bad experience clustering SQL Server with either version 6.5 or version 7.0. My experience with clustering SQL Server goes back to SQL Server 7.0, and I can tell you that clustering was an iffy proposition at best: to do things like apply a SQL Server service pack with SQL Server 6.5 or 7.0, you had to uncluster the nodes, apply the service pack, and then recluster the nodes. Talk about having to cross your fingers! In those days, you were also more likely than not using SCSI-based direct attached storage, which could prove problematic on its own, let alone when used in conjunction with clustering. Then add in the seemingly weird dependence on specific versions of MDAC—believe it or not, this was one of the factors that determined whether failover clustering was able to work. Until SQL Server 2000, which was a fully cluster-aware application, all previous versions of SQL Server failover clustering used a "shim" layer that replaced some DLLs on the server to allow SQL Server 6.5 and 7.0 to work in a clustered configuration. So if you did something to replace one of the DLLs, like install an unsupported version of MDAC, you would break your cluster. Since those early days of clustering with SQL Server, both the hardware and software aspects have improved immensely. While you may have had extremely bad experiences with SQL Server and clustering years ago, you should still consider it for new implementations (if it meets your requirements), because it has changed quite a bit. If your company has a bias due to previous bad experiences, you may want to ask what versions of SQL Server and Windows they are referring to, because clustering Windows Server 2003 with SQL Server 2005 (or SQL Server 2000 with SQL Server 2000 Service Pack 3a or later) is a great experience.

Category Two

As you can probably already tell from the previous three chapters, implementing a cluster is not something you decide to do off the cuff—it takes quite a lot of planning and involves what I refer to as "moving parts." It is human nature that people tend to like more simple, straightforward implementations and shy away from the complexity of a cluster. While I would agree you should not undertake implementing clusters as an afterthought, with the right guidance, planning, and time, you *will* get it right. The end may justify the means if failover clustering meets your availability needs. If need be, for at least your first implementation, find a good consultant to help you and become a sponge—soak up their experience. Just because clustering gets six chapters and quite a bit of space in this book will not turn you into an expert overnight. Gaining experience—especially on your first implementations with someone else more qualified to assist—will help you acquire the practical experience to any "book" learning you may do.

Category Three

Many people are seemingly forced into using SQL Server failover clustering because it is the only high-availability method supported by the application vendor for the program their business chooses to deploy. There is nothing you can do about this other than venting first at the decision maker who wanted the application in the first place, and then contacting the vendor who designed the solution to support other things. No one held a gun to the vendor's head to only support failover clustering, so it is not Microsoft's fault. If you have to, and it is the right thing for your situation, my advice is to find a way to make it work. Fighting it will only make the end implementation much more difficult than it has to be. Over the years, I have had the occasional client try to fight me every step of the way when implementing clusters ("Why do we need to have a specific firmware version on our SAN?," "Why are we spending so much time planning?," "We cannot give the service accounts these rights," and so on). It adds time (and cost if you are paying a consultant for assistance) because you spend more time spinning wheels in "we don't do things this way" arguments than you do just planning it and getting on with things. Consultants who are working with you onsite should be looking out for your best interests. Believe me, they want to get your production environment up and running just as quickly as you do. It isn't any more fun for the consultant to have constant delays when in some cases they could be prevented. There has to be a middle ground that everyone can come to that pushes the implementations forward.

Category Four

Clustering is scary to some. If clustering is new to your organization, it is something that the application and IT teams will have to support and understand inside and out. It changes everything—how you deploy, how you troubleshoot, how you do maintenance. While it's still just an installation of SQL Server when all is said and done, there are still some cluster-specific things you will need to worry about. For example, the IT personnel will have to get used to determining which node owns the cluster resources before trying to solve a problem or possibly do maintenance. If you have test or staging environments that are clustered, they will provide a good training ground and sandbox for your staff.

Category Five

The strict need to adhere to the Windows Server Catalog for hardware configuration is a thorn in many people's sides. Admittedly, it does not make things easier. Remember that it is a Windows requirement, not a direct SQL Server one (guilt by association, I guess). As noted in Chapter 4, the Windows Server Catalog is there to ensure that you have a known good cluster configuration. Unfortunately, I see it cause more strife than happiness with customers. You need to weigh the flexibility of ignoring the rules and doing anything you want to your servers, and thus possibly screwing them up at any time, against having your hands proverbially tied, ensuring that you will be up and running. If it were up to me, I would choose the latter.

New Features of SQL Server 2005 Failover Clustering

For the most part, the failover clustering feature of SQL Server 2005 acts and behaves just like its counterpart in SQL Server 2000. Some enhancements exist, and the most important ones are highlighted in the following list. Some of these enhancements will be discussed in further detail later in this chapter.

- With SQL Server 2000, Analysis Services was not cluster-aware, and installing it in a clustered configuration was only supported via the manual method described in the Microsoft Knowledge Base articles "How to cluster SQL Server 2000 Analysis Services in Windows 2000 and in Windows 2003" (http://support.microsoft.com/kb/308023/en-us) and "How to cluster SQL Server 2000 Analysis Services on a cluster that is running a 64-bit version of Windows" (http://support.microsoft.com/kb/916665/en-us). In SQL Server 2005, Analysis Services is fully cluster-aware like the relational engine, and its installation is integrated with SQL Server 2005 Setup.

- Prior to SQL Server 2005, only the Developer Edition and Enterprise Edition of SQL Server supported failover clustering. SQL Server 2005 introduces support for the failover clustering feature in the Standard Edition.

- SQL Server 2000 supported up to 16 instances in a failover cluster. SQL Server 2005 supports up to 25 instances, which is dependent upon the resources you have available.

- As noted in Chapter 4, mount points are fully supported with SQL Server 2005 failover clustering. You should evaluate whether or not you need to use mount points for your clustered implementations during the planning phase.

- Failover times for an instance are quicker because SQL Server has fast restores, which means the database is available after the redo phase is complete. See the section "Redo Phase" in Chapter 3 for more details on how the redo process works.

- The SQL Mail feature of SQL Server 2000 was not fully supported in clustered configurations. SQL Server 2005's Database Mail feature can be used with all installations of SQL Server 2005, including failover clusters.

- Each SQL Server 2005 cluster resource DLL runs in its own resource monitor instead of sharing a single default resource monitor for all instances, which is how SQL Server 2000 worked.

- SQL Server 2005 Setup introduces support for unattended (scripted) installs for clustered instances of SQL Server 2005.

- Various enhancements were added to ease administration, and I will discuss these throughout this chapter. One example is that you can now rename a clustered instance of SQL Server 2005, whereas with all previous versions of SQL Server failover clustering, you would have to uninstall and reinstall SQL Server to rename your instance.

- With SQL Server 2000, each clustered instance contained a full-text resource that shared the same underlying full-text DLL. In SQL Server 2005, not only does each clustered installation get its own full-text resource, but also installing full-text is completely optional.

- SQL Server 2005 Setup, including the SQL Server 2005 Service Pack and Hotfix setup programs, has the ability to be run against multiple instances at one time—even on a cluster. With SQL Server 2000, you would need to apply service packs on a per-instance basis. Service packs will be covered more in Chapter 16.

- With version 2005, SQL Server is no longer bound to a specific version of MDAC, as was the case in earlier versions of SQL Server. As noted previously, implementing clusters in earlier versions of SQL Server could be difficult if an application required a different version of MDAC. Please do not misunderstand the point here—MDAC is still required for SQL Server, but it is now much easier to independently update and install MDAC without affecting SQL Server.

- The Service Master Key and the Database Master Keys, both of which are used for encryption, are not distributed automatically across all nodes of the cluster.

Planning SQL Server 2005 Failover Clustering Instances

Although planning for installing SQL Server shares some aspects with the Windows portion described in Chapter 4, you must take into account some considerations specific to SQL Server. Although the failover clustering feature of SQL Server 2005 acts and behaves for the most part just like its counterpart in SQL Server 2000, it does have some enhancements (as listed in the section "New Features of SQL Server 2005 Failover Clustering" earlier in the chapter), and the following sections will take a closer look at them.

Number of Instances on a Single Windows Failover Cluster

As mentioned previously, SQL Server 2005 supports up to 25 instances on a single Windows failover cluster. The stand-alone limitation is 50 instances per server, so please note the difference between your clustered implementations and ones on stand-alone servers. That is the only difference. On a single Windows server cluster, you are still limited to only one default instance of SQL Server. This means if you have a total of N instances, one of the N may be a default instance, and the rest of the $N-1$ instances must be named instances. There is no restriction on the number of named instances (up to the supported limit of 25), so you could make all of the instances named instances and never use a default instance.

Caution   Some software that utilizes SQL Server as its database requires that the SQL Server instance be a default instance. Before installing SQL Server, check with the software vendor so that you install SQL Server properly for your needs. There is nothing worse than spending money on what you think will be the "perfect" SQL Server solution only to realize it will not work for you due to an unforeseen product dependency.

Clustered SQL Server Instance Names

SQL Server failover clustering also differs from stand-alone implementations in that the name of the SQL Server instance—even if it is a default instance—must be completely different from the name of any of the nodes themselves or the Windows failover cluster. For example, if you have a Windows server cluster named RUSH and nodes with the names ALEX, GEDDY, and NEIL, you could not install a SQL Server 2005 failover clustering instance with any of those names. It would need to be something unique like BROON.

Because of this, when installing each clustered SQL Server instance on a Windows failover cluster, each instance name must be completely unique not only on the Windows failover cluster itself, but also within your Windows domain. Failover clustering requires the ability to dynamically update DNS, so if you attempt to have an object with the same name twice, the existing object will be overwritten. The named instance portion (which is the part after the slash when you are accessing SQL

Server via its name) must be unique on the same Windows server cluster, but it can be reused on another Windows server cluster. This unique name requirement can potentially cause problems within companies that use some sort of naming scheme for their servers that assumes SQL Server itself takes on that name. For example, say your naming scheme is something like BOSSQLPRD1, where BOS denotes the server location of Boston, SQL denotes the type of server, PRD denotes the category of server such as production or test, and 1 is the sequential number assigned and is incremented for every server. You may need to extend your naming convention or change it slightly to work with names for clustered entities such as the Windows server cluster, the nodes, and SQL Server itself.

When creating named instances, adhere to the following rules:

- Instance names are not case sensitive, so there is no difference between allan, Allan, and ALLAN.

- The words *default*, *MSSQLServer*, or any other SQL Server reserved keyword as defined in the Books Online topic "Instance Name" cannot be used; otherwise, an error will occur during setup.

- A named instance can have a maximum of 16 characters; otherwise, a setup error will occur. For example, MYNAMEDINSTANCE is valid because it does not exceed 16 characters, but MYSECONDNAMEDINSTANCE is not.

- The first character of the named instance must be a letter or an underscore (_). The letter must conform to the Unicode Standard version 2.0, which includes the standard Latin-based characters of A to Z and its lowercase equivalents, and some language-specific characters from various international character sets.

- The instance name must conform to the Windows code page on the nodes. If a Unicode character that is unsupported is used, setup will fail.

- All characters after the first can be any of the characters in Unicode Standard 2.0, numerics, the dollar sign ($), or an underscore.

- Spaces are not allowed; the named instance must be one contiguous string of characters. Other characters disallowed are the backslash (\), the comma (,), the colon (:), the semicolon (;), the single quote ('), the ampersand (&), and the at symbol (@).

Table 7-1 lists examples of both valid and invalid instance names on the same Windows failover cluster.

Table 7-1. *Example Clustered SQL Server Instance Names on a Single Windows Failover Cluster*

Instance Name	Valid	Reason
SQLINS	Yes	This name is not used for any other entity in the domain.
SQLINS\NI	No	SQLINS is already used in the domain, but the named instance of NI would be fine if SQLINS were valid.
SQLINS2\1NI	No	A named instance cannot start with a numeric.
SQLINS2\MY INSTANCE	No	A named instance cannot contain spaces.
SQLINS2\NI	Yes	Both SQLINS2 and NI are unique and conform to the named instance naming conventions.
SQLINS3\NI	No	While SQLINS3 is unique in the domain, NI is not unique on the Windows failover cluster.
SQLINS3\NI2	Yes	Both SQLINS3 and NI2 are unique and conform to the named instance naming conventions.

Clustering Analysis Services

If you need to cluster Analysis Services for availability purposes, as mentioned earlier, it is entirely possible with the release of SQL Server 2005. You do need to make some design decisions for deploying it, though. The recommended configuration for Analysis Services is that it be installed on its own into its own cluster resource group with its own dedicated disk resource, name, and IP address. The name and IP address must be different from anything else in the cluster or the domain, much like SQL Server itself.

However, if you want to conserve a name and an IP address and some disk space, you can install SQL Server and Analysis Services in the same group. You should be aware of the implications of this configuration. First and foremost, while you can still assign the Analysis Services resource its own dedicated disks, any Analysis Services system databases will be on the same drive as the SQL Server system databases. If you lose that disk, you potentially lose both Analysis Services and SQL Server. Analysis Services and SQL Server will also share a name and IP address. Whenever possible, you should install Analysis Services into its own resource group for availability purposes. Realistically, if both SQL Server and Analysis Services are on the same Windows failover cluster, you will have to worry about resource utilization (much as you would with multiple SQL Server instances), but the planning is not a completely different exercise.

The other thing that putting both in the same cluster group ties you to is that you may be forced to upgrade your Analysis Services installation at the same time as your SQL Server installation, even if you don't want to. Ultimately, the goal in your installation should be flexibility, and combining the two in a single cluster group reduces that.

Clustering Other SQL Server Components

Other than clustering the relational engine and Analysis Services, the other SQL Server 2005 features such as Reporting Services, Notification Services, and SQL Server Integration Services are not cluster-aware. If you install them on a cluster, they will be local to each node and would need to be installed per node. Microsoft published an article on how to cluster SQL Server Integration Services (http://msdn2.microsoft.com/en-us/library/ms345193.aspx), but essentially what you are doing is installing it on each node and creating a generic cluster resource to make it clustered. This does not make SQL Server Integration Services cluster-aware. If SQL Server Integration Services is critical for your uses of SQL Server, it is certainly an option worth looking into, but if you want to make any of the non–cluster aware services available, you may want to look at other ways of achieving that. Note that you can place the databases of Reporting Services on a clustered installation of SQL Server and make them available even though Reporting Services itself cannot be clustered. Another solution such as network load balancing may work for Reporting Services. The point is that you have options—you just need to explore what is available to you.

SQL Writer and Failover Clustering

The SQL Writer Service provides functionality for backup and restore of SQL Server 2005 through the Volume Shadow Copy Service (VSS) framework. The SQL Writer Service is installed on each node of the cluster during the installation process, but is disabled by default. If you will be using advanced backup strategies, you may need to enable it.

SQL Server Browser Service

The SQL Server Browser Service directs connection attempts that use instance names to the proper instance on the server. It is installed on each node in the cluster and is not cluster-aware. Unlike a stand-alone install of SQL Server 2005, SQL Server Browser Service is started automatically for a clustered instance of SQL Server.

Dependencies

As you learned back in Chapter 4, SQL Server in a clustered configuration will have resources contained in a single cluster resource group. Some of those resources have dependencies on others. If the parent resource cannot start, the child will not either. Figure 7-1 details the dependencies for a failover clustering implementation of SQL Server 2005.

It is very important that unless directed to in the next two chapters, you do not change how the dependencies are set up for SQL Server. You could potentially break your clustered implementation.

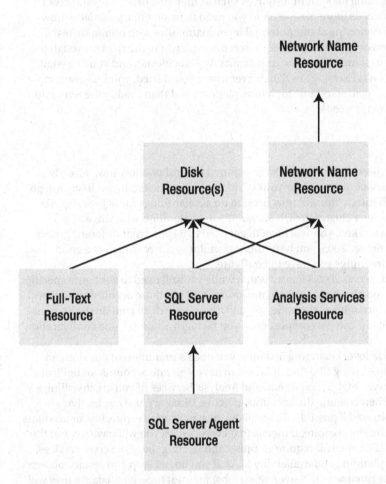

Figure 7-1. *SQL Server resource dependency tree*

Combining SQL Server 2005 and Exchange on the Same Windows Server Cluster

When companies want to maximize their IT budget, and they already have a cluster for either Exchange or SQL Server, they might be tempted to use it for both. While that's great on paper, it's horrible in reality. Think of it this way: would you intentionally put an open flame somewhere near an open gas valve to see if it will blow up? That may seem a bit extreme, but it drives the point home. I cannot comprehend why anyone would put two mission-critical, resource-intensive applications on the same cluster, knowing that they really may not play well in the sandbox together. Is this an unsupported configuration? No, but it is not a recommended one. Microsoft does not prevent you from doing this, much like stove manufacturers do not prevent you from sticking your bare hand on a hot burner. Both are dumb ideas of the first magnitude, but technically possible.

Ask yourself this question: would you combine SQL Server and Exchange on a regular stand-alone server in production? Nine times out of ten, the answer would most likely be no. There is always an exception to the rule, but there is the rule for a reason. The security risks alone should be a red flag. Do you want both fighting for system resources such as memory, processor, and disk I/O? What will you do if SQL Server needs more memory and you need to mix memory models—how will Exchange fare? What about worrying about potential incompatibilities with prerequisites? Combining these two major server applications is definitely one case where the risks outweigh the advantages. If you are looking to standardize how your availability is achieved, and you like what clustering has to offer, whether it is Exchange or SQL Server where you started, you may want to mandate that clustering is your "gold standard" for a base platform and then modify the template to suit your SQL Server or Exchange needs.

Security

If you have read the previous three chapters, you have planned for and possibly have already implemented domain-level service accounts for your Windows server cluster. If you have not, go back and read the Windows chapters. You will now need to do similar things for SQL Server. You cannot use any local accounts for a clustered SQL Server. If you are familiar with the way SQL Server 2000 failover clustering worked, you will have to get used to a somewhat different process in SQL Server 2005. With SQL Server 2005, you have more granular security (which is a good thing), and there are a few more things you have to configure.

The biggest change in SQL Server 2005 security is that while you still need to configure specific accounts at the domain level, you also need to configure groups and put those accounts into them. Instead of adding the individual accounts to the node, you add the groups which contain the accounts. This all sounds pretty simple, but it can get complex once you factor in a side-by-side configuration and/or multiple instances.

For each SQL Server 2005 failover clustering instance, you need a minimum of one domain account and one domain group. Having said that, it is best to have separate accounts for dedicated purposes: one each for SQL Server, SQL Server Agent, and Analysis Services (if you are installing a clustered Analysis Services). When creating the accounts in Active Directory, use names that are easy to remember, like **sqladmin**, and if possible, do not allow the password to expire. If your accounts have a security policy that makes them expire, it means that every N days you will have to reset the password. To change this in SQL Server will require stopping and starting the SQL Server services, so please factor that into your planning and availability SLAs. If you do not stop and restart, objects that use those service accounts (such as SQL Server Agent jobs) may not function because they will be using the old account information until you restart SQL Server.

Once you create your service accounts, you have to create domain groups. Depending on your configuration, you will need up to four groups: one for SQL Server itself, one for SQL Server Agent, one for Full-Text Search, and one for Analysis Services. These groups will contain the domain users that you created. For Full-Text Search, the SQL Server service account must be used and added to the group; otherwise, you will see the error in Figure 7-2 during the install process.

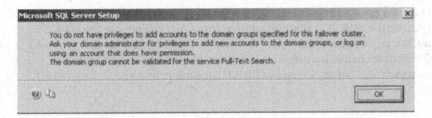

Figure 7-2. *Error during setup if the Full-Text Search group does not contain the SQL Server service account*

Other groups may show a message similar to Figure 7-3. You can avoid such errors if the cluster administrator account has the right privileges at the Active Directory level, but I do not recommend this as it would give the cluster administrator escalated privileges that it does not need. You will see similar messages for the other groups if the right accounts are not in them.

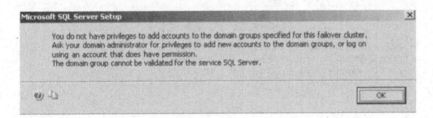

Figure 7-3. *Another group-related error*

The groups need to be placed in the local Administrator group on each node. You will need to assign different local rights depending on the group as listed in Table 7-2.

Table 7-2. *Rights Needed for SQL Server Groups*

Local Security Policy	SQL Server	SQL Server Agent	Analysis Services	Full-Text Search
Act as part of the operating system	Yes	Yes	No	No
Adjust memory quotas for a process	Yes	Yes	No	No
Bypass traverse checking	Yes	Yes	No	No
Log on as a batch job	Yes	Yes	No	No
Log on as a service	Yes	Yes	Yes	Yes
Replace a process-level token	Yes	Yes	No	No

The biggest issue you will now face is if you are going to use multiple instances on a cluster: the reality is that to have security for each instance, you must use separate domain accounts and groups for each instance. So if you plan on having four instances of SQL Server on your cluster, each with SQL Server, SQL Server Agent, and Full-Text Search, that is twelve groups and eight accounts. In my experience, it is hard enough to get one dedicated service account, let alone more than that. You must work with your security administrators to implement security that both protects your server and data, and fits into your corporate security standards.

The cluster must have access to your clustered SQL Server instance to run the LooksAlive and IsAlive checks. To do this, use the BUILTIN\Administrators account. You can remove the BUILTIN\ Administrators account, but you must add the cluster service account to SQL Server first. If you do not add the cluster administrator before moving it and are using only Windows Authentication, you may not be able to access your SQL Server. To remove BUILTIN\Administrators on a clustered SQL Server, see Chapter 8.

Installing SQL Server 2005 Failover Clustering Instances Side-by-Side with SQL Server 2000

A single Windows failover cluster can support both SQL Server 2000 and SQL Server 2005 in what is called a *side-by-side configuration*. Figures 7-4 and 7-5 show an example of such a configuration.

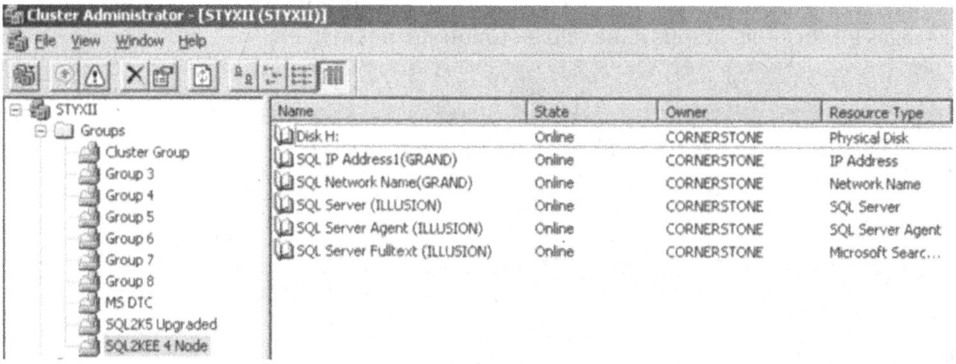

Figure 7-4. *Side-by-side SQL Server failover cluster configuration, SQL Server 2000 instance*

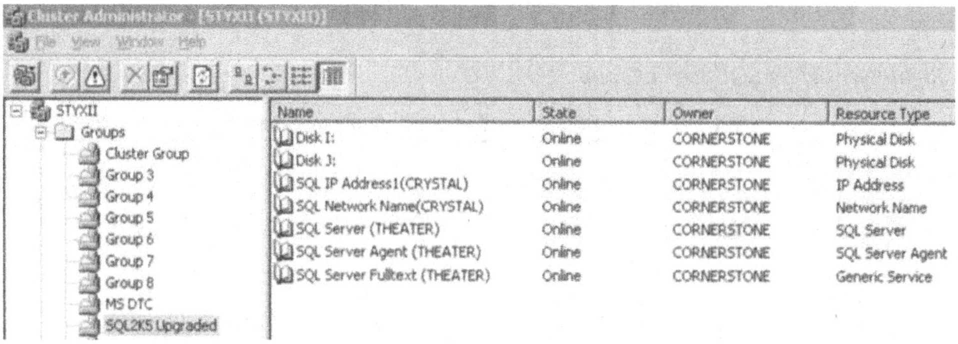

Figure 7-5. *Side-by-side SQL Server failover cluster configuration, SQL Server 2005 instance*

Following are some caveats to take into account when considering deploying SQL Server 2000 and SQL Server 2005 in a side-by-side configuration:

- You are still bound by the standard rules for named and default instances, so if your clustered SQL Server 2000 instance is already a default instance, any SQL Server 2005 instance cannot be a default instance unless you decide at some point to uninstall SQL Server 2000 from your cluster. The next instance installed after SQL Server 2000 is removed may use the newly vacated default instance.

- After installing SQL Server 2005, the SQL Server Native Client replaces the connectivity layer of SQL Server 2000, so you do not have a "pure" SQL Server 2000 implementation. This has been tested by the Microsoft development team and should not cause any problems, but you should fully test such a configuration prior to using it in production to make sure your applications function properly.

- Do not reuse the same domain service accounts for your SQL Server 2000 and SQL Server 2005 instances in a side-by-side configuration. If you do, you will bypass all of the new security enhancements in SQL Server 2005. You must use new domain-based service accounts.

- If you decide to remove the SQL Server 2005 installation(s), you must leave the SQL Server Native Client. Removing the SQL Server Native Client will cause any SQL Server 2000 instance to stop working. If this happens, reinstall the SQL Server 2005 Native Client to bring SQL Server 2000 back to life.

- Using mount points with your SQL Server 2005 instances where you already have a clustered SQL Server 2000 instance results in an invalid configuration. If you want to use mount points, you have to either directly upgrade your existing instance to SQL Server 2005 or install your new instance on new hardware.

- You cannot use the SQL Server 2000 toolset to administer a SQL Server 2005 instance whether the tools are local or remote. You must use the ones installed with SQL Server 2005. If you attempt to use most of the tools, you will see errors. An example is shown in Figure 7-6. You may even encounter "weird" things you should not normally see, such as the node name being displayed in SQL Server 2000 Service Manager as shown in Figure 7-7. These are expected behaviors. Behind the scenes, SQL Server is using a different method of coding called *SQL Management Objects* (SMO) to communicate to SQL Server. Versions of SQL Server prior to SQL Server 2005 used Distributed Management Objects (DMO), which does not support the new features of SQL Server 2005. The only SQL Server 2000 program that works well with SQL Server 2005 is Query Analyzer.

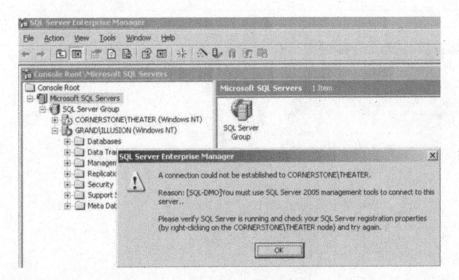

Figure 7-6. *Enterprise Manager and SQL Server 2005 instances*

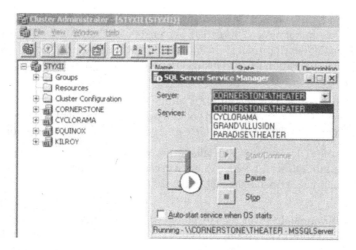

Figure 7-7. *Service Manager on the same node with a clustered SQL Server 2005 instance*

■ **Note** You cannot upgrade existing SQL Server 2000 failover clustering instances (which would be installed using either SQL Server 2000 Developer Edition or SQL Server 2000 Enterprise Edition) to SQL Server 2005 Standard Edition. If you attempt to do this, during the setup process, you will see dialog boxes similar to Figures 7-8 and 7-9. Even though SQL Server 2005 supports failover clustering with Standard Edition, you must also consider that you will be losing functionality by switching from Enterprise Edition in production. Microsoft is essentially blocking your application from using a feature that it relies on in Enterprise Edition when you "down-grade" to Standard Edition. To upgrade or switch to a clustered SQL Server 2005 Standard Edition instance, you can install your new instance of SQL Server 2005 Standard Edition and then migrate your databases using your preferred method, such as backup and restore, log shipping, SSIS, and so on.

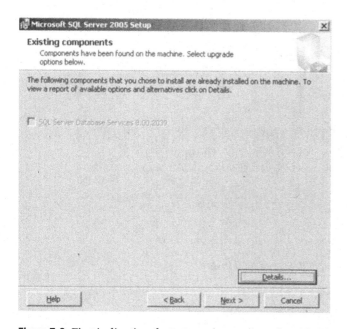

Figure 7-8. *First indication that attemping to upgrade a 2000 instance will be a problem*

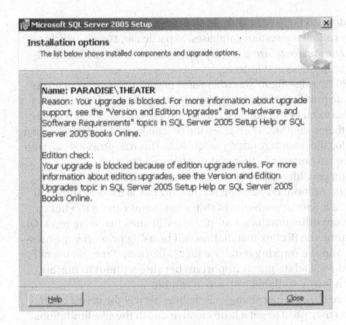

Figure 7-9. *Example error description for an invalid upgrade*

Installing Local Instances and Clustered Instances on the Same Hardware

Installation of local, nonclustered instances of SQL Server on servers that are participating as nodes in a cluster is fully supported. Some exceptions may exist, such as applications that use the desktop versions of SQL Server. The whole purpose of implementing clusters is to make your SQL Servers highly available. It makes no sense to mix and match clustered and nonclustered instances of SQL Server on the same hardware. A good rule to institute is that if you are implementing clusters, all instances must be clustered, as it will make administration easier and reduce confusion.

Disk Configuration

Deciding how you will configure your disks for use with a clustered instance of SQL Server will be one of the hardest configuration choices in this process, with the other being the configuration of a cluster that has multiple instances. You already know that you need drive letters, a single cluster resource group can only contain a single clustered instance of SQL Server, and the drives in a resource group can only be used by that one instance. You also know that at a minimum, four drive letters are most likely already taken: the quorum, the drive for MS DTC, your local system drive, and some sort of optical drive like a CD or a DVD drive. There may be a fifth drive letter unavailable, since many servers still have a floppy drive in them. Out of the gate, you are already at either 21 or 22 possible drive letters that you can use. Some companies map shared drives, so that may take up another drive or two.

As you know, the recommended best practice is to always split data files from their associated log files. Without getting into the direct performance reasons (see Chapter 14 for more information on the performance considerations for disk configurations with SQL Server), think of a consolidated SQL Server that has tens or hundreds of databases: you cannot place each database and its corresponding log on separate disks when you have at most 20 to 23 drive letters available to you. You have to be realistic about what you are trying to achieve in terms of both performance and availability. You will have to share some drives with other databases, so you have to know each database's I/O characteristics to make intelligent decisions. Do not forget about the system databases, in particular, `tempdb`, which may need to be on its own drive for performance reasons. Size is also a problem as described in Chapter 4—you are limited by how big you can make the disks in Windows.

If you are having trouble, use the 80/20 rule—figure out where 80% of your I/O is going in terms of data and logs. Remember that reads do not hit the log file (reads only occur when doing a transaction log backup and would be minimal to no overhead). Place those data and log files that represent 80% of your total I/O requirements on their own disks. Then place the remaining 20% of data files on a single data disk, with their transaction log files sharing another single disk. This rule provides you with a logical starting point, but you may need to perform further optimizations and tuning.

The easiest way to show the design considerations for a clustered instance of SQL Server is by example. Consider a BizTalk implementation. Depending on how BizTalk is used by the application, you will be using different BizTalk databases. Some of those databases can be I/O heavy, which dictates that they be split out from other databases (or placed with ones that have low I/O). For the purposes of this example, assume the BizTalk installation will be using primarily the Message Box database (`BizTalkMsgBoxDb`) and the tracking database (`BizTalkDTADb`). From an overall BizTalk implementation standpoint, the SSO database is important because without it, BizTalk cannot run. It has very low I/O, but if it is not available, you are in trouble.

Knowing these parameters, you need to consider sizing as well: how big will the drives be? If you are creating a 30TB warehouse, you may need to get a little creative due to the size limitations imposed by Windows. Your drive sizes should be manageable, and in the event that `chkdsk` needs to run, it will not take forever to do so. If `chkdsk` needs to run after, say, a failover and a reboot, you may potentially be waiting hours and blow your SLAs out of the water.

You should also keep in mind a drive or two may go to storing backups. These drives need to be dependencies (like all data and log drives) of the SQL Server resource, and will arguably provide the best storage for your backups for a clustered instance of SQL Server.

Configuration Considerations for Multiple SQL Server Instances on the Same Windows Server Cluster

One of the complaints I have heard from many customers over the years in regards to a clustered configuration relates to what everyone seems to refer to as *wasted resources*. You can configure your SQL Server failover clustering instances in one of two ways: in a single-instance configuration or one with multiple instances. A single instance is the easiest configuration: you install one clustered instance of SQL Server on your Windows server cluster, and you should always have the resources to run it on either node because nothing else is consuming resources.

The single instance on a cluster leads to that customer complaint I mentioned. The exchange usually goes something like this:

Customer: So what you are telling me is I am spending all this money to buy two identical N processor servers with M gigabytes of memory, and one of them is going to sit there completely unused, just waiting for the SQL Server to fail?

Me: Yes, that is the case. In the event of a failover of your SQL Server instance, everything will perform at the same level as it did previously.

Customer: Are you serious? That is a waste. I want my servers utilized to their maximum capabilities. I only have so much in the budget available to me, and it needs to stretch as far as it can go.

Believe me, I am not unsympathetic to the fact that budgets are tight, and every server resource and dollar, yen, euro, or whatever local currency you use is precious. It is no secret that getting the maximum value from scaled-down budgets is imperative, but there is a point where continuing to cut costs will impact your availability and performance. You can achieve a well-tuned, multiple-instance SQL Server failover cluster, but it takes quite a bit of planning. If you think you are actually going to get 25 instances on your cluster, I would suggest you rethink your implementation. Just because you technically can do it or are allowed to do it does not mean you can or should. Use your common sense.

The obvious first consideration is your disk configuration, which was discussed in the previous section and to some degree in Chapter 4. Each SQL Server instance will require its own dedicated disk resources as noted in Chapter 4 and earlier in this chapter. They cannot be shared across resource groups, and therefore across instances. Since only 21 or 22 of your drive letters may be available (possibly more if your company maps shared drives on each desktop or server), you are already starting behind the proverbial eight ball. Then you have the quorum and MS DTC drives, which account for two more drives. Your best-case scenario is having 23 drive letters available to your SQL Server instances if you only have the quorum, MS DTC, and a single local drive already using a drive letter.

If you then want to split out all of your data and log files to the *N*th degree for performance reasons—which may be overkill—you may not be able to do it. If you have 12 databases you want to put on that instance, assuming a simple ratio of one data file (no file/filegroup configuration) to one log file, you will need a total of 24 drive letters to split everything out. This does not even take into account the system databases. Do you sense the problem already? The bottom line is that you must put a lot of thinking into your design when implementing a single instance of SQL Server on a cluster, let alone multiple instances. An example of a cluster disk solution is shown in Chapter 14.

Next you have to address both processor and memory contention. The biggest item is that each separate SQL Server instance consumes around 250KB of memory just for its own separate copy of the service—which is something that does not change. While in some ways this is much more of a gray area because everyone has slightly different views of server usage, when it comes to clusters, this is pretty much a case of black and white. What you are designing against is the worst-case scenario where all of your instances will have to run at the same time on a single node. The analogy I have used for years is this: think of a glass of your favorite beverage. The glass has a maximum capacity. Once you exceed that capacity, the excess liquid will spill over the sides. The failover scenario is very much the same.

Consider the following five-instance, four-node configuration:

- Instance 1 requires 4GB of memory and averages 40% CPU utilization on a 4-processor server.

- Instance 2 requires 2GB of memory and averages 23% CPU utilization on a 4-processor server.

- Instance 3 requires 6GB of memory and averages 25% CPU utilization on a 4-processor server.

- Instance 4 requires 3GB of memory and averages 35% CPU utilization on a 4-processor server.

- Instance 5 requires 5GB of memory and averages 43% CPU utilization on a 4-processor server.

Do the simple math. The total amount of memory needed just for all these SQL Server instances in the single-server failover cases is 20GB of memory. The CPU usage adds up to 166%. Clearly, you can throw money at the memory: Windows Server 2003 Enterprise Edition supports up to 32GB or 64GB of RAM depending on your architecture, and Datacenter Edition supports even more. The CPU issue is partially a money problem—you could certainly buy more processors, but is that the right thing to do? There are no real ways around the physics here. Also, keep in mind that you need both memory and CPU for the base operating system as well as any other software and processes running on the node. Even if SQL Server is technically the only application running, there are other things going on.

You can take these five instances, put them on four nodes smartly, and minimize your risk in several ways. First, decide how you want to lay the nodes out. Each node will have 8GB of memory. Following is one valid configuration permutation, also shown in Figure 7-10.

Node 1: Instance 1

Node 2: Instance 2 and Instance 4

Node 3: Instance 3

Node 4: Instance 5

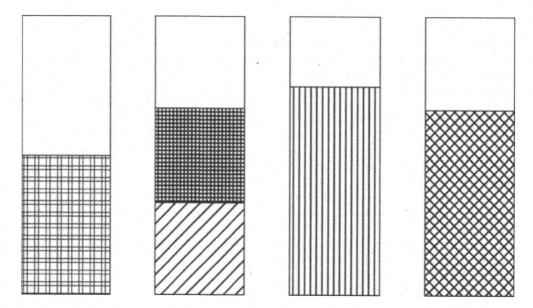

Figure 7-10. *Five SQL Server instances balanced on four cluster nodes*

In a perfect world where no failovers occur, all of these would work because all come in at under 100% CPU utilization and 100% of all memory consumed. If you are not going to buy another node, you can decide in what order you want the instance to fail. For example, for Instance 1, you could set Node 3 as the primary failover node, and then order the others. To allow such scenarios, after installing SQL Server into a cluster, Windows failover clustering allows you to set the failover preferences for each resource group. If you decide to change the preferred failover node for an instance, ensure that no single node will become overburdened by being able to own multiple SQL Server instances at any one time since you are taking the decision-making control away from Windows. To set this, see the section "Setting the Preferred Node Order for Failover" in Chapter 8.

Realistically, for the most part you are still not going to escape the laws of implementing hardware. At some point, you will exceed capacity on a single node in a failover, especially when out of your five instances, one consumes 6GB of memory and all of your nodes have only 8GB of memory. However, there is one way to get around this. You can configure what is known as an *N+1 failover cluster*, where you have a dedicated failover node (the +1) over and above the nodes you are using for your application that will serve as the primary failover node. This is beneficial in the sense that statistically, the chance of all of your instances failing at once is pretty small. You may lose a single server at any given time, but more than that indicates a bigger problem in your ecosystem, such as a full disk subsystem failure. That is something you need to mitigate and plan for whether or not you have multiple instances. You can configure that one failover node with additional memory and processor capacity to ensure that in the worst-case scenario, all instances, or at least most of them, will run smoothly on that one node. For example, you could give that one node eight processors and 24GB of memory. An example of the $N+1$ node cluster is shown in Figure 7-11. The larger node is shown roughly in scale due to capacity.

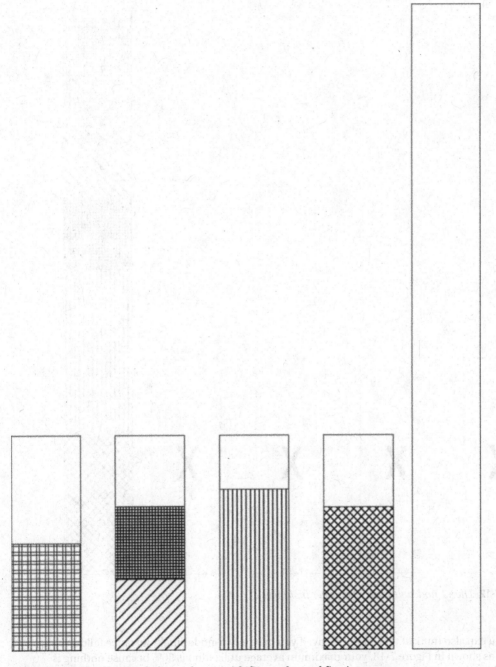

Figure 7-11. *Example N+1 failover cluster with five nodes and five instances*

Figure 7-12 demonstrates the worst-case failover scenario.

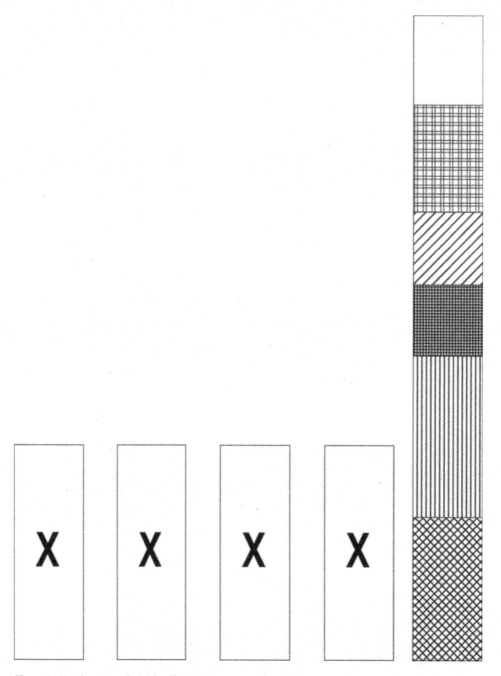

Figure 7-12. *The +1 node with all SQL Server instances*

You can also think of this another way: if you have a two-node single-instance failover cluster as shown in Figure 7-13, your maximum average utilization is 50% because nothing is installed on the second node, and you can have a maximum of 100% utilization on the first node, so 100 – (100+0)/2 = 50. So if you consider the example of a two-node cluster where each node has 8GB of memory and you give 1GB to Windows, you have 7GB of memory available for that one instance, and you can use all available resources with no worry about contention in a failover.

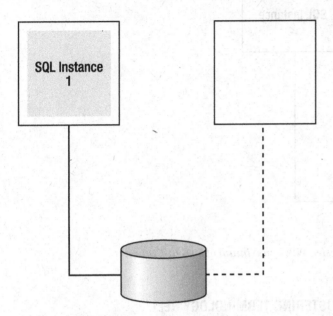

Figure 7-13. *Single-instance cluster with a maximum of 50% utilization*

If you want to better utilize your two nodes and add another instance of SQL Server, you can do that. However, you will discover that if you do things properly, you may not be getting any more utilization. If you are planning properly, at most you will use 50% of each node, taking into account the failover situation for each instance, so (50+50)/2 = 50 (see Figure 7-14). If you translate that into a physical implementation, assume each node has 8GB of memory. Allowing 1GB for the OS on each node, that leaves 7GB available per node for use by SQL Server. If you have two instances that you want to make sure will not starve each other in a failover, you are looking at a maximum of 3.5GB of memory per instance if both are equal. If your memory requirements are more than 3.5GB of memory, you start playing Russian roulette if you do not take into account the failover condition.

Last, but certainly not least, you need to think about anything you do to one instance that may affect another. I am not just referring to a problem occurring on one node causing a failure, which then causes multiple SQL Server instances to fail over to another node. Consider what happens when you install a SQL Server 2005 Service Pack (as described in Chapter 16). A SQL Server 2005 Service Pack updates components that are shared among all instances (including SQL tools for all instances back through SQL Server 7.0) as well as potentially updating or requiring the update of the Windows point version, the Internet Explorer version, the MDAC version, the SQL Server Native Client version, and the MSXML version, and leaves ones dedicated to that instance alone unless they are being updated. This means you will essentially be in a mixed state that is fully supported—your shared components are at one level/version and your dedicated components at another—but is this supported by your application? Assuming you have a dedicated staging and/or test environment, you can prove this beforehand. Not only do you need to worry about compatibility and mixed levels, but what happens if you patch one instance for whatever reason and it requires a reboot? This will affect anything else running on the node.

If you are beginning to get the idea that configuring a failover cluster for SQL Server is not easy, you are correct. It takes a lot of thought to do it right.

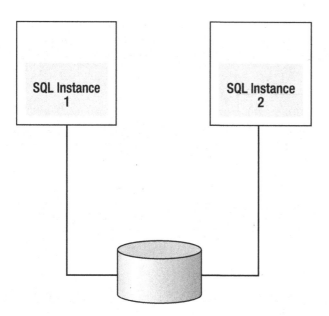

Figure 7-14. *Multiple-instance failover cluster with a maximum of 50% utilization*

FAILOVER CLUSTERING TERMINOLOGY HELL

Over the years, two terms have become linked to SQL Server clustering: *Active/Passive* and *Active/Active*. Those terms are at best loosely accurate, and with SQL Server 2000 (as well as in the book *SQL Server 2000 High Availability* published by Microsoft Press in 2003 and various whitepapers I have written since 2001), I fought hard to change the use of those terms, yet the terminology battle wages on. So I will state my case again here.

The history of Active/Passive and Active/Active stems from about 1998, when with a clustered SQL Server 7.0 installation, you could have at most two installs of SQL Server on a single Windows failover cluster. In that context, Active/Passive and Active/Active both make perfect sense. SQL Server then adopted the instance model in SQL Server 2000, allowing you to break the barrier of two installs per single Windows server cluster with a maximum of 16 instances on a single Windows server cluster. If you only install a single clustered instance of SQL Server in your cluster, Active/Passive is technically still valid because only one node may be active at any given time. But if you have eight instances spread out over four nodes, are you going to call this Active/Active/Active/Active or Active/Active/Active/Active/Active/Active/Active/Active, depending on whether you are addressing the number of SQL Server instances or the number of nodes? If you configure all of your SQL Server instances in one way, this makes sense, but since you are not bound to do it one way, it can become confusing. With SQL Server 2000, the terms *single instance failover cluster* and *multiple instance failover cluster* were introduced. Because people seem to be stuck on the whole "Active" thing, you may hear the terms *single active-instance failover cluster* and *multiple active instance failover cluster*.

The next time you are tempted to use the ever-popular Active/Passive or Active/Active terms, put some thought into what you actually are trying to say because Active/Active can also be applied to Exchange clusters or even Windows itself. When you are referring to SQL Server in a clustered environment, it is always better to include enough information to describe how your cluster is actually configured because Active/Active can mean different things to different people—especially when you now can also go beyond two nodes in a Windows server cluster.

Upgrading to SQL Server 2005 Failover Clustering

The scenarios for upgrading an existing installation of SQL Server to a clustered SQL Server 2005 installation are cut and dry: if you have an existing clustered instance, you can upgrade it, and if you have a stand-alone instance, you cannot. This behavior is changed from SQL Server 2000, which did have the ability to upgrade from a stand-alone instance of SQL Server. With SQL Server 2005, you also have the ability to upgrade a SQL Server 2005 Standard Edition failover clustering instance to Enterprise Edition.

Note This section assumes you are doing your due diligence on testing your databases and applications (such as running Microsoft's Upgrade Advisor) to ensure that they work properly with SQL Server 2005. This section discusses only the technical considerations for an upgrade from a purely IT view.

You can approach a highly available upgrade to a SQL Server 2005 failover clustering instance in multiple ways. If you do an in-place upgrade, which is a direct upgrade of an existing failover clustering instance, your SQL Server 2000 instance must be configured with SQL Server 2000 Service Pack 4. If you are at any other service pack level, you cannot do an in-place upgrade. Keep in mind the following two issues with doing an in-place upgrade:

1. If your only cluster is in production, the first time you will be performing the upgrade will be on your production instance. This is not an ideal situation. You should have a staging environment in which to try it.

2. Doing an in-place upgrade means that you have to be 100% confident that nothing will go wrong. If it does, you will most likely have to reinstall Windows and SQL Server, and then use backups of your databases to get back to your previous state.

If you are upgrading from a stand-alone instance or want a better recoverability scenario, you have a few options. It is always better to get SQL Server 2005 up, running, and tested to ensure that it works right before migrating your databases. Since you can rename a clustered SQL Server 2005 instance (see the next section), it expands your options. If you are in a side-by-side configuration, once you are confident everything works properly and you can uninstall your SQL Server 2000 instance, you can rename the SQL Server 2005 instance to the old SQL Server 2000 name.

The best ways I have found to upgrade to a clustered SQL Server 2005 instance when not doing an in-place upgrade are as follows:

- Detach the databases from your old SQL Server install, copy them to the location on the shared disk array, and attach them in SQL Server 2005.

- Use log shipping (see Chapter 10 for complete information on log shipping).

- Employ the tried-and-true method of using backups of the databases and restoring them on your new failover clustering instance.

Upgrading Analysis Services 2005 in a Clustered Environment

There are a few extra caveats for upgrades to SQL Server 2005 Analysis Services. In these cases, you may need to pick a temporary name for your instance (whether named or default). The upgrade will install this new named instance beside existing instances and perform a *migration* (a copy of the data). Once you are happy that the migration meets your needs, you complete the upgrade by kicking off a separate process outside of setup that removes your original instance and renames your upgraded instance to the original instance's name. This is required due to some underlying changes in the data structures. Note that this is a one-time occurrence, and once up on Analysis Services 2005, you should not need to perform this action again for service pack or hotfix installations for the foreseeable future.

> ## WHY DOESN'T SQL SERVER 2005 FAILOVER CLUSTERING SCALE OUT LIKE OFFERINGS FROM OTHER DATABASE VENDORS?
>
> This question has to rank up there as one of the ones I am most frequently asked since I started using and implementing clustering. Simply put, Microsoft and other software vendors have different design approaches to availability and clusters. Microsoft's approach is just as valid as any other out there.
>
> Microsoft's implementation of a failover cluster in SQL Server is as a software-based availability offering that is built upon the Windows clustering feature. The Microsoft shared-nothing architecture allows only the combination of a single resource group and its resources owned by a node to be able to be accessed by that node. A fully shared architecture would mean that the vendor coding the software to run on the cluster would have to devise some sort of lock mechanism to ensure that things like write order are preserved so that a request coming in from an end user or application from one node does not somehow trump a request from another at the same time. There cannot be chaos at the low level. The other thing to consider is that while such shared architectures allow multiple servers to do processing and create redundancy that way, you are still accessing one copy of the data. Your shared disk, which contains the database and its associated files, is a single point of failure as well as a potential bottleneck for scalability if it is not designed to be highly performing. This is not unlike Microsoft's shared-nothing model, in which your disk subsystem is going to be your single point of failure more often than not.
>
> Microsoft has taken its first strides into the shared database arena with SQL Server 2005. It introduced support for read-only, shared scale-out databases even on clusters. For more information and the steps on how to implement such a solution, consult Microsoft Knowledge Base Article 910378, "Scalable shared databases are supported by SQL Server 2005" (http://support.microsoft.com/kb/910378/en-us).
>
> Oracle's implementation of clustering is known as *RAC*, and while it can increase the availability of your database implementation, it is more of a performance offering. It allows you to scale out by having multiple Oracle servers hitting a single shared database on the back end. This means the workload is distributed among the multiple servers, but your single point of failure and potential bottleneck will become your shared database (as well as your disk subsystem). A locking mechanism is also employed to ensure that the multiple servers hitting the single database do not corrupt or somehow mess up your data. So while the perception is that this is a "better" solution for your databases, you do not necessarily get better availability or scalability than from implementing a traditional Microsoft SQL Server failover cluster and using the methods available to you within SQL Server to scale out. Oracle just gives you an easier scale-out solution out of the box, but it is not a cheap solution. Your basic Oracle implementations generally do not consider RAC. Like Microsoft's clustering, it is an advanced configuration that may require special attention and skilled administrators to know how to deal with it.
>
> SQL Server Analysis Services "clustering" is a different animal entirely (and different from the failover clustering abilities of Analysis Services 2005). It is a data-mining algorithm, first shipped in SQL Server 2000, that sorts through the large amount of data inside your Analysis Services cubes in order to find "groups" of similar areas based on some series of aggregation and prioritization rules you define. Because it's finding groupings of similar data within a statistical set, the algorithm was named "clustering" after the "clusters" of similar data it discovers. Therefore, it is not something that adds performance or availability to your Analysis Services configuration.

Summary

Along with the Windows server cluster information presented in Chapter 4, you have now been presented with the planning building blocks for implementing your SQL Server 2005 failover cluster. The two hardest things to get right at the planning stage are how you will deal with performance issues (memory/CPU) in a multiple instance failover cluster and your disk configuration. Because these two aspects are not easy, it gives the perception that failover clustering is more difficult to implement. Most of the other configuration points are more straightforward. Once you have your plan, which takes into account both Windows and SQL Server, you can then move on to implementation.

CHAPTER 8

■ ■ ■

Failover Clustering: Clustering SQL Server 2005

Y ou have spent the past four chapters preparing for this moment: installing SQL Server in a failover cluster configuration.

■Caution If you have installed one of the beta or CTP editions of SQL Server 2005 on your hardware, you should completely uninstall Windows and reinstall the operating system prior to installing the released version of SQL Server 2005. Some of the early SQL Server 2005 betas included versions of MDAC and the .NET Framework that cannot be uninstalled or replaced and are not compatible with the shipped version of SQL Server 2005.

Step 1: Ensure the Windows Failover Cluster Is Configured Properly

I cannot stress enough that before you install SQL Server, you should check, recheck, and check once more your Windows server cluster configuration, as described in Chapters 4, 5, and 6. If it is wrong in any way, it will wind up causing you a lot of frustration either during the SQL Server install or at some point soon thereafter. Remember that you need to install and configure the Microsoft Distributed Transaction Coordinator. It is required for installing a clustered SQL Server instance. Once you are sure that your Windows server cluster is functioning properly, only then can you move on to the SQL Server–specific tasks.

■Tip If you keep encountering problems, sometimes it is better to start from scratch than it is to spend hours, days, or weeks troubleshooting an issue at this stage. Reinstalling sounds like it may be more time-consuming, but if you missed just one little check mark in a dialog box somewhere, it will be like looking for a needle in a haystack.

Step 2: Create the SQL Server 2005 Failover Clustering Service Accounts and Groups

The first task from a SQL Server standpoint is to create the right users and groups in the domain and then assign them the right permissions on each node so that SQL Server will function properly.

Creating the SQL Server Service Accounts

To create the SQL Server service accounts, follow these steps:

1. Log on to one of the servers as an administrator who has rights to add accounts to the domain.

2. From Administrative Tools, start the Active Directory Users and Computers tool.

3. In the left pane, expand the domain, right-click Users, and select New ➤ User.

4. In the New Object – User dialog box, you must enter at least a first name or a last name, as well as the user logon name. Figure 8-1 shows an example. Click Next.

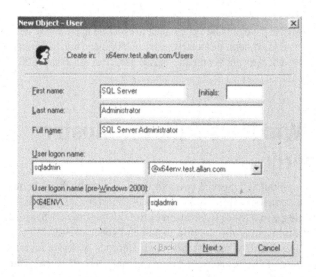

Figure 8-1. *Creating the SQL Server service account*

5. Enter a password for the account in the Password box, and enter it again in the Confirm Password box. Deselect the option User Must Change Password at Next Logon, and if your security policy allows it, select the Password Never Expires option. Figure 8-2 shows an example. Click Next.

6. Click Finish to complete the account creation process, as shown in Figure 8-3.

7. To verify that the account is created, select Users in the left pane of Active Directory Users and Computers. The account you just created will appear on the right side.

8. Repeat steps 3–7 to create a domain account for Analysis Services and SQL Server Agent depending on your implementation needs.

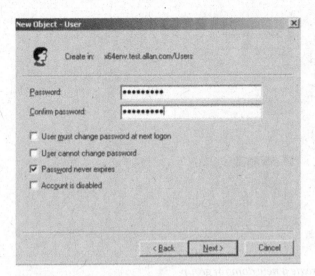

Figure 8-2. *Creating the account password*

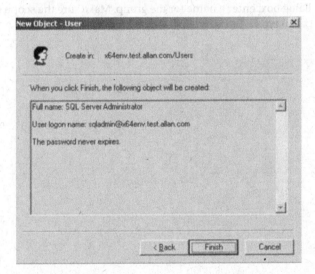

Figure 8-3. *Completing the account creation*

Creating the SQL Server–Related Cluster Groups

To create the SQL Server–related cluster groups, follow these steps:

1. Log on to one of the servers as an administrator who has rights to add accounts to the domain.

2. From Administrative Tools, start the Active Directory Users and Computers tool.

3. In the left pane, expand the domain, right-click Users, and select New ➤ Group, as shown in Figure 8-4.

Figure 8-4. *Menu option to create a new domain group*

4. In the New Object – Group dialog box, enter a name for the group. Make sure the scope of the group is Global and the group type is Security, as shown in Figure 8-5. Click OK.

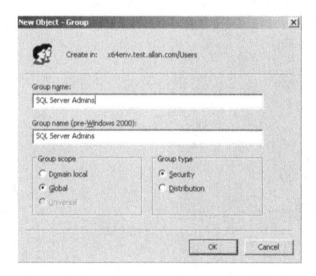

Figure 8-5. *New Object – Group dialog box*

5. Repeat steps 3 and 4 for SQL Server Agent, Analysis Services (if needed), and Full-Text (if needed). Figure 8-6 shows the result of all four groups created.

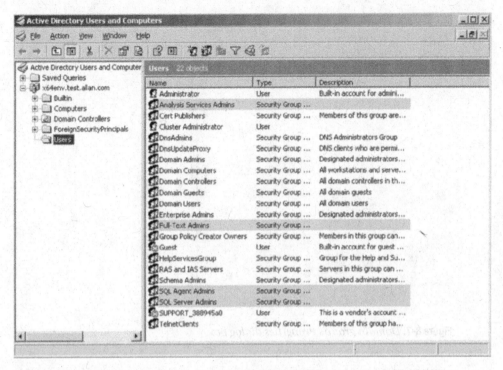

Figure 8-6. *Active Directory Computers and Users after all the domain groups are created*

Adding the SQL Server Service Accounts to the Cluster Groups

To add the SQL Server service accounts to the cluster groups, follow these steps:

1. Log on to one of the servers as an administrator who has rights to add accounts to the domain.

2. From Administrative Tools, start the Active Directory Users and Computers tool.

3. In the right pane, select the group you want to add an account to, right-click, and select Properties; alternatively, double-click the group name. You will see the Properties dialog box for the group, as shown in Figure 8-7.

4. Click Add. In the Select Users, Contacts, or Computers dialog box shown in Figure 8-8, enter the name (or partial name) of the domain user you want to add to the domain group. Click Check Names, and the name will be resolved, as shown in Figure 8-9. Click OK.

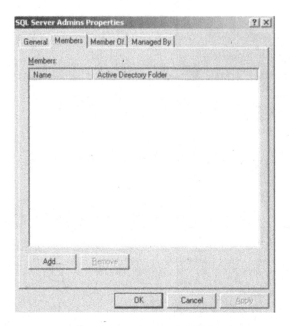

Figure 8-7. *Domain group's Properties dialog box*

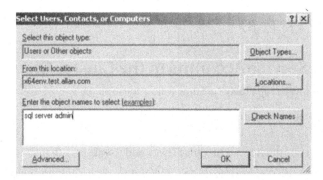

Figure 8-8. *Select Users, Contacts, or Computers dialog box*

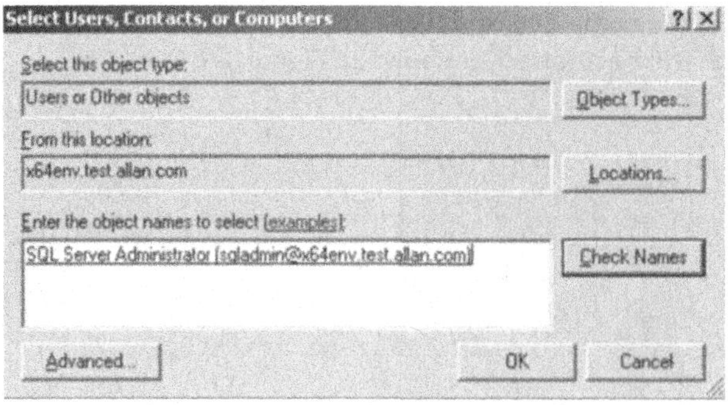

Figure 8-9. *Resolved name*

5. The user will now be part of the domain group, as shown in Figure 8-10. Repeat steps 3 and 4 to add other users to the same group.

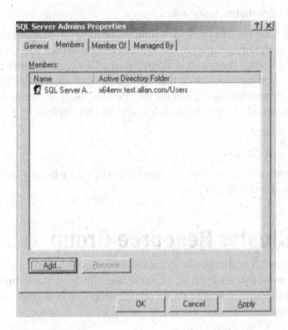

Figure 8-10. *Added user*

6. Repeat steps 3–5 for the other resource groups you created.

Adding the Cluster Groups to Each Node

To add the cluster groups to each node, follow these steps:

1. Log on to one of the servers that will be a node in the cluster with an account that has the administrative access to add and modify users.

2. From Administrative Tools, start the Computer Management tool.

3. Expand Local Users and Groups, and select Groups.

4. In the right pane, select Administrators, right-click, and select the Add to Group option or double-click Administrators.

5. In the Administrators Properties dialog box, click Add.

6. In the Select Users, Computers, or Groups dialog box, verify that the From This Location value is set to the domain. If not, click Locations, and then in the Locations dialog box, select the right domain. Click OK in the Locations dialog box to return.

7. Enter the name of the SQL Server domain group you created earlier in the Enter the Object Names to Select box. Click Check Names. The group will be validated against the domain. Click OK. The Administrators Property will now reflect the addition of the account.

8. Repeat step 7 for all groups needed for your implementation.

9. Click Apply and then OK.

10. From Administrative Tools, select Local Security Policy.

11. Expand Local Policies, and select User Rights Assignment.

12. Refer to the section on security in Chapter 7 to see which policies need to be assigned to each domain group. If the policy is already granted to the Administrators group, you do not need to add it to the domain groups since the group is already part of the local Administrators group. If you need to add a policy, right-click it in the right pane, and select Properties; alternatively, double-click it. The Properties dialog box for the specific policy will be shown and will be similar to the one displayed in step 5. Repeat this step for all policies.

13. Exit Local Security Policy when finished.

14. Log off the node on which you are working.

15. Log on to another node, and repeat steps 2–14 until the domain groups have been added to every node that will participate in the failover cluster.

Step 3: Rename the Cluster Resource Group

For ease of identification and administration, it is always recommended that you rename the cluster resource group in Cluster Administrator to something that makes sense. This is optional, but in the event of a problem, you will lose valuable time trying to figure out which group is the right one you should be viewing. The most common name given is usually the name of the instance.

To rename the cluster resource group, follow these steps:

1. Start Cluster Administrator.

2. In the left pane, expand Groups. Right-click the group that contains the disk that will be used during the installation process for SQL Server, and select Rename. Enter the new name for the resource group to be something logical such as the actual instance name (default or named) or something like **SQL Server 2005 Enterprise Edition**, and hit Enter.

Step 4: Install .NET Framework 2.0

You must now install the .NET Framework 2.0 on each node of your cluster, unless it is already installed. This software is a prerequisite of SQL Server 2005 and will take a little while to install. If it is not installed, SQL Server 2005 will not be able to install or run on the node.

Note Although SQL Server Setup for SQL Server 2005 detects whether the .NET Framework is not present on the node or nodes and would install it for you, what happens is that because the installation takes some time, it appears that the SQL Server Setup is hung. If you see that and then reboot or do something else, your servers will be in an inconsistent state. It is much better to just install this yourself or put it as part of your standard Windows Server 2003 build.

To install the .NET Framework 2.0, follow these steps:

1. Download the .NET Framework 2.0 from http://www.microsoft.com/downloads.

2. Double-click the executable (such as dotnetfx.exe for x86 and NetFx64.exe for x64). On the Welcome to the Microsoft .NET Framework 2.0 Setup page, which will be similar to the one shown in Figure 8-11, click Next.

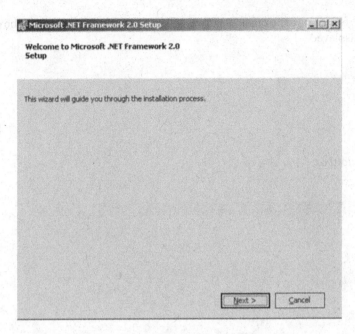

Figure 8-11. *.NET Framework 2.0 Welcome page*

3. On the End-User License Agreement page, read and accept the agreement, as shown in Figure 8-12. Click Install.

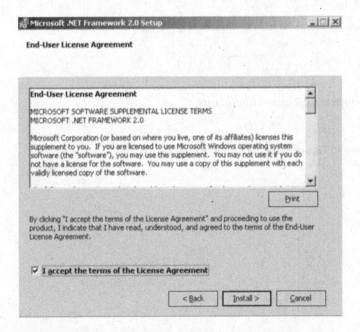

Figure 8-12. *.NET Framework 2.0 end-user license agreement*

You will see a message similar to the one in Figure 8-13, and then the progress dialog box in Figure 8-14 will be displayed.

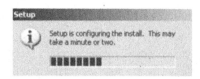

Figure 8-13. *Setup dialog box*

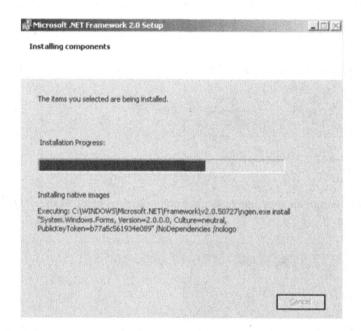

Figure 8-14. *.NET Framework 2.0 installation status*

4. Click Finish, as shown in Figure 8-15, to complete the process.

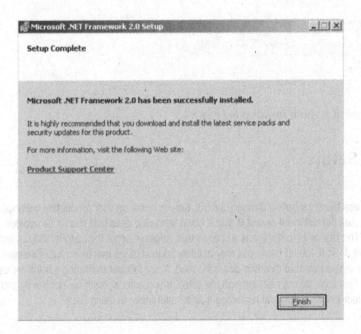

Figure 8-15. *Completed .NET Framework 2.0 installation*

Step 5: Install SQL Server 2005

Here comes the payoff for doing all of the preparation: actually installing SQL Server. You have two ways of installing: the traditional way through a graphic-based setup process or via the command line. You should be aware that the command-line install can potentially be more flexible for customizing your installation, so if you will be deploying multiple instances, you may want to try doing it that way.

One change that you may not like in the setup process is that unlike SQL Server where the install process puts all the SQL Server management tools on every node of the cluster, if you choose to install the management tools as part of the SQL Server 2005 cluster install, you will get the tools only on the node that initiates the install. You will have to install the tools on the other nodes after you install SQL Server.

You should also be aware that the headers of some of the screens during the install may indicate what version you are installing, such as x64.

Caution Although it is fully supported to mix both 32-bit and 64-bit instances on the same cluster with x64, if you install a 32-bit instance first with no other 64-bit components installed and then attempt to install a 64-bit instance after the 32-bit one, you will see the error during setup, as shown in Figure 8-16. It appears at the end during the actual configuration. So if you plan on having mixed-bit versions on your x64 cluster, install a 64-bit instance first. What seems to be occurring is that the 32-bit version of the SQL Server Native Client is installed, and upon initial detection, the 64-bit installer sees that the Native Client is installed, so it proceeds. When it reaches the point it needs to actually use the 64-bit Native Client, it seems to fail. Click OK to continue when you see the error.

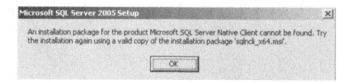

Figure 8-16. *Setup error if 32-bit is installed before 64-bit*

New Installation: Setup

Tip If at all possible, do not use the Back button during your SQL Server install on your production instances. The difference in production versus development or test is that it could introduce risks that should be avoided when high availability matters. The reason is that there is a chance that whoever wrote the installer did not test using Back as much as using Next. So if you hit Back, you may actually undo settings that affect other installation dialog boxes. That is not something you want to discover down the road. Since failover clustering setups are even more important to get right the first time, do not rush through the setup. If you enter something incorrectly and hit Next before you realize it, consider exiting Setup and restarting it as an alternative to using Back.

1. Log on to one of the nodes of the cluster as the cluster administrator account, as shown in Figure 8-17.

Figure 8-17. *Logging on to a cluster node*

2. Start Cluster Administrator, and check to see whether the group you renamed earlier is owned by the node you are logged on to. If it is not, move the group to the node.

3. Insert the SQL Server 2005 installation media into the optical drive of the node you are logged on to, or navigate to the proper network location of the SQL Server 2005 installation point. If you have autorun enabled on your CD or DVD drive, you should see the screen shown in Figure 8-18 if you are installing Enterprise Edition, and the screen shown in Figure 8-19 if you are installing Standard Edition. Click Server Components, Tools, Books Online, and Samples. Conversely, if the screen does not appear or you want to cut to the chase, navigate to the Servers directory of your optical drive, and run setup.exe.

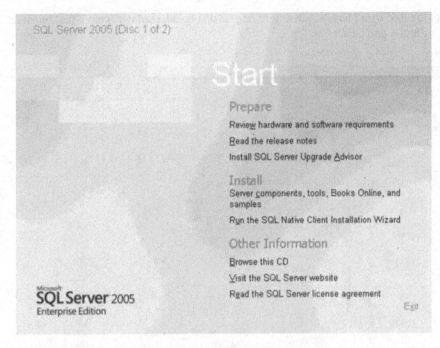

Figure 8-18. *SQL Server 2005 Enterprise Edition start window*

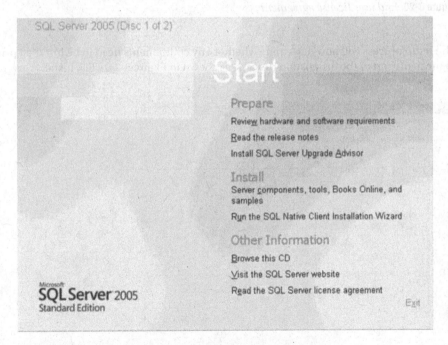

Figure 8-19. *SQL Server 2005 Standard Edition start window*

4. After the End User License Agreement page is displayed, read it, accept it (as shown in Figure 8-20), and click Next.

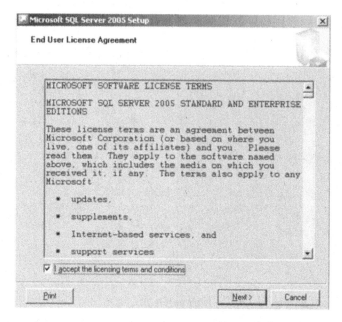

Figure 8-20. *End user license agreement*

5. The setup process will now determine whether any components need to be installed prior to the main part of the installation process, as shown in Figure 8-21. Click Install.

Figure 8-21. *Installing Prerequisites dialog box*

Setup will then install any prerequisites on the node that started the install process. During the process, a green check mark will appear next to completed tasks, and a red arrow pointing right will indicate the current task being executed. When all tasks are completed, as shown in Figure 8-22, click Next to continue.

Figure 8-22. *After prerequisites are installed*

Setup will then scan your configuration, as shown in Figure 8-23.

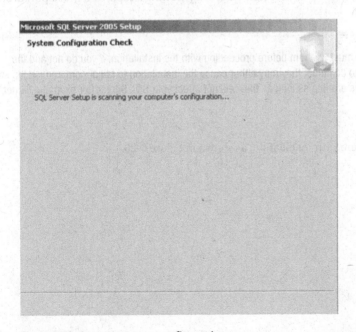

Figure 8-23. *Scanning your configuration*

6. Click Next on the Welcome to the Microsoft SQL Server Installation Wizard page, as shown in Figure 8-24.

Figure 8-24. *Welcome to the Microsoft SQL Server Installation Wizard page*

7. Setup will now do a more exhaustive check of the node that started the installation process, as shown in Figure 8-25. Any warnings or errors will be detected, and you can see them by clicking Messages next to the appropriate item or by viewing a report via the Report drop-down list. Click Next.

Note If there are errors, you must fix them before proceeding with the installation. If you do not and the installation process allows you to continue, they may either cause the installation to fail or compromise the stability of the installation. Warnings are fine as long as they will not affect your SQL Server (for example, IIS not being installed).

Setup will now prepare your installation, as shown in Figure 8-26.

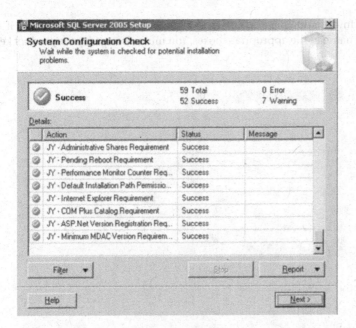

Figure 8-25. *System Configuration Check*

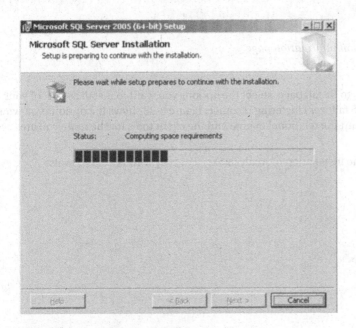

Figure 8-26. *Preparing the installation*

8. On the Registration Information page, as shown in Figure 8-27, enter your name and, if needed, a company name in the appropriate boxes. You must also enter your product key. Click Next.

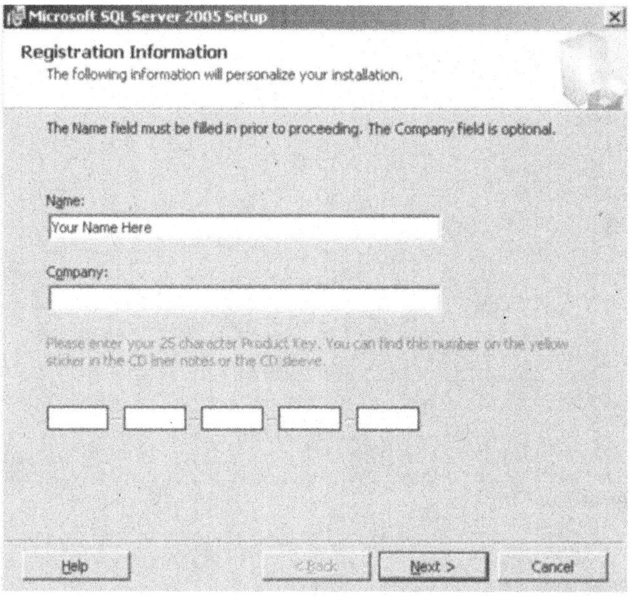

Figure 8-27. *Registration Information page*

9. On the Components to Install page, select the options you want to install as part of your new SQL Server 2005 failover clustering instance. Figure 8-28 shows the options you would choose if you just want the relational engine and the client tools for the node you are installing.

Figure 8-29 shows the installation of Analysis Services only with the client tools.

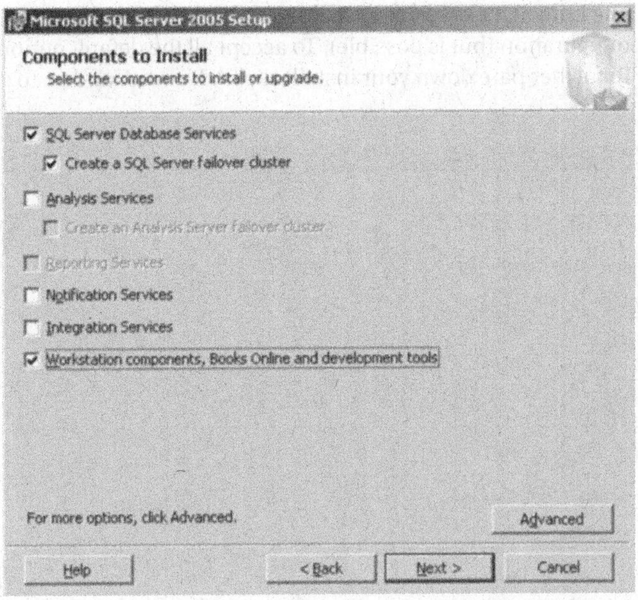

Figure 8-28. *Options needed to install the relational engine*

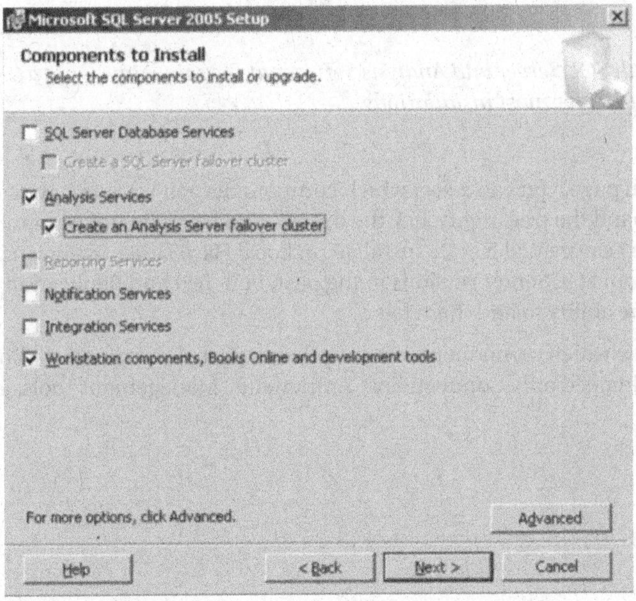

Figure 8-29. *Options needed to install Analysis Services*

Figure 8-30 shows installing both SQL Server and Analysis Services at the same time, which is not a recommended configuration (but is possible). To accept all the default options, click Next, and go to step 11. To further pare down your install, click Advanced, and go to step 10.

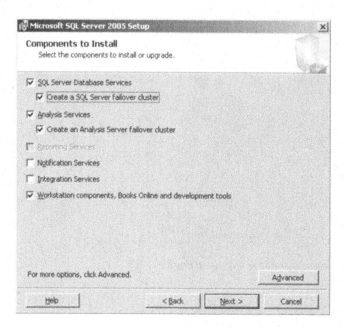

Figure 8-30. *Installing both SQL Server and Analysis Services at the same time—not a recommended configuration for most installations*

10. On the Feature Selection page, you can select which components you want to have as part of your installation. Expand the tree, right-click the option, and if you do not want to have it installed, select Entire Feature Will Not Be Installed on Local Hard Drive, as shown in Figure 8-31. Different from SQL Server versions in the past, Full-Text and Replication are optional. You do have the ability to add them later.

Similarly, you can change which components are installed as part of the client, as shown in Figure 8-32. DBAs should need only Connectivity Components, Management Tools, and Legacy Components.

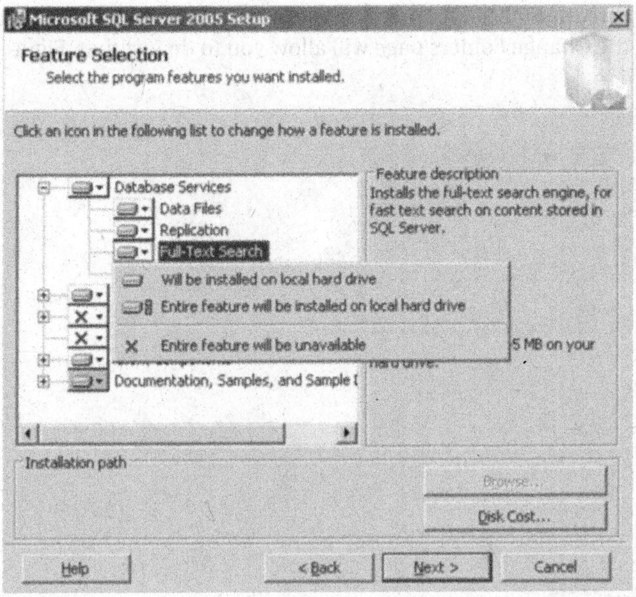

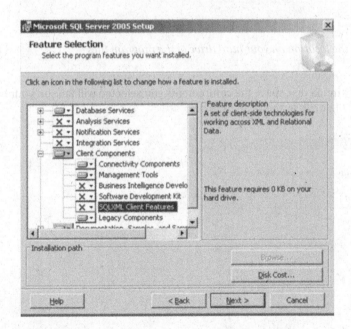

Figure 8-31. *Selecting whether a feature will be installed*

Figure 8-32. *All necessary client components for a DBA*

If you want to change where the SQL Server program files will be installed on your local drive, click Browse, and the Change Folders page will allow you to do just that. Figure 8-33 shows an example.

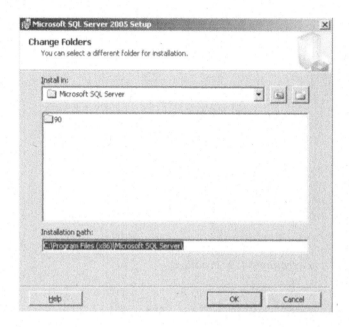

Figure 8-33. *Changing the location on your hard drive of the program files*

If you want to see how much disk space the components you selected will take on your hard drive, click Disk Cost. Figure 8-34 shows an example.

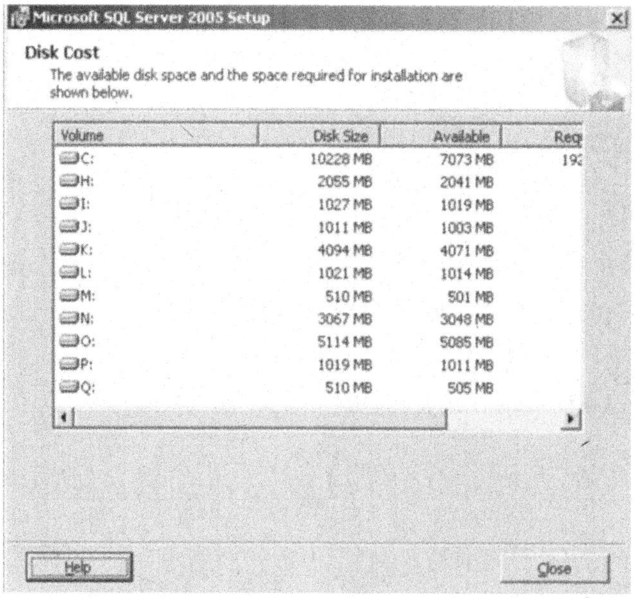

Volume	Disk Size	Available	Req
C:	10228 MB	7073 MB	193
H:	2055 MB	2041 MB	
I:	1027 MB	1019 MB	
J:	1011 MB	1003 MB	
K:	4094 MB	4071 MB	
L:	1021 MB	1014 MB	
M:	510 MB	501 MB	
N:	3067 MB	3048 MB	
O:	5114 MB	5085 MB	
P:	1019 MB	1011 MB	
Q:	510 MB	505 MB	

Figure 8-34. *Disk Cost page*

11. On the Instance Name page, you will select the type of instance that will be installed. If there is already a default instance of SQL Server from an existing installation of SQL Server 2000 in a side-by-side configuration or another SQL Server 2005 installation, you must select a named instance. To install a default instance, select Default Instance, as shown in Figure 8-35.

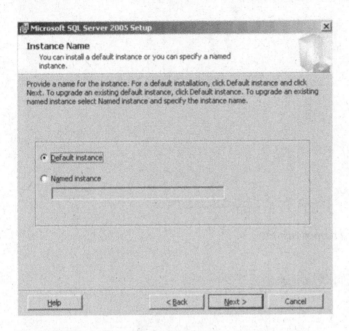

Figure 8-35. *Installing a default instance*

If you are installing a named instance, select Named Instance, and enter the second part of the name (that is, if your named instance will be GEDDY\LEE, enter **LEE** here), as shown in Figure 8-36.

If there are already failover clustering instances installed, you will see Figure 8-37. Click Next.

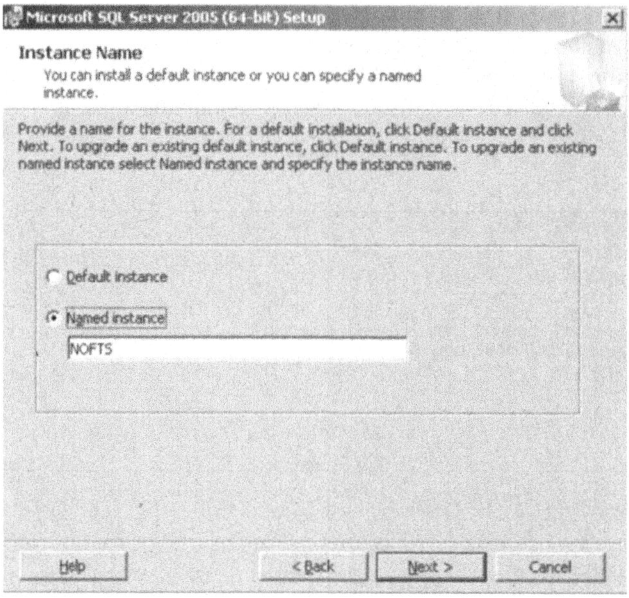

Figure 8-36. *Installing a named instance*

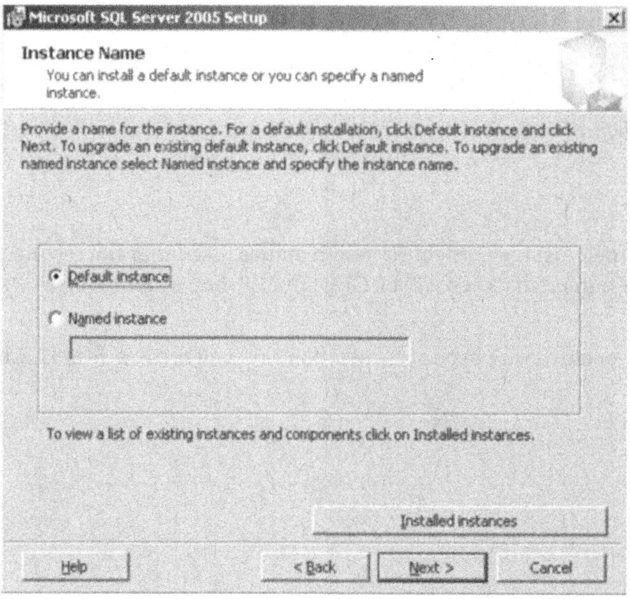

Figure 8-37. *Instance Name page when other clustered instances are already installed. Note the addition of the Installed instances button on the page, which does not appear in Figure 8-36.*

If you enter an invalid instance name for a named instance, you will see the message in Figure 8-38.

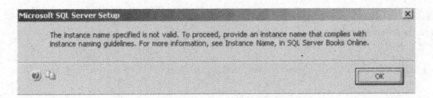

Figure 8-38. *Error if an invalid instance name is entered*

12. On the Virtual Server Name page shown in Figure 8-39, enter the name of the SQL Server that will be registered in DNS. This will be the name used to access SQL Server if it is a default instance; it will be the first part before the backward slash (so enter **GEDDY** in GEDDY\LEE) if it is a named instance. Click Next to continue.

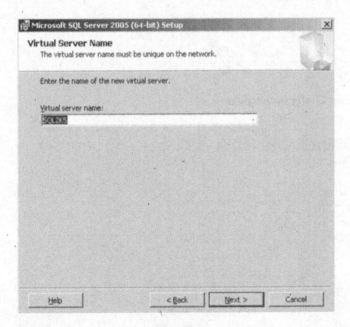

Figure 8-39. *Virtual Server Name page*

13. On the Virtual Server Configuration page shown in Figure 8-40, select the network in the Network to Use list that will be used by SQL Server to allow connectivity from users and applications. This should be an externally (public) facing network in the Windows server cluster. Enter the static IP address that will be used by SQL Server. Click Add.

The information will now appear in the Selected Networks and IP Addresses box, as shown in Figure 8-41. SQL Server may be assigned more than one IP address, so if necessary, repeat this step for all IP addresses that SQL Server will use. Click Next when finished.

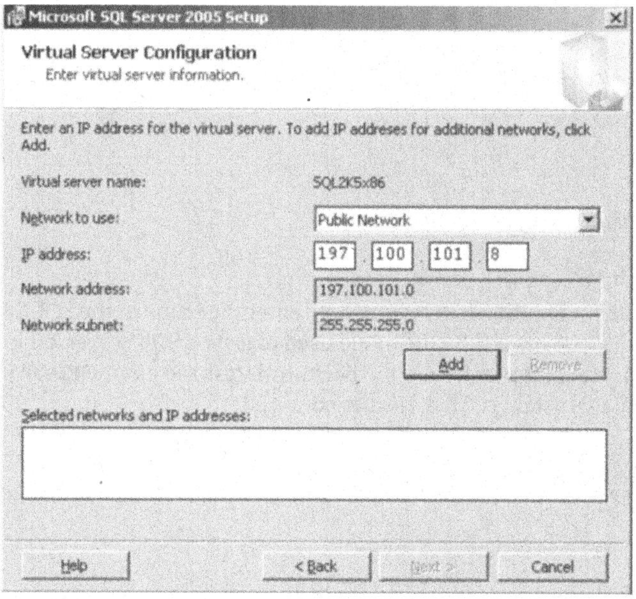

Figure 8-40. *Virtual Server Configuration page*

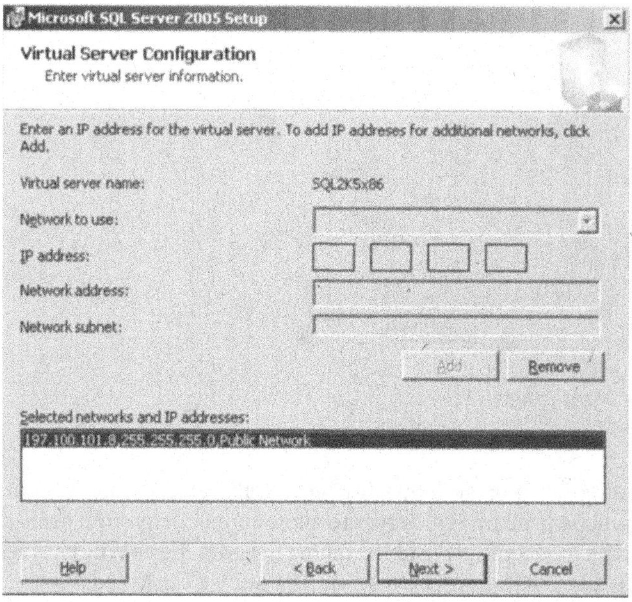

Figure 8-41. *IP address is added.*

14. On the Cluster Group Selection page shown in Figure 8-42, select the cluster group from the Available Cluster Groups list, which contains the disk that this clustered SQL Server installation will use for its system databases. Never select the default cluster group, which contains the quorum disk, or the group that contains the Microsoft Distributed Transaction Coordinator.

Figure 8-42. *Cluster Group Selection page*

If an existing failover clustering installation exists on the server cluster already, the group that contains the existing instance will not be available for selection and will show up in the Unavailable Cluster Groups section. Figure 8-43 shows an example. If you want to change the location of the data files, type the location into the Data Files field. Click Next.

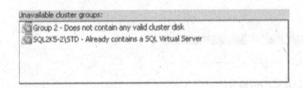

Figure 8-43. *Example informative messages*

15. On the Cluster Node Configuration page shown in Figure 8-44, all available nodes by default will be added to the definition of the failover clustering instance.

    If nodes are unavailable for some reason, there will be an appropriate entry in the Unavailable nodes section, as shown in Figure 8-45 and Figure 8-46.

    If you are using the Standard Edition installer on a cluster that has more than two nodes, you can allow only two nodes in total to be part of the definition of the failover clustering instance. If you try to have more, you will see the error in Figure 8-47. When finished, click Next.

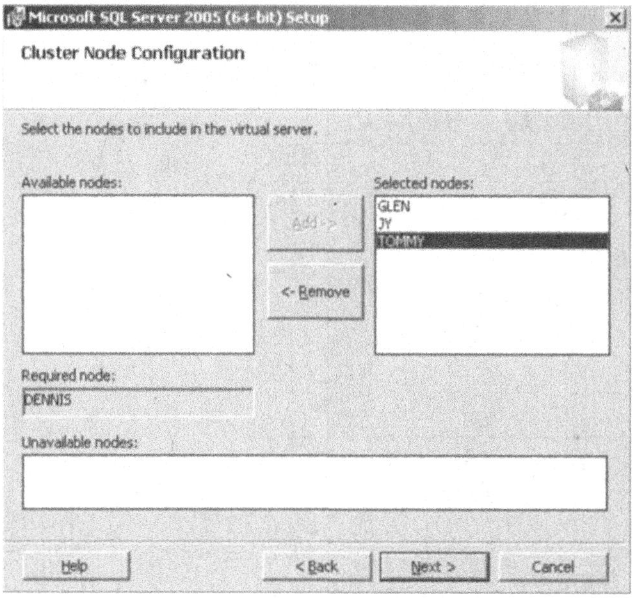

Figure 8-44. *Cluster Node Configuration page*

Figure 8-45. *Example unavailable node message*

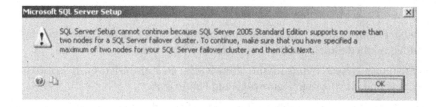

Figure 8-46. *Another unavailable node message*

Figure 8-47. *Standard Edition error if you have too many nodes selected*

16. On the Remote Account Information page shown in Figure 8-48, enter the password of the cluster administrator whom you are logged in as. If you enter the wrong password, you will see the message in Figure 8-49. If the user you are currently logged in as is not an administrator of the cluster nodes, cancel Setup, log off, and log on as the proper user. Click Next.

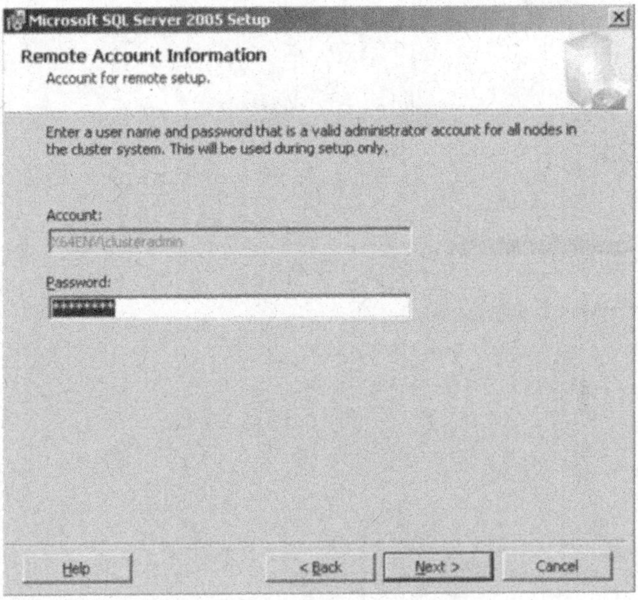

Figure 8-48. *Remote Account Information page*

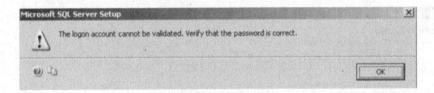

Figure 8-49. *Error if the wrong password is entered for cluster administrator*

17. The Service Account page is where you enter the service accounts and passwords for the various services depending on the configuration you selected. As noted in the section on security in Chapter 7, you should use different accounts for each service. Figures 8-50 through 8-53 show different variations of Service Account depending on the configuration you select. Click Next to continue.

    Figure 8-50 shows the Service Account dialog box when installing both SQL Server and Analysis Services at the same time.

    Figure 8-51 shows the Service Account dialog box when installing both SQL Server and Full-Text at the same time.

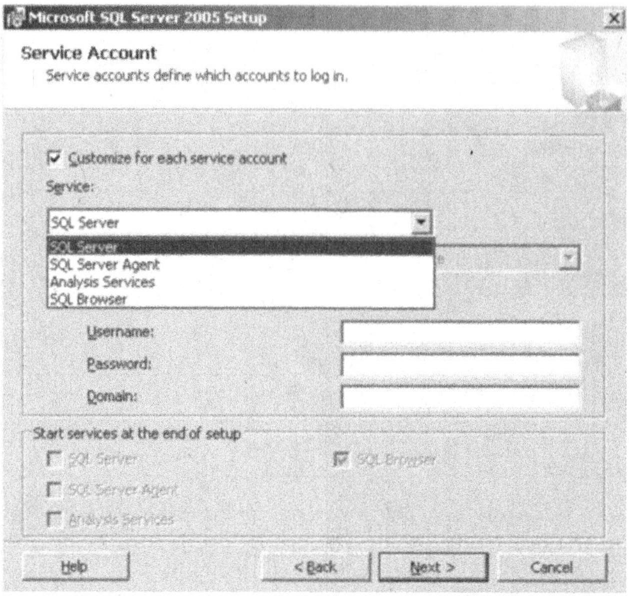

Figure 8-50. *Installing both SQL Server and Analysis Services*

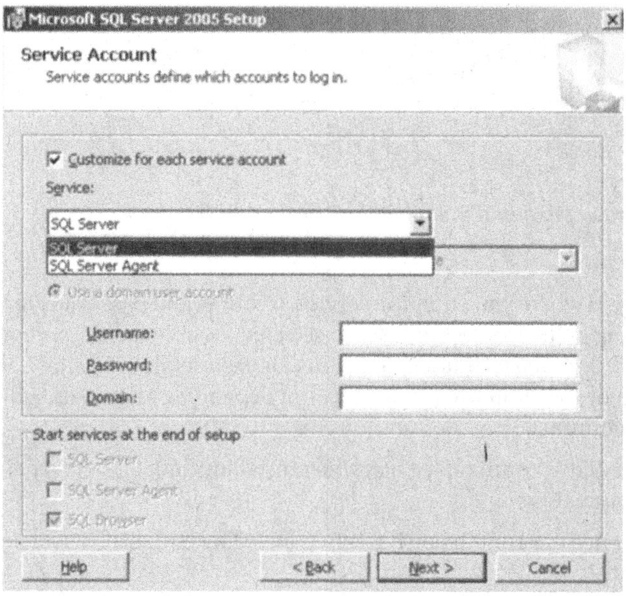

Figure 8-51. *Installing SQL Server only and customizing each account and password. Not customizing each account will appear similar to Figure 8-53.*

Figure 8-52 shows the Service Account dialog box when installing only Analysis Services.

Figure 8-53 shows the Service Account dialog box when installing only SQL Server.

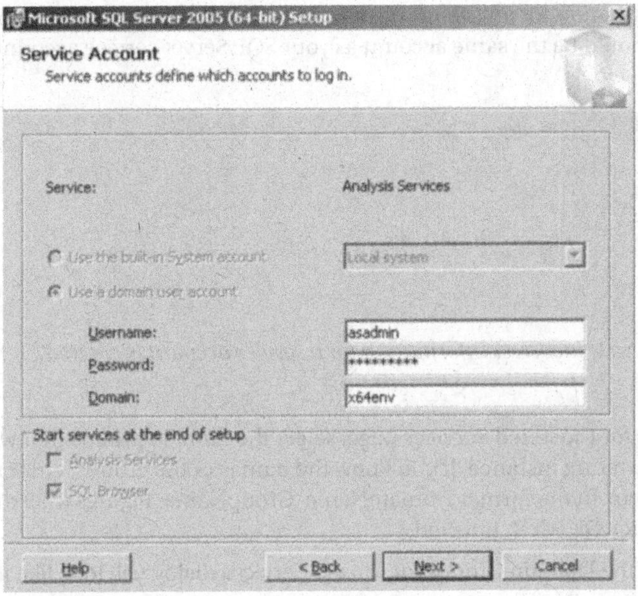

Figure 8-52. *Installing Analysis Services only*

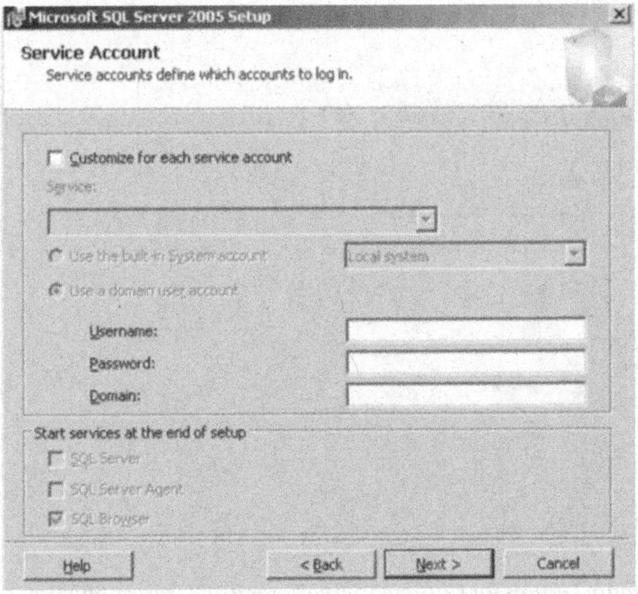

Figure 8-53. *Installing SQL Server only and using the same account and password. Customizing each account will appear similar to Figure 8-51.*

If you enter invalid information for an account, you will see the message in Figure 8-54. The SQL Browser account should be the same account as your SQL Server service account.

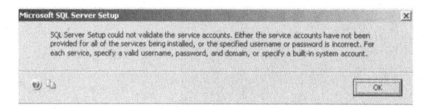

Figure 8-54. *Error displayed if incorrect information for a service account is entered*

18. On the Domain Groups for Clustered Services page, select the domain groups that will be used for the failover clustering instance. If you know the names of the groups, enter them in the appropriate text box in the format DomainName\GroupName. Figures 8-55 through 8-58 show examples. Click OK when finished.

Figure 8-55 shows what the Domain Groups for Cluster Services dialog will look like if you are installing only SQL Server.

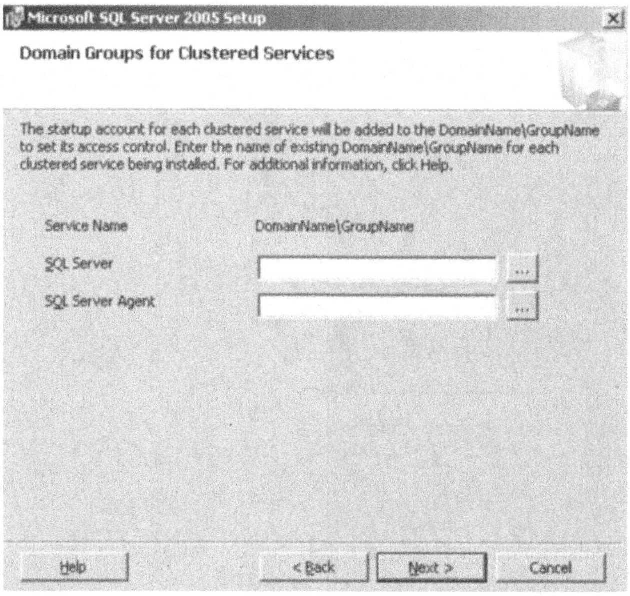

Figure 8-55. *Example Domain Groups for Clustered Services for a SQL Server failover clustering instance with no Full-Text*

Figure 8-56 shows what the Domain Groups for Cluster Services dialog will look like if you are installing SQL Server with Full-Text Search.

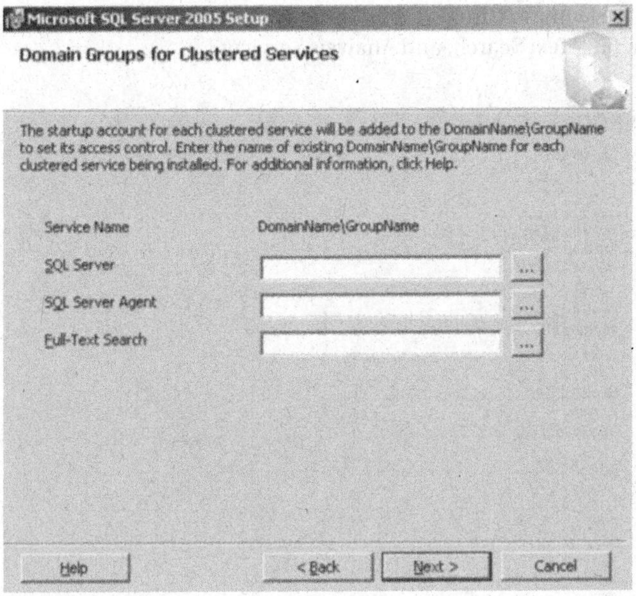

Figure 8-56. *Example Domain Groups for Clustered Services for a SQL Server failover clustering instance with Full-Text*

Figure 8-57 shows what the Domain Groups for Cluster Services dialog will look like if you are installing only Analysis Services.

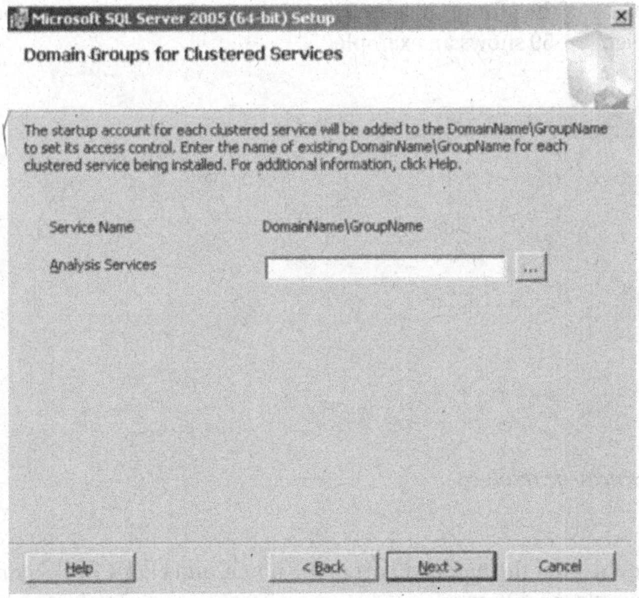

Figure 8-57. *Example Domain Groups for Clustered Services for an Analysis Services–only failover cluster*

Figure 8-58 shows what the Domain Groups for Cluster Services dialog will look like if you are installing SQL Server, Full-Text Search, and Analysis Services.

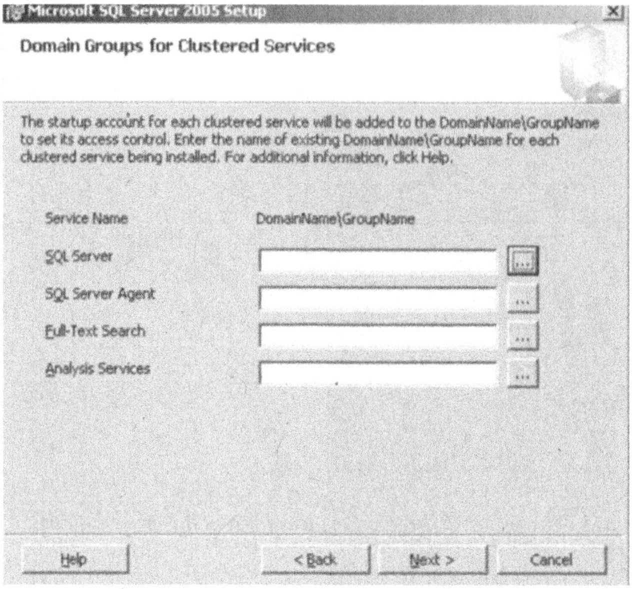

Figure 8-58. *Example Domain Groups for Clustered Services for a SQL Server failover clustering instance with all options*

If you do not know the name of the group, click the ellipsis button, and the Select Group page will be displayed. Figure 8-59 shows an example.

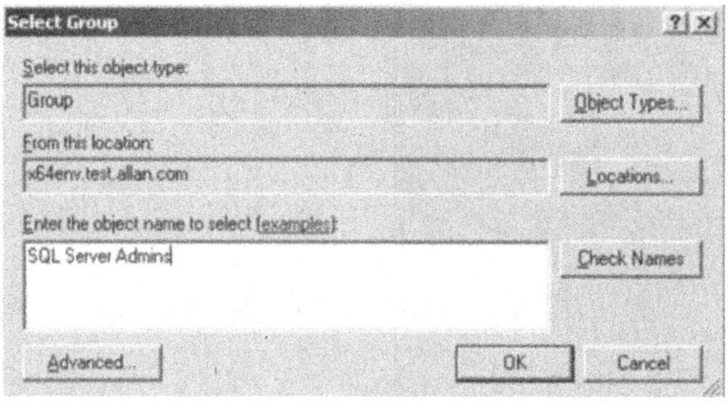

Figure 8-59. *Typing the name to be resolved*

Select the domain to search, enter the name or part of the name, and click Check Names. Figure 8-60 shows an example resolution.

Figure 8-61 shows a completed Domain Groups for Clustered Services page.

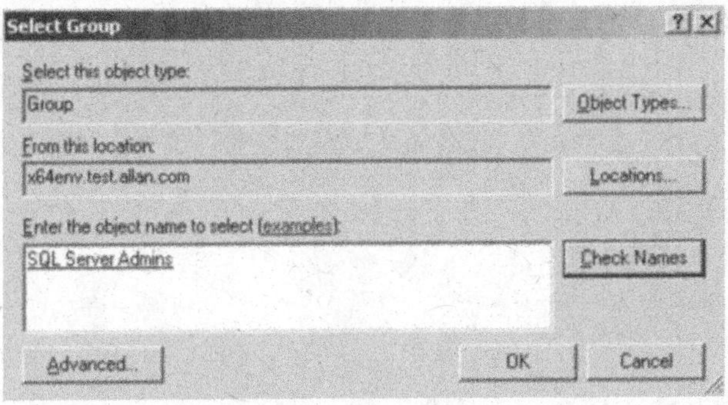

Figure 8-60. *Name that has been checked against the domain*

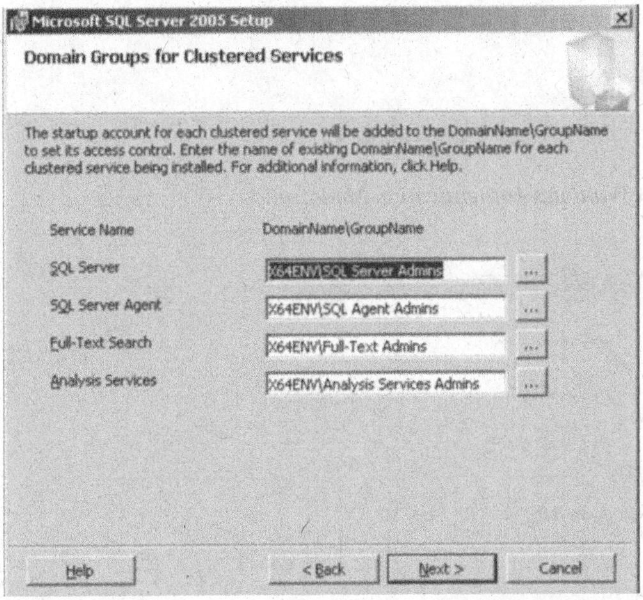

Figure 8-61. *Example of a completed Domain Groups for Clustered Services page*

19. On the Authentication Mode page, click either Windows Authentication Mode, as shown in Figure 8-62, or Mixed Mode, as shown in Figure 8-63. Most installations will use Mixed Mode. If you select Mixed Mode, you will be prompted to enter a password for the sa user. You cannot use a blank password for the sa user in SQL Server. Click Next.

Note If you select Windows Authentication, the sa user will still exist within SQL Server even though it may not be used to access SQL Server. You must set a password for sa once the installation process is complete. This is for your protection—a registry key controls the Mixed Mode setting. So if someone maliciously changes your registry key, they still will not be able to get into SQL Server because you have set a password for sa.

Figure 8-62. *Choosing the Windows Authentication Mode option*

Figure 8-63. *Choosing the Mixed Mode option*

20. Now you have to pick the collation or collations for your configuration. Figures 8-64 through 8-67 show examples of different Collation Settings pages depending on the configuration you are installing. Select the proper collation you need—or leave the defaults—and then click Next.

Note Save yourself a lot of time and trouble down the road by getting your collation right at the beginning. If you get it wrong, it is not always easy to change it without affecting your databases. In some cases, you may even have to do a complete uninstall and reinstall of SQL Server.

Figure 8-64 shows an example of what the Collation Settings dialog will look like when you are only installing SQL Server by itself.

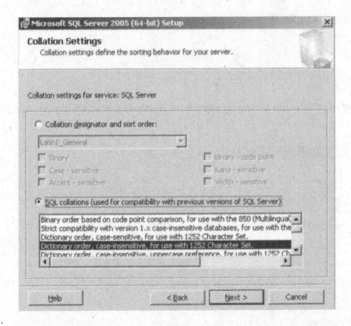

Figure 8-64. *Example of the Collation Settings page for a SQL Server–only install*

Figure 8-65 shows an example of what the Collation Settings dialog will look like when you are only installing Analysis Services by itself.

Figure 8-66 shows an example of what the Collation Settings dialog will look like when you are installing both SQL Server and Analysis Services and want to use the same setting for both installations.

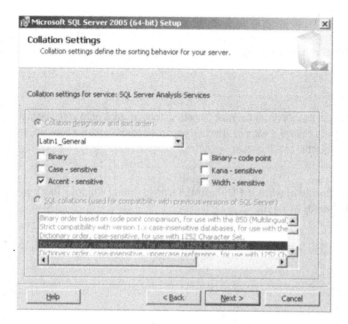

Figure 8-65. *Example of the Collation Settings page for an Analysis Services failover cluster*

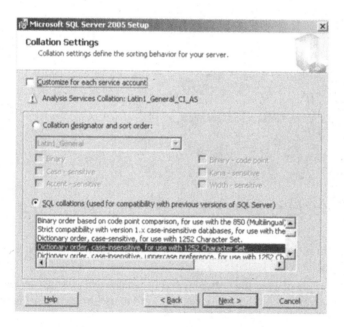

Figure 8-66. *Example of the Collation Settings page when customizing for both SQL Server and Analysis Services in the same failover clustering instance*

Figure 8-67 shows an example of what the Collation Settings dialog will look like when you are installing both SQL Server and Analysis Services and want to use different settings for each installation.

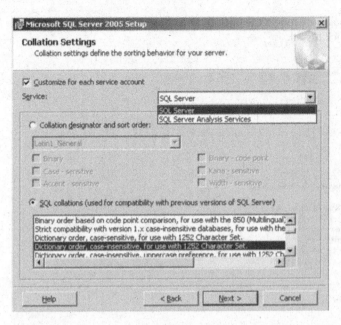

Figure 8-67. *Example of the Collation Settings page when customizing only SQL Server for a failover clustering instance with both SQL Server and Analysis Services*

21. On the Error and Usage Report Settings page shown in Figure 8-68, select the desired options if you want to send error or usage data to Microsoft. These are optional. Click Next.

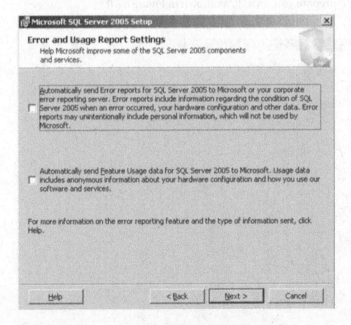

Figure 8-68. *Error and Usage Report Settings page*

22. The Ready to Install page will reflect the options you chose earlier in the install. Figure 8-69 shows an example. Click Install.

Figure 8-69. *Ready to Install page*

Setup will then start to prepare your install, as shown in Figure 8-70.

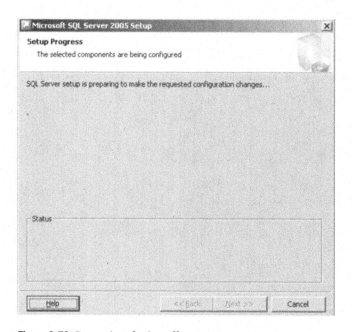

Figure 8-70. *Preparing the install*

During the installation process, unlike previous versions of SQL Server, you can see the progress of the install on each node by selecting the node in the drop-down list, as shown in Figure 8-71. This new feature of the installer is a welcome addition because you can now see what is going on during Setup on each individual node and the progress for each node.

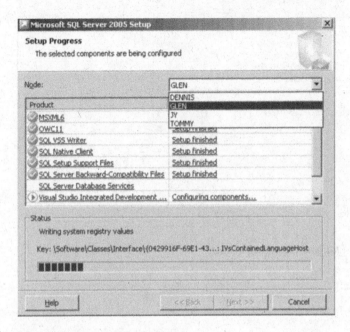

Figure 8-71. *Setup Progress page*

23. When setup is complete, the Setup Progress page shown in Figure 8-72 will show all products with a status of Setup Finished. If a component causes a reboot, it will also be noted. Click Next.

24. On the Completing Microsoft SQL Server 2005 Setup page shown in Figure 8-73, read the information presented, and click Finish.

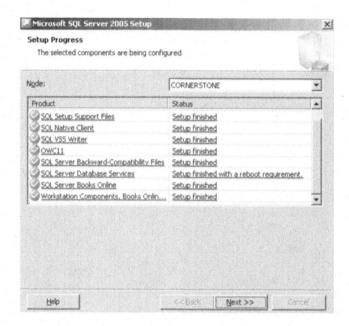

Figure 8-72. *Completed failover clustering install*

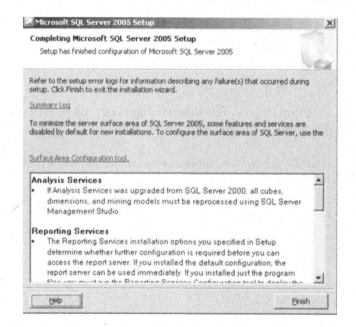

Figure 8-73. *Completing Microsoft SQL Server 2005 Setup page*

25. If you are prompted to reboot as shown in Figure 8-74, click OK, and then reboot all nodes of the cluster.

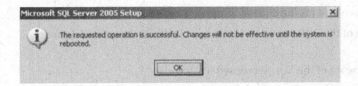

Figure 8-74. *Reboot message*

New Installation: Command Line

A great new addition to SQL Server 2005 is the ability to install a SQL Server 2005 failover clustering instance without having to use the graphic interface. This was not possible with previous versions of SQL Server and could be done only with stand-alone instances. This is probably my new favorite feature for clustering SQL Server because it benefits many environments and allows much more automation of the entire process.

You have two ways to install via command line: you can type everything into a single command and execute it, or you can put it in a file and run against the file. Obviously, creating a setup configuration file with the parameters needed is a much more repeatable process.

■**Note** Any command line–based installation (or update) you do via command line will contain your administrator passwords in plain text. For obvious reasons, this may be a security risk. Microsoft does have a free utility named killpwd.exe that scrubs the password information out of the script files that are usually left behind on the nodes after an installation. You can find more information about killpwd.exe in the Microsoft Knowledge Base article 263968 (`http://support.microsoft.com/kb/263968/en-us`). To download the utility, you can get it from `http://www.microsoft.com/technet/security/bulletin/MS02-035.mspx`; this will always contain the latest version.

The following are the parameters you need (which may vary depending on whether you are installing SQL Server or Analysis Services):

- VS: This is the name of the SQL Server instance (née virtual server) that gets registered in DNS and would be a default instance name (or the part of the name before the slash in the named instance).

- INSTALLVS: This parameter sets the type of installation you will be doing. It can be *SQL_Engine*, *Analysis_Server*, or both (if separated by commas).

- INSTALLSQLDIR: The parameter sets the location of the SQL Server or Analysis Services program files on the local hard drive.

- INSTALLASDATADIR: This parameter sets the location for Analysis Services data used in the install (you can add other disks after it is installed).

- INSTALLSQLDATADIR: This parameter sets the location for SQL Server data used in the install (you can add other disks after it is installed).

- INSTANCENAME: If you are creating a named instance of SQL Server, this is where you will enter the name of the instance (the part that comes after the slash). If your instance is a default instance, you must use the value MSSQLSERVER.

- ADMINPASSWORD: This is the password for the cluster administrator account.

- SQLACCOUNT: This is the name of the SQL Server service account with its associated domain name.

- SQLPASSWORD: This is the password of the SQL Server service account.

- AGTACCOUNT: This is the name of the SQL Server Agent service account with its associated domain name.

- AGTPASSWORD: This is the password of the SQL Server Agent service account.

- ADDLOCAL: This is where you list all of the components you want to install. Consult the Books Online topic "How to: Install SQL Server 2005 from the Command Prompt" for a full list of all the options available to you. You'll see examples in this chapter.

- ASCOLLATION: This is the collation for Analysis Services. Use a valid collation name as found in the Books Online topic "SQL Collation Name (Transact-SQL)."

- SQLCOLLATION: This is the collation for SQL Server. Use a valid collation name as found in the Books Online topic "SQL Collation Name (Transact-SQL)."

- AGTACCOUNT: This is the domain service account that will be used by SQL Server Agent.

- AGTPASSWORD: This is the password for the SQL Server Agent service account.

- ASACCOUNT: This is the domain service account that will be used by Analysis Services.

- ASPASSWORD: This is the password for the Analysis Services service account.

- SQLACCOUNT: This is the name of the SQL Server service account.

- SQLPASSWORD: This is the password for the SQL Server service account.

- SQLBROWSERACCOUNT: This is the domain service account that will be used for the SQL Server browser service. This should be the same as the SQL Server service account.

- SQLBROWSERPASSWORD: This is the password for the Browser service account.

- SECURITYMODE: This is optional. If you want to change your collation, this is where you would use a valid collation name as found in the Books Online topic "SQL Collation Name (Transact-SQL)."

- SAPWD: If you select a SECURITYMODE of SQL, you will need to set the sa password with this parameter.

- SQMREPORTING and ERRORREPORTING: These two parameters correspond to step 21 and Figure 8-68 earlier in this chapter where you decide whether you want to send information to Microsoft. Use 0 for no and 1 for yes.

- ADMINPASSWORD: This is the password of the cluster service account that you should be logged in with to do the install.

- IP: This is the parameter that will contain the public IP address that will be used by SQL Server as well as the public cluster network that it will utilize. The two values are separated by commas.

- GROUP: This is the Windows cluster resource group that will contain the SQL Server or Analysis Services resources.

- ADDNODE: This is the list of nodes that will be used to create the failover clustering instance. Each node must be separated by commas.

- SQLCLUSTERGROUP: This is the domain group you created for the SQL Server service accounts.

- AGTCLUSTERGROUP: This is the domain group you created for the SQL Server Agent service accounts.

- FTSCLUSTERGROUP: This is the domain group you created for the Full-Text service accounts.

- ASCLUSTERGROUP: This is the domain group you created for the Analysis Services service accounts.

- PIDKEY: This is the code Microsoft gave you on your installation media to allow you to install SQL Server.

This is an example Analysis Services file:

```
[Options]
VS=AnSvcs2K5
INSTALLVS="Analysis_Server"
INSTALLSQLDIR="C:\Program Files\Microsoft SQL Server\"
INSTALLASDATADIR="S:\AS Cubes\"
PIDKEY=
ADDLOCAL="Analysis_Server,AnalysisDataFiles,Client_Components,Connectivity"
INSTANCENAME="AS1"
ASACCOUNT="TESTDOMAIN\asadmin"
ASPASSWORD="password"
ASCOLLATION=SQL_Latin1_General_CP1_CI_AS
ERRORREPORTING=0
SQMREPORTING=0
ADMINPASSWORD=password
IP="172.22.10.188,Public Network"
GROUP="Analysis Services"
ADDNODE="CHUCK,JOHN"
ASCLUSTERGROUP="TESTDOMAIN\Analysis Services Admins"
```

This is an example SQL Server file:

```
[Options]
VS=SQL2K5EE
INSTANCENAME="NmdInst1"
INSTALLVS="SQL_Engine"
INSTALLSQLDIR="C:\Program Files\Microsoft SQL Server\"
INSTALLSQLDATADIR="L:\System Databases\"
PIDKEY=
ADDLOCAL="SQL_Engine,SQL_Data_Files,SQL_Replication,SQL_FullText,
Client_Components,Connectivity"
SQLBROWSERACCOUNT="TESTDOMAIN\sqladmin"
SQLBROWSERPASSWORD="password"
SQLACCOUNT="TESTDOMAIN\sqladmin"
SQLPASSWORD="password"
AGTACCOUNT="TESTDOMAIN\sqlagentadmin"
AGTPASSWORD="password"
SECURITYMODE=SQL
SAPWD=password
```

```
SQLCOLLATION=SQL_Latin1_General_CP1_CI_AS
ERRORREPORTING=0
SQMREPORTING=0
ADMINPASSWORD=password
IP="172.22.10.187,Public Network"
GROUP="SQL2K5EE\NmdInst1"
ADDNODE="RICKY,GOWAN"
SQLCLUSTERGROUP="TESTDOMAIN\SQL Server Admins"
AGTCLUSTERGROUP="TESTDOMAIN\SQL Agent Admins"
FTSCLUSTERGROUP="TESTDOMAIN\FTS Admins"
```

To run the setup with files, log on to the node that owns the disk group with the cluster administrator account, and run the following command where *x* is the drive letter of your installation media. If you have the install media on a share, you must enter the full path between \servers and the drive letter. Here is an example:

```
x:\servers\setup.exe /settings c:\install2005.ini /qb
```

You can also execute the commands directly at the command prompt. Each option listed in the .ini file would be typed out minus the [Options] section, as in this example:

```
start /wait d:\servers\setup.exe VS=AnSvcs2K5 INSTALLVS="Analysis_Server"
INSTALLSQLDIR="C:\Program Files\Microsoft SQL Server\"
INSTALLASDATADIR="S:\AS Cubes\"
PIDKEY=
ADDLOCAL="Analysis_Server,AnalysisDataFiles,Client_Components,Connectivity"
INSTANCENAME="AS1"
ASACCOUNT="TESTDOMAIN\asadmin"
ASPASSWORD="password"
ASCOLLATION="SQL_Latin1_General_CP1_CI_AS"
ERRORREPORTING=0
SQMREPORTING=0
ADMINPASSWORD=password IP="172.22.10.188,Public Network"
GROUP="Analysis Services"
ADDNODE="CHUCK,JOHN"
ASCLUSTERGROUP="TESTDOMAIN\Analysis Services Admins"
```

Tip When executing from the command prompt, you can use either the /qn or /qb switch. The /qn switch suppresses any dialog boxes, so if there is a problem, the only way to detect it would be to view the installation logs. The /qb switch displays some of the dialog boxes and errors as if you were running the GUI-based Setup program. /qb is useful especially when running a script for the first time or debugging a script, but once the script is known to work, you may want to consider switching to using /qn.

In-Place Upgrade: Setup

The following step-by-step instructions will work if you are upgrading a previous clustered installation of SQL Server or if you are upgrading a SQL Server 2005 Standard Edition failover clustering instance to Enterprise Edition. Upgrades are not supported through a command-line installation.

1. Ensure that .NET Framework 2.0 is installed on each node as shown in the earlier section "Step 4: Install .NET Framework 2.0."

2. Make sure the SQL Server 2000 failover cluster is configured with SQL Server 2000 Service Pack 4. To check, open Query Analyzer and run a select @@version command, as shown in Figure 8-75. You should be at version 8.00.2039 (SQL Server 2000 with SQL Server 2000 Service Pack 4) or later. If you are at a previous version of SQL Server 2000 prior to Service Pack 4, you may not have the right code because Microsoft made some changes to SQL Server 2000 to ensure that the upgrade to SQL Server 2005 would be successful. This applies to both SQL Server and Analysis Services.

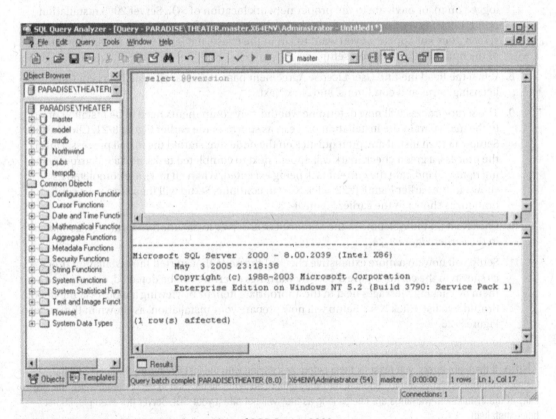

Figure 8-75. *Results of querying the version of SQL Server 2000*

3. Make sure all nodes of the cluster are up and running.

4. Add the existing SQL Server service account to the SQL Server and FTS groups, and add SQL Server Agent service account to the SQL Server Admins group, as described in the earlier section "Step 2: Create the SQL Server 2005 Failover Clustering Service Accounts and Groups." If you do not do this, you may see a dialog box similar to the one in Figure 8-76 later in the install process.

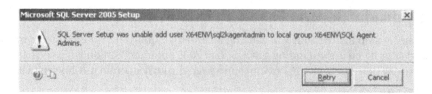

Figure 8-76. *Error*

5. Log on to one of the nodes of the cluster as the cluster administrator account, as shown in the earlier Figure 8-17.

6. Start Cluster Administrator, and check to see whether the group you renamed earlier is owned by the node you are logged on to. If it is not, move the group to the node.

7. Insert the SQL Server 2005 installation media into the optical drive of the node you are logged on to, or navigate to the proper network location of SQL Server 2005 installation point. Click Server Components, Tools, Books Online, and Samples. Conversely, if the screen does not appear or you want to cut to the chase, navigate to the Servers directory of the optical drive, and run setup.exe.

8. When the Read the End User License Agreement page is displayed, read it, accept the licensing terms and conditions, and click Next.

9. The setup process will now determine whether any components need to be installed prior to the main part of the installation process, as shown in the earlier Figure 8-21. Click Install. Setup will then install any prerequisites on the node that started the install process. During the process, a green check mark will appear next to completed tasks, and a red arrow pointing right will indicate the current task being executed. When all tasks are completed as shown in the earlier Figure 8-22, click Next to continue. Setup will then scan your configuration, as shown in the earlier Figure 8-23.

10. Click Next on the Welcome to the Microsoft SQL Server Installation Wizard page, as shown in the earlier Figure 8-24.

11. Setup will now do a more exhaustive check of the node that started the installation process, as shown in the earlier Figure 8-25. Any warnings or errors will be detected, and you can see them by clicking Messages next to the appropriate item or by viewing a report via the Report drop-down list. Click Next. Setup will now prepare your installation, as shown in the earlier Figure 8-26.

Note If there are errors, you must fix them before proceeding with the installation. If you do not and the installation process allows you to continue, they may either cause the installation to fail or compromise the stability of the installation. Warnings are fine as long as they will not affect your SQL Server (for example, IIS not being installed).

---

12. On the Registration Information page shown in the earlier Figure 8-27, enter your name and, if needed, a company name in the appropriate boxes. You must also enter your product key. Click Next.

13. On the Components to Install page, select the options you want to install as part of your new SQL Server 2005 failover clustering instance. The earlier Figure 8-28 shows the options you would choose if you just want the relational engine and the client tools for the node you are installing. Figure 8-29 shows the installation of Analysis Services only with the client tools. Figure 8-30 shows installing both SQL Server and Analysis Services at the same time, which is not a recommended configuration (but is possible). To accept all the default options, click Next, and go to step 15. To further pare down your install, click Advanced, and go to step 14.

14. On the Feature Selection page, you can select which components you want to have as part of your installation. Expand the tree, right-click the option, and if you do not want to have it installed, select Entire Feature Will Not Be Installed on Local Hard Drive, as shown in Figure 8-31. Different from SQL Server versions in the past, Full-Text and Replication are optional. You do have the ability to add them later. Similarly, you can change which components are installed as part of the client, as shown in the earlier Figure 8-32. DBAs should need only Connectivity Components, Management Tools, and Legacy Components. If you want to change where the SQL Server program files will be installed on your local drive, click Browse, and the Change Folders page will allow you to do just that. If you want to see how much disk space the components you selected will take on your hard drive, click Disk Cost. Figure 8-34 shows an example.

15. On the Instance Name dialog box, you will select the type of instance that will be upgraded. To upgrade a default instance, select Default instance, as shown in only Figure 8-37. If you are upgrading a named instance, select Named Instance, and enter the second part of the name (that is, if your named instance will be GEDDY\LEE, enter **LEE** here), as shown in the earlier Figure 8-36. You can also see what instances are installed with what version of SQL Server by clicking Installed Instances. Figure 8-77 shows an example.

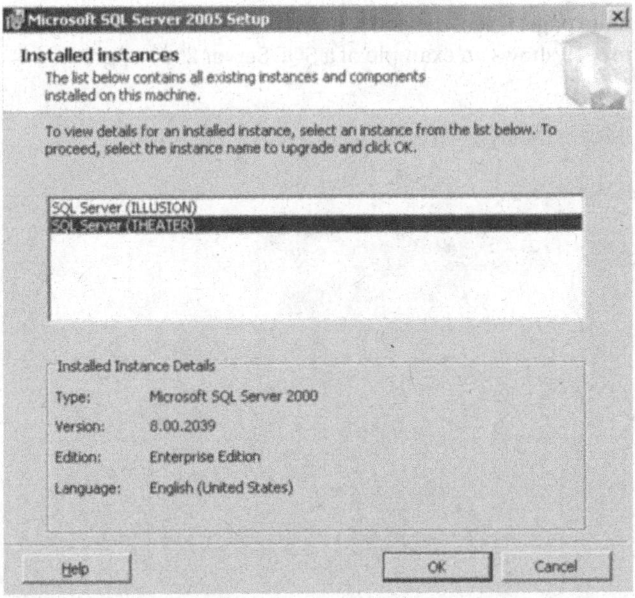

Figure 8-77. *Installed Instances dialog box*

If you don't know the name or type of the instance, select the instance in the Installed Instances dialog, and click OK. The value will be filled in on the Instance Name page, as shown in Figure 8-78. Click Next.

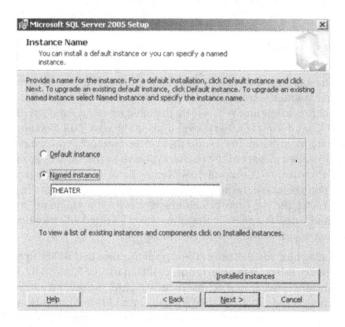

Figure 8-78. *Installed Name page*

16. On the Existing Components page, select the check box next to the instance that you selected in step 15. Figure 8-79 shows an example of a SQL Server 2000 upgrade.

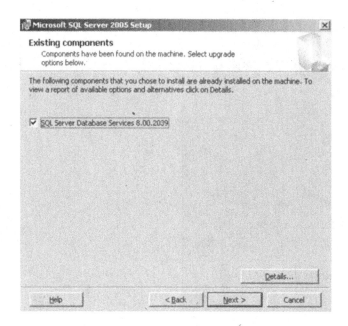

Figure 8-79. *Example of an Existing Components page for a SQL Server 2000 upgrade*

Figure 8-80 shows an example of a SQL Server 2005 Standard Edition upgrade to Enterprise Edition. If you want to see more information, click Details.

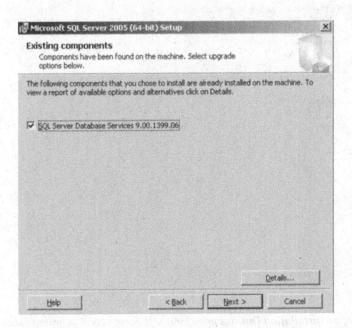

Figure 8-80. *Example of an Existing Components page for a SQL Server 2005 Standard Edition to Enterprise Edition upgrade*

Figure 8-81 shows a SQL Server 2000 upgrade.

Figure 8-81. *Example of an Installation Options page for a SQL Server 2000 upgrade*

Figure 8-82 shows a SQL Server 2005 Standard Edition upgrade.

Figure 8-82. *Example of an Installation Options page for a SQL Server 2005 Standard Edition upgrade*

17. On the Upgrade Logon Information page, click either Windows Authentication Mode, as shown in Figure 8-83, or Mixed Mode, as shown in Figure 8-84. Click Next.

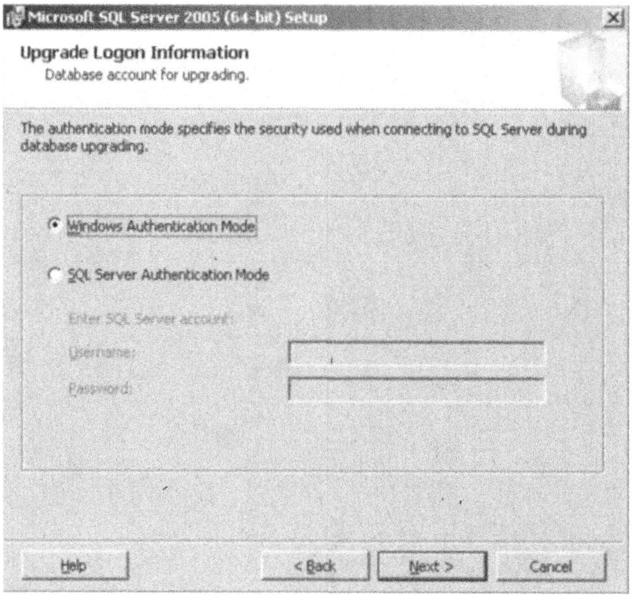

Figure 8-83. *Using Windows authentication during the upgrade*

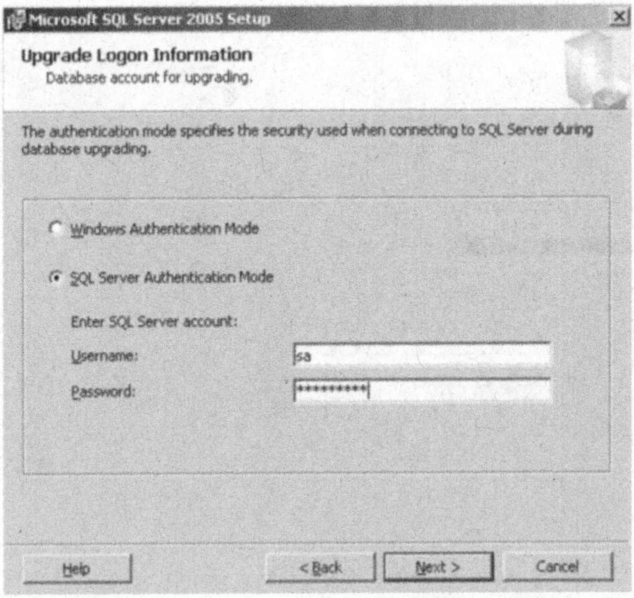

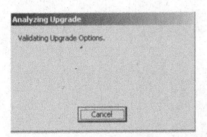

Figure 8-84. *Using SQL Server authentication during the upgrade*

The upgrade will now be verified, and a page similar to Figure 8-85 will be displayed.

Analyzing Upgrade

Validating Upgrade Options.

Cancel

Figure 8-85. *Setup validating the upgrade*

18. On the Remote Account Information page shown in Figure 8-48, enter the password of the cluster administrator whom you are logged in as, which is a domain account with administrator rights on all nodes. If you enter the wrong password, you will see the message in the earlier Figure 8-49. If the user you are currently logged in as is not an administrator of the cluster nodes, cancel Setup, log off, and log on as the proper user. Click Next.

19. The Service Account page is where you enter the service accounts and passwords for the various services depending on the configuration you selected. If you are just upgrading the relational engine, you will see a page similar to Figure 8-86. Note that for SQL Server, you must enter the password for your existing SQL Server service account.

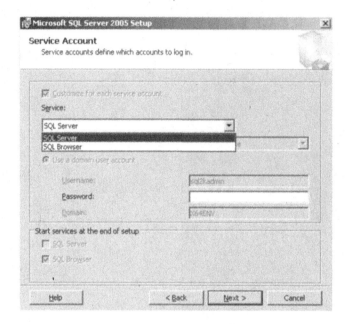

Figure 8-86. *Service Account page during an upgrade*

The SQL Browser account should be the new account created for the SQL Server 2005 service account. Figure 8-87 shows an example. Click Next.

Figure 8-87. *Entering the new SQL Server 2005 service account for SQL Browser*

20. On the Domain Groups for Clustered Services page, select the domain groups that will be used for the failover clustering instance. If you know the names of the groups, enter them in the appropriate text box in the format DomainName\GroupName. If you do not know the name of the group, click the ellipsis button, and the Select Group page will be displayed. Select the domain to search, enter the name or part of the name, and click Check Names. For standard upgrades where the SQL Server relational engine is being upgraded and no new features are being added, you should see Figure 8-56. Click OK.

21. The Ready to Install page will reflect the upgrade as well as the options you chose earlier in the install. Figure 8-88 shows an example. Click Install. Setup will then start to prepare your install, as shown in Figure 8-70. During the installation process, unlike previous versions of SQL Server, you can see the progress of the install on each node by selecting the node in the drop-down list, as shown in Figure 8-71.

Figure 8-88. *Example of Ready to Install page for upgrades*

22. When setup is complete, the Setup Progress page shown in the earlier Figure 8-72 will show all products with a status of Setup Finished. If a component causes a reboot, it will also be noted. Click Next.

23. On the Completing Microsoft SQL Server 2005 Setup dialog box shown in the earlier Figure 8-73, read the information presented, and click Finish.

24. If you are prompted to reboot as shown in the earlier Figure 8-74, click OK, and then reboot all nodes of the cluster.

Performing Post-Installation Tasks

After performing the initial installation steps, you must execute some tasks to finish the configuration of your SQL Server or Analysis Services failover cluster.

Installing SQL Server Service Packs, Patches, and Hotfixes

You should apply any known SQL Server service packs, security updates, and hotfixes. For instructions on installing a SQL Server Service Pack, see Chapter 16.

Adding Additional Disks As Dependencies

Since the installation process allows you to select only one drive during Setup, you must add any other drives that will be used by SQL Server or Analysis Services after the initial installation. It is better to do it before it goes into full production because adding a drive to SQL Server or Analysis Services will cause an availability outage.

1. Start Cluster Administrator.

2. Select the group that contains the disk resource you want to use with SQL Server or Analysis Services.

3. Make sure the disk resource is owned by the node you are currently logged on to. If it is not and you attempt to do the move, you will see the error in Figure 8-89.

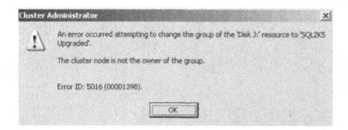

Figure 8-89. *Error if the disk resource is not owned by the node*

4. In the right pane, select the disk resource, right-click, select Change Group, and then select the group that contains your SQL Server or Analysis Services resources. Figure 8-90 shows an example. You can also drag the disk resource to the target group.

5. When prompted to confirm the move action as shown in Figure 8-91, click Yes.

6. Once again, you will be prompted to confirm the disk resource move to the other group, as shown in Figure 8-92. Click Yes.

   The disk will now be moved to the target group and will appear in it, as shown in Figure 8-93.

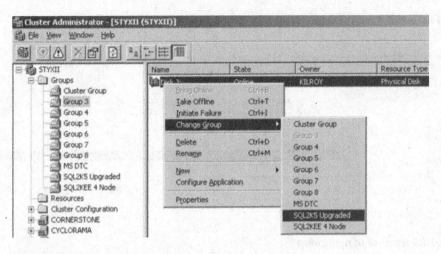

Figure 8-90. *Change Group option*

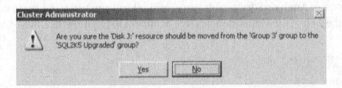

Figure 8-91. *Confirming the disk resource move*

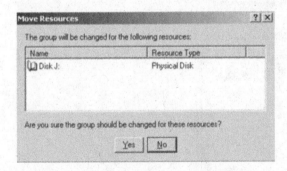

Figure 8-92. *Confirming the disk resource move once more*

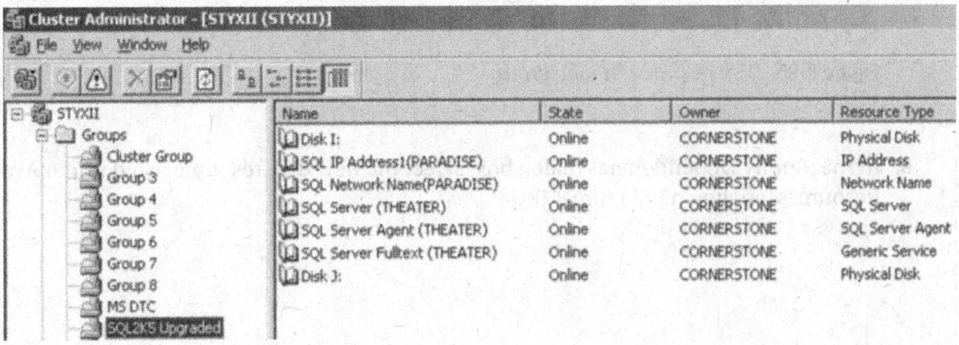

Figure 8-93. *Disk resource in new group*

7. Take the SQL Server resource offline. Once it is, it will appear similar to Figure 8-94.

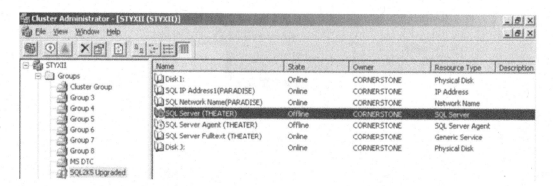

Figure 8-94. *Disk resource in new group*

8. Right-click the SQL Server or Analysis Services resource, and select Properties; alternatively, double-click the resource. Select the Dependencies tab, as shown in Figure 8-95. Click Modify.

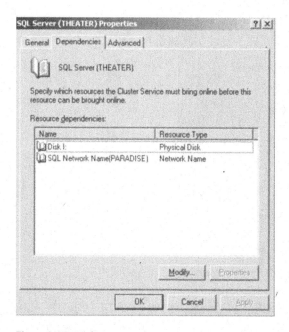

Figure 8-95. *Disk resource in new group*

9. In the Modify Dependencies dialog box, select the new disk resource listed under Available Resources, as shown in Figure 8-96.

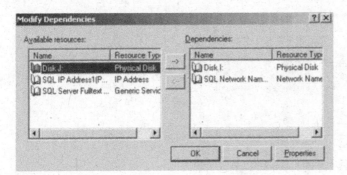

Figure 8-96. *Adding the disk resource as a dependency*

Click the right arrow button to move that resource to Dependencies; it should look like Figure 8-97 when complete. Click OK.

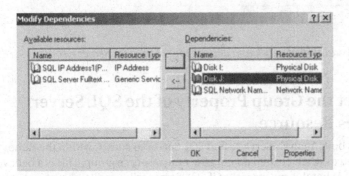

Figure 8-97. *Disk resource added as a dependency*

10. The Dependencies tab will now show that the disk is added as a dependency of the resource, as shown in Figure 8-98. Click Apply. Click OK.

11. Bring the offline resources online. SQL Server and/or Analysis Services will be able to use the newly added disk.

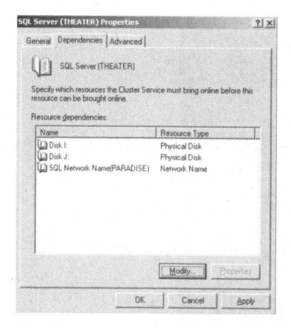

Figure 8-98. *Successful addition of a disk as a dependency to the SQL Server resource*

Changing the Affect the Group Property of the SQL Server or Analysis Services Resource

Since SQL Server 2005 allows both Analysis Services and SQL Server to coexist within the same group, by default those resources when created do not affect the resource group. This is a behavior change from SQL Server 2000. What this means is that if SQL Server fails, it will not automatically fail over to another node. Obviously this is the whole reason for implementing clusters in the first place. To make sure that SQL Server and/or Analysis Services automatically fail over to another node, perform these steps:

1. Start Cluster Administrator.

2. Select the group that contains the SQL Server or Analysis Services resource you want to modify.

3. Right-click the SQL Server or Analysis Services resource, and select Properties; alternatively, double-click the resource. Select the Advanced tab as shown in Figure 8-99, and check the box next to Affect the Group. Click Apply. Click OK.

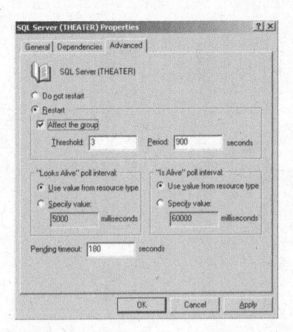

Figure 8-99. *Selecting the SQL Server or Analysis Resource to affect the group in the event of a failure*

Setting the Preferred Node Order for Failover

If your cluster has more than two nodes and your clustered SQL Server uses more than two of the nodes, you can alter the order in which the resource group containing SQL Server or Analysis Services will fail over to other nodes:

1. Start Cluster Administrator.

2. Select the resource group that has the SQL Server or Analysis Services resources, right-click, and select Properties. You will see a dialog box similar to the one shown in Figure 8-100. Click Modify.

3. The Modify Preferred Owners dialog box shown in Figure 8-101 will now be displayed. The right side shows all the possible owners of the resource group. If you want to change the order, select the node, and click the up or down arrows to move it to the order in which you want it to fail over. Click OK when finished to return to the Properties dialog box.

4. Click OK to close the properties of the resource group.

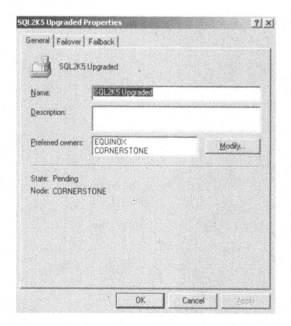

Figure 8-100. *Properties for the resource group*

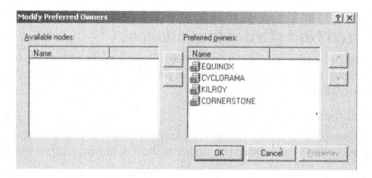

Figure 8-101. *Modify Preferred Owners dialog box*

Installing the Management Tools on the Other Nodes

As noted earlier, if you choose to install the client tools as part of the initial instance install on a cluster, it will put those tools only on the node that initiated the installation. After the install of SQL Server is complete, you now need to add those tools to the other nodes. It is important to note that some of the SQL Server tools are 32-bit, so if you are running a 64-bit server, this will run in WOW mode.

Setup

If you want to use the standard SQL Server Setup process to install the management tools, follow these steps:

1. Ensure that the .NET Framework 2.0 is installed on each node as shown in the section "Step Four: Install .NET Framework 2.0." It should be already installed since it is a prerequisite for SQL Server itself.

2. Log on to one of the nodes of the cluster that does not have the tools.

3. Insert the SQL Server 2005 installation media into the optical drive of the node you are logged into, or navigate to the proper network location of SQL Server 2005 installation point. Click Server Components, Tools, Books Online, and Samples. Conversely, if the screen does not appear or you want to cut to the chase, navigate to the Servers directory of your optical drive, and run setup.exe.

4. After the Read the End User License Agreement page appears, read it, accept the licensing terms and conditions, and click Next.

5. The Setup process will now determine whether any components will need to be installed prior to the main part of the installation process, as shown in the earlier Figure 8-21. Click Install. Setup will then install any prerequisites on the node that started the install process. During the process, a green check mark will appear next to completed tasks, and a red arrow pointing right will indicate the current task being executed. When all tasks are completed as shown in the earlier Figure 8-22, click Next to continue. Setup will then scan your configuration, as shown in the earlier Figure 8-23.

6. Click Next on the Welcome to the Microsoft SQL Server Installation Wizard page, as shown in Figure 8-24.

7. Setup will now do a more exhaustive check of the node that started the installation process, as shown in the earlier Figure 8-25. Any warnings or errors will be detected, and you can see them by clicking Messages next to the appropriate item or by viewing a report via the Report drop-down list. Click Next. Setup will now prepare your installation, as shown in the earlier Figure 8-26.

8. On the Registration Information page shown in the earlier Figure 8-27, enter your name and, if needed, a company name in the appropriate boxes. You must also enter your product key. Click Next.

9. On the Components to Install page, select the Workstation Components, Books Online and Development Tools option, as shown in Figure 8-102. To accept all default options, click Next, and go to step 11. To further pare down your install, click Advanced, and go to step 10.

10. On the Feature Selection page, you can select which components you want to have as part of your installation. Expand the tree, right-click the option, and if you do not want to have it installed, select Entire Feature Will Be Unavailable, as shown in the earlier Figure 8-31. DBAs should need only Connectivity Components, Management Tools, and Legacy Components, as shown in the earlier Figure 8-32. If you are using Analysis Services or doing development work, you may need to install the other tools. If you want to change where the SQL Server program files will be installed on your local drive, click Browse, and the Change Folders page will allow you to do just that. If you want to see how much disk space the components you selected will take on your hard drive, click Disk Cost. Figure 8-34 shows an example. Click Next.

11. On the Error and Usage Report Settings page shown in the earlier Figure 8-68, select the desired options if you want to send error or usage data back to Microsoft. These are optional. Click Next.

12. The Ready to Install page will reflect the options you chose earlier in the install. Figure 8-103 shows an example. Click Install. Setup will then start to prepare your install similar to the dialog box shown in the earlier Figure 8-70.

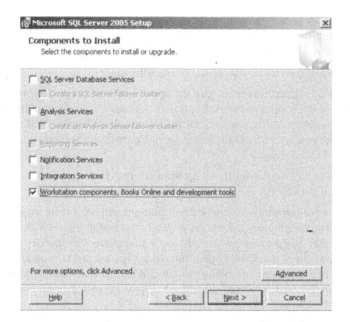

Figure 8-102. *Options needed to install the SQL Server tools*

Figure 8-103. *Ready to Install page*

13. When setup is complete, the Setup Progress page shown in Figure 8-104 will show all products with a status of Setup Finished. If a component causes a reboot, it will also be noted. Click Next.

14. On the Completing Microsoft SQL Server 2005 Setup dialog box shown in Figure 8-73, read the information presented, and click Finish.

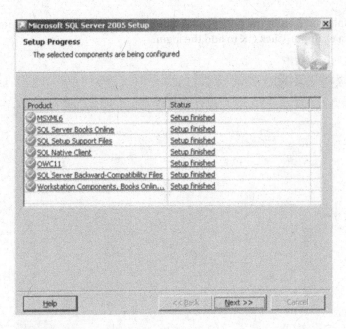

Figure 8-104. *Setup Progress page*

Command Line

Like the installation of SQL Server, you can put all the commands in a single file or execute them all directly from a command prompt. The parameter you need is ADDLOCAL. This is where you list the components you want to install. If you want to add other things such as the extended Business Intelligence tools, consult the Books Online topic "How to: Install SQL Server 2005 from the Command Prompt" for a full list of all options available to you. A DBA should not need more than the options listed in the following snippet:

```
[Options]
ADDLOCAL=Client_Components,Connectivity,SQL_Tools90,SQL_Documentation,
SQL_SQLServerBooksOnline
```

Removing the BUILTIN\Administrators Account

To make your SQL Server 2005 instance more secure, you should probably remove the BUILTIN\ Administrators account from SQL Server. However, since clustering uses BUILTIN\Administrators to access SQL Server, you need to explicitly add the cluster service account to SQL Server:

1. Start SQL Server Management Studio and connect to the SQL Server failover clustering instance.

2. Right-click Security folder, select New, and then select Login, as shown in Figure 8-105.

Figure 8-105. *Adding a login menu option*

3. In the Login – New dialog box, enter the fully qualified domain name for the login name. Figure 8-106 shows an example. Click OK to add the login.

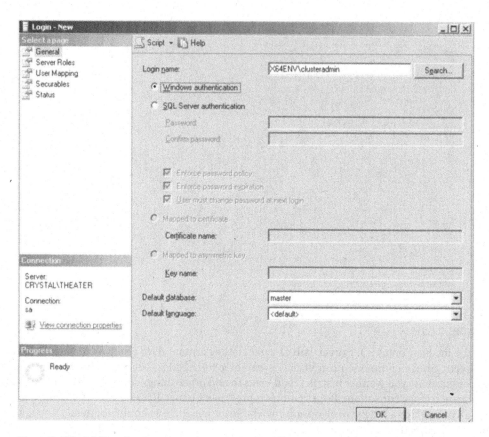

Figure 8-106. *Adding the cluster service account as a login in SQL Server*

4. Expand the Login subfolder of Security. Select the BUILTIN\Administrators account, right-click, and select Delete, as shown in Figure 8-107.

Figure 8-107. *The delete login option*

5. In the Delete Object dialog box shown in Figure 8-108, click OK.

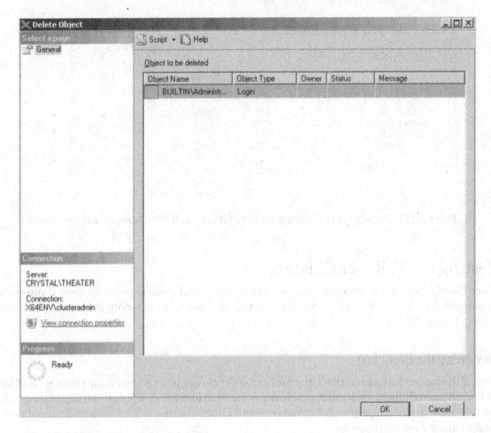

Figure 8-108. *The object to be deleted*

6. You should see a message similar to the one in Figure 8-109. Click OK. Your logins should now look similar to the one in Figure 8-110.

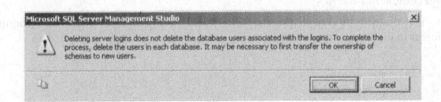

Figure 8-109. *Delete confirmation message*

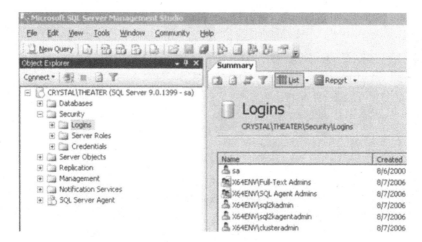

Figure 8-110. *Example of a clustered install that has BUILTIN\Administrators removed*

Testing the Failover Cluster

Once the SQL Server is fully configured, you must ensure that it works properly. Even if you are not prompted at the end of the SQL Server 2005 install, you may want to reboot the nodes. It certainly cannot hurt anything.

Reviewing the Event Log

One of the easiest features to check to ensure that the cluster is up and running properly is to look at Event Viewer. If there are serious problems, more than likely they will first start appearing here. All the messages that appear in Event Viewer should not indicate any problems and should point to the cluster working properly.

Verifying Network Connectivity and Cluster Name Resolution

Now that the SQL Server failover clustering instance is fully configured, you must verify its connectivity:

1. Open a command window.

2. From every node in the cluster, ping the SQL Server IP address. A successful result should be similar to the one in Figure 8-111.

```
C:\>ping 197.100.101.64

Pinging 197.100.101.64 with 32 bytes of data:

Reply from 197.100.101.64: bytes=32 time<1ms TTL=128
Reply from 197.100.101.64: bytes=32 time<1ms TTL=128
Reply from 197.100.101.64: bytes=32 time<1ms TTL=128
Reply from 197.100.101.64: bytes=32 time<1ms TTL=128

Ping statistics for 197.100.101.64:
    Packets: Sent = 4, Received = 4, Lost = 0 (0% loss),
Approximate round trip times in milli-seconds:
    Minimum = 0ms, Maximum = 0ms, Average = 0ms
```

Figure 8-111. *Pinging the SQL Server IP address successfully*

3. From a server or computer outside the cluster nodes, ping the failover cluster IP address to ensure that it can be reached from computers that are not part of the cluster.

4. From every node in the cluster, ping the SQL Server name. This will prove that the name of the cluster can be resolved. A successful result should look like Figure 8-112.

```
C:\>ping paradise

Pinging paradise.x64env.test.allan.com [197.100.101.64] with 32 bytes of data:

Reply from 197.100.101.64: bytes=32 time<1ms TTL=128
Reply from 197.100.101.64: bytes=32 time<1ms TTL=128
Reply from 197.100.101.64: bytes=32 time<1ms TTL=128
Reply from 197.100.101.64: bytes=32 time<1ms TTL=128

Ping statistics for 197.100.101.64:
    Packets: Sent = 4, Received = 4, Lost = 0 (0% loss),
Approximate round trip times in milli-seconds:
    Minimum = 0ms, Maximum = 0ms, Average = 0ms
```

Figure 8-112. *Pinging the SQL Server name successfully*

5. From a server or computer outside of the cluster nodes, ping the SQL Server name to ensure that it can be reached from computers that are not part of the cluster.

Performing Failover Validation

All nodes selected during Setup should be able to access the SQL Server resource group. The easiest way to verify that is to force a failover of the resources to another node:

1. Start Cluster Administrator.

2. In the left pane, expand Groups, right-click the cluster group containing the SQL Server you just installed, select the Move Group option, and finally select a node to move the resource group. If the failover is functioning properly, the owner of the resources will change to the new node name.

3. Repeat step 2 to move the resource to all other nodes of the failover cluster.

Verifying the Disk Configuration

SQL Server 2005 contains a new system dynamic management view (DMV) to be able to see what drives are associated with the clustered SQL Server. This DMV is sys.dm_io_cluster_shared_drives, and it replaces the depreciated function fn_servershareddrives from SQL Server 2000. fn_servershareddrives still is accessible from SQL Server 2005, and to use that function (although you should use the DMV, which gives the same information), you must have VIEW SERVER STATE permissions. Figure 8-113 shows an example of querying sys.dm_io_cluster_shared_drives.

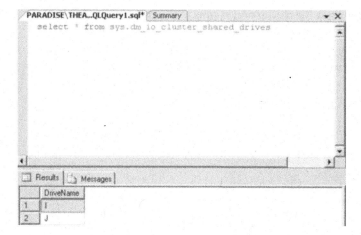

Figure 8-113. *Output of sys.dm_io_cluster_shared_drives*

Verifying the Node Configuration

SQL Server 2005 contains a new system DMV to be able to see what nodes are associated with the clustered SQL Server. This DMV is sys.dm_os_cluster_nodes, and it replaces the depreciated function fn_virtualservernodes from SQL Server 2000. fn_servernodes is still accessible from SQL Server 2005, and to use that function (although you should use the DMV, which gives the same information), you must have VIEW SERVER STATE permissions. Figure 8-114 shows an example of querying sys.dm_os_cluster_nodes.

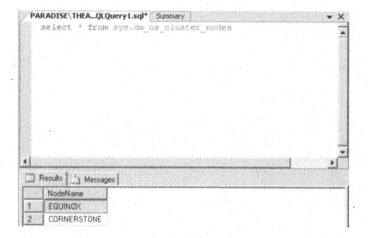

Figure 8-114. *Output of sys.dm_os_cluster_nodes for a two-node cluster*

Upgrade Only: Changing the Service Accounts

To perform the in-place upgrade, you have to add your existing SQL Server 2000 failover clustering instance's administration accounts to your SQL Server 2005 domain groups for clustering. If this is your only SQL Server 2000 instance, you do not have to do anything. However, if you have another SQL Server 2000 instance in a side-by-side configuration that uses the same administrator accounts, you must change the accounts used by the SQL Server instance you just upgraded. For instructions, see the upcoming section "Changing the Service Accounts Used by a Failover Clustering Instance." Once that is done, you must also remove those accounts from the SQL Server 2005 domain groups after changing the service accounts for SQL Server and SQL Server Agent as follows:

1. Log on to one of the servers as an administrator that has rights to add accounts to the domain.

2. From Administrative Tools, start the Active Directory Users and Computers tool.

3. Select Users, and in the right pane, double-click the group that has the old SQL Server 2000 administrator account. Select the SQL Server 2000 service account, as shown in Figure 8-115.

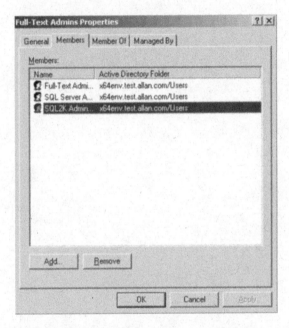

Figure 8-115. *Selecting the SQL Server 2000 service account*

4. Click Remove. You will be asked to confirm the removal of the account from the group, as shown in Figure 8-116. Click Yes.

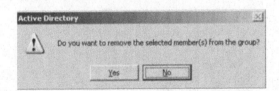

Figure 8-116. *Confirming the removal of the account*

5. Click OK to close the group's properties page.

Summary

In this chapter, you learned how to do the installation of both SQL Server and Analysis Services in a clustered configuration. There is just one last topic you need to understand before being ready to bring your production servers into the world: SQL Server 2005 failover clustering administration.

CHAPTER 9

■■■

Failover Clustering: SQL Server 2005 Failover Clustering Administration

The last part of the puzzle for failover clustering is knowing how to administer SQL Server in a clustered configuration. This chapter will walk you through the various tasks you may need to perform as part of your daily administration of the cluster. The tasks presented are specific to clustering; general administration and best practices as they relate to SQL Server are not the focus of this text.

Querying Failover Clustering Properties

If you are a DBA and either do not have access to Cluster Administrator or want a programmatic way to see which node currently owns the SQL Server resources, issue the query SELECT SERVERPROPERTY('ComputerNamePhysicalNetBIOS'), as shown in Figure 9-1.

You can also run a command via the command-line cluster.exe to see which node owns the cluster resources. Issue the command cluster *clustername* group *groupname* /stat, where *clustername* is the name of the Windows server cluster and *groupname* is the name of the resource group that contains the SQL Server resources. Figure 9-2 shows an example.

If you are a DBA and are not sure whether the instance is clustered or not, you can do one of two things. As with querying to see which node owns the SQL resources, issue the query SELECT SERVERPROPERTY('IsClustered'). If the instance is clustered, it will return a value of 1, and if not, a 0 as shown in Figure 9-3.

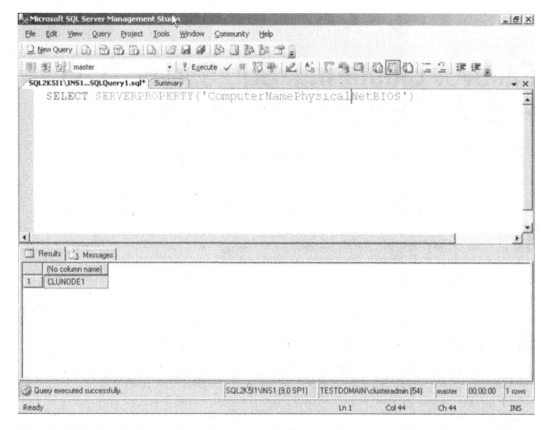

Figure 9-1. *Querying the resource group owner*

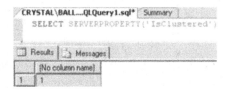

Figure 9-2. *Using the command line to see which node owns the cluster resources*

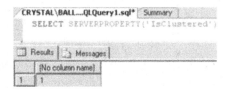

Figure 9-3. *Result of querying to see if the instance is clustered or not*

There are also visual aids you can use to determine that SQL Server is clustered. In SQL Server Management Studio, if you open the Properties of the instance, the IsClustered property is displayed as shown in Figure 9-4.

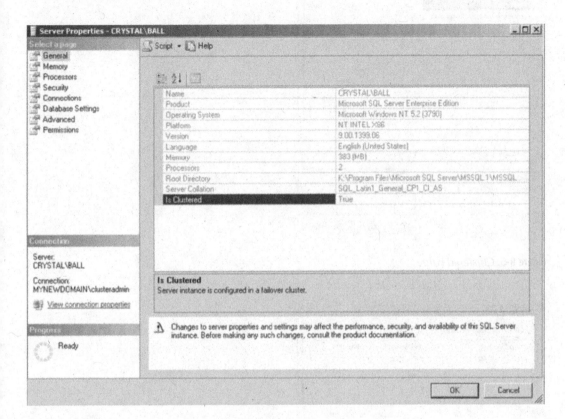

Figure 9-4. *IsClustered on the instance's Properties*

In SQL Server Configuration Manager, if you open the properties of the SQL Server service and select the Advanced tab, there are two places to look. First, look at the Clustered property, shown in Figure 9-5. If it has a value of Yes, the instance you are administering is a failover cluster.

Next, you can scroll down and look at the value for Virtual Server Name. This will only be populated if Clustered has a value of Yes. If this is a named instance, the value for Virtual Server Name will only contain the part before the backslash. In the example in Figure 9-6, the instance name is CRYSTAL\BALL, but the value for Virtual Server Name is just CRYSTAL.

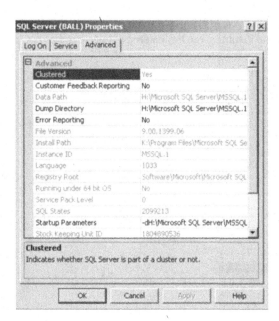

Figure 9-5. *Clustered value*

Figure 9-6. *Virtual Server Name value*

Using SQL Server 2005 Surface Area Configuration with Clustered Instances

SQL Server 2005 Surface Area Configuration is a new tool that ships with SQL Server 2005. It is a tool that allows you to manage both the features and the services of your SQL Server 2005 instance without having to necessarily execute queries or use other tools such as Management Studio. To start Surface Area Configuration, use the path from the Start menu that's shown in Figure 9-7.

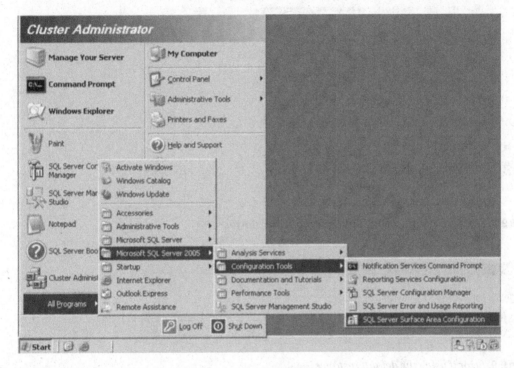

Figure 9-7. *Starting SQL Server Surface Area Configuration*

Although SQL Server Surface Area Configuration is cluster-aware, you must configure it to communicate with a failover clustering instance. When started, the tool will try to connect to a nonclustered local instance—it will default to localhost, as shown in Figure 9-8.

If you try to connect to the clustered instance with the default configuration, you will see the error message shown in Figure 9-9.

To connect to a clustered instance of SQL Server, click the Change Computer link. You will now see the Select Computer dialog box shown in Figure 9-10. Enter the name of the instance that is registered in DNS.

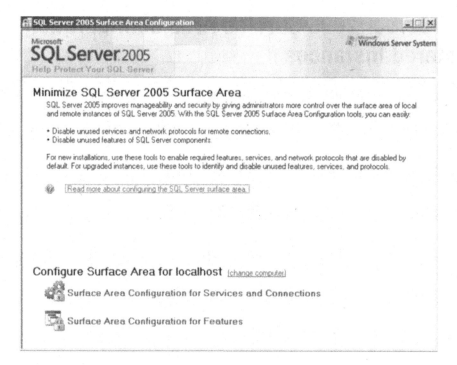

Figure 9-8. *SQL Server Surface Area Configuration after startup*

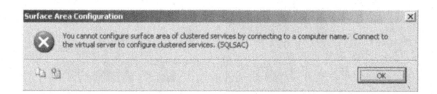

Figure 9-9. *Error if using the default instance*

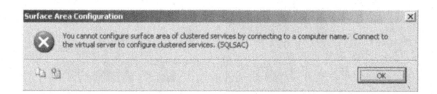

Figure 9-10. *Select Computer dialog box*

For a named instance, it is the part before the slash, so if you had an instance named CRYSTAL\
BALL, you would enter **CRYSTAL**. Click OK. Surface Area Configuration will reflect the change, as
shown in Figure 9-11.

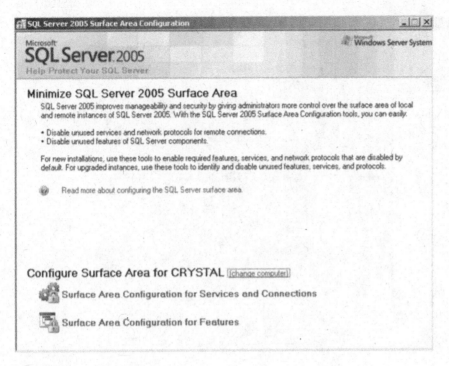

Figure 9-11. *Changed instance*

You can now administer your failover clustering instance via Surface Area Configuration. However, if you have more than one failover clustering instance, you will need to click Change Computer again when you want to administer another instance. You have two options for administration: Surface Area Configuration for Services and Connections and Surface Area Configuration for Features. Surface Area Configuration for Services and Connections will allow you to manage the services and properties that relate to connecting to your SQL Server instance. Figure 9-12 shows an example.

Surface Area Configuration for Features will allow you to select what features (such as xp_cmdshell) are enabled. Figure 9-13 shows an example.

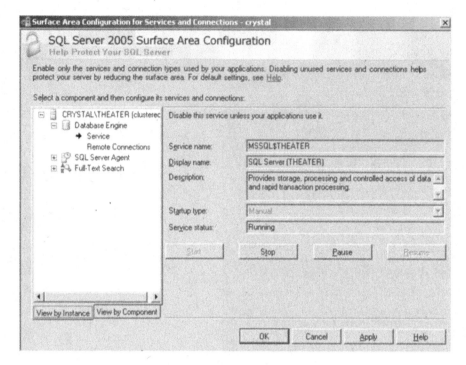

Figure 9-12. *Surface Area Configuration for Services and Connections*

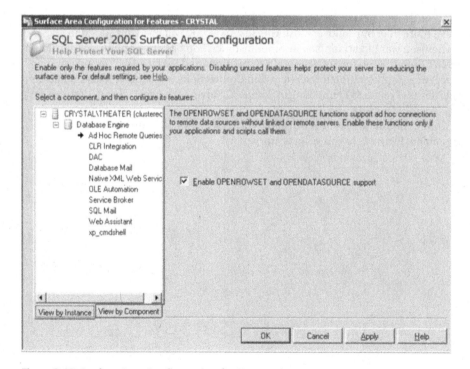

Figure 9-13. *Surface Area Configuration for Features*

Starting, Stopping, and Pausing Clustered SQL Server Services

In a clustered configuration, you have a few options for starting and stopping SQL Server or Analysis Services. One of them, however, is not the Services applet in Windows itself—that is something you should use only if directed by Microsoft Product Support Services. For both the RTM and SQL Server 2005 Service Pack 1 versions of SQL Server 2005, I was unable to start and stop a clustered SQL Server instance in SQL Server Management Studio (although I was told this did work for some). What I would see is shown in Figure 9-14—the options are there but disabled. After installing SQL Server 2005 Service Pack 2, the ability to use SQL Server Management Studio to stop and start SQL Server failover clustering instances seems to have been restored. If you need this functionality, I highly recommend installing SQL Server 2005 Service Pack 2 at your earliest convenience.

The three tools that you can use to stop and start the SQL services are SQL Server Configuration Manager, SQL Server Surface Area Configuration, and Cluster Administrator. Remember that if you stop a parent resource, its children will stop as well. It does not work that way in reverse—if you restart the parent resource, you will need to manually restart the child resource.

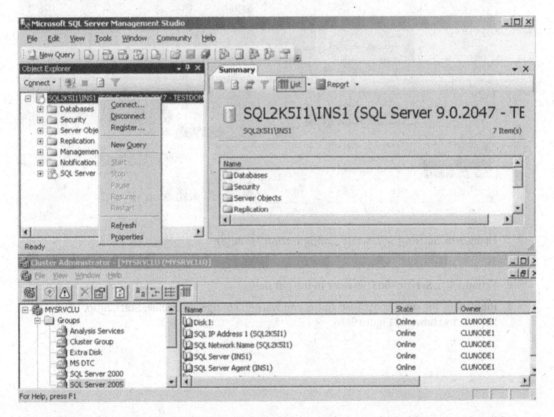

Figure 9-14. *Management Studio's inability to stop and start a failover clustering instance pre-SQL Server 2005 Service Pack 2. Management Studio is on top, while Cluster Administrator is on the bottom, showing that the instance is up and running.*

SQL Server Configuration Manager

SQL Server Configuration Manager is the replacement for SQL Server Service Manager and is the preferred method of stopping and starting all SQL-related services. SQL Server 2005 SQL Server Configuration Manager is fully cluster-aware. SQL Server Configuration Manager does not refresh every second, so you may have to manually refresh it to see the current state of the services. To stop and start a SQL Server 2005 clustered service using SQL Server Configuration Manager, follow these steps:

1. Start SQL Server Configuration Manager, as shown in Figure 9-15.

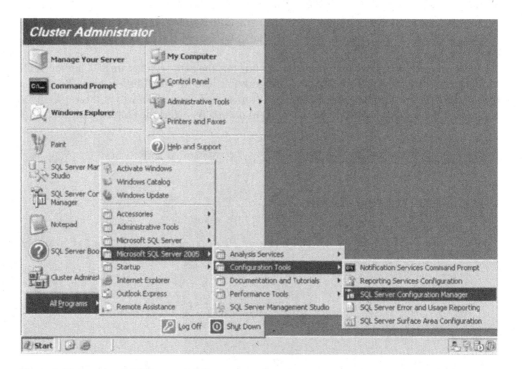

Figure 9-15. *Starting SQL Server Configuration Manager*

2. Expand SQL Server 2005 Services in the left pane.

3. Right-click the resource whose status you want to change, and select Start, Stop, Pause, or Restart, as shown in Figure 9-16.

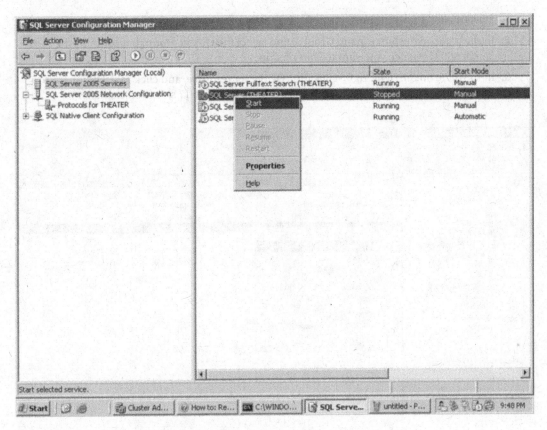

Figure 9-16. *SQL Server Configuration Manager*

SQL Server Surface Area Configuration

SQL Server Surface Area Configuration is the other SQL Server tool that can stop and start the SQL Server–related services in a clustered configuration:

1. Start SQL Server Surface Area Configuration and configure it to connect to the failover clustering instance.

2. Click Surface Area Configuration for Services and Connections.

3. In the left pane, expand the feature (such as Database Engine) that you want to administer, and select Service. Depending on the state of the service as shown in the example previously in Figure 9-16, you can start, stop, pause, or resume the service.

Cluster Administrator

You can use Cluster Administrator to stop and start the SQL Server–related services in a clustered configuration. The account you are using must have administrative rights to run Cluster Administrator and connect to the server cluster. To stop or start a SQL Server 2005 failover clustering instance using Cluster Administrator, follow these steps:

1. Start Cluster Administrator.

2. In the pane on the left, expand Groups, and select the cluster group that contains the SQL Server 2005 instance you want to start or stop.

3. In the pane on the right, right-click the SQL Server resource, and click Take Offline to stop the instance or Bring Online to start the instance. Figure 9-17 shows an example.

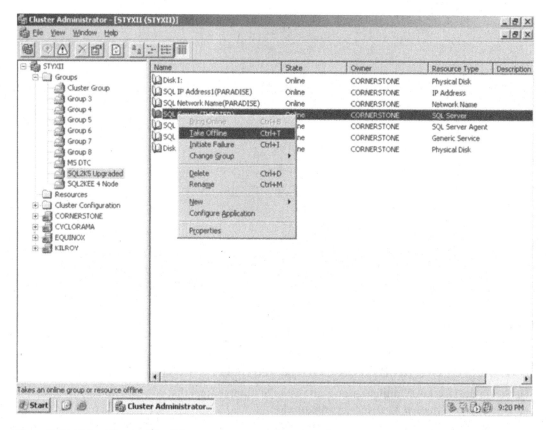

Figure 9-17. *Using Cluster Administrator to start and stop services*

Command Line

You can also use the command-line `cluster.exe` to take a group or resource offline.

Taking a Resource or Group Offline

To take a single cluster resource offline, such as the SQL Server resource, use the command `cluster clustername resource resourcename /off`, where *clustername* is the name of the Windows server cluster and *resourcename* is the name of the resource you will be affecting. If the resource has spaces, use quotes around it. Figure 9-18 shows an example.

```
K:\>cluster styx resource "SQL Server" /off
Taking resource 'SQL Server' offline...
Resource            Group             Node            Status
-----------------------------------------------------------
SQL Server          EQUINOX           NODE1           Offline
```

Figure 9-18. *Example of taking a resource offline with cluster.exe*

To take an entire cluster resource group offline such as the one containing the SQL Server resources, use the command cluster *clustername* group *groupname* /off, where *clustername* is the name of the Windows server cluster and *groupname* is the name of the group you will be affecting. If the group's name has spaces, use quotes around it. Figure 9-19 shows an example.

```
K:\>cluster styx group equinox /off
Bringing resource group 'equinox' offline...
Group               Node              Status
--------------------------------------------
equinox             NODE1             Offline
```

Figure 9-19. *Example of taking a group offline with cluster.exe*

Bringing a Resource or Group Online

To bring a single cluster resource offline such as the SQL Server resource, use the command cluster *clustername* resource *resourcename* /on, where *clustername* is the name of the Windows server cluster and *resourcename* is the name of the resource you will be affecting. If the resource has spaces, use quotes around it. Figure 9-20 shows an example.

```
K:\>cluster styx resource "SQL Server" /on
Bringing resource 'SQL Server' online...
Resource            Group             Node            Status
-----------------------------------------------------------
SQL Server          EQUINOX           NODE1           Online
```

Figure 9-20. *Example of bringing a resource online with cluster.exe*

To bring an entire cluster resource group online such as the one containing the SQL Server resources, use the command cluster *clustername* group *groupname* /on, where *clustername* is the name of the Windows server cluster and *groupname* is the name of the group you will be affecting. If the group's name has spaces, use quotes around it. Figure 9-21 shows an example.

```
K:\>cluster styx group equinox /on
Bringing resource group 'equinox' online...
Group               Node              Status
--------------------------------------------
equinox             NODE1             Online
```

Figure 9-21. *Example of bringing a group online with cluster.exe*

Note Remember that if you take the parent resource offline, its dependencies will go offline as well. When you restart the parent, it does not automatically restart the children, so you will have to restart each dependency manually.

Renaming a Failover Clustering Instance of SQL Server

New to SQL Server 2005 is the ability to rename a clustered instance of SQL Server without having to uninstall and reinstall it. Two caveats are associated with renaming a failover clustering instance:

- If you have a named instance, such as CRYSTAL\BALL, you can rename only the portion that is registered in DNS, which is CRYSTAL. So if you need to do a full rename, you will have to do an uninstall and a reinstall.

Note There is a chance Microsoft will enable the ability to rename a named instance of SQL Server that is clustered in a service pack post–SQL Server 2005 Service Pack 2. Consult the documentation that ships with the service pack to see if this functionality has been added.

- There will be some downtime associated with a rename operation.

Follow these steps:

1. Start Cluster Administrator.

2. Select the resource group that has the SQL Server or Analysis Services resources.

3. Take the SQL Server or Analysis Services service offline.

4. Right-click the SQL Server or Analysis Services Network Name resource, and select Properties; alternatively, double-click the resource.

5. Select the Parameters tab of the resource's properties page, as shown in Figure 9-22. It will reflect the current name.

6. Enter the new name of the failover clustering resource, as shown in Figure 9-23, and click Apply.

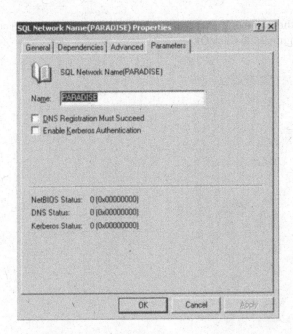

Figure 9-22. *Parameters tab*

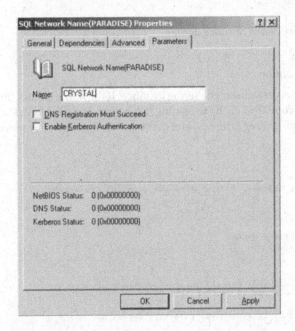

Figure 9-23. *Changing the failover clustering instance name*

7. Select the General tab. Change the name of the resource to include the new name you configured in step 6, as shown in Figure 9-24. Click OK.

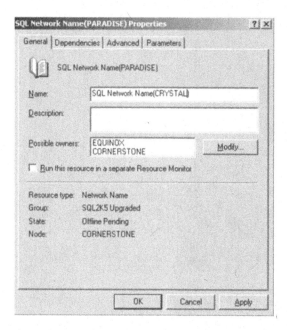

Figure 9-24. *Changing the Network Name resource name*

8. Bring the SQL Server resources online.

9. Ping the new name of the SQL Server failover clustering instance. If the name cannot be
resolved, you will have to flush your DNS cache by issuing these three commands in succession: ipconfig /flushdns, ipconfig /registerdns, and nbtstat -RR. Figure 9-25 shows an
example.

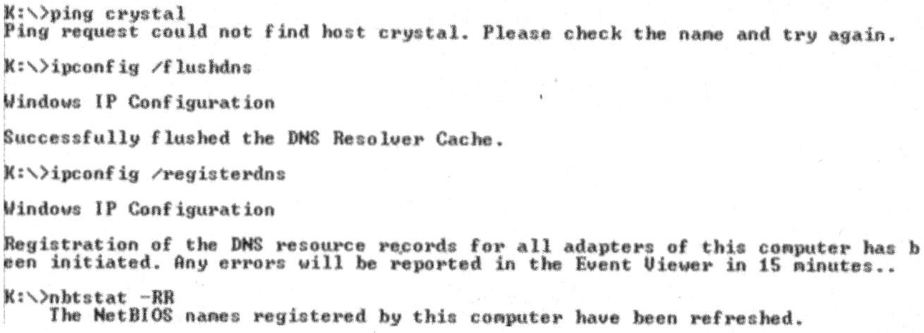

```
K:\>ping crystal
Ping request could not find host crystal. Please check the name and try again.

K:\>ipconfig /flushdns

Windows IP Configuration

Successfully flushed the DNS Resolver Cache.

K:\>ipconfig /registerdns

Windows IP Configuration

Registration of the DNS resource records for all adapters of this computer has b
een initiated. Any errors will be reported in the Event Viewer in 15 minutes..

K:\>nbtstat -RR
    The NetBIOS names registered by this computer have been refreshed.
```

Figure 9-25. *Flushing the DNS cache*

10. Start SQL Server Management Studio, and connect with the new instance name. If this succeeds, the change has been done successfully.

11. For a final verification, you can also run a SELECT @@SERVERNAME query, which should reflect the name change. Figure 9-26 shows an example.

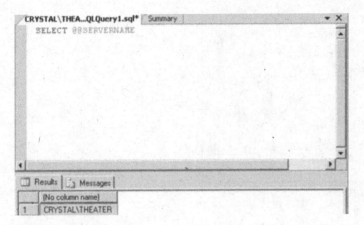

Figure 9-26. *Results of query after changing the name*

Changing the Service Accounts Used by a Failover Clustering Instance

With a SQL Server 2000 failover cluster, you used Enterprise Manager to change the service accounts associated with SQL Server. With SQL Server 2005 (both the relational engine as well as Analysis Services), you do not use its equivalent (Management Studio); instead, you use SQL Server Configuration Manager:

1. Start SQL Server Configuration Manager.

2. Select SQL Server 2005 Services in the pane on the left.

3. In the pane on the right, select the service whose account you want to alter, right-click, and select Properties. The properties page of the resource will be displayed, as shown in Figure 9-27. Make sure the Log On tab is selected.

4. Change the account to the new domain-based service account. Figure 9-28 shows an example. Click Apply. Click OK.

5. When prompted by the Confirm Account Change dialog box, as shown in Figure 9-29, click Yes.

Note Remember that any child resources will be stopped if a parent is restarted. You must manually restart those services.

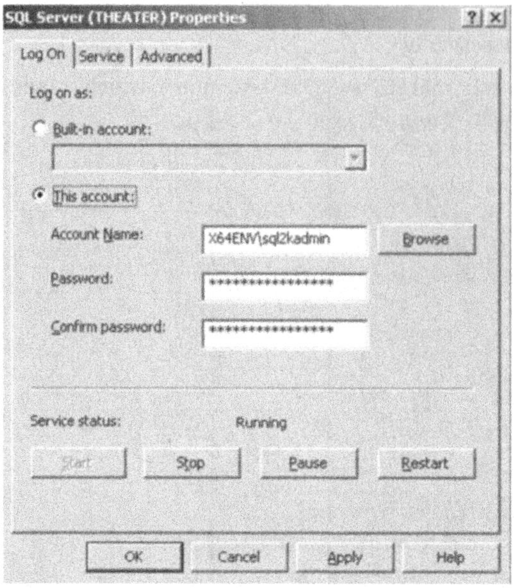

Figure 9-27. *Log On tab of the service properties*

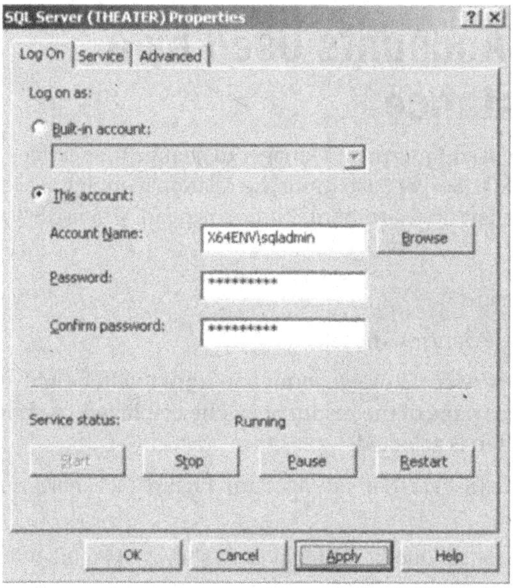

Figure 9-28. *Changing the service account example*

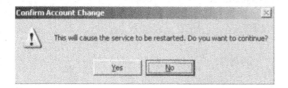

Figure 9-29. *Confirming the change to the service account*

Changing the IP Address of a Failover Clustering Instance

Changing the IP address of a clustered SQL Server instance in SQL Server 2005 no longer requires running Setup as it did in SQL Server 2000—it is much easier. You now can change it within Cluster Administrator. Be aware that there will be an outage of SQL Server when the IP address is changed.

1. Start Cluster Administrator.
2. Select the resource group with the SQL Server or Analysis Services resources.
3. Take the IP address resource that you want to change offline. This will also take all SQL Server or Analysis Services resources dependent upon it offline as well.
4. Select the IP address resource, right-click, and select Properties; alternatively, double-click the resource. Select the Parameters tab, as shown in Figure 9-30.

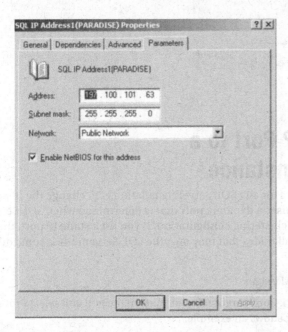

Figure 9-30. *Parameters with the original IP address*

5. Change the IP address. Figure 9-31 shows an example. Click Apply. Click OK.
6. Bring the resources online.
7. Ping the new IP address from all nodes as well as from outside the cluster to make sure the change has been successful.

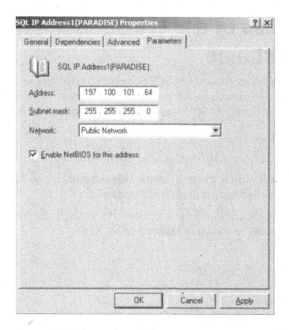

Figure 9-31. *Changed IP address*

Assigning a Static IP Port to a Failover Clustering Instance

One of the recommended best practices for any SQL Server installation is to change the IP port to a static port. By default, SQL Server uses a dynamic port that is determined when SQL Server is started. This is also true in a failover clustering configuration. If you set a static IP port, the port number will remain the same on all nodes that may own the SQL Server unless some other process happens to take that port.

1. Start SQL Server Configuration Manager.

2. Expand SQL Server 2005 Network Configuration in the pane on the left, and select Protocols for <instancename>. Figure 9-32 shows an example.

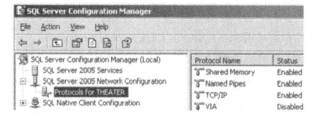

Figure 9-32. *SQL Server 2005 Network Configuration for the failover clustering instance*

3. In the pane on the right, select TCP/IP, right-click, and select Properties.

4. Scroll down to the bottom of the IP addresses, as shown in Figure 9-33. The current dynamic port assignment will be displayed in the section IP All in the category TCP Dynamic Ports.

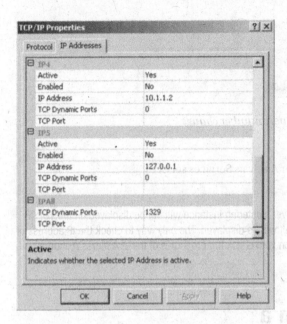

Figure 9-33. *Viewing the dynamic port value*

5. Delete the value from TCP Dynamic Ports, and assign a static port in the parameter TCP Port. Figure 9-34 shows an example. Click Apply. Click OK.

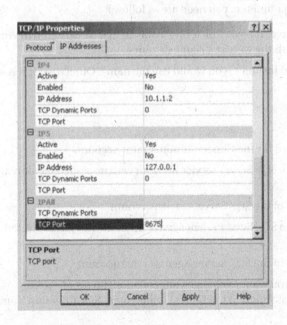

Figure 9-34. *Assigning a static port*

6. You will then be notified that for the change to take effect, you will need to restart SQL Server or Analysis Services, as shown in Figure 9-35. Click OK.

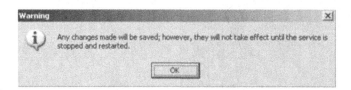

Figure 9-35. *Message to accept the port number change*

7. Stop and restart the SQL Server or Analysis Services services.

Note The actual TCP/IP address of the failover clustering instance will *not* be displayed on the TCP/IP properties page. The nodes and the cluster itself will be displayed. The only way to check the IP address of your SQL Server or Analysis Services installation is to check the properties of the IP Address resource.

Rebuilding master on a Failover Clustering Instance

With SQL Server 2005, Microsoft no longer ships the rebuildm tool to rebuild the master database in the event of a problem or a fundamental reconfiguration. The only way to rebuild master is to do it via the command line. Like installation, you can put all the commands in a single file or execute them all from a command prompt. The parameters you need are as follows:

- VS: This is the name of the SQL Server failover clustering instance that is registered in Windows and is the one associated with the Network Name resource.

- INSTANCENAME: If you have a named instance, you would use the name. Otherwise, if it is a default instance, use MSSQLSERVER.

- REINSTALL: This will be set to SQL_Engine.

- REBUILDDATABASE: This will be set to 1.

- ADMINPASSWORD: This is the password for the Cluster Administrator account.

- SQLACCOUNT: This is the name of the SQL Server service account with its associated domain name.

- SQLPASSWORD: This is the password of the SQL Server service account.

- AGTACCOUNT: This is the name of the SQL Server Agent service account with its associated domain name.

- AGTPASSWORD: This is the password of the SQL Server Agent service account.

- SQLCOLLATION: This is optional. If you want to change your collation, this is where you would use a valid collation name as found in the Books Online topic "SQL Collation Name (Transact-SQL)."

This is an example file:

```
[Options]
VS="SQL2K5I1"
INSTANCENAME="INS1"
REINSTALL="SQL_Engine"
REBUILDDATABASE=1
ADMINPASSWORD="password"
SQLACCOUNT="VALIDDOMAIN\sqlserveraccount"
SQLPASSWORD="password"
AGTACCOUNT="VALIDDOMAIN\sqlagentaccount"
AGTPASSWORD="password"
SQLCOLLATION=SQL_Latin1_General_CP1_CI_AS
```

Adding or Removing a Node

In the event that you need to remove a node because of some sort of failure so you can reconfigure the node, SQL Server provides a method for you to do so. Removing a node is sometimes referred to as *evicting* a node. You can evict a node in two places: from SQL Server, and at the Windows failover cluster later in Cluster Administrator. Unfortunately, most people perform the latter task first, which can damage the SQL Server installation.

The process to add a node uses the same basic process as removing a node and is similar to installing your clustered SQL Server instance.

Using Setup

Using the SQL Server Setup program from your install point, follow these steps:

1. Log in to a node with an account that can administer all nodes of the cluster.

2. Make sure the SQL Server resources are owned by the node you are logged in to.

3. Go to Control Panel, and double-click Add or Remove Programs.

4. Select Microsoft SQL Server 2005 (which may or may not have a 64-bit designation after it). Click Change, as shown in Figure 9-36. *Do not click Remove.* Setup will then scan your configuration like it did during the installation process.

5. In the Component Selection dialog box, select the instance of SQL Server that you want to modify. Figure 9-37 shows an example. Click Next.

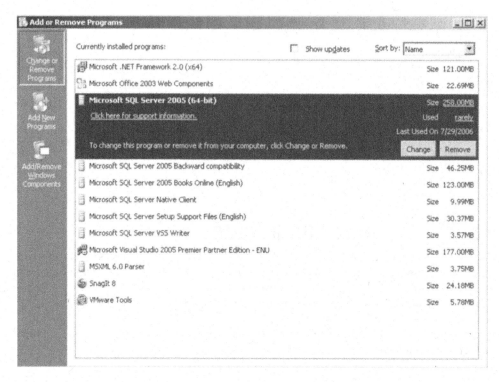

Figure 9-36. *Add or Remove Programs with SQL Server highlighted*

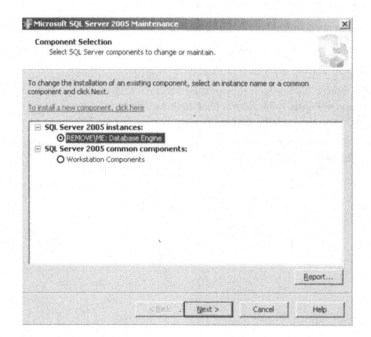

Figure 9-37. *Selecting the instance to change*

6. In the Feature Maintenance dialog box, select the existing component to modify. If you have only one component, it will be automatically selected. Figure 9-38 shows an example. Click Next.

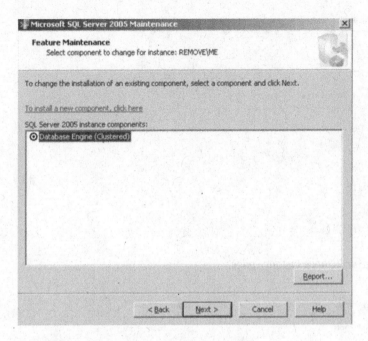

Figure 9-38. *Selecting the component to modify*

7. A scan of your configuration will occur, and then you will see the Welcome to the Microsoft SQL Server Installation Wizard. Click Next.

8. Setup will now do a more exhaustive check not unlike the process of installing a new instance of SQL Server 2005. Any warnings or errors will be detected, and you can view them by clicking Messages next to the appropriate item or by viewing a report via the Report drop-down list. Click Next.

9. On the Change or Remove Instance page, as shown in Figure 9-39, click Maintain the Virtual Server.

10. On the Cluster Node Configuration page, to add a node in the Available Nodes list to the definition of the failover clustering instance, select it, and click Add. To remove a node from the definition, select it from Selected Nodes, and click Remove. Figure 9-40 shows an example.

Figure 9-39. *Change or Remove Instance page*

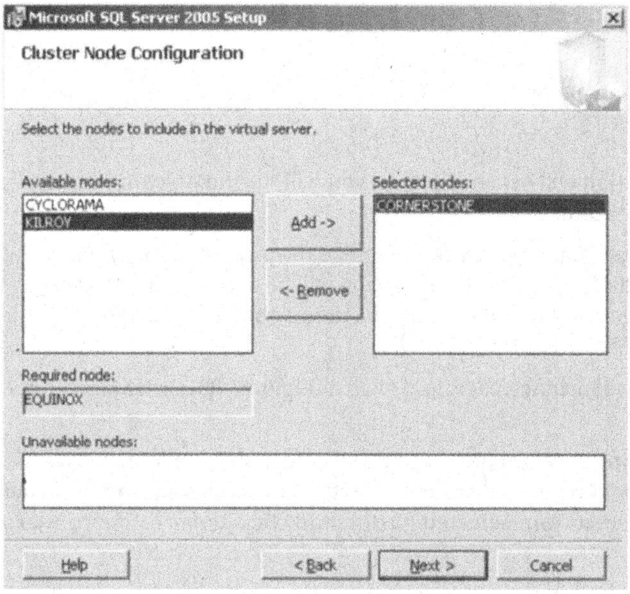

Figure 9-40. *Selecting the nodes to add or remove*

If some nodes are not available, they will be displayed in Unavailable Nodes, as shown in
Figure 9-41. If the nodes are unavailable, they cannot be added or removed from the definition. Click Next.

Figure 9-41. *Example list of nodes that are unavailable to add to the failover clustering instance's definition*

11. If you made changes to your configuration, you will see the Remote Account Information page. Enter the password of the cluster administrator you are logged in as. If the user you are currently logged in as is not an administrator of the cluster nodes, cancel Setup, log out, and log in as the proper user.

12. On the Ready to Update page, if you did not make any changes to the configuration, you will see the page in Figure 9-42. Hit Cancel to exit. If there are configuration changes, you will see the page in Figure 9-43. Click Install. The configuration changes will be made. As with the standard install process, you can see the progress of the configuration. When finished, click Next. If you removed nodes, continue with step 13. If not, you may stop here.

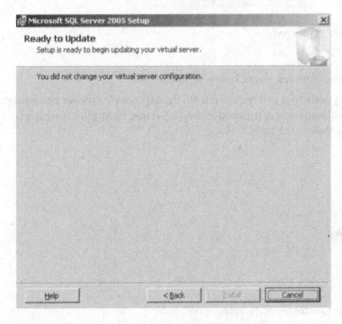

Figure 9-42. *No changes made to the configuration*

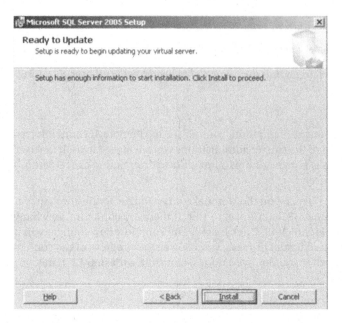

Figure 9-43. *Setup is ready to proceed.*

13. If you removed one or more nodes, start Cluster Administrator.

14. On the left side, select a node that you removed from the SQL Server failover clustering instance. If the node is already down, proceed to step 12. If not, right-click, and select Stop Cluster Service, as shown in Figure 9-44.

Figure 9-44. *Stopping the Cluster Service on a removed node*

15. Once again, right-click the node that is now stopped, and select Evict Node, as shown in Figure 9-45.

16. When prompted to confirm the node eviction, as shown in Figure 9-46, click Yes.

17. Repeat steps 12 through 14 for all nodes removed from the SQL Server failover clustering instance.

Tip See the section in Chapter 5 on adding additional nodes to the cluster to see how to add a node via Cluster Administrator.

Figure 9-45. *Menu option to evict a node*

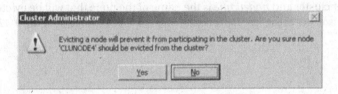

Figure 9-46. *Confirming the node eviction*

Using the Command Prompt

With SQL Server 2005, you can also add and remove nodes via the .ini file method. The parameters that are used are as follows:

- VS: This is the name of the SQL Server failover clustering instance that is registered in Windows and is the one associated with the Network Name resource.

- INSTALLVS: This will be set to SQL_Engine or Analysis_Service (or both separated by a comma) depending on your configuration.

- INSTANCENAME: This will be the name of your instance. If it is a default instance, this will be set to MSSQLSERVER.

- ADMINPASSWORD: This is the password for the Cluster Administrator account.

- ADDNODE: This is the node or list of nodes (separated by commas) to be added from the definition of the failover clustering instance.

- REMOVENODE: This is the node or list of nodes (separated by commas) to be removed from the definition of the failover clustering instance.

- GROUP: This is the cluster resource group that contains the SQL Server or Analysis Services resources.

To add a physical node to the cluster via the command line, follow the section in Chapter 5 on adding additional nodes to the cluster. The following snippet is an example of the right things to put in the file to add a node to the SQL Server definition of the cluster:

```
[Options]
VS="SQL2K5I1"
INSTALLVS="SQL_Engine"
INSTANCENAME="INS1"
ADMINPASSWORD="password"
ADDNODE="CLUNODE2"
GROUP="SQL Server 2005"
```

The following snippet is an example of the right things to put in the file to remove a node:

```
[Options]
VS="SQL2K5I1"
INSTALLVS="SQL_Engine"
INSTANCENAME="INS1"
ADMINPASSWORD="password"
REMOVENODE="CLUNODE2"
GROUP="SQL Server 2005"
```

To remove a node using the command line once you have removed its definition from SQL Server as shown with the previous snippet, use `cluster.exe`. First, you must stop the Cluster Service on that node with the command `cluster` *clustername* `node` *nodename* `/stop`, where *clustername* is the name of the Windows server cluster and *nodename* is the name of the node that will be evicted. Once that is complete, you will execute `cluster` *clustername* `node` *nodename* `/evict`. Figure 9-47 shows an example.

```
K:\>cluster styx node node3 /stop

Attempting to stop the cluster service on node 'node3'
The cluster service has been successfully stopped.

K:\>cluster styx node node3 /evict
Evicting node 'node3'...
```

Figure 9-47. *Evicting a node via the command line*

■**Note** Remember to check the SQL Server definition of the failover clustering instance after evicting a node. See the section on verifying the node configuration in Chapter 8.

Uninstalling a Failover Clustering Instance

Uninstalling a clustered SQL Server 2005 instance is different than in previous versions of SQL Server. It is important to note that removing SQL Server will not remove the client tools or utilities. You have to do those manually. To uninstall SQL Server, you must meet these three criteria:

- The user executing it must have administrative privileges on all nodes. An example would be logging in and running the uninstall Cluster Administrator service account.
- The installation point and/or physical media must be available.
- The process must be initiated from the node that currently owns that instance.

Using Setup

Using the SQL Server Setup program from your install point, follow these steps:

1. Log in to a node with an account that can administer all nodes of the cluster.

2. Start Cluster Administrator, and ensure that the node that you are logged in to is the owner of the SQL Server resources. If not, use Cluster Administrator to move the resources to the node you are on, or log out and log in to the node that owns the resources.

3. Navigate to Control Panel, and select Add or Remove Programs.

4. Select Microsoft SQL Server 2005 (which may or may not have a 64-bit designation after it), as shown in the earlier Figure 9-36. You have two methods: click Change or click Remove.

Change

To Change SQL Server, follow these steps:

1. Follow steps 5 to 9 from the section "Adding or Removing a Node."

2. On the Remove Microsoft SQL Server page shown in Figure 9-48, click Remove.

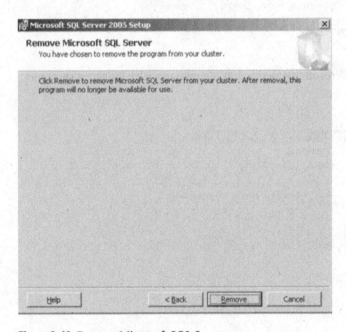

Figure 9-48. *Remove Microsoft SQL Server page*

3. Setup will now remove the cluster configuration and will display the status as it would during the normal installation process. When the process is complete, you will see a page similar to the one in Figure 9-49. Click Next.

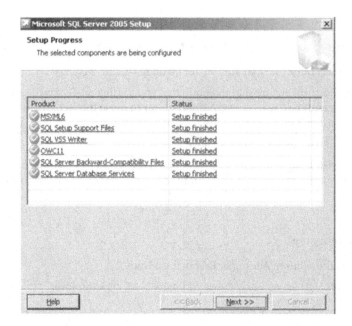

Figure 9-49. *Setup Progress page*

4. On the Completing Microsoft SQL Server 2005 Setup page, click Finish, as shown in Figure 9-50.

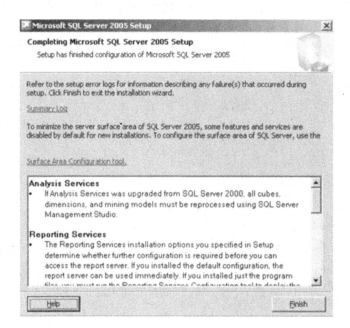

Figure 9-50. *Completing Microsoft SQL Server 2005 Setup page*

Remove

To remove SQL Server, follow these steps:

1. On the Component Selection page, select the option Remove SQL Server 2005 Instance Components, and select the instance to remove. Figure 9-51 shows an example.

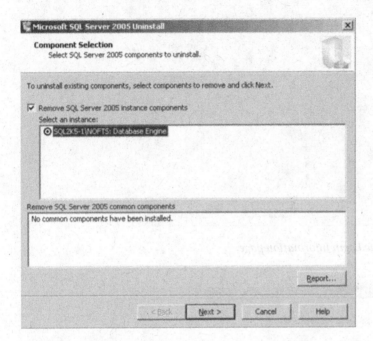

Figure 9-51. *Component Selection page after clicking Remove*

2. On the Remove Login Information page shown in Figure 9-52, enter the password for the account that you are logged in to because that has administrator access to all nodes of the cluster. Click Next.

3. On the Confirmation page shown in Figure 9-53, click Next.

4. On the Welcome to the Microsoft SQL Server Installation Wizard page, click Next.

5. Setup will now remove the cluster configuration and will display the status as it would during the normal installation process. When the process is complete, you will see a page similar to the one in the earlier Figure 9-49. Click Next.

6. On the Completing Microsoft SQL Server 2005 Setup page, click Finish as shown in the earlier Figure 9-50.

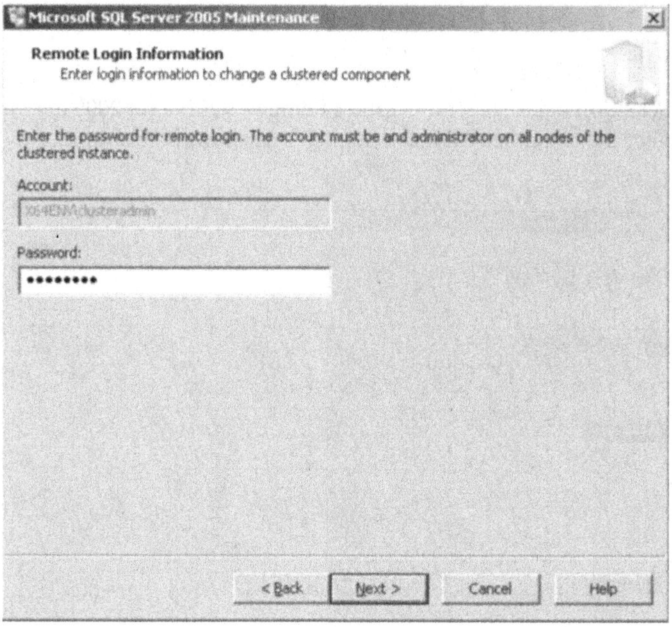

Figure 9-52. *Remote Login Information page*

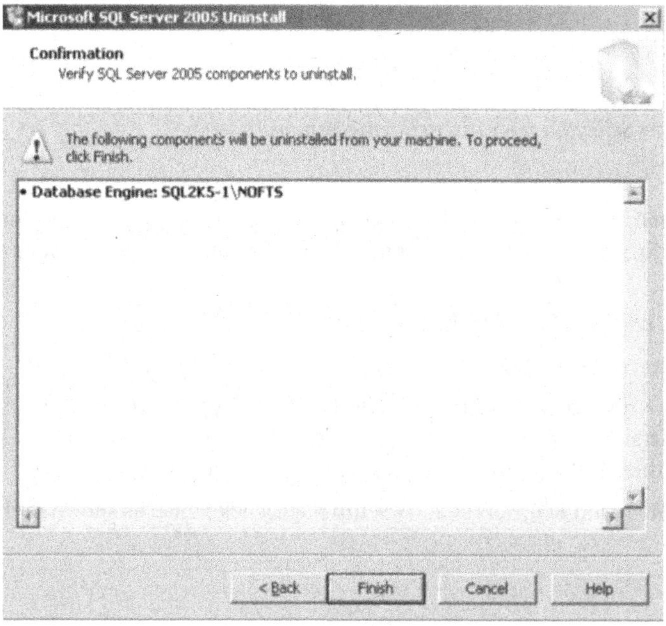

Figure 9-53. *Confirmation page*

Command Prompt

Like installation or adding/removing a node, you can put all the commands in a single file or execute them all from a command prompt. The parameters you need are as follows:

- VS: This is the name of the SQL Server failover clustering instance that is registered in Windows and is the one associated with the Network Name resource.

- INSTANCENAME: If you have a named instance, you would use the name. Otherwise, if it is a default instance, use MSSQLSERVER.

- REMOVE: This will be set to SQL_Engine.

- ADMINPASSWORD: This is the password for the Cluster Administrator account.

Here's an example file to remove Analysis Services:

```
[Options]
VS=SQL2K5AS
INSTANCENAME="AS1"
REMOVE="Analysis_Server"
ADMINPASSWORD="password"
```

Here's an example file to remove SQL Server:

```
[Options]
VS=SQL2K5I1
INSTANCENAME="INS1"
REMOVE="SQL_Engine"
ADMINPASSWORD="password"
```

Changing Domains

Sometimes if you are moving data centers or unifying an infrastructure, you may need to change the domain of your SQL Server 2005 failover clustering instances. This means both the Windows and SQL portions will change. What you have to do will depend on whether your underlying network infrastructure and IP addresses are changing or whether you just need to change service accounts. Both methods require outages, so they will affect your end users and overall availability.

Unfortunately, as of SQL Server 2005 Service Pack 2 (which is the latest version used for testing in the book), the only way to change domains for SQL Server is to do a complete uninstall and reinstall of SQL Server. There is no other way to change SQL Server itself. Believe me, I tried a few methods I thought would work. I spent quite a few days even doing things such as changing registry entries to try to fake either SQL Server or Windows out. I had no luck. This may change in a future revision of SQL Server, so remember to read the readme file that ships with upcoming SQL Server 2005 service packs.

Changing the Domain with No IP Address Changes

If your underlying network infrastructure supporting the failover clustering instance is not changing, this is the easiest scenario to deal with:

1. Back up all SQL Server databases. You may also consider detaching the user databases, but the method is completely up to you. Detaching may be a better option here because you can leave the databases on the shared drives and attach them after reinstalling SQL Server.

2. Script and back up any objects (logins, users, SSIS packages, SQL Server Agent jobs, custom scripts, etc.) from SQL Server.

3. Uninstall the clustered SQL Server 2005 failover clustering instance as per the instructions in the section "Uninstalling a Failover Clustering Instance" earlier in this chapter.

4. Start Cluster Administrator.

5. Start the Services applet. Select Cluster Service, right-click, and select Properties. Set the startup type to Manual, as shown in Figure 9-54.

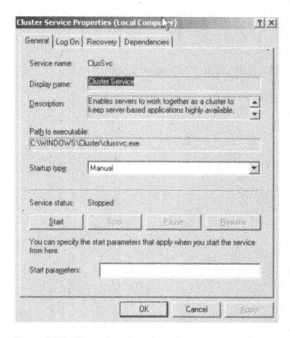

Figure 9-54. *Changing the Cluster Service to start manually*

6. Repeat step 5 for all nodes of the cluster.

7. Select System from Control Panel. Select the Computer Name tab, as shown in Figure 9-55. Click Change.

8. In the Domain entry box shown in Figure 9-56, enter the name of your new domain, and click OK.

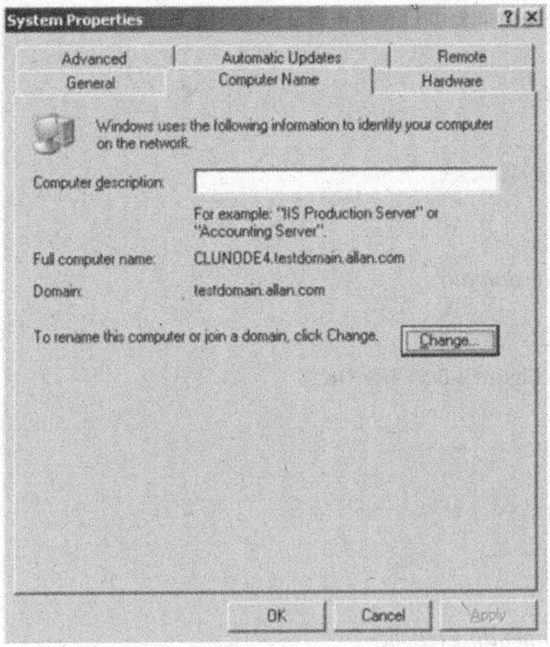

Figure 9-55. *Selecting the Computer Name tab*

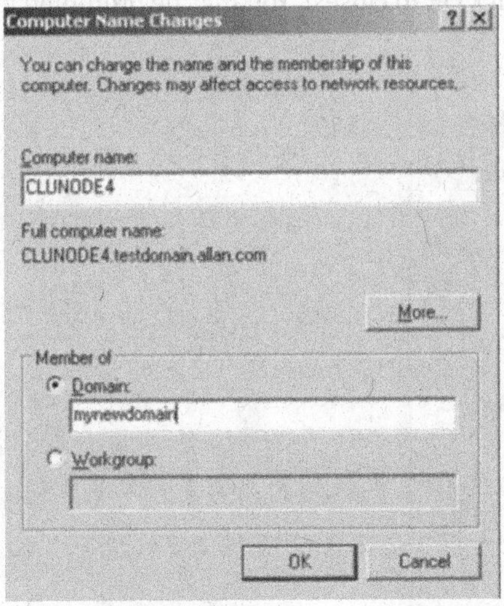

Figure 9-56. *Changing the domain for a node*

If successful, you should see the message in Figure 9-57. Click OK.

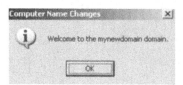

Figure 9-57. *Successfully joining the domain*

You will then see the message in Figure 9-58. Click OK.

Figure 9-58. *Warning you of the impending reboot*

9. The new domain will be reflected in the System Properties dialog box to which you are returned. Figure 9-59 shows an example. Click OK to close it. You may be prompted to reboot. Do not reboot at this time.

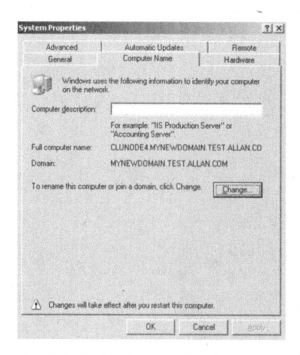

Figure 9-59. *New domain name reflected on System Properties*

10. Repeat steps 7 through 9 on all other nodes.

11. Shut down all nodes. When all nodes are shut down, power on one node only. You may see an error message similar to Figure 9-60 at startup, especially if you did not set Cluster Service to run manually. Log in to the node.

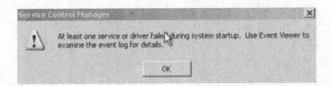

Figure 9-60. *Error that a service has failed*

12. Recreate the Windows server Cluster Service account as detailed in the section on creating and configuring the Cluster Administrator account in Chapter 5. As you are adding the account and assigning it to groups and rights, you may see a dialog box similar to Figure 9-61. This is because in changing domains, the name or group associated with that security identifier (SID) no longer exists. You can delete those as you encounter them.

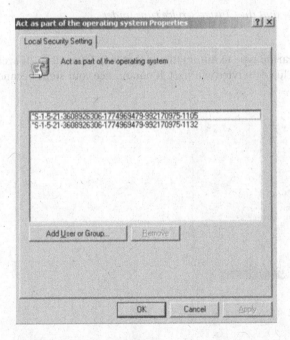

Figure 9-61. *Orphaned SIDs*

13. Start the Services applet. Select the Cluster Service, right-click, and select Properties. Select the Log On tab, and enter the new credentials for the account you just created and added to the node in the previous step. Figure 9-62 shows an example.

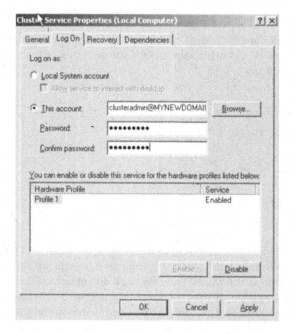

Figure 9-62. *Changing the account that the Cluster Service runs under*

14. Select the General tab. Set the startup type to Automatic, as shown in Figure 9-63. If everything is executed properly, the Cluster Service will start. If not, retrace your steps because you missed something.

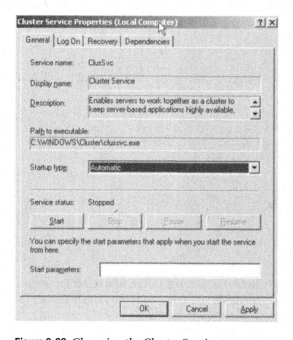

Figure 9-63. *Changing the Cluster Service to start manually*

15. Start Cluster Administrator. Your Windows server cluster should now be online. Check the IP addresses of each existing IP resource to ensure it is using the public network.

16. Power on each of the remaining nodes one by one, and repeat steps 12 to 15.

17. Install and configure your new SQL Server 2005 failover clustering instance by following the instructions in Chapter 8. As with the Windows server cluster, you will need to re-create all service accounts and security.

18. Restore or attach your databases, and synchronize any users, add jobs, and so on, to make your instance ready for use.

Summary

The past six chapters are only part of this book, yet they cover more pages on clustering SQL Server than most other books or papers currently available. Instead of trying to cram everything into one or two chapters, I presented the breadth and depth of planning, implementing, and administering SQL Server 2005 failover clustering. It should be clear at the end of this journey that a lot of planning is involved. This complexity of planning and installing is one of the reasons many shy away from implementing clusters. Once it is up and running, for the most part, it is what I would refer to as *set and forget*—you administer it and treat it as you would a standard SQL Server instance; in the event of a problem, the instance automatically fails over to another node and retains the same name and IP address.

Keep in mind that despite the volume of text given to it in this book, failover clustering is only one option available to you to increase the availability of your SQL Server instances. Read on to understand the other availability technologies in SQL Server and determine for yourself what will be the best option or options for you.

■ ■ ■

CHAPTER 10

Log Shipping

There is one form of SQL Server availability that stems back to version 4.21a: log shipping. The first implementation released by Microsoft appeared as scripts in the *Microsoft BackOffice 4.5 Resource Kit* (Microsoft Press, 1999). In SQL Server 2000, Microsoft officially added it as a feature with a full interface and monitoring capabilities. In SQL Server 2005, log shipping also exists as a feature and is improved from the SQL Server 2000 implementation. Besides Microsoft's own implementations of log shipping through the years, many people have coded custom log shipping scripts and procedures.

This chapter covers not only how log shipping works but the considerations for implementing it as well as how to configure and administer the feature in SQL Server 2005 as well as a custom solution.

How Log Shipping Works

Log shipping provides protection on a per-database, not a per-instance, level. Its concept is very simple: take your transaction logs from a database on one SQL Server and apply them to a copy of the database on another server. The source SQL Server instance is called the *log shipping primary* (or just *primary*), and the destination SQL Server instance is called the *log shipping secondary* (or just *secondary*). The secondary is also known as the *warm standby*. Together, a primary and secondary are known as a *log shipping pair*.

The database on the secondary stays in a state that allows the restoration of transaction logs until the standby database needs to be recovered for use. The process of bringing the secondary online is called a *role change* since the primary server will no longer be the main database used to serve requests. There are two types of role changes: *graceful* and *unplanned*. A graceful role change is when you have the ability to control when the role change happens and can ensure that you back up the tail of the log and have it copied and applied to the secondary. An unplanned role change is where you lose access to the primary and you need to bring your secondary online. The process flow is shown in Figure 10-1.

TERMINOLOGY: ROLE CHANGE VS. FAILOVER

A pet peeve of mine—much like using *active/passive* and *active/active* for failover clustering—is the use of the word *failover* for the process of changing from one instance to another for log shipping. To me, failover implies something more automatic. There is a reason different technologies have different terminology. If you think about the way log shipping works, you really are switching places, or roles, of the servers. I know many of you will still use the term *failover* in conjunction with log shipping, but I can hope one day that everyone will use the right terminology for each technology.

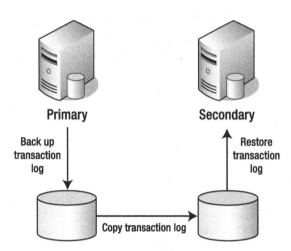

Figure 10-1. *Log shipping flow*

The one concern many have around log shipping is latency: how far behind is my secondary? There are many factors, but some of the most common are how frequently you are backing up your transaction log, copying it to the secondary, and then restoring it. Log shipping is not bound by any distance, so as long as your network supports what you want to do, you can log ship to a server all the way around the planet. From a transactional consistency standpoint, you would only be as current as the following:

- The last transaction completed on the primary database
- The last transaction log backed up for that database
- The last transaction log copied from the primary instance to the secondary instance
- The last transaction log restored to the database on the secondary

Looking at the timeline in more detail, remember that the last transaction log that is backed up may not contain the last transaction completed in the database, so there may be a delta right there. This comes into play when you attempt to go through a role change, but you have the same exposure as if you did not use log shipping and were just doing backups: you can recover to the last transaction log available. Once the transaction log is backed up, a process (manual or automated) would then take that transaction log and copy it to the other server, where it could be restored immediately by a manual (if someone is sitting at the console) or automated process, or possibly stored there for application later during a manual restore process.

Take the example of a database that has log shipping configured with automated processes. There is a job that backs up the transaction log every five minutes and takes two minutes to perform. Another process runs every ten minutes to copy any transaction logs generated, and on average takes four minutes. On the secondary, a process runs every ten minutes to scan for databases to copy to the secondary, and a separate process runs every ten minutes to restore any transaction logs that are waiting. Each transaction log takes three and a half minutes to restore. Based on this configuration, a sample timeline is shown in Table 10-1.

Table 10-1. *Log Shipping Timeline Example*

Time	Action Performed on Server #1	Action Performed on or for Server #2
10:00 a.m.	Transaction log #1 backed up	
10:02 a.m.	Transaction log #1 backup complete	
10:05 a.m.	Transaction log #2 backed up	
10:07 a.m.	Transaction log #2 backup complete	
10:10 a.m.	Transaction log #3 backed up	Transaction logs #1 & #2 copied to the secondary
10:12 a.m.	Transaction log #3 backup complete	
10:14 a.m.		Transaction logs #1 & #2 copy complete
10:15 a.m.	Transaction log #4 backed up	
10:17 a.m.	Transaction log #4 backup complete	
10:20 a.m.	Transaction log #5 backed up	Transaction log #1 restore begins; copy of transaction logs #3 & #4 begins
10:22 a.m.	Transaction log #5 backup complete	
10:24 a.m.		Transaction log #1 restore complete; copy of transaction logs #3 & #4 complete; transaction log #2 restore started
10:25 a.m.	Transaction log #6 backed up	

What this example translates into is that the database loading transaction logs on the secondary will be approximately 24 minutes behind the one on the primary even though you are backing up your transaction logs every 5 minutes. This example demonstrates one important point around latency and log shipping: if your SLA dictates that you can only have 5 minutes of data loss, just doing transaction log backups every 5 minutes will not get you there. If that SLA requires that another database has those transactions and is considered up-to-date, there's much more you have to do to meet that SLA.

Best Uses for Log Shipping

There are a few scenarios that best fit the use of log shipping. Not all may be applicable in your environment.

Disaster Recovery and High Availability

The most common use for log shipping is disaster recovery. Log shipping is a relatively inexpensive way of creating a copy of your database in a remote location without having to worry about getting tied into a specific hardware configuration or SQL Server edition. The considerations listed in this chapter (such as network latency and the ability to redirect your application to the new database server) as well as your SLAs will dictate how effective your disaster recovery solution is, but this has been log shipping's main use over the years.

Log shipping is also a very effective high availability solution for those who can only use a low-tech solution (for whatever reason). I know some of you are probably saying to yourselves that log shipping is not a high availability solution since there is a lot of latency. In fact, that was said to me while I was working on this chapter. Look, log shipping has historically been a disaster-recovery solution, which is arguably its best use. I wholeheartedly agree with that. Not everyone has the budget, need, or expertise to deploy other technologies to make their databases available. I would argue that most people out there who started with log shipping employed it in a *high availability* capacity. Log shipping certainly is not the equivalent of a supermodel you drool over, but may be much more attractive in other ways.

Intrusive Database Maintenance

Assuming that you have no issues with your application after a role change and the secondary has enough capacity to handle the performance needed, another possible use of log shipping is to create your warm standby and switch to it when you need to perform maintenance on your primary database. This would allow minimal interruption to end users in a 24x7 environment. For example, if reindexing your 30 million–row table takes two hours, but a log shipping role change only takes ten minutes if you are up-to-date in terms of restoring transaction logs, what sounds better to you? Having the application unavailable for two hours, or ten minutes? Most people would say ten minutes. This does mean that you may need to have a mechanism of switching back to the primary database at some point (such as configuring log shipping from the new primary—the secondary— back to the old primary instance), but I always argue that with the proper capacity, you should not have to switch back. The whole point is that the end users do not care about where the data lives; you do. They only care about accessing their information in a timely manner. Log shipping may be too much hassle and work for some to consider for this role, and for others it may be a lifesaver.

Migrations and Upgrades

My favorite use of log shipping is to facilitate a server move or a SQL Server version upgrade from one to another where you are also going from old hardware to new hardware. The reason this works so well is that you can start the process at any given point before the switch to the new hardware. At some point, you stop all traffic going to the primary, take the last transaction log backup, make sure it is copied and applied to the secondary, recover the database, and do whatever else you need to do (such as redirecting the application) to make that new database a full copy of your current production database. The switch itself should take under ten minutes, assuming your transaction logs are caught up.

The two biggest pluses of doing a migration or upgrade this way is that first, it provides a fall-back/back-out plan where you can go back to your old configuration, and second, you can start the process way before you do the actual switch; that is why it takes ten minutes. You can take your full backup, restore it on the new hardware, and start log shipping hours, days, or months in advance of your actual cutover date. What is even better is that the process is based on the tried and true method of backup and restore; there is no fancy technology to understand. A log shipping–based migration or upgrade is not for every scenario, but there are very few I have found where it is not applicable.

USING LOG SHIPPING AS A REPORTING SOLUTION

One of the questions I am asked the most when it comes to log shipping is "Can I use the secondary as a reporting database?" Technically, if you restore the database using WITH STANDBY, which allows read-only access while still allowing transaction log loads, you can. You can also stick a fork in your eye, but it does not make it a superb idea. Since sticking a fork in your eye will most likely cause you permanent damage, I would even go so far as to say it is a dumb idea and the pain you will feel is not worth whatever momentary curiosity you are satisfying. Similarly, I would tell you that thinking you can use a log-shipped database for reporting will cause great pain for your end users. A reporting solution is supposed to be available for use. For you to use that log-shipped secondary as a reporting database, as part of your transaction log loading process, you need to make sure that all users are kicked out of the database since the log requires exclusive access to the database to be restored. If you do not kick the users out, the transaction logs will not be applied and your data will be old (and most likely leave you exposed from an availability perspective since you are most likely using this for disaster recovery or high availability). Consider the example with the timeline shown in Table 10-1 earlier in this chapter. Every 10 minutes transaction logs will be restored and take on average 3½ minutes. That leaves 6½ minutes out of those 10 that the database is available; multiply that by 6, and you get at best 39 minutes of availability per hour for reporting if you are only loading one transaction log. Most likely you will have much less availability for reporting since you are doing fairly frequent transaction log loads. Does that sound like an ideal reporting solution to you?

Log Shipping Considerations

The factors detailed in this section will influence the planning and deployment of log shipping in your environment.

Location of the Primary and Secondary

If you are using log shipping for disaster recovery purposes, you should never place the primary and secondary instances on the same server or in the same data center. You would have a single point of failure in your data center or on the server. The whole purpose is to eliminate a single point of failure.

As noted previously, depending on your use for log shipping (such as high availability or doing maintenance and providing an instance to redirect your applications to minimize your downtime), there are legitimate reasons for having a configuration that has the primary and secondary on the same server (or instance) or in the same data center.

Full Database Restoration on the Secondary

To be able to apply the transaction log on the secondary, when you restore the full backup, you must use either WITH NORECOVERY or WITH STANDBY. If you do not restore your database explicitly with one of these options, your database will be restored WITH RECOVERY, and it will not be in a state to be able to restore transaction logs. My recommendation is to use WITH NORECOVERY since you should be using log shipping for some availability purpose. This would also ensure that no one else would be accessing the database inadvertently while you are loading transaction logs (without having some sort of manual control).

Sending Transaction Logs to More Than One Secondary

One of the benefits of log shipping over some of the other technologies is that it can be a one-to-many relationship: you can ship the logs from one primary to many secondary instances. You can even potentially set different copy-and-restore times for each secondary database if you go this route; however, you must keep the same backup schedule. Despite the ability to send transaction logs to multiple secondaries, you do not have the ability to use a secondary as an intermediate and configure log shipping from that log-shipped database that is receiving transaction logs. In other words, you cannot do a double hop. Multiple secondaries must all be sourced from the primary.

Transaction Size

Your transaction size will have an impact on how quickly your transaction logs are restored. If you generate many longer-running transactions, your transaction logs will take longer to apply, and you will be a larger delta off of the primary database. It is in your best interest to optimize your transactions within your application to be as small as possible. The quicker SQL Server can process them, the faster the log is restored (or rolled forward in a stop/start). The next time your developer wants to do some funky insert with 70,000 joins, slap his or her wrist since it will ultimately affect your availability or performance in one way or another.

Transaction Log Backup Frequency and Size

One of the keys to the kingdom with log shipping is how frequently you back up your transaction log size. In Chapter 3 I noted that frequent backup of your transaction log will help you maintain its size (assuming it is sized properly to begin with). What it will also do is create smaller transaction log backup files. Smaller transaction log files equate to faster restore times more often than not. I cannot tell you how many times over the years I have heard that someone's transaction log backup file is unmanageable because they are not backing it up frequently enough. In Chapter 3 I discussed how a transaction log backup works; while it will truncate the data, if the log file has grown, it will stay that large unless you physically shrink the file. Shrinking a file in SQL Server is an operation you want to avoid. Size matters. In this case, it is small that is optimal. Log shipping forces you to think economically.

Copy Frequency and Transaction Log Backup Location

Once you understand the size of your transactions and the size of your transaction log backup file, you need to take into consideration how often you copy the transaction log backup to the secondary. Your copy frequency will depend on a few factors. First is your network latency and speed (which is addressed in the next section), the other is the size of the file itself. If it takes ten minutes to copy each transaction log backup file, it is really going to limit how far behind the secondary will be.

Another aspect of copying is where and how you are copying the file. In the simple case, you back up the transaction log on server A and copy it to a share on server B. This is also arguably the quickest (unless server B is really an instance on the same server as server A, which means you are going across the network to copy to the same drives and that would be like shooting yourself in the foot), but it does not necessarily afford you the best protection. If your primary goes down, you lose all of the files on there. If you copy to an intermediate share or server before going to the secondary, you now have a backup location of your transaction log that the secondary can pull the transaction log from (or push it out, depending on how you set up your preferred method of log shipping). It will obviously add time and latency since your copy stage now has two steps (although the time may be insignificant if you have an efficient network), but only you can determine whether the extra redundancy and protection it provides is worth it for your environment.

Network Latency and Network Speed

Factoring into your ability to copy your transaction logs will be how fast and reliable your network is. The good thing about log shipping is that it can tolerate latencies that other technologies may not be able to withstand, but it is also its flaw to some degree. The simple fact of the matter is that if you have a poorly performing, inefficient network, your copies may not only be slow, there is a chance they may not even work. You cannot afford to have a network that is held together by shoestring and tin cans when you are employing high availability technologies such as log shipping.

Network latency will also factor in. Because log shipping does not lock you into any set distance between locations, even if you are on gigabit Ethernet, the farther the distance is between sites, the longer it will take to copy. This is just how networks work; you cannot escape the limitations of the wire. This has to factor into your thoughts when you are configuring log shipping.

One thing I always recommend if you can do it is to set up a private network between the servers, or the servers and the intermediate location if you use a separate share for the transaction log copies. This is not unlike the private cluster network for a failover cluster. The main reason for doing this is that the pipe will be dedicated for the file copies and will not be affected by the bandwidth of serving requests from the application or other traffic that would come across the public network. For example, if your public network is on the 187.100.101.x network, if you add a network card (or use a dual-homed network card) and configure it to talk on the 188.100.101.x network, which does not share any other traffic, your copies may actually benefit even if the network speed may not be technically as fast as the public network. Deploying a dedicated network may only make sense if you have the budget and actual network bandwidth. It does not come free, so before taking this suggestion as gospel, you should always test in your own environment to see if this configuration will benefit you.

Networks, Domain Connectivity, and Log Shipping

One of the biggest benefits of log shipping is that from a pure backup and restore level, you are not tied into having your primary and warm standby on the same subnet or the same domain. As long as you can configure log shipping to allow server A to talk to server B in some way, shape, or form, log shipping will work. In your environment, this may mean trusts are set up, or some intermediate place for the transaction log backups is configured, but it allows a much more flexible configuration that is not as strict as other SQL Server high availability technologies.

Log Shipping Between Versions of SQL Server

Since log shipping is based on backup and restore, you can log ship from SQL Server 7.0 and SQL Server 2000 to SQL Server 2005 since SQL Server will upgrade those databases in the process, but you cannot log ship to versions of SQL Server other than SQL Server 2005 if your source database is SQL Server 2005. You can configure log shipping between different editions of SQL Server 2005 (e.g., Enterprise Edition to Standard Edition), and between hardware platforms (e.g., an x64-based instance to an x86-based instance, or IA64 to x64). This is one of the best benefits of log shipping: it is hardware agnostic. Your databases can also technically be different versions (e.g., log shipping between SQL Server 2005 RTM and SQL Server 2005 Service Pack 1), but I recommend trying to keep the differences minimal as they may result in different behaviors should you need to recover the log-shipped database. Or as part of your recovery process, you may need to add steps to ensure the servers or databases are at the same version.

Code Page/Sort Order/Collation

While SQL Server allows you to set a different collation per database, ideally the primary and secondary instances should be configured to be the same. If the primary database and the secondary database are configured with different collations, it will potentially cause application-based problems if the warm standby has to be recovered to become the new primary database. For example, each collation tells SQL Server how to deal with sorts (such as case-sensitive or case-insensitive). If the primary database is case-insensitive but the secondary is not, it could potentially yield radically different query results for the same data.

Directory or Share Permissions

An aspect that is easily overlooked in the planning of log shipping is setting up the proper security for all directories and shares on any server that will be participating in log shipping. Not setting up the security right from the start is one of the more common problems with log shipping deployments. Since SQL Server backups are unencrypted text files as noted in Chapter 3, if you do not employ some sort of tool to encrypt your backups, they will be sitting on the file system for anyone who has access to open their favorite text editor and try to read them. Even if you do encrypt the backups, you still need to worry about security, especially these days when you can carry many files on a USB key barely bigger than a stick of gum that can store gigabytes of information. The directories should allow the SQL Server login or logins that are running the individual log shipping jobs (especially the backup and copy ones) and no one else unless there is some valid reason.

Synchronizing Database Logins

One of the challenges with log shipping (as well as with other SQL Server technologies such as backup and restore, database mirroring, and replication) is to synchronize the logins between the primary and warm standby. How to synchronize your logins is covered in Chapter 15.

Objects That Reside Outside the Database

In addition to synchronizing database logins, you will need to worry about other objects such as SQL Server Agent jobs, database maintenance plans, and SSIS packages residing outside of the database you are log shipping. Those objects may be needed to make the secondary a true production-ready copy of the database. Log shipping only applies any changes that are captured either in the transaction log or the initial full backup. Most of the objects are easily scripted or re-created but must be taken into account when considering log shipping because if you miss one thing, it could mean that your applications that rely on the database may not function properly. For example, if a job performs an important data manipulation on a scheduled basis and it is not re-created on the secondary, chances are your reports will not give back the right data.

Log Shipping and Maintaining Consecutive LSNs

Restoring the transaction logs one after another keeps the LSN sequence intact as I discussed in Chapter 3. This sequence, also known as a *log chain*, is what log shipping counts on. If you break the LSN chain, you break log shipping. It is like pushing the reset button on your computer. The easiest way to break the LSN chain is to put your database in Simple recovery mode at some point. Unfortunately, this is not an uncommon occurrence. It is something I have seen happen where the

DBA or other administrator dealing with SQL Server thinks they are doing something good by putting the database in Simple for a bulk load and then changing it back. You cannot allow this to happen. Educate your fellow administrators on the implications of their actions if you are going to use or are already using log shipping.

Log Shipping and Backup Plans

Log shipping should either integrate with or change your existing backup plans. There is no middle ground on this point. If you are using a third-party backup tool to do your backups across the network and you never store them on a disk accessible by the server, it will be virtually impossible to implement log shipping. Log shipping relies on the fact that the database and transaction log backups are available locally to copy or restore. While your third-party tool may allow you to do scheduled restores over the network, I would argue the latency would make log shipping ineffective.

Even if you are already backing up to disk, you can break log shipping by doing either manual or automatic transaction log backups in between the transaction log backups that are scheduled for use with log shipping. If you do transaction log backups that are not part of the log shipping process and do not apply those transaction logs manually to the secondary, you will break the LSN chain since the database will be expecting consecutive LSNs on the restore.

Consider this example. Before deciding on an availability technology, you back up your transaction logs every 15 minutes. You then want to deploy log shipping using a scheme that backs up your transaction log every 7 minutes. You configure log shipping but do not remove or disable the existing transaction log backup job. You have a few issues, the first of which is that at certain times where the two jobs intersect on the recurring schedule, one will fail since you cannot take two transaction log backups at the same time. The second is the issue I mentioned in the previous paragraph: if this transaction log backup is made every 15 minutes and the log shipping configuration knows nothing about this transaction log, at some point the restoration process will fail until you manually apply the transaction log or logs on the secondary to restore the LSN chain.

Another concern of some is that doing other backups (such as daily full or differential, or file and filegroup backups) will break log shipping. This is absolutely false. Full or differential backups do not break the LSN chain; so you can make as many full or differential backups as you want. After you restore the initial full backup, all the log shipping process cares about is that the transaction logs are consecutive and applied in the right order.

Database Maintenance, Updates, and the Secondary

Something I wrote a long time ago in the SQL Server 2000 Resource Kit (http://www.microsoft.com/technet/prodtechnol/sql/2000/reskit/part4/c1361.mspx?mfr=true) in the section "Using the Log Shipped Database to Check the Health of the Production Database" is that you could use the log shipped database on the secondary for doing maintenance. That is 100% wrong, and I apologize for it. That was written nearly ten years ago, when I was really starting to get into high availability. With the database in a state where it can only load transaction logs, you cannot use it to make backups of your database (and take that role away from the primary), nor can you run any commands such as a DBCC CHECKDB. Those commands and tasks require that the database be fully online and available.

If you apply an update (such as a service pack) to your SQL Server instance that has a database in a loading state, it will skip over that database if it needs to apply updates to each individual database. This means that the update will not be applied to the database. This may or may not be a concern to you but it is something to take into account when you are considering log shipping as a possible technology.

Applications and Role Changes

As you may have gathered by now, log shipping involves the changing from one instance to another. Those instances will have different names, different IP addresses, and possibly, different database names for the databases participating in log shipping. This can cause problems for some environments and applications if it is not taken into account up front.

This is a general best practice for all SQL Server–based applications, but if you are going to use any technology that requires the name of the server to change, do not hard-code or embed server names, SQL Server instance names, or IP addresses into the application itself. This makes it virtually impossible to achieve and perform most high availability and disaster recovery. While there are ways of abstracting the name or IP address (such as aliasing in your DNS or configuring Network Load Balancing in a specific configuration), it adds administrative overhead that adds complexity to a role change. All applications should allow flexibility and, if possible, use standard connections that are easy to reconfigure to allow your application to be redirected to the new server. Put another way, it is better to have a mechanism—even though it may complicate your role change—external to your application. Your company would come to a standstill if you needed to recompile your application after a role change if the SQL Server instance name was hard-coded into the application itself or if you had to touch every single desktop to update an ODBC connection.

SQL Server Functionality vs. Custom Log Shipping

Should you use SQL Server's built-in log shipping feature or use your own custom version? As always, it depends on your needs. Obviously, from a pure supportability standpoint, you cannot beat using Microsoft's feature. If you encounter a problem, you can call Microsoft to sort it out. If you code your own and something goes awry, it is up to you to figure it out and fix it. For many organizations, this one thing outweighs nearly every other consideration in this arena.

The reality is that whether you code your own or use Microsoft's implementation, they both have the same basic needs and limitations:

- You can log ship to multiple secondaries with different copy-and-restore schedules, but you only have one backup job for your transaction logs.

- You need to restore the database on the secondary in a state to be able to load transaction logs.

- You need some way to monitor the status of log shipping.

- You need to set up shares with the proper security for the copies of the transaction logs.

- You need to configure the SQL Server Agent jobs performing the copy to run under context of an account that has the rights given to the share.

For the record, Microsoft's implementation of log shipping in SQL Server 2005 is not unlike configuring a maintenance plan for a database. Underneath the covers, the jobs created when you configure log shipping call on a new executable in SQL Server 2005: sqllogship.exe. An example is shown in Figure 10-2. Also, notice that the log shipping job is of the type CmdExec. A CmdExec-based job is run under context of the service account for SQL Server Agent and allows you to execute a program at the OS level. Only system administrators can create CmdExec jobs. If this is a violation of your security policies, the built-in feature is not for you.

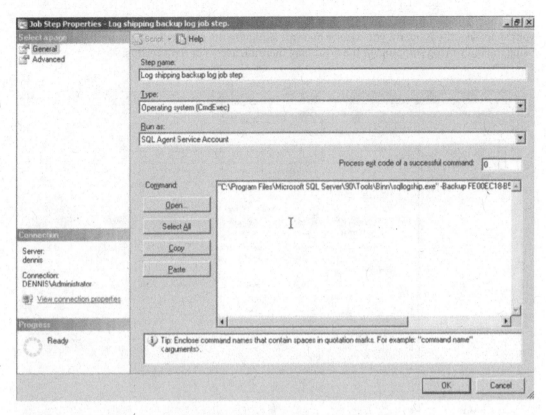

Figure 10-2. *Log shipping job step example showing the use of sqllogship.exe*

If you implement your database maintenance via a maintenance plan versus writing your own Transact-SQL code, you risk dealing with a *black box* (something you have virtually no control over or insight into) if you only use Microsoft's graphical tools. If you code your own backup statements and procedures, you will need to maintain the solution, but it may be much more flexible and understandable. There is no right or wrong answer on this one; you need to decide for yourself.

The one difficulty you may have with the built-in feature is that if you are trying to log ship outside of a domain and you do not specify IP addresses for your server names during the configuration process, log shipping may not work if you cannot resolve the server names. If Server A and Server B are in the same domain or domains that are trusted, or your DNS is not set up in a way that names and IP addresses can be resolved and security can be achieved, this will not even be an issue. However, if your secondary server does not fall into that category, coding your own solution may wind up being a better answer if it conforms to your needs, especially around security.

Configuring Log Shipping

Implementing log shipping is a straightforward setup in SQL Server 2005.

Create the Backup Share(s)

Before you can even configure log shipping, you need to configure the folders as shares on the servers that will be participating in log shipping. As noted earlier, you will need to do it at least on the primary and secondary, and on an intermediate location, if there is one. If you do not configure your share security properly, you will see an error similar to the one shown in Figure 10-3 if you are using the built-in log shipping, or the error may mention access or rights errors.

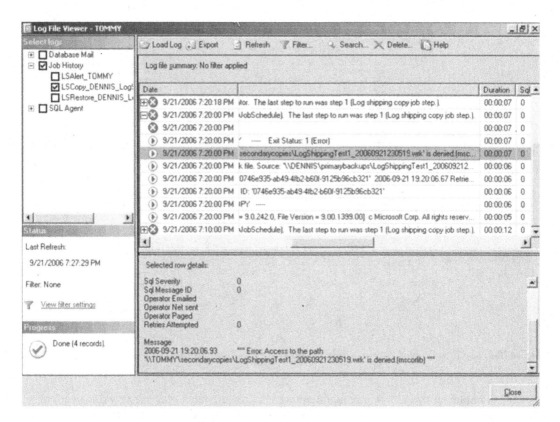

Figure 10-3. *Access denied error for the copy job on the secondary*

Stand-Alone Server Shares

Creating a share for use with log shipping on a server that is not clustered is done with the following steps:

1. Log on to the server that will contain the folder, using an account that has the proper privileges to create a folder and set security on it.

2. Start Windows Explorer.

3. Create a folder with an appropriate name on the target drive, such as MySQL Backups on your C:\ drive.

4. Select the folder you just created, right-click, and select Properties. A dialog similar to the one in Figure 10-4 will appear. Select the Sharing tab.

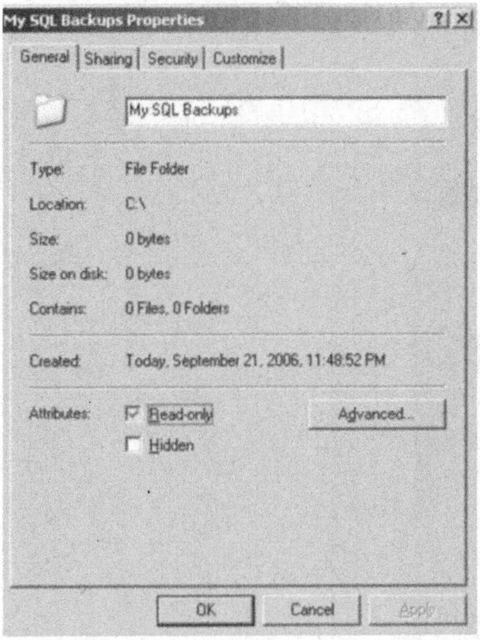

Figure 10-4. *The MySQL Backups folder properties*

5. Select the Share This Folder option, and enter an appropriate name for the share. This will be used to access the files from any other computer. I recommend you use a name that does not involve spaces. An example is shown in Figure 10-5. Using this example, the share that would be accessed is *servername*\backups.

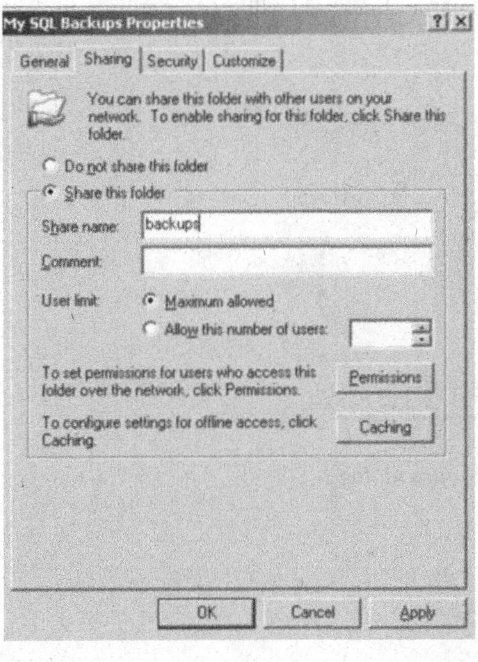

Figure 10-5. *Sharing tab with a name entered for the share*

6. Click Permissions. A dialog similar to the one in Figure 10-6 will be shown.

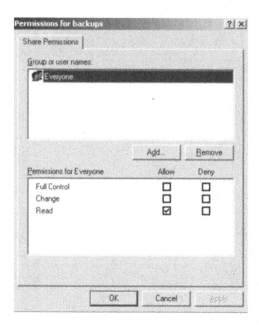

Figure 10-6. *Permissions dialog*

7. Click Add. On the Select Users, Computers, or Groups dialog, enter the name (or part of the name) of the account that needs permissions to write to the share as shown in Figure 10-7. Click Check Names to resolve the name. If you are not logged in as a user who has access to check the names, you will be prompted to enter an account that does have permission, as shown in Figure 10-8. After a successful name check, you will see something similar to Figure 10-9. Click OK.

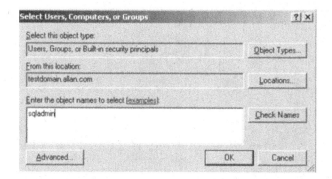

Figure 10-7. *Select Users, Computers, or Groups dialog*

Figure 10-8. *Enter Network Password dialog*

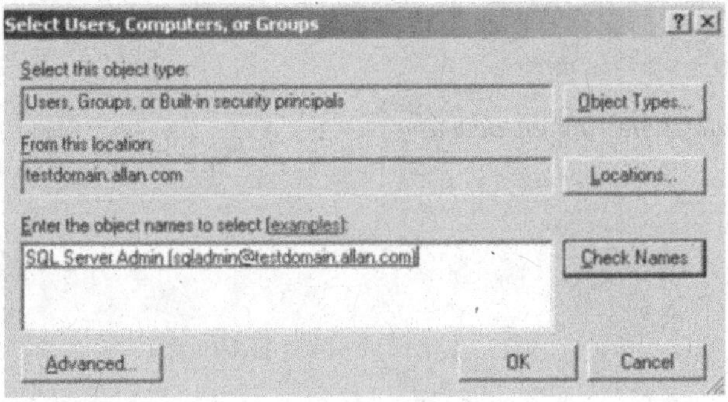

Figure 10-9. *Validated entry for a user or group*

8. After you return to the Permissions dialog, select the user in the Group or User Names section, and select the Full Control check box as shown in Figure 10-10. Click Apply. Click OK. You will now be returned to the dialog shown in Figure 10-5. Click Apply. Click OK. If things are configured properly, in Windows Explorer the folder will have a little hand in its icon as shown in Figure 10-11.

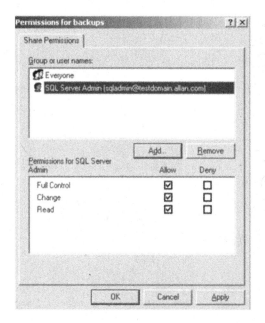

Figure 10-10. *Permissions dialog reflecting the new user*

Figure 10-11. *Shared folder*

9. Now you must test to see that the user can write a file to that share. Log out and log in as the user you just added to the share. An example is shown in Figure 10-12.

Figure 10-12. *Logging in as a user with access to the share*

10. From the Start menu, select Run. Enter the name of the share that you just created and click OK. An example is shown in Figure 10-13.

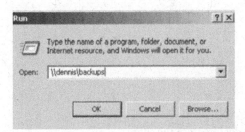

Figure 10-13. *Connecting to the share*

11. When the contents of the folder are displayed, right-click in the window, select New, and then select a type of document to create. An example is shown in Figure 10-14. If you are successful, a document should be created and appear similar to Figure 10-15.

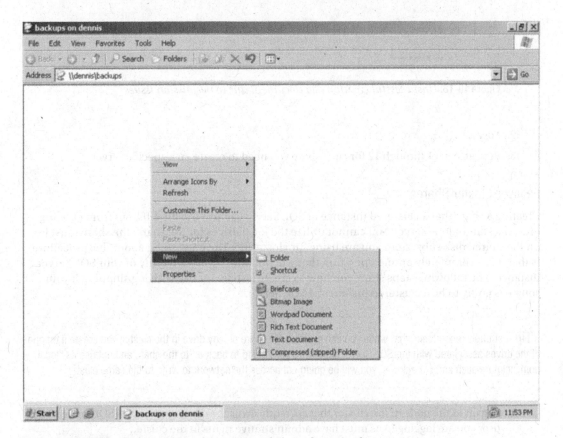

Figure 10-14. *Menu showing types of documents that can be created*

Figure 10-15. *Successful creation of a new document in the share*

If you did not configure your share properly, you will see an error message similar to the one in Figure 10-16 and you will need to go back and fix the permissions for the user.

Figure 10-16. *Unsuccessful creation of a document due to permission issues*

12. Log out.

13. Repeat steps 1 through 12 for each share you need to create on a specific server.

Failover Cluster Shares

Creating a share that a clustered instance of SQL Server can use is a bit different from creating one on a stand-alone server. You cannot utilize the local drives for the share; the share must be on the shared disk subsystem you are using for clustering. The good thing about this procedure is that it is a completely online operation that will not affect the availability of your SQL Server instance. The following steps show you how to create a share for use with log shipping if your source is going to be a clustered instance of SQL Server.

■**Tip** I strongly recommend that while you can create a file share on any drive in the cluster, you create it on one of the drives associated with the SQL Server itself. If you are going to back up to the share and not use its "local" nomenclature such as I:\backups, you will be going out across the network to write to the same cluster.

---

1. Log on to the node of the cluster that currently owns the disk resources for SQL Server. The user you are logging in as must have administrative rights in the cluster.

2. Select the cluster resource group that contains the disk resource that contains the backup folder. Right-click, select New, then Resource. An example is shown in Figure 10-17.

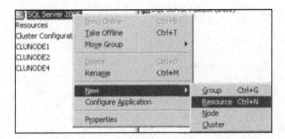

Figure 10-17. *New cluster resource menu option*

3. In the New Resource dialog, enter a name for the resource, and select a resource type of File Share. An example is shown in Figure 10-18. Click Next.

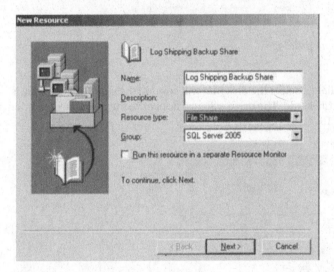

Figure 10-18. *New Resource dialog*

4. On the Possible Owners dialog, make sure all nodes that can own the SQL Server instance can own the resource. An example is shown in Figure 10-19. Click Next.

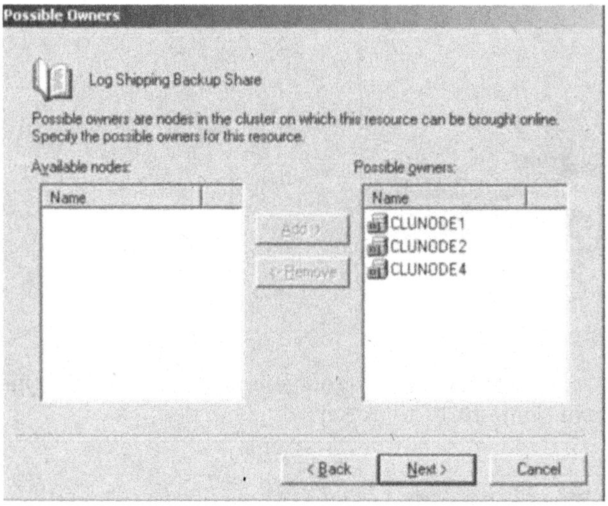

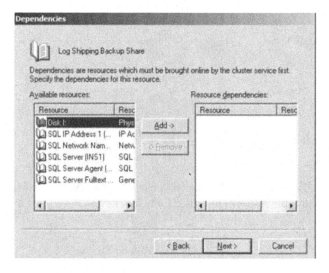

Figure 10-19. *Possible Owners dialog*

5. On the Dependencies dialog, select the disk that will contain the share. An example is shown in Figure 10-20. Click Add. The drive will now appear in the resource dependencies box as shown in Figure 10-21. Click Next.

Figure 10-20. *Selecting the drive with the backup directory*

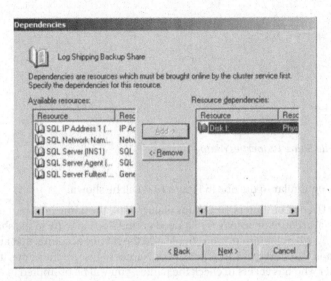

Figure 10-21. *Drive added as a dependency*

6. On the File Share Parameters dialog, enter the name for the share. The share will be accessed with the nomenclature of \\windowsclustername\sharename. Enter the path to the backup directory. An example is shown in Figure 10-22. Click Advanced. Ensure that the option Normal Share is selected on the Advanced File Share Properties dialog as shown in Figure 10-23. Click OK to return to the File Share Parameters dialog.

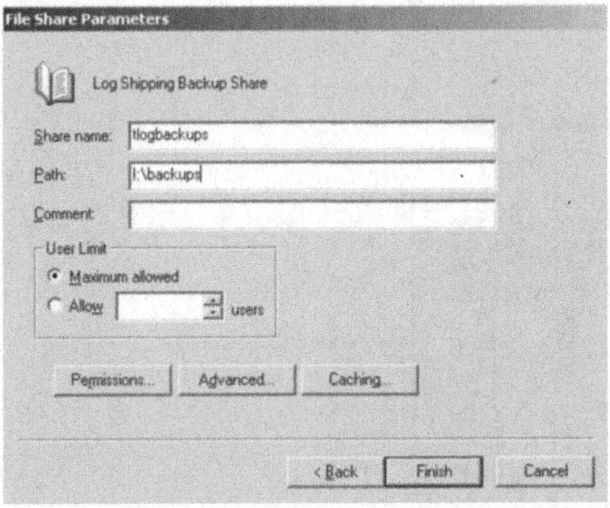

Figure 10-22. *File Share Parameters dialog*

Figure 10-23. *Advanced File Share Properties dialog*

7. Click Permissions. A dialog similar to the one in Figure 10-6 will be shown.

8. Click Add. On the Select Users, Computers, or Groups dialog, enter the name (or a part of the name) of the domain-level account or accounts that need permissions to write to the share as shown in Figure 10-7. At a bare minimum you should add the service accounts that are set up for both SQL Server and SQL Server Agent. Click Check Names to resolve the name. If you are not logged in as a user who has access to check the names, you will be prompted to enter an account that has permission, as shown in Figure 10-8. After a successful name check, you will see something similar to Figure 10-9. Click OK.

9. After you return to the Permissions dialog, select the user in the Group or User Names section, and select the Full Control check box as shown in Figure 10-24. Repeat for all users added to the share. Click Apply. Click OK. You will now be returned to the File Share Parameters dialog as shown in Figure 10-22. Click Finish. Click OK. You should see the success dialog as shown in Figure 10-25. Click OK.

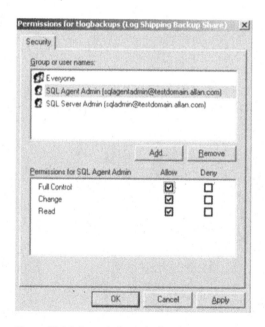

Figure 10-24. *Permissions dialog for a folder*

Figure 10-25. *Successful creation of the file share resource*

10. To use the share, you must bring the newly created resource online. Select it in Cluster Administrator, right-click, and select Bring Online as shown in Figure 10-26. The status should now reflect that the resource is online.

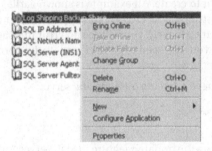

Figure 10-26. *Bringing the file share online*

11. Now you must test to see that the user can write a file to that share. If you are not already logged in as one of the users who you granted permission on the share, log out and log in again as one of the users. An example is shown earlier in Figure 10-12. First check to see if things are configured properly by looking in Windows Explorer. The folder will have a little hand in its icon as shown in Figure 10-27.

Figure 10-27. *Cluster drive with a file share*

12. From the Start menu, select Run. Enter the name of the share that you just created and click OK. The nomenclature of a share via a UNC path is \\windowsclustername\sharename. If the name of your Windows failover cluster is MYSRVCLU, and your share's name is tlogbackups, the path you would enter is \\mysrvclu\tlogbackups. An example is shown in Figure 10-28.

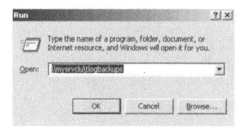

Figure 10-28. *Entering the share name*

13. When the folder contents are displayed in a dedicated window, right-click in the window, select New, and then select a type of document to create. An example is shown earlier in Figure 10-14. If you are successful, a document should be created and appear similar to Figure 10-15. If you did not configure your share properly, you will see an error message similar to the one shown in Figure 10-16, and you will need to go back and fix the permissions for the user.

14. Repeat steps 1 through 11 for each share you need to create on a specific server.

SQL Server Built-in Functionality

There are two options for configuring log shipping using the updated feature in SQL Server 2005. You can either use SQL Server Management Studio or stored procedures. Using the stored procedures to configure log shipping was not possible in SQL Server 2000. Log shipping is included as a feature in the following editions of SQL Server 2005: Developer Edition, Enterprise Edition, Standard Edition, and Workgroup Edition. In SQL Server 2000, log shipping was only available in the Developer and Enterprise Editions.

Like SQL Server 2000, SQL Server 2005 provides a way to monitor the status of your log shipping pair by configuring a monitor server during the configuration of log shipping. The section "Monitoring Log Shipping" later in this chapter shows you how to see the status of log shipping. The only reason I am mentioning it here is that where you place the monitor is a consideration for installation. It can be placed on any available SQL Server 2005 instance that supports the log shipping feature. I do not recommend placing it on your primary, as that would be a single point of failure. I always recommend putting the log shipping monitor functionality on a completely separate server that is not the primary or the secondary. The monitor is optional; so if you choose not to deploy one, there are other ways of monitoring the status of log shipping. One bonus of a monitor that exists on another SQL Server instance is that multiple log shipping configurations can share one log shipping monitor.

■ **Note** If you do not configure a log shipping monitor during the installation, you will not be able to configure it post-installation through the SQL Server Management Studio interface. The option will be disabled as shown in Figure 10-29.

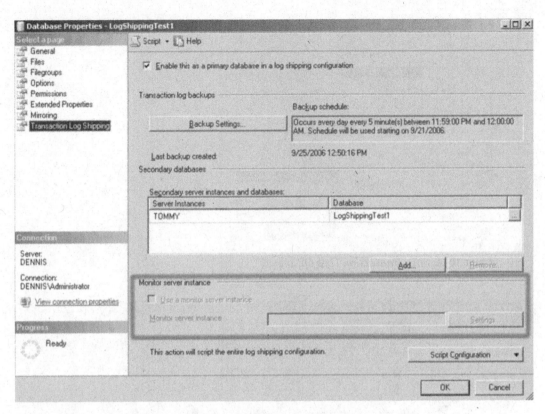

Figure 10-29. *The ability to add a log shipping monitor disabled after configuration*

SQL Server Management Studio

The following steps walk you through the process of configuring log shipping via SQL Server Management Studio:

1. Start SQL Server Management Studio. Expand the Databases folder, select the database that will serve as the primary, right-click the database, select Tasks, then Ship Transaction Logs as shown in Figure 10-30. You can also select Properties, and then when the properties of the database are displayed, select the Transaction Log Shipping option. With either method, you will see the screen displayed in Figure 10-31.

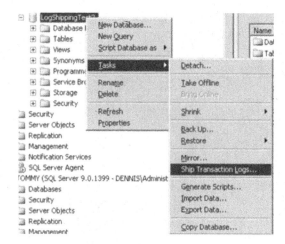

Figure 10-30. *Ship Transaction Logs option*

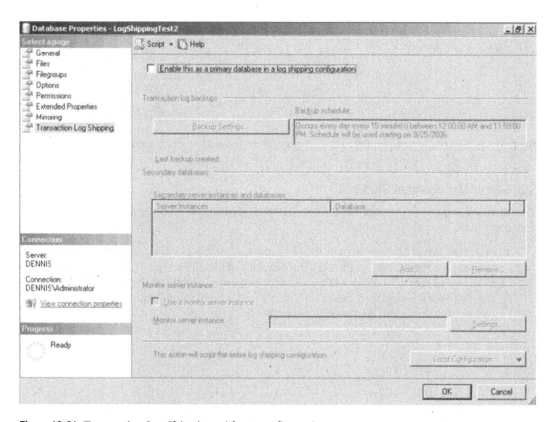

Figure 10-31. *Transaction Log Shipping with no configuration*

2. Select the Enable This as a Primary Database in a Log Shipping Configuration option, as shown in Figure 10-32.

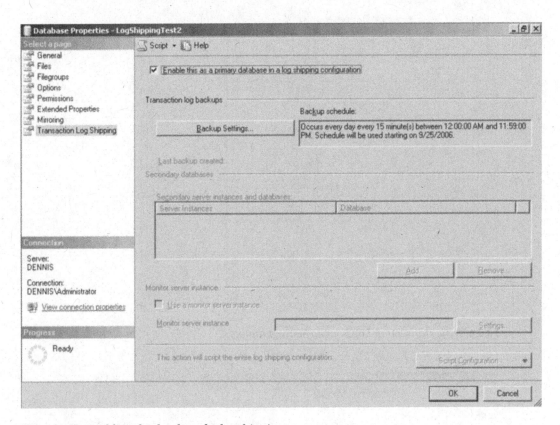

Figure 10-32. *Enabling the database for log shipping*

3. Click Backup Settings. The Transaction Log Backup Settings dialog will be displayed. In the Network Path to Backup Folder text box, enter the share name you created on the primary computer. If you are planning on crossing domains that are not trusted for log shipping, you will have to use the IP address instead of the server name in the share (e.g., \\172.22.10.1\ backups). If the folder is located on the same server as the SQL Server instance containing the primary database, enter the path to the local backup path share. This is not necessary if you are generating backups to another server or share (as I noted previously in the considerations for log shipping). By default, the log shipping functionality will create a backup job on the primary with the name LSBackup_dbname, where *dbname* is the name of the primary database. If you wish to change the name of the backup job, change Job Name, as shown in Figure 10-33. The backup job defaults to a frequency of 15 minutes. If you want to change how often the backup job is executed, click Schedule. You will see a dialog similar to the one in Figure 10-34. The schedule will default to a name that includes the instance name, not the database name. You do not need to change this, but you may want to for clarity's sake. Change the job schedule to the frequency you desire, and click OK to close the job schedule properties. Click OK to close the Transaction Log Backup Settings dialog. The main Transaction Log Shipping dialog will now appear similar to the one in Figure 10-35.

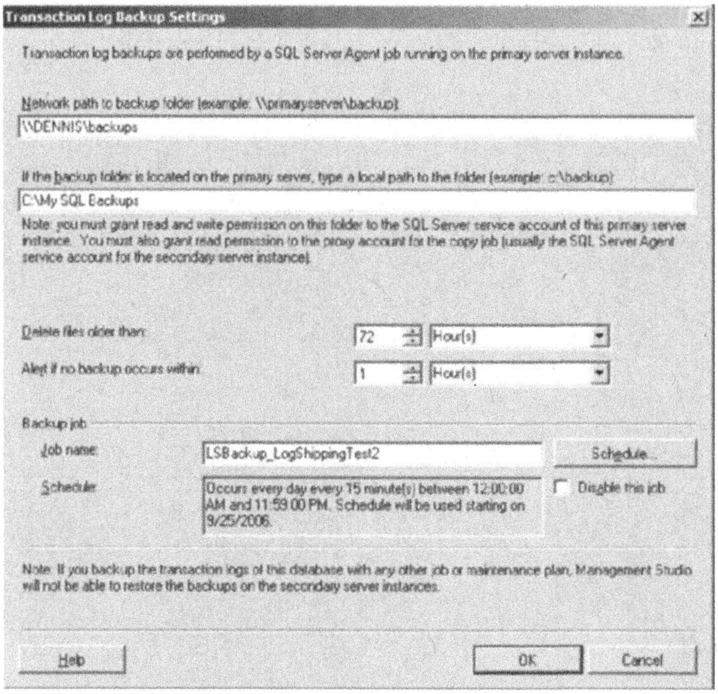

Figure 10-33. *Transaction Log Backup Settings dialog*

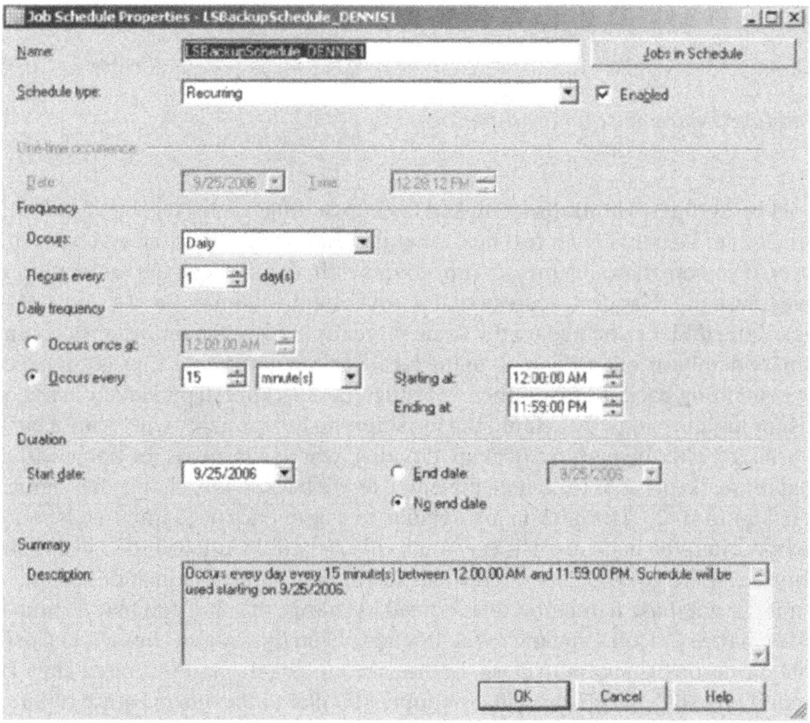

Figure 10-34. *Setting the schedule for the transaction log backup job*

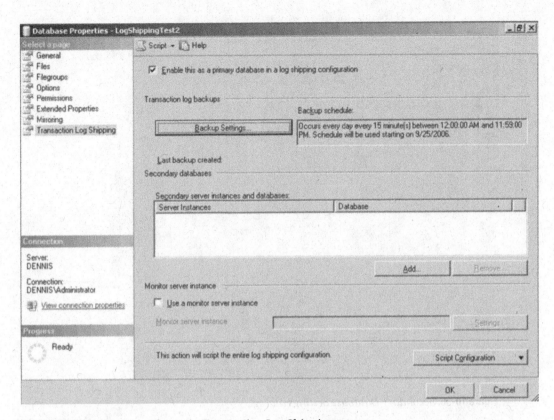

Figure 10-35. *Returning to the main Transaction Log Shipping screen*

4. Click Add to begin the process of adding a secondary. You will see the Secondary Database Settings dialog as shown in Figure 10-36. Click Connect. You will be prompted to connect to the secondary database instance as shown in Figure 10-37. Make sure that you enter the proper name or IP address of the SQL Server 2005 instance that will contain the warm standby database and click Connect.

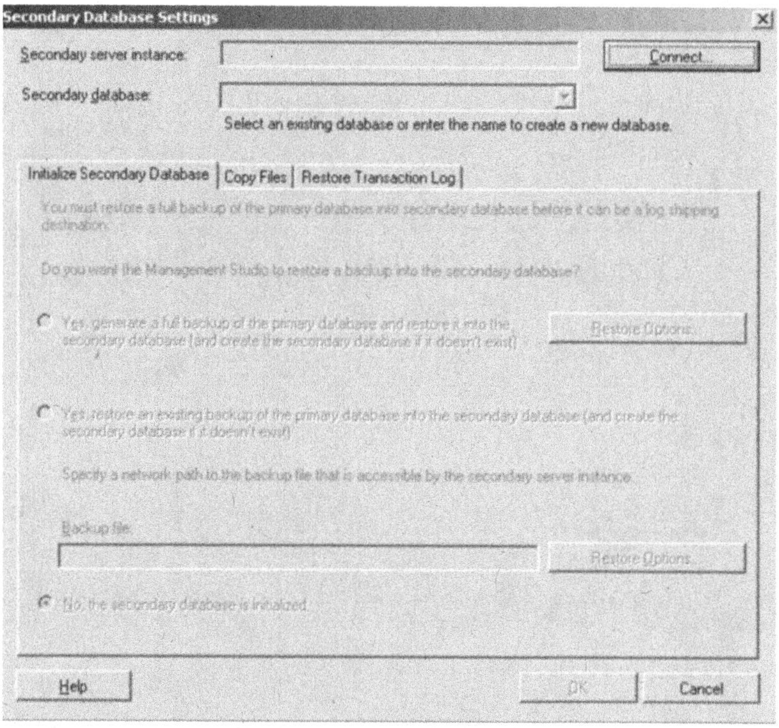

Figure 10-36. *Secondary Database Settings dialog*

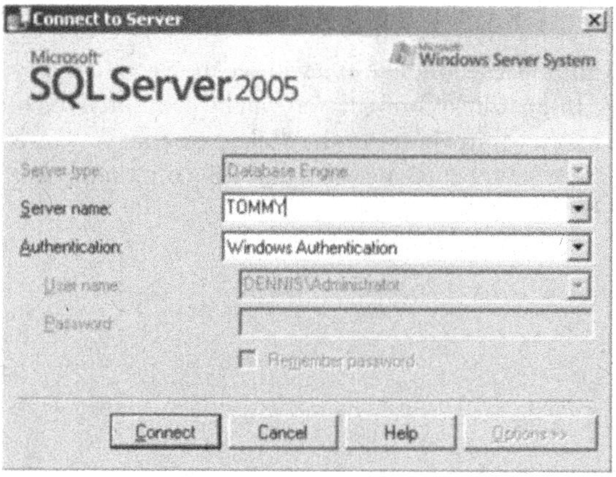

Figure 10-37. *Connecting to the secondary instance*

5. Select the Initialize Secondary Database tab of the Secondary Database Settings dialog. By default, the name of the database that will be used on the secondary SQL Server instance is the same as the one on the primary. You have three options:

- Use the configuration tool to create a full backup of the primary database as shown in Figure 10-38. You cannot control the name of the backup that is generated; it will be *dbname*.bak, and will be placed in the directory or share you configured in step 3. If you want to restore the database to a different path on the secondary, click Restore Options, and enter the new paths for your data and log files in the dialog as shown in Figure 10-39. The paths you enter should be local to the secondary server, such as C:\SQL Data. If you want to restore the database to a different name, enter a new name in the Secondary Database drop-down/entry box.

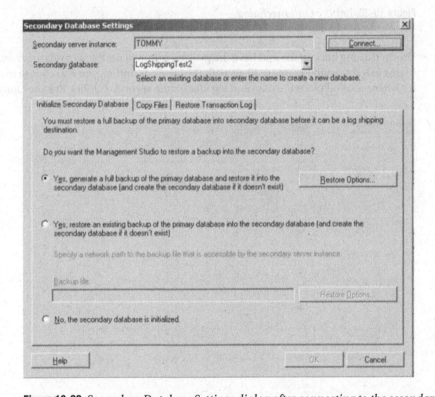

Figure 10-38. *Secondary Database Settings dialog after connecting to the secondary*

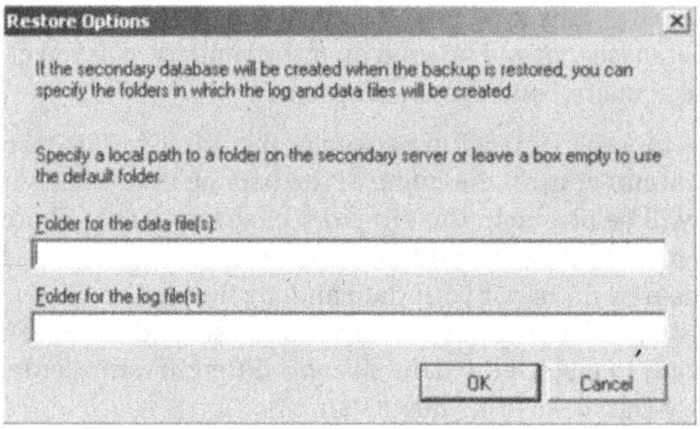

Figure 10-39. *Restore Options dialog*

- Use an existing backup file and have the process restore it on the secondary server. An example is shown in Figure 10-40. As with the previous option, you can choose to customize where you will place the data and log files on the secondary. Click Restore Options.

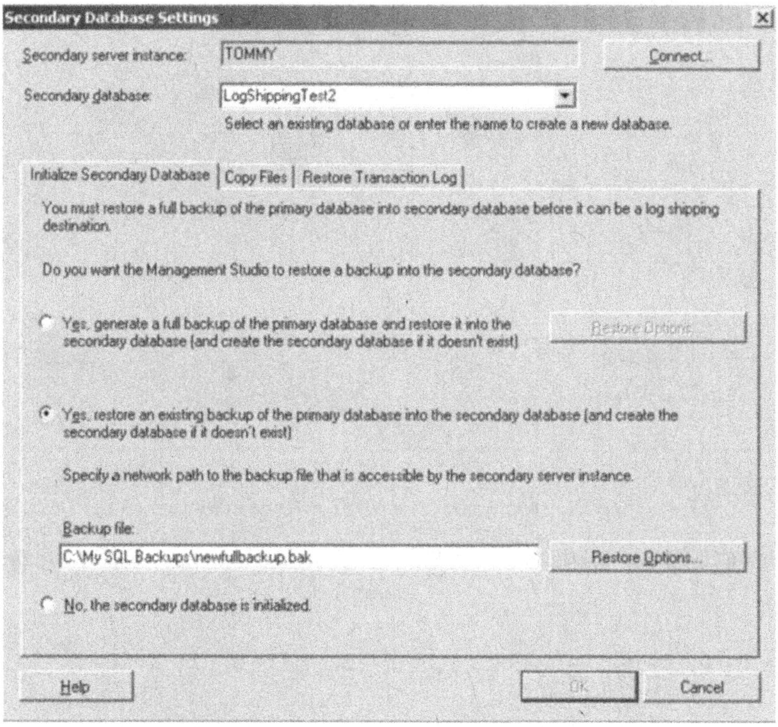

Figure 10-40. *Using an existing backup to initialize log shipping*

Note Both options for initializing your standby database are controlled by the settings you will configure on the Restore Transaction Log tab for restoring your transaction log files. For more information, see step 7.

- Back up, copy, and restore the database on the secondary yourself with either NORECOVERY or STANDBY. Select No, the Secondary Database Is Initialized, as shown in Figure 10-41. You must select the database you restored in the Secondary Database drop-down.

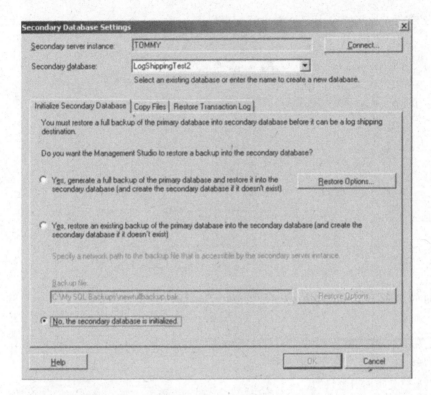

Figure 10-41. *Secondary Database Settings dialog*

6. Select the Copy Files tab. Enter the share name you created on the secondary to receive the backup files. An example is shown in Figure 10-42. The log shipping functionality can also delete the files copied to the secondary. The default is three days (72 hours). The default job created on the secondary (so the copy is a pull, not a push) is named LSCopy_primary_dbname where *primary* is the name of the primary database instance and *dbname* is the name of the database. To modify how often the copy job is run, click Schedule. You will see a dialog similar to the one displayed in Figure 10-43. Click OK when finished modifying the schedule.

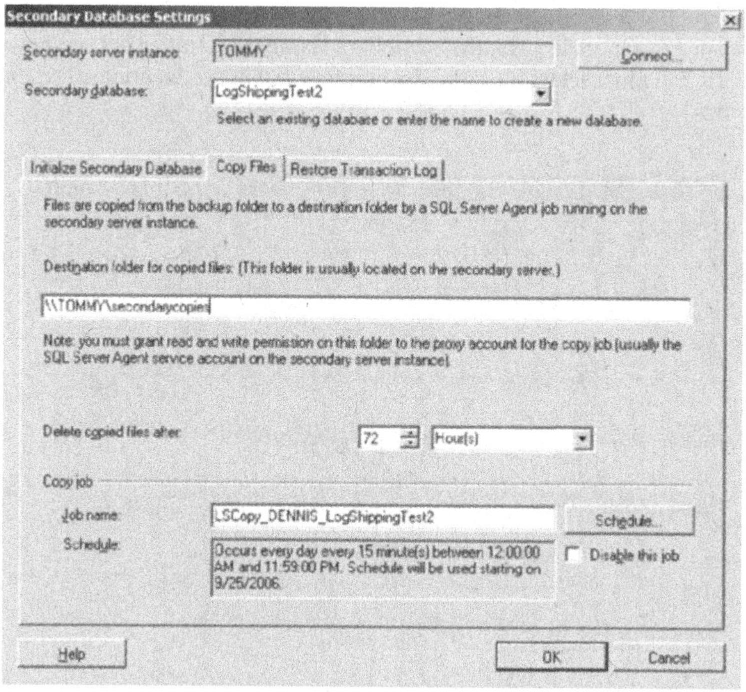

Figure 10-42. *Copy Files tab of the Secondary Database Settings dialog*

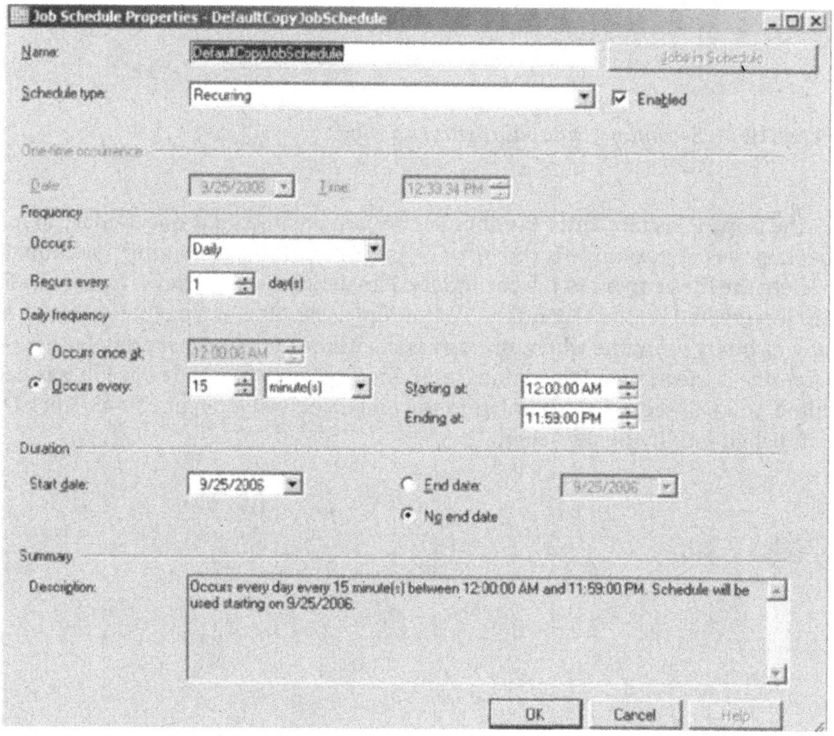

Figure 10-43. *Log shipping copy job schedule*

7. Select the Restore Transaction Log tab. The main option you will select here is to tell the restore job to apply the transaction logs using either WITH NORECOVERY or WITH STANDBY. If you previously selected the option to initialize the database, whatever you selected for the restore state will also be used for the restoration of the full database backup. An example is shown in Figure 10-44. The default job created on the secondary (the copy is a pull, not a push) is named LSRestore_primary_dbname where *primary* is the name of the primary database instance and *dbname* is the name of the database. To modify how often the restore job is run, click Schedule. You will see a dialog similar to the one displayed in Figure 10-45. Click OK when finished modifying the schedule.

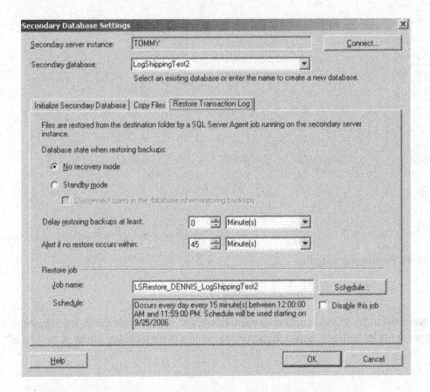

Figure 10-44. *Using WITH NORECOVERY for restoring backups*

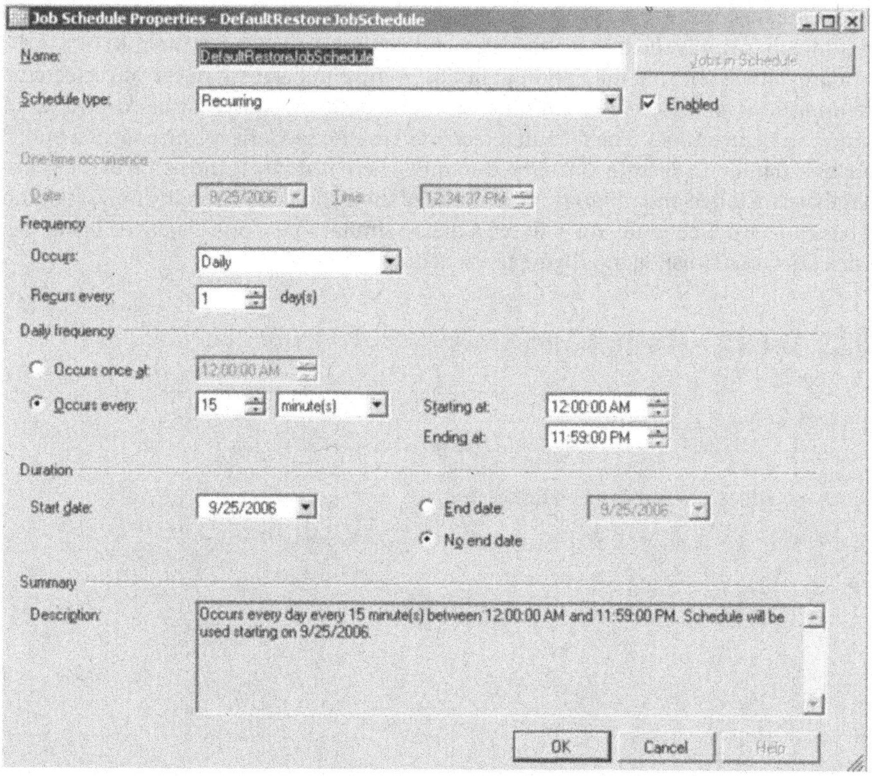

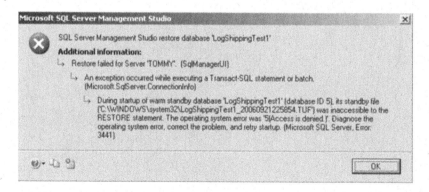

Figure 10-45. *Restore job schedule*

■**Note** If you select the WITH STANDBY option for your restore, and the user configuring log shipping does not have the proper rights for both SQL Server instances, you should see a message similar to the one in Figure 10-46.

Figure 10-46. *Sample error if a restore cannot be done WITH STANDBY*

8. Click OK on the Secondary Database Settings dialog to return to the main transaction log shipping screen. To configure a monitor, select the option Use a Monitor Server Instance. This is optional; however, as noted previously, if you do not create the monitor now, you cannot add it later. The display will be similar to the one in Figure 10-47. If you create a monitor, click Settings. Otherwise, skip to step 10.

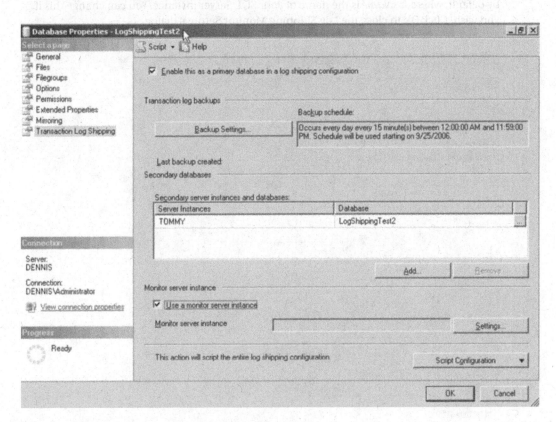

Figure 10-47. *Selecting the option to create a monitor*

9. On the Log Shipping Monitor Settings dialog shown in Figure 10-48, click Connect. You will be prompted to connect to the SQL Server instance that will contain the monitor. An example is shown in Figure 10-49. Click Connect. You should now see the dialog updated, as shown in Figure 10-50. Select how the primary and secondary instances will connect to the monitor. On the monitor, the alert job will be configured with the name LSAlert_InsName by default, where *InsName* is the name of your SQL Server instance. You can change this if you wish. Click OK to close the Log Shipping Monitor Settings dialog.

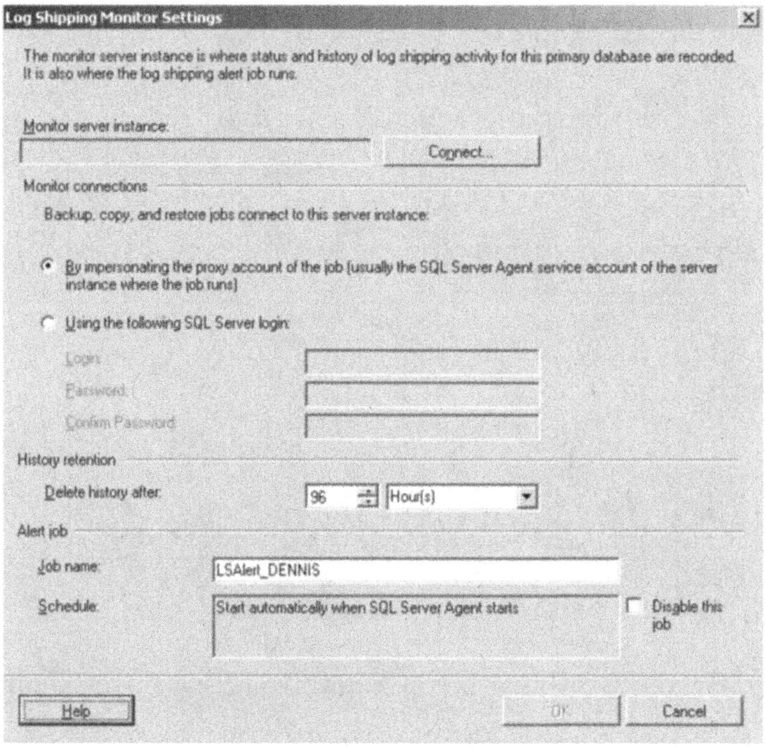

Figure 10-48. *Log Shipping Monitor Settings dialog*

Figure 10-49. *Connecting to the monitor instance*

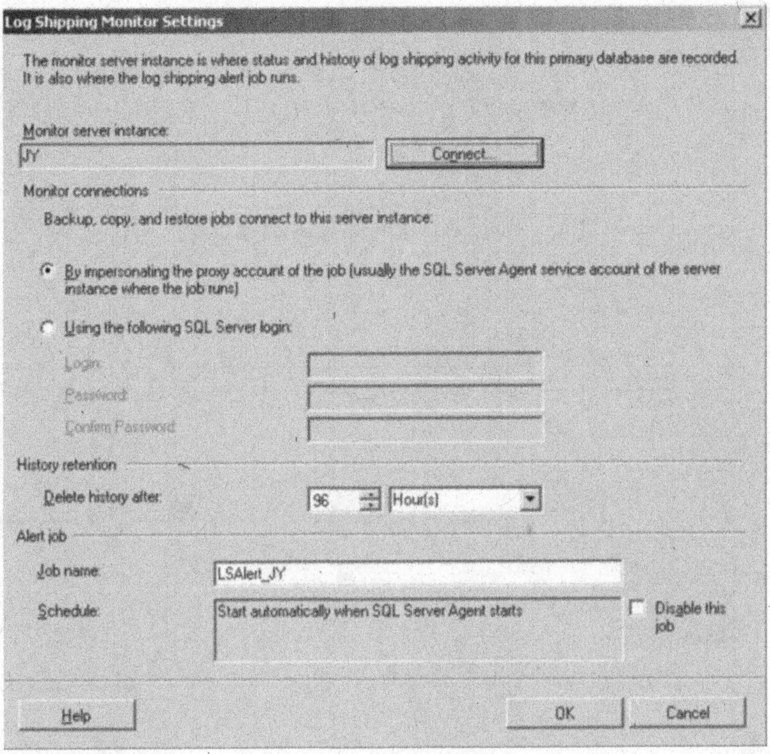

Figure 10-50. *Configured Log Shipping Monitor Settings dialog*

10. Click OK to start configuring log shipping as shown in the dialog in Figure 10-51.

11. Once log shipping is successfully configured, you will see a dialog similar to the one in Figure 10-52. Click Close.

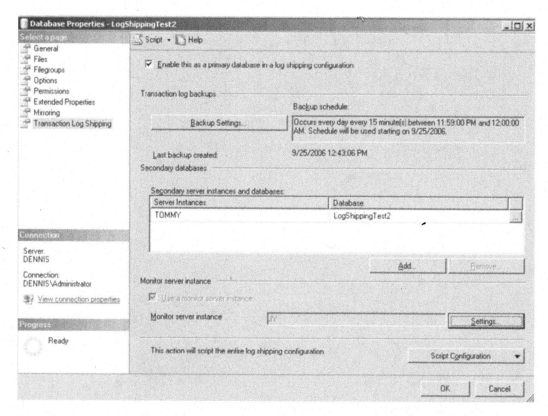

Figure 10-51. *Finished configuration waiting for execution*

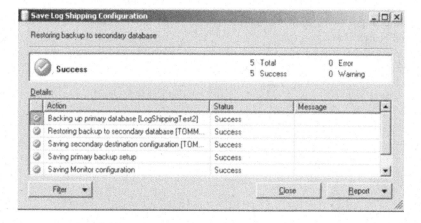

Figure 10-52. *Successful completed log shipping configuration*

Transact-SQL

As with most features in SQL Server 2005, you can set things up either via SQL Server Management Studio or through Transact-SQL. To configure log shipping, you will use the stored procedures Microsoft provides. The stored procedures are listed in Table 10-2.

Table 10-2. *Log Shipping Stored Procedures*

Stored Procedure	Server
sp_add_log_shipping_primary_database	Primary
sp_add_schedule	Primary
sp_add_log_shipping_primary_secondary	Primary
sp_add_log_shipping_alert_job	Monitor (optional)
sp_add_log_shipping_secondary_primary	Secondary
sp_add_jobschedule	Secondary
sp_add_log_shipping_secondary_database	Secondary

> **Note** If you look in both the master and msdb databases, you may see other system stored procedures that relate to log shipping (e.g., sys.sp_processlogshippingmonitorhistory). These procedures are used by log shipping and are called within some of the stored procedures used for installing, running, and maintaining log shipping. These are not documented since you would never actually use them yourself.

The easiest way to see how log shipping is scripted is to do it through SQL Server Management Studio once and then generate a script. The stored procedures listed earlier in Table 10-2 are covered in SQL Server 2005 Books Online, and going through them here does not make a lot of sense.

Custom Log Shipping

As noted earlier, you can also code your own log shipping process. I have written scripts for you to use or use as an example; they can be found on the Apress site in the Source Code/Download section. The log shipping process I wrote is a tad different than but similar to Microsoft's built-in feature. One of the main problems I have with canned features such as the built-in implementation in SQL Server 2005 is that it requires you to change any maintenance you may have in place already. You cannot just hook into an existing transaction log backup that is already being done. The scripts on the Apress site allow you to use your existing transaction log backup job. You also do not have as much control over the copy process since it is pretty much a black box. My scripts are a combination of SQL Server stored procedures and VBScript that is used to perform the copying.

Postconfiguration Tasks

After you configure log shipping, you will need to ensure that all objects that live outside of the primary database are also configured on your secondary (or *secondaries* if you are log shipping to more than one server). If you do not do this, your database may not function properly if you ever need to bring it online. The easiest way to do most tasks is to create scripts, modify them if necessary, and apply them to the secondary instance. Many dialogs in SQL Server 2005 have an option you can click that says Script. An example is shown in Figure 10-53. Many objects can also be scripted as a menu option from Management Studio as shown in Figure 10-54.

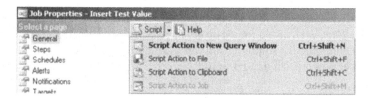

Figure 10-53. *Example dialog with the Script button*

Figure 10-54. *Example of the ability to script the creation of an object*

Once you select the object to script, you will have three options: script to a query window, script to a file, or script to the clipboard. The easiest option is to script the object directly to a file, but if you are trying to create a master script to create all objects, you may want to script it to the clipboard or to a query window and manipulate it that way.

If an object cannot be scripted from Management Studio, such as an SSIS package, you will need to find what the best method is for getting that object over to the secondary. The easiest way is always to get it into some sort of file in Windows and then copy it to the other server and apply it.

Administering Log Shipping

Once you get log shipping set up, you will need to administer and maintain it. There are two methods for hiding the server name change in a log shipping role change: Network Load Balancing and configuring a DNS alias. Since these techniques apply to more than just log shipping, they are covered in Chapter 15. As you learned back in Chapter 4, using Network Load Balancing cannot be configured on the same hardware as a failover cluster; so if any of the instances are nodes of a failover cluster, you cannot use this method to abstract the instance name change.

Monitoring Log Shipping

One major change from SQL Server 2000 Enterprise Edition is the way you monitor log shipping. SQL Server 2000 shipped with a Log Shipping Monitor that when installed showed you in an interface the status of your log shipped pair. SQL Server 2005 removes the graphic interface, but you can query tables or use stored procedures.

Job Status

Arguably the simplest way to first check the status of log shipping for most administrators will be to see the status of the SQL Server Agent jobs involved with log shipping. Those will tell you if the configured jobs are actually running successfully or are failing. You can see an example in the earlier Figure 10-5.

System Tables

If you do not want to use any of the available stored procedures to monitor your log shipping configuration, you can query the system tables (log shipping–specific tables, tables relating to jobs, etc.) that contain information about log shipping directly. All of the tables are located in msdb. The tables specific to log shipping are the following:

- msdb.dbo.log_shipping_monitor_alert: This table contains only one column, which is the SQL Server Agent job ID of the log shipping alert job.

- msdb.dbo.log_shipping_monitor_error_detail: This table contains the specific SQL Server Agent job errors encountered during log shipping.

- msdb.dbo.log_shipping_monitor_history_detail: This table contains the history details for the SQL Server Agent jobs associated with the log shipping plans.

- msdb.dbo.log_shipping_monitor_primary: This table contains configuration information about the primary database, and there is only one record per primary.

- msdb.dbo.log_shipping_monitor_secondary: Similar to the previous table, this contains one record per secondary and has information about the configuration of the secondary.

- msdb.dbo.log_shipping_primaries: This table contains the monitor information for each log shipping plan.

- msdb.dbo.log_shipping_primary_databases: This table contains one record per primary, and has information about the primary database.

- msdb.dbo.log_shipping_primary_secondaries: This table contains one record per primary, and has information about the secondary database.

- msdb.dbo.log_shipping_secondaries: This table has the mappings from the log shipping plan to the secondary instance and database.

- msdb.dbo.log_shipping_secondary: This table contains information about the secondary and its status. There is one record per database.

- msdb.dbo.log_shipping_secondary_databases: This table contains configuration information about the secondary database. There is one record per configuration.

Some examples of using the tables are in the next section. If you want to see the exact columns contained in each table and the explanation of what can be stored in those columns, consult SQL Server Books Online's topics for each of the tables listed.

Stored Procedures

SQL Server 2005 provides you with stored procedures that essentially equate to canned reports to assist you in the monitoring process. All of the stored procedures are located in master:

- master.sys.sp_help_log_shipping_alert_job: This stored procedure returns the unique ID (GUID) associated with the monitoring alert job. You should not really have to execute this stored procedure often, if ever.

- master.sys.sp_help_log_shipping_monitor: This stored procedure is the procedure you would most likely query to get the updated status about what is going on with log shipping. This essentially replaces the graphic monitor functionality that was available in SQL Server 2000. Because this is no longer available in Management Studio as a dialog, you will need to understand what this stored procedure is returning as its values. Table 10-3 explains what each column means when returned.

Table 10-3. *sp_help_log_shipping_monitor Columns*

Column	Explanation
status	This is the overall status of the specified log shipping plan. 0 is healthy with no failures; 1 means that there are failures.
is_primary	This tells you whether the row you are looking at relates to the primary or the secondary. 0 is the secondary; 1 is the primary.
server	This is the name of the primary or secondary server depending on the value of is_primary.
database_name	This is the name of the database on the primary.
time_since_last_backup	This is the time (in minutes) since the transaction log was last backed up on the primary. If the value is NULL, the information could not be retrieved.
last_backup_file	This is the name of the last transaction log backup file made. If the value is NULL, the information could not be retrieved.
backup_threshold	This is the value (in minutes) that has been set that if exceeded will trigger an alert if the transaction log backup has not happened. If the value is NULL, the information could not be retrieved.
is_backup_alert_enabled	If this is set to 0, an alert will not be raised if the value in backup_threshold is exceeded. If it is 1, an alert will be raised. If the value is NULL, the information could not be retrieved.
time_since_last_copy	This is the time (in minutes) since the last transaction log backup was copied to the secondary. If the value is NULL, the information could not be retrieved.
last_copied_file	This is the name of the last transaction log backup file that was successfully copied to the secondary. If the value is NULL, the information could not be retrieved.
time_since_last_restore	This is the time (in minutes) since the last transaction log copied was restored on the secondary. If the value is NULL, the information could not be retrieved.
last_restored_file	This is the name of the last transaction log backup file that was restored on the secondary. If the value is NULL, the information could not be retrieved.
last_restored_latency	This is the time (in minutes) from the time the backup of the file was completed to the time the restore occurred. If the value is NULL, the information could not be retrieved.
restore_threshold	This is the value (in minutes) that has been set that if exceeded will trigger an alert if the restore has not happened.
is_restore_alert_enabled	If this is set to 0, an alert will not be raised if the value in restore_threshold is exceeded. If it is 1, an alert will be raised. If the value is NULL, the information could not be retrieved.

- master.sys.sp_help_log_shipping_monitor_primary: This stored procedure has two parameters: @primary_server, which is the name of the SQL Server instance containing the primary database, and @primary_database, which is the name of the primary database. An example is shown here:

```
exec master.sys.sp_help_log_shipping_monitor_primary
    @primary_server = 'DENNIS'
    @primary_database = 'MyLogShipDB'
```

The values that will be returned are most of the same values as those if you had run `sp_help_log_shipping_monitor` but are only the values that are related to the primary. There are a few added columns, such as `last_backup_date_utc` and `history_retention_period`.

- `master.sys.sp_help_log_shipping_monitor_secondary`: This stored procedure has two parameters: `@secondary_server`, which is the name of the SQL Server instance containing the secondary database, and `@secondary_database`, which is the name of the secondary database. An example is shown here:

```
exec master.sys.sp_help_log_shipping_monitor_secondary
    @secondary_server = 'TOMMY'
    @secondary_database = 'MyLogShipDB'
```

The values that will be returned are most of the same values as those if you had run `sp_help_log_shipping_monitor` but are only the values that are related to the primary. There are a few added columns, such as `last_copied_date_utc`, `last_restored_date_utc`, and `history_retention_period`.

- `master.sys.sp_help_log_shipping_primary_database`: This stored procedure has two parameters: `@database`, which is the name of the primary database, and `@primary_id`, which is the unique identifier associated with the log shipping plan. An example execution is shown here:

```
declare @ls_primary_id as uniqueidentifier
declare @ls_db_name as varchar(500)

set @ls_db_name = 'LogShippingTest1'

set @ls_primary_id = (select primary_id
    from log_shipping_primary_databases
    where primary_database = @ls_db_name)

exec master.sys.sp_help_log_shipping_primary_database
    @database = @ls_db_name,
    @primary_id = @ls_primary_id
```

The values returned are nearly identical to the ones from `sp_help_log_shipping_monitor_primary`.

- `master.sys.sp_help_log_shipping_primary_secondary`: This stored procedure has one parameter: `@primary_database`, which is the name of the primary database. An example execution is shown here:

```
exec master.sys.sp_help_log_shipping_primary_secondary
    @primary_database = 'LogShippingTest1'
```

The values returned will say the name of the secondary server(s) and database(s) associated with that primary.

- `master.sys.sp_help_log_shipping_secondary_database`: This stored procedure has two parameters: `@secondary_database`, which is the name of the secondary database in the loading state, and `@secondary_id`, which is the unique identifier associated with the secondary. An example execution is shown here:

```
declare @ls_secondary_id as uniqueidentifier
declare @ls_db_name as varchar(500)

set @ls_db_name = 'LogShippingTest1'
```

```
set @ls_secondary_id = (select secondary_id
    from log_shipping_secondary_databases
    where secondary_database = @ls_db_name)

exec master.sys.sp_help_log_shipping_secondary_database
    @secondary_database = @ls_db_name,
    @secondary_id = @ls_secondary_id
```

The values returned are nearly identical to the ones from sp_help_log_shipping_monitor_secondary with a few additions such as copy_job_id.

• master.sys.sp_help_log_shipping _secondary_primary: This stored procedure is run on the secondary and has two parameters: @primary_server, which is the name of the primary SQL Server instance, and @primary_database, which is the name of the primary database. An example execution is shown here:

```
exec master.sys.sp_help_log_shipping_secondary_primary
    @primary_server = 'DENNIS'
    @primary_database = 'LogShippingTest1'
```

The values returned will show the configuration of the log shipping pair as it relates to the secondary.

Modifying Log Shipping

If you need to alter the log shipping plan for whatever reason, such as changing the schedule for each job, modify the SQL Server Agent jobs directly. Most modifications are tweaks that are job-related. Log shipping can be modified via the database's properties dialog, and certain tasks from a tool perspective are exclusive to that dialog such as deleting log shipping. Where the properties dialog has an advantage is that if you modify any properties there, they are also altered on any SQL Server instance participating in the log shipping plan versus having to visit each individual instance.

Changing the Monitor Server

There is no graphic way to change the server that is serving as the monitor, or even add the monitor after the fact through SQL Server Management Studio as shown in Figure 10-29. You do have the ability to do both if you update the proper log shipping configuration tables in msdb. These steps are not currently documented by Microsoft and are the same whether you are adding a new monitor or changing an existing one.

Since there is no graphic way to add a monitor server if you did not specify one during configuration, you must execute the commands in the following steps. Only steps 1 and 2 are required if you have already configured a monitor server and are just changing the server. If you want to modify other aspects, continue on.

1. Set the name (or IP address) of the monitor server in the instance containing the primary database. This is the only step required on the primary if you have already specified a monitor server and are changing its location:

```
UPDATE dbo.log_shipping_primary_databases
SET monitor_server = 'Monitor_Server'
WHERE primary_database = 'MyDB'
GO
```

You now have to execute a similar statement on each secondary:

```
UPDATE msdb.dbo.log_shipping_secondary
SET monitor_server = 'Monitor_Server'
WHERE primary_database = 'MyDB'
GO
```

Update the column that tells SQL Server that you configured the monitor when you initially set up log shipping. In essence, you are faking out SQL Server. This step is not necessary if you are just changing the server name:

```
UPDATE msdb.dbo.log_shipping_primary_databases
SET user_specified_monitor = 1
WHERE primary_database = 'MyDB'
GO
```

2. Perform a similar step on each secondary:

```
UPDATE msdb.dbo.log_shipping_secondary
SET user_specified_monitor = 1
WHERE primary_database = 'MyDB'
GO
```

3. Set the security mode for the monitor. You cannot specify a user and a password (or at least I can't find where it's stored) to allow you to use SQL Server authentication. For this reason, you must set monitor_server_security_mode to 1, which is Windows Authentication:

```
UPDATE msdb.dbo.log_shipping_primary_databases
SET monitor_server_security_mode = 1
WHERE primary_database = 'MyDB'
GO
```

4. Do the same step on all secondaries:

```
UPDATE msdb.dbo.log_shipping_secondary
SET monitor_server_security_mode = 1
WHERE primary_database = 'MyDB'
GO
```

5. You should now be able to bring up the properties of the primary database, click Transaction Log Shipping, and see the monitor server.

6. Now you must manually create the alert job to populate the monitor on the primary. The job needs to have a Transact-SQL step with the following syntax: exec sys.sp_check_log_shipping_monitor_alert. It should be scheduled to run every two minutes.

7. Once the job is created, you must update the log shipping configuration with the GUID of the job. Execute the following Transact-SQL command:

```
UPDATE msdb.dbo.log_shipping_monitor_alert
SET alert_job_id =
(select job_id from msdb.dbo.sysjobs
where [name] = 'Name_Of_Alert_Job')
GO
```

8. Repeat steps 6 and 7 for all secondaries.

Disabling Log Shipping

There may be times where you need to disable log shipping. This may need to occur for a variety of reasons, including maintenance on the network that could disrupt log shipping and wanting to avoid "false" errors from being reported to your monitoring software. Remember to reenable log shipping when the task that interrupts it is complete.

Caution Although you have the option of disabling the transaction log backup job in SQL Server Management Studio as shown in Figure 10-55, I do not recommend doing that. As you learned in Chapter 3, backups are the cornerstone of your availability.

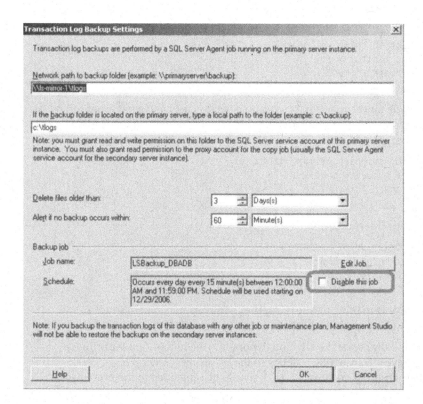

Figure 10-55. *Transaction Log Backup Settings subpage of the Transaction Log Shipping properties*

SQL Server Management Studio

To disable log shipping using SQL Server Management Studio, follow these steps:

1. Start SQL Server Management Studio.

2. Connect to the SQL Server instance containing the secondary database.

3. Expand the SQL Server Agent, then expand Jobs as shown in Figure 10-56.

4. Select the copy job, right-click, and select Properties as shown in Figure 10-57.

5. On the Job Properties dialog, deselect the Enabled check box, shown in Figure 10-58. Click OK.

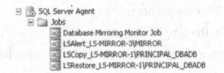

Figure 10-56. *Jobs expanded on the secondary*

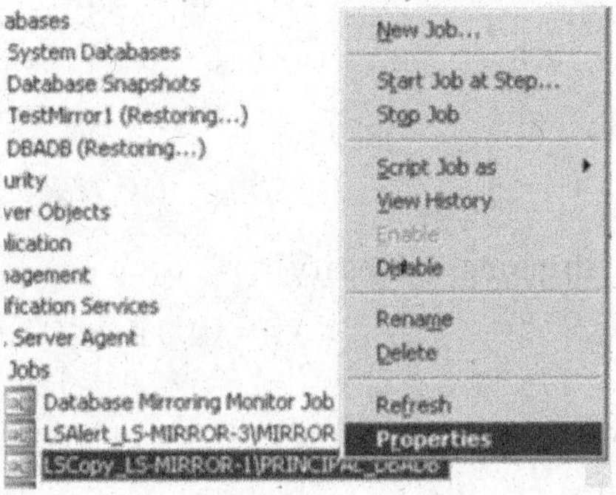

Figure 10-57. *Properties menu option for a job*

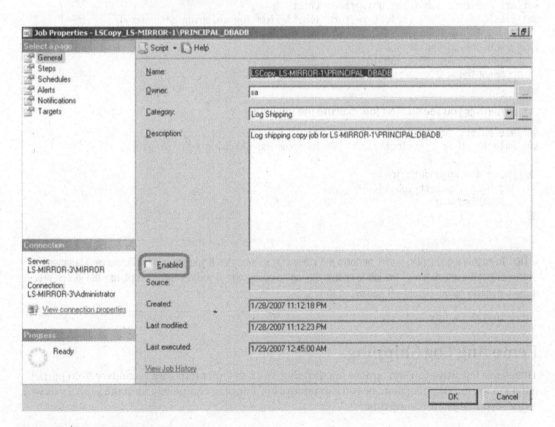

Figure 10-58. *Disabling the job*

6. Select the restore job, and repeat steps 4 and 5 for the restore job.

7. Select the alert job and repeat steps 4 and 5 for the alert job.

8. Connect to the primary and monitor instances, and repeat steps 4 and 5 for any alert job.

Transact-SQL

Use the following Transact-SQL scripts to disable log shipping. First, run this script on the secondary:

```
use msdb
go

-- Disable the copy job
declare @copy_job_id as uniqueidentifier
set @copy_job_id = (select copy_job_id from log_shipping_secondary)

EXEC msdb.dbo.sp_update_job
    @job_id = @copy_job_id
    ,@enabled = 0
GO

-- Disable the restore job
declare @restore_job_id as uniqueidentifier
set @restore_job_id = (select restore_job_id from log_shipping_secondary)

EXEC msdb.dbo.sp_update_job
    @job_id = @restore_job_id
    ,@enabled = 0
GO
```

Wherever you see an alert job, execute the following:

```
declare @alert_job_id as uniqueidentifier
set @alert_job_id = (select alert_job_id from log_shipping_monitor_alert)

EXEC msdb.dbo.sp_update_job
    @job_id = @alert_job_id
    ,@enabled = 0
GO
```

Tip To enable log shipping again, perform the steps in reverse order. If you are using SQL Server Management Studio, select the check box of the job to enable the log shipping jobs. If you are using script, use the stored procedures previously listed, except set @enabled to 1.

Removing Log Shipping

There are a few ways you can remove log shipping. You can either remove a secondary from participating in the log shipping plan, or you can remove log shipping completely from the primary as well as the secondary at the same time.

SQL Server Management Studio: Removing a Secondary

Use the following steps to remove a secondary from a log shipping plan:

1. Start SQL Server Management Studio.

2. Expand Databases, select the database, select Properties, and then select the Transaction Log Shipping page.

3. Deselect the Enable This as a Primary Database in a Log Shipping Configuration option as shown in Figure 10-59. Click OK.

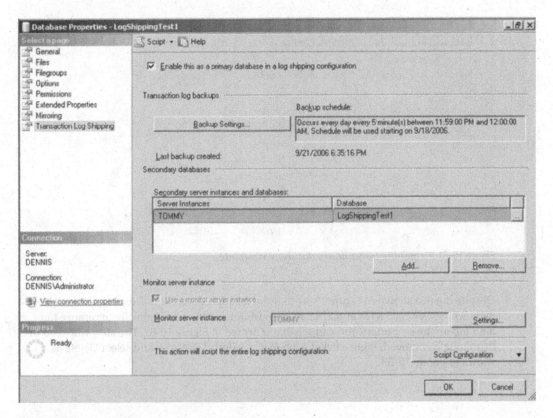

Figure 10-59. *Log shipping properties page*

4. You will be prompted to confirm the removal of the secondary database from the log shipping plan. Click Yes if this is what you want to do. An example is shown in Figure 10-60. If the deletion is successful, you will see a dialog similar to the one in Figure 10-61. Click Close.

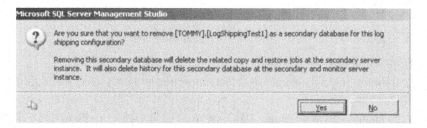

Figure 10-60. *Removing a secondary database confirmation*

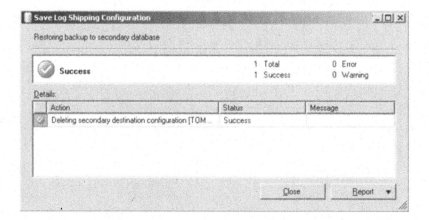

Figure 10-61. *Removing a secondary database complete*

5. Despite the text shown in Figure 10-61 that the deletion is successful, log shipping (at least with SQL Server 2005 RTM and SP1, which is what I used for testing) will not remove the alert job on the secondary. You can see that reflected in Figure 10-62. The alert will need to be manually removed. Right-click the job (e.g., LSAlert_TOMMY), and select Delete as shown in Figure 10-63.

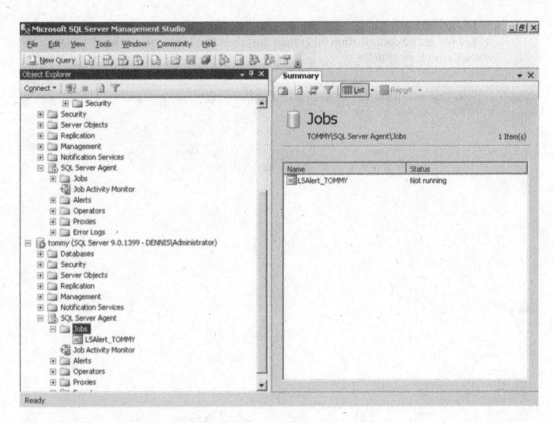

Figure 10-62. *Alert job after the removal of the secondary*

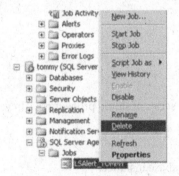

Figure 10-63. *Leftover SQL Server Agent job*

6. On the Delete Object dialog, as shown in Figure 10-64, click OK to finish the deletion of the job. You will get no confirmation other than the job will no longer be displayed in SQL Server Management Studio.

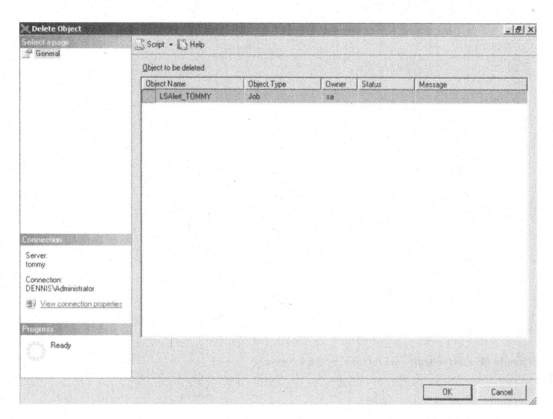

Figure 10-64. *Deleting a job*

Transact-SQL: Removing a Secondary

Deleting the log shipping plan in Transact-SQL is done via a series of stored procedures. They must be executed in the order presented here:

1. Start SQL Server Management Studio.

2. Open a query window connected to the primary database instance.

3. On the primary database instance, run the stored procedure sp_delete_log_shipping_primary_secondary. This removes any entries associated with the secondary from the tables storing information about the log shipping plan on the primary. A sample execution is shown here:

```
exec master..sp_delete_log_shipping_primary_secondary
    @primary_database = 'LogShippingTest2',
    @secondary_server = 'TOMMY',
    @secondary_database = 'LogShippingTest2'
```

The stored procedure has the following parameters:

- `@primary database`, which is the name of the database on the primary that is the source of the secondary database

- `@secondary server`, which is the name of the SQL Server instance containing the standby database

- `@secondary_database`, which is the name of the database on the standby server

4. Connect to the secondary instance and run the stored procedure `sp_delete_log_shipping_secondary_database`. The procedure has one parameter: `@secondary_database`, which is the name of the secondary database. The following is an example:

```
exec master..sp_delete_log_shipping_secondary_database
     @secondary_database = 'LogShippingTest2'
```

Note If there is only one database on the secondary that corresponds to the primary database, the stored procedure `sp_delete_log_shipping_secondary_primary` is automatically run as part of `sp_delete_log_shipping_database`. If it is not the only database, it will be skipped since the log shipping plan is still sending logs to that instance for the specified primary database.

SQL Server Management Studio: Deleting the Entire Plan

1. Start SQL Server Management Studio.

2. Expand Databases, select the primary database, right-click, and select Properties. Select the Transaction Log Shipping page of properties.

3. Deselect the Enable This as a Primary Database in a Log Shipping Configuration option as shown earlier in Figure 10-59. Click OK. You will be prompted to confirm the removal as shown in Figure 10-65. Click Yes. If the removal is successful, you will see a dialog similar to the one in Figure 10-66.

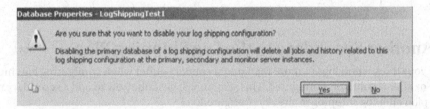

Figure 10-65. *Confirming the disabling of a log shipping plan*

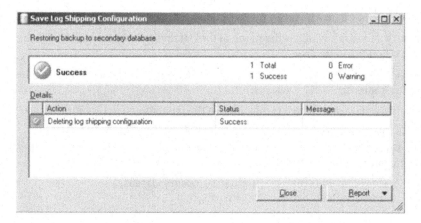

Figure 10-66. *Successful removal of a secondary database*

Transact-SQL: Deleting the Log Shipping Plan

Deleting the log shipping plan in Transact-SQL is done via a series of stored procedures. They must be executed in the order presented here:

1. Follow steps 1 through 4 of the section "Transact-SQL: Removing a Secondary."

2. If necessary, on the primary instance, run the stored procedure sp_delete_log_shipping_ primary_database. The procedure has one parameter: @database, which is the name of the primary database. The following is an example:

```
exec master..sp_delete_log_shipping_primary_database
    @secondary_database = 'LogShippingTest2'
```

Caution Whether you delete the log shipping secondary or you delete the whole plan, SQL Server will not automatically delete the database in the loading state on the warm standby. You must manually delete it.

Adding Another Secondary to the Log Shipping Plan

You can ship your transaction logs to more than one secondary either when configuring log ship-ping initially or after it is already configured. This section will describe how to add a secondary to a log shipping plan after log shipping is already configured.

SQL Server Management Studio

Take these steps to add another secondary to the log shipping plan using SQL Server Management Studio:

1. Start SQL Server Management Studio.

2. Expand Databases, select the primary databases, select Properties, and then select the Transaction Log Shipping page of the database properties.

3. Follow steps 4 to 7 from the section "SQL Server Management Studio Log Shipping Setup" earlier in this chapter.

4. Once you return to the Transaction Log Shipping page, click OK to begin the configuration process.

Transact-SQL

Take these steps to add another secondary to the log shipping plan using Transact-SQL:

1. Manually back up, copy, and restore the primary database on the secondary using WITH NORECOVERY or WITH STANDBY. You can also use an older full backup and restore the subsequent transaction logs to bring the secondary up-to-date.

2. Start SQL Server Management Studio and connect to the secondary database instance.

3. Open a query window.

4. Execute the stored procedure sp_add_log_shipping_secondary_primary. Its syntax is fully described in the Books Online topic "sp_add_log_shipping_secondary_primary (Transact-SQL)."

5. Execute sp_add_jobschedule as described in Chapter 15 to set the schedule of the new copy-and-restore SQL Server Agent jobs created in step 3.

6. Execute the stored procedure sp_add_log_shipping_primary_secondary. The following is an example:

```
exec master..sp_add_log_shipping_primary_secondary
        @primary_database = 'LogShippingTest2',
        @secondary_server = 'NewIns',
        @secondary_database = 'LogShippingTest2'
```

The stored procedure has the following parameters:

- @primary database, which is the name of the database on the primary that is the source of the secondary database

- @secondary server, which is the name of the SQL Server instance containing the standby database

- @secondary_database, which is the name of the database on the standby server

7. Open a query window to the primary instance. Execute the stored procedure sp_add_log_shipping_primary_secondary. The procedure has one parameter: @secondary_database, which is the name of the secondary database. The following is an example:

```
exec master..sp_add_log_shipping_primary_secondary
        @primary_database = 'LogShippingTest2',
        @secondary_server = 'NewIns',
        @secondary_database = 'LogShippingTest2'
```

The stored procedure has the following parameters:

- @primary database, which is the name of the database on the primary that is the source of the secondary database

- @secondary server, which is the name of the SQL Server instance containing the standby database

- @secondary_database, which is the name of the database on the standby server

Manually Killing Database Connections

If you are using your database for reporting purposes and restored your database WITH STANDBY, you will need to manually kill each connection before the transaction log restore can happen. Each connection has a unique system processing identifier (SPID). The Transact-SQL code in the following listing can be executed manually (which defeats the purpose of log shipping since it is an automated process), or you can either put it in a SQL Server Agent job step directly, or in a stored procedure that is called by a job. This script must be run prior to the transaction log restore. You must run it in the context of the master database.

To use the script, substitute the name of your standby database for MyDB. The script will then find all connections for that database and kill them. Use this script wisely; set the proper expectations with any end users:

```
DECLARE @spid_to_kill int
DECLARE @sqltxt varchar(300)

DECLARE kill_spids CURSOR FOR
    SELECT spid
    FROM sysdatabases sd, sysprocesses sp
    WHERE sd.[name] = 'MyDB'
        and sd.[dbid] = sp.[dbid]
    ORDER BY spid

OPEN kill_spids

FETCH NEXT FROM kill_spids INTO @spid_to_kill

WHILE @@FETCH_STATUS = 0
BEGIN
    SET @sqltxt = 'KILL ' + CAST(@spid_to_kill as varchar(6))
    EXEC (@sqltxt)
    FETCH NEXT FROM kill_spids INTO @spid_to_kill
END

CLOSE kill_spids
DEALLOCATE kill_spids
```

Following is an example error you would see (or need to trap in an application) if your connection was disconnected:

```
Msg 233, Level 20, State 0, Line 0
A transport-level error has occurred when sending the request to the server.
(provider: Shared Memory Provider, error: 0 - No process is on the
other end of the pipe.)
```

To verify that all SPIDs have been killed, run the following query. It should return no results:

```
SELECT spid
FROM sysdatabases sd, sysprocesses sp
WHERE sd.[name] = 'MyDB'
    and sd.[dbid] = sp.[dbid]
ORDER BY spid
```

Performing a Role Change

When you have to switch from your primary to your warm standby, you have to perform a role change. The steps in the following sections walk you through the process of promoting your warm standby to the new primary. There are two types of role changes. The first is a graceful role change that is generally planned. You can get the tail of the log from the primary and copy and apply it to the secondary, as well as possibly switch roles where the primary becomes the secondary and vice versa. The second and more common type is when you have some sort of problem or failure on the primary and need to bring the secondary online as the new primary. The second scenario is one where you may incur some data loss.

Tip Some of the following steps may involve running Transact-SQL commands. I would strongly recommend creating a SQL Server Agent job on the warm standby for each database participating in log shipping. Separate each task or command into multiple jobs or multiple job steps (in order) in a single job. The job should be set to be run manually. In the heat of a disaster—or even if it is not a disaster—removing the possibility of human error will minimize your downtime.

Graceful Role Change

To perform a role change in a nondisaster scenario, follow these steps:

1. At a predetermined point in time that has been properly communicated, stop all application traffic and user connections to SQL Server. Allow all transactions to complete in the database. I would strongly suggest that while the traffic is spinning down you disable any existing backup and maintenance jobs on the primary database to ensure that no other work will happen while you are trying to do the role change.

2. Manually back up the last transaction log to capture the tail of the log, and if you wish, leave the database in a loading state. Leaving it in a loading state will allow it to accept transaction logs if you need to reverse the process. For instructions on how to back up the tail of the log, refer back to Chapter 3.

3. Copy all transaction log backups (including the manual transaction log backup you made in step 2) to the share on the secondary that have not yet been copied.

4. Connect to the secondary SQL Server instance via SQL Server Management Studio.

5. Apply all transaction log backups except the last outstanding transaction log available using either WITH NORECOVERY or WITH STANDBY. You can use an existing restore job, but at this point, doing it yourself may prove more efficient. If you do it manually, disable the existing restore job to ensure that you do not allow any automatic restorations. When you reach the last transaction log backup, you must use WITH RECOVERY to bring the database online. If all transaction logs have already been applied, use the command RESTORE DATABASE dbname WITH RECOVERY where *dbname* is the name of your database.

6. Synchronize all logins using the stored procedure sp_resolve_logins. Synchronizing logins are described in more detail in Chapter 15.

7. Make sure all other objects that live outside the database are added to the instance that contains the new primary database as well as the database itself if necessary.

8. Disable any jobs associated with log shipping on the secondary.

9. Redirect the application to the new database instance. Your application may be using some sort of standard connection, such as an ODBC DSN, so you would need to modify that. Never implement solutions such as NLB or add aliases in DNS unless you absolutely have to; your application layer should be coded to be easy to reconfigure.

▪Note If you are using Network Load Balancing or a DNS alias to abstract the server name change, see Chapter 15 for more information on how to use it during the role change.

---

10. Test the application to ensure that everything functions properly after the role change.

11. Allow others to access the application.

Emergency Role Change

These steps assume that the primary server is completely unavailable, therefore you cannot back up the tail of the log or access any resources on it.

1. Using your preferred method, check to see what the last available transaction log backup is, and where it is located. If the share is on the secondary, check there, or if you are using an intermediate server share, check there. Make sure the latest file is actually copied on the secondary. Once you know what your last transaction log backup is, make a note of it.

2. Follow steps 4 through 11 of the previous section to complete the process.

Switching Back to the Old Primary

Unlike SQL Server 2000's log shipping feature that gave you an option to create a job that would make it easy to log ship back to the primary, SQL Server 2005 does not offer such a feature. To log ship back to the original primary, you will need to configure log shipping from the new primary (which is the old secondary) back to the old primary (which will be the new warm standby). Configure this via your preferred method (either the feature in SQL Server 2005 or your own custom log shipping).

If the switch was performed as a graceful role change and you followed the previous instructions, your database should already be in a loading state. Since the secondary was brought online at the point where the primary was, configuring log shipping back to the old primary should be trivial; all you need to do is start the transaction log backups on the new primary (the old secondary) and initiate the copy-and-restore process to the old primary (now the secondary). If the role change was done as part of an emergency role change, you will need to start the process from scratch.

Assuming you have the proper capacity on your secondary, I do not recommend switching back to the old primary unless you have to. It will cause an outage. If that secondary is sized properly, you should be able to run your applications with no slowdown or problems to the end users, which is your ultimate end goal. If you do need to switch back, plan it during a time that will minimize the interruption to your end users.

Summary

Log shipping continues to be one of the best and most popular forms of availability or disaster recovery with SQL Server, and will arguably continue in that role until Microsoft either stops making SQL Server or pulls any backup and restore functionality out of the product. It provides reliable per-database protection that integrates well with other things going on (such as backup plans, failover clustering, database mirroring, and replication), and adds virtually no overhead to the instance.

The main issue with log shipping is that the role change means that you may have a server, an instance, or an IP address change that your application may not be able to tolerate. The other problem some have with log shipping is that the role change is completely a manual process. While you can automate some of it through SQL Server Agent jobs, it is near impossible to completely automate it.

Armed with the pros and cons of log shipping, you can now proceed to learn about the newest availability feature of SQL Server, database mirroring, which is related to log shipping in its mechanisms.

CHAPTER 11

■ ■ ■

Database Mirroring

One of the most touted new features of SQL Server 2005 is database mirroring. Database mirroring is in both the Standard and Enterprise Editions of SQL Server 2005. This feature adds to the already strong arsenal of failover clustering, log shipping, and replication. This chapter will describe how database mirroring works, the things you need to think about before implementing, the steps to implement, and finally, how to administer database mirroring.

Note Although the functionality for database mirroring is technically in the released to manufacturers (RTM) version of SQL Server 2005 and could be enabled with a trace flag, it was not officially enabled and fully supported as a feature until SQL Server 2005 Service Pack 1. If you plan on implementing database mirroring, you must upgrade to at least SQL Server 2005 Service Pack 1 to take advantage of it.

How Database Mirroring Works

Like log shipping, database mirroring provides protection on a per-database, not a per-instance, level. The easiest way to describe database mirroring is that it is transactional replication meets log shipping with a touch of clustering thrown in for good measure. Like log shipping, you take a point-in-time backup of your database and restore it in a state that can load transaction logs. Database mirroring does not work by sending individual transaction log backups—it sends each individual transaction log record to the standby database (like transactional replication, which is covered in the next chapter). Therefore, anything captured in the transaction log will be applied to the copy of the database on the other server. The action of sending transaction log records can happen synchronously or asynchronously. The switch to the other database can happen either manually or automatically, depending on your configuration. Like log shipping, you can only mirror user databases, not system databases.

Most of the terminology for database mirroring is different from the other SQL Server availability technologies. You have a source database, or the *principal*, that then sends the transaction log records to the *mirror*, which is the target database. The instance with the principal and the instance with the mirror are *partners* in a *database mirroring session*. One significant difference from log shipping is that the relationship from the principal database to the mirror database is that it is a 1:1 ratio—you cannot have multiple mirrors for every principal.

Besides the principal and mirror, there is a third optional instance named the *witness*. The witness is required if you want automatic failover and can be shared by different database mirroring sessions. Like clustering, the witness helps create *quorum* to ensure that only one of the partners currently owns the database that is used by end users and applications. Database mirroring has three types of quorum:

- *Full quorum*: A principal, mirror, and witness
- *Witness-to-partner quorum*: Quorum established by the witness and one of the partners
- *Partner-to-partner quorum*: Quorum established between the two partners with no witness involved

The quorum mechanisms used by database mirroring are not unlike the heartbeat for failover clustering. It is part of the mechanism that determines failover for a mirrored configuration. Database mirroring performs a ping across the network once every second. If ten pings are returned as missed, a failure is initiated. However, as you will see, different types of failures (SQL Server or hardware/operating system) will affect the time—it will not necessarily be a ten-second failover. SQL Server failures can generally be quicker than hardware or operating system failures in terms of the ability to switch to the mirror.

Database mirroring requires the use of endpoints that are different from the normal instance endpoints. An *endpoint* is an object created by SQL Server that is bound to a particular network protocol that allows SQL Server to communicate on your network to applications and other servers. An endpoint for database mirroring is known as a *database mirroring endpoint*. This endpoint is a shared endpoint for each database on a particular SQL Server instance, so once it is configured, until you change it, all databases that will use database mirroring will use the same endpoint. The database mirroring endpoint is used for SQL Server to SQL Server communication and uses TCP/IP exclusively. The endpoint must have a unique port number that is different from that of any other TCP/IP service on the server. This functions not unlike the cluster private network in a failover clustering configuration.

Transaction Safety

Database mirroring introduces the concept of transaction safety. There are two ways this can be set: FULL (synchronous) and OFF (asynchronous). The value for transaction safety controls which mode will be used by the database mirroring session. The default value is FULL.

Mirroring State

A database participating in database mirroring can have one of the following *mirroring states*, or status:

- SYNCHRONIZING: This is when the mirror is not caught up to the principal. This would most commonly be seen when database mirroring is first started and is in high performance mode described in the next section.
- SYNCHRONIZED: This is when the mirror is caught up to, or nearly caught up to, the principal. Your transaction safety setting will govern whether there may be data loss. If your transaction safety is set to FULL, there will be no data loss. If it is set to OFF, there is the potential for data loss.
- SUSPENDED: This means that the mirror is unavailable and is not receiving transactions from the principal.
- PENDING_FAILOVER: This state will only occur once a failover from the principal to the mirror is initiated and before the mirror becomes the new primary.
- DISCONNECTED: This is when one partner cannot connect to the other partner.

Database Mirroring Modes

There are two modes for database mirroring: high performance and high safety. Both are related to the combination of the safety level set for the mirroring session and whether a witness is required.

High Performance Mode

High performance mode of database mirroring is simply mirroring asynchronously. This means that any transactions created on the principal will not necessarily be immediately applied to the mirror. This is much like log shipping where there is a delta between the primary and the secondary. However, if you are mirroring asynchronously, you will see better performance and arguably less overhead, but you are trading some availability for that performance. High performance mode requires that transaction safety has a value of OFF.

The witness serves no purpose in high performance mode—only the principal and mirror are needed. In fact, adding the witness to a high performance mode configuration will add risk since its addition to this setup will enforce quorum, which requires two or more SQL Server instances. I would not use a witness in this scenario, as it provides no value. If quorum is lost, there are two scenarios: when the principal is down, you will only be able to manually force the mirror to become the new primary if it can connect to the witness; and when the mirror is down, the principal will be taken offline if it cannot connect to the witness. Therefore, it is recommended that if you plan on implementing high performance mode, you do not configure a witness.

The sequence of events that happens in high performance mode is as follows and is represented in Figure 11-1:

1. An application or end user submits a transaction for the principal, and SQL Server writes that transaction to the transaction log file.

2. SQL Server commits the data on the principal and acknowledges to the application or end user that it "has" the transaction.

3. The principal contacts the mirror, and the transaction is sent.

4. The transaction is written to the transaction log of the mirror.

5. The mirror "handshakes" with the principal to acknowledge that the mirror has the transaction.

6. The data is committed on the mirror.

As you may have already deduced, the process is basically a delayed two-phase commit where you have the possibility of incurring data loss. A *two-phase commit* is a transaction initiated by a host that waits for acknowledgement from the receiver before it is completed. This mode is closer to the way log shipping works. You are only as current as the last transaction sent from the principal, committed, and then acknowledged on the mirror. Depending on factors such as your network and distance, this could be a subsecond response or something much larger than that.

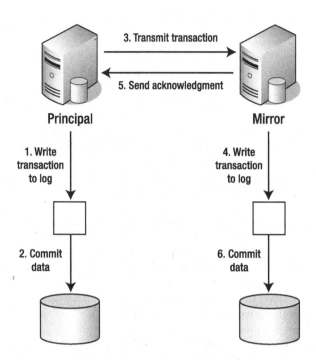

Figure 11-1. *High performance mode database mirroring*

Since high performance mode does not support automatic failover, if the principal is unavailable you have three options:

- Assuming nothing catastrophic happened on the principal, you can wait for it to come back online. For example, someone just rebooted it after performing normal maintenance.

- If something happened to the principal database itself, but the instance that is home to the principal has no damage, you can reinitialize database mirroring by restoring the database from backups.

- You can force the mirror to become the new primary. The mirroring state will be DISCONNECTED or SUSPENDED to allow this to happen.

High Safety Mode

High safety mode is when database mirroring is operating synchronously. The process is similar to high performance mode, except that this is a "proper" two-phase commit: the transaction cannot be committed on the principal until it has been committed on the mirror as well. This ensures both partners are completely in sync. High safety mode requires the use of an instance to contain the witness if you want an automatic failover.

The sequence of events that happens in high safety mode is as follows and is represented in Figure 11-2:

1. An application or end user submits a transaction for the principal, and SQL Server writes that transaction to the transaction log file on the principal.

2. The principal contacts the mirror, and the transaction is written to the transaction log of the mirror.

3. The mirror "handshakes" with the principal to acknowledge that the mirror has the transaction.

4. SQL Server acknowledges to the application or end user that SQL Server "has" the transaction.

5. SQL Server commits the data on the principal.

6. SQL Server commits the data on the mirror.

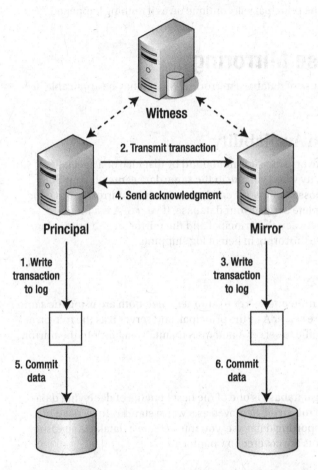

Figure 11-2. *High safety mode database mirroring*

Like failover clustering, high safety mode can support automatic failover from the principal to the mirror if it is configured to do so. This requires that not only is the mirror database synchronized, but that the witness and mirror are still connected when the failure on the principal occurs. Once the automatic failover occurs, the mirror is the new principal database, and when or if the principal comes back online, it will assume the mirror role. If the principal and witness are lost, you will have to force the mirror to become the primary database.

The automatic failover time should take less than 30 seconds in most cases, but it depends on a few factors. The first is when the failure is detected on the principal. This is governed by the database mirroring TIMEOUT value, which defaults to ten seconds. However, depending on the failure (such as a disk failure on the principal), this may actually take longer than the value specified for TIMEOUT. If the witness cannot get the principal to respond in the time set by TIMEOUT, it is considered to be down. The next is ensuring that the principal and mirror are in sync. If they are, there will be no transactions to roll forward on the mirror when the redo process begins to bring the database online. If there are transactions to roll forward, they will be applied and will take as long as necessary to complete. If the principal comes online before the redo phase completes, the mirror does not assume the principal role. Once the mirror is designated as the principal, all incomplete transactions are rolled back and the database comes online.

If the witness is lost in high safety mode, you lose the ability to do an automatic failover and there is no impact on the application or client. The principal will continue on as if nothing happened.

Best Uses for Database Mirroring

There are a few scenarios that best fit the use of database mirroring. Not all may be applicable in your environment.

Disaster Recovery and High Availability

Database mirroring supports disaster recovery since it is not bound by distance or a specialized configuration, and supports high availability when you are in the same data center. If your SLA requires you to have as little data loss as possible for your databases, database mirroring is a good choice since, like log shipping, it is a complete copy of your database. If your SLA is a bit more relaxed and you can tolerate some delta between the principal and the mirror, or you are setting up a server remotely, you can use database mirroring in lieu of log shipping.

Migration to New Hardware

Database mirroring can facilitate moving from one server to another when both are using the same edition of SQL Server 2005. If you configure server A as the principal, and server B as the mirror, at some designated point you can stop all traffic to server A and then manually fail over to the mirror.

Reporting

The ability to use the mirror as a reporting database is one of the best benefits of deploying database mirroring. This allows even database mirroring deployed as a warm standby to be used in other ways. To configure the mirror as a reporting database, you must create a database snapshot on the mirror database. Database snapshots are covered in Chapter 13.

Database Mirroring Considerations

The factors detailed in this section will influence the planning and deployment of database mirroring in your environment.

High Performance Mode vs. High Safety Mode

Deciding whether you want asynchronous or synchronous database mirroring will govern every other decision you make for your database mirroring implementation. Obviously, from a protection standpoint, high safety mode is the way to go, but depending on your system resources, or if your SLAs do not need to be up to the last transaction, you should consider asynchronous (high performance) mode. Keeping your mirror in step via an asynchronous process means your mirror may not be exactly where your principal is, but you are taking into account other factors that influence your implementation. If you have a heavy OLTP system and a poor network, synchronous mirroring may not be realistic.

Edition and Version Configuration

Database mirroring requires that the principal and mirror instances are the same edition of SQL Server. For example, if you are planning on deploying high-safety mode, you cannot have one partner installed with SQL Server 2005 Standard Edition and one partner with SQL Server 2005 Enterprise Edition. Both the primary and the mirror must be the same edition of SQL Server. This is similar to failover clustering but different from replication and log shipping, which are edition-agnostic.

Note If you are using SQL Server 2005 Standard Edition, only high safety mode of database mirroring is supported. This means that you cannot do any form of asynchronous mirroring with Standard Edition.

From a pure technology standpoint, database mirroring should technically work if your partners are at different versions (for example, the principal is Enterprise and the mirror is Standard), but it is not really a supported way of deploying database mirroring. Since you cannot mirror between editions of SQL Server, you cannot use database mirroring as a way to perform what is known as a *rolling upgrade* from one edition to another. A rolling upgrade is one where you configure technologies such as log shipping between two instances to facilitate an upgrade or server move while your primary database is still active. Database mirroring would make this very difficult since its support for editions and versions of SQL Server is limited. However, database mirroring can facilitate a migration from one server to another if you are going to the same edition of SQL Server and want to deploy new hardware.

SQL Server 2005 does not care if the principal and mirror are in a failover clustering configuration or if the instance is stand-alone. You can configure database mirroring between the two types of servers with no issue. You should not, however, configure database mirroring to the same instance of SQL Server. That makes no architectural sense.

Location of the Principal, Mirror, and Witness

If you are using database mirroring for high availability or reporting, there is a high probability that the servers hosting the SQL Server instances will reside in the same data center. In this scenario, location is somewhat relative since your network latency should be good. You are not completely isolated since a complete data center failure will take out any server participating in database mirroring.

If you are using database mirroring for disaster recovery, all of the servers should not reside in the same data center to ensure that the whole ecosystem does not have a single point of failure. If it is configured, the witness can reside in the data center that contains either the principal or the mirror, or even possibly in a third data center. The best place is arguably with the mirror. The reason is that if there is a complete outage of the primary data center that has the principal database, the witness is able to initiate the failover to the mirror. If the witness is in the same data center as the principal, you lose both, and subsequently the ability to do an automatic failover.

Two things ultimately dictate what lives where: your network and your transaction log. This is mostly the case for high safety mode since it is synchronous. If you have good bandwidth and latency, distance should not be a problem for any server participating in database mirroring. If you are using asynchronous database mirroring, location will be dictated more by how you want to individually isolate components of database mirroring since performance will not be an issue.

Mirror Database Recovery Model

You must have your databases participating in database mirroring configured with the Full recovery model. Log shipping supports Bulk-logged in addition to Full, but database mirroring does not. So if you have to use any recovery model other than Full (for whatever reason), do not consider database mirroring. If you configure database mirroring but at some point decide to change your recovery model from Full to Bulk-logged or Simple, you will break database mirroring and you will have to reconfigure it.

Database Restoration and Configuration on the Mirror

To be able to apply the transaction log on the secondary, when you restore the full backup, you must use WITH NORECOVERY. This is a key difference from log shipping, which also supports WITH STANDBY.

The database name and configuration location should remain the same on the mirror. This is yet another difference from log shipping, which does not have such a requirement. If the database name is different on the mirror, it may present problems if the application has the ability to automatically fail over and reconnect. If the location is different, objects that are created through data definition language (DDL) will not get created or not be created properly.

Server Sizing

I am not going to sugarcoat this one: database mirroring will require a fairly robust database server and SQL Server design. First and foremost is the use of SQL Server's worker threads. As of SQL Server 2005 with SQL Server 2005 Service Pack 1, it is recommended that up to ten databases per instance can be mirrored due to the number of threads consumed by each individual mirroring session. This number is not hard-coded in SQL Server, so you can have more or less, depending on your system resources. If your applications use a lot of worker threads, you should consider whether to use mirroring, and if you do, whether you will deploy mirroring for other databases on that instance.

Since database mirroring does have some overhead associated with it, you may want to ensure that your overall processor utilization for SQL Server does not go above what you may consider out of bounds. Most people have a comfort zone of constant processor utilization somewhere between 50% and 70%. The reason you need to keep an eye on your processor utilization is that higher usage may result in the inability to ping the other servers in the database mirroring session and may cause a failover that is not needed.

Disk Design and Performance

If you have a database with a lot of transactional activity, do not place your data files and log file on the same disks. Since database mirroring is a much more granular level of availability as compared to log shipping, and you have the ability to configure it in high safety mode, which could send every transaction as it happens, you easily have the potential of saturating your disk I/O if you do not do some capacity planning upfront. Some companies will undersize a redundant server such as a mirror since they view it as a temporary solution, and that can also translate into a lesser performing disk subsystem. If your disk subsystem is bad, it will affect the speed at which you can apply transactions. If your disk subsystem is slow, even if you are mirroring synchronously, you may still be behind.

Networks, Domain Connectivity, and Database Mirroring

How fast the two-phase commit process occurs is directly related to how fast and reliable your network is. If you are using high safety mode, deploying it on a slow network would not be recommended, and if that network is unreliable, it could even cause things such as unwanted failovers if the mirror is configured for automatic failover. If you are planning on deploying high performance mode, the speed of your network may not be *as* crucial, but it is still important in terms of potential data loss since you assume some latency between the principal and the mirror. With high performance mode, it can tolerate a backed-up queue of transactions, but high latency will cause the queue to get bigger. There needs to be a balance somewhere. You cannot expect the equivalent deployment of a high performance sports car such as a Lamborghini, Ferrari, or Porsche if you are running a four-cylinder engine under the hood (even though the exterior may still say Lamborghini, Ferrari, or Porsche). That car needs a beefier engine such as a V6 or a V8 with a turbo to really scream.

Network latency will also factor into your ability to have a mirror that is completely in sync. Database mirroring, especially in high safety mode, will not be able to tolerate high latency without affecting database mirroring. A slow network means poor performance. Database mirroring does not require that the principal, mirror, and witness have to be even remotely near each other, but the longer the distance, the longer it will take for a transaction to go from point A to point B. You cannot escape any distance limitations related to networking.

If you are using high safety mode, I recommend you set up a private network between the servers, if it is possible. Configuring a dedicated network is similar to the private cluster network for a failover cluster. The main reason for doing this is that the network will be dedicated for the database mirroring traffic and will not be affected by the bandwidth of serving requests from the application or other traffic that would come across the public network. For example, if your public network is on the 187.100.101.x network, and you add a network card (or use a dual-homed network card) and configure it to talk on the 188.100.101.x network, which does not share any other traffic, the transfer of log records may actually benefit even if the network speed is not technically as fast as the public network. Before taking this as gospel, you should always test in your own environment to see whether this configuration will benefit you.

Code Page/Sort Order/Collation

While SQL Server allows you to set a different collation per database and per instance, the partner configurations should be configured to avoid any potential behavior differences. For example, each collation tells SQL Server how to deal with sorts (such as case-sensitive or case-insensitive). If the primary database is case-insensitive, but the secondary is not, it would potentially yield radically different query results for the same data.

Security

Database mirroring requires the use of Windows Authentication and uses it by default. There is no SQL Server Authentication option, so if you do not have domain connectivity (either the same domain or trusted domains for all servers), you must use certificates. If you cannot use either, database mirroring may not be an option for you.

Distributed Transactions

If you are using distributed transactions, they are not supported in database mirroring. So if you are utilizing the Microsoft Distributed Transaction Coordinator as a key component of your architecture, database mirroring may not be the best availability solution for your databases.

Transaction Size

Your transaction size will have an impact on how quickly your transaction logs are processed. If you generate many longer running transactions, the mirror will be a larger delta off of the primary database since it will take longer to send and then apply the transaction. It is in your best interest to optimize your transactions within your application to be as small as possible. The quicker SQL Server can process them, the faster the log is restored (or rolled forward in a stop/start). The next time your developer wants to do some funky insert with 70,000 joins, slap his or her wrist since it will ultimately affect your availability or performance in one way or another.

Transaction Logs and Database Mirroring

Database mirroring is dependent upon a transaction log that is not log bound at the disk level. If you have a poorly performing transaction log, database mirroring will suffer. If everything is working properly, the only things you need to worry about are how the high performance and high safety modes interact with the transaction log.

In either mode, if you pause database mirroring, the database mirroring state is preserved but the transaction log on the principal continues to grow since no transactions are sent to the mirror. Pausing also means that a transaction log cannot be truncated. This obviously affects the ability to back up the transaction log since part of the backup process is to truncate the transaction log.

If the mirror is lost, the transaction log will continue to grow on the principal. If you have enough disk space, it is not a problem, but at some point you may need to break database mirroring and reconfigure it once the mirror is back up if you are in jeopardy of running out of disk space.

Synchronizing Database Logins

Like backup and restore, log shipping, and replication, you will need to worry about synchronizing the logins between the principal and the mirror if you plan on ever using the mirror as the primary database. For more information on synchronizing database logins, see Chapter 3 and Chapter 15.

Objects that Reside Outside the Database

Besides synchronizing database logins, you need to worry about other objects such as SQL Server Agent jobs, database maintenance plans, and SSIS packages that may be needed to make the mirror a true production-ready copy of the database. Like log shipping, database mirroring only applies changes that are captured either in the transaction log or the initial full backup. Most of the objects are easily scripted or re-created but must be taken into account when considering log shipping because missing something may mean that your applications that rely on the database might not function properly. For example, if a job performs an important data manipulation on a scheduled basis and it is not recreated on the mirror, chances are your reports will not produce the right data.

Database Mirroring and Maintaining Consecutive LSNs

Applying the transactions one after another keeps the LSN sequence intact. This unbroken sequence is what database mirroring counts on. If you somehow manage to break the LSN chain, you break database mirroring. The easiest way to break the LSN chain is to put your database in Bulk-logged or Simple recovery mode; so educate your fellow administrators on the implications of their actions if you are going to use or are already using database mirroring. Another way to break the LSN chain is to pause database mirroring. Pausing mirroring allows transactions to occur on the principal that are not sent to the mirror. To resynchronize your mirror, stop allowing transactions to occur on the principal, make a transaction log backup, and then copy and apply it using WITH NORECOVERY to the mirror. You can then reenable database mirroring between the partners.

Database Maintenance, Updates, and the Mirror

Since the mirror has been restored WITH NORECOVERY, it will be unaffected by issues such as service pack installations and hotfixes. The behavior of SQL Server updates is such that they bypass databases they cannot update if they are not active. It also means that no database maintenance can be performed directly on that mirror database until it has been recovered.

Applications and Database Mirroring Failover

If you are using high performance mode or the manual failover capability of high safety mode, you will most likely need to take into account the fact that the database instance your application or end users will be connecting to will change. Your application should be able to tolerate the name change (either via some form of configuration setting or file, or through some standard mechanism such as an ODBC DSN). If it cannot tolerate a name change, like log shipping, you may be able to abstract the name change via NLB or a DNS alias.

If you are using high safety mode, there is the possibility that you may not have to have the applications or end users reconnect to the mirror in a failover. This goes for both the automatic and manual failover. It depends on one main factor: how your application is coded (custom or third-party). Like failover clustering, if you switch from one server to another, the existing connection will be dropped. The question always comes in on the reconnect. Failover clustering has the concept of a cluster-aware application that is coded to understand that the SQL Server on the backend is clustered and can handle the situation. Database mirroring has something similar.

You need to code your application to specifically know about database mirroring to be able to handle the primary and mirror. First, you will need the version of MDAC (or later) that is compatible with SQL Server 2005 as well as either SQL Server Native Client or ADO.NET. If you are coding your own application, use the SqlConnection object's ConnectionString. For detailed information, see the topic "Using Database Mirroring" in the .NET Framework Developer's Guide's "Using the .NET Framework Data Provider for SQL Server" (http://msdn2.microsoft.com/en-us/library/kb9s9ks0.aspx). The bottom line is that the connection string has to contain not only the primary but the mirror. The connection string also assumes the same database name on each partner. The following is a sample connection string:

```
"Server=Principal_Instance; Failover Partner=Mirror_Instance;
Database=MirrorDB;Network=dbmssocn"
```

You should never hard-code this connection string to make it inflexible but should allow the application to be configured so that you can use different partner names or a database name if necessary.

Tip Check with your software vendors to see whether the software you wish to deploy using SQL Server 2005 supports automatic failover with database mirroring. If not, you will need to account for the instance name change with the methods listed previously.

Configuring Database Mirroring

Once you plan your database mirroring implementation, it is time to configure the partners.

Step 1: Back Up and Restore the Database

Before you can configure database mirroring, you must back up the database on the principal, copy the backup to the mirror, and restore the database WITH NORECOVERY. Use your preferred method from Chapter 3 to achieve this task.

Step 2: Set Up Database Mirroring

When the database is restored on the mirror, you can then configure mirroring itself.

SQL Server Management Studio

1. Start SQL Server Management Studio and connect to the SQL Server instance that contains the principal database.

2. Expand Databases and select the database that will serve as the principal. Right-click, select Tasks, and then Mirror, as shown in Figure 11-3. Conversely, you can right-click, select Properties, and then select the Mirror page. Both will lead you to the example shown in Figure 11-4.

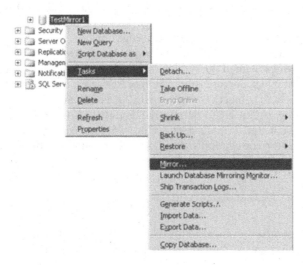

Figure 11-3. *Mirror menu option*

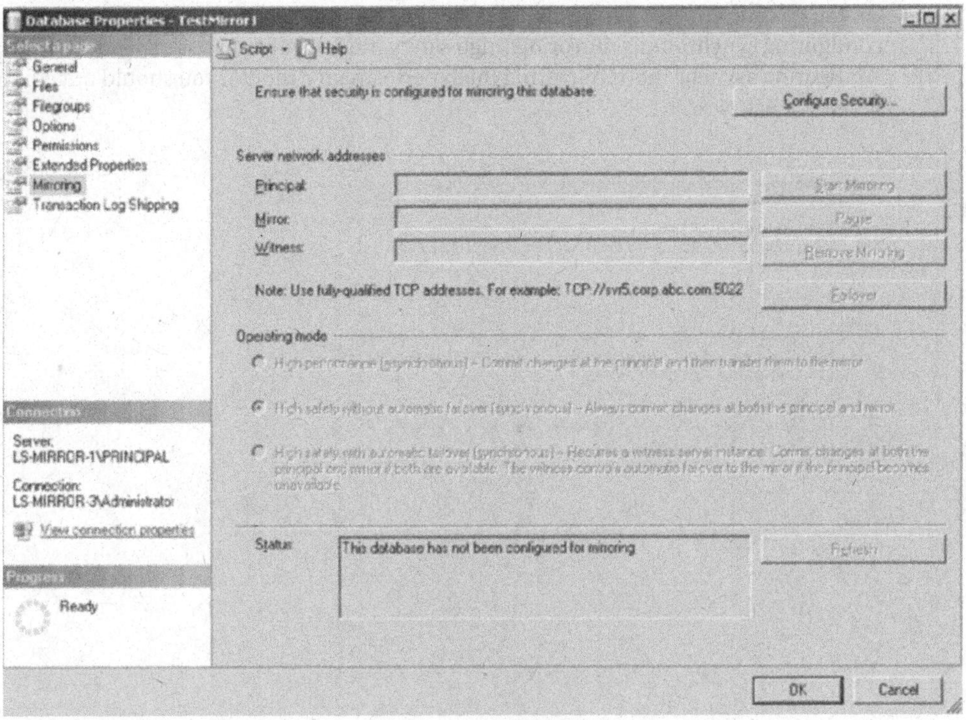

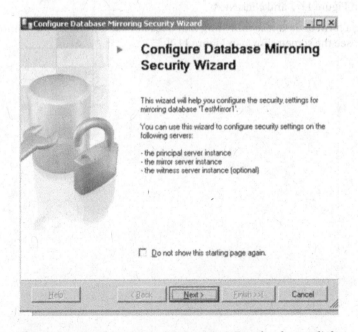

Figure 11-4. *Properties dialog of a database with the Mirroring page selected*

3. Click Configure Security. You will see the Configure Database Mirroring Security Wizard dialog as shown in Figure 11-5. Click Next.

Figure 11-5. *Database Mirroring Security Wizard welcome dialog*

4. On the Include Witness Server dialog as shown in Figure 11-6, select Yes or No. If you are configuring synchronous mirroring (high safety mode), you must use a witness. If you are configuring asynchronous mirroring (high performance mode), you should not configure a witness. Click Next.

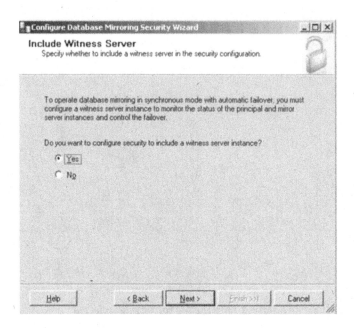

Figure 11-6. *Include Witness Server dialog*

5. On the Choose Servers to Configure dialog, make sure the option Witness Server Instance is selected as shown in Figure 11-7 and click Next.

    If you are deploying a form of database mirroring that does not use a witness or it cannot be configured, you will see the screen shown in Figure 11-8.

CHAPTER 11 ■ DATABASE MIRRORING   439

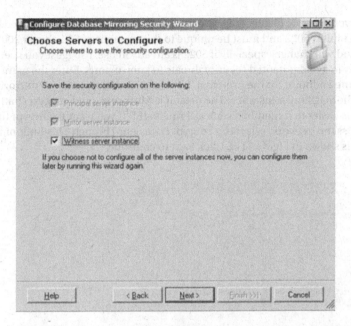

Figure 11-7. *Choose Servers to Configure dialog with the witness option*

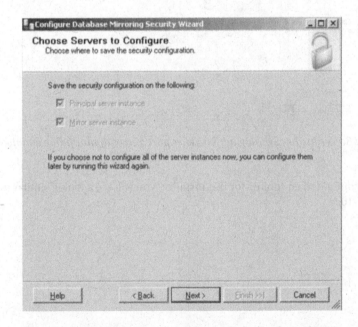

Figure 11-8. *Choose Servers to Configure dialog without the witness option*

6. On the Principal Server Instance dialog, enter the listener TCP/IP port that will be used by the principal. The default is 5022 and must be unique to this instance of SQL Server 2005. It may be different and will change especially if 5022 is already in use. I suggest you use another port number to avoid potential security threats to known ports. Enter the name of the database mirroring endpoint for the principal. It must be a unique database mirroring endpoint name for the SQL Server instance. The default is Mirroring, but I suggest changing it to something that is easier to remember, such as PrincipalEP. If you want to encrypt the data that is sent across the network, select the Encrypt Data Sent Through This Endpoint option. An example is shown in Figure 11-9. Click Next to continue.

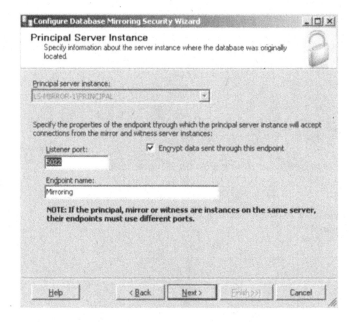

Figure 11-9. *Principal Server Instance dialog with listener port and endpoint name enabled*

If you have already configured endpoints for this instance, you will see a dialog similar to the one in Figure 11-10.

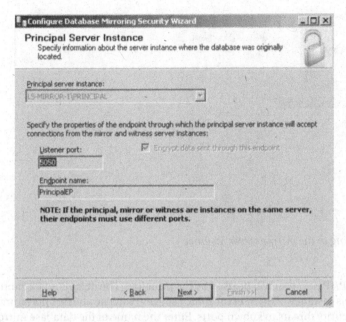

Figure 11-10. *Principal Server Instance dialog with listener port and endpoint name disabled*

7. On the Mirror Server Instance dialog, first select the instance in the Mirror Server Instance drop-down as shown in Figure 11-11. Click Connect, and you will be prompted to connect to the mirror instance as shown in Figure 11-12.

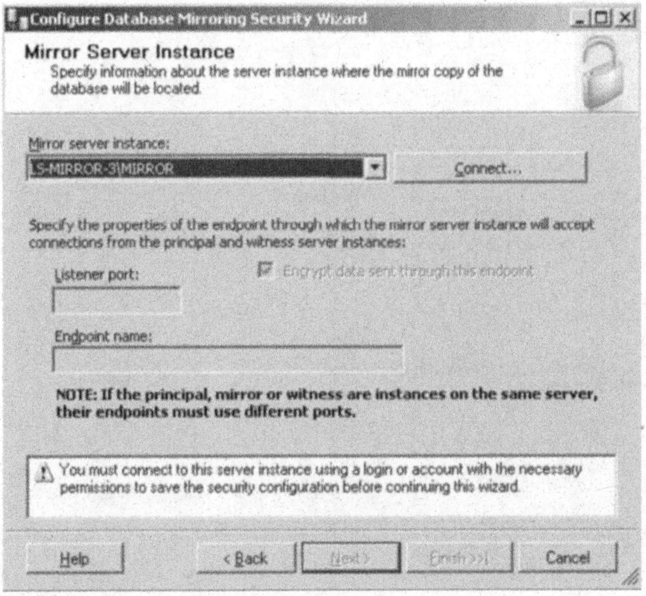

Figure 11-11. *Selecting the mirror server instance*

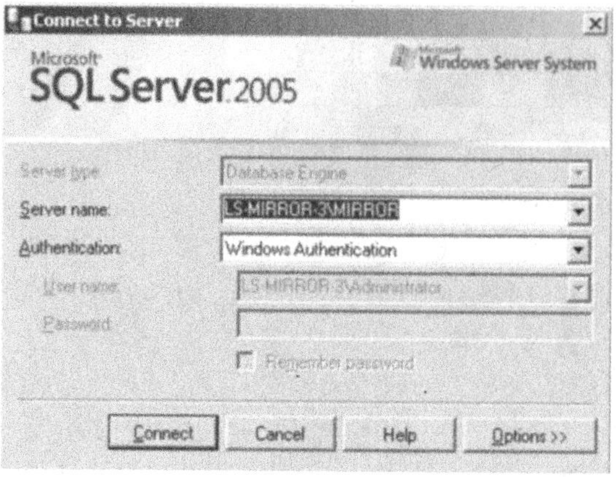

Figure 11-12. *Connecting to the mirror server instance*

Enter the listener TCP/IP port that will be used by the principal. The default is 5022 and must be unique to this instance of SQL Server 2005. I suggest you use another port number to avoid potential security threats to known ports. Enter the name of the database mirroring endpoint for the principal. It must be a unique database mirroring endpoint name for the SQL Server instance. The default is Mirroring, but I suggest changing it to something that is easier to remember, such as MirrorEP. If you want to encrypt the data that is sent across the network, select the Encrypt Data Sent Through This Endpoint option. An example is shown in Figure 11-13. Click Next to continue.

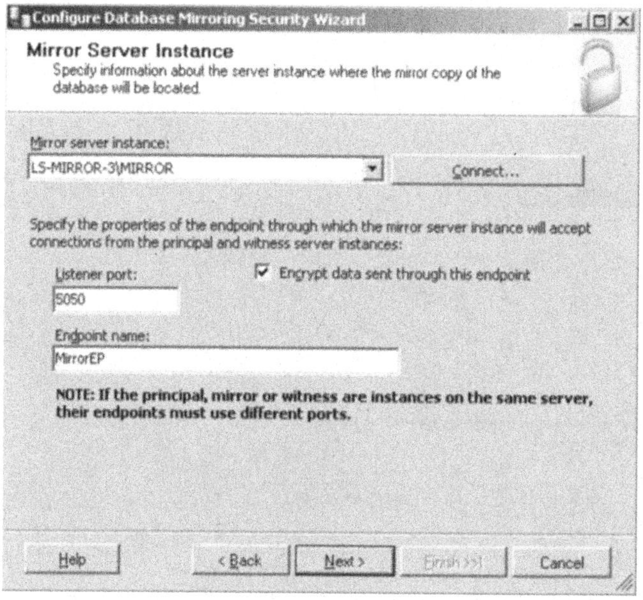

Figure 11-13. *Mirror Server Instance dialog with listener port and endpoint name enabled*

If you have already configured endpoints for this instance, you will see a dialog similar to the one in Figure 11-14.

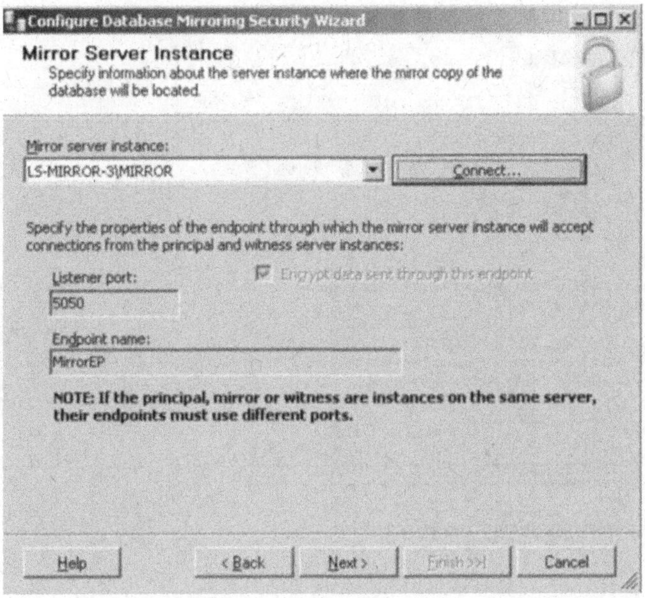

Figure 11-14. *Mirror Server Instance dialog with listener port and endpoint name disabled*

8. If you are creating a witness, you will see the Witness Server Instance dialog as shown in Figure 11-15. Select the instance in the Witness Server Instance drop-down. Click Connect, and you will be prompted to connect to the instance that will assume the witness role as shown in Figure 11-16.

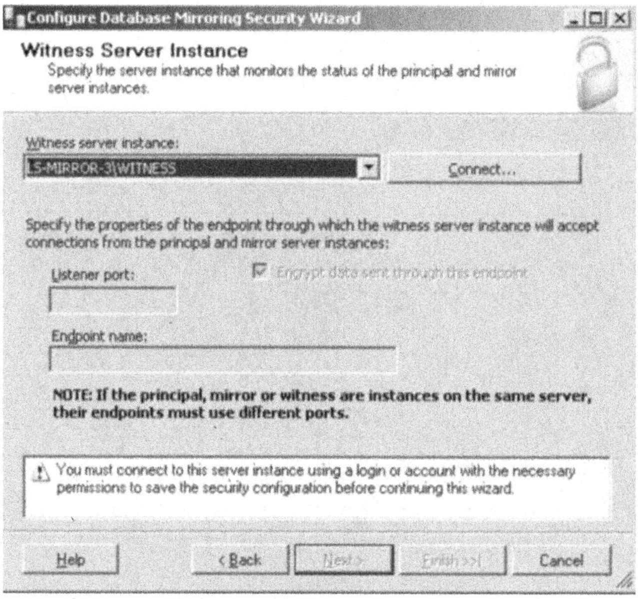

Figure 11-15. *Selecting the witness server instance*

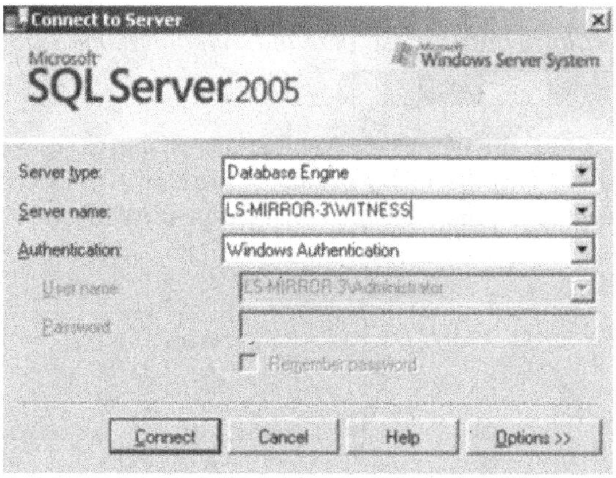

Figure 11-16. *Connecting to the witness server instance*

Enter the listener TCP/IP port that will be used by the principal. The default is 5022 and must be unique to this instance of SQL Server 2005. I suggest you use another port number to avoid potential security threats to known ports. Enter the name of the database mirroring endpoint for the principal. It must be a unique database mirroring endpoint name for the SQL Server instance. The default is the name of Mirroring, but I suggest changing it to something that is easier to remember, such as WitnessEP. If you want to encrypt the data that is sent across the network, select the Encrypt Data Sent Through This Endpoint option. An example is shown in Figure 11-17. Click Next to continue.

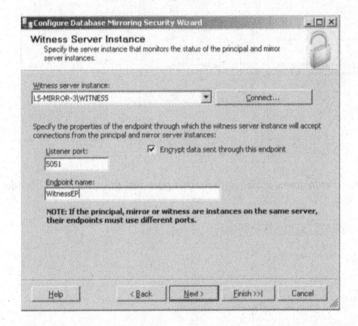

Figure 11-17. *Witness Server Instance dialog with listener port and endpoint name enabled*

If you have already configured endpoints for this instance, you will see a dialog similar to the one in Figure 11-18.

9. On the Service Accounts dialog, enter the names of the service accounts used by SQL Server for each instance (principal, mirror, and witness) as shown in Figure 11-19.

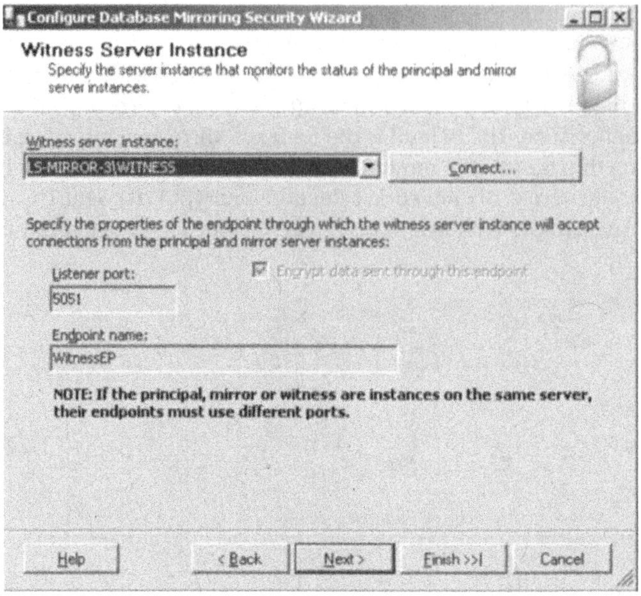

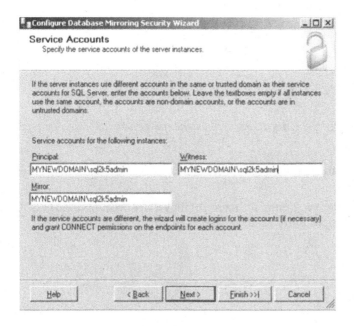

Figure 11-18. *Witness Server Instance dialog with listener port and endpoint name disabled*

Figure 11-19. *Service Accounts dialog*

10. On the Complete the Wizard dialog, shown in Figure 11-20, confirm that the settings are correct, and click Finish. Database mirroring will now be configured for the database. As the install proceeds, status will be displayed. If everything is successful, you will see the dialog in Figure 11-21. Click Close.

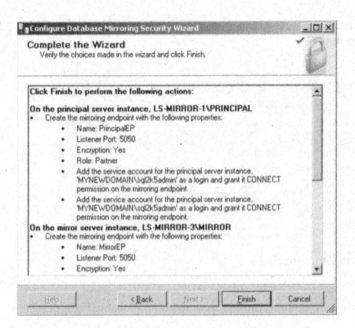

Figure 11-20. *Complete the Wizard dialog*

Figure 11-21. *Successful database mirroring setup*

11. You will then be prompted to either start or not start mirroring as shown in Figure 11-22. Click the appropriate option.

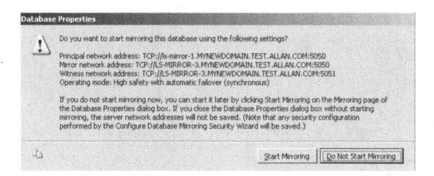

Figure 11-22. *Prompt to start mirroring*

If you started mirroring successfully, you will see something similar to Figure 11-23.

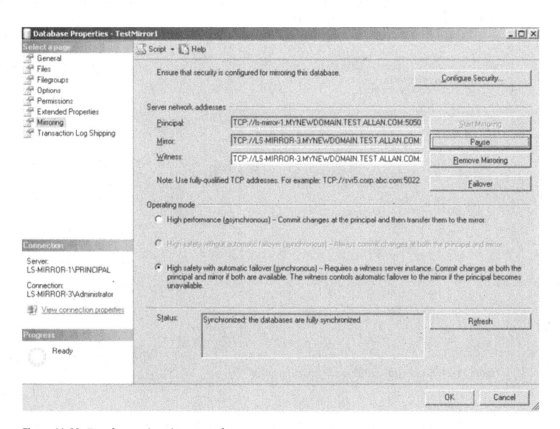

Figure 11-23. *Database mirroring started*

If you choose not to start mirroring, you will see a dialog similar to the one in Figure 11-24. Click OK.

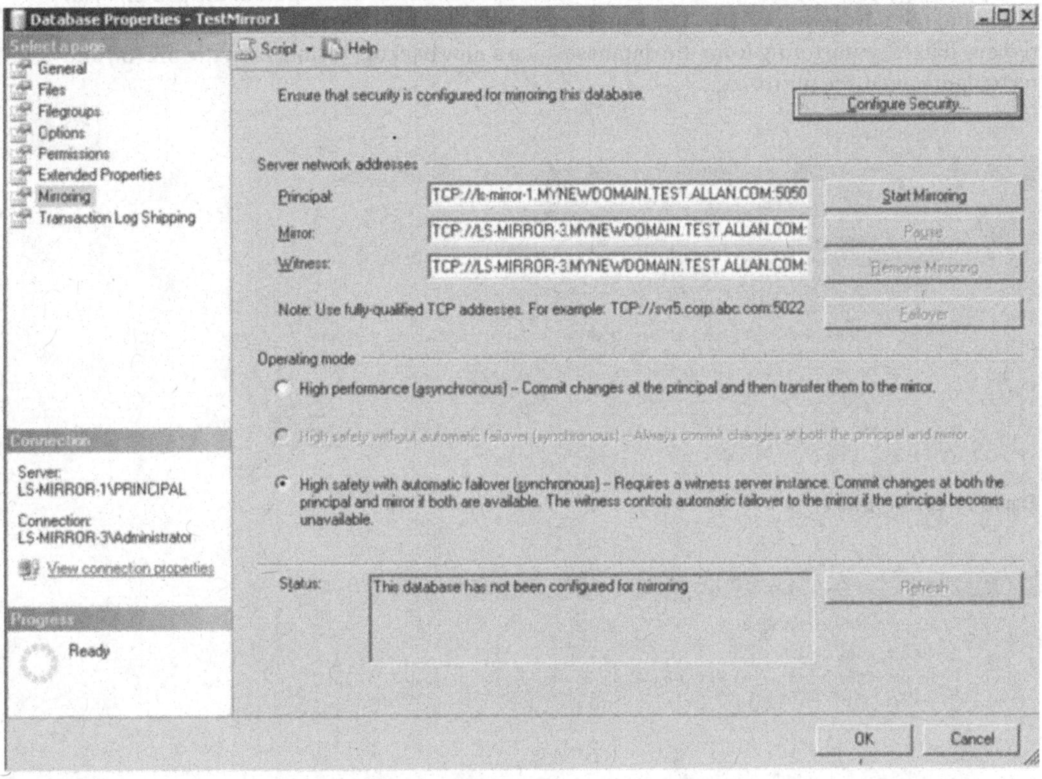

Figure 11-24. *Database mirroring configured but not started*

If you start mirroring, you should see something similar to Figure 11-25, where the principal is reflected and the mirror is reflected in SQL Server Management Studio.

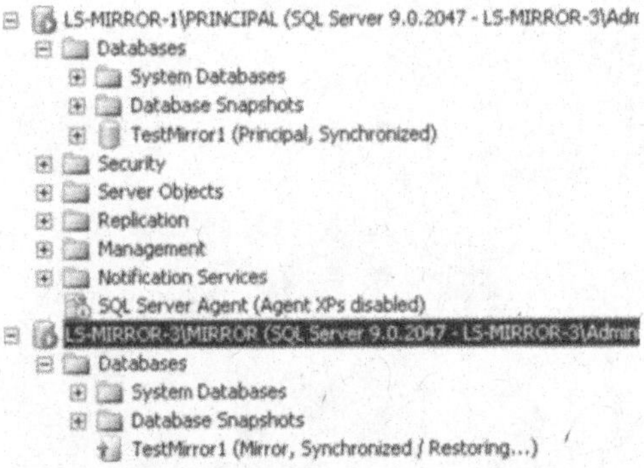

Figure 11-25. *Successful mirroring configuration*

If your database mirroring session fails to start, you will need to investigate why. Example errors are shown in Figures 11-26 through 11-29. For example, the dialog shown in Figure 11-26 tells you that database mirroring could not be started because the principal and the mirror are not at the same starting point. If you have the ability to back up the transaction log from the principal and apply it to the mirror, you can do it and then try to restart mirroring. If you cannot, you will have to remove database mirroring from the database, take a new backup, restore it on the mirror, and reconfigure database mirroring.

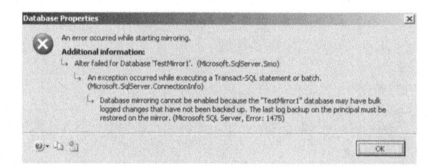

Figure 11-26. *Sample error #1*

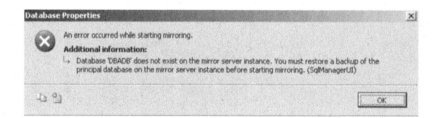

Figure 11-27. *Sample error #2*

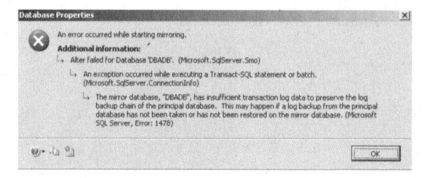

Figure 11-28. *Sample error #3*

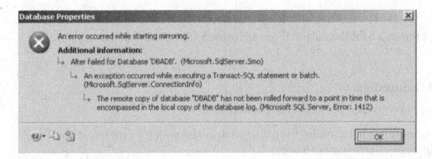

Figure 11-29. *Sample error #4*

Configure Outbound Connections

Take the following steps to configure your outbound connections:

1. Connect to the instance that contains the principal database with your preferred query tool (sqlcmd or SQL Server Management Studio).

2. Make sure that your context is the master database. Issue the following command:

```
USE master
GO
```

3. If you are using a certificate, you must create a master key if one is not already created. To do this, execute the following command. If you are not using a certificate, but using Windows Authentication, skip to step 5.

```
CREATE MASTER KEY ENCRYPTION BY PASSWORD = 'enter_a_password'
GO
```

4. Create the certificate for the principal instance:

```
CREATE CERTIFICATE Principal_Certificate WITH SUBJECT = 'Principal Certificate'
GO
```

5. Create the database mirroring endpoint that will be used by the principal using the following command. Modify the name and port as necessary. ENCRYPTION can have values of DISABLED, SUPPORTED, and REQUIRED. If ENCRYPTION is set to anything but DISABLED, you must specify the specific ALGORITHM you wish to use: RC4, AES, AES RC4, or RC4 AES. The ROLE can have a value of WITNESS, PARTNER, or ALL. For full information, see the topic "CREATE ENDPOINT (Transact-SQL)" in SQL Server Books Online.

```
CREATE ENDPOINT Principal_Endpoint STATE = STARTED
AS TCP (LISTENER_PORT = 5050, LISTENER_IP = ALL)
FOR DATABASE_MIRRORING (
    AUTHENTICATION = CERTIFICATE Prinicpal_Certificate,
    ENCRYPTION = REQUIRED ALGORITHM RC4,
    ROLE = ALL)
GO
```

6. Back up the certificate to a file. Make sure that it is created where only authorized users can access the folder. When finished, copy the certificate to the mirror. Issue the following command to back up the certificate:

```
BACKUP CERTIFICATE Principal_Certificate TO FILE =
'c:\Cert\Principal_Certificate.cer'
GO
```

7. Open a query window to the instance mirror.

8. Repeat steps 2 through 6 for the mirror. If you are using a witness, repeat the steps on the witness.

Configure Inbound Connections

Take the following steps to configure your inbound connections:

1. Connect to the instance that contains the principal database with your preferred query tool (sqlcmd or SQL Server Management Studio).

2. Make sure that your context is the master database. Issue the following command:

```
USE master
GO
```

3. Create a SQL Server Authentication-based login that will be used to access the principal from the mirror:

```
CREATE LOGIN Mirror_Account WITH PASSWORD = 'enter_a_password'
GO
```

4. Set the context to the database that will be the principal.

```
USE TestMirror1
GO
```

5. Create a user in that database that corresponds to the login just created:

```
CREATE USER Mirror_User FOR LOGIN Mirror_Account
GO
```

6. Associate the certificate you copied from the mirror to the principal with that user:

```
CREATE CERTIFICATE Mirror_Certificate
AUTHORIZATION Mirror_User
FROM FILE = 'C:\Mirror_cert.cer '
```

7. Grant the created login permission to the endpoint:

```
GRANT CONNECT ON ENDPOINT::Principal_Endpoint TO [Mirror_Account]
GO
```

8. To allow the mirror to participate in mirroring, you must ensure that the mirror instance has the certificate (if you are using one) before configuring it as part of the solution. Then you will be able to configure it as an endpoint. If you are using a witness, repeat the steps on the witness.

Configure Database Mirroring

Take the following steps to configure database mirroring:

1. Connect to the instance that contains the mirror database with your preferred query tool (sqlcmd or SQL Server Management Studio).

2. Make sure that your context is the master database. Issue the following command:

```
USE master
GO
```

3. Set the principal as a partner. You must use the fully qualified domain name or a valid TCP/IP address. If you are using certificates, you will most likely need to use the TCP/IP address since you may not be able to resolve the name:

```
ALTER DATABASE TestMirror1 SET PARTNER = 'TCP://172.22.10.1:5050'
GO
```

4. Open a query window and connect to the principal. Make sure that your context is the master database. Issue the following command:

```
ALTER DATABASE TestMirror1 SET PARTNER = 'TCP://172.22.10.2:5050'
GO
```

5. Set the safety mode of the mirroring session. It can be FULL for the high safety mode, or OFF for high performance mode:

```
ALTER DATABASE TestMirror1 SET PARTNER SAFETY = FULL
GO
```

6. If you set the safety to FULL, you must configure a witness. On both the principal and mirror, run the following command:

```
ALTER DATABASE TestMirror1 SET WITNESS = 'TCP://172.22.10.1:5050'
GO
```

Transact-SQL for Database Mirroring Using Windows Authentication

Take the following steps to configure database mirroring using Transact-SQL and Windows authentication:

1. Connect to the instance that contains the principal database with your preferred query tool (sqlcmd or SQL Server Management Studio).

2. Make sure that your context is the master database. Issue the following command:

```
USE master
GO
```

3. Create the database mirroring endpoint that will be used by the principal using the following command. Modify the name and port as necessary. The example uses Windows Authentication.

```
CREATE ENDPOINT Principal_Endpoint STATE = STARTED
AS TCP (LISTENER_PORT = 5050, LISTENER_IP = ALL)
FOR DATABASE_MIRRORING (ROLE=PARTNER)
GO
```

4. If you are using a witness, ensure that the Windows user that will connect to the witness has a login on the principal and has permissions on the endpoint. If you are not using a witness, you can skip this step:

```
CREATE LOGIN [DOMAIN\WitnessUserName] FROM WINDOWS
GO
GRANT CONNECT ON ENDPOINT::Principal_Endpoint TO [DOMAIN\WitnessUserName]
GO
```

5. Repeat steps 3 and 4 in a window connected to the mirror with appropriate values for the mirror.

6. If you are using a witness, open a window connected to it and set the context to the master database, and run commands similar to steps 3 and 4. The login used here will need to be able to connect to both instances:

```
CREATE ENDPOINT Witness_Endpoint STATE = STARTED
AS TCP (LISTENER_PORT = 5050, LISTENER_IP = ALL)
FOR DATABASE_MIRRORING (ROLE=WITNESS)
GO
CREATE LOGIN [DOMAIN\SQLAccount] FROM WINDOWS
GO
GRANT CONNECT ON ENDPOINT::Witness_Endpoint TO [DOMAIN\SQLAccount]
GO
```

7. In the query window for the mirror, set the principal server as its partner:

```
ALTER DATABASE TestMirror1 SET PARTNER = 'TCP://PRINCIPAL.MY.DOMAIN.COM:5050'
GO
```

8. In the query window for the principal, set the mirror server as its partner. and if using a witness, the witness as the witness:

```
ALTER DATABASE TestMirror1 SET PARTNER = 'TCP://MIRROR.MY.DOMAIN.COM:5050'
GO
ALTER DATABASE TestMirror1 SET WITNESS = 'TCP://WITNESS.MY.DOMAIN.COM:5050'
GO
```

Step 3: Configure Network Load Balancing or a DNS Alias (Optional)

If you need to abstract the instance name change in a database mirroring failover, follow the instructions for redirecting applications and clients in Chapter 15.

Administering Database Mirroring

Once you configure database mirroring, you will need to make sure it is up and running as well as possibly perform other tasks.

Monitoring Database Mirroring

To monitor database mirroring there are a few options. The easiest to use is arguably the Database Mirroring Monitor. You can also use Transact-SQL to query the DMVs and views that correspond to database mirroring.

Database Mirroring Monitor

The Database Mirroring Monitor is launched from SQL Server Management Studio, as shown in Figure 11-30.

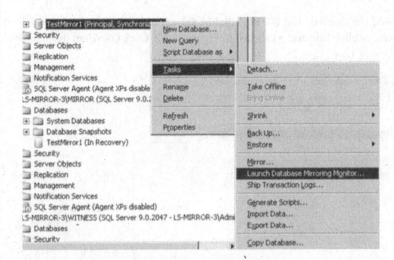

Figure 11-30. *Launching the Database Mirroring Monitor*

To register database mirroring sessions, take the following steps:

1. Click Register Mirrored Database, as shown in Figure 11-31.

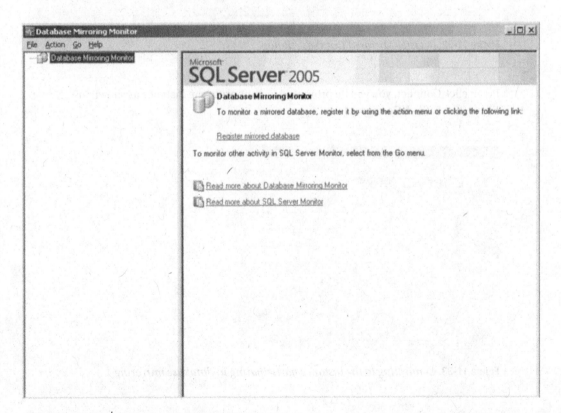

Figure 11-31. *Main Database Mirroring Monitor dialog*

2. On the Register Mirrored Database dialog, if it is available, select either the principal or mirror from the drop-down, or click Connect as shown in Figure 11-32. Click OK when done.

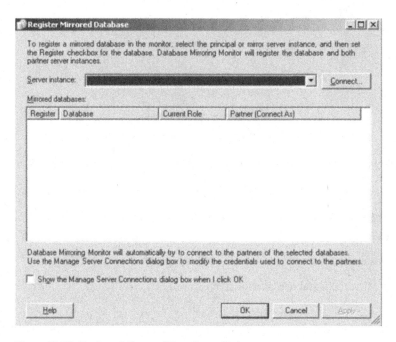

Figure 11-32. *Register Mirrored Database dialog*

If you click Connect, you will be prompted to connect to the instance as shown in Figure 11-33. Click Connect.

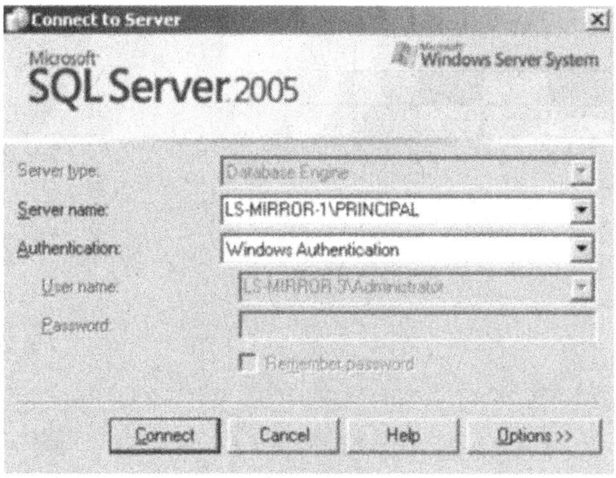

Figure 11-33. *Connecting to the instance participating in database mirroring*

3. After connecting to the principal or the mirror, you will see a display similar to the one shown in Figure 11-34. Select the Register check box next to the database, as shown in Figure 11-35, and click OK.

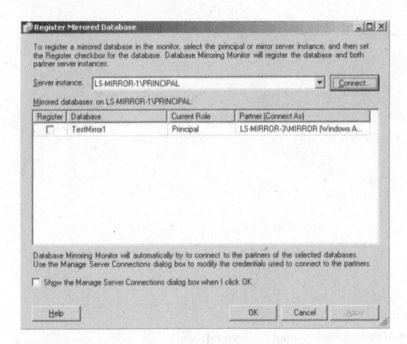

Figure 11-34. *Register Mirrored Database dialog after connecting*

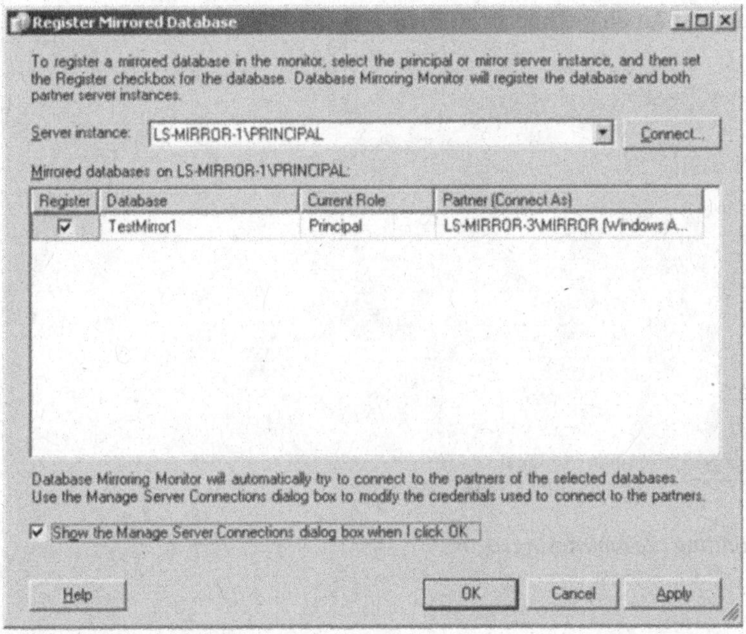

Figure 11-35. *Selecting the database mirroring session*

4. On the Manage Server Instance Connections dialog, the configuration should automatically select the other instances participating in the database mirroring session as shown in Figure 11-36. If not, click Add and connect to the instance. Click OK when done.

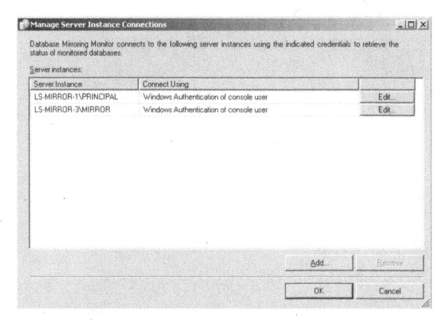

Figure 11-36. *Manage Server Instance Connections dialog*

If you want to change how you connect to the instance for monitoring, click Edit and change the authentication method as shown in Figure 11-37.

Figure 11-37. *Editing the monitoring login*

5. When finished, expand the Database Mirroring Monitor and the database mirroring session will be displayed as shown in Figure 11-38.

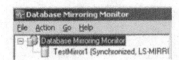

Figure 11-38. *Successful registration*

Select the database mirroring session in the Database Mirroring Monitor. You will see a dialog similar to the one shown in Figure 11-39. You will see quite a few statistics and bits of information about that database mirroring session. The two most important things besides the actual state and connection status are Unsent Log and Unrestored Log. These will indicate delays (for whatever reason). What you can do is set thresholds (see Figure 11-42) and if the threshold exceeds a limit you set, you can be notified.

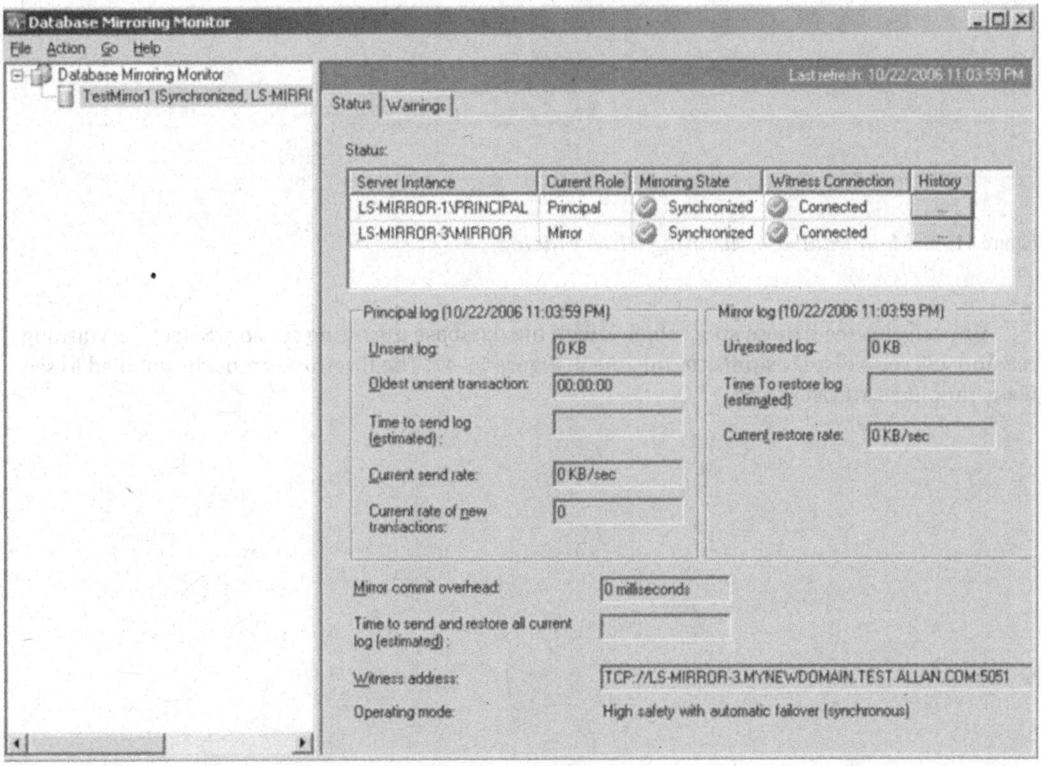

Figure 11-39. *Sample monitoring display*

If you want to see the history of what has transpired on the principal or mirror, click the History ellipsis button in the right row. You will see a display similar to the one in Figure 11-40.

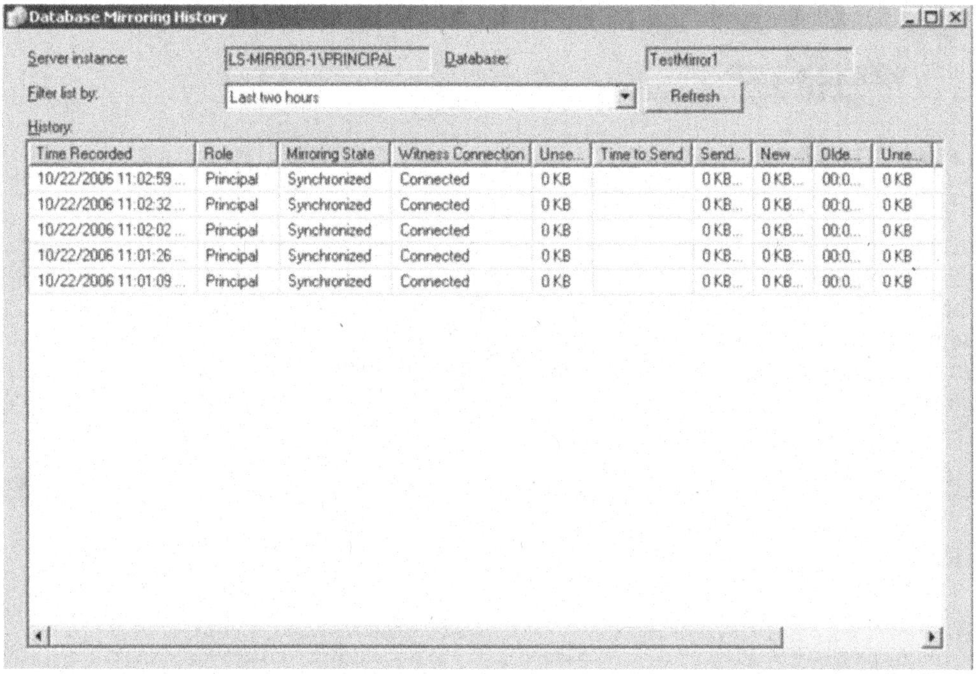

Figure 11-40. *Main Database Mirroring History dialog*

You can also see if there are problems with the database mirroring session. Select the Warnings tab. You will see a display similar to the one in Figure 11-41. The thresholds must be enabled to see if any problems are occurring.

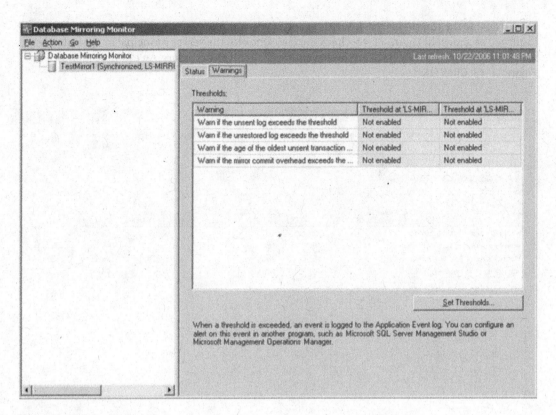

Figure 11-41. *Warnings tab*

To enable the thresholds, click Set Thresholds. When the Set Warnings Thresholds dialog is displayed as shown in Figure 11-42, check the check box for the server (principal or mirror) you want to alter, and then select the numeric value and alter it as necessary. An example is shown in Figure 11-43. Click OK.

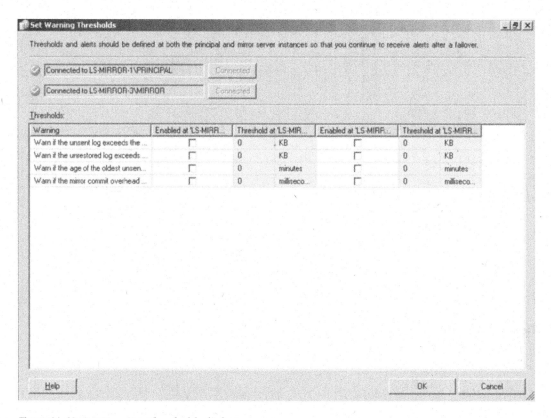

Figure 11-42. *Set Warning Thresholds dialog*

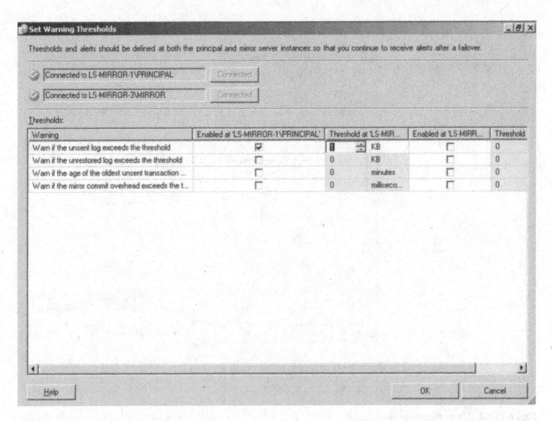

Figure 11-43. *Changing a threshold*

The new values will be reflected on the Warnings tab. An example is shown in Figure 11-44.

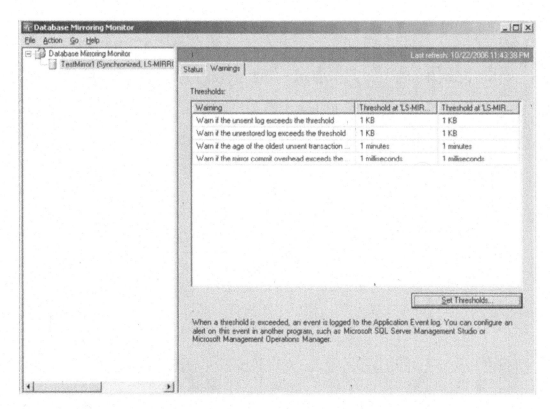

Figure 11-44. *After changing thresholds*

Performance Monitor

There are some counters in Performance Monitor (also known as PerfMon) that can be indicators for database mirroring. The bulk of the counters can be found in the new counter object `SQL Server:Database Mirroring`. Each counter is set per database.

The following is a list of the counters you should monitor on the principal:

- `Bytes Sent/sec`: This is the total number of bytes sent per second.

- `Log Bytes Sent/sec`: This is the total number of transaction log bytes sent per second.

- `Log Send Queue KB`: This is the current queue for mirroring and is measured against your transaction log. If there is a number above 0, it is the amount that has not been transmitted to the mirror. This may or may not represent a problem; so when monitoring, know your thresholds.

- `Pages Sent/sec`: This is the number of pages sent to the mirror per second.

- `Send/Receive Ack Time`: This monitors the mirroring process from a network perspective.

- `Sends/sec`: This is the total number of sends the mirroring process starts every second.

- `Transaction Delay`: This is the delay measured in milliseconds that SQL Server has to wait to hear back from the mirror that a commit has occurred for a transaction. This is a *summed counter*, meaning it represents all transactions currently in process.

The following is a list of the counters you should monitor on the mirror:

- `Bytes Received/sec`: This is the total number of bytes that the mirror is receiving from the primary every second.
- `Log Bytes Received/sec`: This is the amount of transaction log bytes that are received every second.
- `Receives/sec`: This is the total number of actual receives per second.
- `Redo Bytes/sec`: This tells you the rate (in bytes) at which transactions in the transaction log have actually been applied to the database.
- `Redo Queue KB`: This should generally be a low number since it indicates that there is a queue of transactions waiting to be rolled forward. This number is represented in total size, not in terms of number of transactions. If you are doing a data intensive task such as an index rebuild or logged bulk insert, you may see a higher redo queue. You may also see a redo queue if you have a slow (i.e., high latency) network.

Here are some other useful counters that can aid you with database mirroring:

- `Logical Disk Disk Write Bytes/sec`: This tells you how fast your disk is being written to. If this value is not fast enough, it will impact your database mirroring performance. Slow disks are not what you want. You should monitor the log and data disks for both the principal and the mirror.
- `SQL Server:Databases Log Bytes Flushed/sec`: This tells you how fast SQL Server is flushing the log and writing the contents of the transaction log to disk. If this number is high, it means you may have a suboptimal disk subsystem that will impact the performance of your principal.
- `SQL Server:Databases Transactions/sec`: This tells you how many transactions are occurring per second in the selected database.

Figure 11-45 shows the addition of one of the database mirroring counters for a single database.

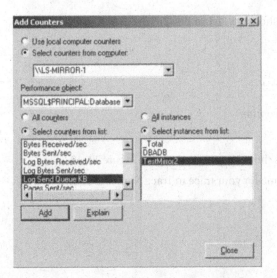

Figure 11-45. *Example of adding a Database Mirroring counter per database*

Here are some helpful calculations using Performance Monitor information:

- Average delay per transaction = (Transaction Delay)/(Transactions/sec)
- Estimated time for the mirror to catch up with the principal = (Log Send Queue KB)/ (Log Bytes Received/sec)
- Estimated time to roll transaction forward = (Redo Queue KB)/(Redo Bytes/sec)

SQL Server Profiler

Within Profiler, you can not only trace any Transact-SQL statement issued that may relate to database mirroring, but you can capture failover events. Using this information, you can determine the time it takes to switch from the principal to the mirror.

1. Start SQL Server Profiler as shown in Figure 11-46.

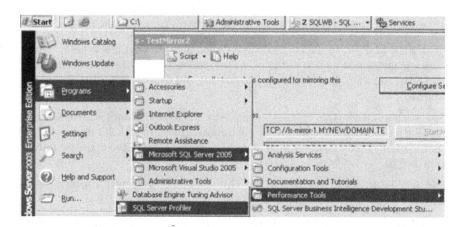

Figure 11-46. *Starting SQL Server Profiler*

2. From the File menu, select New Trace, as shown in Figure 11-47.

Figure 11-47. *Selecting the New Trace menu option*

3. Connect to the database instance that has the principal, as shown in Figure 11-48.
4. On the Trace Properties dialog, enter a name for your trace in Trace Name, as shown in Figure 11-49.

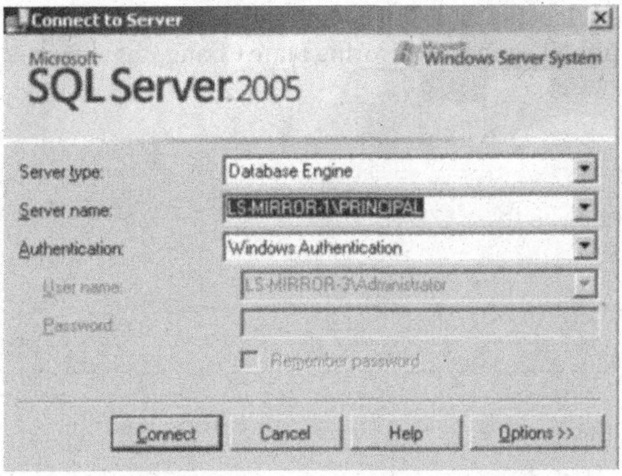

Figure 11-48. *Connecting to the instance with the principal database*

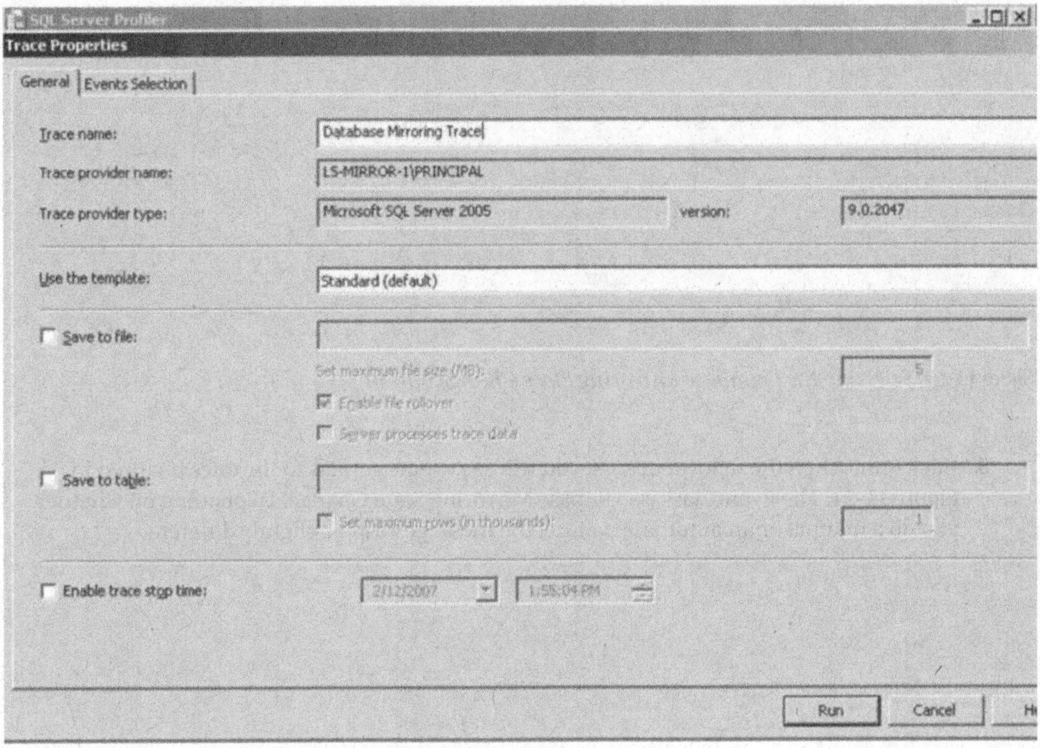

Figure 11-49. *Entering a name for the Profiler trace*

5. Select the Event Selection tab and select the Show All Events check box. Expand the Database menu, and select the option Database Mirroring State Change, as shown in Figure 11-50.

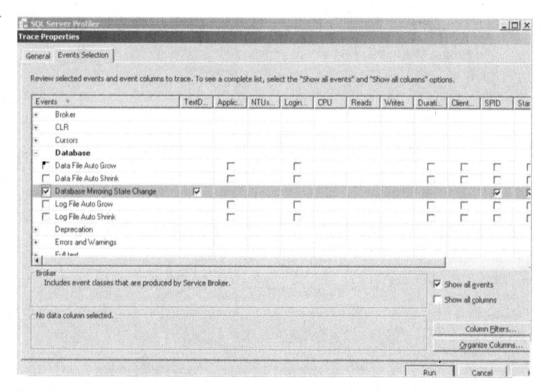

Figure 11-50. *Selecting the Database Mirroring State Change option*

6. Click Run. When the failover occurs, you will see events similar to the ones pictured in Figure 11-51. The EventClass is Database Mirroring State Change. Depending on whether you do a manual or an automatic failure, the messages will be slightly different.

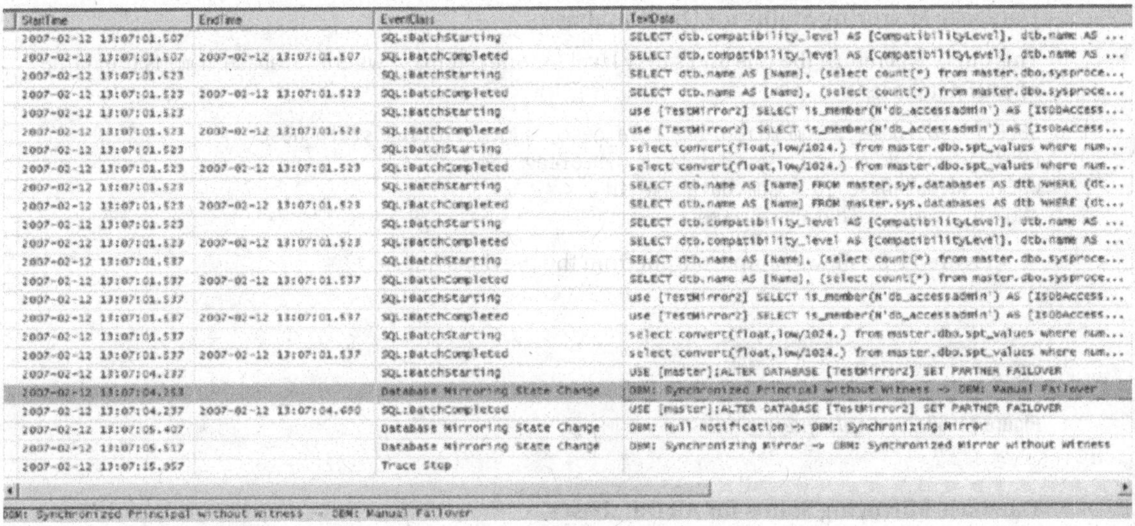

StartTime	EndTime	EventClass	TextData
2007-02-12 13:07:01.507		SQL:BatchStarting	SELECT dtb.compatibility_level AS [CompatibilityLevel], dtb.name AS ...
2007-02-12 13:07:01.507	2007-02-12 13:07:01.507	SQL:BatchCompleted	SELECT dtb.compatibility_level AS [CompatibilityLevel], dtb.name AS ...
2007-02-12 13:07:01.523		SQL:BatchStarting	SELECT dtb.name AS [Name], (select count(*) from master.dbo.sysproce...
2007-02-12 13:07:01.523	2007-02-12 13:07:01.523	SQL:BatchCompleted	SELECT dtb.name AS [Name], (select count(*) from master.dbo.sysproce...
2007-02-12 13:07:01.523		SQL:BatchStarting	use [TestMirror2] SELECT is_member(N'db_accessadmin') AS [ISDBACCESS...
2007-02-12 13:07:01.523	2007-02-12 13:07:01.523	SQL:BatchCompleted	use [TestMirror2] SELECT is_member(N'db_accessadmin') AS [ISDBACCESS...
2007-02-12 13:07:01.523		SQL:BatchStarting	select convert(float,low/1024.) from master.dbo.spt_values where num...
2007-02-12 13:07:01.523	2007-02-12 13:07:01.523	SQL:BatchCompleted	select convert(float,low/1024.) from master.dbo.spt_values where num...
2007-02-12 13:07:01.523		SQL:BatchStarting	SELECT dtb.name AS [Name] FROM master.sys.databases AS dtb WHERE (dt...
2007-02-12 13:07:01.523	2007-02-12 13:07:01.523	SQL:BatchCompleted	SELECT dtb.name AS [Name] FROM master.sys.databases AS dtb WHERE (dt...
2007-02-12 13:07:01.523		SQL:BatchStarting	SELECT dtb.compatibility_level AS [CompatibilityLevel], dtb.name AS ...
2007-02-12 13:07:01.523	2007-02-12 13:07:01.523	SQL:BatchCompleted	SELECT dtb.compatibility_level AS [CompatibilityLevel], dtb.name AS ...
2007-02-12 13:07:01.537		SQL:BatchStarting	SELECT dtb.name AS [Name], (select count(*) from master.dbo.sysproce...
2007-02-12 13:07:01.537	2007-02-12 13:07:01.537	SQL:BatchCompleted	SELECT dtb.name AS [Name], (select count(*) from master.dbo.sysproce...
2007-02-12 13:07:01.537		SQL:BatchStarting	use [TestMirror2] SELECT is_member(N'db_accessadmin') AS [ISDBACCESS...
2007-02-12 13:07:01.537	2007-02-12 13:07:01.537	SQL:BatchCompleted	use [TestMirror2] SELECT is_member(N'db_accessadmin') AS [ISDBACCESS...
2007-02-12 13:07:01.537		SQL:BatchStarting	select convert(float,low/1024.) from master.dbo.spt_values where num...
2007-02-12 13:07:01.537	2007-02-12 13:07:01.537	SQL:BatchCompleted	select convert(float,low/1024.) from master.dbo.spt_values where num...
2007-02-12 13:07:04.237		SQL:BatchStarting	USE [master];ALTER DATABASE [TestMirror2] SET PARTNER FAILOVER
2007-02-12 13:07:04.253		Database Mirroring State Change	DBM: Synchronized Principal without Witness -> DBM: Manual Failover
2007-02-12 13:07:04.237	2007-02-12 13:07:04.680	SQL:BatchCompleted	USE [master];ALTER DATABASE [TestMirror2] SET PARTNER FAILOVER
2007-02-12 13:07:05.407		Database Mirroring State Change	DBM: Null Notification -> DBM: Synchronizing Mirror
2007-02-12 13:07:05.517		Database Mirroring State Change	DBM: Synchronizing Mirror -> DBM: Synchronized Mirror without Witness
2007-02-12 13:07:15.957		Trace Stop	

DBM: Synchronized Principal without Witness -> DBM: Manual Failover

Figure 11-51. *Example of Profiler trace results with a database mirroring failover*

Transact-SQL

There are three views and one DMV for use with database mirroring. If you want to know the status of what is going on with mirroring as well as other information without using any kind of interface, these will be your best bet:

- `sys.database_mirroring`: This view contains the configuration information for the particular instance you are connected to in the query window. For a full listing of what columns this view returns, see the SQL Server Books Online topic "sys.database_mirroring (Transact-SQL)."
- `sys.database_mirroring_endpoints`: This view contains information about the endpoints defined for each database. There is only one row per database. For a full listing of the columns this view returns, see the topic "sys.database_mirroring_endpoints (Transact-SQL)" in SQL Server Books Online.
- `sys.database_mirroring_witnesses`: This view contains information about the witness if one is configured. There is one row per principal. For a full listing of the columns this view returns, see the topic "sys.database_mirroring_witnesses (Transact-SQL)" in SQL Server Books Online.
- `sys.dm_db_mirroring_connections`: This DMV shows current information about the connections involved with database mirroring. There is one row per connection. For a full listing of the columns this DMV returns, see the topic "sys.dm_db_mirroring_connections" in SQL Server Books Online.

The following three sections show example queries with some of the things you can do with the DMVs. If you are having problems with your database mirroring setup, you should query the DMVs to see if they contain the values you expect. For example, if you are having connection problems, query the `sys.database_mirroring_endpoints` DMV to see that the endpoints are properly defined and started.

Database Mirroring Status for One Database

This query will return the role and safety level for one database where database_name is the name of your database:

```
SELECT  sd.[name], sdm.mirroring_role_desc, sdm.mirroring_state_desc
FROM sys.databases sd, sys.database_mirroring sdm
WHERE sd.database_id = sdm.database_id
AND sd.[name] = 'database_name'
```

Figure 11-52 shows sample output from the previous query.

	name	mirroring_role_desc	mirroring_state_desc
1	TestMirror1	PRINCIPAL	SYNCHRONIZED

Figure 11-52. *Example query results*

Database Mirroring Status for All Databases

This query will return the role and mirroring status for each database:

```
SELECT  sd.[name], sdm.mirroring_role_desc, sdm.mirroring_state_desc
FROM sys.databases sd, sys.database_mirroring sdm
WHERE sd.database_id = sdm.database_id
```

Safety Level

This query will return the role and safety level for each database:

```
SELECT  sd.[name], sdm.mirroring_role_desc, sdm.mirroring_safety_level_desc
FROM sys.databases sd, sys.database_mirroring sdm
WHERE sd.database_id = sdm.database_id
```

Controlling Database Mirroring

You can either suspend or resume a database mirroring session.

Suspending Database Mirroring

Suspending the database mirroring session will pause the mirroring from the principal to the mirror. It will cause mirroring to stop sending transactions to the mirror, and the transaction log on the principal will grow until it runs out of space or mirroring is resumed.

SQL Server Management Studio

To suspend database mirroring using SQL Server Management studio, use the following instructions:

1. Start SQL Server Management Studio.

2. Expand the Databases menu, and select the database that will serve as the principal. Right-click, select Tasks, and then Mirror. Conversely, you can right-click, select Properties, and then select the Mirror page. Both will lead you to the example shown earlier in Figure 11-23.

3. Click Pause. You will be prompted as shown in Figure 11-53. Click Yes. The database mirroring session will now be paused, and its new status will be reflected as shown in Figure 11-54.

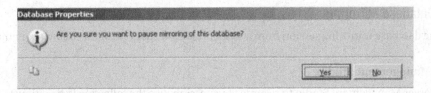

Figure 11-53. *Prompting to pause database mirroring*

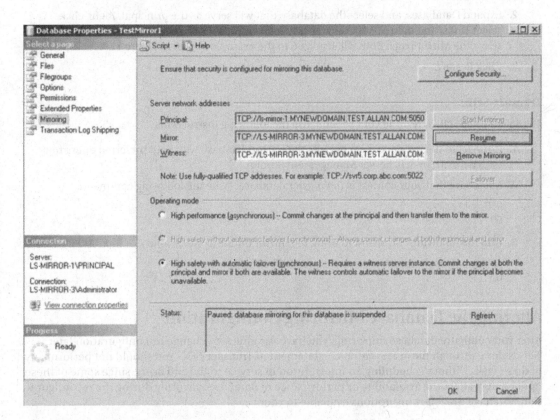

Figure 11-54. *Paused database mirroring session*

Transact-SQL

To suspend database mirroring via Transact-SQL, use the following instructions:

1. Connect to the instance that contains the mirror database with your preferred query tool (sqlcmd or SQL Server Management Studio).

2. Make sure that your context is the master database. Issue the following command:

```
USE master
GO
```

3. Run the following command to bring the mirror online as the primary:

```
ALTER DATABASE database_name SET PARTNER SUSPEND
GO
```

Resuming Database Mirroring

To resume the database mirroring session from a suspended state, use one of the following methods.

SQL Server Management Studio

To use SQL Server Management Studio to resume your session, use the following instructions:

1. Start SQL Server Management Studio.

2. Expand Databases, and select the database that will serve as the principal. Right-click, select Tasks, and then Mirror. Conversely, you can right-click, select Properties, and then select the Mirror page. Both will lead you to the example shown in Figure 11-4.

3. Click Restart.

Transact-SQL

To use Transact-SQL to resume your session, use the following instructions:

1. Connect to the instance that contains the mirror database with your preferred query tool (sqlcmd, osql, or SQL Server Management Studio).

2. Make sure that your context is the master database. Issue the following command:

```
USE master
GO
```

3. Run the following command to bring the mirror online as the primary:

```
ALTER DATABASE database_name SET PARTNER RESUME
GO
```

Altering the Database Mirroring Configuration

After you configure database mirroring, you have the ability to change its configuration later. This is done through the ALTER DATABASE statement of Transact-SQL. You should not perform any of these tasks without scheduling an interruption in service to the end users, since some of these options may affect the availability or performance of database mirroring during the reconfiguration. You have the following options available to you:

- SET PARTNER SAFETY: This sets the mode of database mirroring—high safety or high security. For high safety mode, set a value of FULL. For high performance mode, set a value of OFF. If you set this to OFF, you must also disable the witness as shown here:

```
USE master
GO
ALTER DATABASE database_name SET PARTNER SAFETY FULL
GO
```

- SET PARTNER TIMEOUT: This sets the value that controls how long database mirroring will wait until it decides that the principal is unavailable. The value is an integer and is represented in seconds. You cannot set this below five seconds; SQL Server will use five seconds even if you enter a lower value. You should not alter this unless you are seeing a problem, as a lower value may create false failovers if automatic failovers can occur:

```
USE master
GO
ALTER DATABASE database_name SET PARTNER TIMEOUT 5
GO
```

- SET WITNESS = 'witness_name': This configures the instance that will serve as the witness. This needs to be set if safety is set to FULL:

```
USE master
GO
ALTER DATABASE database_name SET WITNESS = 'mynewwitness'
GO
```

- SET WITNESS OFF: This unconfigures the witness from the database mirroring session:

```
USE master
GO
ALTER DATABASE database_name SET PARTNER WITNESS OFF
GO
```

Removing Database Mirroring

If you decide to remove the database mirroring session from the partners, you can do it either via SQL Server Management Studio or Transact-SQL.

SQL Server Management Studio

1. Start SQL Server Management Studio.

2. Expand the Databases menu, and select the database that will serve as the principal. Right-click, select Tasks, and then Mirror. Conversely, you can right-click, select Properties, and then select the Mirror page.

3. Click Remove Mirroring. You will be prompted as shown in Figure 11-55 to confirm that failing over is the action you wish to perform. Click Yes. Once finished, the display should appear similar to Figure 11-56.

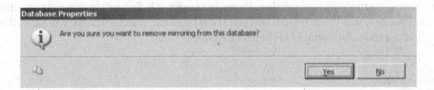

Figure 11-55. *Prompt for removal*

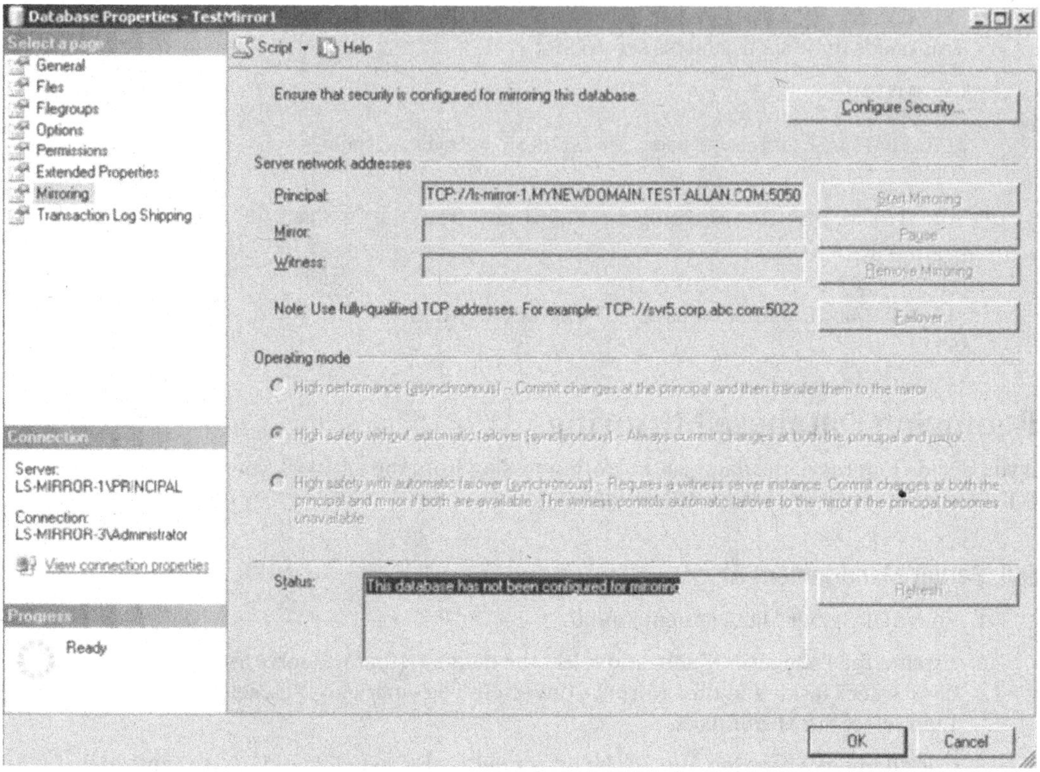

Figure 11-56. *Reversed roles after failing over*

Click OK to close the Properties dialog. To verify, refresh SQL Server Management Studio. The database that was the principal will just show its name, and the mirror will show that it is in a loading state. An example is shown in Figure 11-57.

Figure 11-57. *Database mirroring removed*

Transact-SQL

1. Connect to the instance that contains the mirror database with your preferred query tool (sqlcmd or SQL Server Management Studio).

2. Make sure that your context is the master database. Issue the following command:

```
USE master
GO
```

3. Execute the following command to remove database mirroring. The only response you will get is that the command completed successfully:

```
ALTER DATABASE database_name SET PARTNER OFF
GO
```

Failing Over from the Principal to the Mirror

You configure mirroring in the hopes you will never need to use it, but invariably, there will be cases where you will need to bring the mirror online as the new primary. There are two main scenarios for this: a planned failover, and an unplanned failover. The overall sequence is basically the same:

1. Fail the principal over to the mirror.

2. Synchronize logins as described in Chapter 15.

3. Ensure all objects that reside outside of the database are re-created on the mirror.

4. Synchronize full-text indexes.

5. Redirect clients to the new primary instance of SQL Server (the former mirror). If you are using NLB or a DNS alias, see the section on redirecting applications and clients in Chapter 15.

If you have automatic failover configured in high safety mode, all you need to worry about are steps 2 through 5.

Planned Failover

A planned failover where nothing is wrong with the database mirroring session is the easiest condition to account for.

SQL Server Management Studio

Execute the following command from either the principal or the mirror:

1. Start SQL Server Management Studio.

2. Expand the Databases menu, and select the database that will serve as the principal. Right-click, select Tasks, and then Mirror. Conversely, you can right-click, select Properties, and then select the Mirror page.

3. Click Failover. You will be prompted as shown in Figure 11-58 to confirm that failing over is the action you wish to perform. Click Yes.

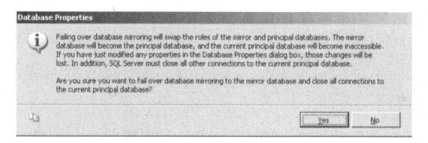

Figure 11-58. *Prompt for failing over*

To verify, refresh SQL Server Management Studio. The roles should be reversed. An example is shown in Figure 11-59.

```
□ 📁 LS-MIRROR-1\PRINCIPAL (SQL Server 9.0.2047 - LS-MIRROR-3\Adm
   ⊟ 📁 Databases
      ⊞ 📁 System Databases
      ⊞ 📁 Database Snapshots
         📁 TestMirror1 (Mirror, Synchronized / Restoring...)
   ⊞ 📁 Security
   ⊞ 📁 Server Objects
   ⊞ 📁 Replication
   ⊞ 📁 Management
   ⊞ 📁 Notification Services
      📁 SQL Server Agent (Agent XPs disabled)
□ 📁 LS-MIRROR-3\MIRROR (SQL Server 9.0.2047 - LS-MIRROR-3\Admin
   ⊟ 📁 Databases
      ⊞ 📁 System Databases
      ⊞ 📁 Database Snapshots
      ⊞ 📁 TestMirror1 (Principal, Synchronized)
```

Figure 11-59. *Reversed roles after failing over*

Transact-SQL

1. Connect to the instance that contains the principal database with your preferred query tool (sqlcmd or SQL Server Management Studio).

2. Make sure that your context is the master database. Issue the following command:

```
USE master
GO
```

3. Execute the following command to bring the mirror online as the primary. The only response you will get is that the command completed successfully:

```
ALTER DATABASE database_name SET PARTNER FAILOVER
GO
```

Unplanned Failover

If the principal instance becomes unavailable in a high performance mode configuration, or if the principal instances become unavailable in a high security mode configuration, you must manually bring the instance containing the mirror database online. This is a disaster recovery operation, so there is always the chance that you may lose data that may exist on the principal. If you are using a witness, to force the mirror online, the mirror must be able to connect to the witness. If not, you must use the steps in the next section.

To bring the mirror online in this scenario, follow these steps:

1. Connect to the instance that contains the mirror database with your preferred query tool (sqlcmd or SQL Server Management Studio).

2. Make sure that your context is the master database. Issue the following command:

```
USE master
GO
```

3. Run the following command to bring the mirror online as the primary:

```
ALTER DATABASE database_name SET PARTNER FORCE_SERVICE_ALLOW_DATA_LOSS
GO
```

Unplanned Failover with No Principal or Witness

If you are using high security mode and you lose both the principal and the witness, you will need to recover the database outside of the context of the database mirroring session:

1. Connect to the instance that contains the mirror database with your preferred query tool (sqlcmd or SQL Server Management Studio).

2. Make sure that your context is the master database. Issue the following command:

```
USE master
GO
```

3. Run the following command to remove the database mirroring configuration:

```
ALTER DATABASE database_name SET PARTNER OFF
GO
```

4. Run the following command to bring the mirror online as the primary:

```
RESTORE DATABASE database_name WITH RECOVERY
GO
```

Full-Text Indexes

One thing you will have to worry about after making the mirror the new primary database is your full-text indexes, if you are using that feature of SQL Server. When you restore the database on the mirror, the full-text catalog is at the same point as the restore. Any index changes that occur on the principal that are not logged operations will not be recorded in the transaction log, and therefore not applied as part of the mirroring process. CREATE FULLTEXT CATALOG, ALTER FULLTEXT CATALOG, and DROP FULLTEXT CATALOG are logged operations that will get rolled forward on the mirror. After the switch, you will need to synchronize your database to its corresponding full-text catalog.

Redirecting Clients to the Mirror

If your application is coded to the SQL Server Native Client and you are using the failover partner setting for database mirroring, the clients will be automatically redirected to the mirror without any intervention needed. If you did not code to the SQL Server Native Client, even if you have automatic failover set, you will need to find a way to abstract the change in SQL Server instance names from the client, or have some other way of redirecting the clients to the instance of SQL Server 2005 containing the new primary database. You can use Network Load Balancing or create an alias as described in Chapter 15, or you can make sure that the application itself can be reconfigured to use another SQL Server instance.

Summary

Database mirroring is an excellent option for high availability or disaster recovery if it meets your needs. It offers granular protection at a per-transaction level, which is a distinct advantage if that is what your SLA requires. Despite the ability to do an automatic failover to the mirror, database mirroring may not meet your needs depending on your configuration. Database mirroring does require a fairly robust hardware design that also goes hand in hand with how you configure database mirroring. Database mirroring may be the new kid on the block, but it compares favorably to other technologies that have been in SQL Server for quite some time, such as replication.

CHAPTER 12

■■■

Replication

Replication is the final member of the quartet of major SQL Server availability features. It has been a feature of SQL Server since version 6.0 and, depending on how you configure it, is a useful availability option. There are two main scenarios for replication: server to server, and server to client, such as a remote worker with a laptop. This chapter focuses on a server to server replication topology.

This chapter covers not only how replication works but also the considerations for implementing it as well as how to configure and administer it once it is up and running.

■**Note** Replication could fill a book on its own since there are so many facets to it. There is not enough room in a single chapter to go into all of the minutiae of each type of SQL Server replication, but the most salient topics as they relate to availability are covered here. If you need to delve into replication more, your best sources of information are SQL Server 2005 Books Online as well as the few published books for SQL Server 2005 dedicated to replication. Two examples are *Pro SQL Server 2005 Replication* by Sujoy Paul (Apress, 2006) and *Microsoft SQL Server 2005 Replication* by Bren Newman and Philip Vaughn (Sams, 2007).

How Replication Works

Simply put, replication allows you to take some of your data and make it available elsewhere. Replication works at a data level. There are three main types of replication within SQL Server:

- Snapshot
- Merge
- Transactional

Each of these types of replication has the same common components: a Publisher, a Distributor, and a Subscriber. The *Publisher* is your source database that has a *publication* and a set of *articles* (the actual selections of data that will be replicated) defined on it to denote what data will be published to the *Subscribers* of that data. The *subscription* that the Subscriber uses can be either *push* or *pull*, meaning it can be sent from the Publisher to the Subscriber, or the Subscriber can grab it itself. The *Distributor* keeps track of the subscriptions and is the hub for the activity between the Publisher and the Subscriber.

As part of its configuration, replication configures various SQL Server Agent jobs as well as possibly creates triggers on the Publisher to capture when changes occur to the data. The reason I mention this is that as a DBA, you will have to be aware of what is added to each SQL Server instance participating in replication. Objects such as triggers can certainly affect the overall performance of your database and the instance containing it. If you have a very heavily used

OLTP database with many inserts, you have to account for the overhead of replication in the sizing of your server; otherwise you may have serious problems down the road.

Replication is similar to log shipping and database mirroring since it offers some protection on a per-database level. With database mirroring and log shipping, you get everything that hits the transaction log at the standby server; with replication, you generally only get what data is defined in the publication. This may be all the data in a table or a database (assuming it does not exceed any limitations of replication), but it is not a guarantee. The ability to be much more focused and deliver a granular set of data to a standby server can be a very helpful feature but it may not be right for you. When disaster strikes and you need to have business continuity, replication is a great way to make crucial data available elsewhere to allow the business to run while you are solving the bigger issue. On the flip side, if you need your entire database at your standby site, replication is not the best or most efficient way to go about achieving that goal; database mirroring and log shipping are far better technologies for that.

Caution Never update or change objects such as the triggers configured during replication unless directed to by Microsoft. I know many people out there do it, but you will not only be in an unsupported position if you need support, you will also need to maintain whatever customizations you deploy. If replication doesn't do what you want, maybe it is the wrong technology for you. Think about it.

Snapshot Replication

Snapshot replication completely refreshes the data of the Subscriber each time a push or pull occurs (according to the subscription that is configured). If any data is updated at the Subscriber, it will be completely overwritten when the snapshot is republished to the Subscriber. Snapshot replication is not for those who need to update data at the Subscriber.

Snapshot replication is generally helpful where data changes infrequently, and it is easier to refresh everything instead of just a portion of it. A good example of the use of snapshot replication is a catalog for an online e-commerce site. Since this database is read-only, you could do a full refresh at a scheduled time each day across all instances.

Arguably the most important use of snapshot replication is that in many cases, it is used to seed the other forms of replication via the initial snapshot. While there are other methods by which this can be achieved in some cases (described later in the section "Step 3: Subscribing to the Publication"), even if you are using merge or transactional replication, chances are you may use snapshot replication in some way.

When it comes to availability, snapshot replication will most likely not be appropriate unless you have a small dataset and refresh frequently enough to meet your SLAs. Since each push and pull is a "one off," there is a lot of autonomy on both sides and there could be a large delta between the Publisher and the Subscriber. The whole goal of availability is to have small deltas of difference. Keep in mind that pushing a snapshot of an entire published database will put quite a resource hit on both Publisher and Subscriber and may take some time to complete.

Figure 12-1 shows the architecture for snapshot replication.

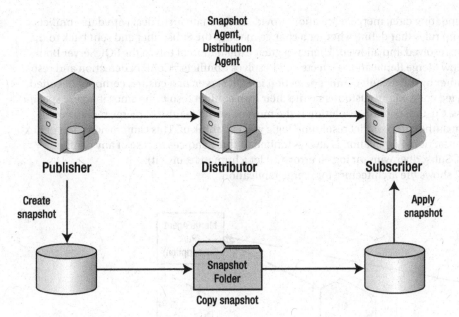

Figure 12-1. *Snapshot replication architecture*

Merge Replication

Merge replication is slightly different from snapshot. After the initial subscription is in place, you can send only the changes made at a scheduled interval. In this way, it is not unlike a differential backup or applying incremental transaction logs. However, one main difference over any other form of SQL Server availability is that with merge replication, you do have the possibility of updating Subscribers, which can send changed data back to the Publisher.

Merge replication works when a transaction occurs at the Publisher or Subscriber; that change is written to change tracking tables. The Merge Agent checks those change tracking tables and writes the changes to the distribution database where the data is then possibly sent out (depending on how merge replication is configured).

It is not a requirement of deploying merge replication that the Subscribers have the ability to update data. Merge replication can be a one-way send of data from the Publisher to the Subscriber. Clearly, a one-way data send is a much easier topology to deal with. However, the ability to have autonomous Subscribers (who are in turn Publishers of data back to the central server, which would be a Subscriber to the data) can be very beneficial in an availability scenario.

Consider this example:

You have a retail store with 1,000 locations across North America. There is a central data warehouse that has all the data from all the stores. Each local retail store has a scaled down version of that database with all of the relevant lookup and company data and the store's local sales information. This architecture allows each individual store to be autonomous in its operation. An individual store is not dependent on the home office (or other stores) for anything other than updates. Periodically during the day, each store sends updated sales figures and other information to the central server. In the event that the central server fails and has a total meltdown, the data can not only be reconstructed from the data in each store, but the largest portion of the business—the retail outlets serving customers nearly 12 hours a day—are unaffected and are able to keep going despite the outage.

If you are updating data, merge replication provides a mechanism to deal with data conflicts. You need to set up rules that define whether a change made at the Subscriber and sent back to the Publisher will be resolved and allowed. There is a great explanation of this in the SQL Server Books Online topic "How Merge Replication Detects and Resolves Conflicts." Conflict detection and resolution occurs either by the default conflict detection in SQL Server, or a custom component coded by you in managed code. Many customers write their own conflict resolution since it is very specific to their business. Custom conflict resolution is the most powerful feature of merge replication because you can author any conflict resolution logic you can think of. This can provide a ton of flexibility where transactional replication is always limited to three choices in case of any conflict (Publisher wins, Subscriber wins, or log an error and let a human resolve it).

Figure 12-2 shows the architecture for merge replication.

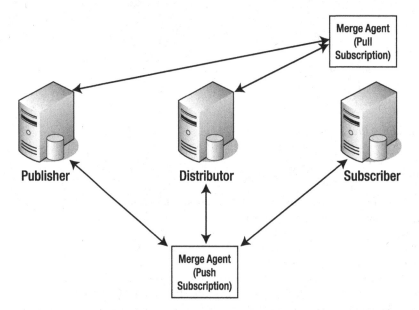

Figure 12-2. *Merge replication architecture*

Transactional Replication

Transactional replication is arguably the most popular form of replication, especially when it comes to availability. It is also the most granular and gives you the lowest latency and often the best throughput. Like its feature name, transactional replication replicates the data from the Publisher to the Subscriber each time a transaction completes at the Publisher. If you have a very high use OLTP system, this could add significant overhead to your instances that you would need to take into account.

When the transaction is written to the transaction log, the Log Reader Agent reads it from the transaction log and writes it to the distribution database. The Distribution Agent then is aware of the new data that will either be pushed to or pulled by the Subscriber.

Figure 12-3 shows the architecture for transactional replication.

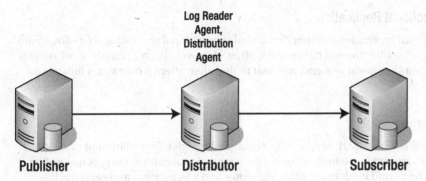

Figure 12-3. *Transactional replication architecture*

Updateable Subscriptions

Like merge replication, you can also have Subscribers that can update data. The two main types of updateable subscriptions are ones that do immediate updating and ones that queue updates. *Immediate* updating is exactly what it implies: before the data change is made at the Subscriber, it is sent back to the Publisher through a two-phase commit. The Publisher then redistributes that change to other Subscribers, including the Subscriber that initiated the change.

Queued updating Subscribers allow latency. The Publisher and Subscriber do not have to be connected. Updates are queued and sent when there is connectivity. The problem comes with conflicts. Since the process can be asynchronous, another Subscriber could update the data in the interim. The data that is sent would overwrite what was already sent. Queued updating Subscribers works best if the transactional replication is applied to Subscribers that own their own data and therefore work within the available conflict resolution choice of Subscriber wins.

Figure 12-4 shows the architecture for an updateable subscription with immediate updates. Queued updates would be similar, except there would be a Queue Agent and MS DTC involved in the chain of publishing from the Subscriber to the Publisher.

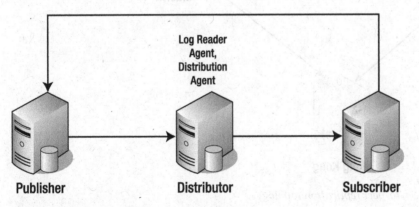

Figure 12-4. *Updateable subscription with immediate updates*

Bidirectional Transactional Replication

Bidirectional transactional replication is a specific form of transactional replication that allows both the Publisher and the Subscriber to send data to each other. However, this is a "dumb" send; there is no validation. When data changes at one end, it is sent to the other where it overwrites the data at the Subscriber.

Peer-to-Peer Replication

Peer-to-peer replication is new to SQL Server 2005. It is actually a specific variation of transactional replication and very similar to bidirectional transactional replication. There is no conflict resolution. It allows you to update data at both a Publisher and a Subscriber and send the updated data to each. Where peer-to-peer differs from bidirectional is that if any of the servers hosting the databases fail, your application (assuming it is properly programmed) can use any one of the other databases participating in peer-to-peer as its primary database. This means that all copies of the data at all Publishers and Subscribers are exactly the same. This is also another case where Network Load Balancing can be used to abstract the name of the servers to provide a single name/virtual IP address to your application. One of the challenges with peer-to-peer is that you will have a hard time knowing where any given transaction is within the replication process at the moment of failure. If you are considering peer-to-peer replication, I would recommend issuing some sort of custom check to see where your databases are in terms of consistency. Figure 12-5 shows a high level peer-to-peer configuration that has three geographically dispersed locations, all of which are replicating to each other.

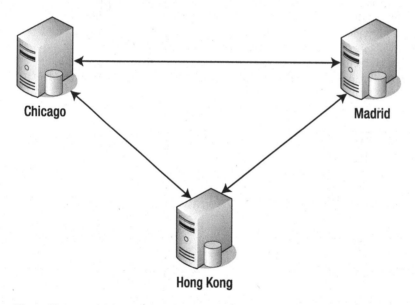

Figure 12-5. *Example peer-to-peer replication topology*

Understanding the Replication Agents

There are quite a few different agents used during replication, namely the following:

- *Snapshot Agent*: This agent prepares schema and initial data files of the tables and stored procedures that are published to a Subscriber. The Snapshot Agent usually is run at the Distributor. Each publication has its own Snapshot Agent and a set of files that will differ depending on the implementation. The possible files you may see are shown in Table 12-1.

Table 12-1. *File by Type of Replication*

Type of File (Extension)	Snapshot & Transactional Replication	Merge Replication
Compressed snapshot files (.cab)	Yes	Yes
Conflict tables (.cft)	No	Yes
Constraints (.idx)	Yes	No
Constraints/indexes (.dri)	Yes	Yes
Data (.bcp)	Yes	Yes
Schema (.sch)	Yes	Yes
System table data (.sys)	No	Yes
Triggers (.trg)	Yes[a]	Yes

[a]Updating Subscribers only

- *Log Reader Agent*: This reads and moves the transactions in the transaction log marked for replication in the publication database to the Distributor. Every publication database has one Log Reader Agent.

- *Distribution Agent*: This sends the changes that are being held at the Distributor to the Subscriber.

- *Merge Agent*: This is the piece of merge replication that deals with all changes that occur at the Publisher and Subscriber by reconciling them. For a pull subscription, it is run at the Subscriber, and for a push, at the Distributor.

- *Queue Reader Agent*: This agent is used when there are queued updating Subscribers in the topology. The Queue Reader Agent, of which there is one per published database, sends and reconciles changes made at the Subscriber to the Publisher.

Table 12-2 lists the agents and the forms of replication they are used by.

Table 12-2. *Replication Agents by Type of Replication*

Replication Agent	Snapshot Replication	Merge Replication	Transactional Replication
Snapshot Agent	Yes	Yes	Yes
Log Reader Agent	Yes	No	Yes
Distribution Agent	No	No	Yes
Merge Agent	No	Yes	No
Queue Reader Agent	No	No	Yes

Each agent will require a service account. For security purposes, it is recommended not to use any existing service account (such as the SQL Server or SQL Server Agent accounts) and to assign each account to a unique domain account with the proper rights. Table 12-3 lists what is necessary for each agent's account.

Table 12-3. *Replication Agents and Their Security Requirements*

Replication Agent	Database	Database Role Required	Other
Snapshot Agent	Distribution	db_owner	Write permissions on snapshot share
	Publication	db_owner	
Log Reader Agent	Distribution	db_owner	
	Publication	db_owner	
Distribution Agent	Distribution	db_owner	Member of the PAL; read permissions on snapshot share
	Subscription	db_owner	
Merge Agent	Distribution	db_owner	Read permissions on snapshot share; member of the PAL; login associated with account (pull subscription only)
	Publication	db_owner	Read permissions on snapshot share; login associated with account; member of the PAL
	Subscription	db_owner (push subscription only)	
Queue Reader Agent	Distribution	db_owner	Write permissions on snapshot share
	Publication	db_owner	
	Subscription	db_owner	

▪**Tip** Each replication agent has its own overhead signature, so you should be aware of where the deployed agent is running to ensure that not only are the agents running properly, but that they are taken into account in the server sizing.

Replication Considerations

There are many factors that will influence the planning and deployment of replication in your environment. This section details the most important ones, including the application, your network, the disk I/O, and the schema for the database itself.

▪**Note** A general rule of thumb applies when planning your replication deployment: keep it simple. Complex replication implementations can lead to manageability problems down the road. In addition, people do not understand the right way to use replication, so they come up with convoluted architectures or they want to make the product do things it is not designed for (such as conflict resolution with peer-to-peer replication). Be smart about how you use replication; a lot of these "smarts" stem from your planning stage.

The Application

All applications are not candidates for replication even though the availability requirements may seem like replication is a natural fit. The DBAs and the developers should definitely be in communication during the requirements and planning stages if the application to be deployed is an in-house, custom application since most forms of replication require that specific things are defined as part of the database schema. Developers should not assume that the DBAs can bolt replication on after the fact.

Similarly, third-party applications are just as difficult, if not more so, to deploy replication against. You do not control the schema; you bought a prepackaged piece of software, even if it allows customizations. This means that the database schema may not be suitable for replication even if you think you may need it. On top of that, there are quite a few vendors that explicitly state that SQL Server's replication feature (any type) is not supported and may invalidate your support contract if you attempt to deploy it. Do not be a hero and try to implement it. Check with the vendor to see that replication is supported. A good example of a third-party application that does not support replication is Siebel.

Component Location, Network Latency, and Network Speed

In a perfect world, you would have great end-to-end throughput on your network and you could stick your Subscriber anywhere in the world. Wouldn't that be great?

Unfortunately, we all live in the real world. I once was talking to a client who wanted to stick a bunch of Subscribers all across Africa where there was intermittent power and only the equivalent of dialup for a network, yet they wanted to use bidirectional transactional replication. Needless to say, that is an architecture that would not work in any way, shape, or form. The infrastructure can barely power the server let alone support sending and receiving transactions.

If your application or solution requires that there is a method of refreshing data at remote sites (or having data flow two ways), it doesn't mean that it is physically possible to achieve. I know these types of scenarios may be "requirements" for you, but you need to be realistic. You are probably not going to get a 10 millisecond delay between New York and Zimbabwe with a bad link (or even with a good link, for that matter). As network packets travel over a longer distance, your latency grows and your speed decreases. That's just the physics behind the scenes. You cannot beat physics no matter how much you try. If you spend a lot of money, you may be able to go faster over a farther distance, but at some point, even money won't solve the issue. The cost would also be astronomical. Is your solution really so important that the network infrastructure alone is worth spending millions? I seriously doubt it.

Having said this, there are possible ways you can "fake" replication out. By that I mean your topology and where you place your various components will impact not only the ability to do replication, but the speed. For example, if you are replicating to Africa, you may be able to do replication but use snapshot or merge along with FTP instead to update the Subscriber; this would tolerate much more latency.

With replication, you can have multiple stops along the way until the data reaches the final destination. SQL Server's replication feature allows you to *republish* data. This means that a Subscriber can also act as a Distributor of data to other locations. Where this comes into play is that as you go farther from the source, you have the ability to use other sources besides the original Publisher to serve the small tributaries.

■**Caution** If it is at all possible, never place the Distributor on the same server as the Publisher. While it is a valid architecture, the instance (and by association, the server hosting the instance of SQL Server) housing both of these components becomes a single point of failure.

Disk Performance and Sizing

The consideration of disk performance, already a general concern for any SQL Server deployment, is magnified with the addition of replication since you are writing to more databases. In the case of transactional replication, where you may be sending a lot of data to the other side, the disks powering your database, and specifically, your transaction logs on the Subscriber, can become a bottleneck very quickly.

You will also need to account for disk space for your databases when it comes to using replication. First, if you are using any form of snapshot replication, even to just initialize a subscription, you must have enough disk space to store the snapshots generated. This disk space is usually accounted for on the Distributor. The distribution database itself can potentially grow to be quite large, especially if you are using transactional replication. The transaction is stored until all Subscribers have received the change, or until the Snapshot Agent is rerun (whichever comes first). The default retention period for a transactional replication subscription is 72 hours; so if data has not been synchronized in that time period, the subscription will be marked as deactivated and will have to be reinitialized. To change this value, use the @max_distretention parameter of sp_adddistributiondb and @retention of sp_addpublication. For merge replication, the defaults for retention are set using the parameters @retention and @retention_period_unit of sp_addmergepublication.

Similarly, any publication database participating in transactional replication may be larger than normal since the records cannot be truncated from the transaction log until they have been moved to the distribution database. If for some reason either the distribution database is unavailable (a good case to make your Distributor highly available) or the Log Reader Agent fails, the transaction log of the Publisher will continue to grow indefinitely—or until you run out of disk space (whichever comes first).

Making Replication Highly Available

One of the most important things you need to do when planning your replication deployment is figuring out how you will make replication itself highly available. If you are doing a global deployment that relies on replicated data occurring 24x7, your primary goal should be to protect both the Publisher and the Distributor. Although it may wind up being a pain, the Subscribers can always resubscribe to a publication or be reinitialized, but if your Publisher fails, no data will get to the Subscriber, and without a Distributor, data will not get to the Subscriber. You would need to employ other SQL Server high availability technologies and techniques such as failover clustering to ensure that these key cogs in the replication works do not fail.

SQL Server Agent and Replication

One thing you will need to ensure is that SQL Server Agent automatically starts when SQL Server is started; otherwise replication will not run since it relies on SQL Server Agent jobs. While this should be the standard setting for most installations of SQL Server, it does not hurt to remind you to check that this setting is configured.

Database Schema

How your actual schema on the Publisher is architected will dictate what, if any, kind of replication may be possible. If your schema does not adhere to the rules dictated by SQL Server, chances are replication may be nearly impossible for you to deploy.

Transactional replication requires that all tables have primary keys. If not, you cannot deploy transactional replication. This is one of the reasons why replication can be difficult with applications in which you do not control the schema. Many vendors do not support the modification to their database schema.

Merge replication requires the use of a globally unique identifier (GUID) for each row. This GUID has a data type of uniqueidentifier with the ROWGUID property and a unique index. If the GUID column does not exist, merge replication will automatically add the GUID during the configuration process. The GUID column will only be removed if replication is deleted and added by the replication setup process. If the column existed before replication was configured, it will not be deleted.

■**Tip** The application should only use the column names for inserting and reading data. The GUID is only used internally by replication.

While timestamp columns are supported for replication with merge, there are some caveats you need to be aware of. A column with a data type of timestamp can be replicated, but the value is regenerated when the data is replicated and applied to the Subscriber. Put simply: the values will be different at the Publisher and Subscriber. This means that not only can a timestamp-based column not be used for validation, if any other values in the database are dependent upon that date to be the same as the original, either in the application or as part of referential integrity, you will have problems at the Subscriber.

text, ntext, and image Data Types

If you are replicating any large object (LOB) data types such as text, ntext, and image, you can potentially affect the available memory of the Publisher's SQL Server instance. If you are using merge replication, set the value for the @stream_blob_columns parameter of the stored procedure sp_addmergearticle to TRUE. If you fail to do this, you could potentially run out of memory on the Publisher since the LOB will need to be built in memory prior to replication. The downside of setting the value to TRUE is that it will affect the performance of the Merge Agent, so use this setting carefully. The reality is that you should most likely avoid replication LOB data unless it is absolutely necessary. The recommendation from Microsoft is to try to use varchar(max), nvarchar(max), and varbinary(max) in place of text, ntext, and image. The recommendation also holds true for transactional replication.

There is a configurable parameter called max text repl size that will tell the SQL Server engine how big a text, ntext, varchar(max), nvarchar(max), or image column can be that can be replicated. The value set is in bytes and is configured via sp_configure. For example, to set the maximum value to 4000 bytes, enter the following command:

```
sp_configure 'max text repl size', 4000
go
reconfigure with override
go
```

Only an UPDATE statement will cause a column with a data type of text, ntext, or image to be marked for replication. If those columns are updated using either WRITETEXT or UPDATETEXT, replication will not detect the change. The application would need to issue a dummy UPDATE statement after the WRITETEXT or UPDATETEXT operation to let SQL Server know that data needs to be replicated. This is a great example of something that would need to be handled by the developers up front. The following is a simple example of code that achieves the task:

```
BEGIN TRAN
DECLARE @mytextpointer binary(16)

- Get the text pointer value for the row
SELECT @mytextpointer = TEXTPTR(ColNm)
FROM TableNm
WHERE ID = '1'

WRITETEXT TableNm.ColNm @mytextpointer 'Domo Arigato'

- Set the value to be the same
- Use the WHERE clause to qualify which row-
- to mark for replication
UPDATE TableNm SET ColNm = ColNm
WHERE ID = '1'
COMMIT TRAN
```

Object and Row Limitations

You also have some limitations on the size of objects when it comes to replication. First and foremost, your row size must be under 8000 bytes if you are using snapshot or transactional replication, and 6000 if you are using merge (the 2000 byte difference is the overhead reserved for conflict detection). In keeping with the theme of making all aspects of your application such as queries smaller and compact, really large row sizes might impact your ability to replicate your data efficiently on a high volume OLTP database. If you are pushing the limits of replication, chances are your schema is inefficient. This is a good example of a design choice that could potentially become a bottleneck to your availability should you decide to implement replication.

Tables can only have a certain number of columns in total if you are going to implement replication. You are limited to 246 per table if you are going to use merge replication, and 1,000 for snapshot or transactional replication. A row filter in merge replication consumes 1024 bytes, and you are limited to a total of 256 articles per publication.

Schema Changes

One of the biggest misunderstandings when it comes to replication is how it deals with schema changes. As noted previously, replication in general is not designed to provide a complete copy of your database somewhere else. However, replication can send out changes to your schema since they may be needed at the Subscribers. The commands ALTER TABLE, ALTER VIEW, ALTER PROCEDURE, ALTER FUNCTION, and ALTER TRIGGER (although ALTER TRIGGER is limited to data manipulation language [DML] triggers only) will tell replication (if it is configured to do so) to send the changes to the Subscriber. Changes are replicated when the new snapshot is applied (the Subscriber gets a complete refresh including the new schema objects), the Distribution Agent is run, or the Merge Agent is run.

To configure replication to automatically send schema changes, set a value of 1 for the @replicate_ddl parameter of sp_addpublication (snapshot or transactional replication) or sp_addmergepublication (merge replication). Also, to alter an article, you can use the replication stored procedures. For snapshot or transactional replication, execute the sp_changearticle stored procedure with the schema_option property. The equivalent stored procedure for merge replication is sp_changemergearticle. If you do not set the right values prior to starting replication, you may need to reinitialize your Subscribers. Some options may require a reinitialization due to the nature of the object being created.

If you attempt to update a table via SQL Server Management Studio, the schema change will fail because, unfortunately, Management Studio actually attempts to drop and re-create the table (as part of how it deals with updating tables). If an object such as a table is published as part of an article, it cannot be dropped. Therefore, you have to make sure that any updates to the schema are via some sort of code or script (Transact-SQL or SQL Server Management Objects). This means that all updates from developers that come through change management cannot be done manually by the DBA in the supplied SQL Server tools.

You should not allow schema updates at the Subscribers if the Subscribers also publish data back to a central repository. While merge replication disallows schema updates at the Subscriber, transactional replication does not. Allowing schema changes in a two-way transactional replication deployment can cause the deployment to ultimately fail since you really only want one master schema.

Constraints (either *foreign key* or *check*) can be ignored if you set the NOT FOR REPLICATION option. NOT FOR REPLICATION can also be used to help replicate identity columns. Using NOT FOR REPLICATION is not the default behavior of replication. Think of it in this way: you want to have all the appropriate checks to ensure the data is valid when it is first added to your Publisher. When you are pushing (or pulling) the data to a Subscriber, you just want to put it there. Why would you need to have it validated twice?

Tip If the schema change you want is not listed here, it is most likely not supported. Check the SQL Server 2005 Books Online topic "Making Schema Changes on Publication Databases" for more information and other rules. If what you want to do is not officially supported through replication, you will have to stop replication, make the change, and then reinitialize replication once the change is complete.

Push or Pull Subscriptions

One of the seemingly innocuous decisions you will have to make is whether you will push your data to the Subscriber, or the Subscriber will pull it. Both are valid, so it will boil down to your requirements. A push subscription puts the entire burden on the Distributor, and depending on how many subscriptions there are, this could add significant overhead that the SQL Server instance may not be able to tolerate. However, configuring a push model also centralizes the management of the subscriptions.

A pull subscription puts the burden on the Subscriber. While this may lighten the load at the Distributor, it could potentially cause administration headaches if the Subscriber is remote and the DBA can't reach it. If it goes down or has a problem, that location might as well fall off the face of the earth. However, one of the benefits of a pull subscription is that even when you have poor connectivity, you can synchronize when you do have connectivity.

Security

Last but certainly not least, your replication deployments must be secure. There are two main aspects that you need to consider. One of the most important things to do is ensure that the data you are sending across the wire is either not sensitive or, if it is, secure it. Anyone who can sniff your network packets could potentially gain access to your data. While this should technically be a concern for both log shipping and database mirroring, the problem is magnified much more in replication since there is usually some sort of tactical use for the replicated data besides high availability and it may enter a public network at some point. SQL Server can be configured with Secure Sockets Layer (SSL) or IP Security (IPSEC). You could also use a virtual private network (VPN) to create a secure tunnel from site to site.

Secondly, secure the directories used for snapshots. Think back to Chapter 3 where I talk about securing your backup directories. This is no different. You must secure the folders used by the snapshots so the snapshots cannot be used by anyone who should not have access. You must grant read access to the accounts for the Merge Agent or Distribution Agent, and write access for the account that the Snapshot Agent runs under.

Configuring Replication

After you figure out what your plan will be for replication, you have to put the plan into action.

Step 1: Configuring the Distributor

The first thing you must do is set up the Distributor. The Distributor configuration might have multiple steps depending on whether the Publisher will also act as its own Distributor. You must set up distribution on the Publisher and the Distributor separately if they are not the same SQL Server instance.

Step1a: Configuring the Instance Serving As the Distributor

Whether this is the same server as the Publisher or a completely separate instance of SQL Server, you need to do this step first before you configure a Publisher to use a remote Distributor:

1. Start SQL Server Management Studio.

2. Select the Replication folder, right-click, and select Configure Distribution as shown in Figure 12-6.

Figure 12-6. *Replication context menu options*

3. On the Configure Distribution Wizard dialog, shown in Figure 12-7, click Next.

4. On the Distributor dialog, select the first option, as shown in Figure 12-8. The instance name will reflect the instance you are connected to in SQL Server Management Studio. Click Next.

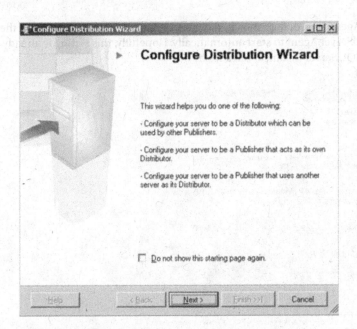

Figure 12-7. *Configure Distribution Wizard dialog*

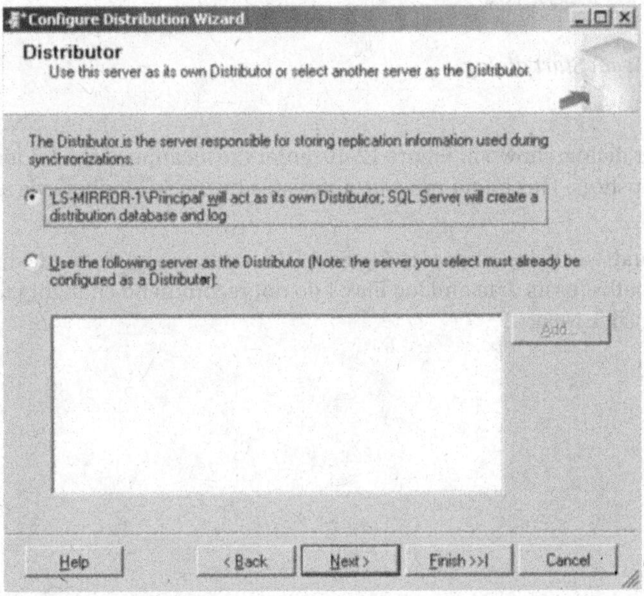

Figure 12-8. *Distributor dialog*

5. On the SQL Server Agent Start dialog, shown in Figure 12-9, you should always select the option to allow SQL Server Agent to start automatically. Hopefully, this setting is already configured for the SQL Server instance. Click Next.

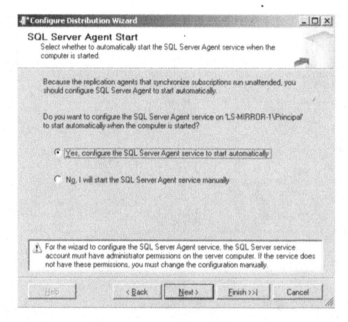

Figure 12-9. *SQL Server Agent Start dialog*

6. On the Snapshot Folder dialog, shown in Figure 12-10, enter the location of the folder that will be used for the snapshots. This folder must be accessible by the Subscribers via a UNC path name. Click Next.

7. On the Distribution Database dialog, shown in Figure 12-11, enter the name of the distribution database and the paths for its data and log files. I do not recommend changing the default name or paths. Click Next.

Figure 12-10. *Snapshot Folder dialog*

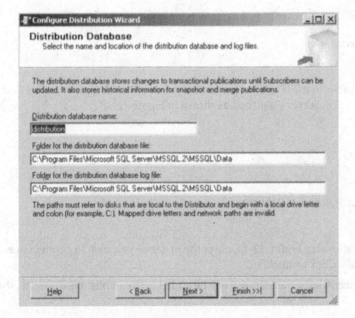

Figure 12-11. *Distribution Database dialog*

8. On the Publishers dialog, shown in Figure 12-12, you will add the servers that can use the Distributor as a Publisher. By default, the instance itself can use the Distributor. When you are done, click Next.

Figure 12-12. *Publishers dialog*

To add another Publisher to the list of instances that can use this Distributor, select Add, and then choose Add SQL Server Publisher, as shown in Figure 12-13.

Figure 12-13. *Adding a SQL Server Publisher*

When prompted, as shown in Figure 12-14, enter the instance you wish to connect to and the proper credentials. Click Connect.

After you connect successfully, the instance will be added to the Publishers dialog, as shown in Figure 12-15.

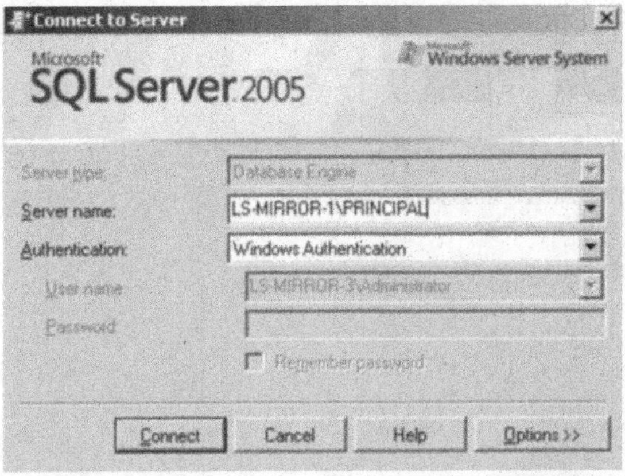

Figure 12-14. *Connect to Server dialog*

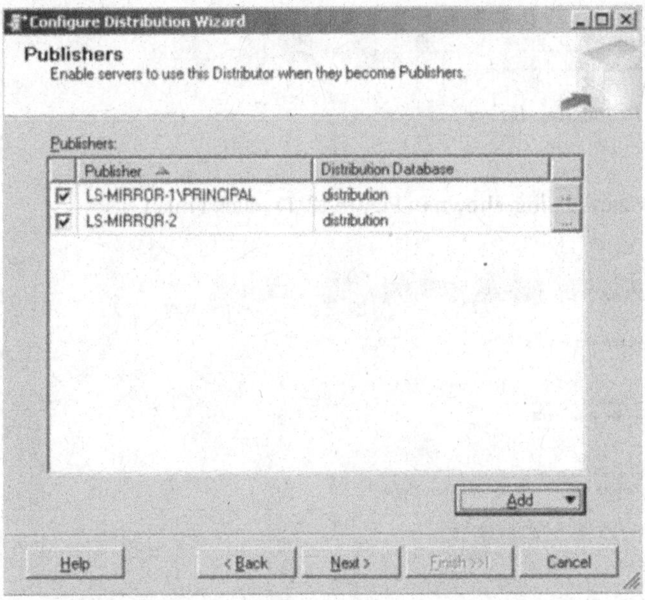

Figure 12-15. *Publishers dialog with an added instance*

9. On the Script File Properties dialog, shown in Figure 12-16, enter the location where you want to place the script for creating the Distributor. Select the options that are relevant for your deployment. Click Next.

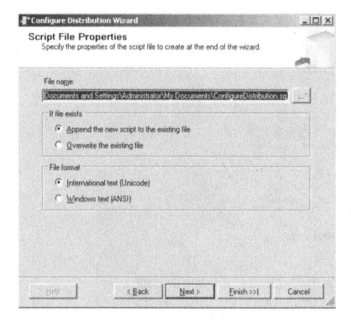

Figure 12-16. *Script File Properties dialog*

10. On the Complete the Wizard dialog, shown in Figure 12-17, click Finish.

Figure 12-17. *Complete the Wizard dialog*

11. SQL Server will now configure the Distributor. During the process, you will be updated, as shown in Figure 12-18.

Figure 12-18. *During the configuration process*

If your configuration is successful, you will see a dialog similar to the one shown in Figure 12-19. Click Close.

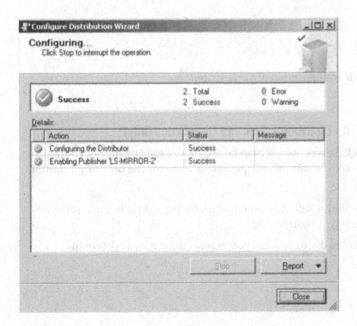

Figure 12-19. *Successful configuration of the Distributor*

Figure 12-20 shows a successful configuration of the Distributor but with errors. Figure 12-21 shows the exact error that occurred.

Figure 12-20. *Successful completion with errors*

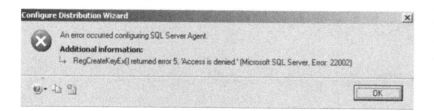

Figure 12-21. *Example error during the configuration of the Distributor*

Step1b: Adding the Publisher to the Distributor (Remote Distributor Only)

If you did not configure the other SQL Server instances to be able to use the Distributor configured in Step 1a, the following steps will walk you through the process of allowing the use of that centralized Distributor:

1. In SQL Server Management Studio, select the Replication folder, right-click, and select Distributor Properties as shown in Figure 12-22.

2. When the Distributor Properties dialog is displayed, select Publishers, as shown in Figure 12-23.

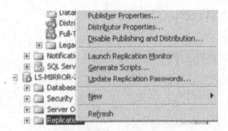

Figure 12-22. *Replication context menu*

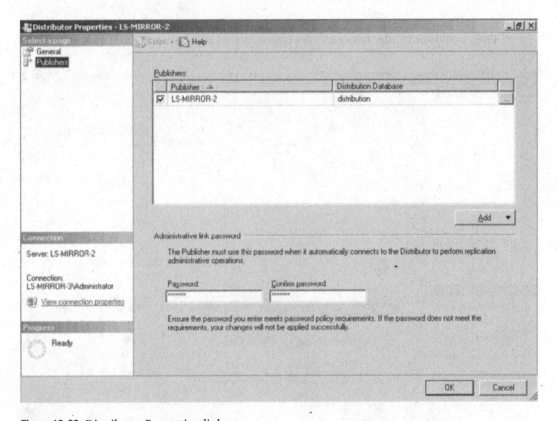

Figure 12-23. *Distributor Properties dialog*

3. To add another Publisher to the list of instances that can use this Distributor, select Add, and then Add SQL Server Publisher as shown earlier in Figure 12-13.

4. When prompted, as shown earlier in Figure 12-14, enter the instance you wish to connect to and the proper credentials. Click Connect.

5. You will see the message shown in Figure 12-24 pop up. Click OK.

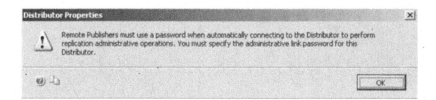

Figure 12-24. *Message after adding the Publisher*

6. Enter a password under Administrative Link Password as shown in Figure 12-25.

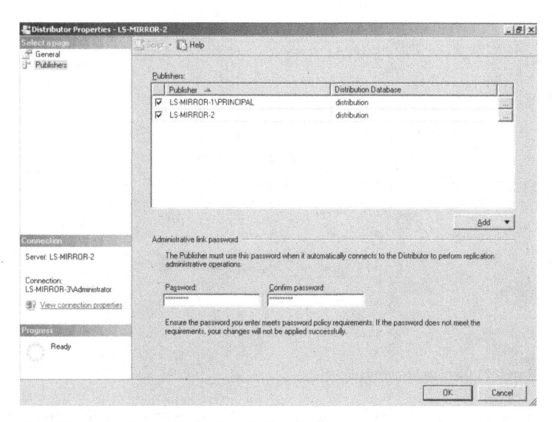

Figure 12-25. *Entering the password for the administrative link*

7. Repeat steps 3 and 4 for all Publishers.
8. Click OK to complete the process.

Step1c: Configuring the Publisher to Use a Remote Distributor

Once the Publisher has been added to the Distributor, you can configure distribution at the Publisher by following these instructions:

1. Start SQL Server Management Studio.

2. Select the Replication folder, right-click, and select Configure Distribution, as shown in Figure 12-6.

3. On the Configure Distribution Wizard dialog, as shown earlier in Figure 12-7, click Next.

4. On the Distributor dialog, select the second option, as shown in Figure 12-26. Click Add. If you failed to add the Publisher correctly in the previous step, you will see Figure 12-27; otherwise, you will be prompted to connect to the remote Distributor similar to the earlier Figure 12-14. If you are successful, the remote Distributor will appear as shown in Figure 12-28. Click Next.

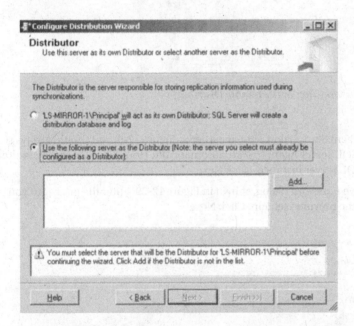

Figure 12-26. *Distributor dialog*

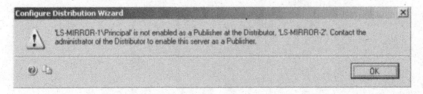

Figure 12-27. *Failure to add the Publisher to the remote Distributor*

Figure 12-28. *Successful addition of the remote Distributor*

5. On the SQL Server Agent Start dialog, shown earlier in Figure 12-9, you should always select the option to allow SQL Server Agent to start automatically. Hopefully, this setting is already configured for the SQL Server instance. Click Next.

6. On the Administrative Password dialog, shown in Figure 12-29, enter the password you entered in step 6 of the previous section. Click Next.

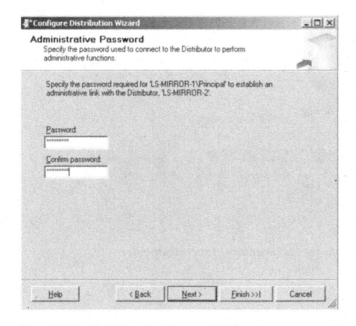

Figure 12-29. *Administrative Password dialog*

7. On the Complete the Wizard dialog, shown in Figure 12-30, click Finish.

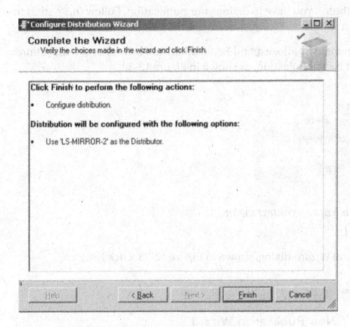

Figure 12-30. *Distribution Database dialog*

8. If the configuration is successful, you will see a dialog similar to the one in Figure 12-31. Click Close.

Figure 12-31. *Successful configuration of a remote Distributor*

Step 2: Configuring the Publication

After you configure the Distributor, you have to define your publication. Follow these steps to create the publication for replication:

1. In SQL Server Management Studio, expand Replication, and select Local Publications. Right-click and select New Publication, as shown in Figure 12-32.

Figure 12-32. *Local Publications context menu*

2. On the New Publication Wizard dialog, shown in Figure 12-33, click Next.

Figure 12-33. *New Publication Wizard dialog*

3. On the Publication Database dialog, select the database that contains the data or objects to publish. An example is shown in Figure 12-34. Click Next.

Figure 12-34. *Publication Database dialog*

4. On the Publication Type dialog, shown in Figure 12-35, select the type of replication to use. Click Next.

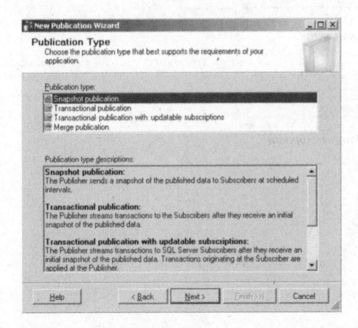

Figure 12-35. *Publication Type dialog*

5. On the Articles dialog, select the tables and objects that will be used as part of the publication. An example is shown in Figure 12-36. If you want to change the properties of the article, click Article Properties and select the appropriate option as shown in Figure 12-37. You will then see the Article Properties dialog as shown in Figure 12-38. Click OK to close when you are finished configuring your properties, and click Next on the Articles dialog when finished.

Figure 12-36. *Articles dialog*

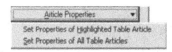

Figure 12-37. *Article Properties options*

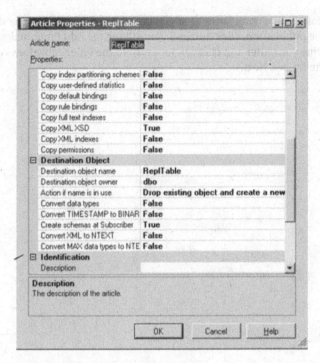

Figure 12-38. *Article Properties dialog*

6. If you selected a merge publication in step 3, you may see the Article Issues dialog, shown in Figure 12-39. Click Next.

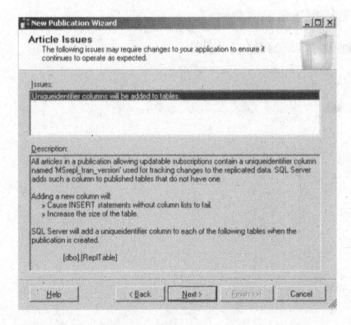

Figure 12-39. *Article Issues dialog*

7. On the Filter Table Rows dialog, shown in Figure 12-40, if you wish to further filter how data will be defined as part of the publication, click Add and you will see the Add Filter dialog shown in Figure 12-41. Define your filter and click OK to return to the Filter Table Rows dialog. The filter will be reflected. Click Next.

Figure 12-40. *Filter Table Rows dialog*

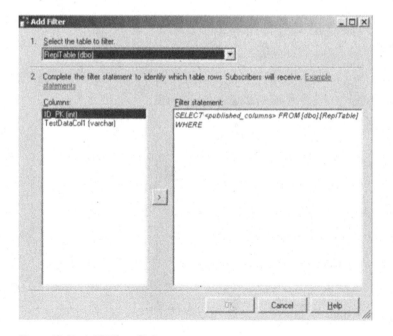

Figure 12-41. *Add Filter dialog*

8. On the Snapshot Agent dialog, shown in Figure 12-42, select the option that is right for you and click Next.

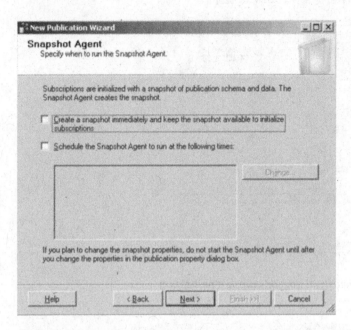

Figure 12-42. *Snapshot Agent dialog*

9. The Agent Security dialog will differ, depending on the type of replication you select. Figure 12-43 shows what it looks like with merge, Figure 12-44 shows snapshot, and Figure 12-45 shows transactional.

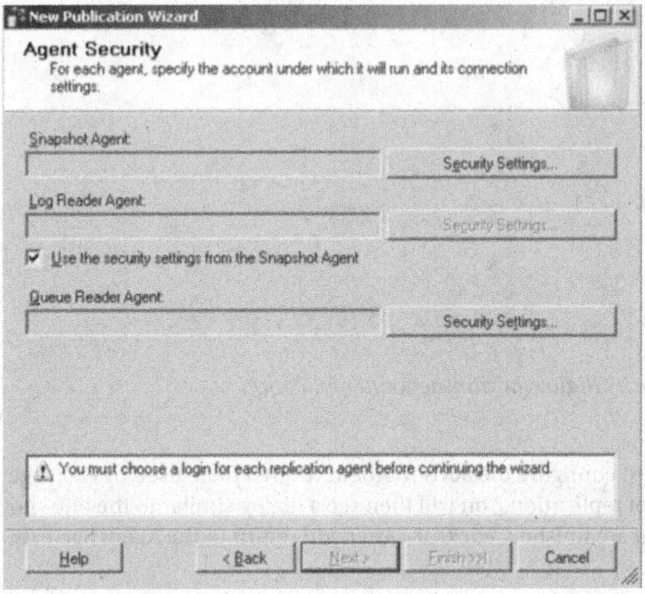

Figure 12-43. *Agent Security dialog for merge replication*

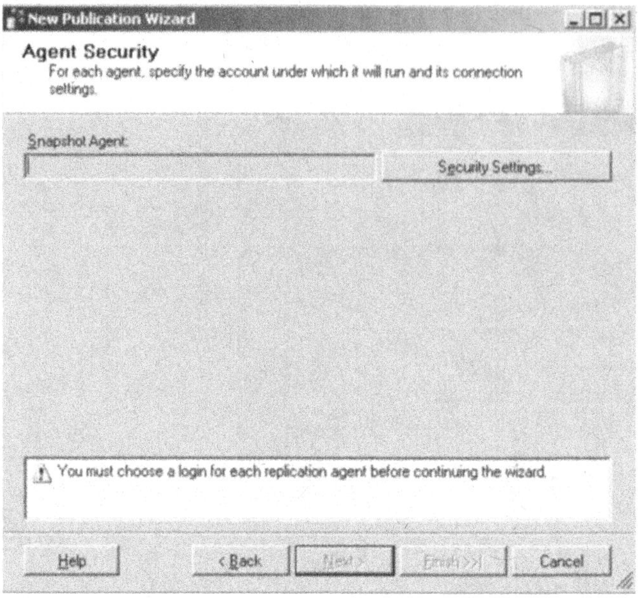

Figure 12-44. *Agent Security dialog for snapshot replication*

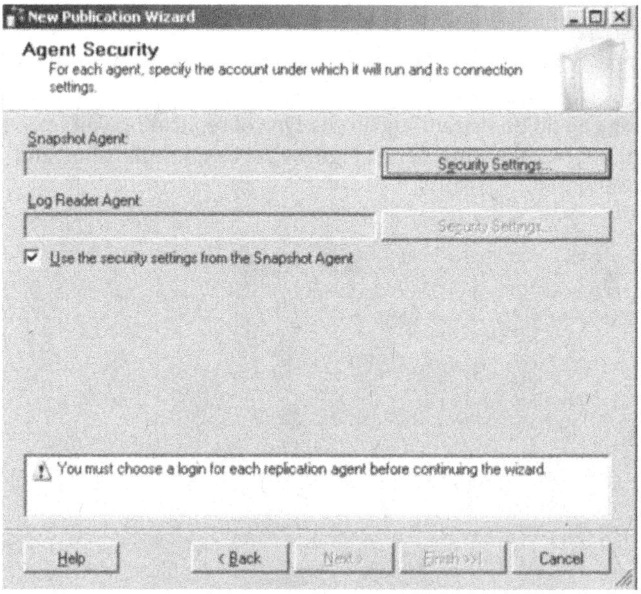

Figure 12-45. *Agent Security dialog for transactional replication*

Click Security Settings to configure the account (or accounts) to be used by each agent applicable to the type of replication. You will then see a dialog similar to the one shown in Figure 12-46. When you are finished, click OK. After you return to the Agent Security dialog, click Next.

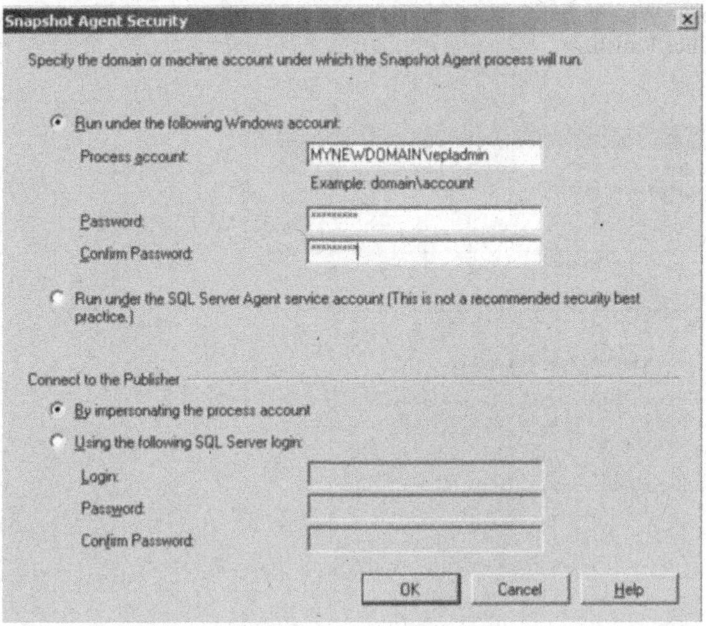

Figure 12-46. *Snapshot Agent Security dialog*

10. If you want to generate a script, click the appropriate option on the Wizard Actions dialog, shown in Figure 12-47, and click Next.

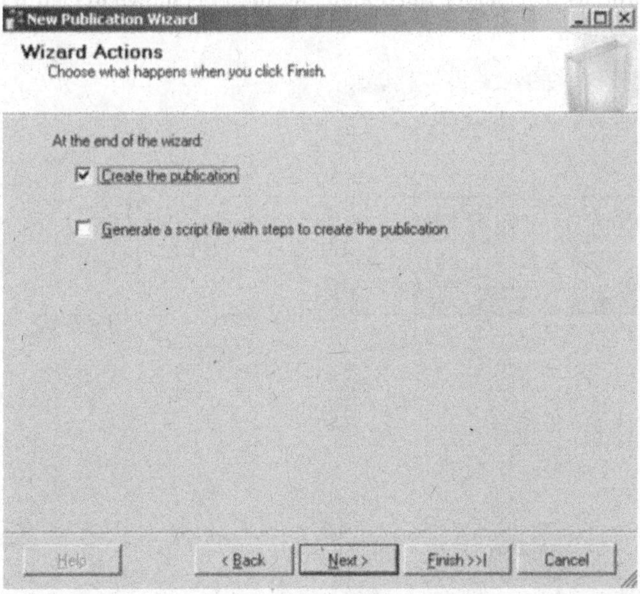

Figure 12-47. *Wizard Actions dialog*

11. On the Complete the Wizard dialog, enter the name of the publication. An example is shown in Figure 12-48. Click Finish.

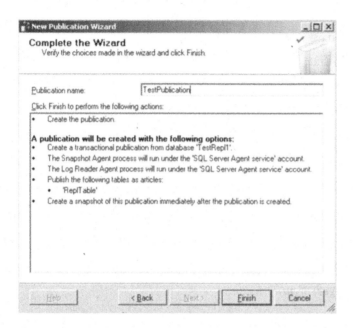

Figure 12-48. *Complete the Wizard dialog*

During the configuration process, SQL Server will update the status as shown in Figure 12-49.

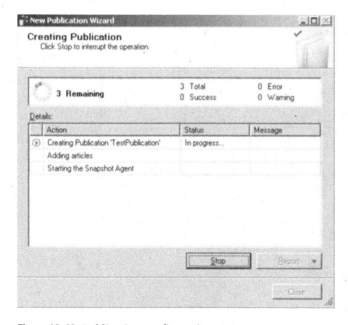

Figure 12-49. *Publication configuration status*

When the process is complete, you will see a dialog similar to the one in Figure 12-50. Click Close.

Figure 12-50. *Successful creation of a publication*

The new publication will be displayed in SQL Server Management Studio, as shown in Figure 12-51.

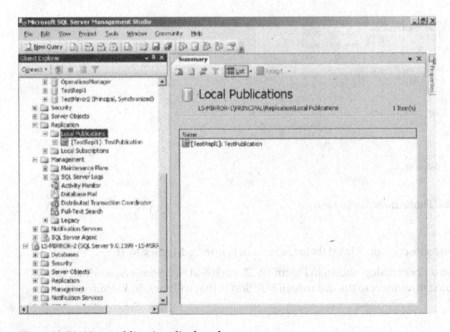

Figure 12-51. *New publication displayed*

Step 3: Subscribing to the Publication

Once you have your publication defined and your distribution channel configured, you need to configure the Subscriber.

You must seed the Subscriber with an initial set of data. There are many ways to go about achieving this. One of the nice things about replication is that for the initial seed of data, which is usually done via a snapshot, you are not limited to one way. You can use an alternate location for the Subscriber to get the snapshot. You can use a network share, removable media (such as a DVD-R), FTP, a USB, or a FireWire hard drive to transfer your snapshot. The following instructions describe how to configure a subscription:

1. Connect to either the Publisher or the Subscriber instance via SQL Server Management Studio.

2. If you are connected to the Subscriber, expand Replication, select Local Subscriptions, and right-click. Select New Subscriptions from the context menu, as shown in Figure 12-52.

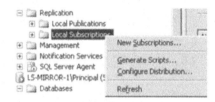

Figure 12-52. *Local Subscriptions context menu*

If you are connected to the Publisher, select the publication under Local Publications, right-click, and select New Subscriptions from the context menu, as shown in Figure 12-53.

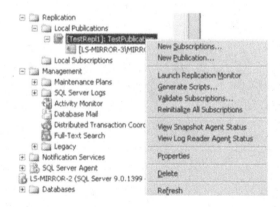

Figure 12-53. *Publication context menu*

3. On the New Subscription Wizard dialog, shown in Figure 12-54, click Next.

4. On the Subscribers dialog, shown in Figure 12-55, click Add SQL Server Subscriber. You will be prompted to connect to the instance of SQL Server that will contain the Subscription.

Figure 12-54. *New Subscription Wizard dialog*

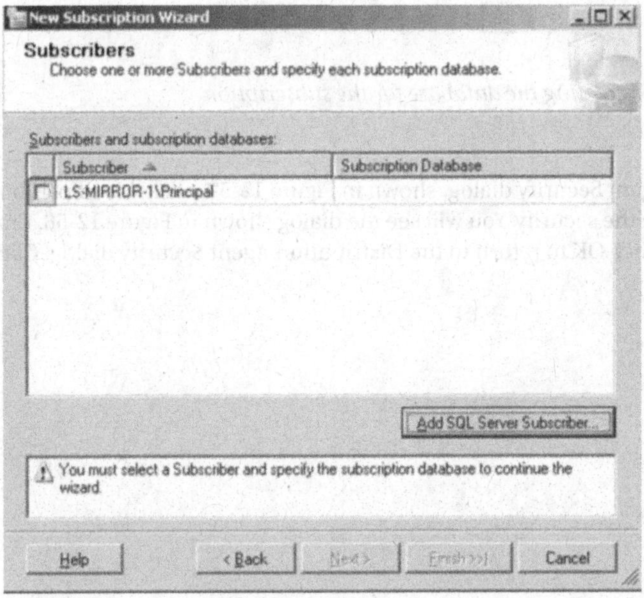

Figure 12-55. *Subscribers dialog*

5. Once you connect to the new Subscriber, you must select which database will be used. If you select the option to create a new database, you will be prompted for the parameters for that new database. An example is shown in Figure 12-56. Once you are finished selecting the database to use, click Next.

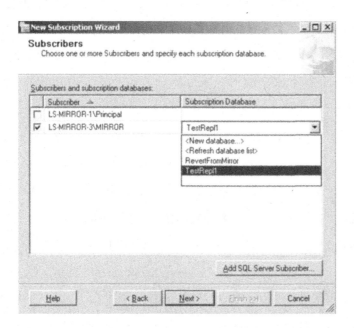

Figure 12-56. *Selecting or creating the database for the subscription*

6. On the Distribution Agent Security dialog, shown in Figure 12-57, click the ellipsis button as prompted to configure the security. You will see the dialog shown in Figure 12-58. Enter your security settings and click OK to return to the Distribution Agent Security dialog. Click Next.

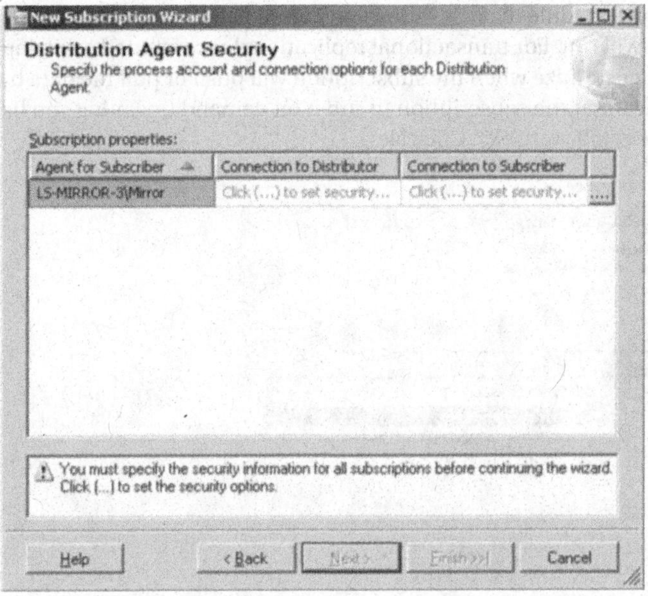

Figure 12-57. *Distribution Agent Security dialog*

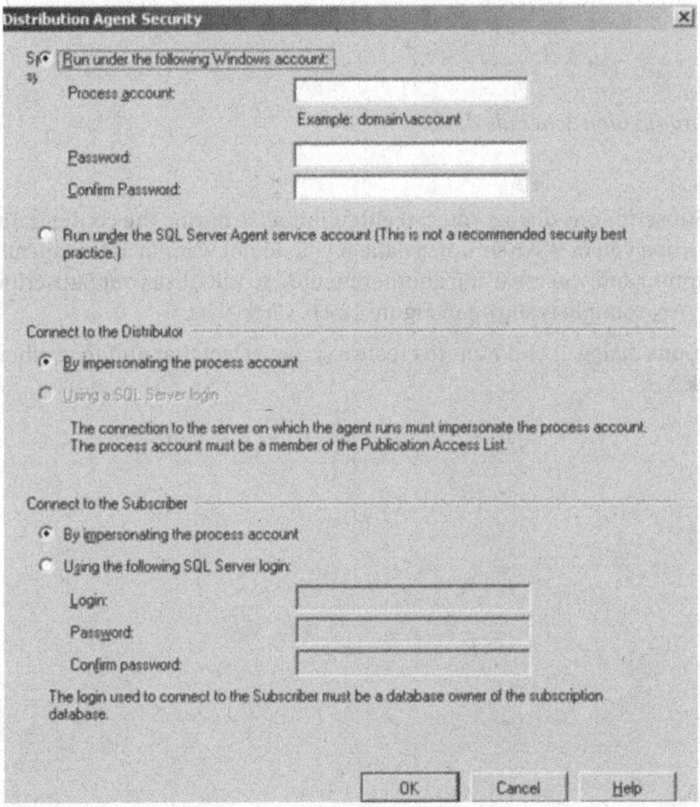

Figure 12-58. *Dialog to specify the security required for distribution*

7. On the Synchronization Schedule dialog as shown in Figure 12-59, you will choose how often the subscription will run. For transactional replication, I recommend selecting Run Continuously. You can customize when the subscription will push or pull the data by defining a schedule, or you can set the subscription to run it on demand (meaning you have to run the SQL Server Agent job yourself). Click Next.

Figure 12-59. *Synchronization Schedule dialog*

8. On the Initialize Subscriptions dialog, you can either initialize during the configuration (immediately) or when you first synchronize data. If you do not want to automatically initialize the subscription and you are using another method to initialize your Subscriber, deselect Initialize. An example is shown in Figure 12-60. Click Next.

9. On the Wizard Actions dialog, if you want to create a script, select that option, as shown in Figure 12-61. Click Next.

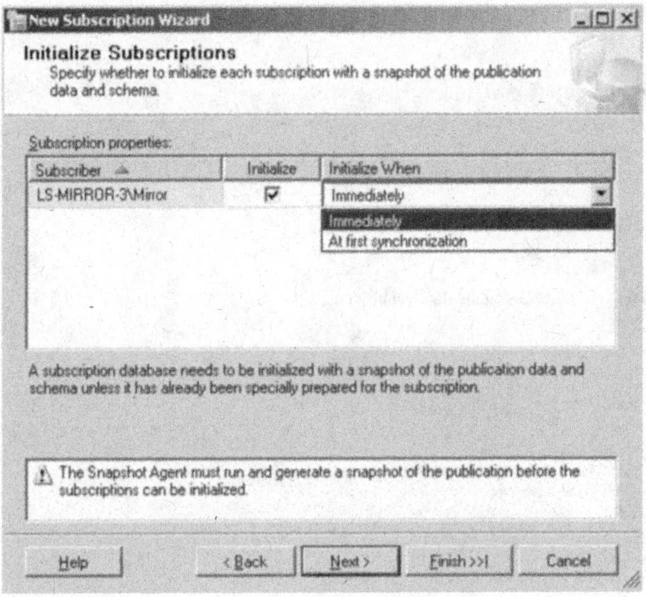

Figure 12-60. *Initialize Subscriptions dialog*

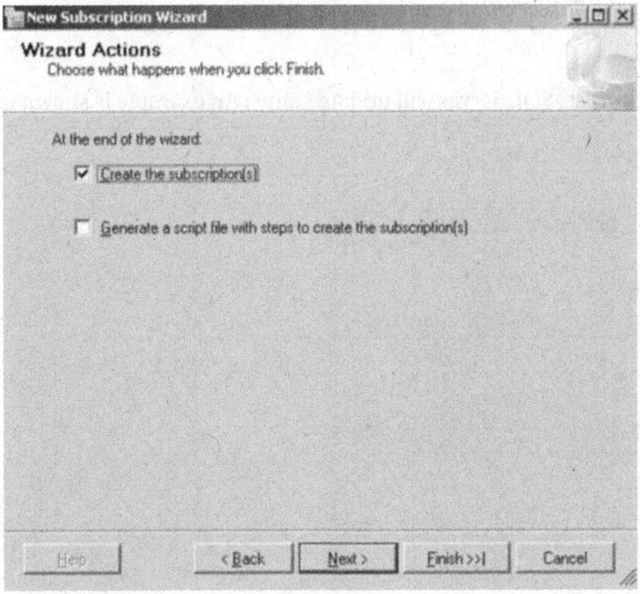

Figure 12-61. *Wizard Actions dialog*

10. On the Complete the Wizard dialog, shown in Figure 12-62, click Finish.

Figure 12-62. *Completing the Subscription configuration process*

During the configuration process, SQL Server will update status. An example is shown in Figure 12-63.

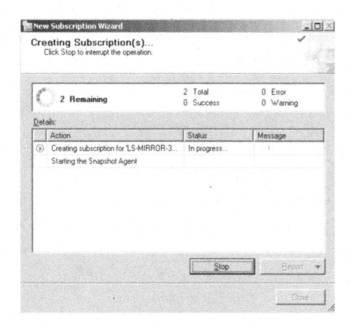

Figure 12-63. *Displaying the progress of the Subscription configuration*

When the configuration is successful, you will see a dialog similar to the one in Figure 12-64. Click Close.

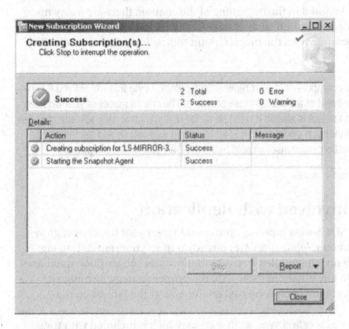

Figure 12-64. *Successful completion of adding a Subscriber*

PROGRAMMING AND REPLICATION

SQL Server gives you the ability to write code to configure, maintain, and monitor replication through some of your own custom applications. For example, if you have a replication topology that has a server-to-client portion, and you want to give the client—which may be a server, laptop, or workstation—the ability to resynchronize the data via a snapshot, you can use the programming functionality built into SQL Server to achieve that. It is outside the scope of this book and definitely outside the scope of this chapter to get into programming with replication using managed code or some other sort of formal programming language. You will notice that I do cover some scripting via Transact-SQL and stored procedures. This is something I would expect DBAs to encounter. I have not covered all of the possibilities even with Transact-SQL. See the topic "Replication System Stored Procedures (Transact-SQL)" in SQL Server 2005 Books Online for a full list of all of the stored procedures that are used or can be used with repli- cation. I don't expect every DBA to be using stored procedures such as sp_register_custom_scripting or sp_lookupcustomresolver, nor do I expect them to be coding custom code (in Visual Basic or some other lan- guage) to create a component for conflict resolution. For complete information on coding for replication, consult the SQL Server 2005 Books Online topic "Planning for Replication Programming."

Administering Replication

Once you configure replication, you will need to make sure it is up and running, as well as possibly perform other administrative tasks. As noted in the beginning of the chapter, there are many more in-depth resources for information on replication such as the SQL Server Books Online topic "Administering Replication." This section covers the most relevant topics that relate to availability.

Tip It is imperative that you script *every* component in your replication topology. Doing this will aid you if you need to reconfigure replication, and in the event of a disaster, these scripts will be crucial pieces of your disaster recovery plan. This means that any time an object is altered it must be scripted. If you have daily schema changes, you are generating new scripts after the schema is updated. This is a big reason why you should get things right as much as possible up front in any application; otherwise, it could make the DBA's life a living nightmare.

Backing Up Databases Involved with Replication

Once replication is involved in your SQL Server topology, you need to treat your backups slightly differently. As noted earlier in this chapter, replication may already impact your transaction log, which will affect how you can back it up. The publication, distribution, and subscription databases should all be backed up as you would any other database with the proper strategy. Although it should already be done, if it was not, you must back up master and msdb at the Publisher, the Distributor, and all Subscribers.

One option you should be aware of is called sync with backup, which is included with transactional replication. If you do not set this option on the publication or distribution databases (or one but not the other), you are at risk of them being inconsistent. With this option, you could still incur data loss, but you will at least be consistent, which is crucial. For example, while you would lose all transactions since the last transaction log backup if the drive containing the transaction log of the Publisher fails, since those transactions would not be at the Distributor yet, your publication and distribution databases would still be in sync. If you set sync with backup on the publication database, there may be some latency since the transactions will not move to the distribution database until they are backed up at the publication database. So if you never take a transaction log backup and you set sync with backup, your Subscriber will never get updated. Unless you have a valid reason to not set sync with backup on the distribution database, it should always be configured. To check whether sync with backup is set on your publication or distribution databases, execute the following command:

```
select databasepropertyex('db_name', 'IsSyncWithBackup')
```

An example output is shown in Figure 12-65. If the value is 0, sync with backup is not set. If the value is 1, sync with backup is set. If sync with backup is not set, as shown in Figure 12-65, enter the following Transact-SQL command to configure it:

```
sp_replicationdboption @db_name = 'db_name',
    @optname = 'sync with backup',
    @value = 'true'
```

Once you run the command and get back the response Command(s) completed successfully, rerun the query to check to see that the option is set.

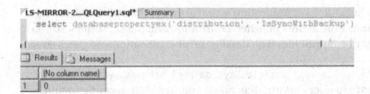

Figure 12-65. *Checking to see if sync with backup is set*

Tip For more information and specific steps, see the SQL Server Books Online topics "Strategies for Backing Up and Restoring Snapshot and Transactional Replication" and "Strategies for Backing Up and Restoring Merge Replication." Pay attention to the restoration portions of these topics because they can guide you through the right way to restore a replicated environment.

Monitoring Replication

Arguably the most important aspect of administering replication is ensuring that it is up and running. The biggest portion of this is monitoring all of the components of the topology. I am not just talking about seeing that SQL Server itself is up, but checking every job, every agent, and so on.

The first place you should probably look to see if everything is functioning properly is in Replication Monitor, shown in Figure 12-66. Replication Monitor will tell you a great deal of information about your publications.

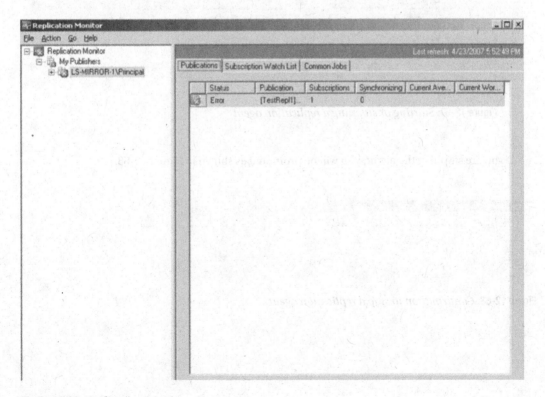

Figure 12-66. *Replication Monitor*

Another important place to check status of replication is the history of the SQL Server Agent jobs that replication uses. These may exist at the Publisher, Distributor, and the Subscriber, so you should look everywhere. There may be output files with detailed error explanations, so check your directories to see if those exist.

Finally, you can use the DMVs sys.dm_repl_articles, sys.dm_repl_schemas, sys.dm_repl_tranhash, and sys.dm_repl_traninfo to query information about your replication configuration. Many monitoring tools such as Microsoft Operations Manager and System Center Operations Manager have the ability to monitor replication as well.

Starting and Stopping a Replication Agent in SQL Server Management Studio

The following instructions tell you how to start and stop the replication agents in SQL Server Management Studio:

1. On the Publisher, as shown in Figure 12-53, select the publication, right-click, and select the option to view the status of the appropriate replication agent.

2. On the dialog with the status of the replication agent, select either Start or Stop. An example is shown in Figure 12-67.

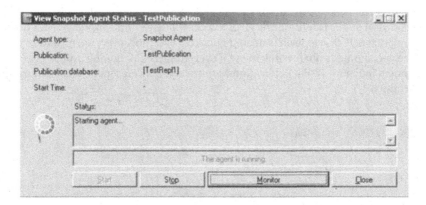

Figure 12-67. *Starting or stopping a replication agent*

If you are stopping the agent, you will be prompted as shown in Figure 12-68.

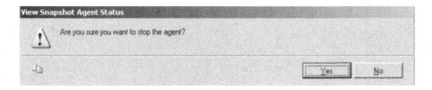

Figure 12-68. *Confirmation to stop a replication agent*

Starting or Stopping a Replication Agent in Replication Monitor

Use the following instructions to start or stop a replication agent using Replication Monitor:

1. Start Replication Monitor.
2. Expand all trees until you find your publication. Select the publication.
3. In the right pane, select the Warnings and Alerts tab.
4. Right-click the agent, and from the context menu select either Start Agent or Stop Agent. An example is shown in Figure 12-69.

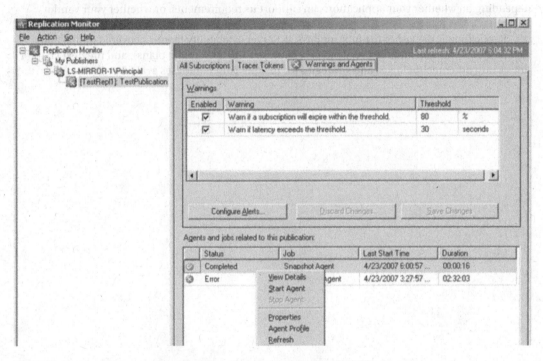

Figure 12-69. *Starting or stopping a replication agent in Replication Monitor*

■**Tip** Always remember to set alerts and thresholds for your replication jobs and other aspects of replication so you can be notified when a problem occurs. You don't want to discover after the fact that replication is failing, because the mess will be much worse.

Summary

Replication is somewhat different than pure availability features such as failover clustering, log shipping, and database mirroring since you can control at a much more granular level what data you make available. Replication is somewhat misunderstood since it does have so many uses that do not relate to availability and is frequently confused with and compared to log shipping and database mirroring. In the right architecture, replication can complement your SQL Server deployments and enhance the value of your application. Whether you choose snapshot, merge, or transactional replication, you will need to take into account the different set of considerations, challenges, and administration points for each. The reality is also that replication may not be an option for you, depending on whether your application can support its requirements, or whether your vendor allows it.

Replication is the last of the four major SQL Server availability features covered in this book (in addition to backup and restore, which is common to all availability plans), and the next chapter delves into other technologies and strategies for making your databases available.

■ ■ ■

CHAPTER 13

Making Your Data Available

Besides the standard SQL Server high availability technologies that consumed the bulk of the chapters before this one, there are other methodologies you can use to make your data available. Some may not seem like obvious choices, such as the applications you use, partitioning, database snapshots, and using multiple read-only databases. When it comes to availability, you should explore every option. This chapter will guide you through some of the not-so-obvious ways to make your data available.

Note Some of these methods are more developer-specific, and I will not go into extreme detail since developing applications for SQL Server is outside the scope of this book, which is IT-focused. This chapter provides the information you need to work with your developers or if you are a developer, things to think about.

The Application

One of the easiest ways to help make your databases available is to ensure that you understand how the application layer interacts with the database back end. The biggest barrier I often see is the flexibility (or lack thereof) in the application itself. You are probably asking yourself, if you are more of an infrastructure person or a DBA, why you would care about the application when you only implement and administer the back end. If you are a developer, you may have the misguided impression that high availability is only an IT problem. Unfortunately, your application is only as good as its weakest link; and in my experience, the weakest link can be (and often is) the application that the back end uses. The back end may not be perfect, but it will be the equivalent of a paperweight if the application cannot take advantage of it. Even worse, what if it cannot work with your existing infrastructure?

There are two ways applications make their way into your ecosystem: they are either developed in-house, or they are acquired. These applications may also use other packaged products or middleware as part of the overall application architecture, so even in a custom application there may be acquisitions. This means that your availability will only be as good as your weakest subcomponent, which may not even be written by you. If you purchase your application from a third-party vendor, you have little control over how it is designed, except for customizing some superficial parts such as the interface or adding columns to a database schema. There are two main challenges you are facing:

- As an administrator, you are rarely (if ever) involved in the decisions around the purchasing of the application, so you have little insight into how the application works.

- As a consequence of the previous point, you are forced to make the application work in your environment. Deployment is obviously easier said than done, and you always have to make the best of a bad situation if you have no involvement early on.

Making Third-Party Applications Available

Third-party applications are what they are—you did not make them, so you are stuck with how the application is designed and can be deployed. It is in your best interests to either be involved in the decision-making process to influence what is purchased, or at least be in the loop early enough so that you can understand how you need to architect your infrastructure to meet your availability needs in a way that is compatible with the application and fits into your way of doing business. The application choice will absolutely limit what technologies you can use. For example, if the standard in your environment for primary SQL Server availability is failover clustering, and this new application does not support its application deployed with a clustered back end, what are you going to do? While the application may work on a clustered back end, do you take the chance and possibly end up in a state where you are unsupported by the vendor? If you do that, you put your company (and possibly your job) at risk. You may need to develop a new standard that uses as much of your existing processes and standards while changing them where appropriate.

When I am onsite with a client, I am often asked to help them do exactly what I described in the previous paragraph: just make it work. I am always amazed at how stubborn some companies are in their drive to stick to the party line. They seem hell-bent on disregarding the vendor's documentation and best practices on how the software must be deployed. Instead, they insist that it *has* to work in the way they deploy things now, based on their own internal standards.

I will admit that sometimes you can make the square peg fit through the round hole (with a lot of effort and risk involved), but 9.9 times out of 10, it is impossible. The best example of this I find often is how some software integrates with your existing administration processes, such as doing your backups. As I noted in Chapter 3, BizTalk has its own way of doing backups, and if you deviate from it, you could potentially put yourself in an unsupported position. This is not something the DBAs and backup administrators should find out as an "oh by the way" when the software is about to be deployed. They may have no choice in supporting it, but the more time that is spent evaluating the solution will allow for more discovery and proper planning for these types of issues.

The ultimate decision should be influenced by those who actually do the implementation to determine what the appropriate solution is and the risks involved if they decide not to implement what is supported. As a consultant, all I can ever do when I go onsite is make recommendations and it is up to the customer to make the ultimate decision to do their own thing, follow my suggestion, or come up with some other way. All I can tell you is that it is much easier to know your restrictions and work with them than fight them.

Making Custom Applications Available

Custom applications are a whole different ballgame. Since you theoretically have control over all aspects of the design, it should be a perfect fit for your database back end, right? Wrong. How many times do you see the system administrators or DBAs involved in the design phase? It is definitely a small percentage of the time since deployment is just an IT problem, right? Most companies do not foster communication between developers and IT, and neither group tends to initiate it either. That's a problem only you can solve.

However, what developers can do is build high availability into the application. The following list describes some ways you can do that. The items listed are general high availability application development best practices since technology-specific material has been covered in the previous chapters:

- Never hard-code anything into the application itself such as server names, SQL Server instance names, protocols, database names, usernames, passwords, authentication methods, or IP addresses. This makes your application inflexible and can possibly prevent you from using a standby server with another name. Use standard technologies such as ODBC DSNs or secured configuration files for connections since they allow for easy reconfiguration. The flip side of this is that if you are coding an application that is installed on every desktop, you may have to touch every desktop or implement some magic mechanism to allow the desktops to search for a new configuration in a server-down situation to repoint the application to the new data source, so you should make every effort possible to keep these types of configurations at a server level. For example, you may have a Registry key that points to a server application that provides a downloaded table for all the proper IP addresses or server names of the application. The worst-case scenario for this example is that you can send an e-mail containing a new .reg file that the user can just click to update the Registry key to regain access to the application.

- Create solid requirements to guide the development process and encourage everyone to ask questions if you do not understand something. Words on a page are just that—words on a page. If you interpret them wrong, it could be an expensive mistake to have to completely redo all of your work. A developer must understand the business requirement that is driving the technical requirement that dictates how the code will be written.

- Code your application so it can play nicely with other databases; or if you do not, make sure it is well-documented in the design and requirements documents as to why this database needs to be on its own and cannot exist in a shared SQL Server environment. To assume that your application will get its own dedicated SQL Server instance, let alone its own server may not be something your company wants. There are some cases where this cannot be avoided, but do your best since it leads to problems down the road for administrators. The one database, one instance, one server mentality is old-school SQL Server thinking and needs to be updated. Remember that even if this is the current plan, the future may involve server consolidation that would affect your application's database.

- Design the application for performance. Performance is a key aspect of availability, and poor performance can lead to perceived availability problems. Allow the DBAs to help you set up your development and test environments so they resemble what the back end might really look like. Do you really think that all applications should have their databases deployed to the C:\ drive in the default data and log locations along with every other database? Do you see where that could be a problem?

- Make the application flexible enough to do tasks such as handling back end failures gracefully and have some sort of retry logic to allow the application to reconnect to the back end without having to restart the application. Too many applications I see out there die if there is a failure on the back end, which creates an unpleasant end user experience. Making the application fault tolerant can be anything from a lightweight retry to a full application workflow implementation, whatever is most appropriate for your needs. Also, remember to create application-level logging, and possibly also monitor alerts for these failures along with the application's ability to automatically try to reconnect to the database server.

- Understand that every feature and function you add may mean a headache on the back end. For example, if you decide to employ replication as part of the application, talk to the DBAs to see what kind of impact it may have on them. If you work with them to ensure that the technology is not implemented in a way that causes them anguish, chances are they will not be blaming you for the pain you have made them feel once the application is in production.

- Make it easy in a disaster scenario to identify where you are at from a data perspective. This means that within your application, you need to quickly determine who has the latest copy of the data. Finding out whether any specific server has any transactions stored that have not been applied to all places arguably represents the most important first step in the disaster recovery. The DBA generally is not as intimate with your application and its data. After a problem, the business also wants to know what data may have been lost. Application-level logging can assist here, so you may want to consider building it into your custom applications. The fact still remains that there needs to be a straightforward way to ensure that after a disaster you know where you are and the business has confidence in the data being used.

- If you know you are using a specific availability technology on the back end, code the proper support for it into the application. For example, it is not the cluster's fault if your application goes belly-up in a failover. The cluster did what it is supposed to; your application did not. Putting in retry logic in this case may work, but a better option would be to code the application to use the clustering API of Windows.

Caution Although I talk about security in Chapter 15, this seems like an appropriate time to caution anyone developing custom applications to not use any accounts with sa privileges in SQL Server. It infuriates me to see applications that require full administrative (sa) privileges or database owner (dbo) membership in SQL Server to work. No application should require these escalated rights in SQL Server. That is horrible coding and indicates that no effort was put into making the application use the lowest amount of privileges needed. Security is a key aspect of maintaining availability, and if you are unnecessarily escalating rights because you developed the application on your own machine, shame on you. You may also be guilty of other violations, such as not being SOX compliant since you are giving logins and users rights that they do not really need.

I apologize to the developers who are availability-savvy, but to be honest, most developers I have encountered over the years are so worried about delivering features and functions that they have no time to think about (or learn about) how to develop code to easily and safely deploy an application. Forget about patching or updating an application without affecting availability; this is usually never baked into the requirements and is more often than not an afterthought. It is one thing to build an application that works well with high availability technologies, but part of that has to be how it is deployed and patched later on.

A lot of downtime is caused by application updates that are poorly thought out. The ones that are really bad have no way to be backed out and your only recourse is to restore the entire database from your backups. I've seen it happen. In Chapter 1 I talked about the importance of having proper development, testing, and staging environments to complement a production environment. I cannot stress enough how important this is since those are your last lines of defense before the application's data and its operations become your problem. One client I worked with had a process for updating data in the tables where they had to drop the database and recreate it in a version upgrade, thereby losing all their current data. Until we tried to get it to work in production, no one had thought that design would be a problem.

Getting In on the Ground Floor

Here's the bottom line: if you are an administrator (DBA or not), you must find a way to insert yourself into the process much earlier. I would venture to guess that you are only involved as the application is nearly ready to be deployed in production. By then it is too late; you will most likely be making a ton of compromises or trying to make something work that is not matched to the task and you wind up with a fragile deployment waiting to fail.

If you are a developer or someone who is involved in the acquisition of a third-party application, have some compassion on your IT staff; make it a point to get them involved or at least give them a heads-up on what will be coming their way. I dare you to sit in with the DBAs and watch them try to administer your handiwork. I'll bet you would view your code in a much different light if you saw how difficult the application is to support day in and day out.

Partitioning Your Data

One of the most overlooked ways to make your data available is *partitioning* your data—breaking it up into smaller chunks in a logical way. Partitioning data is far from a new concept, but a very powerful one when used properly. Partitioning is traditionally used for scale-out solutions and usually is not thought of when it comes to availability. If you use a form of partitioning for your data, it will absolutely affect how you administer and configure your databases and servers. The reality is that as databases become VLDBs, it will be nearly impossible to get any kind of performance or availability without doing some sort of partitioning. You can split your database by placing objects on a specific filegroup; partitioning the schema of the database; using partitioned views; and using data dependent routing.

Note If you are considering partitioning your databases, it is something that must be taken into account in the design stage. Developers cannot assume that the DBAs have the ability to partition a database after it is already in production. Partitioning also has to be supported in the application for it to work. If you want to partition using a third-party application, check with the vendor to ensure it supports what you are trying to do. Also, note in the following sections that certain features will require the use of SQL Server 2005 Enterprise Edition to work. If you are planning on using the features that require it, it will absolutely impact what version of SQL Server 2005 is eventually deployed.

Creating Objects on a Specific Filegroup

SQL Server has included the ability to create an index or a table on a specific filegroup. When you create a table with CREATE TABLE or an index with CREATE INDEX, there is an ON clause that you can use that tells SQL Server which filegroup to place a table or index in. While this is not technically partitioning in the traditional sense, it is a valid method of splitting out an index or a table to create better availability. Performance is usually the reason for going down this road since using a different physical filegroup on separate disks will allow you to split out and isolate your I/O.

The benefit of doing this is discussed in Chapter 3 with regard to file and filegroup backups. If you are physically creating an object on another filegroup, chances are it is your most used table or index. In the backup and eventual restore of the data, it is arguably this table or index that will be one of if not the most important thing to restore along with the primary filegroup. Or you could do the reverse and create all important objects in the primary filegroup and all of the "nonessential" tables in other filegroups. Either way, this method will allow you to control what is backed up and how it can be restored.

One nice thing about this methodology is that it is something that can be implemented even after the database is in place. While you cannot have two objects with the same name in one database, there are ways that you can get around it, such as creating the object with another name and renaming it after you have moved the data from the old object. Other SQL Server features are not as flexible.

For example, you have a B2B order processing system. Your WEB_ORDERS table is not only the most heavily hit table but you must be able to recover the information in that table, otherwise you could potentially lose millions of dollars' worth of transactions. It would be in your best interest to make sure that, if possible, you could find a way to not only make access to the table perform better, but protect it as well. This is where using the ON clause of CREATE TABLE buys you something. The syntax would look something like this:

```
CREATE TABLE MyTable
    (
        <columns go here>
    )
ON [MyNewFilegroup]
GO
```

Figure 13-1 shows how the architecture may actually look. In this example, the MyNewFileGroup filegroup has two physical data files to allow you to evenly spread the I/O load over multiple physical LUNs.

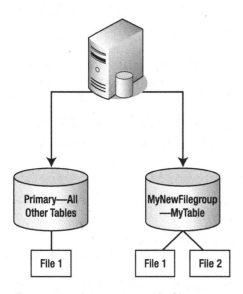

Figure 13-1. *Object on a specific filegroup*

■**Tip** For more information, see the SQL Server 2005 Books Online topics "CREATE INDEX (Transact-SQL)" and "CREATE TABLE (Transact-SQL)".

Partitioning Databases and Indexes with Transact-SQL

New to SQL Server 2005 is the ability to partition tables and indexes when you create the schema. Partitioning your indexes and tables via Transact-SQL is only a feature of SQL Server 2005 Enterprise Edition or Developer Edition. This means that if you plan on implementing any other edition as part of your final deployment, even if you create the application with this feature in mind, it will not work with your deployment.

To partition when your schema is created, you first need to figure out how you want to partition your database. You can have up to 1,000 partitions per table. First, you must create a *partition function*. The partition function tells SQL Server how to place the data in a partition. Assume you are going to partition via last name. Your schema looks like this for a table named App_Names:

```
CREATE TABLE [dbo].[App_Names](
    [NameID] [int] IDENTITY(1,1) NOT NULL,
    [Last_Name] [varchar](30) NOT NULL,
    [First_Name] [varchar](30) NOT NULL
) ON [PRIMARY]
GO
```

You decide that you want the divisions to be A–G, H–N, O–T, and U–Z. What you need to think about here is that when SQL Server partitions its data, these definitions become the ranges. Here is the sample code that defines the ranges:

```
CREATE PARTITION FUNCTION MyPF (varchar(30))
AS RANGE LEFT FOR VALUES ('G','N','T')
```

Now when you create a table that will use this function, your data will be stored in the following manner:

- All values less than or equal to G will be in the first partition.

- All values greater than G but less than or equal to N will be in the second partition.

- All values greater than N but less than or equal to T will be in the third partition.

- All values greater than T will be in the last partition.

Once you create your partition function, make sure that you have a 1:1 ratio of filegroups to partitions. In this case, you have four partitions, so you will need four data filegroups to store the partitioned data. An example is shown in Figure 13-2. These filegroups should be located on physically separate spindles if possible.

Once your filegroups are created, the next step is to create the *partitioning scheme*. The partitioning scheme maps the partitioning to the physical filegroups. The following is the syntax for the partitioning example:

```
CREATE PARTITION SCHEME MyPS
AS PARTITION MyPF
TO ([PRIMARY], SECONDARY, THIRD, FOURTH)
```

At this point, the partitioned table is ready to use. Since the partitioning is based on files and filegroups, you can use a file/filegroup backup scheme and take advantage of a piecemeal restore should that need to happen. There is no easy way to update this partitioning scheme after it is implemented (such as making it A–C, D–F, etc.) other than deleting it and reconfiguring it, so make sure you get it right the first time. Deleting the partition by first using DROP PARTITION SCHEME and then DROP PARTITION FUNCTION is not possible if data has been inserted into the table. You must create a new table or database to accommodate your request.

The biggest benefit is that behind the scenes it is all transparent to the application or the end user. There are no special names or views or other things involved; you just access the table as if it is not partitioned.

Tip For more information, see the topic "Partitioned Tables and Indexes" in SQL Server 2005 Books Online. Also, understanding how hashing algorithms work in SQL Server will help when you are creating your partitioning schemes.

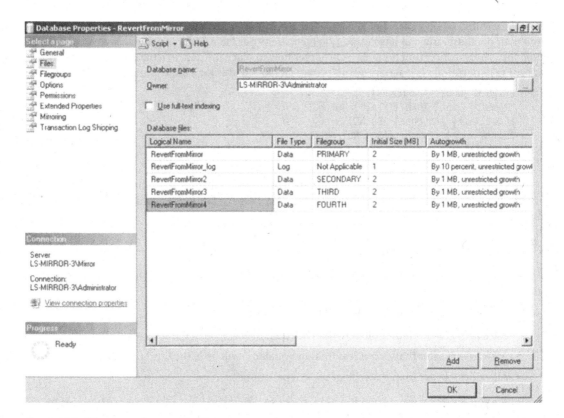

Figure 13-2. *Filegroups for partitioning*

Partitioned Views

Partitioned views have been a feature of SQL Server for quite some time and have been the built-in method for achieving scale-out with SQL Server. The name of the feature gives away how it works: you create a view that encompasses multiple databases (whether they are in the same instance of SQL Server or across multiple instances that could be on the same or different physical servers). If it spans more than one SQL Server instance, a partitioned view is known as a *distributed partitioned view* (DPV). A DPV is also known as a *federation* of database servers. Since we are talking availability, you would not want all of your databases taking part in a partitioned view in a single instance of SQL Server anyway; that defeats the entire purpose. DPVs can only be configured with the Enterprise (or Developer) Edition of SQL Server 2005. Local partitioned views can be configured with any edition. When using partitioned views for availability, I am really talking about using DPVs since it allows you to distribute your data in a way to not create a single point of failure.

Creating a partitioned view is done first by creating linked servers to the other SQL Servers that will be participating in the view. This is done on all instances of SQL Server that will have parts of the view, not just on one. Then use a CREATE VIEW statement that incorporates a UNION ALL as part of the SELECT statement that makes up the view. The following example shows a DPV that spans three different instances of SQL Server:

```
CREATE VIEW MyView
AS
SELECT Col1, Col2
FROM INSTANCE1.MyDB.Owner.MyTable_To100
UNION ALL
SELECT Col1, Col2
FROM INSTANCE2.MyDB.Owner.MyTable_To200
UNION ALL
SELECT Col1, Col2
FROM INSTANCE3.MyDB.Owner.MyTable_To300
GO
```

Tip For this to really work well, you need good network connectivity and bandwidth between the servers.

The underlying tables should be set up with CHECK constraints to limit the values that can be placed in them. Using the previous DPV example definition, you have three tables on three SQL Server instances: MyTable_To100, which contains values up to 100; MyTable_To200, which contains values from 101 to 200; and MyTable_To300, which contains values from 201 to 300. The table creation would look similar to this:

```
CREATE TABLE MyTable_To100
    (
        PartitioningColumn int primary key
        CHECK (PartitioningColumn BETWEEN 1 AND 100)
        <other columns go here>
    )
GO
```

Figure 13-3 is a graphic representation of what a distributed partition view looks like.

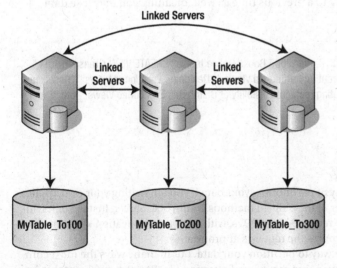

Figure 13-3. *Distributed partition view*

As with creating an object on a specific filegroup, the most common usage of partitioned views is for performance. All tables that are part of the DPV should have the same structure but a different set of data. The application may request data on the entire data range (0–300) from any of these instances. The SQL Server instance will then use the DPV cache information to determine which data lives where and then send a transaction to the other two servers to gather any information required to satisfy your request. After the other instances respond, their data is aggregated with the local data and is finally passed back to the application. The benefit is obvious, but the back end servers wind up doing more work to respond when the data is stored across multiple servers with a DPV.

Because of the way DPVs work, the application should query the server in the federation that actually contains the most data you are looking for. This is usually the difference between an application that performs well and one that does not. If you do not do this, the consequence is that you may actually take an incredibly large performance hit (some colleagues of mine have seen up to a 10x hit) if you are waiting for one of the UNION ALL queries to come back with its results.

If you are a DBA, one of the biggest challenges you have is directly caused by the primary benefit of a DPV: dealing with physically separate entities. How do you make the entire DPV solution highly available when it is really just databases on different instances of SQL Server? How will you restore the individual components of the DPV? With DPVs, if one of the database servers that is defined as part of the view goes down, the DPV is completely unavailable.

The best way to keep your DPV available is to arguably use failover clustering as your primary defense. This way if there is a failure, another node can immediately start the SQL Server instance and you have minimal (if any) interruption to your application. Some may say that failover clustering will not buy you much because failover clustering gives you no scale-out capabilities; but if you are implementing DPVs, most other technologies do not make sense. Does it add a bit of complexity? Yes, but everything has a price.

Because there is no built-in method of synchronization, backing up and restoring the databases is going to be a challenge. If you completely lose one of the databases, you will have the issue I outlined in Chapter 3: how do you restore your databases to one consistent point? Unless you are employing a technique such as log marking, there is no way to do it. It may involve rolling back the other databases taking part in the DPV to a previous time as well, meaning you may lose data across the board.

■**Tip** For more information, consult the SQL Server 2005 Books Online topics "CREATE VIEW (Transact-SQL)," "Creating Distributed Partitioned Views," "Creating Partitioned Views," "Designing Partitioned Views," "Resolving Distributed Partitioned Views," "Troubleshooting Metadata Visibility of Distributed Partitioned Views," and "Federated Database Servers."

Data Dependent Routing

Data dependent routing (DDR) is a way of partitioning your data if you are writing your own application code and do not want to use either of the built-in methods within SQL Server. Instead of having SQL Server track all the data and route requests as in DPVs, with DDR the application keeps track of what data is where and subsequently routes the requests appropriately.

DDR is arguably the most flexible way to partition your data, but in many ways the most complex. With DDR, you would need to have some sort of configuration file, Registry entry, or table in a database that would tell the application where the partitioned data resides. I do not recommend using a Registry entry, but I have seen it done. A file should be placed in a directory that has been locked down; only the application should be able to access it. You do not want anyone coming along and seeing how to get at your data. Putting the routing information in a database table is straightforward, but what happens if the database or server goes down?

When you employ DDR, it means the only link between your databases is the application itself and your routing table or file. If you look at Figure 13-4, it looks similar to what a DPV would look like minus the linked servers. Unlike the built-in methods of partitioning in SQL Server, it allows you to add another database or server easily since all you have to do is update your configuration file or table. Since you have the ability to update the configuration on the fly, you should incur no downtime to update your partitioning scheme. While this method of partitioning can potentially be a lot of work, it could also be very rewarding.

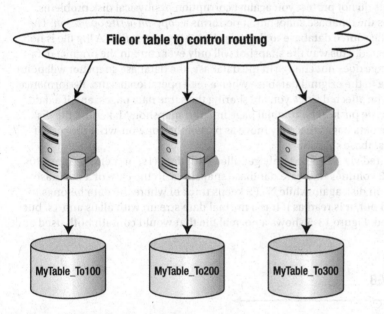

Figure 13-4. *Data dependent routing*

You also have similar issues as with DPVs: how do you make each instance of SQL Server in a DDR configuration available and easy to recover? Since each instance is completely independent, you do not have any linkage other than your definition file or table. You can use whatever method of availability you want to use for each individual instance of SQL Server, but the fact remains that you need to manually synchronize your data to ensure consistency. By no means is that an easy task; and do not assume that the DBAs will know how to understand which data is right and which data is wrong. The application developers should provide scripts to assist in the verification process.

■**Tip** For more information on DDR, see http://www.microsoft.com/technet/prodtechnol/sql/2005/scddrtng.mspx.

Database Snapshots

Database snapshots is a new feature of SQL Server 2005 Enterprise and Developer Editions only. A database snapshot is a read-only, point-in-time "copy" of the source database. This should not be confused with making a hardware-based snapshot as described in Chapter 3. The database snapshot, like a photograph, represents a specific moment in time of your data and is perfect for reporting purposes. This means that when a snapshot is created, it contains all committed transactions in the database up until the point of creation.

From an availability perspective, you can roll your database back to the specific point in time of the snapshot to take into account human error. Although SQL Server 2005 Books Online also lists using database snapshots to create a test database, it is impractical for any tests unless they are read-only. Database snapshots do not protect you against corruption or physical disk problems.

When SQL Server creates the database snapshot, it performs a *copy-on-write operation*. The data pages are copied from the source database to the snapshot using *sparse files*. A log file is not created; only a data file is created. This way the snapshot will only ever contain the original data pages. However, if the data page does not change in the database, the database snapshot will point back to the original data page in the original database when a read operation occurs. Performance on your source database will be affected since you are sharing the same data pages, and if a data page changes, the copy-on-write pushes the original page into the snapshot. Make sure the disk has enough room to store the data pages that may move as part of the copy-on-write process. If not, you will invalidate the database snapshot.

Sparse files are files created via NTFS but only get filled with data (1s), not empty space (0s). You cannot use FAT or FAT32 volumes to create database snapshots. In the case of a database snapshot, the data is stored on disk again while NTFS keeps track of where the data belongs in the file. So when data is read out, it is read as if it is a normal data stream with all 0s and 1s, but only the 1s are actually stored. Figure 13-5 shows a normal file that would contain both used and unused space.

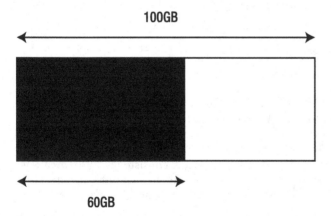

100GB

60GB

Figure 13-5. *Normal file*

Figure 13-6 shows the same file represented as a sparse file, where it would only contain the data. The dotted lines show what the file size would be if it contained the 0s as well.

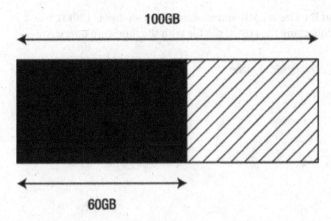

Figure 13-6. *Sparse file*

Sparse files grow in 64KB increments, so you should always format disks that are going to have database snapshots with at least a 64KB block size. To reinforce the concepts that the sparse file only contains the original data pages that have changed, if you look at the properties of the sparse file, you will see its maximum file size on disk is not actually what is stored. In Figure 13-7 you will see two database snapshot files: RFM.ss and RFM2.ss.

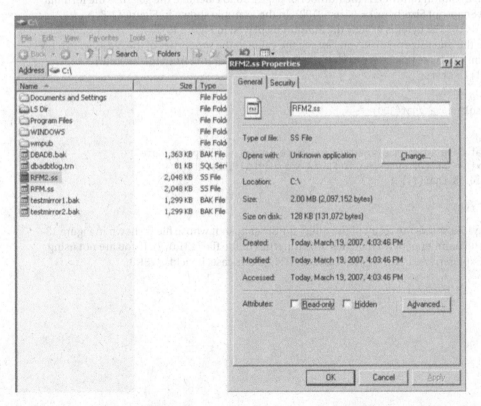

Figure 13-7. *Database snapshot files*

The properties of RFM2.ss show that the size is 2MB; but its actual size on disk is 128KB. You can also calculate the maximum size by querying the size of the file with the following query. An example is also shown in Figure 13-8.

```
select b.[name], a.file_id, a.[size], a.physical_name
from sys.master_files a, sys.databases b
where b.database_id = a.database_id
and b.[name] = 'Snapshot_Name'
```

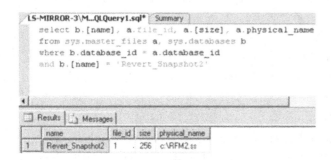

Figure 13-8. *Results of querying the file size*

The size column returned is the number of pages. So to calculate the size, use the formula Maximum Snapshot Size(bytes) = (size * 8192). In the example shown in Figure 13-8, 256 * 8192 = 2097152 bytes is exactly the amount displayed in Figure 13-7.

To see the exact size on disk, you can see the value in the properties of the file as shown previously, or you can issue this query to view the BytesOnDisk column from the function fn_virutalfilestats:

```
DECLARE @db_id int
DECLARE @sqltxt varchar(300)

SET @db_id =
(select database_id from sys.databases where [name] = 'Snapshot_Name')
SET @sqltxt = 'SELECT BytesOnDisk FROM ::fn_virtualfilestats(' +
CAST(@db_id as char(1)) + ',1)'

exec (@sqltxt)
```

Figure 13-9 shows the result of the query for the snapshot whose file is shown in Figure 13-7. Note that the number of bytes matches the properties of the file (131,072). If you are not using Windows Explorer, size in KB = BytesOnDisk/1024. In this case, it yields 128KB.

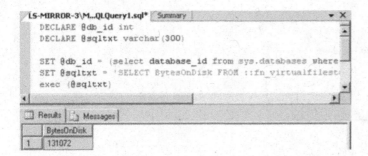

Figure 13-9. *Results of querying fn_virtualfilestats for a database snapshot*

Creating a Database Snapshot

The only way to create a database snapshot is to use Transact-SQL. The syntax for creating the database snapshot is similar to creating a database. The following syntax sums up how to do it. You cannot drop, detach, or restore a database while a database snapshot is in place on the source database, nor can you create a database snapshot on the system databases:

```
CREATE DATABASE Snapshot_Name ON
(
    NAME = Data_File_For_Source_Database,
    FILENAME = 'Path_and_file_name_for_sparse_file'
)
AS SNAPSHOT OF Source_Database
GO
```

So if you have a database named MyDB whose data file is MyDB_Data, your syntax would look like this:

```
CREATE DATABASE MyDB_Snapshot ON
(
    NAME = MyDB_Data,
    FILENAME = 'c:\SQLData\MyDB_Snapshot.ss'
)
AS SNAPSHOT OF MyDB
GO
```

Once the snapshot is created, you can view it and the objects in it as you would a regular database. It can be found under the Database Snapshots folder in SQL Server Management Studio. An example is shown in Figure 13-10. If you want a text-based list of the database snapshots, you can execute the following query:

```
SELECT a.[name] as Snapshot, b.[name] as Source_DB
FROM SYS.DATABASES a, SYS.DATABASES b
WHERE a.database_id = b.source_database_id
```

You can create as many database snapshots on a given database, provided you have the physical storage available to do so. It also means that the storage you use for the database snapshot must be attached to the instance that contains the source database, so you cannot create a snapshot of a source database on another instance. This also means that when applications or end users access the database snapshot, it will consume resources on the same instance. This could be a potential problem for instances that are already overloaded, so performance has to be a consideration when you want to deploy a database snapshot. As noted in Chapter 12, this is one of the best features of database mirroring: you can create a database snapshot on the mirror. An example is shown in Figure 13-11.

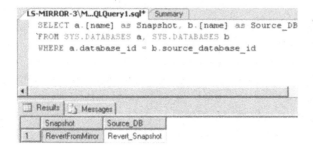

Figure 13-10. *Querying the snapshots*

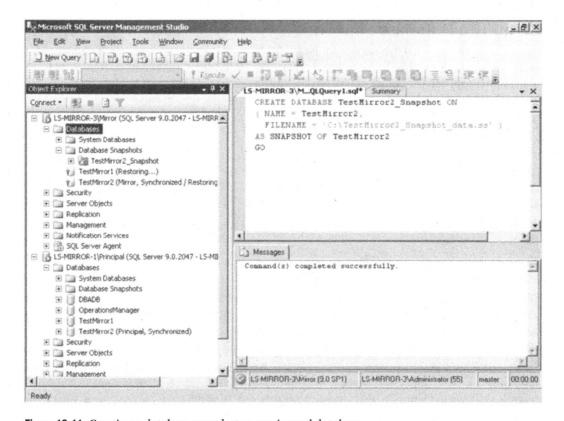

Figure 13-11. *Creating a database snapshot on a mirrored database*

Database Snapshot Administration

This section documents the various tasks you may need for administering your database snapshot.

Deleting a Database Snapshot

You have two ways of deleting a snapshot: either through Management Studio or Transact-SQL.

SQL Server Management Studio

To delete a snapshot using SQL Server Management Studio, follow these instructions:

1. Start SQL Server Management Studio and connect to the instance with the database snapshot.

2. Expand the Database Snapshots folder.

3. Select the snapshot you would like to delete. Right-click, and select Delete as shown in Figure 13-12.

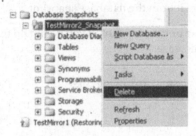

Figure 13-12. *Delete menu option*

4. On the Delete Object dialog, shown in Figure 13-13, click OK.

5. Refresh the Database Snapshots folder to verify that the database snapshot no longer exists.

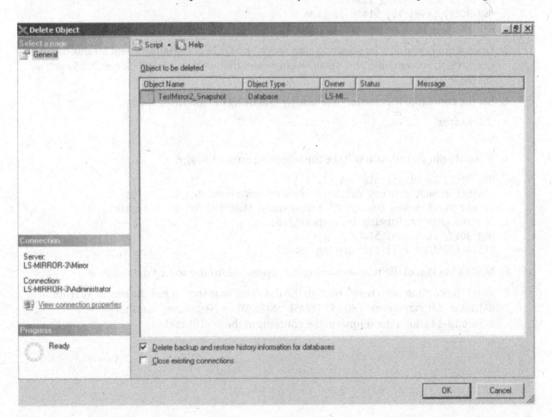

Figure 13-13. *Delete Object dialog*

Transact-SQL

To delete a snapshot using Transact-SQL, execute the following:

```
DELETE DATABASE Snapshot_Name
GO
```

Reverting the Source Database to an Earlier Point Using a Database Snapshot

If you encounter a data problem in your database and you are using database snapshots, instead of restoring the database from a backup file, you can restore it from the database snapshot.

1. Ensure all users are not using the source database or the snapshot. If you do not do this, you will see something similar to this sample error message:

```
Msg 5070, Level 16, State 2, Line 1
Database state cannot be changed while other users are using the
database 'RevertFromMirror'
Msg 3013, Level 16, State 1, Line 1
RESTORE DATABASE is terminating abnormally
```

2. Delete all snapshots on the database that you will not be restoring from. If you do not delete additional snapshots, you will see this error message during the restore process:

```
Msg 3137, Level 16, State 4, Line 1
Database cannot be reverted. Either the primary or the snapshot names
are improperly specified, all other snapshots have not been dropped,
or there are missing files.
Msg 3013, Level 16, State 1, Line 1
RESTORE DATABASE is terminating abnormally.
```

3. Open a query window by selecting New Query in SQL Server Management Studio, or connect to SQL Server using your favorite query tool that works with SQL Server 2005 such as sqlcmd.

4. Set the context to the master database by executing the following query:

```
USE master
GO
```

If you do not do this, you will see the following error message:

```
Msg 3102, Level 16, State 1, Line 1
RESTORE cannot process database 'RevertFromMirror' because it is
in use by this session. It is recommended that the master database
be used when performing this operation.
Msg 3013, Level 16, State 1, Line 1
RESTORE DATABASE is terminating abnormally.
```

5. Make a backup of the transaction log if it is possible for the source database.

6. Enter the command to revert back to the database snapshot. It has the syntax `RESTORE DATABASE database_name FROM DATABASE_SNAPSHOT = 'Database_Snapshot_Name'`. Figure 13-14 shows the output of the contents of the NewTbl table.

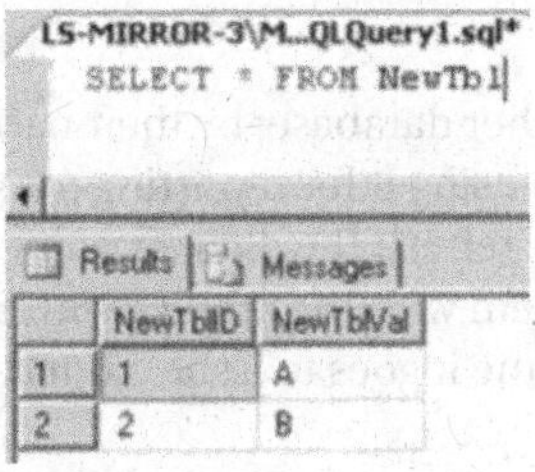

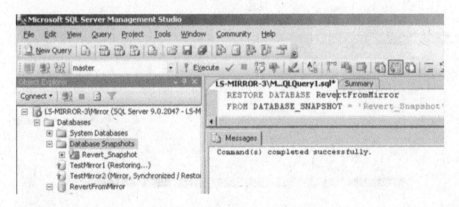

Figure 13-14. *Output of the table contents prior to creating the database snapshot*

Figure 13-15 inserts a row into the table and displays the results after the insert. At this point, I created a snapshot.

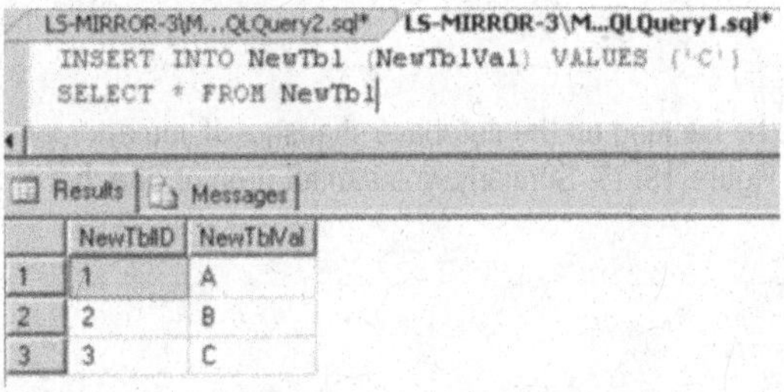

Figure 13-15. *Inserting a new value into the table*

Figure 13-16 reverts the database back to the database snapshot. If you query the results after reverting, it looks just like the output in Figure 13-14.

Figure 13-16. *Reverting to the point prior to the snapshot where the row was not inserted*

Applications and Database Snapshots

Applications access database snapshots just like they would any other database: by their names. The problem is that because it is a static view of the data, if you are using it for reporting purposes, at some point the data will become stale. You will have to manually refresh the data, or come up with an automated process to refresh the snapshot data. The problem with the application is that it is probably expecting the same database snapshot name every time it goes to issue a query. The only way to do this is to follow these steps:

1. Create a SQL Server Agent job.
2. For the first job step, delete the existing snapshot.
3. For the second job step, recreate the snapshot.

Schedule the job to run as frequently as you need it to, taking into account how long it actually takes to create the snapshot, but realize that during these times, applications dependent upon the snapshot for data will not work properly.

■**Note** It is not possible to back up the source database by backing up the database snapshot. If you attempt to do it, you will see something similar to the message in Figure 13-17. Similarly, you cannot drop or attach a database snapshot.

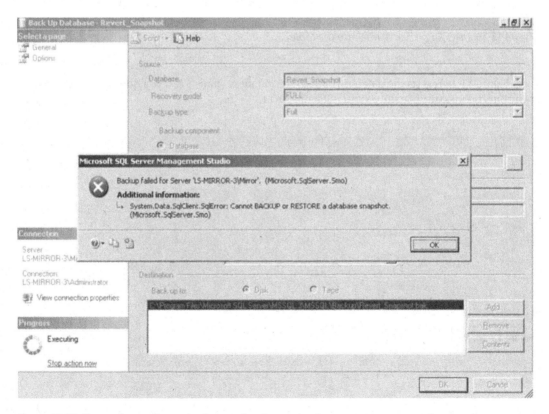

Figure 13-17. *Error when trying to back up a database snapshot*

Using Multiple Read-Only Databases

Up to this point, you have seen various methods for making your databases and applications more available. The last method I will describe is one that you may not think of using: multiple read-only databases. Each database would be an exact copy of the other and it would not matter which one users or applications use to query data. This method has specific scenarios where it can be appropriately used. A good example of such a scenario is a catalog server for an e-commerce site, or some sort of company intranet where you have the same data accessed by many people. While the databases themselves would need to be updated and written to periodically, from an end-user application access method, they are read-only. This means that you can scale out to the maximum ability of the technology you use to employ your multiple read-only databases.

The biggest benefit to this scenario (assuming your application supports it) is that if part of your SQL Server farm goes down, your application would still be able to function. This means that you could also perform maintenance, such as applying service packs, in a selected fashion and not have a total outage of your application and database farm. It would mean that not all of your servers would be completely at the same patch level; but for read-only data, it would be a small risk, as long as all servers could be accessed.

The problem with using multiple read-only databases is this: how do you synchronize all of the databases? There are definitely challenges involved in this process. First of all, what technology would you use to synchronize the database copies? The two most logical technologies are backup/ restore and replication. Backing up the source database on a frequent basis, copying it to multiple destinations, and then restoring the database is a lot of work, especially if the database size is fairly large. Snapshot or merge replication make the most sense for updating these read-only databases since you either want a full refresh or a partial refresh. Because this read-only database is most likely a subset of the source database, you don't need to worry about having every bit of data that exists in the source database also in the read-only copy.

For your application to be able to access the multiple databases, you need to use some sort of load balancer (such as Microsoft's own Network Load Balancing clusters in Windows or a hardware-based load balancer) placed in front of the SQL Server farm. The architecture would look similar to the one shown in Figure 13-18.

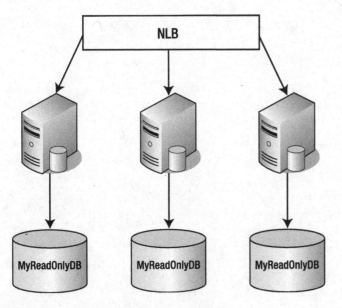

Figure 13-18. *Multiple read-only databases*

Caution Remember that each of these databases is read-only. You should only have one master copy of the data where inserts, updates, and deletes are allowed. Do not accidentally update data at one of the databases that gets overwritten.

Summary

While backup/restore, failover clustering, log shipping, database mirroring, and replication may be at the top of the food chain in terms of mindshare, there are other ways to make your data available. Partitioning, multiple read-only databases, and database snapshots all can be used to increase the availability of your databases outside the realm of the obvious availability features. When it comes to availability, all of your options should be on the table, and some should even be considered at design time, such as partitioning and database snapshots. This chapter ends the section of the book that is focused specifically on features. The rest of the book focuses on deploying and administering a highly available solution.

PART 3

■ ■ ■

Administration for High Availability

Now that you have learned about individual technologies, it is time to put the pieces of the puzzle together. You do not live in a world where you are only dealing with, say, failover clustering or log shipping. You design, administer, and maintain solutions. This last section of the book will now take you on the journey of how to turn the past 13 chapters into a true 24x7 environment.

CHAPTER 14

▰ ▰ ▰

Designing High Availability Solutions

This chapter is where the payoff happens: where you can put all your knowledge to work for you. One of the reasons I spent the past few hundred pages concentrating on the technical is that by the time you got here, you would understand how each of the technologies works, as well as their deployment, implementation, and administration. Without that foundation, you cannot even begin to put together your solution. This chapter will do its best to convey the thought processes that I go through when working with clients, but it is hard to cram all my years of experience into a few pages of text. This chapter will not cover every single individual SQL Server feature such as Notification Services and SSIS. I am focusing more on the database and full instance level, which is where most people need the protection.

What High Availability Technology Should You Use?

If I had a dollar for every time I'm asked by a customer what they should use to make their SQL Servers highly available, I'd be independently wealthy. The answer is the one I keep stressing all throughout this book: it depends on your situation. I apologize to those who may be a bit put off by that, but it is 100% honest. No one technology is necessarily better than another; it just depends on what you are trying to achieve and what rules govern your implementation.

Before I give any examples or implementation considerations, you will notice that I pretty much avoided direct technology comparisons in the other chapters. That was on purpose; I wanted the comparison piece of the puzzle to be presented in one place, after you have a full understanding of the various individual technologies. Had I done comparisons earlier in the book, it would have taken focus from the content.

I'm sure many of you have seen the Microsoft slide decks that compare most of the main technologies presented in this book. I do have to be honest here—I've had some difficulty with some of that content over the years. While it's accurate in a literal and absolute sense, I have never found it to be a true reflection in all cases of where, when, and how the technologies are deployed in the real world. My major problem with most of the content out there is that it tries to label the technologies with such terms as *instant*, *hot*, *warm*, and so on. You are not making a hot drink where those adjectives would be appropriate. In my opinion they are slightly inaccurate because they leave a lot open to interpretation and can make you assume something is valid when it really is not. For example, as noted in Chapter 10, you can *technically* use log shipping for reporting purposes, but only those who are masochists should attempt it. There is the spirit of the law, which is following the core of the rule and adapting it to your situation, and then there is the letter of the law, which is taking something and doing exactly as it states but possibly causing you a lot of pain in the process. I tend to follow the spirit of the law because there are no absolutes when it comes to implementing these types of solutions.

I want to be upfront since parts of this chapter may deviate from some of the standard Always On messaging from Microsoft. This chapter represents my views on this topic—someone whose job, day in and day out, is to assist customers with the problem of how do you configure a highly available solution with SQL Server?

Comparing the SQL Server High Availability Technologies

This section compares the main Always On technologies against each other and some other technologies that are similar. Table 14-1 provides a comparison of what I deem to be the salient points.

Table 14-1. *SQL Server High Availability Technology Comparison*

Attribute	Failover Clustering	Log Shipping	Database Mirroring	Replication
Distance	Limited[1]	No distance limitations[2]	No distance limitations[2]	No distance limitations[2]
Server switch	Automatic or manual	Manual	Automatic or manual	Manual
Server switch time (average)	30 seconds–2 minutes	Minutes	10 seconds– 1 minute (+/–)	Minutes
Protects	Full instance of SQL Server	Individual database	Individual database	Individual database
Granularity	Entire instance	Per transaction log	Per transaction	Depends on type of replication
Individual database restrictions	None	Bulk-logged or Full recovery only	Full recovery only	Depends on type of replication
Special hardware considerations	Yes[3]	No	No	No
Data loss in server switch	No[4]	Likely[5]	Maybe[6]	Likely[7]

1. *Limited by any restrictions of fiber.*

2. *Limited by your network as well as your disk subsystem.*

3. *Solution must be in the Windows Server Catalog as a cluster solution.*

4. *Databases are always consistent to the point of failover, meaning any transactions completed will be rolled forward and any incomplete transactions will be rolled back.*

5. *Unless it is a graceful role change where you back up the tail of the log, you will only be able to restore to the last transaction in the last transaction log backup available.*

6. *If you are in high safety mode, you should not have any data loss. If you are mirroring asynchronous, there is a chance you will lose data.*

7. *When using replication, you are most likely not replicating your entire database, and if you are not using transactional replication, you are most likely losing data.*

Attribute	Failover Clustering	Log Shipping	Database Mirroring	Replication
Single point of failure	Disk subsystem	None	None	None
Worry about objects that reside outside the database	No	Yes	Yes	Yes
Redundant server(s) can be used for reporting	No[8]	Maybe[9]	Yes[10]	Yes[11]
Coexists/works with SQL Server 2000	Yes[12]	Yes[13]	No	Yes[14]
Works with other SQL Server 2005 editions	N/A	Yes[15]	No[16]	Yes[17]
Number of possible failover/mirror/ standby servers	Up to 8	Unlimited	1	Unlimited
Editions supported	Developer, Enterprise, Standard	Developer, Enterprise, Standard, Workstation	Developer, Enterprise, Standard	All
Full-text indexes automatically accounted for in switch	Yes	No	No	No
Server name change abstracted	Yes	No	Maybe[18]	No

8. *One node owns all resources associated with a particular instance.*

9. *Technically, the secondary, if it is restored* WITH STANDBY *can be used for reporting purposes, but it would be unavailable during transaction log restores.*

10. *If you create a database snapshot, the mirror can be used for reporting.*

11. *This is most likely the purpose for using replication in the first place.*

12. *A SQL Server 2005 failover cluster can be configured in a side-by-side configuration with a SQL Server 2000 failover cluster.*

13. *You can log ship using custom scripts from SQL Server 2000 to SQL Server 2005, but not from SQL Server 2005 to SQL Server 2000.*

14. *Replication can populate older versions of SQL Server.*

15. *Log shipping has no restrictions on the edition of the primary or secondary.*

16. *While technically you can mirror if you are in high safety mode from Standard to Enterprise or vice versa, it is not recommended.*

17. *Replication has no edition restrictions.*

18. *If you are using high safety mode and your application is coded properly, the server name change during the server switch will be abstracted.*

Failover Clustering vs. Other Technologies

The following sections compare failover clustering with database mirroring, log shipping, replication, and third-party clustering.

Database Mirroring

Database mirroring has become the one technology that is most asked about in comparison with failover clustering because on the surface they sound similar. But they are very different implementations. In some of its early marketing material, it seemed as if Microsoft was positioning database mirroring to replace failover clustering. Database mirroring is by no means a cluster killer, at least how it has been implemented in SQL Server 2005. In reality, they are two different technologies focusing on different aspects of availability.

Architecturally, both have the concept of quorum. Endpoints in database mirroring are similar to the cluster's private network. Both require that the servers participating are using the same edition of SQL Server. Both support automatic and manual failover options. By default, failover clustering is designed to take advantage of an automatic failover, whereas database mirroring depends on which mode you implement. The trade-offs of the different operating models of database mirroring are discussed in Chapter 11. Both may or may not force applications and end users to reconnect, depending on the application.

Both give you excellent availability, but their main difference is that failover clustering protects your entire instance, while database mirroring protects a single database. This is a huge difference. It means that in a failover for a clustered instance, you will have to worry about reconnecting to the instance, but everything will still be there. With database mirroring, logins will need to be added and synchronized, and anything that resides outside of the database that is not captured as a transaction (such as jobs, maintenance plans, etc.) will need to be created on the mirror.

The one major aspect that database mirroring has over failover clustering is that the whole implementation can be done on commodity hardware with no specific requirements around a solution, such as the cluster solution in the Windows Server Catalog, and every little detail that goes along with clustering (multiple network cards, networks, etc.). This is one reason why I think most people will look for an "easier" solution, even if it may not totally meet their needs. Clustering is perceived as being difficult, or maybe you had a bad experience with it in the past for one reason or another. This is not the right way to evaluate a technology. Where it may have been wrong in the past it may be right now. As your needs change, so does technology (and usually for the better). It is never a bad thing to reevaluate it again if you need to implement a new solution.

Another aspect that is easier with database mirroring is spanning distance. With failover clustering, you need a specialized geographically dispersed cluster solution that most likely has some sort of physical limitation (e.g., fiber is only rated at certain distances), which you cannot avoid. Database mirroring involves two separate installations that can reside on any supported hardware (clustered or not), and is not bound by distance but by the limitations of your network bandwidth and the speed of applying the transactions.

Last but not least, with failover clustering, you have a definite single point of failure in your disk subsystem. Configuring your disks with some sort of RAID gives you some redundancy, but if you are not deploying a geographically dispersed failover cluster, your disks are all part of the same set of enclosures in one data center and become your single point of failure. Database mirroring's architecture enables redundancy across distance to another data center.

Log Shipping

Log shipping is hard to compare to failover clustering in a meaningful way, as it does not act or feel like clustering at all. Log shipping is based on a core functionality of the SQL Server engine: backup and restore. It only protects a single database, has no options for automatic failover, and the server switch is not abstracted from the client connections. The one thing that log shipping has on failover clustering is that it is easy to implement over long distances. Can log shipping provide the same availability as failover clustering? In some cases the answer is absolutely yes, but your deployment would need to know all the caveats that go along with log shipping. Log shipping works much better as a disaster recovery technology than as a high availability technology and can complement failover clustering in this capacity.

Replication

Replication is an effective data availability solution that allows you to possibly take all of the data in your database or a subset of the data and make it available elsewhere. Failover clustering defends your databases as a whole since its unit of protection is the entire instance. Like database mirroring and log shipping, replication can be configured on an instance that is deployed as a failover cluster. Like log shipping, you really cannot directly compare replication to failover clustering because the mechanisms and what they provide are two completely different things, and depending on what type of replication you are using, things change even more. The main differences are similar to those of log shipping.

Third-Party Clustering

Third-party clustering products are now being used by some to "cluster" SQL Server. They generally use a completely different mechanism and approach than a standard SQL Server failover cluster. Some are hardware-only. Some are purely software-based. Others are tied into both a hardware and a software solution in one way or another and act more like Microsoft's implementation, but they have a few features that companies may find desirable. Some are widely used, others are up-and-coming. They all work fairly well and as advertised, and you should do your homework to see if they will meet your needs.

The biggest issue with most of these products is that if you encounter a problem, the manu-facturers will be the first point of contact—not Microsoft—since it most likely is not a Microsoft-certified solution. As a consultant, one of my biggest responsibilities to my customers is to identify risk and mitigate it. I certainly cannot force a customer to use or not use a technology or a solution (Microsoft or non-Microsoft), but supportability is a concern since the last thing you want to hear from a support engineer is "sorry, have a nice day" when your system is down. You know your organization better than I ever will. You know what risks your business is willing to accept and what it won't tolerate.

As you go through the process of evaluating products, especially ones that would be a primary form of availability or disaster recovery, keep supportability in mind. You should consult with those in the trenches—the administrators who live, eat, sleep, and breathe your SQL Server administra-tion and implementations. They will most likely be able to tell you if they have firsthand knowledge of the technology in question and whether the vendor you are considering is good. You may have implemented another product from a vendor and had a bad experience, either with the technology, or worse, the support. Know all of your facts before you spend a lot of money on something that could be the equivalent of a technology paperweight.

As noted in the chapters on clustering, for a geographically dispersed failover cluster solution, it is always best to consider solutions that are certified and appear in the Windows Server Catalog. Any other solution—no matter how reputable the vendor—may cause you some support headaches down the road.

Log Shipping vs. Other Technologies

The following sections compare log shipping directly with the other SQL Server availability technologies.

Database Mirroring

Database mirroring and log shipping are both based on some of the same technologies. Using synchronous database mirroring with automatic failover is a huge benefit over either asynchronous database mirroring or log shipping where you would need to switch to your other server manually. Database mirroring is also more granular than log shipping since it sends transactions to a standby server per transaction, not per transaction log backup. Database mirroring also has the ability to abstract the server name change if your application is coded properly; log shipping has no such option. There is also the chance that database mirroring may perform better than log shipping. Disk I/O for log shipping can potentially be highly serialized. As with database mirroring, performance of the disk on the receiver will impact performance of the data load, but instead of waiting for a whole log to load, you will have more granular applications and be more in sync, even if you are using a high-performance mode of database mirroring.

Failover Clustering

Log shipping versus failover clustering is described in the previous "Log Shipping" section.

Replication

Since there are different forms of replication, I will compare log shipping to the main three: snapshot, merge, and transactional. In general, log shipping is much better for availability or disaster recovery because it protects your whole database, whereas replication is generally only used for a subset of data. If you need a reporting solution, replication beats log shipping hands down because even if you restore your secondary database WITH STANDBY, your users will have to be knocked out of the database each time a transaction log is loaded. If they are not, your database cannot be updated.

Snapshot replication does not really compare to log shipping since it is refreshing the whole thing. Merge replication, in its own way, is like log shipping since it only pushes changes since the last time data was replicated. It only sends over changes as defined as part of the publication. Transactional replication is potentially more granular than log shipping since it is at the per-transaction level. Log shipping, however, is much more robust in terms of a disaster solution since it is designed to capture everything in the transaction log (not just what is defined in the publication) and it is geared for these types of solutions.

Finding your transactions with transactional replication is a bit more challenging if you switch to your standby server. Is it still sitting in the original transaction log and not read yet? Is it waiting to be replicated sitting at the distributor? Has it been picked up by the log reader as a transaction to be replicated but not yet run? When it comes to disaster recovery, you want to know that your data is right and absolute. You would have to compare your data to know what is there and not there, or monitor your replication more carefully to know the state of your standby. With log shipping, you know at what point your primary fails, and what the last transaction log to be loaded is. Replication is reliable, but the nature of how it works is fundamentally different than log shipping.

Database Mirroring vs. Other Technologies

The following sections compare database mirroring directly with the other SQL Server availability technologies.

Failover Clustering and Log Shipping

For a comparison of database mirroring with failover clustering and log shipping, see the previous sections.

Replication

This is an interesting comparison. You can't really compare database mirroring to any form of replication other than transactional, as they are the most similar; you may even have questions about when to use one versus the other. Both protect at the individual database level; and transactional replication and database mirroring work per transaction. So what is the difference? Database mirroring is designed more for disaster recovery since it takes all transactions, whereas transactional replication is based on whatever you set up for your publications. Database mirroring is also set up to handle your failovers, whereas with transactional replication you must create all of those processes yourself. Both transactional replication and database mirroring require you to get all objects and logins in sync manually.

In the simple case, database mirroring may have the edge over replication in the sense that once you set it up, it works with the sole purpose of creating a standby server. Replication will need much more monitoring and setup (such as defining your publications) and is not really my go-to solution for availability.

Hardware-Based Disk Mirroring

I get this question often: how does SQL Server's database mirroring feature stack up against hardware-based disk mirroring? The answer is they are two entirely different mechanisms for providing availability, each with its own strengths and weaknesses. A hardware disk mirror doesn't know one change from another and sends all altered disk bits as disk updates. Database mirroring can potentially be more efficient on the disk subsystem at the cost of more processing time where costs are regularly driven down by Moore's Law (just think about the servers you can buy today that are a fraction of the cost and way more powerful than ones you bought even five years ago).

A hardware-based solution will always be more costwise since you generally need an exact copy of your disk subsystem in another location. The methods by which the disks are mirrored are usually proprietary to a vendor, and you may be limited in ways (such as distance) by a component such as fiber. Both solutions can be configured synchronously or asynchronously.

Hardware-based disk mirroring is transparent to SQL Server, but it protects in a completely different way: you are most likely mirroring at the block or page level of the disk, which has no conception of transactions. You are literally sending disk bits across the wire. In the event of having to use the standby server, SQL Server will behave as it should: a completed transaction will always be rolled forward, incomplete rolled back. You need to determine if this form of mirroring is better for you than database mirroring, which is based on SQL Server transactions. You do have the advantage of hardware-based disk mirroring where it will not impact your transaction log, nor should it impact SQL Server performance. The one way that a hardware-based solution is inferior is that if you ever want to reverse the process after a switch, it is not a trivial task.

Replication vs. Other Technologies

For a comparison of replication with database mirroring, failover clustering, and log shipping, see the previous sections.

Combining the SQL Server High Availability Technologies

In the previous section, I mainly compared the technologies in the context of high availability. This section shows how the various SQL Server availability technologies can be used in conjunction with others and the specific implementation considerations for doing so.

Failover Clustering with Other Technologies

The following sections describe how failover clustering can be used with the other SQL Server availability technologies.

Database Mirroring

While failover clustering and database mirroring complement each other, there are some things you should look out for. The main problem with using database mirroring for a database in a clustered instance of SQL Server is that if you are using high-safety mode and have automatic failover set up for mirroring, it may wind up conflicting with the failover mechanism for the cluster. This is because if you have a failover of the instance, mirroring may detect the problem and then switch to have the mirror become the new main database and server. This behavior is not what most people want. You would in most cases want the failover of the instance to occur, and if the cluster itself fails, to then have mirroring pick up the slack. If this is what you want to achieve, you will have to set database mirroring to not allow an automatic switch to the mirror.

Another aspect of configuration you will need to worry about is that when you are configuring your endpoints and one or both of the instances participating in database mirroring are configured as clusters, remember to use the clustered IP address and not one of the IP addresses from the nodes. If you are using name resolution, this will not apply but it is something to keep in mind. Figure 14-1 shows what this architecture may look like.

This combination is starting to emerge as a popular choice since your remote data center will be potentially synchronized with your principal database at a fairly low cost. Either this configuration or failover clustering with log shipping will most likely be your starting point as combination high availability/disaster recovery solutions.

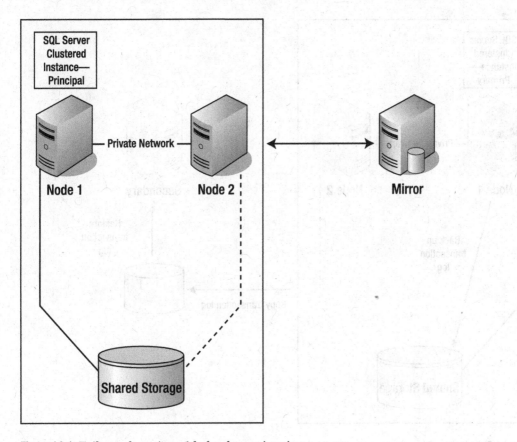

Figure 14-1. *Failover clustering with database mirroring*

Log Shipping

Combining log shipping with failover clustering is arguably the most common configuration I have seen for years at customer sites and looks something like Figure 14-2.

Until database mirroring was introduced in SQL Server 2005, it was my favorite solution and remains a no-brainer even though mirroring is available. As noted in Chapter 10, if your primary or secondary is a failover cluster, you will have to create shares on one of the disks that SQL Server is dependent upon. Other than that, log shipping should "just work"—and that is what you want. It is based on technology (backup and restore, copying files) that is easy to grasp. There's no magic. One of the reasons that log shipping is so popular with clustered deployments of SQL Server is that it may also balance out the cost of buying the cluster, which can be considerable for some, depending on the implementation. And why not? You have to back up your databases anyway, and chances are you have to do transaction log backups, so it is a natural fit.

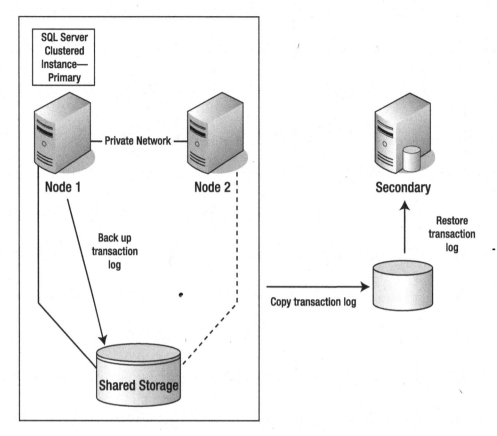

Figure 14-2. *Failover clustering with log shipping*

Replication

Using replication with failover clustering is also a standard configuration. SQL Server does not care if your source, distributor, and destination are clustered, some are clustered, or none are. If you are planning a remote distributor, you may want to think about whether to put it in another instance on the same cluster with your source or destination if they are clustered, put it on the same instance, or put it in a completely separate location. All are valid architectures. It boils down to what you think gives you the most flexible deployment and best performance while maintaining availability. Figure 14-3 shows a sample architecture containing both failover clustering and replication.

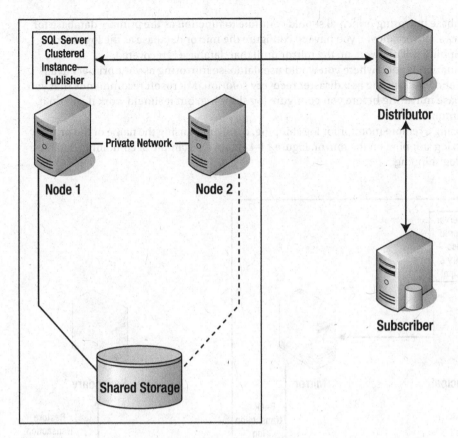

Figure 14-3. *Example of failover clustering with replication and a remote distributor*

Log Shipping with Other Technologies

The following sections describe how log shipping can be used with the other SQL Server availability technologies.

Database Mirroring

Since your principal database in a database mirroring session is in Full mode, it can be used with log shipping. Similarly, if your primary database for log shipping is in Full and not Bulk-logged mode, it can be configured as the principal in a mirror. If you are in synchronous mode for database mirroring, you should generally have no problems with log shipping since your transaction log backups can occur without transactions that may need to stay in the transaction log and cannot be committed. If you are in asynchronous mode for database mirroring, I would argue that you should not combine log shipping and database mirroring since you may essentially be doing the same thing, depending on your latency. I would only suggest combining the two if you are using synchronous mode.

One problem you will definitely encounter is that your editions of SQL Server may not match. Since database mirroring is only supported with Standard or Enterprise editions of SQL Server 2005, your combinations will be limited to those versions. And since database mirroring really wants both the principal and mirror to be the same edition, you are tied into either Standard or Enterprise, but probably not both.

If your database mirroring principal should continue to function as the primary database for log shipping after a mirror failover, you have to configure the mirror database as the log shipping primary. Log shipping will not work on the mirror until that database is recovered.

This combination is good where you would use database mirroring as your primary availability solution and log shipping as a disaster recovery solution. Microsoft recommends that you configure database mirroring before you configure log shipping, but it should work if you do it the other way around.

If you are using a remote monitor for log shipping, configure it using the name of the primary when you set up log shipping on the mirror. Figure 14-4 shows an example of combining database mirroring with log shipping.

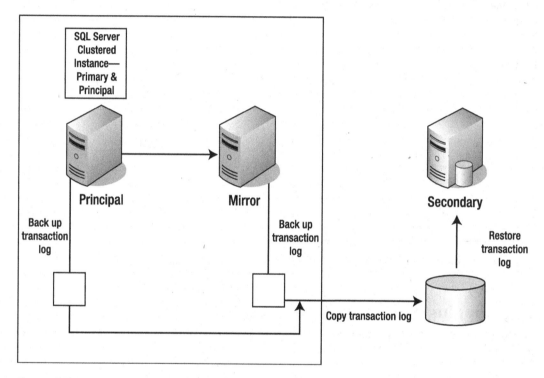

Figure 14-4. *Log shipping with database mirroring*

Failover Clustering

To see how log shipping can be used in conjunction with failover clustering see the previous "Log Shipping" section.

Replication

Log shipping can work with both merge and transactional replication. However, you must take into account the following:

- All databases must be log shipped to the same secondary if you plan on deploying log shipping where an instance has more than one publication database.

- You must ensure that the KEEP_REPLICATION option is used for all transaction log restores.

- All paths for SQL Server must be configured to be the same during install and for the database locations.

- You must back up the service master key on the primary with the following command and restore it on the secondary. The service master key is the root of SQL Server's encryption hierarchy:

```
BACKUP SERVICE MASTER KEY TO FILE = 'file_path'
ENCRYPTION BY PASSWORD = 'use_a_password'
```

- You may encounter some data loss.

When using log shipping with transactional replication, you need to worry about the sync with backup option of replication as discussed in Chapter 12. Enabling this option means that the primary and secondary would be in sync because the distribution database would not have transactions that the original publisher would have. All places would be consistent. Whether or not you are using the sync with backup option, here is what you need to do:

1. Perform a role change from the primary to the secondary.

2. Take backups from the primary's master and msdb databases and restore them on the secondary. This may cause problems if you have more databases than just the databases you were log shipping to that instance since you are going to essentially overwrite the existing record of the current configuration.

3. Rename your computer to match the original primary. This is going to be a problem if the original primary is still on the network. If you are on a cluster, this will also be a problem since you cannot rename a named instance of SQL Server. If you did not use sync with backup, you may see errors that the publication database and the distribution database are not synchronized.

4. Restore the service master key with the following syntax:

```
RESTORE SERVICE MASTER KEY FROM FILE = 'file_path'
DECRYPTION BY PASSWORD = 'use_a_password' [FORCE]
```

5. If you did not use sync with backup, you must also perform the following:

   a. Execute sp_replrestart.

   b. Restart the Log Reader Agent after sp_replrestart runs successfully.

   c. Set up replication such that if a transaction is reapplied to a subscriber, distribution will not fail. Use the distribution agent profile Continue on Data Consistency Errors.

If you are going to use merge replication with log shipping, follow steps 1 through 4 and then you must manually synchronize the publication with one or more of the subscribers.

If you don't perform the previous steps, combining replication and log shipping is not a good idea.

Database Mirroring with Other Technologies

The following sections describe how database mirroring can be used with the other SQL Server availability technologies.

Failover Clustering and Log Shipping

To see how database mirroring can be used in conjunction with failover clustering and log shipping, see the previous sections on these topics.

Replication

The best use of database mirroring with replication is to protect the source, or *publication*, database. It really has no business protecting any other database such as the distributor or the subscriber. You should be worried about your source since if it goes, where is your data coming from?

Combining the two has the following constraints:

- Since database mirroring is only supported by SQL Server 2005, the servers that act as the publisher and the distributor must be using SQL Server 2005.

- As of the writing of this book, only merge replication and transactional replication with either read-only subscribers or queued updating subscribers are supported for use with database mirroring. Any other form of replication, including snapshot and peer-to-peer, is not supported.

- The principal and mirror must share the same distributor.

The steps to configure database mirroring with log shipping are the following:

1. Configure the publisher.

2. Configure database mirroring on the publisher ensuring it uses the same distributor as well as the same snapshot folder.

3. Set the mirror name for the -PublisherFailoverPartner with the following syntax:

   ```
   exec sp_add_agent_parameter @profile_id = 6,
   @parameter_name = N'-PublisherFailoverPartner',
   @parameter_value = N'<Failover Partner Name>'
   ```

4. Configure both the principal and Mirror in the Replication Monitor.

Replication with Other Technologies

The following sections describe how replication can be used with the other SQL Server availability technologies.

Database Mirroring, Failover Clustering, and Log Shipping

To see how replication can be used in conjunction with database mirroring, failover clustering, and log shipping, see the previous sections on these topics.

Designing Your Solution

Now comes the fun part: putting the individual components together to form your solution. There are many aspects that will influence what the final design will look like, and they will be discussed in this section.

Performance

A key component to any deployment of SQL Server is its performance. What good would it do anyone to have a highly available solution that underperforms and creates the perception that things are unavailable? Performance and availability are joined at the hip. You may have noticed that not much of this book has been focused on performance directly. This is not a book dedicated to performance tuning of SQL Server 2005—this is *SQL Server 2005 high availability*. As you know, performance is worth a book on its own, and I would not do it justice in a book dedicated to availability. I address performance in this chapter as it relates to general SQL Server design.

Performance encompasses many aspects: processor (speed, number of cores, and number of physical processors), disk I/O, physical architecture, logical architecture, and most importantly, the application or applications you are running. You cannot design a hardware architecture and infrastructure without knowing anything about the application. Let me take that back—you can, but it will be based on a lot of guesswork and may cost you more in the end.

Sizing Processor and Memory and Purchasing Servers

One of the hardest things to do is size your servers. As a consultant, I am frequently asked by customers to help them size the servers that will be purchased, or to assess whether current servers are big enough to handle the current workload (or the future workload). In theory, this should be easy. In practice, it is very, very hard.

The first challenge that you will always face in your deployments before you even rack a server, deploy an operating system, or carve up disks on a shared disk array is dealing with the manufacturer and the lead times for acquiring the hardware. For example, if your company places an order for hardware on the first of the month, and your hardware vendor of choice tells you it will take three weeks to fill your order, chances are it will be at least a month before you even do the basics for preparing your servers, such as racking them and installing an operating system. Server orders generally take a few days (or weeks) to process and get shipped to you. Common server configurations may be in stock and can ship within a few days, but if you are ordering a larger server or a nonstandard configuration, you are going to add to your lead time. It is crucial to know your vendor's lead times since that bit of information will influence your overall project and deployment dates.

Tip The previous advice applies to all software vendors. Make sure you have all software procured and properly licensed in plenty of time for your rollouts. Do not install a trial, personal, developer, or desktop-type edition of SQL Server (or any other nonlicensed products for that matter) because you may encounter issues down the road. Deploy only what you intend to use in production. (Ironically, a few weeks before writing this tip, a customer of mine encountered this situation. SQL Server would not restart one night after some routine maintenance. I tried rebooting the server but it didn't work. We went to the data center and saw that a keyboard was not hooked into the KVM. Once we solved that, we realized that the reason SQL Server was not starting was because it was a 120-day trial installation that had actually expired years before. It had never been shut down beyond day 120. That was not a happy discovery. I wish I was making this up, but I'm not.)

Once you realize you already have a lead time challenge that may place you behind schedule before you get started (you didn't think your timeline was realistic, did you?), you can think about your actual server needs. The problem I usually encounter with clients, and it has happened many times, is that I am asked to provide hardware specifications before I have gathered all of the proper information to make that decision. I may not even know the budget. I am just asked to come back with server totals and specs that will meet the needs.

On a recent SQL Server consolidation project that was happening around the time I was writing this book, I had to put a hardware order in two months before deployment and one month before my solution was even close to being finalized. Fortunately or unfortunately, this is where experience comes in. You will not get it just from reading this book. It takes quite a few deployments under your belt to make reasonably accurate guesstimates.

So how do you estimate your hardware needs when you don't have the experience or knowledge of how SQL Server will be used? My general rule of thumb when it comes to the servers themselves is to always start out with at least four processors (hopefully dual-core at this point) and a minimum of 4GB of memory. That configuration is about as standard as you get in the server world these days. With the newer servers, especially the dual-core ones (which are the latest and greatest as of the time of writing this book; quad cores are just starting to hit the market and have yet to prove themselves in terms of cost-to-performance ratio), people are getting much better scalability out of a similarly priced and sized server than they did a few years ago. More cores and processors means SQL Server's engine has more choices for deciding how to run workloads. Less than 4GB of memory for the most part does not give you much growth and headroom and may limit your scalability.

A four-way server may now perform better than that eight-way you procured two years ago. I am seeing less and less need for larger servers with eight, sixteen, or more processors unless you really are doing some heavy lifting. In fact, many hardware vendors are not making those larger servers since there really is no demand for them. The reality is that blade servers can handle four (or more) processors these days in a fraction of the space, with a smaller power and cooling requirement.

Do you still need a 4U rackmount server? There may not be one anymore. With the advent of 1U servers as well as blades, you can get great performance in a smaller package that requires less power, cooling, and space. Do not mistake my words; I have worked on and still implement solutions that absolutely need more horsepower than four processors and require a larger 4U server, but they are generally for the most complex tasks and largest implementations.

A lot of processors come with hyperthreading, and SQL Server 2005 will work with it, but I have seen where hyperthreading can potentially affect performance in a negative way. If your processor supports hyperthreading, I suggest you do testing under load before you go into production, and if it is causing problems, disable it in the server's BIOS.

Memory is a whole different ball game. Where new dual-core four-way servers can handle a lot of processing, I see a lot of SQL Servers that increasingly need 8, 16, or more gigabytes of memory due to the size of the databases and tasks asked of them. One of the main things to consider is that memory used as cache can "act like" additional disk power. SQL Server includes a very powerful self-tuning cache that allows 1GB of memory to take a lot of potential workload off your disk array. This is especially true for a heavy read-based database but can help write-intensive databases as well.

32-BIT VS. 64-BIT

Another reason SQL Server 2005 is seeing such great scalability is the wider adoption of the 64-bit platform. SQL Server 2005 comes in two major flavors of 64-bit: x64 (both AMD and Intel) and Intel's Itanium (IA64). There is also your familiar friend, the x86 32-bit version. Does it make sense for you to go 64-bit? It depends. Using a 64-bit processor, operating system, and application does not mean 2x in terms of performance just because the number of bits are doubled. You may see better performance, you may see the same performance, or in some cases, worse performance. Yes, you read that right: worse performance.

If you are using the version of Analysis Services that ships with SQL Server 2005, I can say without hesitation that in most cases the 64-bit version will give you better performance than its 32-bit counterpart, especially since it natively can handle the larger amounts of memory supported by SQL Server. Besides that, Analysis Services and the nature of what it does lends itself well to a 64-bit architecture. The relational engine of SQL Server's answer to the 32- vs. 64-bit debate is not as cut-and-dry.

SQL Server 2005 is the first version of SQL Server to have native 64-bit support in most editions. The mobile version of SQL Server (and I'm sure Microsoft will consider making a 64-bit mobile version of SQL Server when there are 64-bit consumer devices like phones and PDAs), SQL Server 2005 Workgroup Edition, and SQL Server 2005 Express Edition do not have 64-bit versions. SQL Server 2000 had a special edition released post–SQL Server 2000 Service Pack 3 that supported Intel's Itanium chips only. There were no real tools that worked on 64-bit—just the server software itself. It needed to be managed from 32-bit clients with the 32-bit management tools.

Do you get better scalability with the 64-bit versions of Windows and SQL Server 2005? On paper, absolutely you do. In fact, in most cases you should. Due to the server's hardware architecture, you will most likely have a pure 64-bit path from processor out to the I/O subsystem, so you should get full bandwidth of most if not all components. You will not completely eliminate bottlenecks, but you can certainly reduce them.

No matter what, I will caution you not to be a spec-head; do not buy into marketing hype. The 32-bit version of SQL Server 2005 is still a viable platform and may still be the right one for you. If you are still confused or unsure, run your own "bake-off." Set up a 32-bit server and a 64-bit server, each with its native version of SQL Server, and run a bit of your load against it. It does not matter which edition of SQL Server you test with, per se, but you should keep the general hardware configurations the same to do as close to an apples-to-apples comparison as you can. This means you need the same disk setup, nearly similar hardware (such as iSCSI or HBA cards), and so on. Document your test results, review them, and make an informed decision. The test results may even come in handy when you go to the business asking for the money since you have proof to back up your requests.

Sizing, Purchasing, and Designing Disk Subsystems

Oh, how I wish I had the time to write a companion book right now on disk subsystems (although keep your eyes peeled . . .). I would argue that your disk purchase will be your most important purchase for SQL Server—period. Your hardware and the solution architected on top of it controls the keys to your performance, growth, and flexibility for your SQL Server implementations. I will do my best in a limited amount of space to give you my high-level thinking around disk.

Forget about things such as RAID levels and such for the moment. Why? Sure, it's important, but what you don't realize is that you may have no control over your end design. Many companies have a centralized storage group and do not acquire a new disk storage system for every application. That centralized group "owns" all storage. When the DBAs get a request for a new database, they ask the internal client how much space they will need. The DBAs tell the storage group their "storage needs"—in this case meaning the amount of space needed—and the storage group carves it up and presents it most likely to the Windows group who then adds that storage to the server. That all sounds idyllic, doesn't it? There is one fundamental flaw in that equation: performance.

SQL Server and its performance is linked to how much I/O you can process. That is not just your mainline data; if you become either log or tempdb bound, you might as well kiss your performance goodbye. If you are on a shared disk subsystem that may be housing Exchange or is being used as a file server, you are sharing overall I/O (which is now comprised of different mixed workloads) and cache. And if I hear another storage engineer say "Don't worry, we have a ton of cache. Performance will be fine," I think I will scream. Cache only helps for things that stay in cache. When you have tons of things sharing the same disk subsystem, there is no guarantee that your data will stay there and the storage will not have to go back and physically read from the disk (which can be an expensive operation).

Although it is not usually done this way, you should do some benchmark testing with a version of your application to understand its I/O requirements, and then go size your disk solution. Some disk vendors require some sort of I/O number from you. Unfortunately, most people order their disk subsystem in the hopes it will scale since they do not have these numbers.

To get you started, those of you who do a large amount of reading in your workload will know that more physical disks and possibly even more memory in your servers are good directions to head in. What you need to get over is that this may mean having more physical disks—and disk space—than are actually used. You may have a 10MB table that is a hot spot and requires 15 physical disks to get the performance you need from it. Do not let the size of your tables fool you; it is their usage that dictates their layout on your physical architecture.

If, however, you have a high percentage of writes in your average workload, faster disks (such as 15,000 rpm) and more controller channels with a large amount of cache talking to the disks may be more important than a large number of physical disks. You would always want to separate your transaction log I/O from your main data I/O since writing to both on the same set of spindles would cause contention.

Growth is another factor that many forget about. Before you size your LUNs or tell your storage group what you need, you have quite a few things to take into consideration:

- The short-term view of the world: how much storage do you need to get you through the initial phases of the deployment?

- Once you figure out your short-term, how long will the system actually be in use? One year? Two years? Five years? Once you know that number, what is the projected growth expected for the solution? How easy or hard will it be to expand your current solution, and what is the turnaround time from the vendor to do this?

- If you know that your amount of disk I/O growth is of more concern than your space growth, consider the advantages of trying to ensure that data and log are written to the outermost tracks of the physical disks if possible.

- If you have regional offices, chances are you may need to deploy either a centralized solution or have some sort of disk solution at each office. That can get very expensive if your requirements are to have exact duplicates of your primary solution.

- If you have iron-clad hardware contracts that cannot be altered, it may limit what you can purchase, deploy, and design.

- When calculating growth, you now need to look at your hot spots. Most databases are a mixture of very static (usually lookup-type) tables and ones that change often. You should know what those are, or the developer/vendor needs to help you with that. Similarly, the developer/vendor needs to tell you calculations on how to properly estimate the size of the database based on the growth patterns you are told and the number of years the system will be in place.

Note Refer back to Chapters 4 and 7 where I talk about disk configuration for clustering. Most of the information presented there, such as using DISKPART and formatting to the proper block size, is relevant even for nonclustered solutions. There is no need to rehash all of the information presented in those chapters.

Keywords

There are certain keywords you can use to assist you when you are designing your solution:

- If you hear the word *reporting*, you should immediately rule out log shipping as an option. Can log shipping technically be used to create a reporting solution if you restore the database on the secondary WITH STANDBY? Sure, but you can also stab yourself with a kitchen knife because it sounds like fun, too. (If you haven't already gotten the hint from this chapter and Chapter 10, I really hate log shipping as a reporting solution.) Use either database mirroring with a database snapshot or replication. You may even want to consider a SQL Server Reporting Services solution that may be based on Analysis Services or another relational database.

- If you hear the words *automatic failover*, both failover clustering and database mirroring immediately pop into mind. No other technologies besides other solutions from third-party vendors support automatic failover at the unit it protects.

- If you hear *very large databases* (VLDBs), you may need to consider alternative methods of administration and backups since normal methods may not meet your needs. You may need to look at things like split-mirror backups. I cannot stress enough that when you grow from the hundreds of gigabytes into the terabyte range for your databases, you will need to throw a lot of the rules you traditionally use with your smaller databases out the window. I mean, are you really going to copy a 1TB backup file to a tape device? Another hard disk? How long is that going to take? Probably longer than you have time for it to take. You have to be smart and use technology to help you. Your job as a DBA is only going to get more challenging as data sets grow in size and your SLAs are shorter and shorter.

How Features and Functionality Affect Deployment

Some features of SQL Server or the hardware you plan on using require you to build them into the design from day one. You cannot retrofit them without redesigning the entire solution. An example of a hardware-based solution is a geographically dispersed cluster. Another is using a hardware-based backup solution such as a split-mirror since it usually entails being taken into account in your disk design. SQL Server's new partitioning feature in SQL Server 2005 also requires upfront planning since it too affects your disk design. It is also your responsibility to make management aware of this since they may not know the impact of deploying something and they may think it is an easy add-on later.

Designing with Disaster Recovery in Mind

One thing that is usually talked about by many of my clients is disaster recovery. After the initial shock of implementing high availability, there is not much time or money left over for implementing a disaster recovery solution, even though SLAs and other requirements may dictate the need for such a solution. If you fall into this category, make sure that whatever you implement now will not be impossible to add a disaster recovery component to later. This is easier said than done. See Chapter 16 for more information on disaster recovery.

LICENSING FOR STANDBY SERVERS

This is probably the best chapter to discuss the topic of licensing and how it affects standby servers because it will impact your design—especially if what you are planning winds up being deemed "too expensive." As of the writing of this book, Microsoft's policy at `http://www.microsoft.com/sql/howtobuy/activepassive.mspx` states that if your failover node/mirror/warm standby is only being used for the purpose of switching to it in an emergency (meaning it has no active processes running on it), you do not specifically need a SQL Server license for it since it is not doing any processing. If you do switch to that failover node/mirror/warm standby, you are legally entitled to run that server as the main database server for up to 30 days. After that it must get its own license. However, if you are using your mirror or warm standby server for reporting purposes, you will need to acquire a license since you are actually using the mirror or standby for some purpose other than availability or disaster recovery. I am by no means a licensing expert, so please consult with your local Microsoft sales representatives to ensure that you get the correct answer for your deployments.

Example Solution for an Existing Environment

Consider this scenario. Your company has deployed SAP. Due to the cost of deploying SAP and the army of consultants you brought in, management decides to worry about availability later to ensure the rollout date is met. The database will be used for normal SAP functionality as well as reporting since a "large" server was purchased and the IT manager feels that it is large enough to handle both the normal SAP traffic as well as reporting.

Your SAP system is worth roughly $10,000 an hour to your business. Three months into the system in production, the SAN experiences a catastrophic failure. All nearline backups are on the SAN, and the last backup made to tape was two weeks ago—a possible loss of $3,360,000. That tape backup was not verified since your company does not believe in testing backups because they have never had a reason to. Two days later, the SAN vendor has completed all repairs and luckily the tape backup used to restore the database is valid (although the consequences would be dire if the reverse were true; consider yourself lucky).

Your company, due to regulatory constraints, keeps copies of the actual transactions elsewhere and your company has to now manually recreate two weeks worth of transactions. While you ultimately can make back some of that $3,360,000, you were still down for three days, which affected your business an additional $720,000. That is an expensive outage.

You are where most companies find themselves at some point. The sad truth is that many do not see the value of availability until it is too late. It only takes one massive outage (and it may not be massive from a time perspective, but in other ways) to see the value of what they said no to earlier. (It may also make you realize keeping an updated resume around is not a bad idea because someone may wind up being the fall guy for the problem.) There is always an excuse when you initially deploy your solution: "it's too expensive," "it's too complex," "we don't have the time." All of a sudden when an outage like the one I describe occurs, an epiphany happens and management has a lightbulb moment. So how do you now retrofit availability onto an existing solution?

In this specific scenario, I can tell you that clustering is not an option available to you since it is really something you must do at design time. That leaves database mirroring, log shipping, and replication. For something like SAP, I would also rule out replication since you do not want a subset of your database that may not be supported by the software vendor. You want the whole thing redundant. We are down to database mirroring and log shipping. In this scenario for availability I would deploy database mirroring in high safety mode. If you are deploying SAP, you are serious about what you are doing. A small mom-and-pop shop is not paying the cost to implement an enterprise-class SAP deployment unless it has deep pockets (and even if it did, would it make sense?). High-safety mode gives you the most granular protection you can get at a database level.

You now just need to ensure that from an I/O and a network perspective you can handle it. This also means you may be buying more hardware to set up the mirror server and additional disk capacity. One huge benefit of this new configuration is that the mirror can be used for reporting purposes and you can offload that functionality elsewhere. Even though you may not have seen any performance problems due to reporting and normal activity on the same database, it is never a bad thing to separate the two. If additional storage costs you $150,000, and a server $25,000, that $175,000 is less than the cost of the time your business is down and the effects of that downtime.

To take things one step further, I would also suggest that because SAP is such a mission-critical application, you may want to also configure log shipping to a remote data center for disaster recovery purposes. Even if your data center blows up, which is definitely a more catastrophic failure than the one you encountered with your SAN, you still have business continuity elsewhere. Again, this may require additional hardware and disk, but what is the cost to the business? Even if it is the same as that mirror server you just got and the storage, it is still cheaper than losing $10,000 an hour. If you are down for 18 or more hours due to your catastrophic outage, it pays for itself.

Example Solution for a New Deployment

Consider this scenario. Your company is going to be implementing a new customer relationship management (CRM) system that is expected to initially grow about 10% per month and then ramp up from there. You don't know the future growth rate after the system is in production and your organization grows. Since this system is for the global sales force and will be driven by data in the database, it needs to be available as close to 24x7 as possible.

First Things First

Since this is a new application, sometimes known as a *greenfield*, you have a blank canvas to start with in terms of your solution. In many ways it is both a blessing and a curse. Management wants something robust, but they are not looking to break the bank if they can help it. Like the previous example, the first thing you need to do is quantify the business side of things: if this system ever goes down, what is the actual cost to the business? Even though the company may want to go cheap, it may not be possible. Since your company has never implemented a CRM system before or a system of this magnitude, you have no internal projects to use as a basis for gathering numbers. What you do know is that the entire sales force will be crippled once this system is deployed if it goes down.

At this point, you also need to ensure that you have your executive sponsorship and are gathering together your implementation leads. Once those are solidified, you should then have the budget discussions. Even though the number may change, it is always best to go in with some sort of number. Why propose a $5,000,000 solution when your company is only willing to spend $500,000? You are eventually given a starting budget of $750,000 and any other expenditures would need to be approved.

Requirements

Now that the basics are in place from a business perspective, it is time to start gathering the requirements that will drive the design. You talk to end users, management, and the IT staff. Here is a list of things you will be designing to:

- Automatic failover to the standby server (manual failover is not acceptable).

- Both a local availability solution and a disaster recovery solution that will span distances. This is not negotiable.

- A manageable solution (many people forget this aspect).
- An unplanned outage (nondisaster) of five minutes.
- An initial database size of 500GB for year one.

The Architecture

Because you need automatic failover and a solution that minimizes your downtime, you really only have two choices for availability: failover clustering and database mirroring. Your company has mentioned that you are not allowed to consider a geographically dispersed cluster solution because it is not implementing the fiber needed to achieve it, nor is it willing to take on the expense.

If I was designing this solution, I would put failover clustering in your primary data center and then use database mirroring for your disaster recovery solution. Why? For your unplanned outage, you are protecting your entire instance and not just a single database. Your single point of failure will be your disk subsystem, and your backup plan will have to account for that.

Your disk subsystem is estimated to cost $300,000 upfront for a single unit, and since you need disaster recovery, that means two units. That leaves $150,000 left over for licensing, servers, and support contracts. None of the expense costs account for consultants or other experts that you will need to help plan and deploy the solution. You must go back to the business and set that expectation. You must also go back to the business because that initial $750,000 does not cover development, testing, or staging environments. When all is said and done, you are looking at probably a $1.5 million investment.

I know that number sounds high, but if your sales organization is supposed to drive $20 million in business every quarter and be more efficient, that $1.5 million all of a sudden looks like a drop in the bucket over the lifetime of the deployment.

Planning and Deployment

Because you have a distance requirement for disaster recovery, that brings log shipping into the mix as well. For your local availability in your main data center, deploying clustering is the easiest solution since not only is it an automatic failover, but it protects the entire instance. As long as not much is hanging around in the transaction log, you will meet your five-minute SLA. The disaster recovery solution is not as cut-and-dry. Both database mirroring and log shipping would work. You then go back to the business and ask about your disaster tolerance; how much data can you afford to lose in a disaster? The answer it gives you is ten minutes. That gives you some play.

If you do log shipping every five minutes, and copy the log, which takes three minutes, and the log restore takes two minutes, your standby would be—with no problems or delays—exactly ten minutes off of your primary database. That would do the trick, but what happens if something changes and you unknowingly go to fifteen minutes? You have broken your SLA. In this case, deploying database mirroring would be a better option. Since you are using clustering, you can use synchronous with no witness. This gives you a manual failover and will not do a false failover if you fail over in clustering.

Now that the design is complete, you need to devise your plans and test them. In this case, having a staging environment allows you to set up the solution and walk through your implementation plan before you actually go to do it. I cannot stress how important this is. Any implementation issues must be worked out ahead of time, and any gotchas identified so you can handle them during the deployment.

For the actual rollout and go-live, staff appropriately. Put the right people on, not just warm bodies. There is *always* a flurry of activity, whether something goes wrong or not. There is also going to be some confusion from end users when you roll out something new, such as they cannot access it, they get an error on screen, and so on. You create a lot of goodwill with the business and end users if you step up to the plate. Implementation is not just about installing SQL Server and getting it up and running.

Administration

First and foremost, let's talk about backup and restore. On day one you will not be facing 500GB, but if you hit that number at the end of year one, that is just over 40GB a month. A traditional SQL Server backup scheme may work for a while, but once you start getting into the 500GB or more range, you may need to consider a hardware-based backup solution that would need to be designed when you deploy the solution since it will most likely affect your disk design. Table 14-2 shows a projected database size if you grow 10% per month starting in year two based on an initial size of 500GB at the end of year one.

Table 14-2. *Projected Database Growth*

Month	Size (in GB)
January	550
February	605
March	665.5
April	732.05
May	805.26
June	885.78
July	974.36
August	1071.79
September	1178.97
October	1296.87
November	1426.56
December	1569.21

So as you can see, you will be well over 1TB and on your way to 2TB by the end of year two. If you cannot afford to get more disk or design a hardware-based backup solution, you should look at building partitioning into your design, if possible, and if *that's* not possible, you would definitely need some sort of archive solution. You are most likely looking at the most recent data, not necessarily historical data, so you can come up with a scheme where data will be considered "out of date" and design a history solution where the data is available for querying; it will just not be in your primary database on the fastest disks.

There is also the day-to-day administration you need to worry about besides backups: monitoring, performance, and so on. You must be aware of the types of administration and maintenance that will affect your availability. You must put mechanisms in place for coordinating with the business and making sure that end users are aware of any scheduled maintenance that will occur and possibly affect them. I cannot stress how important this is. It is overlooked by most companies initially, and causes pain and perception problems.

Change control must also be hardened and in place at this point. When CRM systems are initially deployed, they are designed to meet your needs at the time. As the company grows and trends change over time, so does the application and its functionality. If you are upgrading any component or rolling out an application change, it must be fully tested and documented before IT even sees it.

You must address staffing. If you are not used to a 24x7 application and supporting it, you will be in for a rude awakening. You need to devise your staffing plans to accommodate business hours as well as off-hours and weekends. Staffing only 9 to 5 from Monday through Friday leaves the entire weekend, as well as an additional 80 hours a week where your environment is a black hole. You are a global corporation, so you must do what it takes to service each geographic region. This may mean a centralized and possibly offshore call center. This may mean support professionals in each region. It definitely means escalation layers. The point is, you need to plan for this.

Most of the monitoring needs to be automated. This means that alerts and information are sent out by the software you invest in, especially when something appears to be abnormal. Thresholds need to be established. For example, if your drives reach 70% capacity, start sending alerts. I have been in plenty of environments where these messages are routinely ignored or, worse, shut off because employees don't want to deal with the e-mail. If that is the case, then why did you hire employees who are not going to do the job? They are putting your environment at risk by potentially ignoring a message (or stopping the message from being generated) that could be telling you something is wrong.

A last item to consider is external dependencies. You've got your servers and disk storage all set up with great technology and processes. However, there are many components that are dependencies of your servers and that may be shared with other production and test environments with lower SLAs than your solution. Take the time to create your list of dependencies and talk with the appropriate people to ensure you are covered when a problem on those items affects your solution. Some highly relevant external dependencies to look into are DNS, Active Directory, your monitoring solution (such as MOM or System Center, and physical backup devices [tape]).

■**Note**   Just because your company will not be deploying a +$1 million dollar solution does not mean you are not facing the same challenges at a smaller level if your budget is $20,000. Change the numbers to what you want, but the scenario stays the same. The challenge arguably gets harder with less money and overall resources. It is hard coming up with scenarios that are one size fits all, and ones that are a bit larger are easier to make the point.

Example Solution for Disk Configuration for a Failover Cluster

A disk configuration is not a whole solution but a very specific configuration point for a failover clustering implementation. This example walks you through the thought process of devising a disk subsystem for your clusters.

Requirements

The disk subsystem will power all databases used by your company's finance department in a consolidation effort. There are 14 databases, 2 of which are heavy hitters when it comes to disk I/O. The other 12 databases have relatively low I/O and are not used as much. The following lists your known basic requirements and known issues:

- One disk is needed for the quorum.
- One disk is needed for MS DTC.
- You will need 30 days of on-disk retention for making backups to disk.
- One of your applications uses `tempdb` heavily.
- You have no control over the low-level configuration of the shared disks; you can only control size.

Here are your unknowns:

- You do not know the growth patterns of each database.
- When you run out of space on your current drives, you don't know how to size a new environment properly.

- You have intermittent I/O performance issues on your current database servers and do not know the root cause.

- You do not know your I/O requirements.

Planning and Deployment

The previous requirements are not much to go on (but are often all I know when I assist customers). The last bullet point is crucial: you have *no* control over how your disks are configured at the physical level. While this may result in your disks not being able to handle your I/O load (you do not know your I/O requirement anyway), it is not something you will find out until it is too late. In these cases, I always recommend documenting this fact so that if performance problems occur, you have documentation that states that it is known and you had nothing to do with it.

Think back to the clustering chapters; you need drive letters with failover clustering. You could use mount points under them, but that may or may not be the right architecture. In this case, if you want to split the data and log for each database, you are looking at 28 drive letters— two more than the alphabet. You also don't really have 26 drives available to you. On your servers, C (OS), D (DVD-ROM), and X (the mapped drive for the user that is logged in) are already used, leaving you 23. Two disks are already being used for MS DTC and the quorum, so you're down to 21. So what is the best use of those 21 disks?

Your goal should not be to use every single drive letter. What happens if you need to deploy another instance of SQL Server on the cluster, or you need some future expansion? Be smart—leave yourself some headroom. Also keep in mind that if you are considering mount points, it is a LUN attached to Windows; it may not have a drive letter but it still has overhead.

One disk should definitely be your dedicated backup disk (down to 20). This will arguably be your largest disk in size since you will be doing all backups to this drive. Because you have a 30-day retention policy, you will also need to get smart about your backup strategy. Doing full backups every night of every database may not be possible, and to get 30 days worth of backups on a single disk, you may need to look into third-party products that compress the database backups—even with compression, that may be a challenge.

The basic system DBs (master, model, and msdb) can be placed on a single small-size disk with low I/O. You already know that you have high tempdb utilization and you dedicate a single disk for it. The tempdb disk will have both data and log since you do not know if you are log bound with tempdb; you can always change it later. You also need to size the tempdb disk appropriately since you are now combining the workload of 14 databases onto a single instance of SQL Server.

Since you are combining 14 databases under a single instance of SQL Server, you cannot assume they will all play nicely with each other in terms of disk I/O. It is best to know something about the database's characteristics in determining where it will ultimately be placed. Is it heavy read? Is it heavy write? Is it used for reporting? Is it mission-critical and has to be separate from others at a physical level? Those are just some of the questions you need to ask yourself.

Once you know a bit more about the databases, you are going to want to spread the load out somewhat evenly if possible. You know you have two huge databases and each one of those should get their own dedicated data and log disks for a total of four drive letters. That leaves the other twelve databases. This is where things get interesting. They are of generally low I/O consumption and not very big, so you decide to spread the load—you will put them across three drives (four databases per drive). The drives for the databases will contain both data and log, since you will get no benefit from a dedicated log drive because the disk head will have to pick up for each of the four databases when a write occurs.

When it comes to exact size for the drive, I'm avoiding it in this example because not only is it discussed in the previous example with the 10% growth as shown in Table 14-2, the exact size is irrelevant for purposes of this discussion. The bottom line is that without growth numbers, no matter what you do, you're just guessing. You already have disk space issues on your current servers.

Going to this cluster is supposed to make you more available and give you flexibility. You won't have it if you undersize your disks. If you are maxed out of your current storage, at a minimum you should plan for doubling the size of the disks to accommodate 100% growth. Will that be expensive? Most likely, but it is probably better than having an unusable system that does not even come close to meeting your needs.

The final configuration would look like Table 14-3. You are left with 12 drives to use for other purposes or later expansion.

Table 14-3. *Failover Cluster Disk Configuration*

Drive Letter	Location	Purpose
C	Internal drive	OS
D	Internal drive	DVD-ROM
E	Shared disk subsystem	System databases (`master`, `model`, `msdb`)
F	Shared disk subsystem	`tempdb` data and log
G	Shared disk subsystem	Large database #1—data only
H	Shared disk subsystem	Large database #1—log only
I	Shared disk subsystem	Large database #2—data only
J	Shared disk subsystem	Large database #2—log only
K	Shared disk subsystem	4 databases—data and log
L	Shared disk subsystem	4 databases—data and log
M	Shared disk subsystem	MS DTC
N	Shared disk subsystem	4 databases—data and log
Q	Shared disk subsystem	Server cluster quorum
X	Mapped drive	user files

Summary

If designing solutions for availability were easy you wouldn't be reading this book, and the information presented in this chapter would be common knowledge (and I'd probably be a jazz musician playing bass somewhere instead of doing SQL Server for my day job). Designing a solution is not paint by numbers—taking a technology and implementing it, and that is it. The decisions that influence the solution and its final design come from everywhere: budget, technical, process, people, and so on. Any solution implemented is going to be a trade-off in one way or another. At the same time, the solution must meet your availability, performance, and growth needs. What looks good on paper has to work well when implemented, otherwise you will have a nightmare solution to administer day in and day out. I cover 24x7 administration in the next chapter.

CHAPTER 15

24x7 Database Administration

Although marketing material may lead you to believe SQL Server administers itself (and in some cases it can (e.g., automatically updating statistics), the truth is that if you implement a mission-critical SQL Server–based solution that requires around-the-clock uptime, you will need to be hands-on in one way, shape, or form. Is automation a big part of a well-run 24x7 environment? Absolutely. This chapter walks you through the various administration tasks put in place to ensure that your availability will not suffer. As you may know, administration is a much bigger topic than can be covered in just one chapter. This chapter covers the topics relevant to a 24x7 environment and references other material should you want to go deeper.

Testing and Change Management

I cannot start discussing anything else in this chapter before I mention testing and change management. Although these topics have hopefully been beaten into your head by this point, it bears repeating that the cornerstone to any implementation or administration is testing before you implement a change and ensuring that you have a process to handle the change. You do not want your production environment to be the first place you try *anything*. As a DBA, it's up to you to ensure that your availability goals are met. Part of that is testing your changes and other mainte-nance tasks in another environment first. This is where a staging environment is so crucial. It costs money but gives you a lot of peace of mind.

Change management is huge when it comes to administration and maintenance; it's all about the plan, the people executing the plan, and communication. Nothing—and I literally mean *nothing*—should ever be done in a production environment on the fly with no thought or notifica-tion. Even if what you need to do is an emergency change, there needs to be proper coordination and communication. Making hasty decisions rarely adds to your availability.

Installing and Configuring SQL Server

Arguably the first thing you can do as a DBA or system administrator is to ensure that the SQL Server and the databases contained in that instance are installed and configured properly. Without that solid foundation, you will potentially have stability issues that will show up intermittently.

Installing SQL Server

If you think back to the clustering chapters, I talked about how you should not install the SQL Server portion if the Windows portion is not installed properly. This also applies to all installations of SQL Server—clustered or stand-alone. This section goes through the steps you should take to ensure that your SQL Server installations are stable and to note if there are considerations that are specific to a version of SQL Server or types of installations. These recommendations are based on best practices from Microsoft Product Support Services (PSS). Take the following steps in order; if you don't you may have problems (unless you are directed to skip a step).

Note Some of these tasks may not be familiar to DBAs, so involve your system administrators where necessary.

---

1. Read any additional information needed for installing SQL Server. There are two main resources I will point you to: the Microsoft Knowledge Base article 910228 "SQL Server 2005 Readme and Installation Requirements" (http://support.microsoft.com/default.aspx?scid=kb;EN-US;910228) and KB 907284 "Changes to the Readme File for SQL Server 2005" (http://support.microsoft.com/default.aspx?scid=kb;EN-US;907284). Similarly, consult any readme files for all patches and hotfixes if that is what you are installing.

2. Make sure that security is set up properly for the service accounts that will be used with the various SQL Server services. Chapters 4, 5, 7, and 8 talk about security for a failover cluster. A stand-alone server is not much different. Make sure you work with your security administrators to get all accounts provisioned ahead of time so as to not delay your implementations. For more information, see the aforementioned chapters as well as the section on security later in this chapter.

3. On each server if it is a node of a failover cluster (or a single server solution if it is a stand-alone install), open the Registry and navigate to the key HKEY_LOCAL_MACHINE\SYSTEM\CurrentControlSet\Control. The Registry is a place where most of your configuration information is stored for your operating system and applications. Select Session Manager in the left pane. Then double-click the value PendingFileRenameOperations in the right pane. If the value is not empty, reboot your server before attempting to install SQL Server. An example is shown in Figure 15-1.

4. Make sure that networking is configured properly and the server can connect to the rest of the environment. See Chapters 4, 5, 7, and 8 for clustering-specific networking tasks.

5. Make sure that both long and 8.3 format (short) names are supported on the server. To verify, open a command prompt where there are longer-named folders and files and enter the command **DIR /X**. If you do not see both types, as shown in Figure 15-2, in the Registry, set the value for HKEY_LOCAL_MACHINE\ SYSTEM\CURRENTCONTROLSET\CONTROL\FileSystem\Ntfs\Disable8dot3NameCreation to **0**. If this value has to be set, log out and log back into the server as another administrator account and delete the directory created with your name under C:\Documents and Settings. Make sure you back up or copy all files you may have created first.

6. Before installing SQL Server, make sure that all of the services in Table 15-1 are up and running. Any other services should be stopped unless they are required by components such as your shared disk subsystem. Especially make sure you disable programs such as antivirus. If you have default server configurations that disable some of these services by default, they will need to be modified.

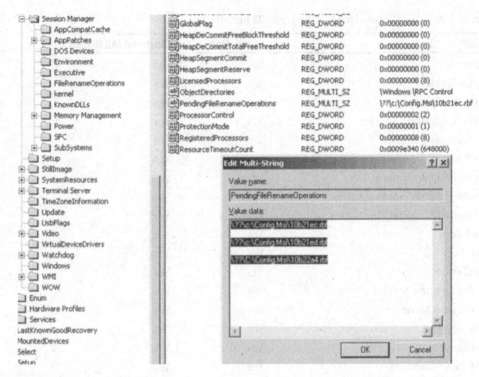

Figure 15-1. *Server with pending files needing a reboot*

```
C:\>DIR /X
 Volume in drive C has no label.
 Volume Serial Number is A012-5E40

 Directory of C:\

10/27/2005  12:52 PM                 0                AUTOEXEC.BAT
10/27/2005  12:52 PM                 0                CONFIG.SYS
02/12/2007  08:20 AM         1,395,200                DBADB.bak
02/12/2007  08:25 AM            82,432 DBADBT~1.TRN   dbadbtlog.trn
10/22/2006  06:55 PM       <DIR>      DOCUME~1        Documents and Settings
01/29/2007  03:02 AM       <DIR>      LSDIR~1         LS Dir
05/11/2007  07:15 PM       <DIR>      PROGRA~1        Program Files
05/11/2007  06:55 PM         2,097,152               RFM.ss
05/11/2007  06:55 PM         2,097,152               RFM2.ss
10/22/2006  08:45 PM         1,329,664 TESTMI~1.BAK   testmirror1.bak
02/12/2007  01:47 PM         1,329,664 TESTMI~2.BAK   testmirror2.bak
10/22/2006  06:40 PM       <DIR>                      WINDOWS
10/27/2005  12:53 PM       <DIR>                      wmpub
               8 File(s)      8,331,264 bytes
               5 Dir(s)   2,595,409,920 bytes free
```

Figure 15-2. *Directory listing with both long file and 8.3 name support*

Table 15-1. *Services Required for SQL Server 2005 Installation*

Service	Stand-Alone	Clustered (All Nodes)
Alerter	Yes	Yes
Cluster Service	No	Yes
Computer Browser	Yes	Yes
COM+ Application Service	Yes	Yes
Cryptographic Service	Yes	Yes
DHCP Client	Yes	Yes
Distributed File System	Yes	Yes
Distributed Link Tracking Client	Yes	Yes
Distributed Link Tracking Server	Yes	Yes
DNS Client	Yes	Yes
Event Log	Yes	Yes
IPSEC Policy Agent	Yes	Yes
License Logging Service	Yes	Yes
Logical Disk Manager	Yes	Yes
Messenger	Yes	Yes
Net Logon	Yes	Yes
Network Connectors	Yes	Yes
NT LM Security Support Provider	Yes	Yes
Plug and Play	Yes	Yes
Process Control	Yes	Yes
Remote Procedure Call (RPC)	Yes	Yes
Remote Procedure Call (RPC) Locator	Yes	Yes
Remote Registry	Yes	Yes
Removable Storage	Yes	Yes
Security Accounts Manager	Yes	Yes
Server	Yes	Yes
Spooler	Yes	Yes
Task Scheduler	Yes	Yes
TCP/IP NetBIOS Helper	Yes	Yes
Telephony	Yes	Yes
Time (Windows 2000)	Yes	Yes
Windows Management Instrumentation Driver Extensions	Yes	Yes
Windows Time (Windows 2003)	Yes	Yes
Workstation	Yes	Yes

7. Delete everything including folders from the X:\Documents and Settings\login_name\local settings\temp, where *X* is the letter of your system drive. If you are doing a 64-bit installation, make sure that all files and folders are deleted from X:\temp. Finally, delete all files and folders from %systemroot%\temp.

8. Delete any files (not folders) under %systemroot% that have a prefix of sql and a file type of log (sql*.log). From the same directory, also delete all files with a type of iss (*.iss) as well as any files that start with sql and have a file type of mif (sql*.mif).

9. If you have other installations of SQL Server (either failed or successful), first archive then delete all files from X:\Program Files\Microsoft SQL Server\90\Setup Bootstrap\LOG, where *X* is the letter of the drive that contains the files for SQL Server. Also, delete all files from X:\Program Files\Microsoft SQL Server\90\Setup Bootstrap\LOG\Files. Before deleting the files, if you need to keep records of installation for auditing purposes, make sure you copy them elsewhere.

10. Flush your DNS prior to installation. Issue these three commands in succession: ipconfig /flushdns, nbtstat -rr, and ipconfig /registerdns. An example is shown in Figure 15-3.

```
C:\>ipconfig /flushdns

Windows IP Configuration

Successfully flushed the DNS Resolver Cache.

C:\>nbtstat -rr

    NetBIOS Names Resolution and Registration Statistics
    ----------------------------------------------------------

    Resolved By Broadcast    = 220
    Resolved By Name Server  = 0

    Registered By Broadcast  = 4
    Registered By Name Server = 0

    NetBIOS Names Resolved By Broadcast
    ----------------------------------------------------------
            NEWDC
            NEWDC
            NEWDC
            NEWDC
            NEWDC
            NEWDC
            NEWDC
            NEWDC

C:\>ipconfig /registerdns

Windows IP Configuration

Registration of the DNS resource records for all adapters of this computer has b
een initiated. Any errors will be reported in the Event Viewer in 15 minutes..
```

Figure 15-3. *Flushing the DNS and resolver cache*

11. Check to see that the value returned for the server's logonserver value matches the other ones in your environment; and if you are installing a failover cluster, especially make sure all nodes are pointing to the same domain controller. To check, type **set logonserver** in a command window. An example is shown in Figure 15-4.

```
C:\>set logonserver
LOGONSERVER=\\LS-MIRROR-3
```

Figure 15-4. *Checking the value for logonserver*

If it is not set properly, enter the command **set logonserver=\\Domain_Controller**. Then enter **set logonserver** again to verify the change. An example is shown in Figure 15-5.

```
C:\>set logonserver=\\newdc

C:\>set logonserver
LOGONSERVER=\\newdc
```

Figure 15-5. *Setting a new value for logonserver*

12. Check to see that the times for each server are synchronized to the domain controller. At a command prompt, enter the command set time **%logonserver% /SET**. When prompted, enter **Y**. An example is shown in Figure 15-6.

```
C:\>net time %logonserver% /SET
Current time at \\newdc is 5/14/2007 2:43 AM

The current local clock is 5/14/2007 2:43 AM
Do you want to set the local computer's time to match the
time at \\newdc? (Y/N) [Y]: Y
The command completed successfully.
```

Figure 15-6. *Synchronizing the time*

13. Verify that there are no errors in the various Event Viewer logs that would adversely affect the installation process. If you make an error during the installation process, while you can use the Back button, I always recommend starting over since it only takes a minute or two and you ensure nothing is "hanging around."

14. Install the .NET Framework 2.0 prior to installing SQL Server.

15. If you have a failed installation, you should download and install the Windows Installer CleanUp Utility as per KB 290301 (http://support.microsoft.com/default.aspx?scid=kb; EN-US;290301).

■**Tip** The best thing you can do to ensure that you have high-quality builds is to have a consistent, reliable, and repeatable process that is as automated as possible. A lot of these checks can be automated; example scripts can be found in the Source Code/Download section of the Apress web site: http://www.apress.com.

Configuring SQL Server Instances

After SQL Server is up and running, you have to ensure that it is configured properly. This section focuses on some of the more important settings; others are discussed in other sections of this chapter. There are many more settings and configuration points you can have, but I will only tackle memory since it is one of the most misunderstood concepts.

With most options in SQL Server there are multiple ways to set values. The easiest way I find to set instance settings is via the tried-and-true system stored procedure sp_configure. This also allows you to have a very repeatable process across all servers. There are also different places you can change most, if not all, options via an interface either in SQL Server Management Studio or in Surface Area Configuration. The choice is yours. If you are going to use sp_configure, make sure that you can see all options by entering the following command first. It only needs to be done once, but keep in mind some options may require a restart of the SQL Server service, affecting your availability:

```
sp_configure 'show advanced options', 1
GO
RECONFIGURE WITH OVERRIDE
GO
```

Table 15-2 shows a comparison of server options between SQL Server 2000 and SQL Server 2005.

Table 15-2. *Server Configuration Options*

Option	SQL Server 2000	SQL Server 2005
Ad Hoc Distribution Queries	No	Yes
affinity I/O mask	No	Yes
affinity mask	Yes	Yes
Agent XPs	No	Yes
allow updates	Yes	Yes
awe enabled	Yes	Yes
blocked process threshold	No	Yes
c2 audit mode	Yes	Yes
clr enabled	No	Yes
cost threshold for parallelism	Yes	Yes
Cross DB Ownership Chaining	Yes	Yes
cursor threshold	Yes	Yes
Database Mail XPs	No	Yes
default full-text language	Yes	Yes
default language	Yes	Yes
default trace enabled	No	Yes
disallow results from triggers	No	Yes
fill factor (%)	Yes	Yes
ft crawl bandwidth (max)	No	Yes
ft crawl bandwidth (min)	No	Yes
ft notify bandwidth (max)	No	Yes
ft notify bandwidth (min)	No	Yes
index create memory (KB)	Yes	Yes
in doubt xact resolution	No	Yes
lightweight pooling	Yes	Yes
Locks	Yes	Yes
max degree of parallelism	Yes	Yes
max server memory (MB)	Yes	Yes
max text repl size (B)	Yes	Yes
max worker threads	Yes	Yes
media retention	Yes	Yes

Continued

Table 15-2. *Continued*

Option	SQL Server 2000	SQL Server 2005
min memory per query (KB)	Yes	Yes
min server memory (MB)	Yes	Yes
nested triggers	Yes	Yes
network packet size (B)	Yes	Yes
Ole Automation Procedures	No	Yes
open objects	Yes	Yes
PH timeout (s)	No	Yes
precompute rank	No	Yes
priority boost	Yes	Yes
query governor cost limit	Yes	Yes
query wait (s)	Yes	Yes
recovery interval (min)	Yes	Yes
remote access	Yes	Yes
remote admin connections	No	Yes
remote login timeout (s)	Yes	Yes
remote proc trans	Yes	Yes
remote query timeout (s)	Yes	Yes
Replication XPs	No	Yes
scan for startup procs	Yes	Yes
server trigger recursion	No	Yes
set working set size	Yes	Yes
show advanced options	Yes	Yes
SMO and DMO XPs	No	Yes
SQL Mail XPs	No	Yes
transform noise words	No	Yes
two digit year cutoff	Yes	Yes
user connections	Yes	Yes
user options	Yes	Yes
Web Assistant Procedures	No	Yes
xp_cmdshell	Yes	Yes

■**Caution** I never recommend changing the values for max degree of parallelism or priority boost. They can have an adverse effect on your performance (and subsequent availability). Only change these if you are directed by PSS or do a full complement of testing prior to changing your production servers.

Setting Memory Values

One of the most common missed configuration points I see with SQL Server is how memory is configured for an instance. In my book Microsoft *SQL Server 2000 High Availability* (Microsoft Press, 2003), we did a great description of how memory works. Unfortunately I can't reproduce that content here, but most of it is still valid today, so I suggest you look it up for reference. I will do my best to summarize in this section a good deal of that information and how it affects you.

With SQL Server, depending on your desired configuration, you can install either a 32-bit or a 64-bit version. All memory under a 64-bit operating system using a 64-bit SQL Server is dynamic. That is a good thing, as it allows SQL Server to police itself and adjust memory as needed. But 32-bit is a different story. By default, SQL Server 32-bit versions can only use up to 2GB of memory with no special options set in the operating system. With SQL Server 2000 32-bit, to allow SQL Server to use more than 4GB of memory, you would have to set both awe enabled and set working set size to 1. You would also need to set your maximium and minimum amounts of memory to be the same thing, essentially hard-coding the amount of memory SQL Server would use. The final piece of the puzzle is that you need to add the /PAE to boot.ini as shown in Figure 15-7.

```
[boot loader]
timeout=30
default=multi(0)disk(0)rdisk(0)partition(1)\WINDOWS
[operating systems]
multi(0)disk(0)rdisk(0)partition(1)\WINDOWS="Windows Server 2003, Enterprise" /noexecute=optout /fastdetect /PAE
```

Figure 15-7. *boot.ini with /PAE*

With 32-bit SQL Server 2005 and Windows Server 2000, the the same basic rules apply, except set working set size is no longer valid. However, if you are using 32-bit SQL Server 2005 with Windows Server 2003, all memory above 4GB is dynamic. You still have to set /PAE in boot.ini and set awe enabled to 1, but you do not need to do the other configuration steps. This is a huge improvement and makes things much easier to deal with. As with SQL Server 2000, you can set a fixed maximum and minimum amount of memory to ensure that SQL Server grabs a chunk of memory (e.g., hard coding it). You do not have to allow the memory to be dynamic if you do not want it to be.

If you will not be using memory above 4GB, to scale beyond 2GB of memory but not use more than 4GB with a 32-bit edition of SQL Server, you have to use the boot.ini switch /3GB instead of /PAE. Otherwise, SQL Server will be limited to 2GB of memory.

One question that always comes up is this: can you combine /PAE and /3GB on the same 32-bit server? The answer is yes; but the reality is you should pick one memory model and stick to it. The two can possibly play nice up to somewhere between 12GB and 16GB of memory. After that, you will have problems and you should not combine the two. The two types of memory work differently (read the memory parts of my Microsoft book), and some applications can take advantage of /3GB but still need /PAE. A good example is Siebel. If you are using a 64-bit edition, unless you are installing a 32-bit SQL Server instance for use under Windows on Windows (WOW), you should not have to worry about these boot.ini switches.

If you are scaling beyond 4GB of memory (either 32- or 64-bit), I recommend setting a minimum so the SQL Server instance cannot dip below that point. While there is a chance, depending on available server resources, that you could go below the amount configured, you reduce your chances by setting this option, and you will know your SQL Server instance will perform at a minimum level. The sp_configure setting is min server memory and is measured in megabytes (MB). Here is an example where you are setting the minimum amount of memory to 2GB:

```
sp_configure 'min server memory', 2048
go
reconfigure
go
```

You also have the option of limiting the maximum amount of memory a SQL Server instance can take with the sp_configure option max server memory. It functions exactly the same as min server memory. To limit the total amount of memory to 4GB that a SQL Server instance can use, execute the following:

```
sp_configure 'max server memory', 4096
go
reconfigure
go
```

The options for setting memory in SQL Server Management Studio are shown in Figure 15-8 and correspond to their equivalent sp_configure option.

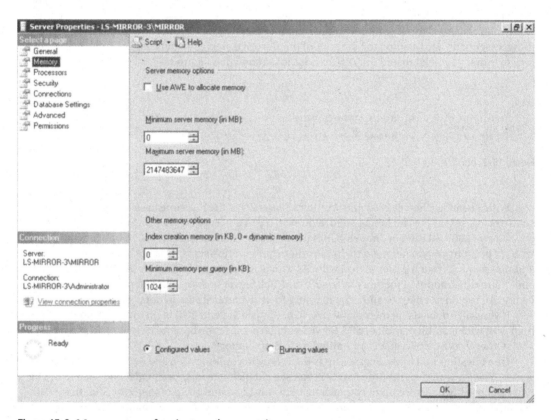

Figure 15-8. *Memory page of an instance's properties*

Tip Even if you are not going to implement failover clustering, I suggest you read the section in Chapter 7 on configuring multiple instances on a cluster since the same concepts apply for memory here.

Configuring Databases

After SQL Server is up and running and you have added databases, you need to ensure that they are also configured properly. While there are many settings that you can configure, I will focus on a few main ones. As with sp_configure for server options, there is an equivalent stored procedure for each database sp_dboption. Its use is similar to sp_configure except most values are TRUE or FALSE. You can also configure the settings in SQL Server Management Studio as shown in the example in Figure 15-9.

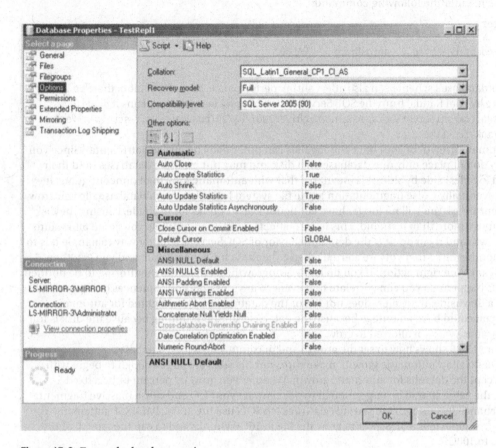

Figure 15-9. *Example database options*

Sizing Your Databases Properly

One of the more common problems I see at nearly every client site for an individual database is that it is sized improperly. I am not just talking about the data files, but the log files as well. As I have alluded to in parts of the book and will call out specifically here, the idea of one database, one disk per data and log file for each database, and one SQL Server instance all on one physical server is just unrealistic. While it may actually be what you need from a performance standpoint, when the mantra is to do more with less, this architecture will not fly. Unfortunately, no customer I have ever worked with has had complete and proper I/O isolation, which in turn means that you have some challenges that get introduced with your disk configuration such as disk fragmentation.

Never enable the ability to automatically shrink your database data or log files. It is one of the most misused and dangerous options that is exposed in SQL Server. It also says that you have done something to create large growth that may have not been needed (or needed and unaccounted for in your original sizing), and now you have a lot of free space that will come and go like the tide. Many DBAs and administrators think that if you allow the database to shrink itself and free up disk space, it's a good thing, right? Wrong. All you are doing is causing a lot of unnecessary disk I/O that happens every 30 minutes on databases that have that parameter set to TRUE.

You cannot set the schedule. Would you want to kill your disk I/O every half hour? I know I wouldn't. It also winds up contributing to physical disk fragmentation. If for some reason autoshrink is enabled (which is not the default behavior unless the model database is changed), to disable it, enter the following command:

```
USE master
GO
EXEC sp_dboption 'mydb', 'autoshrink', 'FALSE'
GO
```

Your database's schema can also affect shrink performance. For information, there's a great blog entry by Paul Randal from the SQL Server storage engine team that explains it at http://blogs.msdn.com/sqlserverstorageengine/archive/2007/03/29/how-does-your-schema-affect-your-shrink-run-time.aspx.

Automatic growth of your data and log files can potentially be just as detrimental. Since you generally do not place only one database on a disk and may put multiple databases (and their data and log files) side by side, it is inevitable that with automatic growth of noncontiguous files you will eventually cause fragmentation at the file system level since each database file will grow at different times. You will no longer have contiguous disk chunks for each file, causing the disk head to move more than it should. This in turn affects performance. While you could allow automatic growth and most do (it *is* the default behavior of SQL Server), a better way to handle it is to set up monitoring so that you are alerted when a database file is nearly full, and you can then manually take the right action. If you do allow autogrowth, set up some monitoring to be notified when this happens so you can correlate that event to any possible consequences or support calls. There is a downside: if the alert does not fire or the database is not configured for automatic growth, you could have an outage because the database stopped running because the disk is full or the database was not allowed to grow.

Figure 15-10 shows how to set the growth and maximum sizes for a database.

If you do allow automatic growth, make sure your file sizes are large enough to begin with. Never accept the defaults for automatic growth. Whether you grow by percent or by a fixed amount, the value should be large enough to not saturate your I/O and cause massive fragmentation. To change the autogrowth settings via Transact-SQL, use the ALTER DATABASE statement. The following example tells SQL Server to grow the file in 10GB chunks and to cap the growth of the database to 100GB:

```
ALTER DATABASE TestRepl1
MODIFY FILE
(
    NAME = Data_or_Log_File,
    FILEGROWTH = 10GB,
    MAXSIZE = 100GB
)
```

I've seen automatic shrink and automatic growth in action. It can become a vicious cycle that can cause internal fragmentation inside the database as well as on the physical disks. Automatic shrinking and growth of databases would not really be necessary if you sized them properly to begin with. Sizing will always be a challenge since most administrators are not trained in the ways to size a database, manage the size of database files (including log files), or ask the right questions of the business and the application owners/developers/vendors; even if they ask the right questions, there is a lack of information to assist them in the process. At some point you need to make your best guess and start from there. My recommendation is to have databases and files that are possibly too large or take into account years of growth versus undersizing and subsequently causing availability and performance problems.

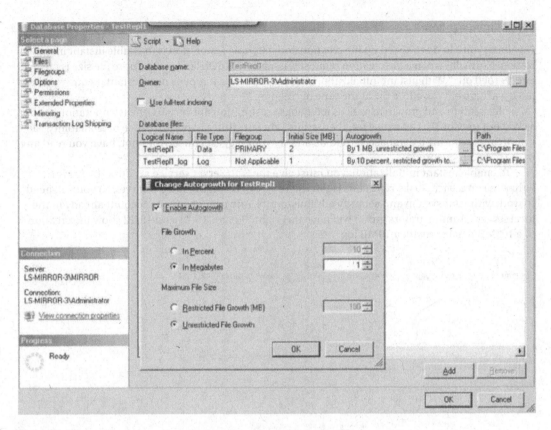

Figure 15-10. *Setting automatic growth options for a particular file*

I'm not saying to never shrink your databases. At my last client, they were disk-space challenged, and when they tried to do tasks such as index rebuilds, the transaction log would grow to be very large and fill up the disk. At that point, we had to manually truncate the transaction log and shrink the file using DBCC SHRINKDATABASE or DBCC SHRINKFILE. Trust me when I say doing that on a regular basis gets very old very quick. We eventually did a few things to combat this, such as breaking up the maintenance into smaller chunks and sizing the transaction log properly, but it takes a bit of experimentation to get to that place when the processes and information are not there to begin with. When you size your transaction logs, remember to take into account the way the relational engine of SQL Server handles maintenance tasks (or tasks the engine does automatically) and whether this will cause your transaction log to grow. A good example is the rebuild of an index, which is a fully logged operation and may increase your transaction log immensely if you use clustered indexes that could potentially be the size of your tables. In this example, your transaction log file could wind up being the same size as your data file if you do not watch it carefully. Don't expect that your disk won't be filled if you have a billion rows and a 100MB transaction log that you are not doing the proper maintenance on.

The same could be said for the data portion as well. If you do a ton of inserts, you should know your growth rates. Size your data files appropriately. Some of this is covered in Chapter 14 where I go through the data sizes for the cluster disk configuration. The less information you have, the more likely you will be the victim of autogrowth. Like automatically shrinking, continually allowing unmoderated growth of your database will eventually fill your disk and most likely cause fragmentation on the physical level. Dealing with physical disk fragmentation is covered in Chapter 16.

Instant Initialization

One thing you can do to speed up file creation and database restoration is to enable instant initialization. Normally, when a file creation request is issued from SQL Server, the entire file size is created and "zeroed out." With instant initialization, the file allocation happens near instantaneously without having to zero out the entire file at the time of creation.

File creation and growth as well as a database restoration are very I/O-heavy operations and, as laid out previously, can cause fragmentation. When it comes to performance or availability, file growth and restoring a database should be among your biggest concerns (if not, have you read any of the previous chapters?).

To enable instant initialization, you must give the SQL Server service account the Perform Volume Maintenance Tasks right; this is not a setting you configure in SQL Server, so you will need to work with your system and security administrators. Any user or service account already in the local server's Administrators group will have this right. Figures 15-11 and 15-12 show the creation of a 100MB database with a 10MB log.

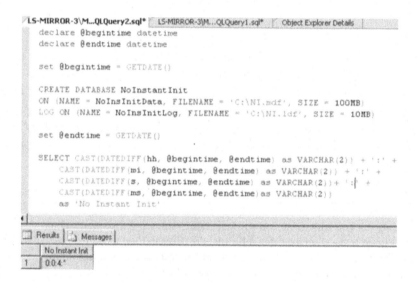

Figure 15-11. *Creating a database without instant initialization*

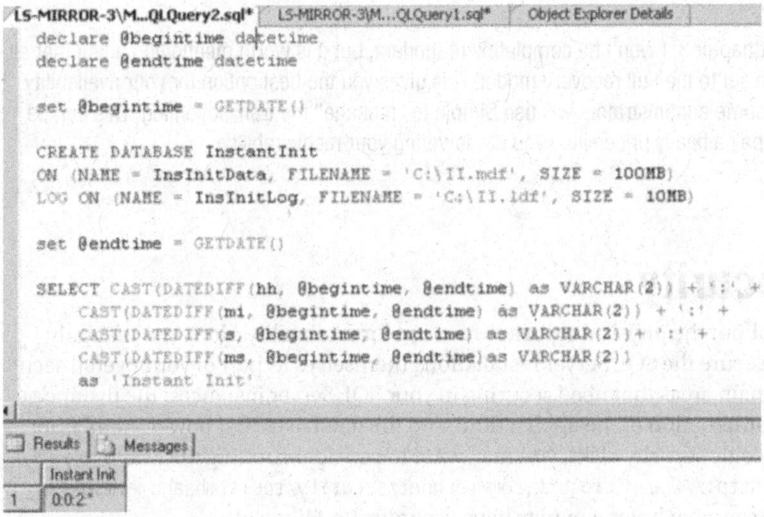
LS-MIRROR-3\M...QLQuery2.sql*
LS-MIRROR-3\M...QLQuery1.sql*
Object Explorer Details
declare @begintime datetime
declare @endtime datetime
set @begintime = GETDATE()
CREATE DATABASE InstantInit
ON (NAME = InsInitData, FILENAME = 'C:\II.mdf', SIZE = 100MB)
LOG ON (NAME = InsInitLog, FILENAME = 'C:\II.ldf', SIZE = 10MB)
set @endtime = GETDATE()
SELECT CAST(DATEDIFF(hh, @begintime, @endtime) as VARCHAR(2)) +':'+
CAST(DATEDIFF(mi, @begintime, @endtime) as VARCHAR(2)) + ':' +
CAST(DATEDIFF(s, @begintime, @endtime) as VARCHAR(2))+':'+
CAST(DATEDIFF(ms, @begintime, @endtime)as VARCHAR(2))
as 'Instant Init'
Results
Messages
Instant Init
1
0:0:2:*

Figure 15-12. *Creating a database with instant initialization*

While it's not the most scientific test (it was done within a virtual machine with limited disk space, which was all that was available to me at the time), you can see it was 50% quicker with instant initialization. On a SAN with larger files, you may see a more dramatic difference. Kimberly Tripp in a blog posting (`http://www.sqlskills.com/blogs/kimberly/2007/03/04/InstantInitializationWhatWhyAndHow.aspx`) has some eye-opening numbers. As she notes, creating a 20GB database was 64,846% faster (14 minutes, 3 seconds vs. 1.3 seconds), and restoring an 11GB backup was 50% faster (38 minutes, 28 seconds vs. 19 minutes, 42 seconds). When seconds count, this is an easy tweak.

Updating Statistics

Many of you may know that SQL Server has its own internal algorithm for updating the statistics for your database and that by default it is automatic. With SQL Server 7.0, I can remember instances where the algorithm did not work for some people and they had to disable automatic statistics and manually update with an `UPDATE STATISTICS` or `CREATE STATISTICS` command via a SQL Server Agent job. Some people still think they need to manually update statistics by default. They do not. What I see a lot out there in the wild is that there is a job to update statistics but automatic statistics is not disabled so the DBA is allowing the database to trip over itself. The DBA would not be able to ascertain which update of the statistics is working, if one is working at all. My recommendation is that with SQL Server 2005, you let SQL Server handle the automatic updating of statistics. If you determine that it is not working for you, disable the feature and code your own Transact-SQL to do the job. An example of disabling automatic updating of statistics follows:

```
USE master
GO
EXEC sp_dboption 'mydb', 'auto create statistics', 'FALSE'
GO
EXEC sp_dboption 'mydb', 'auto update statistics', 'FALSE'
GO
```

■**Note** Since it is covered in Chapter 3, I won't be completely redundant, but it is worth mentioning again that all production databases should be set to the Full recovery model. This gives you the best option for your availability and recovery. With file growth, some administrators will use Simple to "manage" the transaction log. This can be done to a degree, but you may pay a heavy price since you are lowering your recoverability.

SQL Server Security

In the first chapter I talked about the physical security you need for availability. However, that only gets you so far. You need to secure the SQL Server installations themselves as part of your overall security strategy. There are two main areas that need securing in your SQL Server instances: the instances themselves, as well as the combination of the applications and the databases that power them. Prior to doing any SQL Server–specific security tasks, you may want to consider running the Microsoft Baseline Security Analyzer (http://www.microsoft.com/technet/security/tools/mbsahome.mspx) as part of your server builds to see what holes you may have according to Microsoft.

■**Caution** There's secure, and then there is *secure*. I have seen customers cripple themselves in trying to either perform an installation of Windows or SQL Server or attempt to perform administrative tasks because they lock down servers to the point they are basically useless. I know there are corporate security policies that you must adhere to, but sometimes you may need to have exceptions. There should not be a "one size fits all" mentality when it comes to security. That can do more harm than good. Similarly, you should be vigilant about how you manage your Active Directory users or groups. If the wrong user or group is added to the SQL Server administrators, it will unnecessarily escalate privileges.

Securing the Instance

Before the SQL Server instance is used by anything, lock it down as best you can to ensure that no one will have improper access to it. There are various methods an administrator can employ to secure the instance, including using certificates and Kerberos, auditing logins, using Common Criteria, and implementing password protection. Many of these options can be set with sp_configure or in the Surface Area Configuration for Features option of SQL Server 2005 Surface Area Configuration. How to access this is shown in Chapter 9. An example screenshot is shown in Figure 15-13.

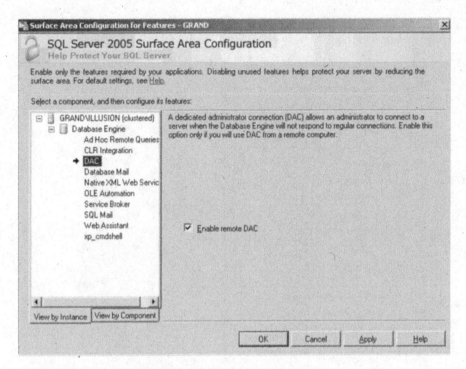

Figure 15-13. *Surface Area Configuration for Features*

Some of the security features can also be set on the Security page of the Properties dialog for the instance itself, as shown in Figure 15-14.

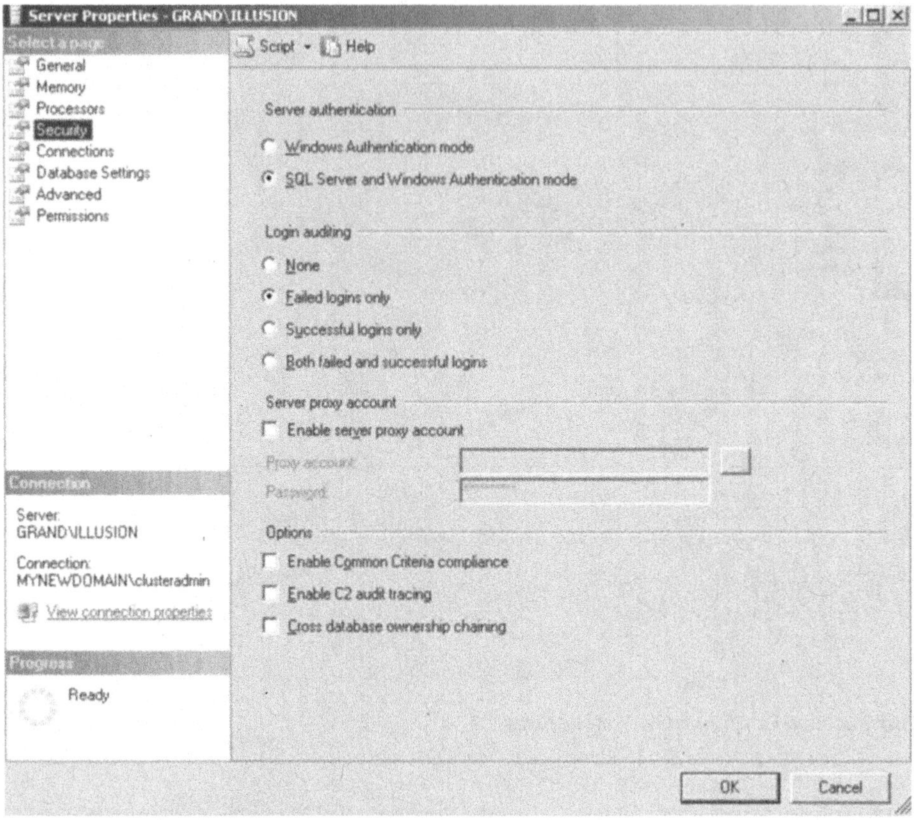

Figure 15-14. *Security page of an instance's Properties dialog*

Antivirus Programs and SQL Server Instances

Although this topic was mentioned in the clustering chapters, it bears repeating here: unless you absolutely have to, do not place an antivirus program on your SQL Servers. They can be deadly to the health and well-being of your SQL Server instances and databases and can cause potential performance issues. While this is a nice sentiment, the reality is that antivirus programs are required by nearly every company out there. Make sure that you take the proper precautions and configure exclusions on each server containing SQL Server. You should exclude the extensions for all data and log files, full-text index files, and most likely your backup files, too. This will help prevent possible corruption of these files and unwanted I/O spikes if an attempt is made to scan a file. If you do not get these exclusions in place, make sure that you have good backups and a résumé handy.

Using Domain-Based Service Accounts

To ensure that your SQL Servers are secure, you should use domain accounts for all service accounts for SQL Server, SQL Server Agent, Full-Text Search, and Analysis Services. Domain accounts are definitely required for clustered installations but technically optional for installations on stand-alone servers that may not be part of a domain. Using domain-based service accounts allows you to centralize management of service accounts and standardize how SQL Server is deployed across your enterprise. However, you may want to consider different service accounts for different purposes (i.e., one each for SQL Server, SQL Server Agent, Full-Text Search, and Analysis Services) and possibly change them up for each instance. That may wind up being a lot of accounts, but it would offer you the best isolation and security.

If you have sensitive information in some SQL Server databases but not others, and you have one master service account for all SQL Servers, anyone who has access to that service account password can access the sensitive data. Play it smart. Apply the same logic to your file shares that contain SQL Server files, especially your backups. Don't go super nuts and have 10,000 service accounts, but don't settle for one, either. These accounts must have the proper permissions to work. Again, I have seen more customers cripple themselves by trying to fight tooth and nail to not give an account a permission because it's "not their standard." Change your standard—have an exception. You bought the solution, implement it properly or pay the consequences when something does not work. For more information, see Chapter 7 as well as the Books Online topic "Setting Up Windows Service Accounts."

Tip You may want to consider removing the BUILTIN\Administrators account from SQL Server. The reason many remove it is that it prevents Windows administrators from easily accessing SQL Server. This is more prevalent in clustered installations since BUILTIN\Administrators is also used by the cluster. How to remove BUILTIN\Administrators in a failover cluster is covered in Chapter 8. The process for removing BUILTIN\Administrators on a stand-alone instance of SQL Server is basically the same.

Using Static TCP/IP Ports and Disabling Network Protocols Not Used

The entire world at this point knows that port 1433 is the default port for SQL Server. Unless your application requires it, I highly recommend changing the port to something unique for each instance. While this will not completely guarantee prying eyes from seeing that SQL Server is there, at least you are not making it easy for a hacker. To see how to set a static TCP/IP port number for a SQL Server instance, follow the instructions in Chapter 8.

Another security configuration point you may want to consider is to disable any connectivity protocols that you are not using (if they are not disabled already).This is done via SQL Server Configuration Manager by connecting to the instance, expanding SQL Server 2005 Network Configuration, and then selecting Protocols for <INSTANCE>, where <INSTANCE> is your instance name (MSSQLSERVER if it is a default instance of SQL Server 2005). The protocols will be displayed on the right, as shown in Figure 15-15, and you can enable or disable as necessary. However, I would not recommend changing any of the default settings unless you have to.

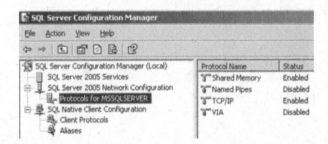

Figure 15-15. *SQL Server instance protocols for a stand-alone installation*

Using SSL Certificates and Kerberos

By default, SQL Server is not configured to use SSL certificates or Kerberos. You can use either or both if you want—or neither. There is no requirement from Microsoft to use them. Your applications and solutions may even dictate that they are used. DBAs will most likely not be performing the Windows portion of an SSL certificate or Kerberos, so you must work with your server administrators to ensure that things are installed and configured properly prior to installing and configuring SQL Server and these advanced security features. You cannot and should not configure certificates and Kerberos after the fact to avoid potential problems, including preventing SQL Server from being allowed to be installed.

To configure Kerberos, follow the instructions found in the Microsoft Knowledge Base article 319723 "How to Use Kerberos Authentication in SQL Server" (http://support.microsoft.com/kb/319723/en-us). There is also the topic "How to Enable Kerberos Authentication on a SQL Server Failover Cluster" in Books Online. If you do not follow the instructions properly, you may have incorrectly registered Service Principal Name (SPN) and will most likely see errors as documented in KB 303411 "You Receive a 'Warning SuperSocket Info' Warning Information When a SQL Server Service Account Is a Domain User" (http://support.microsoft.com/kb/303411/en-us). You will also prevent the need to manually change the SQL Server SPN if the TCP/IP address or DNS entry for SQL Server is changed.

To configure SSL certificates, use the instructions in KB 316898 "How to Enable SSL Encryption for an Instance of SQL Server by Using Microsoft Management Console" (http://support.microsoft.com/kb/316898/en-us). Also consult the Books Online topics "Encrypting Connections to SQL Server" and "How to Enable Encrypted Connections to the Database Engine (SQL Server Configuration Manager)" for more SQL Server–specific information.

■**Caution** If you do not implement certificates or Kerberos properly, you may potentially damage the installation to the point you will not only have to reinstall SQL Server but possibly reinstall the operating system.

Auditing

Part of knowing that your data integrity is not compromised is keeping track of who is accessing SQL Server. SQL Server can keep track of login failures, and it is simple to implement. Unfortunately, the only way you can set it is via SQL Server Management Studio, as shown in Figure 15-14 under the section Login Auditing. My recommendation is to leave the default of Failed Logins Only. This means that any failed login attempt will be logged and will be reported in the SQL Error Log. A good example of this is if you encounter a 18456 error in SQL Server, which is related to a login failure, you will not see the reason. If you look at the actual server logs, you will see the actual reason. An example is shown in Figure 15-16.

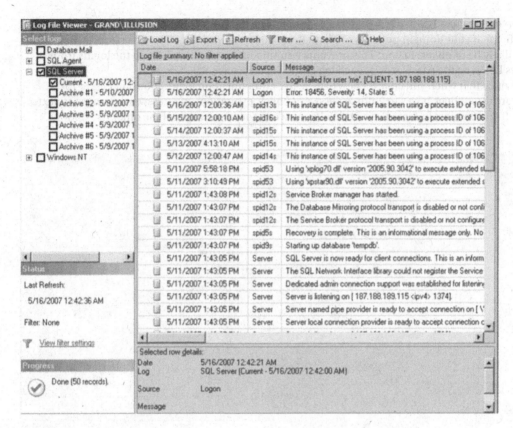

Figure 15-16. *Example login failure*

Common Criteria

Microsoft introduced support for the Common Criteria security standard in SQL Server 2005 Service Pack 1. This supersedes the older C2 audit mode that earlier versions of SQL Server used (and is also implemented in SQL Server 2005 to ensure backward compatibility). For full information on how SQL Server uses this standard and is certified against Common Criteria, consult http://www.microsoft.com/sql/commoncriteria/2005/sp1/default.mspx. To enable this via SQL Server Management Studio, use the Security page, as shown in the earlier Figure 15-14. To enable this via Transact-SQL, enter the following command:

```
sp_configure 'common criteria compliance enabled', 1
GO
RECONFIGURE WITH OVERRIDE
GO
```

Implementing Password Security for Logins

Another new feature of SQL Server 2005 is the ability to hook into your existing domain policies to enforce password complexity for all logins using SQL Server authentication. This only works with Windows Server 2003. You can also force the user to change his password on his next login. Prior to SQL Server 2005, there was no way to enforce password complexity or expiration for SQL

Server–only logins. The catch is that you cannot have a different complexity that is SQL Server–specific, so if your domain policy is inadequate or does not work for SQL Server, this feature will most likely be of no use to you. This prevents administrators who have set up the logins from always knowing the passwords of each login once users access SQL Server.

Notice that when you create a new SQL Server authentication login, shown in Figure 15-17, there are three check boxes to enforce password policy, expiration, and password changes at next login. If you deselect Enforce Password Policy, you cannot select either of the other two options.

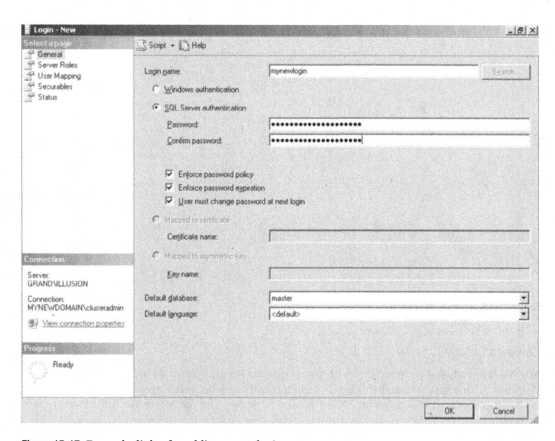

Figure 15-17. *Example dialog for adding a new login*

If you try to create a login that violates the domain policy for passwords, you will see the message shown in Figure 15-18.

To create a new login via Transact-SQL, you will use the CREATE LOGIN statement instead of sp_addlogin. An example statement follows that enforces both the password and the expiration policies, and forces a password change upon login:

```
CREATE LOGIN newtestsql
WITH PASSWORD = 'p@ssw0rd' MUST_CHANGE,
CHECK_EXPIRATION = ON,
CHECK_POLICY = ON
```

If you try to log into the SQL Server instance with your old password, you will get a 18488 error, as shown in Figure 15-19.

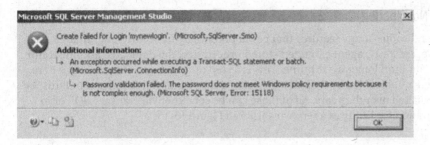

Figure 15-18. *Error if a password violates the domain policy*

```
C:\>sqlcmd -SGRAND\ILLUSION -Umynewlogin -Pp@ssw0rd
Msg 18488, Level 14, State 1, Server GRAND\ILLUSION, Line 1
Login failed for user 'mynewlogin'.  Reason: The password of the account must be
 changed.
```

Figure 15-19. *Error when logging in with old password*

If you are forcing a password change, and if you log in via the SQL Server tools, you will see the following prompt upon login, as shown in Figure 15-20.

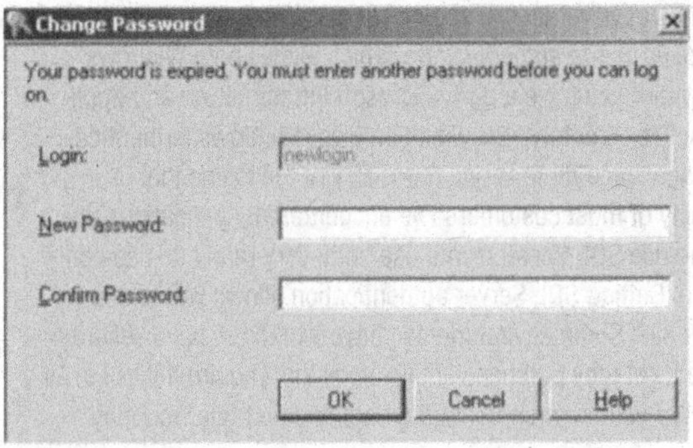

Figure 15-20. *Changing a password*

To change a login's password at a command prompt, use sqlcmd with the -z option to designate the new password. An example is shown in Figure 15-21.

```
C:\>sqlcmd -SGRAND\ILLUSION -Umynewlogin -zP@$sw0rd -Pp@ssw0rd
1>
```

Figure 15-21. *Changing a password using sqlcmd*

■ **Caution** Be careful when forcing a password change. I did not test it with a third-party application, and I would think that unless you can properly trap the error, there will be issues. Only enforce it if you know that there will not be problems. Remember that if the developers and DBAs/installers did not confer, the developer may have no idea that this password change option is selected and it may cause havoc for users.

Disabling Features Not Needed

By default, SQL Server disables many features that could potentially be security nightmares, such as the ability to use xp_cmdshell, agent extended stored procedures, the dedicated administrator connection, and the common language runtime. This is a step up from previous versions where features like these were not disabled by default and violated many internal security standards for a lot of clients I have visited over the years. All of these can be set either via Transact-SQL or in Surface Area Configuration for Features as shown earlier in Figure 15-13.

Caution Do not attempt to remove system stored procedures or extended stored procedures unless directed by Microsoft. In versions prior to SQL Server 2005, I remember reading a lot of documents (non-Microsoft) that advocated removing these potential security problems without thinking of either a) how it would affect the company's supportability from Microsoft if they encounter a problem after removing those objects, or b) what features may actually use something that is removed, thus breaking SQL Server. You most likely have bigger security issues than removing extended stored procedures. If you properly design access to SQL Server, issues such as xp_cmdshell should not be a problem.

WINDOWS AUTHENTICATION VS. SQL SERVER AUTHENTICATION

One of the classic debates when it comes to security and SQL Server is this: should you use Windows authentication or SQL Server authentication (otherwise known as *mixed-mode authentication*, which allows both Windows and SQL Server-only authentication)? In a perfect world where you have a pure Microsoft infrastructure and applications that are designed properly to take advantage of Active Directory, you would only use Windows authentication. Windows authentication is technically easier to manage since there is one repository of the logins that is managed centrally in the environment. This is not the reality of most customers I've encountered. Applications are all over the map; some use Windows authentication, some use SQL Server, some use both. Very rarely do I see only Windows authentication or only SQL Server authentication. Setting SQL Server authentication allows you to use either or, and I recommend this setting since it is a "catch all." Some environments I have worked in have security policies that dictate that SQL Server logins cannot be used, yet they purchase applications that require their use. As with many other things, you should not have every aspect of your environment be a hard and fast rule. You may need to make exceptions from time to time.

Securing the Application and Databases

As a DBA, you are ultimately responsible for administering and securing your SQL Server instances and databases. Unfortunately, unless what is implemented in production has been coded in-house and you are consulted, you most likely have no control over how an application's security is designed. That means you are stuck with someone else's idea of what security should be, and that may even include escalated rights and privileges. There is not much you can do about this situation except voice your concerns and find ways to mitigate the risks that it may cause. Chapter 13 deals with some of these issues.

It is in your best interest to be brought into the process as soon as possible. Whether that is in the requirements phase for a custom application, during the decision-making process for a third-party application, or being told immediately after the decision is made (assuming you are not part of the decision process) so you can do the proper research to find out how this application will have to be configured in SQL Server. Good, mediocre, or horrible, at least you know what you will be dealing with. If you have concerns, raise them immediately. Where this comes into play is if you are asked to make an implementation compliant with a certain set of rules such as SOX or ISO and you cannot because you have no control over changing the application. If this is a third-party application, you may even violate your support agreements if you change the privileges of any object or account used by the application. I see these struggles all the time at client sites, and it is always painful.

One thing DBAs and developers can consider is encrypting the data in a database. This is something that should be taken into account in the planning stages. If you do this after the fact when the system is in production, you may wind up having issues. Up until SQL Server 2005, the only way to do this was via third-party tools. In SQL Server 2005, you can encrypt a column of a table. To see how to achieve this, read the Books Online topic "How to Encrypt a Column of Data."

While encryption may seem like a fairly straightforward and obvious solution, there are some dangers and risks associated with implementing encryption. First, are you impeding the job of the DBA, who may need to actually access the data quickly for some administrative purpose? There are instances where the quick ability to verify data may be needed. Second, what is the potential overhead of the encryption and decryption process? Was it taken into account in server sizing? Was it tested under heavy load? Finally, how will you deal with the data in a standby situation?

Dedicated Administrator Connection

A new feature of SQL Server 2005 is the dedicated administrator connection (DAC). This is a feature that could really save you in a dire situation. As long as there are server resources, the DAC allows an administrator to connect to SQL Server even if you cannot get in any other way. This is turned off by default and is something that should be enabled, but used only in emergency situations. There is only one DAC allowed per instance at any given time. Unless you allow it, you will not be able to have a remote DAC connection. Chances are your server will be unresponsive, so you may need to log into the SQL Server instance from somewhere else.

The DAC is an excellent availability and disaster recovery feature that is very welcome. Remember in the glory days prior to SQL Server 2005 (especially the old days of SQL Server 6.0 or SQL Server 6.5) that once your SQL Server went to lunch, it took a long time (if ever) to come back and allow you to run even a simple sp_who or sp_who2 statement?

To use the DAC, you must first enable the feature either in Surface Area Configuration for Features as shown earlier in Figure 15-13, or use Transact-SQL. Use the following syntax:

```
sp_configure 'remote access', 1
GO
RECONFIGURE WITH OVERRIDE
GO
sp_configure 'remote admin conncection', 1
GO
RECONFIGURE WITH OVERRIDE
GO
```

Once you enable the DAC, you can use it. The best way is to use a command-line utility such as sqlcmd with either the –A option that specifies to use a dedicated administrator connection, or instead of –A, when you specify a SQL Server instance after –S, use the prefix of admin: before entering the instance name. Three examples are shown in Figure 15-22.

```
C:\>sqlcmd -SGRAND\ILLUSION -A
1> exit

C:\>sqlcmd -SGRAND\ILLUSION -A -dmaster -Umynewlogin -Pp@ssw0rd
1> exit

C:\>sqlcmd -Sadmin:GRAND\ILLUSION -dmaster -Umynewlogin -Pp@ssw0rd
```

Figure 15-22. *Using the DAC*

■**Tip** Microsoft has published a white paper "SQL Server 2005 Security Best Practices—Operational and Administrative Tasks" (http://www.microsoft.com/technet/prodtechnol/sql/2005/ sql2005secbestpract.mspx). It should prove a good resource that goes into more depth in certain areas than I can in the space I have in this book. Other security-related white papers and articles can be found under the Security and Protection sections of http://www.microsoft.com/technet/prodtechnol/sql/2005/ technologies/dbengine.mspx.

Monitoring SQL Server

One of the best things you can do to ensure the health and availability of your servers and SQL Server instances is to monitor them. Monitoring them should not consist of glorified trained monkeys to watch a line go across the screen and wait for a blip (although I have seen that in action). Monitoring is much more involved and complex than watching a screen. The process of gathering information should be automated, and if there is a problem, whoever needs to be should be notified automatically. Monitoring mission-critical applications and servers in a 24x7 environment is a whole different world, and if you are not used to it, you are in for a possible rude awakening.

What Should You Monitor?

I'm sure you have done some sort of basic monitoring with Windows. There are a lot of counters you can potentially look at. How do you narrow that down to something that is manageable and easy to understand? While you should not have to monitor every counter that exists, you will need to monitor SQL Server instances and their databases in isolation as well as the underlying systems.

While you will be monitoring individual components, when problems arise, you will have to coordinate events across all components of the solution: the application, the operating system, SQL Server, the disk subsystem, and so on. This is not an easy task since the components may not be on the same server or even in the same data center. Monitoring tools can help you automate the entire process and coordinate these events across different applications and subsystems. This becomes especially important if you do encounter a problem and need to contact a vendor's support organization. If you can give them the information they need quickly, the faster your problem will get solved.

Unfortunately, what I find is that the right monitoring only gets put in place after a problem occurs. This means that all pertinent information that could help diagnose a problem is missed and may not get captured until the problem occurs again. I am always amazed that customers expect miracles when they can't provide the basic information to make sure they get the help they need. Monitoring should never be a burden.

Log Files

Your first line of defense is to monitor *all* application and server logs for errors, including the Windows Event Log. These events can later be correlated back to other numbers and events on that system as well as others to get a snapshot of the problem. SQL Server and SQL Server Agent both have their own logs. They can be found under the Management folder in SQL Server Management Studio under SQL Server Logs, as shown in Figure 15-23. On disk, the logs can be found in the SQL Server installation directory for the instance (such as `C:\Microsoft SQL Server\MSSQL.1\MSSQL\LOG`). On a clustered installation, this will be on the shared drive that contains your databases.

Figure 15-23. *Location of the SQL Server log in Management Studio*

Although many companies do not do this, you should consider archiving older log files for every application and server. SQL Server will continue to enumerate and cycle log files. The default number of log files is six. For auditing purposes—especially if you are bound by rules such as SOX—you should periodically copy the older log files to a safe drive just in case they need to be referenced. To change the number of total log files on disk, right-click SQL Server Logs and select the option Configure. You will then see the Configure SQL Server Error Logs dialog, as shown in Figure 15-24. If you wish to change the default value of six log files, check the check box and enter the maximum number of log files. You should also be careful to monitor the usage of your Windows Event Log since the individual logs can get full and stop logging.

Here is an excellent example of why you should monitor your logs. Quite a few years ago a client was having ongoing availability problems with their SQL Server installation. It was going down if someone looked at the SQL Server sideways. A whole army descended upon the client's location for the better part of a few months to try to solve the issues, which were multifaceted. One of the biggest problems they were having was that the database server kept failing. There were many late nights with PSS on the other end of the phone. One night around 2 a.m. I was going through the Event Log of the database server and lo and behold I noticed there was a nice little message that told me the disk subsystem was failing. This message went back quite a ways. No one was monitoring it. Guess what the problem was with the database? Corruption. Had the client been monitoring the server properly, there is a pretty high chance they could have avoided their summer of pain (and mine as well).

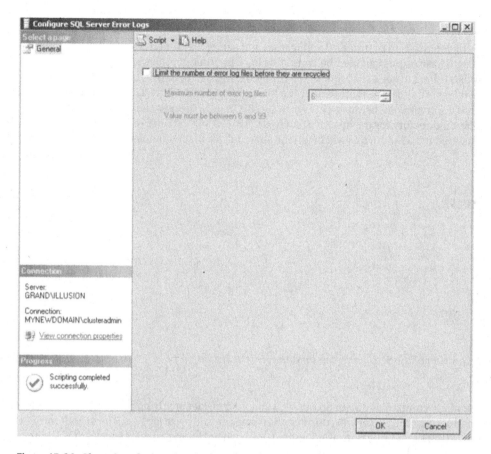

Figure 15-24. *Changing the maximum number of log files*

Services

Unless you are certain that your application services and executables are actually started, you might as well cross your fingers that it is actually up and running. It is easy to detect if a service is stopped or started, and in many ways is one of your first lines of defense when it comes to monitoring. A stopped service is a clear indication of a problem. In certain cases, such as with a cluster, you need to ensure that all of the required services for the Windows server cluster, as well as the SQL Server services, are all up and running to ensure that the entire ecosystem is functioning properly. The second a service fails, you should know about it.

Drive and File Space

A crucial thing to monitor is the usage of your disk subsystem: how full is it at any given time? How much is free? You need to monitor this for each disk of your disk subsystem and set up alerts to notify you when you hit and go beyond a threshold you can tolerate. If you get your notification when you hit 90% and something is filling the disk up quickly, you will not have a lot of time to react.

Similarly, you should also monitor the used and free space in your data and log files. This is just as important and often overlooked by many. Monitoring just the physical disk space is not enough when it comes to SQL Server. SQL Server has dynamic management views (DMVs) and counters where these are exposed. Often when I am onsite at a client, they will find themselves in a situation where the data and/or log files keep growing to the point they fill up the disk, in turn bringing the database to a halt since nothing else can be stored in the data files or written to the transaction log. This is a situation you do not want to find yourself in.

Counters

A *counter* is a single item you will measure. A counter is usually part of a group of related counters under a single category. The easiest way to demonstrate this is to show the Add Counters dialog from Performance Monitor (more commonly known as PerfMon), as shown in Figure 15-25. If you are monitoring a default instance of SQL Server, there will be either a SQLAgent: or SQLServer: before the name of the category. If you are monitoring a named instance of SQL Server, it will either be SQLAgent$Instance_Name: or MSSQL$Instance_Name:.

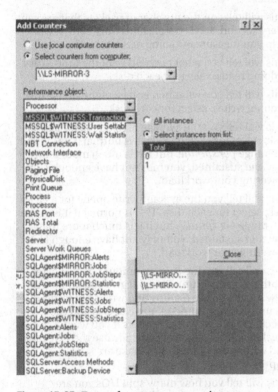

Figure 15-25. *Example counter categories*

Table 15-3 shows the counters I usually start with. If you have multiple instances, you will have to select the SQL Server counters more than once. You can always monitor more counters than what is listed in the table, but it is a great starting place. Every environment has slightly different needs. You may also change some counters if you are monitoring for performance or other reasons specific to your needs.

Table 15-3. *Counters to Monitor*

Category	Counter	Description
Memory	Available MBytes	This will tell you the available amount of memory on the server. Even if you are using a fixed amount of memory for SQL Server, this is always a good counter to monitor.
Memory	Pages/sec	This will tell you if your system is paging and could be an indicator that you do not have enough physical memory in your system to run all processes properly. Only use if all of your memory is dynamic.
Network Interface	Packets Received/sec	This will tell you the number of packets that are received every second; select this for each network card. It will help you measure incoming network traffic.
Network Interface	Packets Sent/sec	This will tell you the number of packets that are sent every second; select for each network card. It will help you measure outgoing network traffic.
PhysicalDisk	% Disk Read Time	This will tell you what percentage of the time a disk is doing reads; select for each disk.
PhysicalDisk	% Disk Write Time	This will tell you what percentage of the time a disk is doing writes; select for each disk.
PhysicalDisk	Avg. Disk Read Queue Length	This will tell you the average read queue for a given disk; select for each disk. This is normal if it is in the 2–5 range *per spindle*, but if it is much more than that *and* sustained, you may not have enough I/Os powering your workload.
PhysicalDisk	Avg. Disk Write Queue Length	This will tell you the average write queue for a given disk; select for each disk. This is normal if it is in the 2–5 range *per spindle*, but if it is much more than that *and* sustained, you may not have enough I/Os powering your workload.
PhysicalDisk	Avg. Disk Bytes/Transfer	This will tell you the average amount of disk bytes (both read and write). This will give you an idea of how much you are reading and writing in terms of quantity from your disks. You can also add the specific read and write counters if you want a breakdown, but you can generally use the % read and write times with this to make an approximation.
PhysicalDisk	Split IO/Sec	This will tell you how many split I/Os you are encountering for a given disk; select for each disk. Split I/Os is something you do not want to see and is an indication of physical fragmentation of your disks.
PhysicalDisk	Disk Reads/sec	This will tell you how many reads you are doing per second for a given disk; select for each disk. This will help you track the type of activity being done.
PhysicalDisk	Disk Writes/sec	This will tell you how many writes you are doing per second for a given disk; select for each disk. This will help you track the type of activity being done.

Category	Counter	Description
Process	% Processor Time	This will tell you what percentage of the overall processor time a certain process is taking; select for each SQL-related service (which will be enumerated and will appear as sqlservr, sqlservr#1). A generic processor utilization counter that is not specifically told to monitor SQL Server will only give you generic information that may not be useful.
Process	IO Read Operations/sec	This will tell the number of read I/Os for a given process; select for each SQL-related service (which will be enumerated and will appear as sqlservr, sqlservr#1). This is important to help you measure the I/Os needed.
Process	IO Write Operations/sec	This will tell the number of write I/Os for a given process; select for each SQL-related service (which will be enumerated and will appear as sqlservr, sqlservr#1).This is important to help you measure the I/Os needed.
Process	Page Faults/sec	This will tell you the number of page faults for a given server process; select for each SQL-related service (which will be enumerated and will appear as sqlservr, sqlservr#1). This may indicate a memory problem.
Processor	% Processor Time	This will tell you the amount of processor that all processes are consuming; add this counter for each individual processor as well as add the total summation of all processors. This will help you put the SQL Server utilization in context of whatever else is going on in the server.
SQLAgent:Jobs	Active Jobs	This will tell you the number of jobs running at a given time for the selected SQL Server instance. This may help you determine concurrency problems with your SQL Server Agent jobs if you are having problems.
SQLServer:Access Methods	Page Splits/sec	This will tell you the number of page splits due to data not fitting on an index page. This will indicate problems internally in the database.
SQLServer:Buffer Manager	Buffer Cache Hit Ratio	This will tell you the success rate of how many times the buffer cache is hit. This should generally be a high number.
SQLServer:Databases	Transactions/sec	This will tell you the number of transactions per second you are generating; select for each database. This will help with capacity planning and give you snapshots of your growth.
SQLServer:General Statistics	Processes Blocked	This will tell you the number of currently blocked processes and may indicate problems with the application or that you need to do database maintenance.

Continued

Table 15-3. *Continued*

Category	Counter	Description
SQLServer:General Statistics	User Connections	This will tell you the total number of users connected to SQL Server; select for each database. This will help you track how many users are actually using a given database at any given time.
SQLServer:Locks	Average Wait Time(ms)	This will tell you the amount of time in milliseconds that a lock request waits to be served. Small locks happen all the time, but if this is a high number, it may ultimately indicate a more serious deadlock situation occurring.
SQLServer:Locks	Lock Timeouts/sec	This will tell you the number of locks that time out per second. This should not be a high value, and again would indicate locked or blocked processes.
SQLServer:Locks	Lock Waits/sec	This will tell you the number of locks waiting. Some waits are normal, but this should not get to be excessively high.
SQLServer:Locks	Number of Deadlocks/sec	This will tell you that there are deadlocks occurring and should be immediately investigated.
SQLServer:Memory Manager	Connection Memory(KB)	This will tell you the total amount of memory SQL Server is using for the connections. This is often forgotten in capacity planning since each connection to SQL Server does consume a small amount of memory.
SQLServer:Memory Manager	Optimizer Memory(KB)	This will tell you the amount of memory being used by SQL Server's optimizer.
SQLServer:Memory Manager	SQL Cache Memory(KB)	This will tell you the amount of memory being used by SQL Server's dynamic SQL cache.
SQLServer:Memory Manager	Total Server Memory(KB)	This will tell you the amount of memory that SQL Server is currently using.
SQLServer:Plan Cache	Cache Hit Ratio	This will tell you how often the cache is hit. This should normally be a high number (above 90%), but if you do not use a lot of stored procedures or objects that use cache, this will not be large.
SQLServer:SQL Statistics	SQL Recompilations/sec	This will tell you how many stored procedures are being recompiled per second. If this is a lot, you may be having issues in your application.
SQLServer: Transactions	Free space in tempdb(KB)	This will tell you how much space is left in tempdb. A threshold should be placed on this to ensure that once it is passed, the problem is addressed.
SQLServer: Transactions	Transactions	This will tell you the total number of transactions going on in SQL Server, whether they are related to a database or not (i.e., MS DTC, etc.).
SQLServer:Wait Statistics	Log write waits	This will tell you if you are potentially log bound if SQL Server is waiting to write to the transaction log.

Querying sys.sysperfinfo will give you the exact same information as you get from using the SQL Server–specific counters and is arguably more accurate since you are doing a query at an exact moment of time. Besides using the DMVs, using SQL Server to query Performance Monitor statistics is very effective. If you execute

```
select object_name, counter_name, cntr_value
from sys.sysperfinfo
order by object_name, counter_name
```

all counters and values will be returned. However, you can customize your query. This example shows the return of a single value:

```
select object_name, counter_name, cntr_value
from sys.sysperfinfo
where object_name = 'SQLServer:Buffer Manager'
and counter_name = 'Buffer cache hit ratio'
```

■**Note** Some hardware vendors provide counters that integrate with most popular monitoring tools. Others provide their own monitoring tools that do not integrate out of the box or may possibly require you to do your own integration with your existing monitoring solution. A good example are the proprietary tools provided by SAN and NAS vendors to monitor the disks. This will require you to be smart and look at different tools to get your arms around the complete environment.

Define 'Normal'

The only way to truly tell when something is wrong is to be able to identify an abnormality. The way to achieve this is deceptively simple: establish *baselines*. Baselines are not unlike benchmarking in a way, but their purpose is slightly different. A *benchmark* is often a one-time test that is meant to prove something, such as excellent performance. A *baseline* is used to determine what performance on your system should look like. Before the solution is deployed in production, perform the following tasks:

- Document measurements for each component of the system when there is no activity or minimal activity to understand what it looks like when it is at rest or when there is not much going on.
- Document measurements for the system during certain tasks or application events.
- Document measurements for the system under key times for the business.
- Document measurements for the system under full load to see the system stressed to its maximum capacity.

These measurements would be your initial baseline, which is what you will measure against. However, your work is not done. This is a continual process because your usage of the application and systems will change over time. Once the system is in production, measure the same things at various intervals and update the baselines if necessary. What is defined as normal at day one will always change. Very rarely are there absolutes when it comes to your baselines because what is normal for one server or system may be completely abnormal for another. As you update your baselines, you should update your monitoring thresholds and alerts accordingly since the alert you may get based on an old value may no longer be valid.

Although you will be continually updating your baseline values, do not just discard them. You should keep them around for historical purposes to track where you have been and to remind you of problems you have encountered so they can be prevented in the future. This historical information is a crucial step in capacity planning and will allow you to predict future trends and growth. This is the data I am often lacking when I go onsite and try to assist customers.

Using a Monitoring Application to Monitor SQL Server

There are many third-party monitoring tools that can monitor SQL Server properly. Some examples include IBM's Tivoli, Computer Associates' Unicenter, Hewlett-Packard's OpenView, NetIQ AppManager, Microsoft Operations Manager (MOM), and System Center Operations Manager (SCOM). All of these programs have the same concept: you "discover" servers and applications, and then deploy agents that report information to a central repository. That repository can then be used not only for near real-time alerting for problems (I say "near real-time" since there will always be a slight delay from when the problem is detected to when it hits the central server even if it is milliseconds), but also for analyzing (reporting trends, monthly reports, etc.) and coordinating the effect of events across multiple servers and locations. The latter is a very tough thing to do without a tool that has access to all of the data. You may have to mine to get that data yourself, but at least it's all there.

There are a few considerations you need to think about if you deploy some vendor's monitoring program. First, your monitoring solution needs to be made highly available and redundant, and you need to not only monitor the monitor, but monitor the agents to ensure they are running properly. Next, you need to think about how much and how frequently you are going to monitor for each server. If you are monitoring hundreds or thousands of servers, it is no easy feat since the counters or other aspects you will be monitoring need to be stored in that central repository, which is most likely a database of some sort. That database will not only continue to grow, but it needs to be on disk fast enough to handle thousands of inserts per second. Growth cannot be infinite, so you will most likely need to implement some sort of archiving or purging process to keep the database a manageable size. Finally, you need to ensure that every server or application deployed has the agent installed, configured, and working. Not all programs will have integration with your monitoring tool. You may need to come up with custom monitoring using standard Simple Network Management Protocol (SNMP) messages generated from the application, Windows Management Instrumentation (WMI) events, or Event Log entries. Implementing a monitoring solution—especially one that is based on an existing tool—is not a set-and-forget proposition.

One of the best things about a tool is that most, if not all, allow you to have your own repository of solutions that can serve as an internal knowledge base. This can prove invaluable to your support staff since someone may have seen the problem before. If a common problem is encountered, you can also have the monitoring tool take corrective action automatically with no human intervention and notify you after the action is completed. This can be an immense benefit to a company that is staff-challenged, assuming the tool is set up properly.

Having said this, I wholeheartedly recommend using a third-party program to do the basic monitoring for all of your servers (SQL Server or not) because it is a centralized way to manage the process. A true enterprise 24x7 environment dictates the need for these tools, which usually do not come cheap. You cannot effectively monitor hundreds or thousands of servers in your worldwide data centers using Performance Monitor (which is described in the next section).

■ **Note** DBAs or those responsible for SQL Server must ensure that SQL Server is monitored correctly because enterprise-wide monitoring tools are generally not used only for monitoring SQL Server. Many of the tools have templates or presets for SQL Server, but they may not always be right for your environment or may have too many counters enabled.

Using Performance Monitor to Monitor SQL Server

If you cannot afford or do not want to use a more advanced tool, use the built-in Performance Monitor (PerfMon) tool that exists in Windows. It isn't the sexiest tool out there, but it does the job. PerfMon does not have some advanced features such as setting up complex alerting, so there are some things you will have to do manually or automate in another way.

I am also not talking about starting Performance Monitor and watching the line go across the screen. The following instructions will direct you on how to gather performance statistics. The data will be stored to your medium of choice (a flat file or a SQL Server database), and you will have to build your own solution on top of that for analysis:

1. Start Performance Monitor from Start ➤ Administrative Tools ➤ Performance, as shown in Figure 15-26.

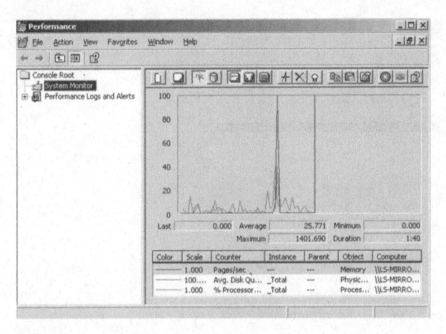

Figure 15-26. *Main Performance Monitor screen*

2. Expand Performance Logs and Alerts, right-click Counter Logs, and select New Log Settings, as shown in Figure 15-27.

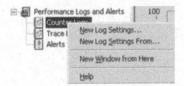

Figure 15-27. *New Log Settings menu option*

3. On the New Log Settings dialog, enter a name. An example is shown in Figure 15-28.

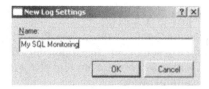

Figure 15-28. *Entering a name for your settings*

4. When the dialog in Figure 15-29 comes up with the name you entered in step 3, select the General tab. Click Add Counters to bring up the Add Counters dialog, shown in Figure 15-30, and add all counters that you wish to capture. Click Close when complete.

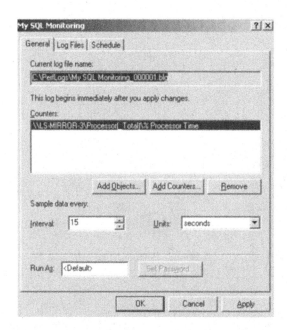

Figure 15-29. *Example dialog for configuring your PerfMon settings*

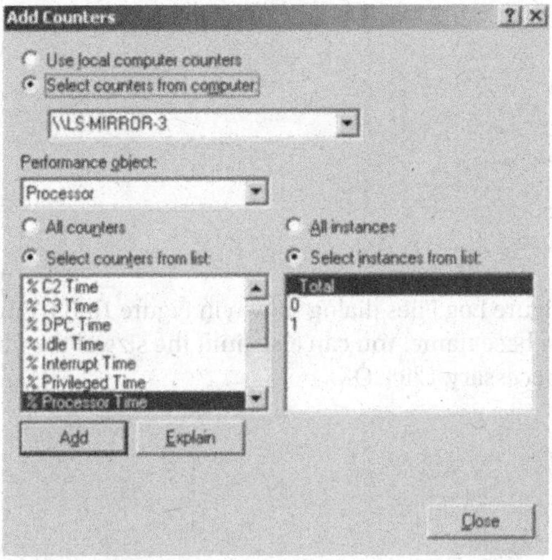

Figure 15-30. *Add Counters dialog*

5. When you return to the dialog shown in Figure 15-29, enter an appropriate interval. I recommend somewhere between 30 seconds and one minute. Much more or less than that will either mean too much or too little is captured.

6. Select the Log Files tab, as shown in Figure 15-31. In the Log File Type drop-down, shown in Figure 15-32, select the type of file you wish to generate. My recommendation is to generate a delimited text file (either tab or comma) since it will be the most compatible. While you can log to a SQL Server database directly, I do not recommend it; if you are logging too much to a log file on a poorly designed disk subsystem, there is a chance your SQL Server may not be able to keep up.

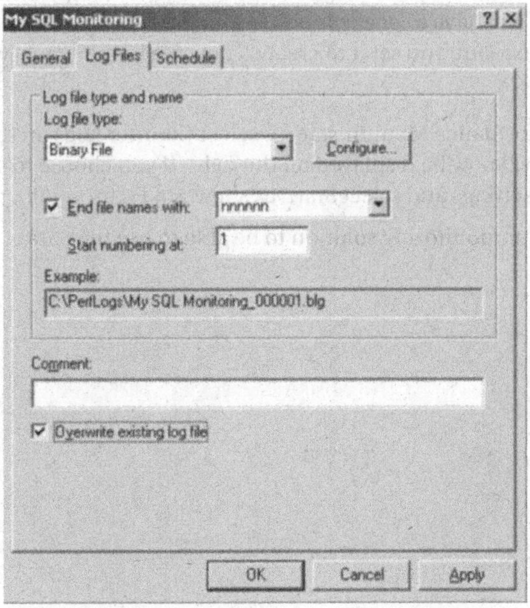

Figure 15-31. *Log Files tab*

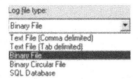

Figure 15-32. *Log File Type drop-down*

7. Click Configure to bring up the Configure Log Files dialog shown in Figure 15-33. Enter a valid location for the files, as well as a base name. You can also limit the size of the file, but I would suggest letting it expand as necessary. Click OK.

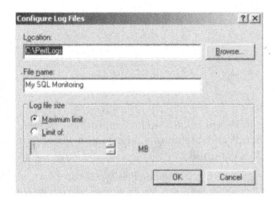

Figure 15-33. *Configure Log Files dialog*

8. Select the Schedule tab, as shown in Figure 15-34. Set a start time and end time for the log file. Make it something reasonable like every few hours or one day (depending on the size of the file) so that the file size you will have to deal with is reasonable. Since PerfMon will be your primary monitoring tool, make sure you set it to create a new file immediately when one is closed. Click Apply. Click OK.

9. When you return to the main Performance Monitor screen, select Counter Logs on the left. The settings you just configured will now be displayed on the right. If you choose to start the process manually, right-click the settings and select Start, as shown in Figure 15-35.

10. Import the files generated into your monitoring solution to be able to use the data.

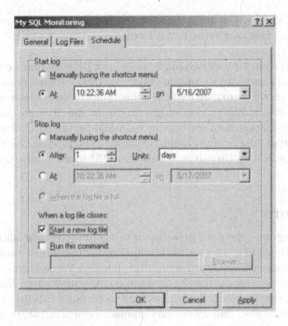

Figure 15-34. *Schedule tab*

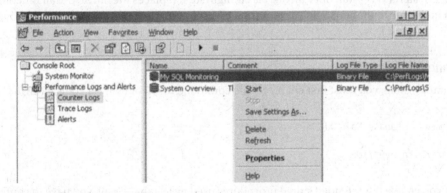

Figure 15-35. *Starting a PerfMon via saved settings*

Using SQL Server Dynamic Management Views to Monitor SQL Server

Besides using a tool, you can query the SQL Server 2005 DMVs to get information from Performance Monitor or a monitoring tool that is properly designed to monitor SQL Server, as well as more granular information. The data you can get via DMVs is more up-to-date since it is accurate at the time of the query execution, whereas a monitoring tool gathers data at a specified interval. Some of the DMVs and their usage have been showcased throughout the book. For a link to all DMVs in SQL Server 2005, see the Books Online topic "Dynamic Management Views and Functions."

The nice thing about using the DMVs is that you can come up with queries and information that means something to you and your environment and then use the output of the queries to be displayed on a web page or stored in a database or in a report that you can pass along to superiors.

Is it more work to monitor this way? Absolutely—I'm not going to lie. While it does mean you need to maintain whatever solution you put in place long-term, it may be more agile than a straight monitoring tool.

The other aspect of using DMVs that comes into play is more tangible for DBAs; at many clients I have visited, DBAs have no visibility into a company's monitoring because the solution is done by a third-party program that does not alert them if there is an issue. The first time they hear or see anything is when someone screams. If there is an existing monitoring solution and the DBAs are getting the right alerts, using DMVs can augment that solution and provide more SQL Server–specific information for the DBA. If the DBA is not part of the existing monitoring solution and process, this can be the DBA's way of doing SQL Server monitoring. There is no excuse for a DBA to say, "I have no idea what is happening on my SQL Server."

Getting Notified of Problems

Monitoring events with no way of finding out if there is a problem (or just getting a regular status report saying everything is okay) is like trying to drive a car while blind. If you are going to monitor but not have any way to react, you might as well not do any monitoring because the end result will be the same (and you should probably have a résumé handy when something goes wrong). The flip side of being notified is that an inbox can get overloaded with messages to the point that they are ignored. I have seen this in action, so you need to find a way to differentiate critical messages from informative ones that are telling you everything is just fine.

The new Database Mail feature of SQL Server 2005 is the underlying functionality that allows you to receive alerts via e-mail once an alert is configured. It replaces the old SQL Mail functionality, which had some limitations, such as requiring a MAPI-compliant client, and it was not cluster friendly.

Configuring Database Mail

To use Database Mail, you must first enable it. The command to enabling it via Transact-SQL is as follows:

```
sp_configure 'Database Mail XPs', 1
go
reconfigure with override
go
```

After you enable the extended stored procedures used by Database Mail, you have to configure Database Mail in SQL Server Management Studio.

1. Under Management, double-click Database Mail. You will see the Welcome to the Database Mail Configuration Wizard dialog shown in Figure 15-36. Click Next.

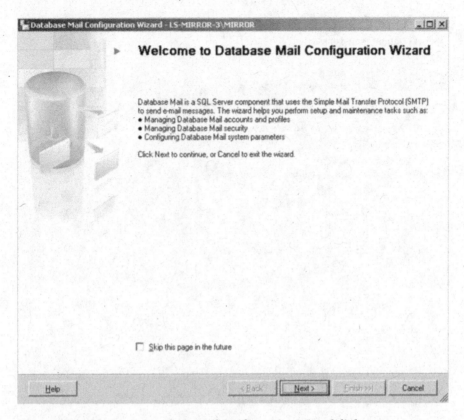

Figure 15-36. *Welcome to Database Mail Configuration Wizard dialog*

2. On the Select Configuration Task dialog, shown in Figure 15-37, select the option to set up Database Mail. Click Next.

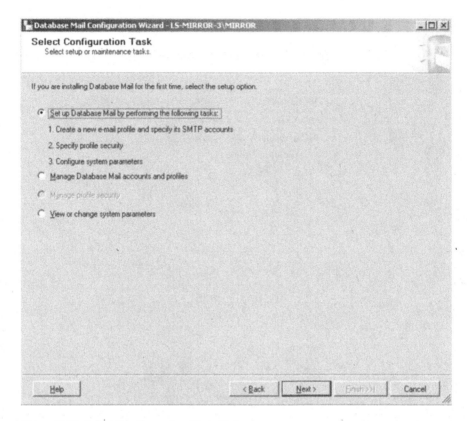

Figure 15-37. *Select Configuration Task dialog*

3. If you have not previously enabled the extended stored procedures for Database Mail before running the wizard, you will be prompted by the dialog shown in Figure 15-38 to enable the feature. Click Yes.

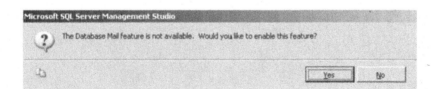

Figure 15-38. *Enabling Database Mail*

4. On the New Profile dialog, shown in Figure 15-39, enter a name for the profile. A description is optional. Click Add.

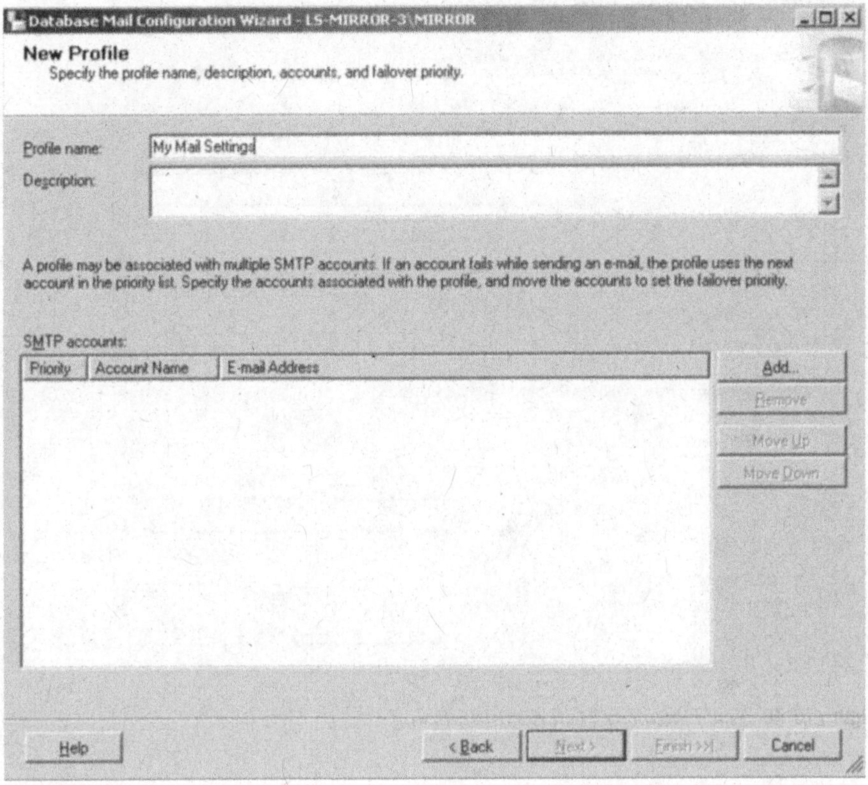

Figure 15-39. *New Profile dialog*

On the New Database Mail Account dialog, shown in Figure 15-40, enter all the information for the account that will be used to send mail from SQL Server. When finished, click OK.

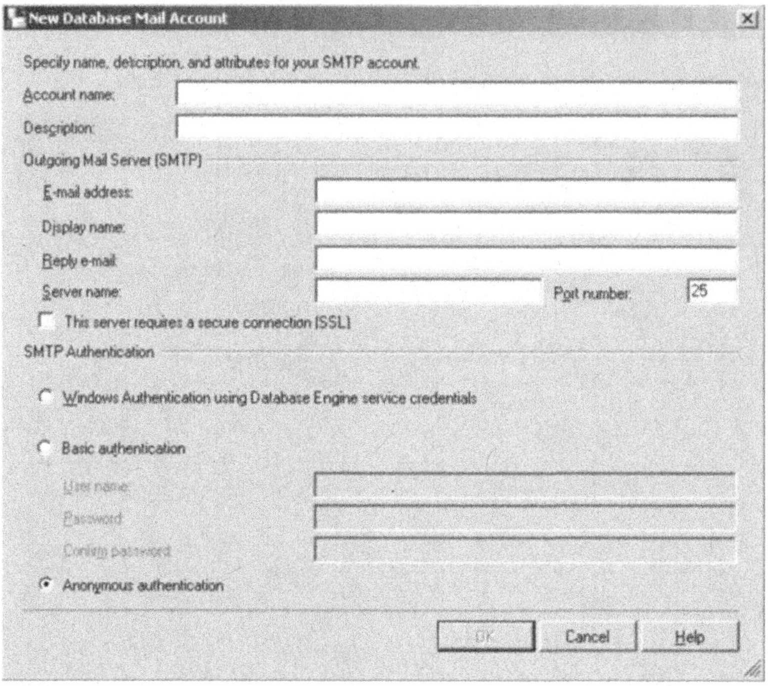

Figure 15-40. *New Database Mail Account dialog*

The profile you just configured will now be reflected on the New Profile dialog shown in Figure 15-41. Click Next.

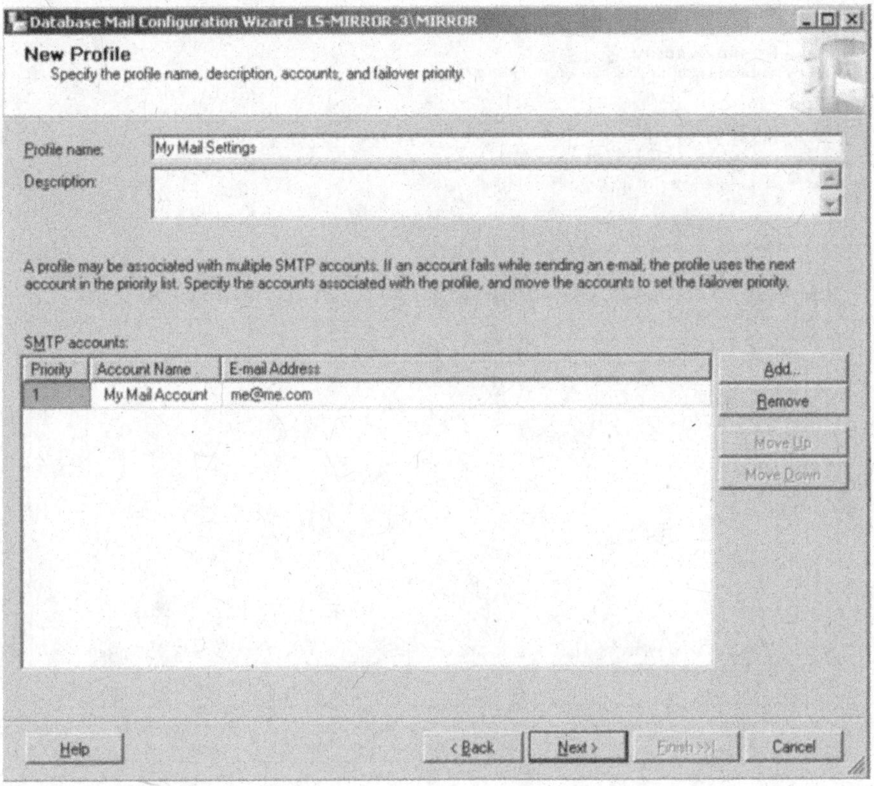

Figure 15-41. *New Profile dialog after adding a mail profile*

5. On the Manage Profile Security dialog, shown in Figure 15-42, you can set a profile as the default profile. Click the check box next to your desired profile. Click Next.

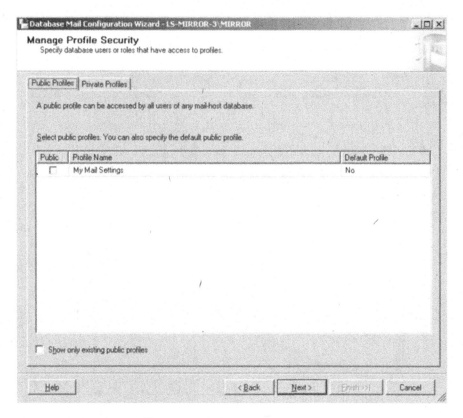

Figure 15-42. *Manage Profile Security dialog*

6. On the Configure System Parameters dialog, shown in Figure 15-43, alter the parameter values as you see fit. Click Next.

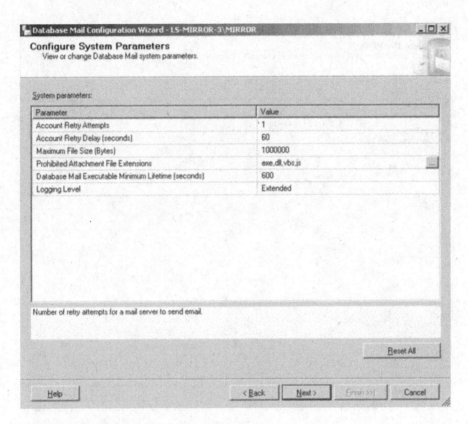

Figure 15-43. *Configure System Parameters dialog*

7. On the Complete the Wizard dialog in Figure 15-44, click Finish. Database Mail will now be configured.

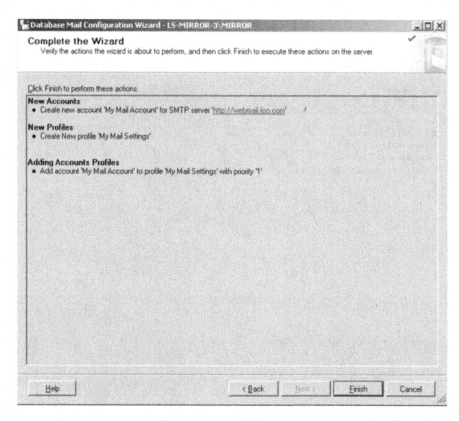

Figure 15-44. *Complete the Wizard*

8. When finished, you will see something similar to Figure 15-45. Click Close.

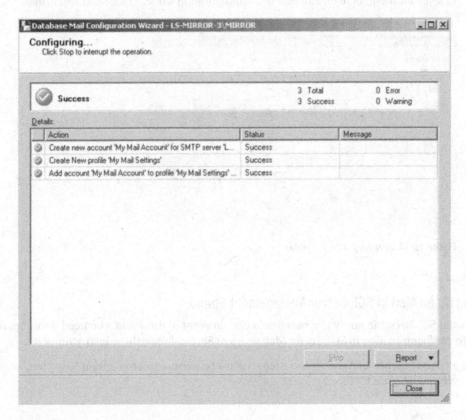

Figure 15-45. *Completed configuration of Database Mail*

9. Right-click Database Mail in SQL Server Management Studio and select Sent Test E-mail from the menu, as shown in Figure 15-46.

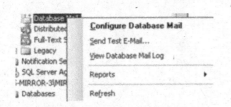

Figure 15-46. *Database Mail context menu*

10. On the Send Test E-mail dialog, shown in Figure 15-47, enter an e-mail address in the To box to send a test e-mail to ensure that your configuration works. Click Send Test E-mail.

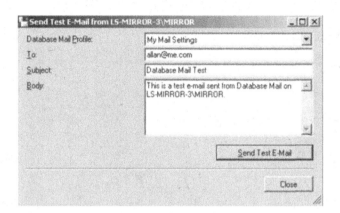

Figure 15-47. *Sending a test e-mail*

Setting Up an Alert in SQL Server Management Studio

If you want SQL Server to notify you based on a certain event or threshold, you need to configure an alert. To configure an alert in SQL Server Management Studio, follow these instructions:

1. Expand SQL Server Agent, select Alerts, right-click, and select the option New Alert, as shown in Figure 15-48.

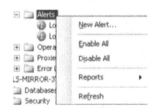

Figure 15-48. *Alerts context menu*

2. On the New Alert dialog, enter a name for the alert. Figure 15-49 shows an example of an alert that would be triggered when SQL Server event generates a severity of 001. This same alert could be configured to be triggered off of specific message text or an exact error number.

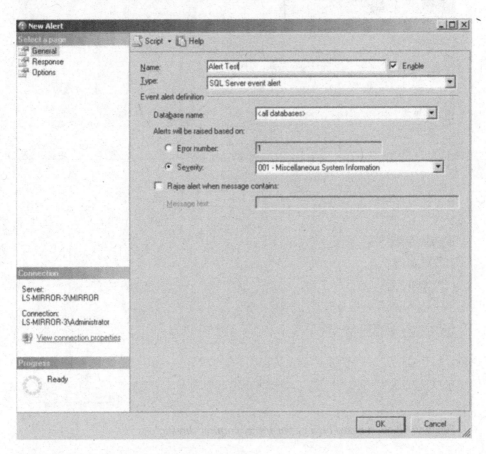

Figure 15-49. *Alert based on a SQL Server event*

Figure 15-50 shows an example of configuring an alert based on a specific performance counter threshold.

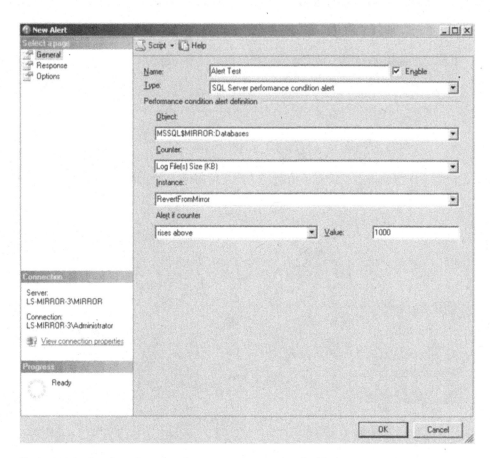

Figure 15-50. *Alert based on a performance counter threshold*

Figure 15-51 shows what you would need to configure to have an alert based on a specific WMI event.

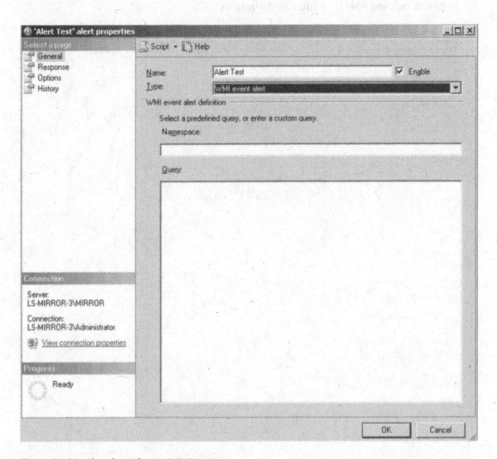

Figure 15-51. *Alert based on a WMI event*

3. Select the Response page of the New Alert dialog, as shown in Figure 15-52. You have two options: you can kick off a SQL Server Agent job to correct the problem, or you can send a note to a defined operator. You can do both as well.

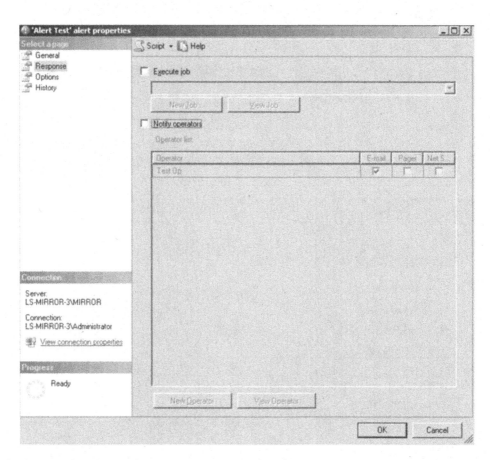

Figure 15-52. *Selecting the Response page*

To be able to send an e-mail based on the event, you have to set up an operator. Click New Operator. You will then see the dialog shown in Figure 15-53. Enter the proper information.

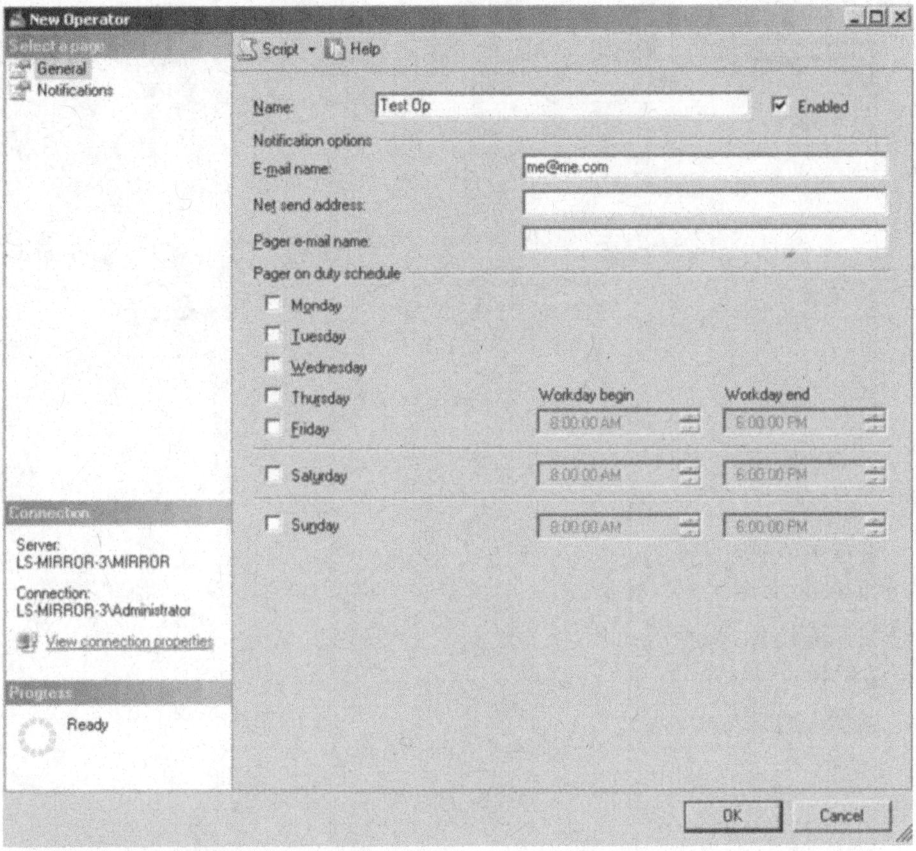

Figure 15-53. *Creating a New Operator*

Optionally, select the Notifications page of the New Operator dialog, as shown in Figure 15-54, and define which alerts this operator should know about and how they should be contacted. Click OK.

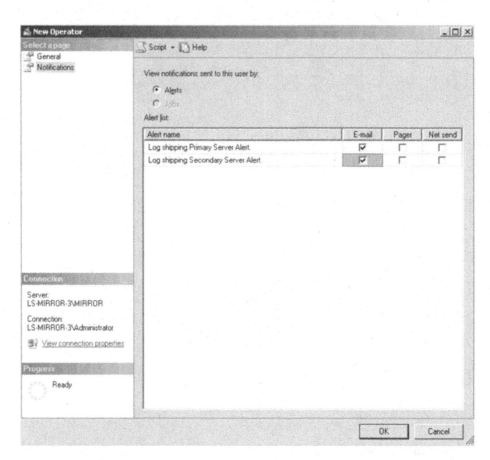

Figure 15-54. *New Operator dialog*

When you return to the Response page, shown in Figure 15-55, select how to notify the operator.

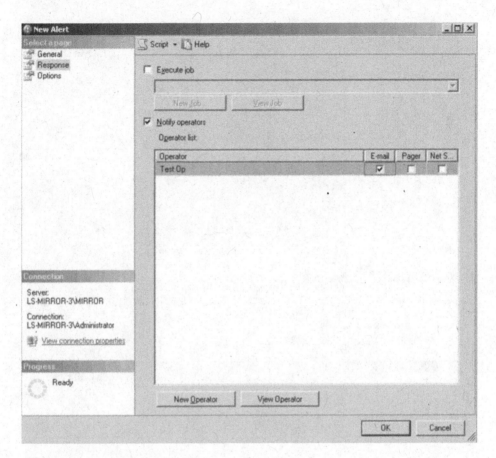

Figure 15-55. *Notifying an operator*

4. Select the Options page of the New Alert dialog, shown in Figure 15-56. Select how the error text will be displayed and enter any additional text you may want to see. Click OK.

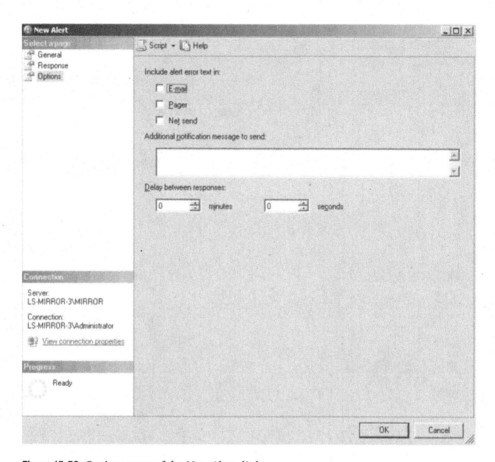

Figure 15-56. *Options page of the New Alert dialog*

The newly configured alert will now be displayed in SQL Server Management Studio. An example is shown in Figure 15-57.

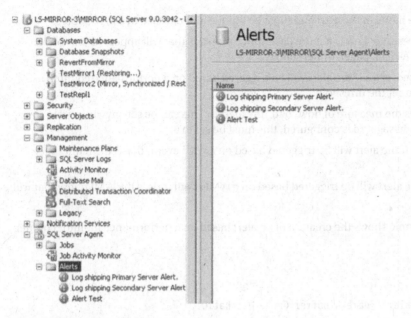

Figure 15-57. *Newly added alert*

Setting Up an Alert Using Transact-SQL

To set up an alert using Transact-SQL, use the stored procedure sp_add_alert, described in this section. Other stored procedures that may come in handy are sp_add_notification, sp_delete_alert, sp_help_alert, and sp_update_alert. Information on those stored procedures can be found in SQL Server Books Online.

sp_add_alert has the following parameters and is always executed in the context of the msdb database where alerts are stored:

- @category_name: This is an optional parameter that will help categorize the alert.

- @database_name: This ties the alert to a specific database. If this parameter is not specified, it will be triggered any time the condition is met for any database.

- @delay_between_responses: Measured in seconds, this controls how often an alert will be repeated over time or a job will be executed. If this is set to something above 0, it may stop the spamming of your inbox.

- @enabled: This defines whether the alert is or is not enabled. A value of 1 means enabled, 0 disabled.

- @event_description_keyword: This is used to help filter and narrow down what the alert will be triggered on. It is similar to LIKE in Transact-SQL.

- @include_event_description_in: This parameter sets how the event will be reported. Values are 0 (not included), 1 (e-mail), 2 (pager), 4 (net send), and 5 (e-mail and net send).

- @job_id: If the alert will trigger a job, use this parameter to input the job ID. This can be used in lieu of the job's name.

- @job_name: If the alert will trigger a job, use this parameter to declare the name of the SQL Server Agent job. It can be used in lieu of the job's ID.

- @message_id: This corresponds to the error message that will trigger the alert. This cannot be used if @severity is set and must be set to 0 in that case.

- @name: This is the name of the alert and must be unique and encased in single quotes.

- @notification_message: This is a more descriptive message that will appear as part of the text received via e-mail, pager, or net send.

- @performance_condition: If the alert will be triggered based on a performance counter, use this parameter to set the threshold.

- @severity: This is the measure of how "bad" the alert is. This can be set anywhere from 1 to 25. However, if @message_id is configured, this must be set to 0.

- @wmi_namespace: If the alert will be triggered based on a WMI event, this is the namespace that will be used.

- @wmi_query: If the alert will be triggered based on a WMI event, this is the WMI query that will be executed.

The following example shows the creation of an alert based on a performance monitor counter and a threshold:

```
USE msdb
GO

EXEC msdb.dbo.sp_add_alert @name=N'Buffer Cache Hit Ratio',
    @enabled=1,
    @delay_between_responses=0,
    @include_event_description_in=1,
    @notification_message=N'Test text',
    @performance_condition=
    N'SQLServer:Buffer Manager|Buffer cache hit ratio||<|90',
GO
```

WHO IS MONITORING THE MONITOR?

I know the question "who is monitoring the monitor?" sounds silly, but it actually is something you need to be concerned with. If your monitoring solution goes down, how will you be notified of problems? Will you even know that the monitoring solution is down? Redundant systems are not just for your mainline application solutions. Your monitoring solution is your first line of defense when it comes to availability. I know that you're probably shaking your head and wondering how all of this is going to happen since you can barely monitor your existing environment, but if you care about your availability, you'll find a way to do it. It's one thing to walk onsite and find certain items (such as Event Logs) are not being monitored, but it is a whole other thing to discover that the monitoring solution isn't working. That is a message no one wants to hear.

Attaching and Detaching Databases

Since it was introduced in SQL Server 7.0, attaching and detaching databases has become another tool in the arsenal of DBAs. Some like to try to use it as their backup-and-restore strategy. I hate to burst your bubble if you fall into this category, but sp_detach_db and CREATE DATABASE ... FOR ATTACH are not even equivalent to doing a traditional backup and restore. Detaching the database does what it sets out to do: it cleanly allows you to physically detach the database and its files from SQL Server. Obviously, this causes an outage: while the database is detached, it is not available to SQL Server for use. Once you detach, you can then make copies at the operating system level of those files (both data and log) and then do what you want with them, including copy them elsewhere.

The best use for detach and attach in my experience is for upgrading the database when your file sizes are manageable and the time to copy the files from one server to another is relatively short (moving a terabyte of data over a small network pipe that takes 24 hours may not be optimal). Another option is when your database server fails, but the files are still available, you can attach them to a new instance so you can most likely "recover" to the last transaction in the database.

Depending on the options used in the detach process, after the database is attached, you may have to manually update the statistics. If you are using full-text search, you also must specify whether you want to detach the full-text index. With a traditional SQL Server backup scheme, the full-text indexes are accounted for.

sp_detach_db has three options:

- @dbname tells SQL Server which database to detach.

- @skipchecks tells SQL Server to either skip or run UPDATE STATISTICS before detaching the database. This is set to true to skip, or false to run it.

- @KeepFulltextIndexFile tells SQL Server whether to detach the corresponding full-text search files with the database or to drop them. The default value is true, which keeps the full-text components. You can set it to false.

The following is an example execution of detaching a database that forces an UPDATE STATISTICS but drops the full-text index:

```
sp_detach_db @dbname = 'mydatabase',
@skipchecks = 'false',
@KeepFulltextIndexFile = 'false'
```

Detaching also differs from backup in other important ways:

- A database that is marked as suspect cannot be detached.

- You must disable publication if the database is the publisher in a replication scenario prior to detaching.

- If you are using any snapshots, a new feature of SQL Server 2005, they must be dropped prior to detaching.

- You must stop database mirroring to allow the database to be detached.

Attaching a database has changed in SQL Server 2005. With SQL Server 7.0 and 2000, you had the options of using the stored procedures sp_attach_db and sp_attach_single_file_db. These two procedures have been depreciated in SQL Server 2005, so while they are still usable, they will be removed in a future version of SQL Server. You should update your syntax to use CREATE DATABASE *database_name* FOR ATTACH or CREATE DATABASE *database_name* FOR ATTACH_REBUILD_LOG where database_name is the name of the database you are attaching. FOR ATTACH will attach the database and all of its associated files and assumes you have all .mdf, .ndf, and .ldf files. FOR ATTACH_REBUILD_LOG allows you to attach all .mdf and .ndf files from a clean detach where the log file (.ldf) is unavailable. This will break the LSN sequence, so you will need to start with a new set of backups to reinitiate once you have attached the database. Also be aware that FOR ATTACH_REBUILD_LOG will create the log file where the primary data file is located, so you may have to move it immediately after attaching the database.

Following are two example statements, the first of which attaches a database with a single data and log file, and the second attaches a database with two data files and re-creates the log file:

```
CREATE DATABASE Precision ON PRIMARY
(name = 'Primary',
FILENAME = 'c:\MySQLData\precision_datamdf')
LOG ON (FILENAME = 'd:\MySQLLogs\precision_log.ldf')
FOR ATTACH

CREATE DATABASE StingRay ON PRIMARY
(NAME = 'Primary',
FILENAME = 'c:\MySQLData\StingRay_data.mdf'),
Filegroup Secondary
(NAME = 'Secondary',
FILENAME = 'd:\MySQLData\4String_data.ndf'
FOR ATTACH_REBUILD_LOG
```

Detaching a Database via SQL Server Management Studio

To detach a database using SQL Server Management Studio, follow these instructions:

1. Start SQL Server Management Studio.

2. Expand Databases.

3. Select the database, right-click, select Tasks, then Detach, as shown in Figure 15-58.

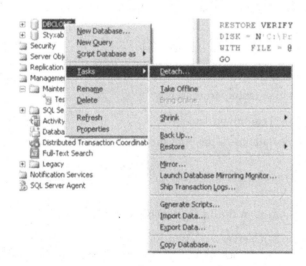

Figure 15-58. *Detach option*

4. On the Detach Database dialog, shown in Figure 15-59, I recommend selecting the Drop Connections and Update Statistics check boxes.

5. Click OK to detach. The database will no longer appear in SQL Server Management Studio.

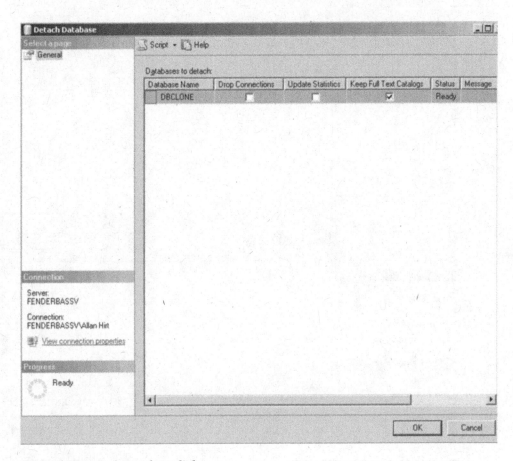

Figure 15-59. *Detach Database dialog*

Attaching a Database via SQL Server Management Studio

To attach a database using SQL Server Management Studio, follow these instructions:

1. Start SQL Server Management Studio.

2. Right-click Databases, and select Attach, as shown in Figure 15-60. You will see the Attach Databases dialog as shown in Figure 15-61.

Figure 15-60. *Attach option*

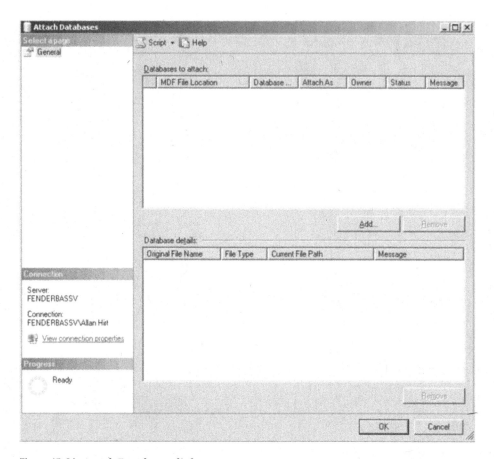

Figure 15-61. *Attach Databases dialog*

3. Click Add. On the Locate Database File dialog, select the main data file for the database you wish to attach. An example is shown in Figure 15-62. Click OK. The Attach Databases dialog will now reflect the database selected, as shown in Figure 15-63.

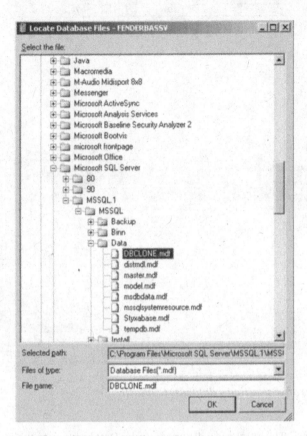

Figure 15-62. *Locate Database Files dialog*

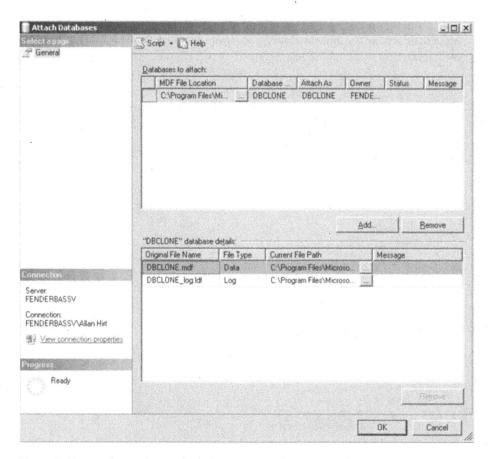

Figure 15-63. *Attach Databases after selecting a database to attach*

4. Click OK to attach the database. The database will appear under Databases once the attach process is complete.

SCRIPTING IS FOR ADMINISTRATORS, TOO

A trend that I am seeing more and more with the DBAs I encounter is the inability to write Transact-SQL code. I'm not talking about writing stored procedures for doing queries in applications; I'm talking about using Transact-SQL for administrative purposes. It is frustrating at times, but then again I come from a background where I cut my teeth using Sybase and Oracle on various flavors of UNIX. Command windows and manually entering commands are not scary to me. I hope by now I've emphasized the point that scripting objects sometimes is the only way to recover them in a disaster scenario. In this day and age where not everyone has a long history and all they have used are graphic tools, a command prompt can be daunting. I understand that. You will only make yourself a better SQL Server professional by furthering your skills.

Where I've had time as well as the space in this book, I've included both the graphic tool way to do a task and the Transact-SQL way to do the same task. Most, if not all, "knobs" and tasks exposed in SQL Server Management Studio can be done via script. Besides Transact-SQL, another language you may want to get familiar with as an administrator is Windows Management Instrumentation (WMI). WMI can be incorporated into operating system–level scripts written in a language such as VBScript and can help you achieve tasks.

Some gray area now comes in with the CLR built into SQL Server. Will DBAs be responsible for maintaining and performance tuning code other than Transact-SQL? I don't know the answer to that, and I suspect it will vary from company to company. Long term, I think it will definitely fall into the realm of the DBA. DBAs will certainly need to be aware of the CLR, the security issues around it, and how it is used. None of my clients to date have used it. I'm sure this will change over time. This also speaks to how an application will be developed and where you will want to place the logic for your application. There needs to be a balance, and you have to know what logic goes best where (application vs. SQL Server).

Using SSIS to Transfer Logins and Objects

Many of the previous chapters refer to a task to transfer logins to another server to create a proper standby server. This can be done one of two ways: via script (see the tip at the end of this section) or via SQL Server Integration Services (SSIS). SSIS is the replacement for the older Data Transformation Services (DTS) in SQL Server 7.0 and SQL Server 2000. Unfortunately for DBAs, using SSIS is not straightforward. It requires you to install the SQL Server Business Intelligence Development Studio even if you will not be using Analysis Services. Using SSIS is not integrated with SQL Server Management Studio as DTS was in Enterprise Manager. SQL Server Business Intelligence Development Studio is really a customized version of Visual Studio, so if you are not a developer by nature, the interface will seem foreign.

Tip While you can do different transfer tasks in a single SSIS package (see the list at the end of this section for the transfer task types other than logins), my recommendation is to do each one in a separate package. Not only will it be easier to copy and reproduce, but if you have to only do one task, you don't have to figure out how to disable (if at all possible) the other tasks or run just part of the logic embedded in the SSIS package. If one item fails, it should not necessarily affect others unless there is a dependency.

The following steps instruct you on how to create an SSIS transfer task:

1. Start the SQL Server Business Intelligence Development Studio from the Start menu, as shown in Figure 15-64.

Figure 15-64. *Starting SQL Server Business Intelligence Development Studio*

2. Under the File menu, select New then Project, as shown in Figure 15-65.

Figure 15-65. *Creating a new project*

3. On the New Project dialog, shown in Figure 15-66, select the Integration Services Project under the Templates. Enter a name for the project and a solution name, and click OK.

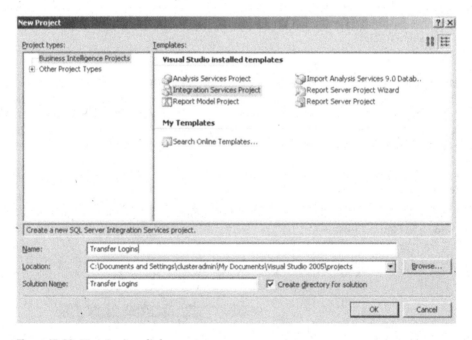

Figure 15-66. *New Project dialog*

The screen will now appear similar to the one in Figure 15-67.

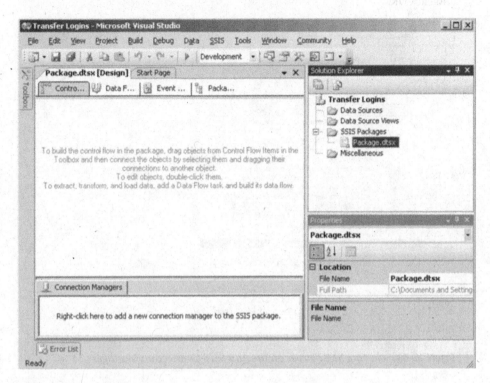

Figure 15-67. *New SSIS package*

4. In the Connection Managers section of the screen, shown in Figure 15-68, right-click and select New Connection.

Figure 15-68. *Connection Managers context menu*

5. On the Add SSIS Connection Manager dialog, select SMOServer, as shown in Figure 15-69, and click OK.

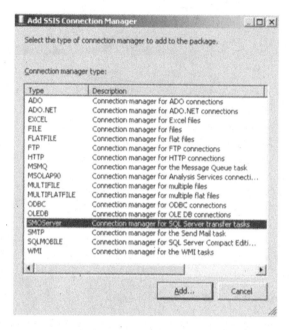

Figure 15-69. *Selecting SMOServer on the Add SSIS Connection Manager*

6. On the SMO Connection Manager Editor, shown in Figure 15-70, enter the name of the SQL Server instance, which is the source under server name, and select the authentication method.

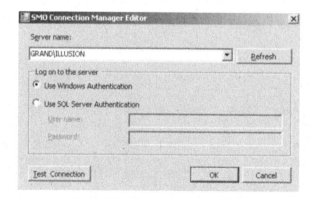

Figure 15-70. *SMO Connection Manager Editor dialog*

Click Test Connection. If you configured things properly, the dialog in Figure 15-71 will be shown. Click OK to close the message, and click OK on the SMO Connection Manager Editor to continue.

Figure 15-71. *Successful test connection dialog*

7. Repeat steps 4 through 6 for the destination instance of SQL Server. When complete, your screen should look like Figure 15-72.

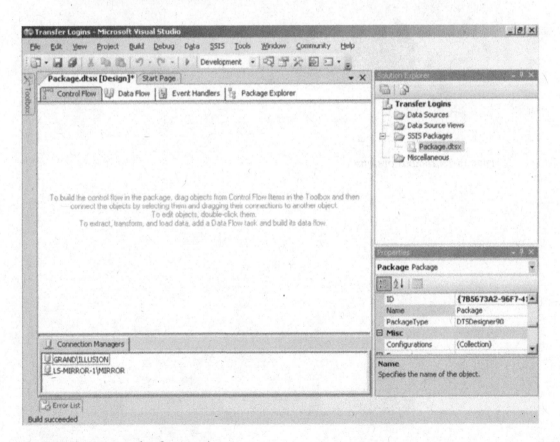

Figure 15-72. *Two completed connections*

8. On the left, click Toolbar, and the Toolbox options will be expanded, as shown in Figure 15-73. Select the appropriate transfer task you wish to configure.

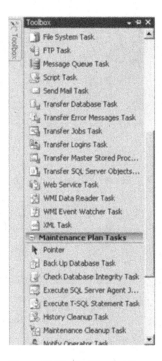

Figure 15-73. *Toolbox options*

9. Double-click on the transfer task you added. The example in Figure 15-74 shows a Transfer Logins Task.

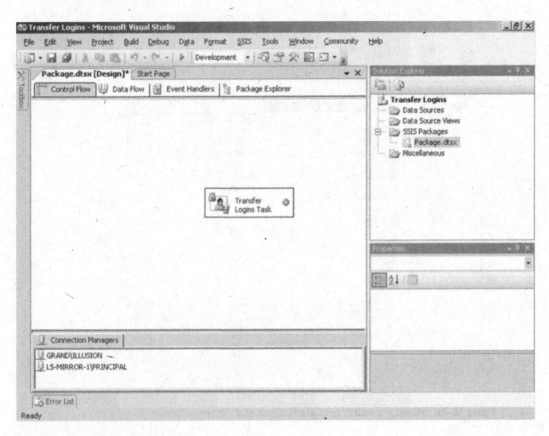

Figure 15-74. *Added transfer task*

10. On the Transfer Logins Task Editor, select the Logins page from the left. First you must select the source and the destination SQL Server instances. An example is shown in Figure 15-75.

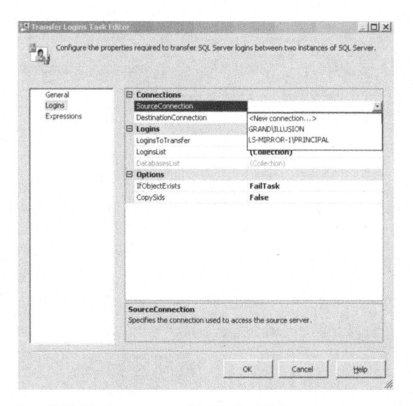

Figure 15-75. *Selecting a source and destination SQL Server instance*

Under Logins, for LoginsToTransfer select the option SelectedLogins and click the ellipsis button next to LoginsList, as shown in Figure 15-76.

When the Select Logins dialog is shown, check the logins that you wish to transfer from the source to the destination, as shown in Figure 15-77. Click OK.

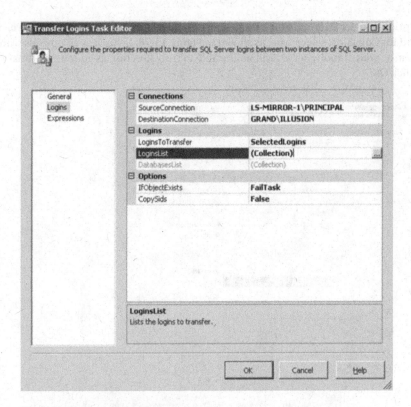

Figure 15-76. *Setting the Logins options*

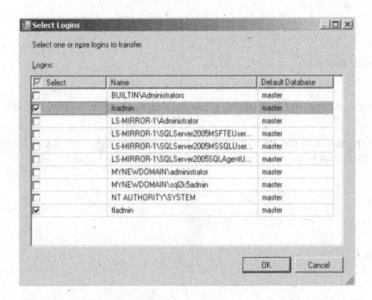

Figure 15-77. *Select Logins dialog*

Under Options, select Overwrite for IfObjectExists to allow the object to be created even if it exists, and for CopySids, select True, as shown in Figure 15-78. If you leave CopySids with a value of False, your standby server will not be able to truly function as your new primary server. Click OK.

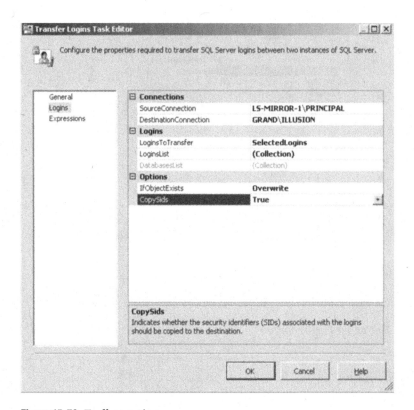

Figure 15-78. *Toolbar options*

11. Under the File menu, shown in Figure 15-79, select Save All to save the package and the project.

    You may be prompted to rename the SSIS package to the more recognizable name (such as Transfer Logins Task) that you defined earlier. Click Yes, as shown in Figure 15-80.

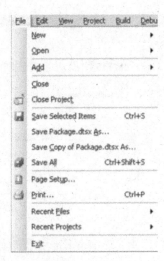

Figure 15-79. *File menu*

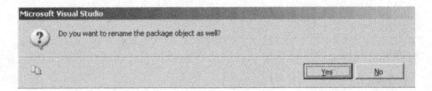

Figure 15-80. *Prompt to rename the SSIS package*

When the save is complete, you will see a screen similar to the one in Figure 15-81. Note the change in the package name on the right and the status at the bottom.

12. To test the new SSIS package, select it on the right, right-click, and select Execute Package, as shown in Figure 15-82.

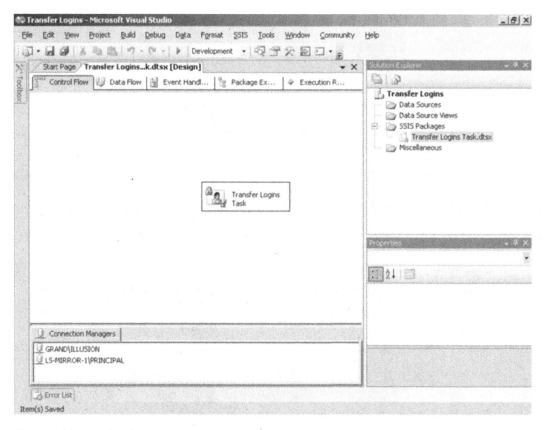

Figure 15-81. *Completed SSIS save*

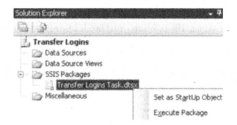

Figure 15-82. *Package context menu*

If you configured the SSIS package successfully, you will see a status on the left similar to the one in Figure 15-83.

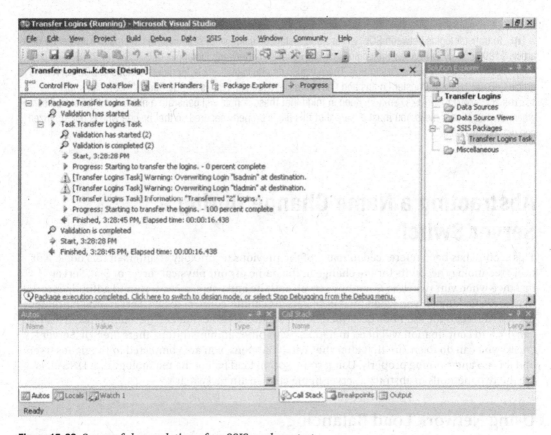

Figure 15-83. *Successful completion of an SSIS package test*

To create SSIS packages for other transfer tasks, as shown earlier in Figure 15-73, the steps are the same except you would see different screens for the different tasks. The tasks you would want to create SSIS packages for would be the following:

- *Transfer Error Messages Task*: If you have custom error messages, use this task to transfer them to your standby server.

- *Transfer Jobs Task*: Instead of scripting each job from your SQL Server instance, you can use this task to transfer your jobs.

- *Transfer Master Stored Procedures Task*: Although you should not be placing anything in the master database, if you place stored procedures there, you can use this task to transfer from a source to a destination.

- *Transfer SQL Server Objects Task*: This task is generally used for transferring objects within a database. You should not have to use this unless you have objects such as stored procedures that exist in one place and do not in another. I have seen this where some stored procedures exist in one place because of replication.

> ■**Tip** To transfer logins between SQL Server 2005 instances using scripts, consult the Microsoft Knowledge Base article 918992 "How to Transfer the Logins and the Passwords Between Instances of SQL Server 2005" (http://support.microsoft.com/kb/918992/). There is also an equivalent article for older versions of SQL Server, KB article 246133 "How to Transfer Logins and Passwords Between Instances of SQL Server" (http://support.microsoft.com/kb/246133/en-us). Keep in mind that these scripts will generate a file that will be stored somewhere on one of your disks. You must ensure that this file is properly secured so that no one who is unauthorized can get a copy of it.

Abstracting a Name Change During a Server Switch

This section has been referenced in many of the previous technology chapters in this book. Not every technology accounts for the change in the name of your physical server or SQL Server instance when you switch to a standby server, and the end users, managers, and administrators may come looking for you when their applications cannot connect to SQL Server after a problem occurs. Although the methods described in this section may be outside the realm of what a DBA can do, and coordination will need to happen with other administrators, there are SQL Server checks you can do to ensure that after the switch happens, you are connected to the right server and it is up and running properly. Using some sort of load balancing technology or a DNS alias are the two methods to abstract a server name change after a switch.

Using Network Load Balancing

One way of hiding the server name change is to use Network Load Balancing (NLB). There are two types of load balancers: hardware and software. Windows has its own built-in version of load balancing. If you use this feature of Windows, as you learned in Chapter 4, NLB cannot be configured on the same hardware as a failover cluster. If any of the instances are nodes of a failover cluster, you cannot use this method to abstract the instance name change. You will have to use a hardware-based solution or DNS aliasing, which is covered in the next section.

Configuring the First Node of an NLB Cluster

This section shows you how to configure the first node of the built-in NLB feature of Windows to abstract a name change in a server switch. For more information on the Windows NLB feature, see Chapter 3, as well as this web page: http://technet2.microsoft.com/windowsserver/en/library/1611cae3-5865-4897-a186-7e6ebd8855cb1033.mspx?mfr=true. Follow all Microsoft best practices when it comes to NLB. One recommendation I strongly suggest is to use two network cards so that both nodes of the NLB cluster can see each other, and you can effectively manage both nodes in Network Load Balancing Manager. If you do not, you may have to manage each node independently of each other, which in turn may cause confusion. The following steps describe how to configure the first node of the NLB cluster:

1. Start Network Load Balancing Manager, as shown in Figure 15-84. You will see the main dialog shown in Figure 15-85.

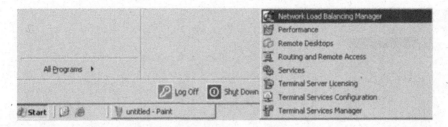

Figure 15-84. *Network Load Balancing Manager menu option*

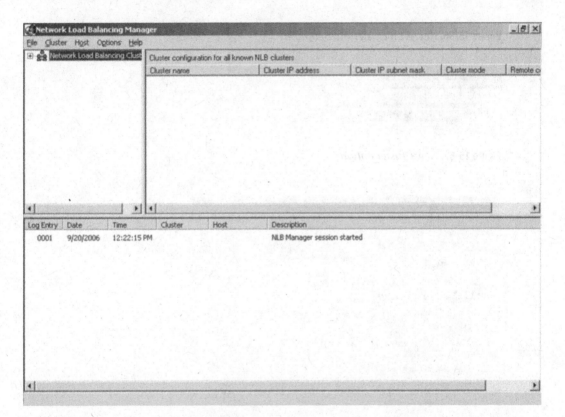

Figure 15-85. *Network Load Balancing Manager*

2. From the Cluster menu, select New, as shown in Figure 15-86, or right-click Network Load Balancing Cluster and select New Cluster, as shown in Figure 15-87.

3. On the Cluster Parameters dialog, enter an IP address and name for the NLB cluster. The name has to be the fully qualified domain name, such as **styx.testdomain.allan.com**. Select Unicast for the operation mode because you will only be using a single host at a given time. Optionally, you can select to allow remote control, but I would recommend just using the Network Load Balancing Manager tool. An example is shown in Figure 15-88. Click Next.

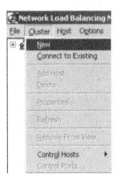

Figure 15-86. *New NLB cluster menu option*

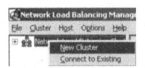

Figure 15-87. *New Cluster option*

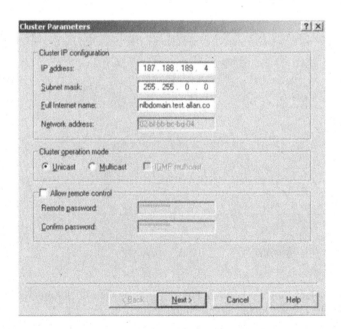

Figure 15-88. *Cluster Parameters dialog*

4. Unless you are going to add another IP address to the NLB cluster, click Next on the dialog shown in Figure 15-89.

5. On the Port Rules dialog as shown in Figure 15-90, click Edit.

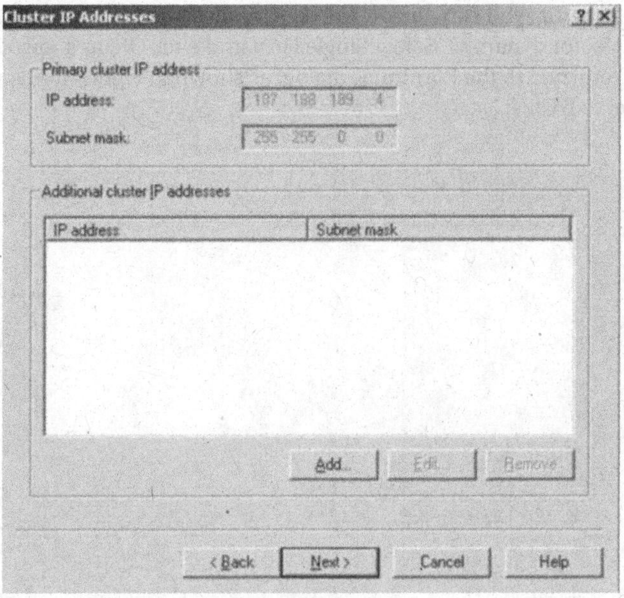

Figure 15-89. *Cluster IP Addresses dialog*

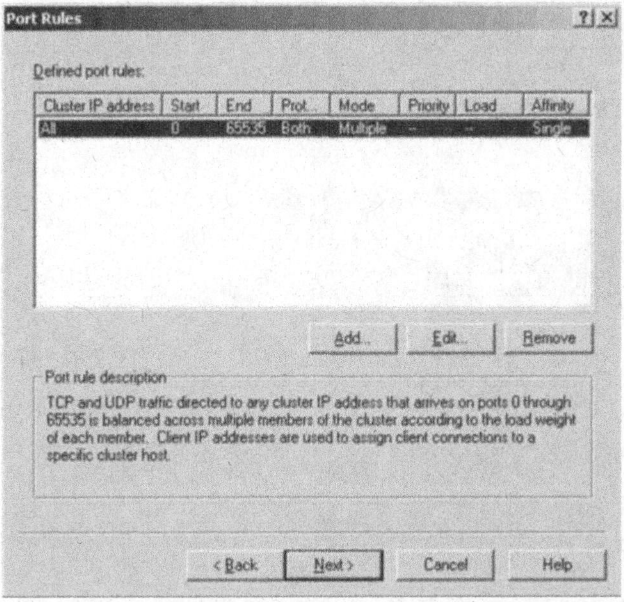

Figure 15-90. *Port Rules dialog*

6. On the Add/Edit Port Rule dialog, you can narrow the port range if you know the exact port of your SQL Server (i.e., it is not dynamic). Select Single Host and click OK, as shown in Figure 15-91. You will be returned to the Port Rules dialog, as shown in Figure 15-92, where your changes will be reflected. Click Next.

Figure 15-91 *Add/Edit Port Rule dialog*

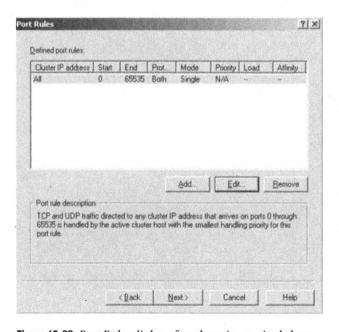

Figure 15-92. *Port Rules dialog after changing to single host*

7. On the Connect dialog, shown in Figure 15-93, enter the name of the first node of the cluster in the Host entry box and click Connect. The lower portion of the dialog will now display the possible network adapters to bind NLB to. Select one, as shown in Figure 15-94, and click Next.

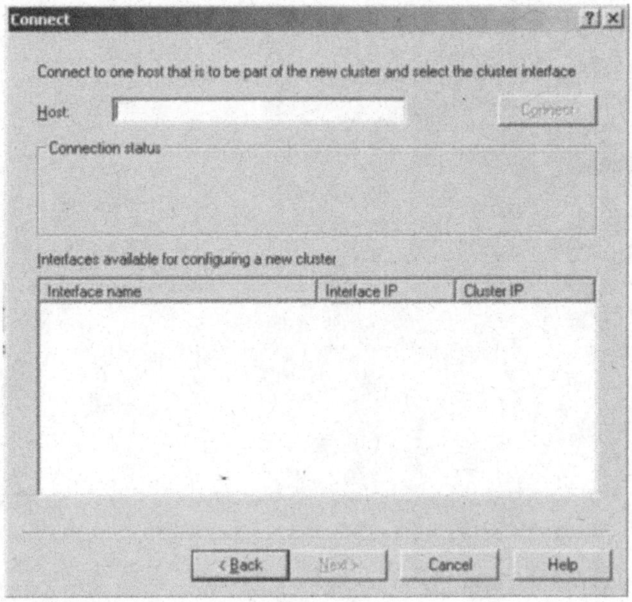

Figure 15-93. *Connect dialog*

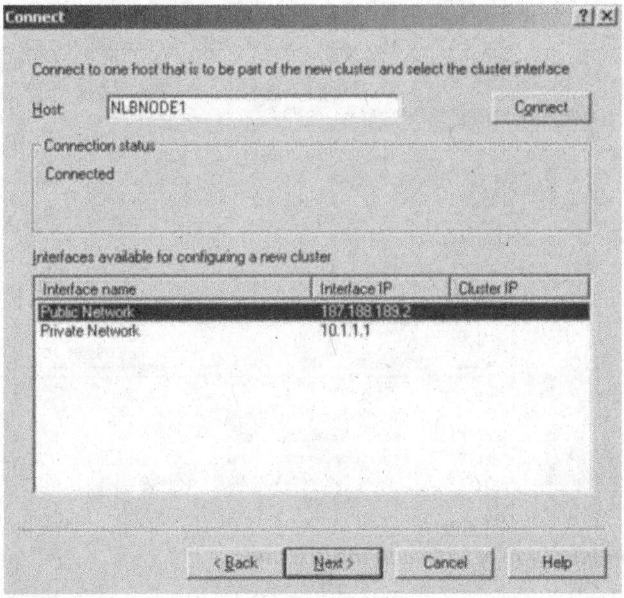

Figure 15-94. *Connect after discovery*

8. On the Host Parameters dialog, the priority will default to 1 for the first node. If you wish, you can change it. An example is shown in Figure 15-95. Click Finish. The new NLB cluster will be configured, and when finished you should see the new configuration similar to the one shown in Figure 15-96.

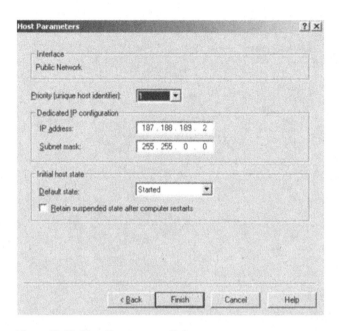

Figure 15-95. *Host Parameters dialog*

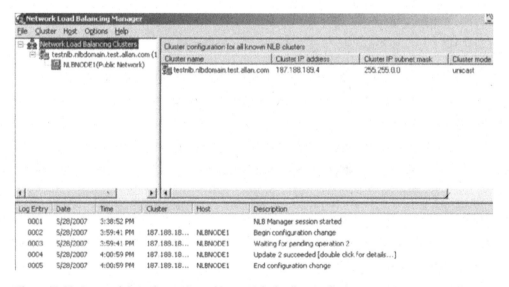

Figure 15-96. *Successful configuration of NLB with the first node*

Configuring Additional Nodes of an NLB Cluster

The following steps show you how to configure all additional nodes for a Windows-based NLB cluster:

1. To add another node to the NLB cluster, either select the cluster name, right-click, and select Add Host to Cluster, as shown in Figure 15-97, or from the Cluster menu, select Add Host, as shown in Figure 15-98.

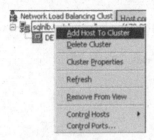

Figure 15-97. *Add Host to Cluster option*

Figure 15-98. *Add Host menu option*

2. On the Connect dialog, enter the name of the computer you wish to join the NLB cluster to in the Host text box. Click Connect. After the host is found, select the network interface you would like to use. An example is shown in Figure 15-99. Click Next.

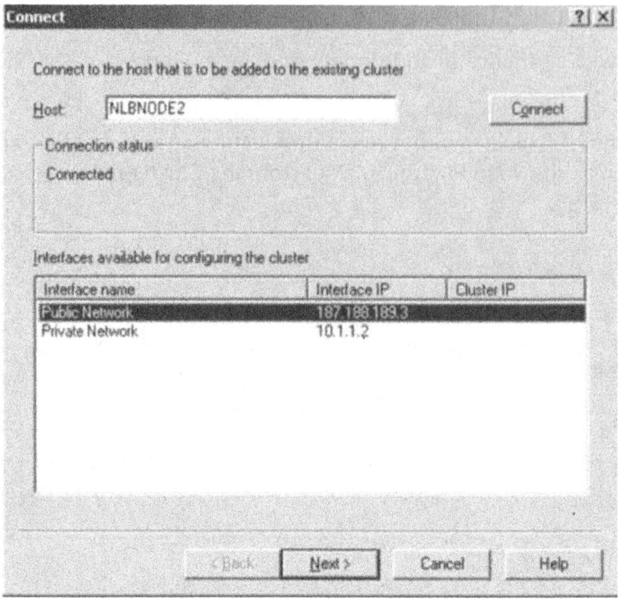

Figure 15-99. *Connect dialog*

3. On the Host Parameters dialog, select the priority of the new host. Select a default state of Stopped. An example is shown in Figure 15-100. Click Finish. The node will be added to the NLB cluster. When finished your result should look similar to Figure 15-101.

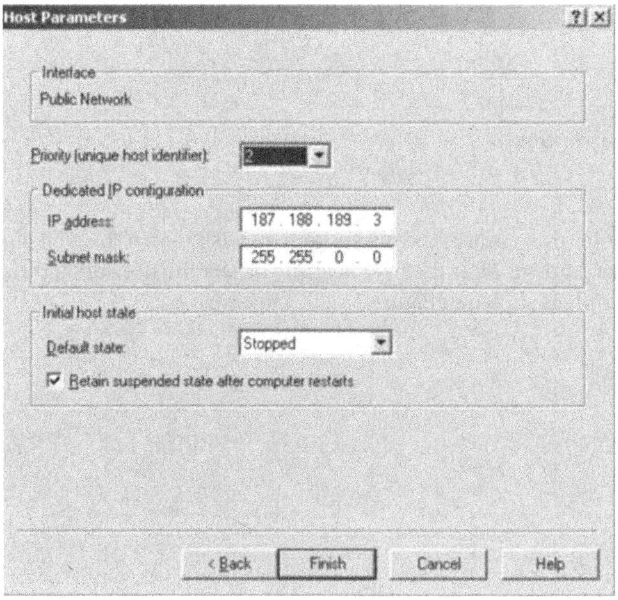

Figure 15-100. *Host Parameters dialog*

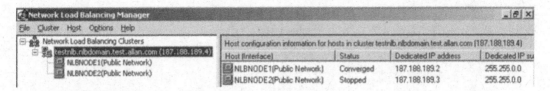

Figure 15-101. *Completed NLB configuration example*

Adding the NLB Cluster Name to DNS

Once the NLB cluster is configured, you have to add it manually to your DNS. For full instructions, follow steps 1 through 5 of the section "Using a DNS Alias to Abstract a Server Name Change."

Testing and Performing a Server Switch Using NLB

To either test your NLB configuration or do the server switch itself, you must follow the instructions in this section.

Emergency Server Switch

To perform an emergency server switch using NLB, follow these steps:

1. Start Network Load Balancing Manager.

2. Right-click the standby node, and select Control Host ➤ Start, as shown in Figure 15-102.

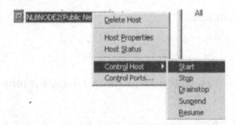

Figure 15-102. *Control Host context menu*

3. Perform the steps required by the technology to bring the database out of a standby state and verify what is required on that instance of SQL Server.

4. Using SQL Server Management Studio, connect to the NLB-fronted SQL Server instance, as shown in Figure 15-103. If you are successful, the Object Explorer will show the aliased SQL Server instance, as shown in Figure 15-104.

5. Open up the database for full testing by the application or solution.

Figure 15-103. *Connecting to the NLB-fronted SQL Server instance*

Figure 15-104. *Connected to the NLB-fronted instance*

Planned Server Switch or a Basic NLB Test

These steps walk through the process of testing your new NLB configuration or doing a planned server switch:

1. If this is just a test, create a table in a database (new or existing) that contains the same column and basic data, but has one thing changed to specify that you are connected to one node or the other.

2. Using SQL Server Management Studio, connect to the NLB-fronted SQL Server instance, as shown in Figure 15-103. If you are successful, the Object Explorer will show the aliased SQL Server instance, as shown in Figure 15-104.

3. Issue two queries. First, verify that the unique data you created is displayed. Next, query the MachineName option of SERVERPROPERTY to verify that the aliased instance is running on the correct NLB node, as shown in Figure 15-105.

4. Make sure that no one is connected to the SQL Server instance that is currently considered the primary instance.

5. Start Network Load Balancing Manager.

```
TESTNLB.maste...SQLQuery1.sql*  Summary
    SELECT test_id, test_data
    FROM testdb..test_table
    GO

    SELECT CONVERT(varchar(20),SERVERPROPERTY('MachineName'))
    go
```

	test_id	test_data
1	1	Node 1

	[No column name]
1	NLBNODE1

Figure 15-105. *Verifying the first NLB node*

6. Using the context menu shown earlier in Figure 15-102, select the active NLB node and select Stop.

7. Using the context menu shown earlier in Figure 15-102, start the other NLB node.

8. Using SQL Server Management Studio, connect to the NLB-fronted SQL Server instance, as shown earlier in Figure 15-103. If you are successful, the Object Explorer will show the aliased SQL Server instance, as shown in Figure 15-104.

9. Issue two queries. First, verify that the unique data you created is displayed. Next, query the MachineName option of SERVERPROPERTY to verify that the aliased instance is running on the correct NLB node, as shown in Figure 15-106.

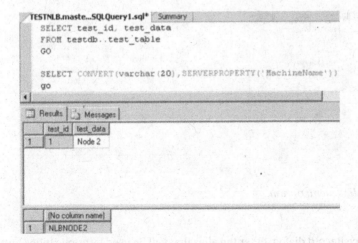

Figure 15-106. *Verifying the second NLB node*

USING NLB FOR READ-ONLY SQL SERVER DATABASES

NLB is a great way to achieve setting up a read-only database farm. If one server fails, another can pick up the slack. This method is described in Chapter 13. Configuring is nearly identical to setting up NLB for abstracting a server name change, except you allow multiple hosts, as shown in the earlier Figure 15-91, instead of directing to a single host. You also set all additional nodes to Started instead of Stopped as you do for abstracting a name change.

Using a DNS Alias to Abstract a Server Name Change

To use DNS to abstract a server name change, use the following instructions. You will need to repeat the steps each time you do a switch of servers. This method does work with failover clustering. The instructions to configure a DNS alias are as follows:

1. Log onto a machine with the proper domain administrator privileges that has the DNS tool.

2. Start the DNS tool found under Administrative Tools.

3. Expand the DNS tree. When you reach the domain, right-click, and select New Alias, as shown in Figure 15-107.

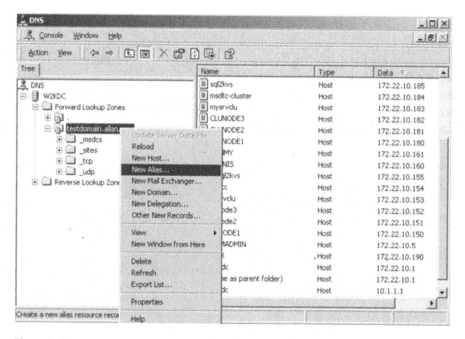

Figure 15-107. *New Alias menu option*

4. On the New Resource Record dialog, enter the alias that will be used by applications and end users as well as the fully qualified name of the underlying server hosting the SQL Server instance. An example is shown in Figure 15-108. Click OK.

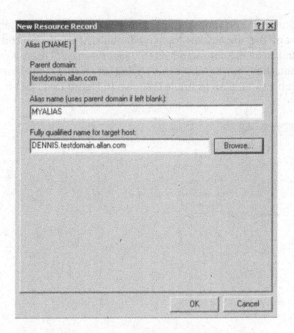

Figure 15-108. *New Resource Record dialog*

5. To test at a network level whether the alias has worked, open a command window and
   enter the command PING aliasname where *aliasname* is the name of the alias you created
   in step 4. A successful example is shown in Figure 15-109. If the ping is unsuccessful, you
   may have to flush your DNS cache by first issuing these two commands in succession:
   ipconfig /flushdns and ipconfig /registerdns. An example is shown in Figure 15-110.
   Ping the alias again to see if it fixes the problem.

```
C:\>ping myalias

Pinging dennis.testdomain.allan.com [172.22.10.160] with 32 bytes of data:

Reply from 172.22.10.160: bytes=32 time=10ms TTL=128
Reply from 172.22.10.160: bytes=32 time<10ms TTL=128
Reply from 172.22.10.160: bytes=32 time<10ms TTL=128
Reply from 172.22.10.160: bytes=32 time<10ms TTL=128
```

Figure 15-109. *Successful ping of the new alias*

```
C:\>ipconfig /flushdns

Windows IP Configuration

Successfully flushed the DNS Resolver Cache.

C:\>ipconfig /registerdns

Windows IP Configuration

Registration of the DNS resource records for all adapters of this computer has b
een initiated. Any errors will be reported in the Event Viewer in 15 minutes..
```

Figure 15-110. *Clearing the DNS cache*

6. Start SQL Server Management Studio. When prompted to connect to the database engine, enter the name of the new alias and the appropriate login credentials. After you are connected, open a new query tab and issue the command SELECT @@servername. This not only proves you can connect to the alias but shows you the underlying server that is running the SQL Server instance the alias is abstracting. An example is shown in Figure 15-111.

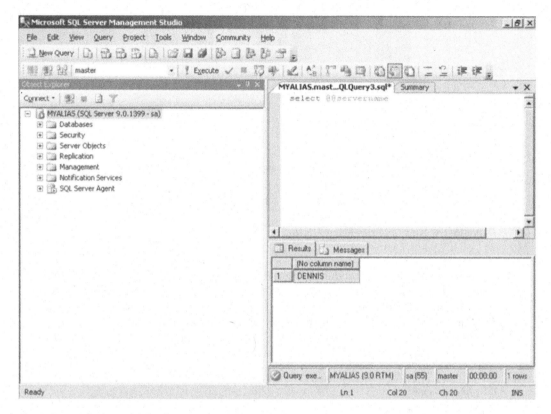

Figure 15-111. *Querying which server is under the alias*

Summary

A key component of ensuring SQL Server availability is not only to ensure that the instances and databases are configured properly, but that you perform the normal day-to-day administration of SQL Server and its databases such as monitoring. Other administrative tasks such as using NLB and attaching and detaching databases may not be common tasks, but they are vital tools in a DBA's arsenal. Besides the 24x7 administration, there is one more component to your offense that will be discussed in the next chapter: database and server maintenance.

CHAPTER 16

■ ■ ■

24x7 Database Maintenance

Routine maintenance on your servers, SQL Server instances, and databases is the final piece of the puzzle for your technology solution. Some maintenance will require a bit of downtime—including downtime of the instance—possibly affecting the availability of the database. This is the challenge in a 24x7 environment and is but one reason why achieving 99.999% uptime is close to impossible even for well-run IT shops. You can certainly minimize the downtime and impact in many cases, but completely avoiding it is not likely. This chapter walks you through the most common maintenance tasks associated with SQL Server and points you to more information where applicable.

Performing Database Maintenance

Proactive database maintenance is one of the best things you can do to ensure the health and availability of your databases. Reacting after the fact is like closing the barn door after the animals have escaped. This section shows you how to automate your maintenance (and administrative tasks) through SQL Server Agent jobs and walks you through the routine maintenance you will need to perform on a frequent basis. The frequency will differ for every SQL Server installation, so you need to figure out when is right for you.

Tip A great source of information on the workings of the SQL Server storage engine, disaster recovery, Database Console Commands (DBCCs), and other topics relevant to high availability can be found at http://blogs.msdn.com/sqlserverstorageengine/. Paul Randal, the main blogger for that site, has some deep, informative, and fun to read insights into how SQL Server works.

Creating SQL Server Agent Jobs

Creating a SQL Server Agent job to schedule and automate a tasks is something I have mentioned a lot in this book. This is one of the best features of SQL Server and has been for quite some time.

Creating a Job Using SQL Server Management Studio

When creating your own database backup plans, you will have to do all of the work yourself. Job creation has changed slightly in SQL Server Management Studio. These steps walk you through that process, but they only cover the basics of creating a job:

1. In SQL Server Management Studio expand SQL Server Agent. Select Jobs, right-click, and select New Job, as shown in Figure 16-1.

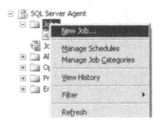

Figure 16-1. *New Job option*

2. On the New Job dialog, enter a name for the job that is easily understood by any DBA or administrator who may need to use it or edit it. Select an owner under whose context the job will be run. Optionally, you can select a Category, which may help you in your DBA task organization, and you can write a longer description, as well. An example is shown in Figure 16-2.

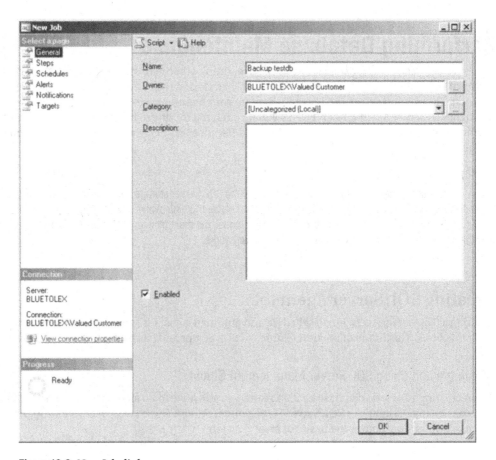

Figure 16-2. *New Job dialog*

3. Select Steps under Select a Page. You will see the dialog shown in Figure 16-3. Click New to start the process of adding a job step.

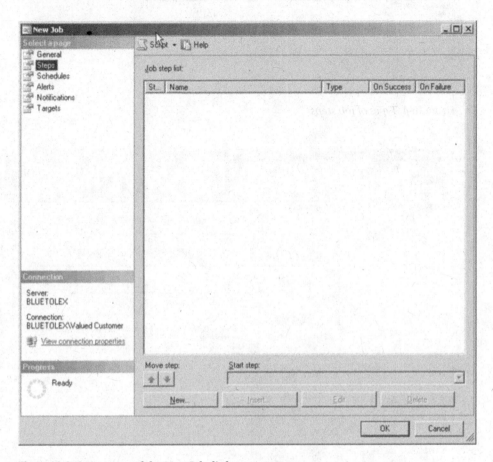

Figure 16-3. *Steps page of the New Job dialog*

4. On the General page of the New Job Step dialog, enter a name for the step. Next you must select what kind of job step this will be, as shown in Figure 16-4. Depending on the type of job step you are creating, you may see different things on the page. A Transact-SQL job is shown in Figure 16-5.

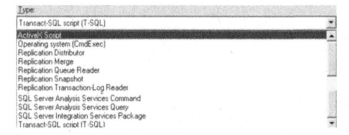

Figure 16-4. *Types of job steps*

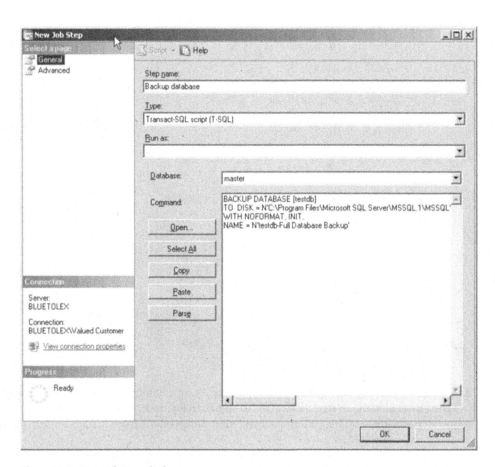

Figure 16-5. *New Job Step dialog*

5. Select the Advanced page of the New Job Step dialog, and you will see the dialog in Figure 16-6.

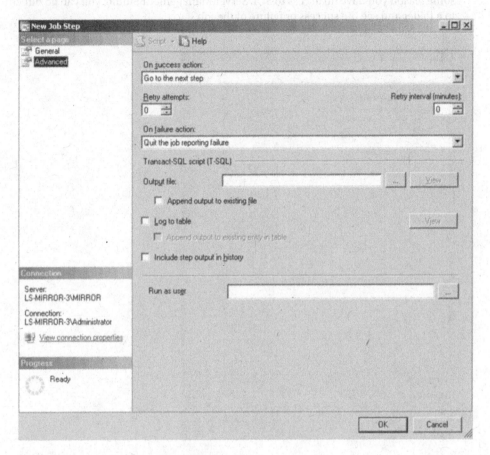

Figure 16-6. *Advanced page for a job step*

If the job is going to have multiple job steps, you must use the On Success Action drop-down to select the action to perform when the job step is complete. Your options are shown in Figure 16-7.

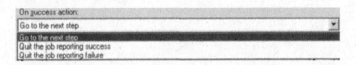

Figure 16-7. *Options for what to do upon a job step completion*

If the job step fails, select the appropriate option, as shown in Figure 16-8. I recommend saving the output of the job to your file system by filling in a value for Output File. If for some reason you have no access to SQL Server Management Studio, you can go directly to a folder and see the success or failure of the job.

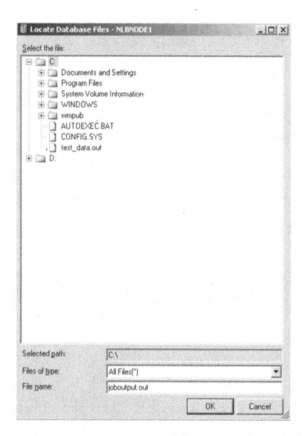

Figure 16-8. *Selecting an output file location for the job*

Click OK when finished, and you will see that the job step has been added, as reflected in Figure 16-9.

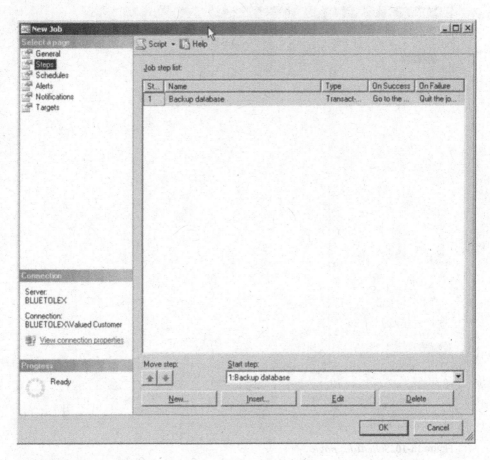

Figure 16-9. *Job step created*

6. Select Schedules from Select a Page, as shown in Figure 16-10. Click New.

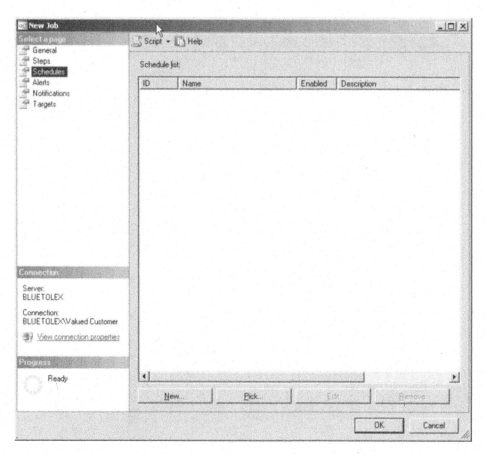

Figure 16-10. *Schedules page*

7. On the New Job Schedule dialog shown in Figure 16-11, enter a name for the schedule, and configure when the job should be run. Click OK.

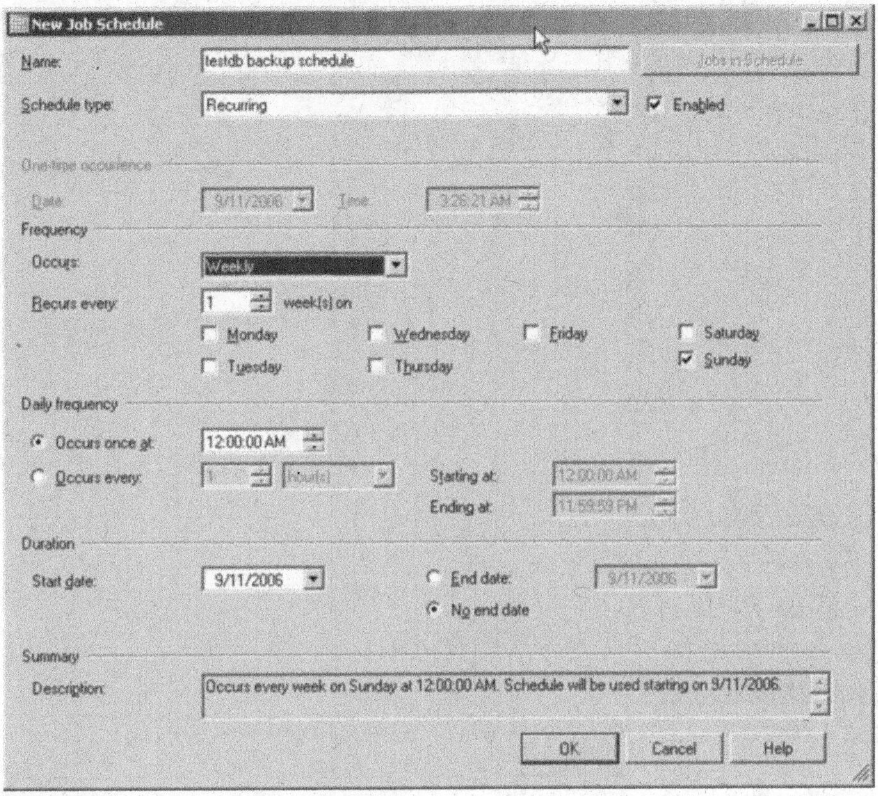

Figure 16-11. *New Job Schedule dialog*

8. The schedule you just created will now be displayed. An example is shown in Figure 16-12. Click OK.

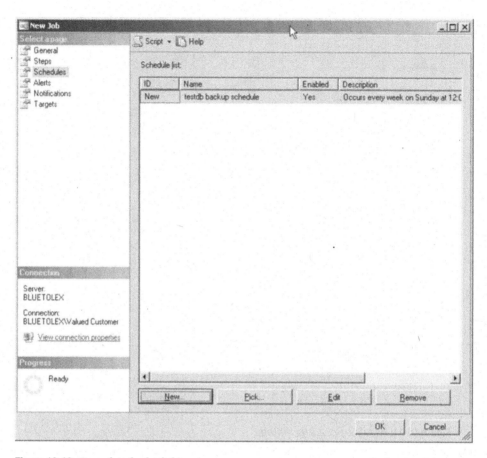

Figure 16-12. *Completed schedule*

9. If you want to create an alert for the job, select Alerts from Select a Page, as shown in Figure 16-13. Click New. You will then be prompted to create an alert, as described in Chapter 15.

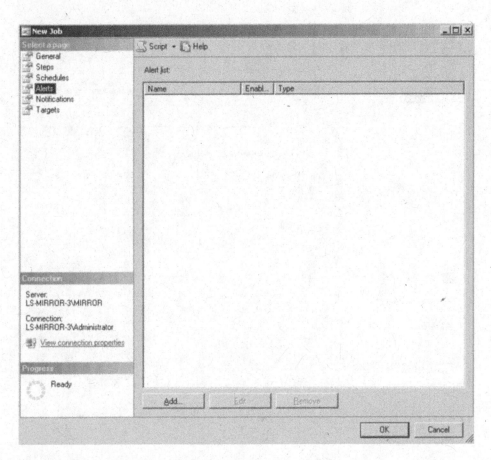

Figure 16-13. *Alerts page for a SQL Server Agent job*

10. If you want to be notified about the status of the job, select Notifications from Select a Page, as shown in Figure 16-14. Select your preferred method of notification and enter the information as needed. An example is shown in Figure 16-15.

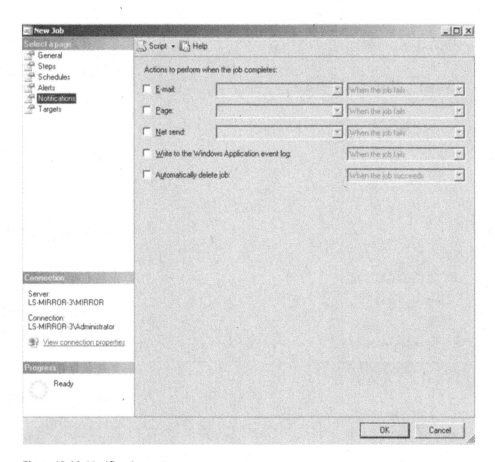

Figure 16-14. *Notifications page*

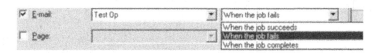

Figure 16-15. *Configuring to be notified by e-mail*

11. Click OK to complete the process.

Creating a Job Using Transact-SQL

To create a SQL Server Agent job via Transact-SQL, you would use a combination of system stored procedures: sp_add_job, sp_add_jobserver, sp_add_jobschedule, and sp_add_jobstep. All of these are described in detail with each parameter in SQL Server Books Online.

The following example creates a full backup job with no notifications:

```
USE msdb
GO

EXEC  msdb.dbo.sp_add_job @job_name=N'Backup testdb',
    @enabled=1,
    @notify_level_eventlog=0,
    @notify_level_email=2,
    @notify_level_netsend=2,
    @notify_level_page=2,
    @delete_level=0,
    @category_name=N'[Uncategorized (Local)]',
    @owner_login_name=N'sa'

EXEC msdb.dbo.sp_add_jobserver
    @job_name=N'Backup testdb',
    @server_name = N'NLBNODE1'
GO

EXEC msdb.dbo.sp_add_jobstep
    @job_name=N'Backup testdb',
    @step_name=N'Full Backup',
    @step_id=1,
    @cmdexec_success_code=0,
    @on_success_action=1,
    @on_fail_action=2,
    @retry_attempts=0,
    @retry_interval=0,
    @os_run_priority=0,
    @subsystem=N'TSQL',
    @command=N'BACKUP DATABASE testdb
        TO DISK = ''C:\backup.bak''',
    @database_name=N'master',
    @output_file_name=N'C:\joboutput.out',
    @flags=0
GO

EXEC msdb.dbo.sp_add_jobschedule
    @job_name=N'Backup testdb',
    @name=N'Full Backup Schedule',
    @enabled=1,
    @freq_type=8,
    @freq_interval=1,
    @freq_subday_type=1,
    @freq_subday_interval=0,
    @freq_relative_interval=0,
    @freq_recurrence_factor=1,
    @active_start_date=20070530,
    @active_end_date=99991231,
    @active_start_time=0,
    @active_end_time=235959,
GO
```

Performing Routine Maintenance

Databases need care and feeding, too. If an automobile goes without oil changes, you can damage the engine. You can apply the same principle here; preventative maintenance goes a long way. Some maintenance is easier to do than others, and some will also affect the availability of the database itself. You need to understand what needs to be done and then figure out when you may need to perform the task in your environment. Maintenance is getting more and more challenging as the size of databases grow, and I do not see it getting any easier. SQL Server self-manages to a point, but not when it comes to checking the health of your databases, rebuilding indexes, or checking for fragmentation.

Checking Database Health

Checking the health of your databases is what I would deem a no-brainer. Think of it another way. Cars have sensors that notify you of a problem. If your check-engine light comes on, are you really going to drive until the car stops working? No, you are going to take it into a repair shop and have it diagnosed. The health checks you do will let you know if there is no problem, or a big problem. Standard monitoring may not catch issues such as database corruption. You need SQL Server tools to do that.

The Transact-SQL command most people know about is DBCC CHECKDB. DBCC CHECKDB is a consistency checker for SQL Server and can be intrusive or nonintrusive, depending on the options you use with it. There are two levels of checks that DBCC CHECKDB does: *physical* and *logical* (meaning inside the database itself). DBCC CHECKDB runs three other DBCC commands as part of its work: DBCC CHECKALLOC, DBCC CHECKTABLE, and DBCC CHECKCATALOG, as well as a few other checks. DBCC CHECKDB can also attempt to repair the errors found if you allow it.

I'll say this upfront: DBCC CHECKDB can potentially be one of the most intrusive checks that you run against your database. You want to make sure that unless you are doing a less stringent check that this is run at a time when there is minimal to no activity to ensure that the process will not be affected by usage of the database. Unless you are using DBCC CHECKDB with the WITH PHYSICAL_ONLY option, it's going to be intrusive. Plan accordingly.

One of the main uses of running DBCC CHECKDB is to detect corruption. If you have corruption, you have big problems. I didn't write that large chapter on backup and restore (Chapter 3) for nothing. If you encounter corruption, your backups will be your saving grace. While DBCC CHECKDB can attempt to repair the corruption with the REPAIR_ALLOW_DATA_LOSS option, it still will most likely not fix your data. REPAIR_ALLOW_DATA_LOSS is exactly what it says it is; it will attempt to repair the corruption, but you will most likely encounter data loss. That may be unacceptable to the business. Manually repairing the data, which will need to occur once the corruption is fixed, will not be easy. The reality also may be that the corruption cannot be fixed and you will have to go to your backups. What you need to figure out in that case is if the corruption was introduced into your backups and when that may have occurred. Chances are if you are being vigilant about running DBCC CHECKDB, you would notice this as soon as possible and have minimal to no data loss.

There is a great multipart series on DBCC CHECKDB posted on the SQL Server storage engine blog I referred to earlier: http://blogs.msdn.com/sqlserverstorageengine/archive/tags/ DBCC+CHECKDB+Series/default.aspx.

Figure 16-16 shows what the output of running a sample DBCC CHECKDB may look like. At the end of the verbose output, a summary (which is easily seen in Figure 16-17) is displayed as well.

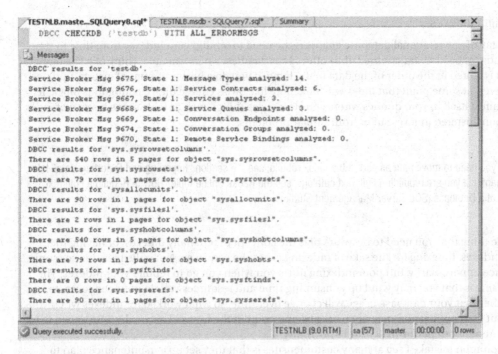

Figure 16-16. *Sample DBCC CHECKDB execution*

Note I know your multi-terabyte database is large and hard to manage, but just because it is big does not give you the excuse to not run health checks. That is absolutely suicide. At worst, run DBCC CHECKDB WITH PHYSICAL_ONLY. An example is shown in Figure 16-17. It will at least detect problems with the pages, and assuming you have page checksums enabled (as described in Chapter 3), corruption will be detected. If your database is partitioned (as described in Chapter 13), you could run a DBCC CHECKFILEGROUP and get consistency checks file by file. It's not a big bang, but it does the job. You could even just run DBCC CHECKTABLE and do it table by table, or just run DBCC CHECKALLOC to check the disk consistency. So you have options.

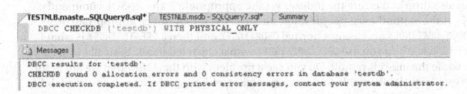

Figure 16-17. *Example of running DBCC CHECKDB WITH PHYSICAL_ONLY*

Rebuilding Indexes

A mainstay of any relational database engine is the need to rebuild your indexes from time to time. When indexes become fragmented, they affect your database's performance. Think of a clustered index; it is stored in the order of the data in the table. If you do a heavy amount of inserts, updates, and deletes, at some point that index will look more like Swiss cheese than a contiguous block. It will manifest itself in your queries where you start to see things such as table scans instead of index seeks. Nonclustered indexes suffer from similar problems.

Tip If you need to move data as part of the index rebuild, see the section "Importing and Exporting Data" later in this chapter. If you are rebuilding Full-Text catalogs, see the Books Online topic "How to Rebuild a Full-Text Catalogs of a Database (SQL Server Management Studio)".

One thing that you need to be aware of is the concept of too many indexes, or having the wrong indexes. Indexing for the sake of indexing is not the way to go. Not only does this consume disk space unnecessarily, but poor indexing hurts you when you go to rebuild your indexes. The bottom line is that you may wind up consuming time and resources you do not need to waste. Remember that your database usage will change over time, so what worked for indexes when you rolled out your application may not work at some point in the future. This is why DBAs need to be vigilant about both performance and availability.

A common mistake I see at many customer sites is that they set up a maintenance plan to rebuild every index of every database in a single SQL Server instance. When you have some small databases that are not mission critical or 24x7, this may be no big deal. Even still, it is not the right thing to do. Not every index needs to be rebuilt all the time, and depending on the size of the table and type of index, the operation could take quite some time and eat up a lot of disk space (your transaction log will grow because an index rebuild is a fully logged operation, and depending on how your Transact-SQL statement is coded, you may also use `tempdb` for sorting).

The smartest way to go about rebuilding your indexes is to determine which ones actually need to be reindexed and only do those. That takes some planning and experience, and even if you have the experience, there are no absolutes. Many companies wind up not doing a big bang for all indexes but staggering the rebuilds at different times to ensure that not only they get done but that the maintenance can fit within a maintenance window—a crucial point to remember.

Depending on the indexes and what needs to be done, there are a few ways to go about rebuilding them. You can use `DBCC DBREINDEX` or `DBCC INDEXDEFRAG`, or do online index maintenance. You can also drop and create the indexes via the appropriate Transact-SQL commands. `DBCC DBREINDEX` is the method most people know and use, but it may not be appropriate in all cases. Using `DBCC DBREINDEX` and using a normal `DROP INDEX` and then a `CREATE INDEX` is what I would deem intrusive. When you use `DBCC DBREINDEX` with a clustered index, basically your table is unavailable while the index is rebuilt. Do you see a problem with that? Now that we are in the age of VLDBs (very large databases) it could be a real killer for both performance and availability. Dropping and re-creating the index is pretty much just as bad; even if the table is accessible, there may be no index, so performance will be in the dumps. Unfortunately, you cannot completely avoid these operations from time to time. If you need to do one of these, make sure it is appropriately scheduled and the right parties are notified.

`DBCC INDEXDEFRAG` is not as brute force as either `DBCC DBREINDEX` or dropping and re-creating the index. `DBCC INDEXDEFRAG` is run per index, so you would need to write scripts to execute it against all of your indexes at once in a given database. If your index spans more than one data file, it will index the data one file at a time. `DBCC INDEXDEFRAG` essentially trawls through and defragments the index while the database is online and should not affect end users. This also means that it may also take longer to complete the job.

A new Transact-SQL command in SQL Server 2005 is ALTER INDEX. It allows you to modify an existing index and can disable, rebuild, or reorganize the index specified. ALTER INDEX is a command you will want to get familiar with when you start using SQL Server 2005, and you may want to replace some of your existing index operations with it. It works with both regular and XML indexes.

Also new to SQL Server 2005 is the concept of doing index operations such as a rebuild or a drop while the database is fully online. Online index rebuilds is only a feature of SQL Server 2005 Enterprise Edition. The ability to rebuild an index while the system and databases are completely online and usable is obviously invaluable for a 24x7 system. Enterprise Edition may be more expensive, but if your SLAs dictate tight time frames and this feature will help you, I strongly suggest considering implementing it. A good example of where this should be mandatory is if you will be administering VLDBs. There is virtually no way you will make your SLAs without this new feature of SQL Server 2005.

Mark Souza did an excellent overview of this in a session at SQL PASS a few years ago. If you can find a copy, I would suggest viewing it. SQL Server Books Online "How Online Index Operations Work" provides excellent background. Behind the scenes, an online index rebuild uses only an Intent Share lock, not a table lock that will block usage of the table. There is always the possibility of unavailability of the data in the table at points, but it is akin to doing a snapshot (the disk kind, not the database snapshot) for backup purposes. It should not really be noticeable to end users. Before implementing online index operations, you should consult the Books Online topic "Guidelines for Performing Online Index Operations." One caveat you should be aware of upfront is that doing online index rebuilds means that no changes can be made to the table (i.e., making a schema change, dropping the table, or truncating the data) while the index rebuild is going on.

Online index operations are achieved through ALTER INDEX. Here is an example of an online index rebuild:

```
USE AdventureWorks
GO
ALTER INDEX PK_Employee_EmployeeID ON HumanResources.Employee
REBUILD WITH ONLINE;
GO
```

Reindexing absolutely affects your transaction logs as well as potentially tempdb, so they should be sized to accommodate the rebuild of your largest indexes. If you are using log shipping or database mirroring, take index rebuilds into account because they will affect the size of the transaction log. This will be especially important for log shipping since the size of your transaction log backups may dramatically increase because rebuilding an index is a fully logged operation. This is yet another case for staggering your index rebuilds to not overwhelm your solutions at any given time to keep your SQL Server deployment manageable. You may even want to consider suspending database mirroring or log shipping for a VLDB clustered index rebuild because the hit to those two availability technologies may be so large it would take a considerable amount of time to catch up. tempdb is used to do the sorting for the index, so if you have very large databases, you would want to ensure that tempdb is on physically different spindles than your log files or your data to ensure the performance of your disk subsystem during an index rebuild.

Caution Your production environment should not be the first place you try the reindexing of a clustered index in your 10TB VLDB. You absolutely need test systems to ensure that what you are trying to do is going to work and to know approximately how long it will take. You do not want to have to roll back an index operation that could take a considerable amount of time.

Performing Server and Instance Maintenance

Besides maintaining your databases, you also need to maintain your SQL Server instances and Windows servers. This section will cover disk fragmentation and the patching, updating, and upgrading of your servers and instances.

Handling Physical Disk Fragmentation

As mentioned earlier in the "Performing Database Maintenance" section, there are two kinds of fragmentation when it comes to SQL Server: logical and physical. This section deals with the *physical*. If you allow automatic growth and/or automatic shrinking of your databases, you will most likely have some sort of fragmentation of your physical disk. Compounding that problem is that you also most likely do not have one database or transaction file per disk; you most likely have multiple files and combinations of data and log files, all of which were added at different times and have grown or shrunk.

If you have any of these conditions, you most likely have some sort of fragmentation at the physical disk layer that is not a SQL Server problem per se, but it absolutely can affect the performance of your SQL Server databases. Light fragmentation is usually not a big deal, but heavily fragmented disks can become serious issues. The reason is that for files on disk to perform, you want the chunks of disk that comprise that file to be contiguous, not broken up. If the chunks are broken up, the disk head needs to move much more to get to the data, thus causing fragmentation. The more fragmented your database files are, the worse your performance can be.

Defragmenting disks with SQL Server data and log files will involve downtime. You must stop SQL Server so that the defragmentation process does not work against the active data and log files because this can potentially introduce corruption in the database. Sometimes system administrators (not DBAs) will automatically defrag all disks in or attached to a server without thinking it will cause problems. Any DBA should ask about the systems he or she is responsible for because ultimately you're responsible for the resulting mess.

Tip Always back up your databases prior to shutting down SQL Server and subsequently running any kind of defragmentation process on your disks. If anything goes wrong, you can always restore from backups.

Performing Maintenance to the Server Itself

It is inevitable that your physical servers will need some sort of maintenance that is not related to SQL Server. Some of these items that may require maintenance may include but are not limited to the following:

- Operating system service packs and hotfixes
- Installation, patching, and maintenance of other software installed on the SQL Server
- BIOS and firmware updates
- Updating of drivers for hardware components
- Hardware upgrades such as processor or memory
- Hardware replacement for failures

It is outside the scope of this book to explain how to do each of these tasks. The problem that DBAs will encounter is that they are most likely not involved in, nor do they have any control over, these updates. Many times they will find out after the fact, when they get notifications that the system was offline for a period of time or a problem has already occurred. Updating system components outside of SQL Server is important, but not when it will break SQL Server or introduce stability. A patch that is right for your IIS server may not be applicable to your SQL Server servers. Take the time to do the research since that one-minute installation of a seemingly innocuous patch may cause hours or days of downtime.

The most common thing I see at client sites is that administrators feel the need to install the "latest and greatest" driver for the various server components—especially disk controller cards such as host bus adapters (HBAs). I can't tell you how many times a client was having problems, the administrators swore up and down that nothing changed, and I find out later they updated the disk drivers the week before. It's not a SQL-related change, so how could it affect SQL Server, right? (I'm rolling my eyes as I type this.) Think back to the six chapters of clustering: you must have a certified solution.

Disabling Automatic Windows Updates

Despite behavior I've seen to the contrary at client sites, servers are not desktop computers. This means that they should not be someone's main computer where they read e-mail, surf the Internet, and so on. I don't care if you live in the data center; you need somewhere else to do your daily business. The server itself, although it may have a connection to the Internet, should be "hands off." Yet I have seen IT departments that are short staffed, allowing the operating system to automatically update itself, like a desktop system does. While in theory this may seem like a good idea, in reality (I'm not going to sugarcoat things) it could be an unmitigated disaster for many reasons. Your server is not your desktop and should be reasonably protected from malware. The main reason you do not want to allow automatic updates is to ensure that there are no surprises.

Aside from ensuring that your server builds are all the same (which has been addressed multiple times in this book), you do not want to introduce patches automatically that may break something. One recent client of mine had automatic updates turned on for some of their database servers. Not only were the servers getting updated, which means that the servers were not maintained at an equal patch level with other servers, but a server was pending reboots they were unaware of. As an administrator, you need full *manual* control over your servers.

To disable automatic updates, navigate to the Automatic Updates applet found under Control Panel, and select the option Turn off Automatic Updates, as shown in Figure 16-18.

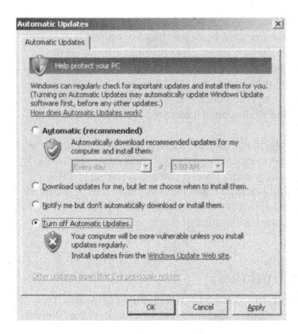

Figure 16-18. *Disabling automatic updates*

Applying a SQL Server 2005 Service Pack

This section covers how to install a SQL Server 2005 Service Pack. The examples show SQL Server 2005 Service Pack 2 and will not reflect any changes that may occur in a service pack released past this version.

Tip Make sure you read the readme file and all instructions before attempting the installation.

---

1. Log into the server as an account that has privileges to install the service pack. On a failover cluster, this must be the cluster service account or a domain account that has administrative privileges on each node of the Windows server cluster.

2. If you are running the installer on a failover cluster, ensure the SQL Server instances you are going to upgrade (either a single failover clustering instance or multiple instances if you are upgrading more than one at the same time) are owned by the node that will launch the process. If you do not, after starting the install, the option to upgrade the SQL Server instance will be disabled and you will see the message shown in Figure 16-19. You can use Cluster Administrator (as described in Chapters 5 and 6) or the command line cluster.exe, shown in Figure 16-20.

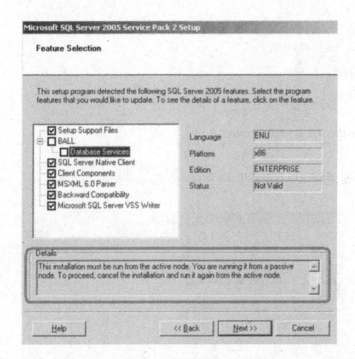

Figure 16-19. *Message if the clustered SQL Server resources are not owned by the node*

```
K:\>cluster STYX GROUP "GRAND\ILLUSION" /MOVE:NODE1
Moving resource group 'GRAND\ILLUSION'...
Group                   Node            Status
--------------------    -----------     -----------
GRAND\ILLUSION          NODE1           Online
```

Figure 16-20. *Moving the resources to the node executing the service pack*

3. Double-click the executable you downloaded from Microsoft's web site (http://
www.microsoft.com/downloads). For example, the SQL Server 2005 Service Pack 2 executable
for English x86 is named SQLServer2005SP2-KB921896-x86-ENU.exe. The files will unpack on
your hard drive, as shown in Figure 16-21, and will detect the instances of SQL Server, as
shown in Figure 16-22.

Figure 16-21. *Unpacking the files*

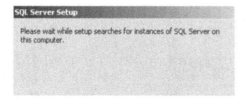

Figure 16-22. *Detecting the SQL Server instances*

4. On the Welcome dialog, shown in Figure 16-23, click Next.

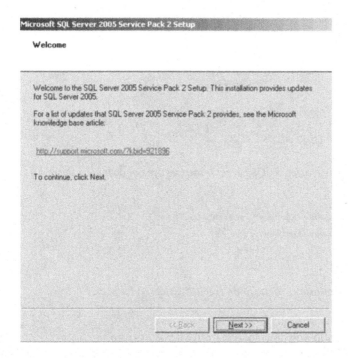

Figure 16-23. *Welcome dialog*

5. On the License Terms dialog, shown in Figure 16-24, select I accept the Agreement, and click Next.

6. On the Feature Selection dialog, you have to select which components you will be upgrading. You cannot deselect any required updates. An improvement over all previous versions of SQL Server is that you can patch more than one instance of SQL Server at the same time as long as they are on the same server. You can even patch SQL Server and Analysis Services at the same time, as shown in Figure 16-25. A selective service pack install example is shown in Figure 16-26. Click Next.

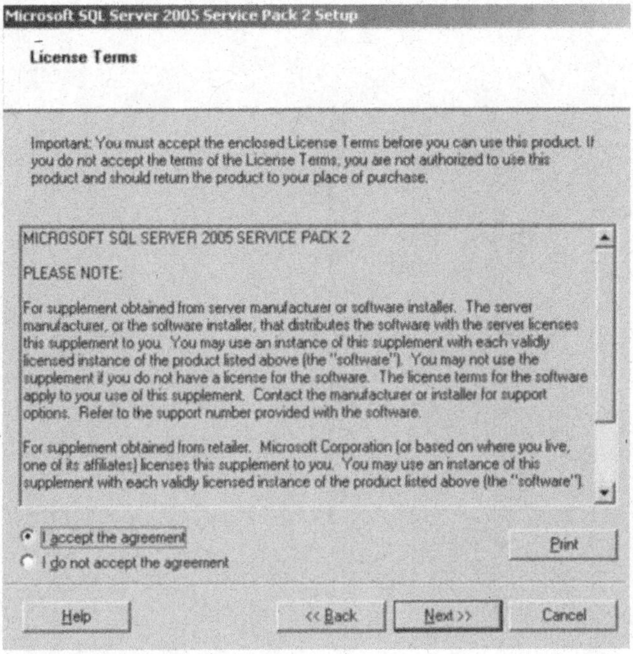

Figure 16-24. *License Terms dialog*

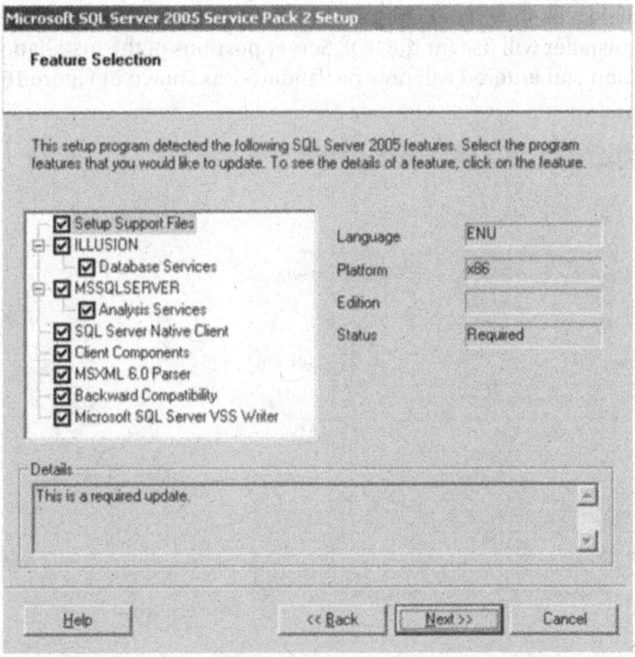

Figure 16-25. *Feature Selection with all options selected*

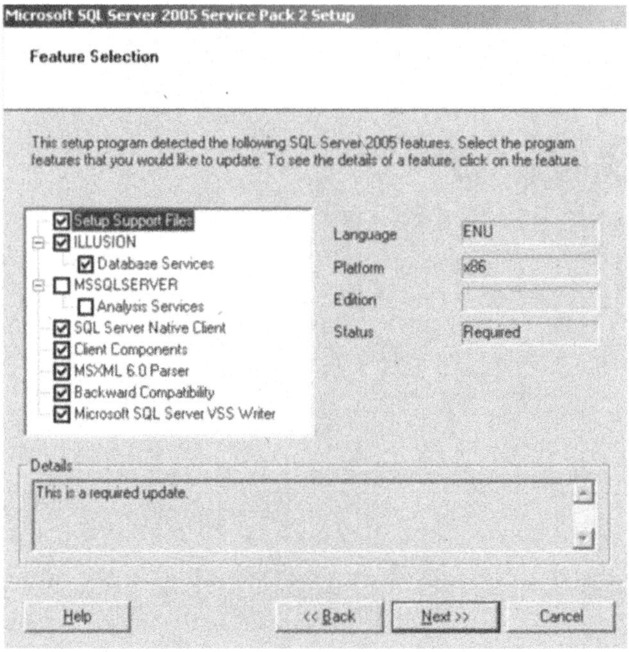

Figure 16-26. *Feature Selection with a partial upgrade*

7. On the Authentication dialog, as shown in Figure 16-27, select the appropriate authentication method, which the installer will use for the SQL Server portions of the installation. Click Next. The information you entered will now be validated, as shown in Figure 16-28.

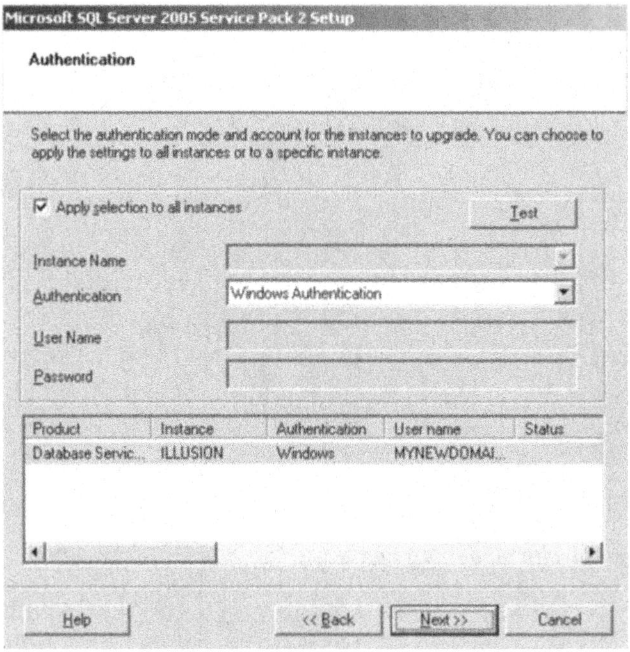

Figure 16-27. *Authentication dialog*

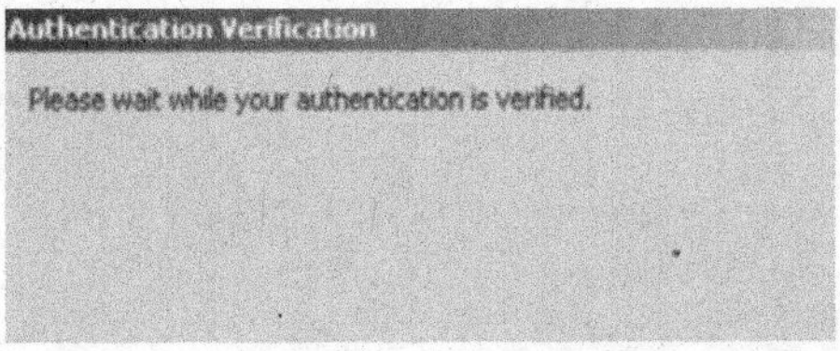

Figure 16-28. *Authenticating the account used for the service pack install*

8. If this is an install for a failover cluster, you will see the Remote User Account dialog shown in Figure 16-29. If this is a stand-alone, skip to the next step. Enter the credentials for the account that has administrative privileges on each node, which is generally the Windows server cluster service account. Click Next.

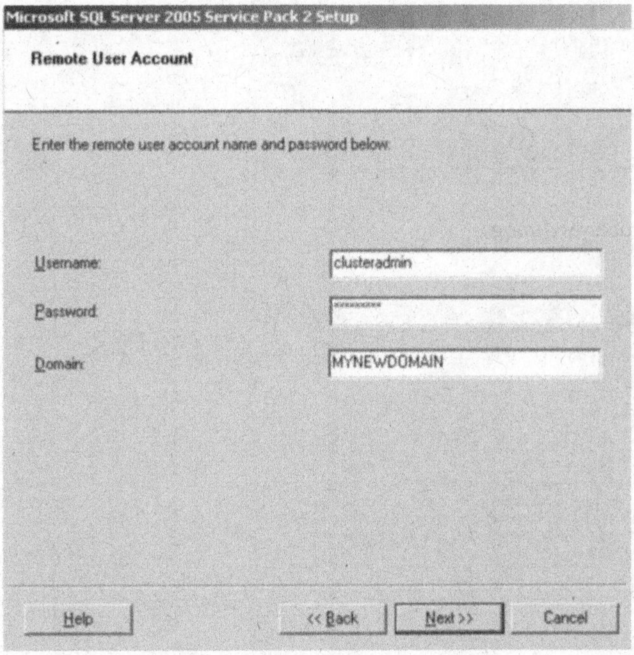

Figure 16-29. *Remote User Account dialog*

9. On the Running Processes dialog, shown in Figure 16-30, the installer is reporting whether there are processes in use and will require a reboot after the service pack is installed. Click Next.

10. On the Error and Usage Reporting Settings dialog, shown in Figure 16-31, check the boxes if you wish to share information with Microsoft. Click Next.

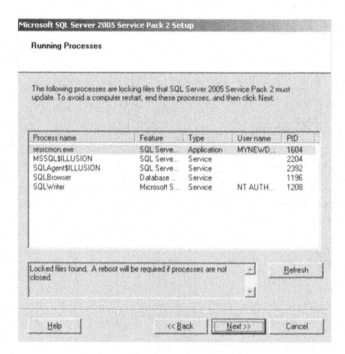

Figure 16-30. *Running Processes dialog*

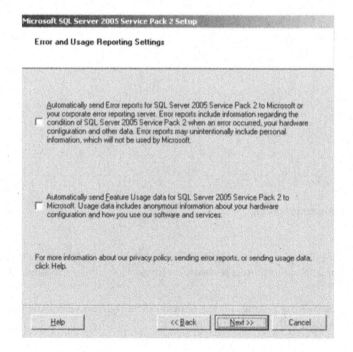

Figure 16-31. *Error and Usage Reporting Settings dialog*

11. On the Ready to Install page, shown in Figure 16-32, click Install.

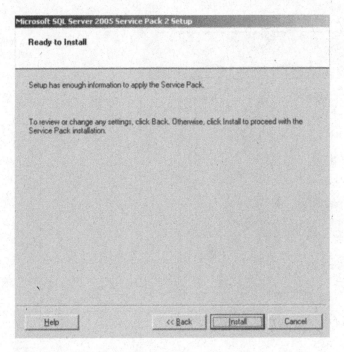

Figure 16-32. *Ready to Install dialog*

The service pack will now be installed. The Installation Progress dialog will indicate the install process and what has been completed. It will also tell you whether a reboot will be required. An example is shown in Figure 16-33.

12. When the installation is complete, you may see the message box in Figure 16-34 informing you that a reboot is required. If a reboot is required and you installed this on a cluster, you will have to reboot all nodes. Click OK.

Figure 16-33. *Progress of the service pack install*

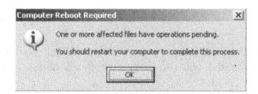

Figure 16-34. *Reboot message*

13. On the Installation Progress dialog, shown in Figure 16-35, click Next.

Figure 16-35. *Completed installation of the service pack*

14. On the Installation Complete dialog, shown in Figure 16-36, you can view the summary of what was done by clicking View Summary. An example is shown in Figure 16-37.

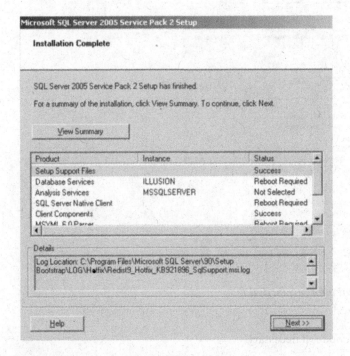

Figure 16-36. *Installation Complete dialog*

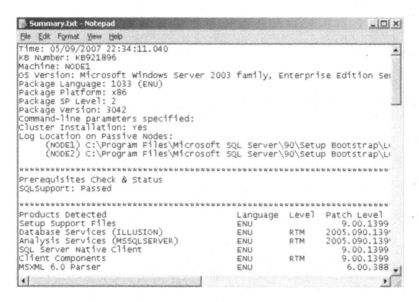

Figure 16-37. *Summary of the service pack install*

15. Click Finish on the Additional Information dialog, shown in Figure 16-38.

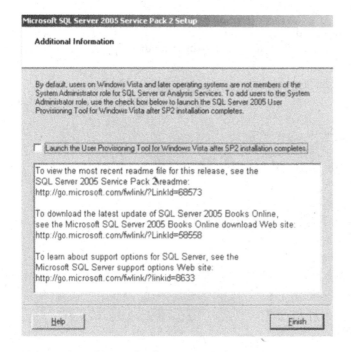

Figure 16-38. *Additional Information dialog*

16. Reboot your server or nodes if necessary.

If this service pack will be installed on a cluster, it will patch the executables and shared files on all nodes. If you choose to also update the tools and utilities, the installer will only update them on the node from which the service pack was launched. If you have installed the SQL Server 2005 tools and utilities on other nodes, you must run the installer from those nodes to patch the tools and utilities.

WHEN SHOULD YOU APPLY HOTFIXES, PATCHES, OR SERVICE PACKS?

There are a lot of opinions out there on when you should apply patches and service packs to your operating systems, drivers, and software. The vendor will most likely say to do it as soon as they are released, or as soon as possible. That's nice in theory, but a bad idea in reality.

Unless it is an emergency hotfix, anything going into your production environment needs to be fully tested and implemented in a way not to break production; or if something breaks, you need to know how to mitigate it or fix it. Not only that, but will the act of patching one server versus another (or all of them) make administration harder? Is it even supported by the software? (By that I mean that just because SQL Server 2005 can be patched to the latest and greatest does not mean that the software vendor who makes your application supports running its software against it.) What is the rollout plan to apply the patch/service pack/hotfix to the other servers?

I will also say this: there's a tried-and-true adage out there—if it ain't broke, don't fix it. If your production environment is stable, and the update does not give you new functionality or fix problems, why install it for the sake of doing an update? Do not misconstrue my words: staying up-to-date, such as on drivers for your hardware and service packs for your software, is absolutely essential. If you are too out-of-date it could also affect your availability, as well as your supportability from the vendor. There has to be a middle ground where this gets done and you don't feel a lot of pain doing it, since the likelihood is that you need to patch tens, hundreds, or thousands of servers, not one. If a patch takes 15 minutes to apply and requires a reboot, and you need to do it to a total of 500 servers, that is a minimum of 125 hours of work, not including the time it takes to reboot the systems, copy the software to each server, coordinate the resources to perform the work, and so on. Bottom line: go into any change with eyes wide open because it is never as simple as clicking the installation program and letting it run.

Importing and Exporting Data

Although it is hard to classify as either an administrative task or a maintenance task, there will be times you may need to move parts of a data set elsewhere, and you will not employ any of the technologies explored in the previous chapters. Two technologies in SQL Server allow you to either copy the data directly, or generate files you can later import into another database or instance. Using these methods to create data files that can then be stored securely can also serve as another form of protection. These two methods are using bcp or SQL Server Integration Services (SSIS) (covered in another way in Chapter 15).

Using bcp to Import and Export Data

bcp is a command-line utility that has been in every version of SQL Server to date. While it has been enhanced over the years (e.g., the ability to use format files was added), its core purpose remains the same: to get data in and out of SQL Server via flat files. There are many command-line switches, and I will not cover them here because they are covered in depth in the Books Online topic "bcp Utility."

bcp is one of the unsung tools of the DBA. I've used it to do everything from loading test databases to exporting data to be used by systems other than SQL Server, and everything in between. It has also saved me once or twice when backups did not work for me. I know there is a big aversion to command-line tools for some, but this is one utility that you want to be familiar with if you are running a highly available SQL Server environment.

■ **Caution** You should be careful if you also have the SQL Server 2000 tools on your system where you are executing bcp.

Figure 16-39 shows an example of executing an export using bcp.

```
C:\>bcp testdb.dbo.test_table out test_data.out -c -SNLBNODE1 -Usa -PP@ssw0rd

Starting copy...

1 rows copied.
Network packet size (bytes): 4096
Clock Time (ms.) Total      : 1        Average : (1000.00 rows per sec.)
```

Figure 16-39. *Export of data using bcp*

Using SSIS to Import and Export Data

As you learned in Chapter 15, SSIS is the replacement for the Data Transformation Services (DTS) functionality in SQL Server 2000. Most DBAs will not want to deal with the complexity of the Business Intelligence Studio to do a simple data transfer. Microsoft has thought of the DBA and kept a simple wizard-based interface into SSIS in SQL Server Management Studio to allow the importing and exporting of data. Follow these instructions to import and export data using this wizard:

1. Select a database in SQL Server Management Studio, right-click, select Tasks, and then select either Import Data or Export Data, as shown in Figure 16-40.

Figure 16-40. *Import Data and Export Data menu options*

2. On the Welcome to SQL Server Import and Export Wizard dialog, shown in Figure 16-41, click Next.

Figure 16-41. *SQL Server Import and Export Wizard welcome dialog*

3. On the Choose a Data Source dialog, shown in Figure 16-42, select the type of source (use SQL Native Client for SQL Server 2005), the instance name, the type of authentication to use, and the database that will be the source of the data. Click Next.

4. On the Choose a Destination dialog, shown in Figure 16-43, select the type of source (use SQL Native Client for SQL Server 2005), the instance name, the type of authentication to use, and the database that will be the destination of the data. Click Next.

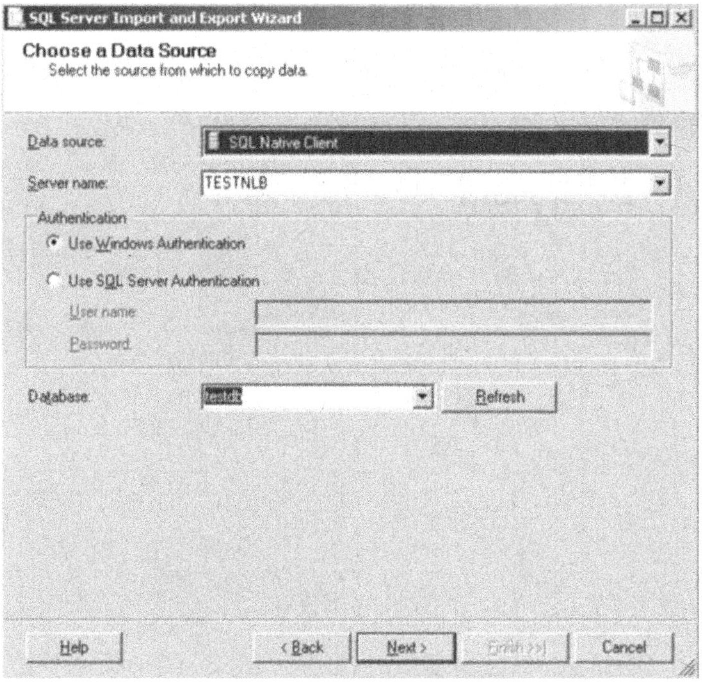

Figure 16-42. *Choose a Data Source dialog*

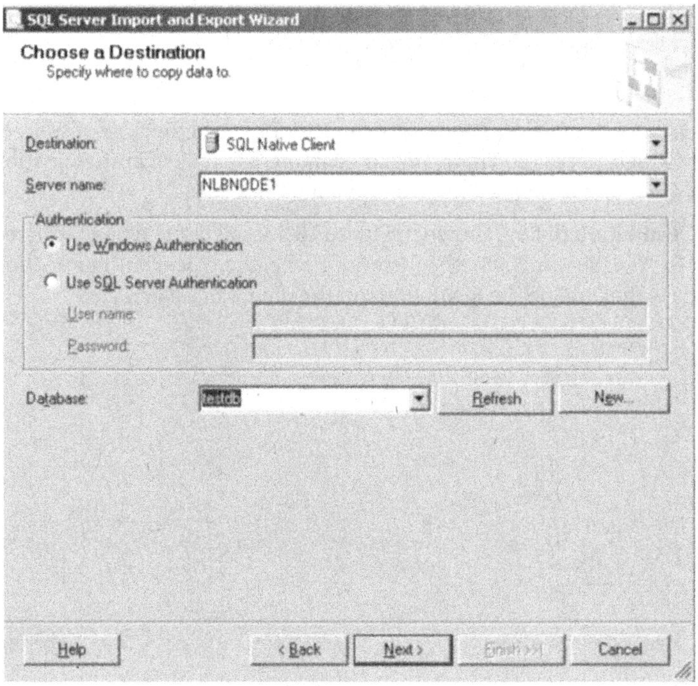

Figure 16-43. *Choose a Destination dialog*

5. On the Specify Table Copy or Query dialog, shown in Figure 16-44, choose whether you will use a query to specify the data to be exported from the source, or whether you will choose a set of tables and columns. Click Next.

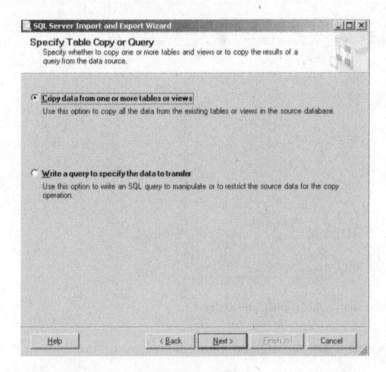

Figure 16-44. *Specify Table Copy or Query dialog*

6. If you are going to select tables or views, you will see the Select Source Tables and Views dialog shown in Figure 16-45. Click Next and skip to step 8.

   If you have special needs, such as remapping columns, enabling identity inserts, and so on, click Edit. You will see the Column Mappings dialog shown in Figure 16-46. Click OK to close and return to the Select Source Tables and Views dialog.

Figure 16-45. *Select Source Tables and Views dialog*

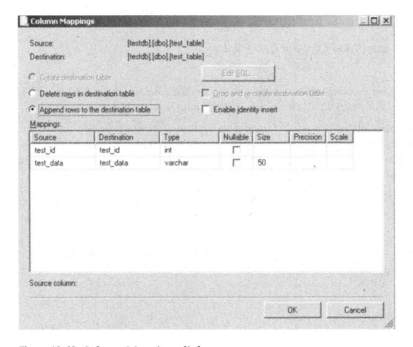

Figure 16-46. *Column Mappings dialog*

7. If you are going to select the data via a query, you will see the Provide a Source Query dialog shown in Figure 16-47. Enter the query, and click Next.

Figure 16-47. *Provide a Source Query dialog*

8. On the Save and Execute Package dialog, chances are you are not going to execute the package immediately. By default, Execute Immediately is checked. Since what you are creating will most likely be run more than once, check Save SSIS Package. You can save the package to SQL Server or to the file system. I recommend the file system, as shown in Figure 16-48, because it makes the package much more portable. Click Next.

9. You will then be prompted to select how you will want to protect the SSIS package, as shown in Figure 16-49. Select the proper option in the drop-down and, if necessary, enter a password. Click OK.

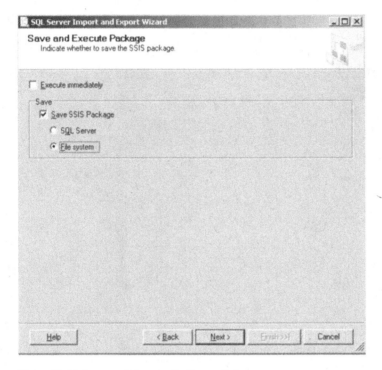

Figure 16-48. *Save and Execute Package dialog*

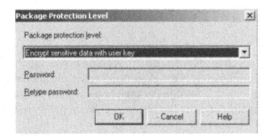

Figure 16-49. *Package Protection Level dialog*

10. On the Save SSIS Package dialog, enter a name for the new SSIS package you are creating as well as a location for the package. An example is shown in Figure 16-50. Click Next.

11. On the Complete the Wizard dialog, shown in Figure 16-51, click Finish to start the generation of the SSIS package.

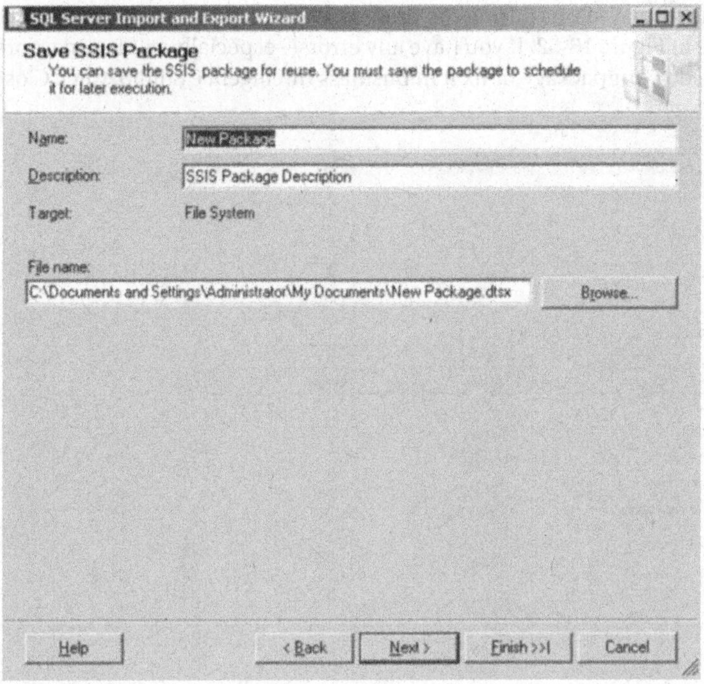

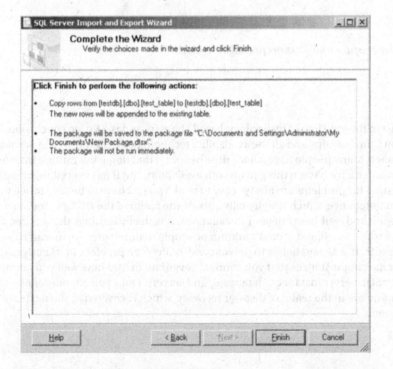

Figure 16-50. *Save SSIS Package dialog*

Figure 16-51. *Complete the Wizard dialog*

12. The execution will display status during the process. When complete, you will see a dialog similar to the one in Figure 16-52. If you have any errors—especially validation errors—go back and either redo your package or fix it in Business Intelligence Studio. Click Close.

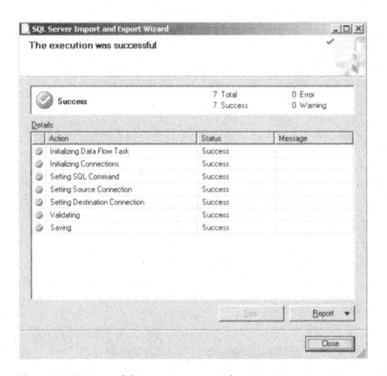

Figure 16-52. *Successful import/export package creation*

Summary

This chapter is the last in the long line of technology-based chapters and is a fitting conclusion. The journey has taken you from backups and all the availability technologies right through to administration and maintenance. Many people have a hard time believing that doing the routine maintenance such as index maintenance has anything to do with availability, but it has everything to do with it. The warning signs for problems are always easy to read; you just have to be able to see them.

Normal server maintenance, which usually falls outside the realm of the DBA's scope, also contributes to the health and well-being of your installations. It is the little things that matter. One missed step along the way—whether it is configuration or simple maintenance—can lead to a lot of downtime in the future. It is always better to prevent and/or detect a problem in its early stages. However, there are some circumstances that you cannot prevent no matter how well you administer and maintain your SQL Server instances, databases, and servers. Once you encounter one of these circumstances, you are in the realm of disaster recovery, which is covered in the next (and final) chapter of the book.

CHAPTER 17

■ ■ ■

Disaster Recovery

Last, but by no means least, is your worst-case scenario: disaster recovery. The topic has been addressed to a lesser degree in earlier chapters and is a subject that can, and has, filled up books. My goal here is not to write a book on disaster recovery alone since it has been addressed where necessary in this book (and many of the technologies presented here such as log shipping and backup and restore will most likely play a part in your disaster recovery plans), but to present you with the essential topics and talking points with which you can approach your own disaster recovery solutions and plans. Planning for disaster recovery is not unlike planning for availability—there are just other challenges you need to overcome, such as distance, time, and that ever popular disaster recovery SLA.

Expect the Unexpected

You've architected the perfect availability solution. Its deployment was flawless, you have the right people in place, and your processes are airtight. Everything that has been thought of is accounted for. What could go wrong? The one thing you did not account for. You have now entered the disaster recovery zone. No one should be smug about their high availability strategy. Do you think all of the financial companies impacted by what happened on 9/11 sat around and were complacent? No. Despite the human tragedy that unfolded, many were prepared with business continuity plans that had them switch to alternate sites. 9/11 is a lesson that proves it is only a matter of time before something goes wrong—not *if* something goes wrong. A good high availability solution would never withstand two buildings collapsing if your redundant systems were only located in those two buildings.

Disaster recovery is an elusive thing: how do you account for something when you really cannot determine all possible permutations? Did anyone really think two planes would come in and take out two of the world's most famous skyscrapers? How do you protect yourself against an unknown enemy? The Boy Scouts have a motto that holds true for disaster recovery: be prepared.

Preparing for Disaster Recovery

Preparing for disaster recovery is more about reducing chaos than preventing the event from happening—or at least it is in my experience. In most cases, you cannot stop the sequence of events that leads to catastrophe. You may even see that train coming down the tracks ahead of time. The question you need to ask yourself is, what you will do when its headlights are almost upon you? That is the real crux of the problem. If you miscalculate, it is a lot of pain. If you have the right pieces on the chessboard, the train will speed right by with you suffering only minor injuries.

Hurricane Katrina unfortunately is a great example of needing to be as prepared as you can be for a disaster and what to do (or not to do, as the case may be) in its aftermath. People were warned, but people are stubborn. Those who wanted to leave and could leave most likely did. Some stuck it out thinking they would be fine. Others could not leave for one reason or another. Add to that people and agencies that were woefully unprepared for a disaster of that magnitude and Katrina wound up being a perfect storm for not only a natural disaster but also a multidimensional tragedy that encompassed many factors such as human, financial, logistics, communications, authority, and so on. I cannot think of one area not affected.

Arguably the biggest failure in Katrina was communication. Katrina wiped out many of the emergency systems put in place to assist in such a disaster, which in turn made coordinating resources, at best, a challenge, at worst, a nightmare. In my experience with disaster recovery scenarios in the IT world, the experience is mirrored. Once the proverbial bomb goes off, you call out the troops and everyone is running in different directions like chickens with their heads cut off. With a lot of soldiers on the ground, there can be no coordination and no communication. This lack of leadership worsens the situation when everyone is stepping on each other's toes. In an IT organization, this can mean the difference between minutes or hours of downtime and days of downtime.

In using Katrina as an example, I am by no means trying to trivialize it or equate its magnitude with that of a data center going down. A data center going down may be catastrophic to your business, but in the grand scheme of life, it only affects your business. However, you should treat your disaster recovery planning with great care and respect. It should not be an afterthought.

Data Loss

Before I talk about anything else, let me deal with this upfront: there is a high probability if you are in a disaster recovery scenario, you will encounter data loss. I see no point in sugarcoating this message. You may get lucky, but in the disaster recovery scenarios I have been involved with either directly or indirectly, all have encountered data loss. This is why I said early on in the book that you need to determine your tolerance for data loss and manage to that stated requirement to the best of your abilities and available resources. Never set the business' expectation that when you are up and running again that everything will be where it was at the point of failure and that there will be no data loss. Chances are there will be minimal to no data loss, but a major part of disaster recovery is setting proper expectations.

Plan in Advance

It goes without saying that there is a reason it is called *disaster* recovery. You never expect your car to run out of gas. That is easy to mitigate—monitor your gas gauge, and when it gets below your comfort level, fill the tank. However, you do not expect the car's drive train to fall off. That is something you cannot easily mitigate unless you can magically carry a spare drive train in your trunk as well as a full car lift and a set of repair tools. Since you can't completely avoid that scenario, you do things like carry emergency supplies, have a charged cellular phone, and join an automobile club to assist you should the need arise.

Think back to the SLAs and guiding principles you established early on for your project: do they apply for disaster recovery? In some cases you can use the same set of rules, but are they realistic? For example, a two-hour recovery window may be possible for high availability, but if you need to switch data centers in the event of a catastrophe, would it be possible? If not, you may need to have an additional set of SLAs that govern your disaster recovery process that are similar to the established SLAs but take into account the different circumstances.

You need to be able to mitigate what you envision as your worst-case scenario and variations of it. Even if you come up with your worst-case scenario, I would contend there is one much worse that you never dreamed of. The problem with the worst-case scenario is that mitigating it can be very, very expensive. If you think achieving high availability is difficult and expensive, disaster recovery is a whole new ball game.

Think about it. If you need two copies of your servers, two copies of your storage array, and redundant networks, it is not something every business can afford. Or even if they can afford it, is it worth the investment? That is a question you must answer for yourself. If your disaster recovery solution costs you $500,000, and without it you would be down for a week, costing you $1,000,000 in lost business, I would say it is money worth spending.

Data Center Access

When you pick a location for your disaster recovery site, make sure you have the access you need when you need it. If your disaster recovery site is in a remote data center (most likely a hosting company) with gated access it makes disaster recovery nearly impossible. If your servers crash at 2 a.m., you should be able to roll up to the remote data center at 2:01, walk in, and put your plan into action.

Also, if your remote disaster recovery site is not close to you or your staff, you need to take that into account during your preparation and plans. Of course, it is a bad idea to have your primary and secondary data centers in close enough proximity to each other that if a natural disaster strikes, it could take out both locations. So your data centers should be far enough away from each other that they will hopefully not be affected by the same event, while maintaining a distance that allows you to be there in a reasonable amount of time.

Depending on the location of the primary and remote data centers, you may also need to factor in flying and renting cars and the resulting time and cost. Your company may have policies for travel, but in a disaster recovery window, you cannot fret about a ticket booked one hour in advance costing you an arm and a leg. That is just penny-wise and pound-foolish. This also has to factor into your SLA; how can you set a two-hour recovery window if it is going to take you four to even get to the door of the remote location?

Once you know that your logistics are set and how to approach them, it should make things much easier. It is these types of "little" things—airplane tickets, access to the remote data center, remote location, budget—that can cause paralysis and cost you crucial time. The order of the day should be "get it done," not "how cheap is that flight?"

Have More Than One Plan

Do not think that one disaster recovery plan is enough. If your main plan (plan A) is not able to be executed for whatever reason, you need a plan B, or maybe a plan C or more. Each scenario you are mitigating may have a different set of circumstances, so you need to treat them differently, and possibly have multiple plans per scenario.

Documentation and the Run Book

One of the biggest keys to a successful disaster recovery operation is that ugly word *documentation*. It is given a lot of lip service in many organizations. Many even write documentation, but no one reads it or keeps it up-to-date. It never matters until you actually need it, then you are in a world of hurt. The other part about documentation is that it is not write once, file somewhere, and forget about it. Documents need to be a living archive of what it will take to get your environment back up and running. If your architecture changed in the past year and the documentation was not updated accordingly, how are you going to execute any plans using or referencing outdated documents? What you do not know will kill you in this case. I know it is hard to find the time, and it is easy to become very lax when it comes to this, but if you are serious about disaster recovery, or just making sure that others have the most current information about your environment, you need to keep things up-to-date.

The most common document created for and used during disaster recovery is called a *run book*. The run book is your life support system. It may be one big document or a collection of many smaller documents. The run book needs to be a living document that grows and changes with your organization, not a static document created once and thrown in a drawer. The best way to think of the run book is to think of it as the fire extinguisher in the box mounted on the wall and behind glass. Break it open only in the case of emergency. You never have just one fire extinguisher, so make sure you have multiple copies of your run book in different locations and possibly in different formats (Microsoft Word, Adobe PDF, database, text file). If you have one copy and it's lost in a data center disaster, what will you do? When writing and compiling information, make sure it is written in a clear, concise manner. Writing $100 words that the person executing the plan may not understand is pointless. If the author is not available or has left the company, someone has to comprehend what to do.

The following sections cover some samples of what you should put in your run book.

Server Configurations

Documentation of each server—not just your SQL Servers—will prove crucial if you need to restore your servers from scratch. One missed documentation point around the configuration could make it function improperly. Here is a set of things that you should include per server:

- The operating system and version with a list of all service packs and hotfixes applied.

- A list of operating system and registry settings specific to that server.

- A list of all firmware and BIOS versions on the system.

- The disk configuration for the server both physical and logical, including all settings for any disk controllers, drivers needed for the disk controllers, RAID settings, storage array configuration (such as write cache settings), and so on.

- Full documentation of the network configuration.

- The SQL Server version with a list of all service packs and hotfixes applied.

- The SQL Server instance name and whether it is a default or a named instance.

- The SQL Server network configuration, including the IP addresses and ports used.

- The SQL Server instance's configuration options, including locations of all relevant objects (user databases and transaction logs, system databases, backups, any shares used by features such as replication).

- A list of all service accounts, SQL Server logins, and passwords. This will be one of the harder things to secure since you may document them in plain text, so you must give this due diligence.

- A list of all permissions to any directories or shares used by SQL Server.

- All database-specific configurations, including linked servers, SSIS packages, SQL Server Agent jobs, backup schedules, maintenance schedules, and so on.

- A list of any special tasks with full instructions that are performed by administrators (DBA or not) who use the databases.

- The output of `sqldiag.exe` or SQL Server MPS reports. This should be run on a scheduled basis, with all changes stored to see the changes in the system over time. Make sure you know what to look for in this file. If not, manually script out the relevant portions.

- Scripts for creating everything from the server configuration, database schemas, and database creation to the SQL Server logins and everything in between. This will not only speed up and automate the rebuilding process, but it will take out much of the element of failure that can happen due to having to type commands manually.

- A list of all software license keys required to rebuild the server, as well as the location of the installation media.

- Any relevant documentation on any specific configurations to the server. For example, disks on different shelves plugged into the same array controller, or special features in use such as XML support for IIS, Active Directory support, and so on. This will be useful in reconstruction.

- The manufacturers and formats of tapes if you are restoring from tape. One vendor's tapes may be incompatible with another's, so you must ensure that what is in your main production environment is available elsewhere.

- A basic test plan that can be executed by anyone who would have steps to ensure that the base servers, platforms, and options (such as clustering) are working properly after the failure.

- A list of all software installed on the server and its versions.

Application Configurations

Not only is it necessary to document the servers but the applications themselves. I am still amazed after all these years in the IT industry that many of my clients cannot rebuild their applications from scratch because some consultant or an employee who has long since left never documented how to set up the application server or the application itself. It might as well be a black box. When it comes time to consolidate or move data centers, there is no fallback plan; either it turns on and works, or it doesn't. Software that captures an "image" of the operating system may work, but it still will not document the configuration. As with the servers, you will need to document the following for each application:

- The application version and any patches applied to it.

- A list of all configuration information for the application, such as where it is installed on disk, all servers involved in the application (Web, database, middleware, etc.), configuration needed for clients (database connectivity components and configuration, etc.).

- A list of all application settings.

- All application dependencies (servers and other objects) that comprise the whole solution.

- An ordered list that details the proper steps to bring the solution online and to validate that it is working properly.

- A documented test plan to ensure that the application is functioning properly. This test plan must be able to be executed by someone who is not an expert on the application.

- A copy (printed or electronic) of all manuals for the application, especially installation manuals.

Contact Information

Having a list of the people who will need to be part of the plans to execute disaster recovery is the most crucial bit of information you can have in your run book. If you have all the other relevant documentation, as long as there are people to carry it out, you are fine. If no one can do it, you are in trouble. You should automate as much of this as possible. Most of this information should be available in your e-mail or HR systems, so a daily, weekly, or monthly pull from those systems to a document, database, or some other method should be able to happen. The following is a list of the essential contact information you will need to gather:

- A list of all employees who are relevant to the disaster recovery plan. This list should indicate not only names and ways to contact them (home and cellular phone numbers, addresses, e-mail addresses, etc.), but their titles and roles. Why would you call someone if you have no idea what they do or why they are on the list?

- A list of all support contract information, support phone numbers, and contacts for the vendors (sales people, etc.).

- A list of all internal application owners and department heads who need to be notified that their systems are down. These people can also notify relevant application folks (such as developers and testers) to be on alert to start validating systems as soon as they are ready.

- A list of all external resources (companies or individuals) that would be affected by the solution or system being down and must be notified.

- A list of all contact information for the remote site/hosting company and how to access the facility.

Staffing and Chain of Command

For any disaster recovery effort, the right people have to be in the right place doing the right job. It is as simple as that. Think back to the first two chapters. In light of all you have read in this book, do you want that junior DBA with his hands on the keys when your business is losing $10,000 a minute? The answer as stated earlier is most likely no, unless your more senior DBAs are unavailable.

So who do you need on staff for a disaster recovery? You do not necessarily need everyone, or at least everyone all at once, since too many hands may be a bad thing. All key players should be on the "list"—DBAs, network engineers, storage engineers, system administrators, application owners. Anyone who has anything to do with the systems involved should be potential candidates.

Coming up with the list is easy. Assigning roles is much more difficult. When you need to do disaster recovery, you do not want everyone to be a jack-of-all-trades; you want someone to be a master of one. If you distract one person with too many tasks, he or she may be scattered and not know what to prioritize first. That could lead to a longer time to recovery. Your staff should also be made painfully aware that they may be asked to do things they do not normally do. For example, your senior SQL Server architect may have to (gasp!) do what the more junior day-to-day DBAs do, such as restore databases. Ego needs to be left at the door.

Besides knowing roles, there needs to be a clear chain of command. If everyone thinks they are a boss because their day-to-day title is manager or supervisor, they may be wrong. Running a disaster recovery operation is like running a military operation. It must be done precisely with no room for back talk. If the leader says jump, ask him or her how high. I was once part of a disaster recovery scenario where the guy in charge was ex-military, and while there was some chaos (it is unavoidable), things ran smoothly. Do not put people in charge who do not function well under pressure and cannot lead. Someone may be a great people-person and a swell manager, but there is a difference between that and someone who can lead the drive down the field for a touchdown. Besides chain of command, managers must also be willing, ready, and able to augment existing worker bees while troubleshooting and recovery processes are in play. Twenty people sitting in a centralized command center with only five people doing the work is counterproductive.

■ **Note** One thing I am seeing more and more of is the drive to do more with less: to cut operational costs by reducing staff and possibly moving a lot of operations offshore. Offshore DBAs cannot help you when your data centers are in your home state and the only way you can access them is by actually going there. Not only does that give you fewer options for a disaster recovery, but going to a bare-bones staff also generally inhibits the updating of documentation and maintaining processes that are crucial for success in a disaster recovery operation. You should always maintain a staff that meets all of your needs.

Supplies and Contingencies

Those of you who remember the worries around the year 2000 and how it was going to affect computer systems worldwide may also recall the kinds of precautions taken on New Year's Eve 1999. Many companies had large amounts of staff on hand or on-call. Because of the fear of the power grid shutting down, precautions were taken, such as securing diesel generators for data centers to keep systems up and running for a period of time, or at least to allow a graceful shutdown.

We're no longer worried about Y2K, but you still need to make sure that when your staff is on the ground, they not only have what they need, but what the business needs to "survive" for some specific period of time. Backup power generators are still a welcome idea. I can remember sitting in a customer's cafeteria on a sunny day and the lights went out in the building and all I could think about was what happened to the systems. The cafeteria faced the power plant and you could see a puff of smoke. That did not give me a warm and fuzzy feeling.

For your staff, make sure that they are given the same amount of care and feeding as your servers. Having staff onsite 24x7 means that people need at a bare minimum food and drink. The last thing you want is a bunch of already overtired, overworked staff members about to drop because they are starving or parched. That is not productive. I know sometimes budgets are an issue, but how expensive is it to order some pizzas and some bottles of soda, juice, and water? The $50 it may cost you is much cheaper than losing an employee. A happy staff is a productive staff. Disasters are stressful enough without denying people even 15 minutes to take a breather and grab a slice of pizza or a sandwich.

There are other supplies that you may need, such as cots, blankets, and pillows. Some disasters will require people to stay around for an extended period of time where they may not be able to go home. When they are on their off rotation, have a comfortable place for them to relax and try to decompress for a little bit. I know it does not seem like much to you, but to your exhausted minions, it's another way to show them that you care about their well-being and they are more than a warm body to you, even if you may not feel that way deep down inside. A little bit of kindness goes a long way. You want people to feel needed, not used. I have been in situations where I have been awake and onsite for just under 30 hours a stretch with minimal amounts of food and water (except maybe some candy out of a vending machine and the water fountain), and definitely no place to close my eyes for 15 minutes. When you are at the end of that, all you want to do is throw up your arms and have a conversation with someone above you that you will most likely regret. Do not put yourself or, if you are an employer, your employees in that situation.

Then again, if you are having multiple outages of this type of duration and depth of problems where employees are constantly on 24-hour shifts, there is something seriously wrong with your processes, your hardware, your software, your solution, or all of it. Everyone has the occasional "glitch," but if disaster recovery is a way of life, start asking questions. That is not a healthy work environment for an IT staff.

Test the Disaster Recovery Plans

I cannot stress how important it is to test your disaster recovery plans. These tests are sometimes known as *fire drills*. It is not good enough to only have a plan, because you will have no confidence if you have never tried it. I had a customer quite a few years ago who was using log shipping as their primary disaster recovery solution. The problem was that they had never tested the switch from one server to another, so when it came time to pull the trigger and do the switch to the standby server, they could not because they were unsure that the standby was valid. We waited for hours for the database to come out of suspect mode and then attempted to restore it from a backup. Instead of being up and running in minutes, we were essentially down for many hours twiddling our thumbs. Does that sound like a good plan to you? It didn't to me at the time, and it still is just as bad of a decision to me many years later. Another example that a colleague related to me is a customer whose only backup was from their test machine that had data that was made anonymous for security reasons. He was asked to help his client convert the anonymous data to real data. This happened because they had access to the wrong database backup that had the same name and size as the regular production backup.

An interesting twist to a disaster recovery test is that unless you've got a complete duplicate of your current production site, you will have to think about how it will be executed. If you do not have that duplicate site to use as a sandbox, the only valid test will be on your actual production hardware (and I think I just heard a few of you call me crazy out there). That will affect your overall availability since it will be a scheduled outage (not unlike planned maintenance); but how can you get any confidence in your plan if it is tested in an environment that is not at all representative of your current production environment? I know some companies that do exactly this, and you can be sure that those administrators know better than to do something stupid in production since they have regular disaster recovery drills and know how bad it can get. That first test is always a trial by fire.

There are two ways you can think about performing a test: doing it at a planned time and date, or doing a surprise test. I would argue that the latter is much more effective. The whole point of disaster recovery is that it is something unexpected. If you do a scheduled test, it gives all involved time to "prepare." The fire drill should not only prove that your plans are rock solid and up-to-date, but that your staff is competent enough to execute them as designed. When the test is complete, hold a postmortem to see what worked and what failed, to determine what needs to get updated in documentation, staffing, and so on.

Check Your Support Contract

I cannot stress enough the need to not only buy a support contract with all of your vendors but to make sure they are valid and you know when they expire, so you can get them renewed in time. Just because you paid for one two years ago does not mean it is still active. You do not want to find this out from your hardware vendor when your motherboard dies and you cannot get anyone to come out until next week since you do not have the appropriate level of coverage, such as 24x7 support with four-hour onsite from the vendor's engineers.

Another aspect of the support contract you will need to consider is who the named contacts are in your company who can contact the vendor on your behalf. If named contacts leave, make sure they are replaced or removed. You do not want to pick up the phone only to find out that you are not authorized to talk to support. It would eventually get sorted out I'm sure, but that is time you do not have.

When Disaster Strikes

As I was typing the title for this section, I was getting the image in my head of those animal documentaries that show some predator attacking suddenly; that is how a disaster sneaks up on you. One minute you're living an idyllic, peaceful life, and the next minute you are thrown into utter chaos.

If you have heeded the advice laid out previously in this chapter, there should be only a brief time of chaos before things come back to a more calm state. Calm is relative, of course, since it is a recovery scenario. I do not want anyone to think that things will all of a sudden be a cakewalk. If you have not done any of the prework needed to make a disaster recovery operation successful, I predict you will have a major amount of pain before things get better.

Assessing the Situation

The first thing you want to do when setting your plan in motion is to assess what is going on. What happened? What is the initial damage assessment? What do the logs say? Just because it seems like Rome is burning does not mean you can't keep your wits about you. Troubleshooting is troubleshooting, and the steps are the same. I have seen way too often cases where people are being pressured to implement a solution well before they have a clue what the problem may even be, and subsequently make things worse . . . not better. Don't be that person. I know you are probably managing to a specific SLA and the CxO is standing over your shoulder (breathing down your neck, calling your cell phone every ten seconds . . .) asking you when the server will be up, but keeping your wits about you is the smartest thing anyone can bring to the table in such a situation. You need to remember to keep any communications truthful and succinct. Do not offer any information that is not needed or asked for that could distract from the situation at hand. It is very easy to let your pride get in the way. I have seen this in action, and it confuses everyone. If you guess or make an assumption and it is incorrect, you may not only cause a longer outage, you may call into doubt how people perceive you in your organization. Know when to keep your mouth shut and, more importantly, know what you do not know.

Contacting Support

Once you have an idea of what happened (but not why or how), it would be a smart idea to do one of two things: call a support professional, or set a fixed time to allow your organization to do some troubleshooting before you set a "go/no go" point where you contact a support professional. I know some of you out there (and I am guilty of it sometimes in my own way) want to figure things out, but this is not something you can waste hours on. This is a server-down situation. If you waste hours and get nowhere, it is literally wasted time. Support professionals (whether they are from Microsoft or some other vendor that is part of your solution) are trained to help customers through difficult situations and may have seen your issue before and know how to solve it immediately. Swallow your pride, pick up the phone, and get the ball rolling. You will thank yourself later.

Implementing the Plan

Once you figure out what the problem is, either on your own or with support, come up with an appropriate corrective course of action and set it into motion. This plan may already be predefined as part of the work you have done before, or it may be something completely new. The plan should have complete sign-off by those in management and/or the chain of command. In scenarios where you may be doing a lot of changes in a short period of time with many different people touching the servers, there needs to be a coordinated plan of attack where there is handoff and knowledge of what is going on, who is doing what, and when things are getting done. You do not want to accidentally rebuild a server (if that is part of the plan) that was working perfectly fine because someone was in a rush and mistyped the server name in a console window. I know you are already working against the clock and your SLA, but will taking a step back for ten seconds to think before you act kill you? Management may hate that ten seconds if they see you sitting there in deep thought, but they will appreciate it when you do not reimage the wrong server.

Maintaining Your Cool

It is inevitable that tempers will flare and it goes without saying that tensions will be high. There is no avoiding it. The problem is that while we all know it happens, it can make an already tense situation worse if you say the wrong thing to someone at the exact wrong moment. I know that things will be moving a mile a minute, but it does not excuse you from saying something stupid that may come back and haunt you. Even the best of us with years of experience slip up. Think of it another way: you are all in the same lifeboat together, so it is better to work together to row at the same time in the same direction instead of everyone going their own way.

Shadowing and Documenting

Always have someone shadowing what someone else may be doing. Another set of eyes may prove crucial since you could be at it for hours and may be a bit weary. Having someone who is validating what you are doing and can point out the typo in your RESTORE command is invaluable. The other purpose of having someone shadow is that the person can be documenting what happens so that when you compare what was done to what is actually documented, the processes and procedures can be updated based on what actions were taken, so no one else has to figure them out again should the disaster strike again. One problem that I often see because things are happening so quickly is that if things are not documented, they are lost. Those executing the plan are so "in the moment" that when things calm down, they can't remember half of what they had to do. There is nothing worse than a lost opportunity for knowledge and improvement. This can and should be a learning experience for all involved.

When the Dust Settles

When the problem is solved and you have a chance to catch a breath, you have to document what happened—the good, the bad, and the ugly. I can guarantee you there is probably a lot more bad and ugly than good. I do not hear many happy disaster recovery stories. They are not affectionately known as "war stories" because you went to an amusement park.

One of the main reasons you need to go through a postmortem is to improve the process. If you went off a plan and it did not work, you would not want to do it exactly the same way again. If it is broken, fix it. Even if it is not broken, chances are things can be tweaked and improved. I highly doubt any plan is so perfect it could never be made better. Another key reason to analyze what happened is to improve some of your processes and procedures to prevent the event from happening again. Do not just concentrate on the problem and the plan. You must also look to improve issues such as communications, the team structures, staffing, chain of command, and so on. No aspect should get an automatic pass. For example, if there was one person so crucial to the recovery that if he were hit by lightning you would never be able to execute the plan, you would need to find a way to get others skilled in his knowledge. What is discussed should be formally documented, and if things need to be changed or modified as a result, come up with the resulting action plan and put a schedule on it.

Fences may need to be mended as well. If you ruffled someone's feathers, be prepared to eat some humble pie. Everyone knows these situations are pressure cookers. You are all professionals, and yes, there may be some residual feelings that need to get smoothed out over time, but you have to get beyond whatever happened. What you do not want to happen is to avoid the difficult conversation, let something fester, and then have it come back and bite you at a later point in time. You could not ask for a worse situation since it will make your workplace a difficult place to be.

SQL Server Disaster Recovery Features

There are some SQL Server technologies that lend themselves to disaster recovery. The most obvious one is backup and restore. You should always have a scenario that includes a "bare metal" restore, beginning with laying down the operating system, installing SQL Server, and restoring your databases. That is as basic a disaster recovery plan as you can get, and everyone should have it in their arsenal whether you are a company of 3 employees or 30,000 employees.

The next technology that lends itself well to disaster recovery is log shipping. Disaster recovery is arguably log shipping's No. 1 use. It is based on tried and true disaster recovery method No. 1: backup and restore. It is cheap to implement and is not an administrative burden. You do need to monitor the log shipping process to ensure that the secondary server is kept in sync and that your transaction logs are backed up. You should not assume that things are working; you don't want to be surprised when you go to switch and you are a week behind. While I'm sure your company will be grateful they are up and running, losing a week's data due to carelessness probably won't be looked upon favorably.

Database mirroring could also be used in a similar fashion to log shipping. If you set up high-safety mode, assuming your infrastructure can handle the volume of transactions being sent across the network to a remote location, you may not lose any data. That is news the business would love to hear.

Replication is not as good as log shipping and database mirroring for disaster recovery since its purpose is more to have data available elsewhere, not the whole database. Having said that, it is a great business contingency plan because if you are using it to maintain either a reporting solution or some other kind of data store, you may have data available to you that you can point users and applications to while you get the environment back up.

Failover clustering is not an ideal disaster recovery solution unless you have a lot of money to burn. I love clustering, but you need a robust network infrastructure and a certified geographically dispersed hardware solution. Most of my customers who have considered a geographically dispersed cluster—which would, like high-safety mode of database mirroring, ensure you had no data loss—ultimately balk at the cost or do not have the infrastructure to support it. If you can implement it, geographically dispersed clusters are a viable option, but it is out of reach for most of you out there.

■**Caution** The one thing I will caution you on with any of the previous technologies is to ensure that you test that the switches from Environment A to Environment B work. The biggest issue is not so much the switching of SQL Servers, but getting the applications reconnected to them and synchronizing the users (as documented in Chapter 15), and so on. As I noted earlier in the chapter, I have seen the paralysis when these procedures have not been tested. I have seen people waiting to see if their VLDB will be fine after being marked as suspect. Do not take that risk. Disaster recovery is as much about getting the business back up and running as it is about confidence that your process works.

Summary

Up until this chapter, you've heard mainly about high availability. All of these techniques apply to disaster recovery as well, which is the last piece of the fault-tolerance puzzle. Not everyone has a plan, but everyone should. Even if your disaster recovery is to use your backups and installation media to rebuild and restore your servers, it is better than no plan at all. However, disaster recovery, like high availability, is more about people, process, and communication than it is about technology. Documentation will be crucial for your success. Disaster recovery will be a pressure cooker, and will truly test your company's resources. Patience needs to be the order of the day; hastily made decisions may wind up costing you more in the end. Business continuity is not easy. If it were, why did you just read 17 chapters?

Index

Numbers and Symbols

4U rackmount servers, 568
8.3 format (short) file names, support for, 580
24x7 environments
    automation in, 579
    availability in, 3
32-bit instances, 259–260
32-bit operating systems, 122
    memory settings, 587
    vs. 64-bit, 568–569
64-bit instances, 259–260
64-bit operating systems, 122
    memory settings, 587
    vs. 32-bit, 568–569

A

.abf file extension, 96
access control, 19
Active Directory connectivity, 127
Active Directory users, managing, 594
Active/Active, 244
Active/Passive, 244
Add Filter dialog, 510
ADDLOCAL parameter, 292
ADDNODE parameter, 292, 349
administrator passwords, 291, 502
ADMINPASSWORD parameter, 292, 342, 349, 355
administrators, isolation of from users, 21
Affect the Group property, 308–309
Agent Security dialog, 511
AGTACCOUNT parameter, 292, 342
AGTCLUSTERGROUP parameter, 293
AGTPASSWORD parameter, 292, 342
alerts, setting up
    in SQL Server Management Studio, 628–637
    in Transact-SQL, 637–638
ALTER DATABASE statement, 472–473
ALTER FUNCTION command, 490
ALTER INDEX command, 689
ALTER PROCEDURE command, 490
ALTER TABLE command, 490
ALTER TRIGGER command, 490
ALTER VIEW command, 490
Always On technology. See high availability technology
Analysis Services, 246
    backing up and restoring, 5296–103
    changing Affect the Group property, 308–309
    cluster aware, 227
    clustering, 230

installing, 267–268, 278–279
starting, stopping, and pausing, 329, 333–334
    from command line, 332–334
    with Cluster Administrator, 331–332
    with SQL Server Configuration Manager, 330–331
    with SQL Server Surface Area Configuration, 331
upgrading, in clustered environment, 245
antivirus programs
    clustering and, 205–206
    SQL Server instances and, 596
application configuration, in run book, 717
application layer, data availability and, 529–533
application programming interface (API), clustering, 109
applications
    availability and, 38
    backup strategy and, 60
    cluster-aware, 114, 435
    change management and, 12
    custom, making available, 530–532
    database mirroring and, 435
    database snapshots and, 548
    for monitoring, 612
    for replication, 487
    retry logic in, 115
    role changes and, 372
    securing, 602–603
    third-party, making available, 530
Article Issues dialog, 509
Article Properties dialog, 509
articles, 479
Articles dialog, 508
ASACCOUNT parameter, 292
ASCLUSTERGROUP parameter, 293
ASCOLLATION parameter, 292
ASPASSWORD parameter, 292
attaching databases, 54
    changes to, in SQL Server 2005, 639
    via SQL Server Management Studio, 641–644
audit logs, 21
auditing, 598
authentication
    password security, 599–601
    Windows vs. SQL Server, 602
Authentication Mode page, 283, 285
automatic failover, 435, 571
automatic growth, of database, 590–591
automatic shrink, of database, 589–591

Automatic Windows updates, disabling, 691–692
autoshrink enabled, 590
availability, 3–4
    application layer and, 38, 529–533
    of backup files, 61–62
    barriers to, 30
    building blocks of, 4–13
    business continuity and, 3–4
    capabilities for, 32
    cost of, 13
    data partitioning and, 533–539
    database snapshots and, 540–548
    dedicated administrator connection, 603–604
    defining, 15
    merge replication and, 481
    multiple read-only databases and, 549–550
    needs, 32–33
    snapshot replication and, 480
    See also high availability
availability percentage, calculating, 16
availability service level agreements, 32–33
awe enabled option, 587

B
Back button, 260
back-end failures, application response to, 531
backup and restore, 12
    Analysis Services databases, 52, 96–103
    attaching and detaching databases, 54
    automating retention policy, 103–104
    availability of, 61–62
    basics, 41–57
    battery, 22
    business goals and, 58
    configuring, 395–399
    custom scripts, 104
    DBMP Wizard for, 73–75
    devices for, 41
    differential, 42–43, 79, 88
    disaster recovery and, 723
    to disk, 61
    failure and recovery scenarios using, 64–67
    file compatibility, 54–57
    file, 79
    filegroup, 80
    frequency of, 69
    full-text indexes, 51, 80
    human error and, 58–59
    importance of, 41
    log shipping and, 371
    managing transaction logs through, 67–68
    Microsoft way, 105
    mirroring, 46
    plan implementation, 68–104
    setting recovery interval, 52
    to mirrored media, 79
    over network, 61

    OS-based file-level, 68
    querying information about, 54
    requirements for, 69
    retaining, 53–54
    retention of, 60
    securing, 20
    of SQL Server databases, 75–83
    with SQL Server instances, 68
    with SQL Server Management Studio, 81–84
    strategy planning, 58–68
        applications and, 60
        availability of backups, 61–62
        database configuration and, 59–60
        goals and, 58
        human error and, 58–59
        media type, 61
        recoverability paths, 64–67
        zero data loss and, 59
    synchronizing, 63–64
    systemwide tape options, 57
    table, 46
    tape, 61
    testing, 62–63
    transaction log, 80, 88
    types of SQL Server, 41–46
        differential database backups, 42–43
        file and filegroup backups, 45
        full database backups, 42
        hardware-assisted, 46
        third-party software–based backups, 45–46
        transaction log backups, 43–45
    viewing status of, 81
    with Transact-SQL, 75–81
    zero data loss and, 59
backup devices
    creating, 78
    full backup to, 79
    restores from, 87
backup expiration, setting, 79
backup files, transaction log, 368
backup media, monitoring, 72
backup security, implementing, 69–70
backup shares
    creating, for log shipping, 373–386
    failover cluster, 380–386
    stand-alone, 374–380
BACKUP statement, 75–78
backup status, monitoring, 72
backup_threshold column, 406
.bak file extension, 75
barriers to availability, 30
baselines, establishing, 611
batteries, monitoring, 22
battery backups, 22
bcp command, importing and exporting data with, 703–704
BCP tool, 46
bidirectional transactional replication, 484

BixTalk, backups of, 60
black boxes, 373
BLOCKSIZE parameter, 76
boot.ini, /PAE option, 587
budget considerations, 29–30
BUFFERCOUNT parameter, 76
BUILTIN\Administrators account, 313–316, 597
Bulk-logged mode, LNS sequence and, 434
Bulklogged recovery model, 49–50
business continuity, 3–4
business problem
    defining the, 27
    existing solutions for, 28

C

cables, 22–23
capacity planning, network and, 23
certifications, value of, 4
chain of command, during disaster recovery,
        718–719
change management, 10–13, 579
changes, rolling back, 51
CHECKPOINT command, 45
checkpoints, 44–45, 52
CHECKSUM parameter, 76, 85
Citrix, 20
Cluster Administrator, 205
    adding additional nodes using, 175–180
    adding first node using, 166–174
    adding new disk, 216–218
    changing quorum disk, 221–223
    configuring cluster networks with, 188–190
    mount point configuration, 214–216
    starting and stopping services with, 331–332
cluster administrator password, 276–277, 301
cluster administrator service account, 128–129
Cluster Configuration Validation Wizard
        (ClusPrep), 156–166
    installing, 157–159
    using, 159–166
Cluster Disk Driver, 112
Cluster Group Selection page, 274–275
cluster groups, 109
    adding SQL Server service accounts to,
        253–255
    adding to nodes, 255–256
    bringing online, 333
    creating SQL Server–related, 251–253
    renaming, 256
    taking offline, 332–333
cluster name resolution, verifying, 200–201,
        316–317
cluster networks, configuring, 188–190
Cluster Node Configuration page, 275–276
cluster nodes, 108–112
    adding additional, to server cluster, 175–181
    adding cluster groups to, 255–256
    adding cluster service account to, 135–141

adding first, to new server cluster, 166,
        170–175
adding or removing, 343–350
    using command prompt, 349–350
    using SQL Server Setup, 343–348
as domain controllers, 127
logging on to, 260
setting preferred order of, in failover, 309
verifying resource access, 201
cluster resources
    bringing online, 333
    querying owner of, 321–322
    taking offline, 332–333
Cluster Service, 111–112, 359
cluster service accounts
    adding to each node, 135–141
    changing password, 206–211
    creating, 132–141
cluster-aware applications, 114, 435
CLUSTER.EXE, 205–211, 332–334
clustered instances
    assigning static IP port to, 340–342
    changing domains of, 355–361
    changing IP address of, 339
    changing service accounts of, 337
    installing, on same hardware as local
        instances, 237
    rebuilding master database on, 342
    renaming, 334–337
    uninstalling, 350–355
        using command prompt, 355
        using SQL Server Setup, 351–353
    using SQL Server 2005 Surface Area
        Configuration with, 325–328
clustering/clusters. See also failover
        clustering/clusters
    API, 109
    client connections and, 114–115
    configuring networks, 188–190
    defined, 107–115
    disk signatures and, 112
    geographically dispersed, 108, 129–130, 571
    high-performance computing and, 116
    Network Load Balancing (NLB), 107–108
    RAC, 246
    requirements for, 108
    resources, 109
    server, 107–130
        planning for, 116–130
        workings of, 108–113
    shared-nothing, 108
    selecting solutions, 118
    virtualizing, 1–8, 181–187
clustering administration (Windows server
        cluster)
    antivirus programs, 205–206
    changing cluster service account password,
        206–211

disk management, 211–224
 adding new disk, 216–218
 changing quorum disk, 221–224
 configuring mount points, 211–216
 expanding disks via DISKPART, 218–220
 remote connectivity, 205
Collation Settings page, 285–287
command line
 adding additional nodes using, 180–181
 adding first node to server cluster using, 175
 adding or removing nodes with, 349–350
 changing quorum disk from, 223–224
 formatting disks via, 154
 installing management tools from, 313
 installing SQL Server with, 259, 291–294
 managing Analysis Services from, 329–334
 querying resource owner via, 321
 rebuilding master database via, 342
 starting and stopping services from, 332–334
 uninstalling instances with, 355
Common Criteria security standard, 599
communication, 7–9
 end-user expectations, 8–9
 intergroup, 7–8
 intragroup, 8
communication systems, 23
compatibility levels, database, 54–57
components
 location of, and replication, 487
 scripting, of replication topology, 524
Components to Install page, 297
compromise, 35–36
Compute Cluster operating system, 116
Compute Cluster Pack, 116
Computer Management, formatting disks via,
  152–153
Configure Distribution wizard, 493
conflict resolution
 merge replication and, 482
 queued updating and, 483
connection strings, database mirroring failover
  and, 435
connectivity protocols, disabling, 597
contact information, in run book, 717–718
contingencies, in disaster recovery plan, 719
CONTINUE_AFTER_ERROR parameter, 78, 87
copy-on-write operations, 540
COPY_ONLY parameter, 76
corporate espionage, 19
corruption, detecting database
cost, of availability, 13
counters, monitoring, 607–612
CREATE DATABASE … FOR ATTACH statement,
  638–639
CREATE INDEX statement, 533–534
CREATE LOGIN statement, 600
CREATE STATISTICS statement, 593
CREATE TABLE statement, 533–534
CREATE VIEW statement, 536

custom applications, making available, 530–532
custom backup scripts, 104–105
custom log shipping, 403
custom restore scripts, 104
customers, expectations of, 8–9

▌D

DAC. See dedicated administrator connection
data
 importing and exporting, 703–712
  using bcp, 703–704
  using SSIS, 704–712
 partitioning, 533–539
  creating object on specific filegroup, 533
  data dependent routing, 538–539
  views, 536–538
  with Transact-SQL, 534–535
 republishing, 487
 updating, 481–483
data center
 access, 19, 715
 cabling, 22–23
 communication systems, 23
 fire suppression systems, 18
 location for, 18
 mentality, 16–25
 networking, 23
 outsourcing, 23–24
 planning the, 17–18
 power supply, 21–22
 racks, 18
 securing, 19–21
  access control, 19
  audit logs, 21
  data and backups, 20
  password policies, 21
  remote administration, 20
  server racks, 20
  surveillance equipment, 19
  systems, 19
 size of, 18
 technology, 25
data conflicts
 merge replication and, 482
 queued updates and, 483
data copy phase, of recovery process, 51
data definition language (DDL) objects, 432
data dependent routing (DDR), 538–539
data disks, formatting, 126
data encryption, 603
data files, moving location of, during restore, 87
data loss
 during disaster recovery scenario, 714
 zero, 32, 59
Data Transformation Services (DTS), 645
database backups, 12, 524–525
database connections, manually killing, 420
database instances, 435
database logins, synchronizing, 421, 434, 370

Database Mail, 227
    configuring, 618–628
    receiving alerts via, 618–638
database maintenance
    checking database health, 686–687
    creating SQL Server Agent jobs, 673–686
        using SQL Server Management Studio,
            673–684
        using Transact-SQL, 684–686
    log shipping and, 366, 371
    outsourcing, 23–24
    performing, 673–689
        routine, 686–689
    rebuilding indexes, 688–689
Database Maintenance Plan (DBMP) Wizard, 73
Database Master Key, 228
database mirroring
    administering, 454–477
        Database Mirroring Monitor, 454–464
        Performance Monitor, 464–466
        querying safety level, 470
        querying status for all databases, 470
        querying status of one database, 470
        SQL Server Profiler, 466–468
        Transact-SQL, 469–470
    applications and, 435
    collation, 433
    combining with failover clustering, 560
    combining with log shipping, 563–564
    combining with other technologies, 565–566
    comparing with other high availability
            technologies, 554–555
    configuring, 431–454
        altering, 472–473
        back up and restore database, 436
        DNA alias, 454
        errors, 450–451
        inbound connections, 452
        network load balancing, 454
        outbound connections, 451–452
        SQL Server Management Studio, 436–451
        using Transact-SQL and Windows
            authentication, 453–454
    counters to monitor, 464–466
    database maintenance and, 435
    database restoration and configuration, 432
    disaster recovery and, 723
    disk design and performance, 432
    distributed transactions, 433
    domain connectivity and, 433
    endpoints, 426
    vs. failover clustering, 556
    failovers, 426, 475–477
        planned, 475–476
        unplanned, 476–477
    full-text indexes and, 477
    functionality, 425
    vs. log shipping, 425, 558
    LSN sequence and, 434

    mirroring states, 426
    mode comparison, 430
    modes, 427–430
    networks and, 433
    objects outside of database and, 434
    vs. other high availability technologies,
            558–559
    planning and deployment considerations,
            430–435
    quorum, 425–426
    recovery model, 432
    redirecting clients to server, 477
    removing, 473–475
    vs. replication, 480, 559
    for reporting, 430
    resuming, 472
    security, 433
    server locations, 431
    server sizing, 432
    sessions, 425
    starting, 448–450
    suspending, 470–471
    synchronizing logins, 434
    transaction logs and, 434
    transaction safety, 426
    transaction size and, 434
    updates and, 435
    uses of, 430
    workings of, 425–430
Database Mirroring Monitor, 454–464
Database Mirroring Security Wizard, 437
@database parameter, 407, 418
DATABASE parameter, 76, 85
database recovery. See recovery
database restoration. See backup and restore
database schema, replication and, 488–491
database snapshots, 540–548
    administration, 544–548
    applications and, 548
    creating, 543–544
    deleting, 544–546
    querying, 543–544
    reverting database using, 546–547
database statistics, updating, 593–594
database status, checking, 70–72
database updates, log shipping and, 371
DATABASEPROPERTY, 72
DATABASEPROPERTYEX, 72
databases
    attaching and detaching, 54, 638–645
    automatic growth/shrinking of, 589–590
    backup strategy and layout of, 59–60
    checking health of, 686–687
    configuring, 588–594
    corruption detection, 686
    creating within instant initialization, 592–593
    encrypting data in, 603
    securing, 602–603
    sizing properly, 589–591
    using multiple read-only, 549–550

database_name column, 406
dba_GenerateBackupCommands stored
    procedure, 66
DBCC CHECKALLOC command, 686–687
DBCC CHECKCATALOG command, 686
DBCC CHECKDB command, 686–687
DBCC CHECKDB WITH PHYSICAL_ONLY
    command, 687
DBCC CHECKFILEGROUP command, 687
DBCC CHECKTABLE command, 686
DBCC DBREINDEX command, 688
DBCC INDEXDEFRAG command, 688–689
DBCC SHRINKDATABASE command, 591
DBCC SHRINKFILE command, 591
db_backupoperator, 70
DDR. See data dependent rating
dedicated administrator connection (DAC),
    603–604
default instances, 228, 234
    installing, 271
    upgrading, 297
deferred transactions, 95
defragmentation, 690
dependencies
    failover clustering, 231
    starting and stopping, 334
deployment, features and functionality
    affecting, 571
DESCRIPTION parameter, 76
design solutions
    choosing technology, 553–554
    combining high availability technologies,
        560–566
    comparing technology for, 554–559
        database mirroring, 558–559
        failover clustering, 556–557
        log shipping, 558
    deployment issues, 571
    disaster recovery and, 571
    disk subsystems, 569–570
    example solution
        for disk configuration for a failover cluster,
            576–578
        for existing environment, 572–573
        for new deployment, 573–576
    hardware specification, 567–569
    keywords, 571
    performance, 566–567
    purchasing servers, 567–569
    sizing server, 567–569
detaching databases, 54
    vs. backing up, 639
    via SQL Server Management Studio, 640
development environment, 10
devices, 41
DHCP. See Dynamic Host Configuration
    Protocol
.dif file extension, 75
differential backups, 42–43, 79, 88

DIR /X command, 580
disaster recovery, 4
    custom application design and, 532
    database mirroring for, 430–431
    dedicated administrator connection for,
        603–604
    designing for, 571
    log shipping for, 365–366
    performing role change in, 422
    postmortem, 722–723
    preparing for, 713–720
        checking support contract, 720
        data center access, 715
        data loss, 714
        documentation, 716–718
        multiple plans, 715
        staffing and chain of command, 718–719
        supplies and contingencies, 719
        testing plan, 720
    recovery scenario, 532, 721–722
    site, 715
    SQL Server features for, 723
disconnected state, 426
disk array
    configuration of disks on shared, 149–155
    shared cluster, 108
disk backups, 61. See also backup and restore
disk configuration
    clusters and, 122–127
    for failover cluster, 576–578
    for SQL Server failover clustering, 237–238
    multiple instances and, 239
    verifying, 155, 317
Disk Cost page, 270
disk design
    backup strategy and, 59–60
    for database mirroring, 432
disk drives
    adding additional, as dependencies, 304–307
    updating, 691
disk fragmentation, 589, 592, 688–690
disk management
    Windows server clusters, 211–224
        adding new disk, 216–218
        changing quorum disk, 221–224
        configuring mount points, 211–216
        expanding disks via DISKPART, 218–220
DISK parameter, 76
disk partitioning, 124, 571
disk performance, replication and, 488
disk semantics, checking, 202
disk signatures, 112
disk sizing, replication and, 488
disk subsystems, 123–124
    performance, 432
    sizing, purchasing, and designing, 569–570
DISKPART.EXE tool, 149–151, 213–220

disks
    adding new, to cluster, 216–218
    changing quorum, 221–224
    configuration of shared, 149–155
    defragmenting, 690
    expanding, via DISKPART, 218–220
    formatting, 152–154
    full backup to, 79
    mirroring, 130, 559
    sector aligning, 126, 149–151
Distributed Management Objects (DMO), 235
distributed partitioned view (DPV), 536–538
distributed transactions, database mirroring
        and, 433
Distribution Agent, 482, 485, 518
distribution database, size of, 488
Distribution Database dialog, 495
Distributor, 479
    adding Publisher to, 500, 502
    configuration of, 492–505
    disk space and, 488
    location of, 487
    remote, 503–504
Distributor dialog, 493, 503
Distributor Properties dialog, 501
DMV. See dynamic management views
DNS (domain name system), 583
DNS alias, abstracting name change using,
        670–672
documentation
    in disaster recovery plan, 715–718
        application configuration, 717
        contact information, 717–718
        server configurations, 716–717
    of recovery scenario, 722–723
    of server installations, 18
domain accounts, for failover clustering, 127
domain connectivity
    database mirroring and, 433
    log shipping and, 369
domain controllers
    cluster nodes as, 127
    redundant, 127
domain groups, 232–233
    adding service accounts to, 253–255
    configuring, in upgrade, 303
Domain Groups for Clustered Services page,
        280–283, 303
domain service accounts, 232–235, 596–597
domains, changing, 355–361
downtime
    costs associated with, 3
    defining, 14
    nines and, 15–16
    planned, 14
    unplanned, 14
drive space, monitoring, 606
drivers, 123–124
DTS. See Data Transformation Servces

dynamic disks, 124
Dynamic Host Configuration Protocol (DHCP),
        121
dynamic management views (DMVs), 607,
        617–618

E
employee training, as building block of
        availability, 5–6
employees
    disgruntled, as security threats, 19
    security issues and, 20
    soft skills of, 6
ENABLE_BROKER parameter, 85
encryption, 126, 603
end user license agreement, 262
end-user expectations, 8–9, 29
endpoints, database mirroring, 426
Enterprise Edition, 236
Error and Usage Report Settings page, 287
Error and Usage Reporting Settings dialog, 697
error messages
    from improperly configured backup shares,
        374
    for invalid service account, 280
ERRORREPORTING parameter, 292
errors, fixing before installation, 264, 296
ERROR_BROKER_CONVERSATIONS
        parameter, 85
Event Log entries, 612
event logs, reviewing, 200, 316
Exchange, combining with SQL Server on same
        cluster, 231–232
Existing Components page, 298–299
EXPIREDATE parameter, 77, 79
extents, 43
external dependencies, 576

F
failover cluster shares, 380–386
failover clustering
    Active/Active, 244
    Active/Passive, 244
    Analysis Services, 230
    cluster-aware applications, 435
    combining SQL Server and Exchange,
        231–232
    combining with log shipping, 564
    combining with other technologies, 560–564
    compared with other high availability
        technologies, 554–557
    configuration of multiple instances, 238–243
    vs. database mirroring, 556
    dependencies, 231
    disaster recovery and, 723
    disk configuration, 237–238
    example disk configuration for, 576–578
    installing local and clustered instances on
        same hardware, 237

vs. log shipping, 556–558
new features of, 227–228
number of instances on, 228
planning instances, 228–245
process, 112–113
vs. replication, 557
resistance to, 225–226
security, 232–234
server virtualization and, 181–187
setting preferred node order, 309
side-by-side configuration, 234–237
SQL Server, 108
    adding cluster groups to each node,
        255–256
    adding service accounts to cluster groups,
        253–255
    Analysis Services, 230
    combining with Exchange, 231–232
    configuration of multiple instances,
        238–243
    creating cluster groups, 251–253
    creating service accounts, 250
    dependencies, 231
    disk configuration, 237–238
    in-place upgrade of SQL Server 2005,
        295–303
    install .NET framework 2.0, 256–259
    install SQL Server 2005, 259–303
    installing SQL Server 2005 side-by-side
        with SQL Server 2000, 234–237
    new features of SQL Server 2005, 227–228
    number of instances on, 228
    planning instances, 228–245
    rename cluster resource group, 256
    resistance to, 225–226
    scaling out, 246
    security, 232–234
    time of, 426
    upgrading to, 245
    Windows cluster configuration and, 249
SQL Server Browser Service, 230
SQL Server components, 230
SQL Writer Service, 230
testing, 316–318
vs. third-party clustering products, 557
See also server clusters; Windows server
    clusters
failover clustering administration
    adding or removing nodes, 343–350
        using command prompt, 349–350
    using SQL Server Setup, 343, 345–348
    assigning static IP port, 340–342
    changing domains, 355–361
        with no IP address changes, 355–356
    changing IP address, 339
    changing services accounts, 337
    querying properties, 321, 324
    rebuilding master database, 342
    renaming instances, 334–337

SQL Server 2005 Surface Area Configuration,
    325–328
starting, stopping, and pausing services,
    329–334
    with Cluster Administrator, 331–332
    from command line, 332–334
    with SQL Server Configuration Manager,
        330–331
    with SQL Server Surface Area
        Configuration, 331
uninstalling instances, 350–355
    using command prompt, 355
    using SQL Server Setup, 351–353
failover manager, 113
failover times, 227
failover validation, 317
failovers
    applications and, 114–115, 435
    database mirroring, 426, 475
        planned, 475–476
        unplanned, 476–477
    role changes vs., 363
    worst-case scenarios, 241–242
fast recovery, 51
fat fingering, 58–59
Feature Selection page, 297
features, disabling unneeded, 602
federation of database servers, 536
file backups, 45, 79. See also backup and restore
file compatibility, of backups, 54–57
file creation, instant initialization, 592–593
FILE parameter, 76, 85
file restores, 88, 94. See also backup and restore
file size, querying, 542
file space, monitoring, 606
file types, 485
filegroup backups, 45, 80
FILEGROUP parameter, 76, 85
filegroups
    creating objects on specific, 533–534
    restoring, 89, 94
Filter Table Rows dialog, 510
financial considerations, 29
fire suppression systems, 18
firewalls, Windows server cluster and, 129
FOR ATTACH, 639
FOR ATTACH_REBUILD_LOG, 639
FORMAT parameter, 77
formatting disks, 152, 154
forms, for change management, 12
FROM DATABASE_SNAPSHOT parameter, 85
FROM DISK parameter, 85
FROM TAPE parameter, 85
FTSCLUSTERGROUP parameter, 293
full backups, 42, 87–88
full quorum, 426
Full recovery model, 49, 432, 594

full-text indexes
    backing up and restoring, 51, 80
    database mirroring and, 477
full-text resources, 227

G

geographically dispersed clusters, 108, 129–130, 571
globally unique identifier (GUID), merge replication and, 489
globally unique identifier (GUID) partition table (GPT), 124
go/no go point, 13
government regulations, 28
graceful role changes, 363, 421–422
greenfield, 573
grounding, 22
GROUP parameter, 292, 349
growth, designing for, 570, 575

H

hard-coding, 531
hardware, 123–124
    database mirroring for migration of, 430
    installing and configuring for clustering, 131
hardware-assisted backups, 46
hardware-based disk mirroring, 559
HBA drivers, 123
high availability, 4
    database mirroring for, 430–431
    defined, 1
    versus disaster recovery, 4
    log shipping for, 365–366
    planning for, 27–38
    replication and, 488
high availability technology
    choosing, 553–554
    combining, 560–566
    comparisons among, 554–559
    See also specific technologies
high performance mode, 427–428
    vs. high safety mode, 430
    network latency and, 433
high safety mode, 428–430
    vs. high performance mode, 430
    network latency and, 433
high-performance computing, 116
hiring decisions, 4–5
hotfixes
    installing, 304
    when to apply, 703
human error, 58–59
Hurricane Katrina, 713–714
hyperthreading, 568

I

I/O isolation, 589
image data type, replication of, 489

implementation, timeline for, 36
Include Witness Server dialog, 438
index backups, 80
indexes
    creating on specific filegroup, 533–534
    partitioning, 534–535
    rebuilding, 688–689
    See also full-text indexes
industry standards, 28
information, demand for, 3
information access, 24x7, 3
Information Technology Infrastructure Library (ITIL), 10
INIT parameter, 77
Initialize Subscriptions dialog, 520
INSTALLASDATADIR parameter, 291
Installation Options page, 299
installations, failed, 584
INSTALLSQLDATADIR parameter, 291
INSTALLSQLDIR parameter, 291
INSTALLVS parameter, 291, 349
Instance Name dialog box, 297
Instance Name page, 271
instance names, 228–229
INSTANCENAME parameter, 291, 342, 349, 355
instances
    choosing type of, to install, 271
    configuring, 584–586
    default, 228, 234
    failover times for, 227
    installing local and clustered on same hardware, 237
    installing SQL Server 2005 Service Pack, 692–703
    maintenance of, 690–703
    multiple, 233, 238–243
    name changes, 435
    named, 228–229, 271–273, 297, 334
    number of, on Windows failover cluster, 228
    planning, for failover clustering, 228–245
    querying, 321, 323
    renaming, 227, 336–337
    securing, 594–602
        auditing, 598
        domain-based service accounts, 596–597
        Kerberos, 598
        password security, 599–601
        SSL certificates, 598
        using static TCP/IP ports, 597
    serving as Distributor, configuring, 492–500
    side-by-side configuration, 234–236
    See also cluster instances
instant initialization, 592–593
intergroup communication, 7–8
International Standards Organization (ISO), 28
intracluster network, 110
intragroup communication, 8

IP addresses
    changing domains without changing,
        355–356
    changing, of clustered instances, 339
    clustered, 109
IP parameter, 292
IP ports, assigning static, to clustered instances,
        340–342
IsAlive process, 110, 113, 234
IsClustered property, 323
iSCSI-based arrays, 123
is_backup_alert_enabled column, 406
is_primary column, 406
is_restore_alert_enabled column, 406

▊K

KEEP_REPLICATION parameter, 85
Kerberos, 598
killpwd.exe, 291
Knowledge Base, 37

▊L

large object (LOB) data types, replication of, 489
last_backup_file column, 406
last_copied_file column, 406
last_restored_file column, 406
last_restored_latency column, 406
latency, 433
    log shipping and, 364–365, 369
    network, 369
    queued updating and, 483
    replication and, 487
licenses, for standby servers, 572
load balancers, types of, 658
load balancing. See network load balancing
LOADHISTORY parameter, 85
local accounts, 232
local instances, 237. See also instances
Local Subscriptions context menu, 516
log chain, 370
log files
    automatic growth of, 590
    automatically shrinking, 589
    changing maximum number of, 605
    managing size of, 589–591
    monitoring, 605
    moving location of, during restore, 87
LOG parameter, 76, 85
Log Reader Agent, 482, 485
log sequence numbers (LSNs), 43
log shipping
    administration, 404–422
        adding another secondary to log shipping
            plan, 418–419
        changing monitor server, 408–409
        disabling, 410–412
        manually killing database connections,
            420
        modifications, 408

    monitoring, 404–408
    performing role change, 421–422
    removal, 412–418
    backup frequency and, 368
    backup plans and, 371
    between versions of SQL Server, 369
    combining with other technologies, 561–565
    comparing with other high availability
        technologies, 554–555, 558
    configuration of, 373–404
        creating backup share, 373–386
        custom, 403
        post-configuration tasks, 403–404
        SQL Server built-in functionality, 386–403
    database maintenance and, 371
    vs. database mirroring, 425, 432, 558
    disabling, 410, 412
        with SQL Server Management Studio,
            410–412
        with Transact-SQL, 412
    disaster recovery and, 723
    domain connectivity and, 369
    enabling, after disable, 412
    vs. failover clustering, 556–558
    flow of, 364
    full database restoration, on secondary, 367
    latency and, 364–365, 369
    location of primary and secondary, 367
    LSN sequence and, 370
    modifying, 408
    monitoring, 386–387, 404–408
        job status, 404
        stored procedures, 405–408
        system tables, 405
    network speed and, 369
    outside objects and, 370
    permissions and, 370
    removing, 412–418
        deleting entire plan, 417–418
        with SQL Server Management Studio,
            413–416
        with Transact–SQL, 416–417
    vs. replication, 480, 558
    role changes and, 372
    sending transaction logs to multiple
        secondaries, 368
    server collation and, 370
    server name resolution and, 373
    SQL Server built-in vs. custom, 372–373
    stored procedures, 403
    synchronizing database logins, 370
    timeline example, 365
    transaction log backups, 368
    transaction size, 368
    uses of, 365–367
    workings of, 363–365
    See also transaction logs
log shipping pair, 363
log shipping primary, 363

log shipping secondary, 363
logical errors, in database, 686
logical units (LUNs)
    reset, 123
    sizing, 126
logins
    implementing password security for, 599–601
    synchronizing, in log shipping, 370
    tracking failures, 598
    transferring, using SSIS, 645–658
logonserver value, 583–584
long file names, support for, 580
LooksAlive process, 110, 113, 234
LSBackup_dbname, 389
LSNs. See log sequence numbers
LSN sequence
    database mirroring and, 434
    log shipping and, 370

M

maintenance. See database maintenance
maintenance plans, 373
Majority Node Set (MNS) server cluster,
    109–110
management, 16
management tools, installing on other nodes,
    310–313
manual port number, 115
marked transactions, 63–64
masking, 123
master boot record (MBR) partition-style disks,
    124
master database, rebuilding, 342
master file table (MFT), 126
master service account, sensitive information
    on, 597
master.sys.sp_help_log_shipping
    _secondary_primary stored procedure,
    408
master.sys.sp_help_log_shipping_alert_job
    stored procedure, 405
master.sys.sp_help_log_shipping_monitor
    stored procedure, 405–406
master.sys.sp_help_log_shipping_monitor_pri
    mary stored procedure, 406
master.sys.sp_help_log_shipping_monitor_seco
    ndary stored procedure, 407
master.sys.sp_help_log_shipping_primary_data
    base stored procedure, 407
master.sys.sp_help_log_shipping_primary_seco
    ndary stored procedure, 407
master.sys.sp_help_log_shipping_secondary_d
    atabase stored procedure, 407
max degree of parallelism value, 586
max server memory setting, 588
max text repl size parameter, 489
MAXTRANSFERSIZE parameter, 77
MDAC, versions, 228
media retention, 53–54

MEDIADESCRIPTION parameter, 77
MEDIANAME parameter, 77, 85
MEDIAPASSWORD parameter, 77, 85
memory, sizing, 567–569
memory counters, 608
memory requirements, of SQL Server instances,
    239–243
memory settings, 587–588
Merge Agent, 481, 485
merge replication, 481–482, 489, 558
Microsoft
    backup and restore strategy at, 105
Microsoft Baseline Security Analyzer, 594
Microsoft BizTalk, 115
Microsoft Cluster Configuration Validation
    Wizard, 156, 161, 164, 166
    installing, 157–159
    using, 159, 161, 164, 166
Microsoft Cluster Server (MSCS), 108
Microsoft Distributed Transaction Coordinator
    (MSDTC), 122, 249
    configuring, 191–200
        creating resources, 191–198
        enabling access, 198–200
        sizing, 124
Microsoft Operations Framework (MOF), 10
Microsoft Product Support Services (PSS), 580
Microsoft Solutions Framework (MSF), 10
Microsoft Virtual Server, 181–187
min server memory setting, 587
minimum LSN (MinLSN), 44
miniport drivers, 123
mirror database, 425
mirror server
    configuring instances, 441–443
    database maintenance and, 435
    database restoration and configuration on,
        432
    location, 431
MIRROR TO parameter, 76
mirrored media set, backups to, 79
mirroring. See database mirroring
mirroring backups, 46
mirroring modes, 427–430
mirroring states, 426
mission-critical systems, researching other,
    28
Mixed Mode option, 283–284, 300
monitor server
    changing, 408–409
    configuring, 386–387, 399–401
monitoring, 604–638
    applications for, 612
    baselines for, 611
    counters, 607–612
    with DMVs, 617–618
    drive and file space, 606
    log files, 605
    with Performance Monitor, 613–616

problem notification, 618–638
redundant systems for, 638
services, 606
monitor_server_security_mode, 409
mount points, 227
configuring, 211–216
side-by-side configuration and, 235
mouse points, 127
MOVE parameter, 86
MPIO, support for, 123
MSDTC. See Microsoft Distributed Transaction Coordinator
msdb.dbo.log_shipping_monitor_alert table, 405
msdb.dbo.log_shipping_monitor_error_detail table, 405
msdb.dbo.log_shipping_monitor_history_detail table, 405
msdb.dbo.log_shipping_monitor_primary table, 405
msdb.dbo.log_shipping_monitor_secondary table, 405
msdb.dbo.log_shipping_primaries table, 405
msdb.dbo.log_shipping_primary_databases table, 405
msdb.dbo.log_shipping_primary_secondaries table, 405
msdb.dbo.log_shipping_secondaries table, 405
msdb.dbo.log_shipping_secondary table, 405
msdb.dbo.log_shipping_secondary_databases table, 405
multiple environments, setting up, 10–11
multiple instances
security issues, 233
of SQL Server, on same Windows Server Cluster, 238–243
multiple servers, 108

▊N

name changes
abstracting, during server switches, 658–672
using DNS alias, 670–672
using network load balancing, 658–669
NAME parameter, 77
name resolution, verifying cluster, 200–201, 316–317
named instances, 228–229
installing, 271–272
invalid names, 273
renaming, 334
upgrading, 297
.NET framework 2.0, installing, 256, 258–259
network attached storage (NAS), 126
network backups, 61
network cards, 121
network connectivity, verifying, 200–201, 316–317
network interface counters, 608
network latency. See latency

network load balancing (NLB)
to abstract name change, 658–669
clusters, 107–108
adding names of, to DNS, 667
adding additional nodes to, 665–667
configuring first node of, 658–659, 662–664
performing server switch using, 667–669
using with read-only databases, 670
Network Load Balancing Manager, 658
network protocols, disabling unused, 597
network speed, 369, 487
networking/networks
configuring, 141–148, 188–190
private network, 145–148
public network, 141–145
setting network priorities, 148
database mirroring and, 433
redundant, 23
server clusters and, 120–122, 141–148, 188–190
new deployment, example design solution for, 573–576
New Job Schedule dialog, 681
New Subscription Wizard dialog, 517
NEW_BROKER parameter, 86
nines, 15–16
NLB. See network load balancing
nodes. See cluster nodes
NOFORMAT parameter, 77
NOINIT parameter, 77
NORECOVERY parameter, 77, 80, 86
NOREWIND parameter, 78, 86
NOSKIP parameter, 78
NOT FOR REPLICATION option, 491
Notification Services, clustering, 230
NOUNLOAD parameter, 78, 87
NO_CHECKSUM parameter, 76, 85
NO_LOG parameter, 77
NO_TRUNCATE parameter, 77
ntext data type, replication of, 489
nvarchar(max), 489

▊O

object size, replication and, 490
objects
creating on specific filegroup, 533–534
transferring, using SSIS, 645–658
offline piecemeal restores, 95
online index rebuilds, 689
online piecemeal restores, 95
operating system (OS), installing and configuring for clustering, 131
operational level agreements (OLAs), 34–35
Oracle, 246
OS-based file-level backups, 68
outsourcing, server hosting and maintenance, 23–24

P

packet sniffing, 491
/PAE option, 587
PAGE parameter, 85
page restores, 90
PARTIAL parameter, 86, 96
partial restores, 95. See also piecemeal restores
partition function, 535
partitioned views, 536–538
partitioning data
    for high availability, 533–539
        creating objects on specific filegroup,
            533–534
        data dependent routing, 538–539
        with Transact-SQL, 534–535
        views, 536–538
partitioning features, 571
partitioning scheme, 535
partner-to-partner quorum, 426
partners, 425
PASSWORD parameter, 78, 86
passwords
    changing cluster service account, 206–207,
        210–211
    changing, 601
    cluster administrator, 276–277, 301
    expiration of, 127
    policies, 21
    security, 291, 599–601
patches
    installing, 304
    when to apply, 703
peer-to-peer replication, 484
pending_failover state, 426
people
    as barrier to availability, 30
    as building block of availability, 4–5
perceived unavailability, 14
performance
    designing for, 531, 566–567
    I/O processes and, 569–570
performance counter threshold, alerts based
    on, 630
performance issues, backup strategy and, 60
Performance Monitor (PerfMon) tool
    database mirroring indicators, 464–466
    using, 613–616
performance service level agreements, 33–34
permissions, log shipping and, 370
phone lines, 23
physical disk counters, 608
physical disk fragmentation, 690
physical errors, in database, 686
PIDKEY parameter, 293
piecemeal restores, 95–96
planned downtime, 14
planned obsolescence, 37

planning process, 27–38
    budget considerations, 29
    compromise, 35–36
    defining problem, 27
    end-user requirements and, 29
    operational level agreements, 34–35
    realistic solutions, 28
    regulations and, 28
    researching solutions, 28
    risk mitigation, 29–30
    service level agreements, 31–34
    timeline, 36
Platform SDK, 115
policies, communication of, 7
port 1433, 597
ports
    client connectivity and, 115
    opening, for failover clustering, 129
post-installation tasks, 188–202, 304–319
    adding additional drives as dependencies,
        304–307
    changing Affect the Group Property, 308–309
    changing service accounts, 318–319
    install service packs, patches, hotfixes, 304
    installing management tools on other nodes,
        310–313
    removing BUILTIN\Administrators account,
        313–316
    setting preferred node order, 309
    testing failover cluster, 316–318
power supply, 21–22
@primary_database parameter, 406–408, 417,
    419
@primary_id parameter, 407
primary keys, transactional replication and, 489
primary server, 363, 367, 422
@primary_server parameter, 406, 408
principal database, 425
principal server, 431
Principal Server Instance dialog, 440–441
prioritization
    of cluster networks, 188–190
    of networks, 148
priority boost value, 586
private cluster network, 110, 120
private cluster networks, configuring for server
    cluster, 145–148
private networks, between servers, 369
problem, defining the, 27
problem notification, 618–638
process counters, 609
processes
    as barrier to availability, 30 as building block
        of
    availability, 6–13
    change management, 10–13
    communication, 7–9
    testing, 9

processor requirements, of SQL Server
    instances, 239–243
processor utilization, 432
processors, sizing, 567–569
product life cycle, 37
professional organizations, 28
program files, changing location of, 270
programming, replication and, 523
Properties dialog, 595
public networks 110, 121, 141–145
Publication context menu, 516
publication database, 566
Publication Database dialog, 507
Publication Type dialog, 507
publications, 479
Publisher, 479
    adding to Distributor, 500
    configuration of, 503–515
    location of, 487
    remote Distributor and3–504
Publishers dialog, 496–497
pull subscriptions, 491
push subscriptions, 491

Q
/qb switch, 294
/qn switch, 294
Query Analyzer, 235
query window
    setting compatibility level in, 57
    setting media retention in, 54
Queue Reader Agent, 485
queued updating, 483
quorum, 109, 112
    creation, 425
    types of, 425–426
quorum arbitration process, 112
quorum disk
    changing, 221–224
    mirroring, 130
    sizing, 124
quorum log, resizing, 190

R
RAC, 246
racks, 18–20
RAID, 46, 126
read-only databases, using multiple, 549–550
Ready to Install page, 288, 303
READ_WRITE_FILEGROUPS parameter, 76, 85
realistic ideas, 28
REBUILDDATABASE parameter, 342
RECONFIGURE WITH OVERRIDE statement, 52
recoverability paths, 64–67
recovery
    goals for, 58
    understanding, 51
recovery interval, setting, 52

recovery models, 47, 51, 432
    Bulk-logged, 49–50
    changing, 50–51
    choosing, 50
    Full, 49
    setting, 47
    Simple, 50
    viewing, 48
RECOVERY parameter, 86
recovery process
    data copy phase, 51
    redo phase, 51
    vs. restore, 51
    understanding, 51
    undo phase, 51
redo phase, 51, 227
redundancy, 25
redundant domain controllers, 127
redundant networks, 23
Registration Information page, 296
Registry, configuration information in, 580
regulations, 28
REINSTALL parameter, 342
released to manufacturers (RTM) version, 425
Remote Account Information page, 276–277,
    301
remote administration, 20
remote connectivity, for administration of
    cluster nodes, 205
Remote Desktop Connection, 205
REMOVE parameter, 355
REMOVENODE parameter, 349
REPAIR_ALLOW_DATA_LOSS option, 686
REPLACE parameter, 86
@replicate_ddl parameter, 490
replication
    administration of, 524–527
        database backups, 524–525
    applications for, 487
    combining with log shipping, 564–565
    comparing with other high availability
        technologies, 554–555
    complex implementations, 486
    component location and, 487
    components of, 479
    configuration of, 492–523
        adding Publisher to Distributor, 500–02
        Distributor, 492–504
        Publisher, 506–15
        Publisher to use remote Distributor,
          503–504
        subscribing to publication, 516–523
    considerations for deployment of, 486–492
    vs. database mirroring, 480, 559
    with database mirroring, 566
    database schema and, 488–491
    disaster recovery and, 723
    disk performance and, 488
    disk sizing and, 488

vs. failover clustering, 557
with failover clustering, 562–563
of LOB data types, 489
vs. log shipping, 480, 558
making highly available, 488
merge, 481–482, 558
monitoring, 525, 527
network latency and, 487
network speed and, 487
object size limitation, 490
with other technologies, 562–563, 566
programming and, 523
row size limitation, 490
schema changes and, 490–491
security, 491
snapshot, 480–481, 558
SQL Server Agent and, 488
subscriptions, push or pull, 491
table size limitation, 490
transactional, 482–484, 558
types of, 479
workings of, 479–480
replication agents, 485–486
    by type of replication, 485
    Distribution Agent, 485
    Log Reader Agent, 485
    Merge Agent, 485
    Queue Reader Agent, 485
    security requirements, 486
    service accounts for, 486
    Snapshot Agent, 485
    starting and stopping, 526–527
Replication context menu, 492, 501
Replication Monitor, 525–527
replication stored procedures, 490
reporting, 571
reporting database, using secondary log
        shipping as, 367
Reporting Services, clustering, 230
reservations, breaking, 123
resource dependencies, 109, 231
resource failover, verifying, 201
resource group owner, querying, 321–322
resource groups, 309
resource monitors, 227
resources, 109, 238
RESTART parameter, 78, 86
RESTORE FILELISTONLY, 91
RESTORE HEADERONLY, 91
restore information, querying, 54
restore jobs, configuring, 397–399
RESTORE LABELONLY, 91
restore process, 51–52
RESTORE REWINDONLY statement, 90
RESTORE statement, 85–87
RESTORE VERIFYONLY statement, 62–63, 90
restores
    Analysis Services databases, 96–103
    custom scripts, 104

from a device, 87
from differential backup, 88
disaster recovery and, 723
file, 88
filegroup, 89
from full backup, 88
from full backup on disk, 87
Microsoft way, 105
moving locating of data and log files during,
        87
piecemeal, 95–96
querying system tables for backup
        commands, 65–67
resuming, 88
SQL Server database, 84–96
synchronizing, 63–64
to point in time, 89
with SQL Server Management Studio, 91–94
from tape, 87
transaction log, 64, 88
using Transact-SQL, 85–87
See also backup and restore
restore_threshold column, 406
RESTRICTED_USER parameter, 86
RETAINDAYS parameter, 78–79
retention policy, automating, 103–104
retry logic, 115, 531–532
REUNCATE_ONLY parameter, 77
REWIND parameter, 78, 86
risk mitigation, 12, 29–30
role changes, 363
    applications and, 372
    emergency, 422
    vs. failovers, 363
    performing, 421–422
        emergency, 422
        graceful, 421–422
        switching back to old primary, 422
roll-forward phase, 51
roll-forward set, 51
rolling upgrades, 431
row size, replication and, 490
run books, 715–718
Running Processes dialog, 697

■S

sa privileges, 532
SANs (storage area networks), 126
SAPWD parameter, 292
Sarbanes-Oxley (SOX), 28
schema changes, replication and, 490–491
scope creep, 36
scripts
    for administrative purposes, 644–645
    for configuration of outside objects, 403–404
    for disabling log shipping, 412
    for manually killing database connections,
        420
    transfer logins using, 658

SCSI bus reset, 123
SCSI commands, support for, 123
secondary databases, 363
  creating, 391–397
  doing maintenance on, 371
  full database restoration on, 367
  location of, 367
  sending transaction logs to multiple, 368
@secondary_database parameter, 407, 417, 419
@secondary_id parameter, 407
@secondary_server parameter, 407
secondary server
  adding another, to log shipping plan,
      418–419
  configuring outside objects on, 403–404
  removing
      with SQL Server Management Studio,
          413–416
      with Transact-SQL, 416–417
@secondary server parameter, 417–419
sector aligned disks, 126
security
  application, 602–603
  backup, 69–70
  data center, 19–21
  data encryption, 603
  database, 602–603
  database mirroring and, 433
  failover clustering, 232–234
  instances, 597
  replication and, 486, 491
  for server cluster, 127–129
  SQL Server, 594–604
    antivirus programs, 596
    auditing, 598
    Common Criteria, 599
    disabling unneeded features, 602
    domain-based service accounts, 596–597
    password security, 599–601
    using static TCP/IP ports, 597
    user rights status, 532
security identifiers (SIDs), 359
SECURITYMODE parameter, 292
SELECT @@SERVERNAME command, 110
SELECT DATABASEPROPERTYEX command,
    47–48, 71
September 11, 2001, 3
server clustering/clusters, 107–116
  32-bit and 64-bit Windows, 122
    disk configuration, 122–124, 126–127
    geographically dispersed, 129–130
    networking, 120–122
    security configuration, 127–129
    Windows Server Catalog, 116–118
  client connections and, 114–115
  disk configuration considerations, 124–126
  firewalls and, 129
  mixed Windows versions and, 122
  mouse points and, 127

  planning for, 116–130
  primary networks, 110
  split brain, 112
  testing, 200–202
  types of, 109–110
  virtualizing, 181–187
  workings of, 108–113
  See also failover clustering/clusters;
      Windows server clusters
server column, 406
server configurations, in run book, 716–717
server hosting, outsourcing, 23–24
server installations, documentation of, 18
server racks, securing, 20
server shares
  creating backup, 373–386
  failover cluster, 380–386
  stand-alone, 374–380
server switches
  abstracting name change during, 658–672
    using DNS alias, 670–672
    using network load balancing, 658–669
  emergency, 667
  planned, 668–669
  using NLB, 667–669
server upgrades, log shipping and, 366
servers
  disabling automatic updates of, 691–692
  maintenance of, 690–703
    applying SQL Server 2005 Service Packs,
        692–693
    physical disk fragmentation, 690
  migration, using log shipping, 366
  purchasing, 567–569
  sizing, 567–569
  standby, licensing, 572
  virtual, 109, 273–274
Service Account page, 277–280, 301–302
service accounts, 232–233
  changing, in upgrade, 318–319
  changing, used by clustered instances, 337
  for cluster, 132–141
  configuring, 445
    in upgrade, 301–302
  creating SQL Server, 250
  domain-based, 596–597
  for replication agents, 486
  in side-by-side configuration, 235
  setting up, 277–280
service level agreements (SLAs), 31–34
Service Master Key, 228
service packs
  installing, 304, 692–703
  running against multiple instances, 227
  when to apply, 703
services, monitoring, 606
Session Manager, 580
SET PARTNER SAFETY option, 472
SET PARTNER TIMEOUT option, 472

SET WITNESS option, 473
set working set size option, 587
Setup Progess page, 303
shared cluster disk array, 108
shared disk arrays, 123, 149–155
shared storage, connecting multiple servers to, 123
shared-nothing configuration, 108
shrink performance, 590
side-by-side configuration, of failover clustering, 234–237
Simple Network Management Protocol (SNMP), 612
Simple recovery model, 50, 434
single instances, wasted resources and, 238
SKIP parameter, 78
Snapshot Agent dialog, 484, 511
Snapshot Agent Security dialog, 513
Snapshot Folder dialog, 495
snapshot replication, 480–481, 558
software, life cycle, 37
software RAID, 126
solutions, 28
source database, 425
SPID, 420
sparse files, 540–541
split brain, 112
split–mirrors, 571
sp_addmergearticle stored procedure, 489
sp_addmergepublication stored procedure, 490
sp_addpublication stored procedure, 490
sp_add_alert stored procedure, 637–638
sp_add_job stored procedure, 684
sp_add_jobschedule stored procedure, 419, 684
sp_add_jobserver stored procedure, 684
sp_add_jobstep stored procedure, 684
sp_add_log_shipping_primary_secondary stored procedure, 419
sp_add_log_shipping_secondary_primary stored procedure, 419
sp_add_notification stored procedure, 637
sp_attach_db, 639
sp_attach_single_file_db, 639
sp_changearticle stored procedure, 490
sp_changemergearticle stored procedure, 490
sp_configure stored procedure, 587–588, 594
sp_dbcmptlevel stored procedure, 57
sp_dboption stored procedure, 589
sp_delete_alert stored procedure, 637
sp_delete_log_shipping_primary_database stored procedure, 418
sp_delete_log_shipping_primary_secondary stored procedure, 416
sp_delete_log_shipping_secondary_primary stored procedure, 417
sp_detach_db stored procedure, 638–639
sp_help_alert stored procedure, 637
sp_replrestart stored procedure, 565
sp_resolve_logins stored procedure, 421

sp_update_alert stored procedure, 637
SQL Browser account, 302
SQL Mail, 227
SQL Management Objects (SMO), 235
SQL Server, 16
  antivirus programs and, 205
  audit logs, 21
  backups. See backups
  built-in log shipping feature, 372–373
    configuration of, 386–403
  collations of, 370
  combining high availability technologies for, 560–566
  comparing high availability technologies for, 554–559
    database mirroring, 558–559
    failover clustering, 556–557
    log shipping, 558
  default port for, 597
  disaster recovery features, 723
  failover clustering, 108
  in-place upgrade of, 295–303
  installing, 579–584
  log shipping between versions of, 369
  monitoring, 604–638
    applications for, 612
    baselines for, 611
    counters, 607–612
    with DMVs, 617–618
    drive and file space, 606
    log files, 605
    with Performance Monitor, 613–616
    problem notification, 618–638
    services, 606
  physical disk fragmentation, 690
  security, 580, 594–604
    antivirus programs, 596
    application and database, 602–603
    Common Criteria, 599
    disabling unneeded features, 602
    instances, 594–602
    password, 599–601
  setting memory values, 587–588
  statistics algorithm, 593–594
  upgrades, 318–319
SQL Server 2000
  clustering, 227–228
  configuration options, 585–586
  side-by-side cluster configuration, with SQL Server 2005, 234–237
  upgrading (failover clustering), 236–237
SQL Server 2000 Service Pack 4, 295
SQL Server 2005
  beta versions, 249
  clustering requirements, 108
  configuration options, 585–586
  failover clustering. See failover clustering installation (failover clustering)
    adding IP addresses, 273–274

authentication mode, 283–285
collation settings, 285–287
command line, 259, 291–294
domain groups, 280–283
error and usage report settings, 287
installing instances, 271–272
installing prerequisites, 262–263
logging on to cluster node, 260
preparing, 288
scanning configuration, 263–265
seeing progress of, 289
selecting cluster group, 274–275
selecting cluster nodes, 275
selecting options, 266–270
service accounts setup, 277–280
setup for new, 260–291
Virtual Server setup, 273–274
management tools, 259
mount points and, 127
post-installation tasks (failover clustering),
304–319
adding additional drives as dependencies,
304–307
changing Affect the Group property,
308–309
changing service accounts, 318–319
install service packs, patches, hotfixes, 304
installing management tools on other
nodes, 310–313
removing BUILTIN\Administrators
account, 313–316
setting preferred node order, 309
testing failover cluster, 316–318
recovery models, 47–51
Bulk-logged, 49–50
changing, 50–51
choosing, 50
Full, 49
setting, 47
Simple, 50
viewing, 48
services required for, 582
Windows Compute Cluster Server 2003 and,
116
SQL Server 2005 Service Packs, applying,
692–703
SQL Server 2005 Surface Area Configuration,
325–328
SQL Server Agent
jobs for restore syntax, 69
replication and, 488
startup of, 69
SQL Server Agent jobs
alerts for, 683–684
checking status of, 526
creating, 673–686
using SQL Server Management Studio,
673–684
using Transact-SQL, 684–686

modifying, 408
monitoring status of, 404
SQL Server Agent Start dialog, 494
SQL Server Analysis Services, 246
SQL Server authentication
password security, 599–601
vs. Windows authentication, 602
SQL Server Browser Service, 230
SQL Server Business Intelligence Development
Studio, 645–655
SQL Server Configuration Manager
changing service accounts with, 337
starting and stopping services with, 330–331
SQL Server databases
backing up, 75–83
restoring, 84–96
SQL Server failover clustering. See failover
clustering
SQL Server groups, 232–233
SQL Server instances
antivirus programs and, 596
backups with, 68
configuring, 584–586
maintenance of, 690–703
processor and memory requirements,
239–243
securing, 594–602
SQL Server Integration Services (SSIS), 46
clustering, 230
importing and exporting data with, 704–712
transferring logins and object using, 645–658
SQL Server Management Studio
adding another secondary to log shipping
plan, 418
for Analysis Services backups, 97–100
for Analysis Services restores, 100–103
attaching databases, 641–644
backups with, 81–84
checking database status with, 70
configuring log shipping with, 386–402
creating SQL Server Agent jobs with, 673–684
deleting snapshots using, 545
detaching databases, 640
disabling log shipping using, 410–412
log shipping removal, 413–418
planned failovers, 475–476
removing database mirroring with, 473
restores with, 913–94
resuming database mirroring with, 472
setting compatibility level in, 56–57
setting up alerts in, 628–637
suspending database mirroring with, 470
table updates and, 491
using media retention in, 53
SQL Server Native Client, 235, 477
SQL Server Profiler, 466–468
SQL Server Publisher, 496
SQL Server Setup
adding or removing nodes with, 343–348
uninstalling instances with, 351–353

SQL Server Standard Edition, 227, 236
SQL Server Storage Solution Review Program, 122
SQL Server Surface Area Configuration, 331
SQL Server–based applications, clustered, 114–115
SQL services
    starting, stopping, and pausing, 329–334
        with Cluster Administrator, 331–332
        from command line, 332–334
        with SQL Server Configuration Manager, 330–331
        with SQL Server Surface Area Configuration, 331
SQL Writer Service, 230
SQLACCOUNT parameter, 292
SQLAgent counter, 609
SQLBROWSERACCOUNT parameter, 292
SQLBROWSERPASSWORD parameter, 292
SQLCLUSTERGROUP parameter, 293
sqlcmd, 601
SQLCOLLATION parameter, 292, 342
sqllogship.exe, 372–373
SQLPASSWORD parameter, 292, 342
SQLServer counters, 609–610
SQMREPORTING parameter, 292
SSIS. See SQL Server Integration Services
SSIS packages, creating, 657
SSL certificates, 598
staffing, during disaster recovery, 718–719
staging environment, 11
standard server cluster, 109
STANDBY parameter, 77, 80, 86
standby servers, licensing for, 572
static ports, 115, 340–342, 597
statistics, updating database, 593
STATS parameter, 78, 86
status column, 406
STOPAT parameter, 64, 86
STOPATMARK parameter, 64, 86, 89
STOPBEFOREMARK parameter, 64, 86, 89
STOP_ON_ERROR parameter, 78, 87
storage area networks (SANs), 126
Storage Foundation, 124
stored procedures
    configuring log shipping with, 386, 403
    monitoring log shipping with, 405–408
    removing, 602
    See also specific stored procedures
@stream_blob_columns parameter, 489
Subscribers, 479
    configuration of, 516–523
    reinitialization of, 490
    table updates and, 491
subscriptions, 479
    push or pull, 491
    retention of, 488
    updateable, 483
supplies, for disaster recovery plan, 719

support, contacting during recovery scenario, 721
support agreements, 36–37
support contracts, checking, 720
support drivers, 123
Surface Area Configuration, 325–328, 594
Surface Area Configuration for Features option, 594
surveillance equipment, 19
suspect_pages table, 90
suspended state, 426
sync with backup option, 524, 565
Synchronization Schedule dialog, 520
synchronized state, 426
synchronizing state, 426
sys.database_mirroring view, 469
sys.database_mirroring_endpoints view, 469
sys.database_mirroring_witnesses view, 469
sys.dm_db_mirroring_connections DMV, 469
sys.dm_os_cluster_nodes, 318
sys.sysperfinfo, 611
system administrator (SA) privileges, 21
system components, updating, 691
system processing identifier (SPID), 420
system tables
    monitoring log shipping with, 405
    querying, to generate backup commands, 65–67
systems, keeping in data center, 19

T

table size, replication and, 490
tables
    backing up, 46
    creating on specific filegroup, 533–534
    partitioning, 534–535
tail of the log, 43, 49, 80
tape, restores from, 87
tape backups, 57, 61, 79
TAPE parameter, 76
TCP/IP addresses, 121, 342
TCP/IP ports, static, 597
TCP/IP settings
    for private cluster network, 145
    for public cluster network, 142
technology, 25
tempdb, reindexing and, 689
Terminal Services, 20
testing, 9, 579
    backups, 62–63
    changes, 12–13
    of disaster recovery plan, 720
    environment, 10
text data type, replication of, 489
third-party applications
    backup strategy and, 60
    making available, 530
third-party clustering products, vs. failover clustering, 557

third-party software–based backups, 45–46
time, as barrier to availability, 30
time synchronization, of servers, 584
timeline, 36
timestamp columns, merge replication and, 489
time_since_last_backup column, 406
time_since_last_copy column, 406
time_since_last_restore column, 406
TO parameter, 76
torn pages, 130
training, as building block of availability, 5–6
Transact-SQL, 72, 75
   adding another secondary to log shipping
      plan, 419
   for administrative purposes, 644–645
   ALTER DATABASE statement, 472–473
   backups with, 75–81
   configuring database mirroring with,
      453–454
   configuring log shipping with, 403
   creating database snapshots, 543–544
   creating SQL Server Agent jobs using,
      684–686
   database mirroring administration, 469–470
   deleting log shipping plan, 418
   deleting snapshots using, 546
   disabling log shipping with, 412
   partitioning databases and indexes with,
      534–535
   planned failovers, 476
   removing database mirroring with, 475
   removing log shipping with, 416–417
   restores with, 85–87
   resuming database mirroring with, 472
   setting up alerts in, 637–638
   suspending database mirroring with, 471
Transact-SQL query, 110
transaction logs
   backups, 43–45
      applying, before role change, 421
      to device, 80
      to disk, 80
      disabling, 410
      frequency of, 368
      importance of, 58
      location, 368
      restores from, 88
   copy frequency of, 368
   database mirroring and, 425, 434
   in failover, 115
   Full recovery model and, 49
   managing, through backups, 67–68
   marked, 63–64
   network latency and speed and, 369
   reindexing and, 689
   restoring, 64
   sending to multiple secondaries, 368
   sizing, 591
   transaction size and, 368
   truncating, 80–81

transaction safety, 426
transaction size, database mirroring and, 434
transactional replication, 482–484, 558
   bidirectional, 484
   peer-to-peer, 484
   primary key requirement of, 489
   updateable subscriptions, 483
Transfer Error Messages Task, 657
Transfer Jobs Task, 657
transfer logins, using SSIS, 645–658
Transfer Master Stored Procedures Task, 657
transfer objects, using SSIS, 645–658
Transfer SQL Server Objects Task, 657
.trn file extension, 75
Try for Minutes option, 57
Try Once option, 57
two-phase commits, 64

U
underpinning contracts, 37
undo phase, 51
uninterruptible power supply (UPS), 22
UNLOAD parameter, 78, 87
unplanned downtime, 14
unplanned role changes, 363
UPDATE statement, LOB data type replication
   and, 489
UPDATE STATISTICS command, 593, 639
upgrades, 318–319, 431
user accounts, with sa privileges, 532
User Datagram Protocol (UDP), 129
user permissions, log shipping and, 370

V
varbinary(max), 489
varchar(max), 489
vendors, support agreements with, 37
version control, change management and, 12
very large databases (VLDBs), 45, 571
views, partitioned, 536–538
Virtual Device Interface (VDI), 45
virtual LANs, 130
virtual log files (VLFs), 43
virtual server, 109
Virtual Server Configuration page, 273–274
Virtual Server Name page, 273
Virtual Server Name property, 323–324
virtualization, failover clustering and, 181–187
VMware, 181–187
Volume Shadow Copy Service (VSS), 230
VS parameter, 291, 342, 349, 355

W
Wait Indefinitely option, 57
warm standby, 363
wasted resources, 238
Windows, mixing versions of, 122
Windows 2000 Server, 131, 174

Windows authentication
    configuring database mirroring with,
        453–454
    vs. SQL Server authentication, 602
Windows Authentication Mode, 283–284, 300
Windows Compute Cluster Server 2003, 108,
        116
Windows domain connectivity, 127
Windows Hardware Compatibility List (HCL),
        116
Windows Installer CleanUp Utility, 584
Windows Management Instrumentation (WMI)
        events, 103, 612, 644
Windows NLB feature, 658
Windows Platform SDK, 109
Windows Server Catalog, 116–118, 226
Windows server clusters
    32-bit and 64-bit Windows, 122
        disk configuration, 122–127
        geographically dispersed clusters, 129–130
        networking, 120–122
        security configuration, 127–129
        Windows Server Catalog, 116–118
    administration, 207–211
    antivirus programs and, 205–206
    configuration, 131
        adding additional nodes, 175–181
        adding first node, 166–175
        checking, 249
        Cluster Configuration Validation Wizard,
            156–166
        cluster networks, 188–190
        installing and configuring hardware and
            OS, 131
        of multiple SQL Server instances on,
            238–243
        of networking, 141–148
        of shared disks, 149–155

    creating cluster service account, 132–141
    disk management, 211–224
        adding new disk, 216–218
        changing quorum disk, 221–224
        configuring mount points, 211–216
        expanding disks via DISKPART, 218–220
    firewalls and, 129
    hotfixes, 131
    introduction to, 108–113
    number of instances on, 228
    planning for, 116–130
    post-installation tasks, 188–202
    primary networks, 110
    testing, 200–202
    types of, 109–110
    workings of, 108–113
Windows servers, maintenance of, 690–703
Windows-on-Windows 64 (WOW) mode, 122
WITH clause, 96
WITH clause, RESTORE command, 85
WITH NORECOVERY option, 43, 51, 367, 397,
        432
WITH STANDBY option, 43, 367, 397–398
witness server, 425, 431
witness server instances, configuring, 443–446
witness to partner quorum, 426
Wizard Actions dialog, 513, 520
worst-case scenarios, planning for, 3, 714

X

XML for Analysis (XMLA), 96–100
xp_cmdshell, 602

Z

zero data loss, 32, 59
zero scope creep, 36
zoning, 123

You Need the Companion eBook

Your purchase of this book entitles you to buy the companion PDF-version eBook for only $10. Take the weightless companion with you anywhere.

We believe this Apress title will prove so indispensable that you'll want to carry it with you everywhere, which is why we are offering the companion eBook (in PDF format) for $10 to customers who purchase this book now. Convenient and fully searchable, the PDF version of any content-rich, page-heavy Apress book makes a valuable addition to your programming library. You can easily find and copy code—or perform examples by quickly toggling between instructions and the application. Even simultaneously tackling a donut, diet soda, and complex code becomes simplified with hands-free eBooks!

Once you purchase your book, getting the $10 companion eBook is simple:

❶ Visit **www.apress.com/promo/tendollars/**.

❷ Complete a basic registration form to receive a randomly generated question about this title.

❸ Answer the question correctly in 60 seconds, and you will receive a promotional code to redeem for the $10.00 eBook.

2560 Ninth Street • Suite 219 • Berkeley, CA 94710

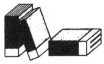

eBookshop

Offer valid through 1/23/08.